Y0-AGC-066

POWERBUILDER 4

A DEVELOPER'S GUIDE

DAVID MCCLANAHAN

M&T BOOKS

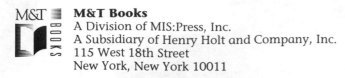

M&T Books
A Division of MIS:Press, Inc.
A Subsidiary of Henry Holt and Company, Inc.
115 West 18th Street
New York, New York 10011

© 1995 by M&T Books

Printed in the United States of America

All rights reserved. No part of this book may be reproduced or transmitted in any form or by any means, electronic or mechanical, including photocopying, recording, or by any information storage and retrieval system, without prior written permission from the Publisher. Contact the Publisher for information on foreign rights.

Limits of Liability and Disclaimer of Warranty
The Author and Publisher of this book have used their best efforts in preparing the book and the programs contained in it. These efforts include the development, research, and testing of the theories and programs to determine their effectiveness.

The Author and Publisher make no warranty of any kind, expressed or implied, with regard to these programs or the documentation contained in this book. The Author and Publisher shall not be liable in any event for incidental or consequential damages in connection with, or arising out of, the furnishing, performance, or use of these programs.

All products, names and services are trademarks or registered trademarks of their respective companies.

Library of Congress Cataloging-in-Publication Data

McClanahan, David.
    PowerBuilder 4 : a developer's guide / David McClanahan.
        p. cm.
    Includes index.
    ISBN 1-55851-417-1
    1. Application software.   2. PowerBuilder   I. Title.
QA76.76.A65M42   1995
005.2--dc20   95-5247
                                                                                   CIP

98 97 96 95   4 3 2 1

Editor-in-Chief: Paul Farrell
Managing Editor: Cary Sullivan
Development Editor: Alla Efimova
Production Editor: Patricia Wallenburg
Copy Editors: Jack Donner and Shari Chappell

DEDICATION

This book is dedicated:

*To all those who work to make the world
a better place for our children.*

and

To the memory of Kirpal Singh, who did make it better.

FOREWORD

I would like to thank the people who have helped to make this book possible. First, my thanks must go to Rachael Stockton at Powersoft for her help and assistance through my never-ending series of requests over the last two years.

I would also like to thank Technalysis Corporation for its support throughout this project, and especially Bill Schmidley, the manager of the Cincinnati branch. I would like to thank Mary Epp and Tom Martin for their contributions to Chapters 19 and 20.

...M&T books: Paul Farrel, Alla Efimova, Patricia Wallenburg, Shari Chappell, and Brian Oxman.

TABLE OF CONTENTS

INTRODUCTION

PREFACE

If you would like to quickly increase your value as a client-server developer and ensure your employability, becoming proficient with PowerBuilder is probably the best step you can take at this time. The intent of this book is to get the developer, who is already proficient in at least one other language, up to speed on PowerBuilder as quickly as possible.

USING THIS BOOK

The material in this book is based on the PowerBuilder seminars that I have been teaching since the release of PowerBuilder 3.0 and on a number of the other Client/Server and database-related seminars that I have been teaching over the last few years. My approach in this material is very much a hands-on development approach. I believe that you learn best by doing and that you only really understand that which you have actually experienced. My goal is to get you up to speed as quickly as possible, with the information that you need and with a well-rounded set of examples.

In this book, I present more than a dozen sample applications, each focused in a specific area of PowerBuilder development. These examples are included on the diskette that came with this book. The intent is for the budding PowerBuilder developer (you) to first read the material presented before each example application. You should then run the associated example, try all of the options, and think about how you would create a similar application. Once you understand the application, you should create your own duplicate of the application (as closely as possible). The complete source code is provided for each of the examples, and I provide walk-throughs for creating several of the examples. When you need a hint, you can refer to the example's code. The examples are also intended to serve as a source for future development. You may use the code in your own applications without limitation (except that you may not use this code for training or for another PowerBuilder book).

The examples have been carefully designed to cover all the essential areas of PowerBuilder development and to stay focused in the area that each is demonstrating. When you have completed the examples, you will have acquired real, hands-on experience with the most important details of PowerBuilder. You will, for example, have created at least one of every type of object in the Window painter. You will also have a large amount of source code and example objects that you can reuse in your PowerBuilder applications. It is highly recommended that you take time to work through each example.

THE POWERSOFT TOOLS

Powersoft markets a number of application tools for developing client/server applications. Powersoft has taken the lead in market share for client/server front-end development systems, and with its purchase of the Watcom Company, has strengthened both its database and language areas. I believe that the Watcom compiler technology will help PowerBuilder to create faster, and better-performing applications, and that the software methodology and experience from both Watcom and Sybase will result in a more robust development environment. So with these developments, I am sure that PowerBuilder is well positioned for growth and will remain in the forefront of client/server development tools.

This book's examples use the Watcom database engine that is included with both PowerBuilder and PowerBuilder Desktop. To run the examples, you must have installed the Watcom engine. If you did not, you should run the PowerBuilder installation and install just the database engine.

POWERBUILDER 4

PowerBuilder is a powerful object-oriented client/server front-end development system for Microsoft Windows (UNIX Motif and Macintosh versions are in development). This is generally considered to be the best product currently available; its main competitors are SQLWindows, ObjectView, and Visual Basic.

PowerBuilder is best known for its intuitive user interface, ease-of-use, and powerful high-level constructs, all of which make development with PowerBuilder highly productive. You define much of your application by creating PowerBuilder objects (such as windows and controls) with the various PowerBuilder Painter utilities.

Visual Basic is a more general programming tool and is generally a more suitable choice for nondatabase-oriented applications. Visual Basic is a compiled language and is therefore considerably faster than

PowerBuilder (which is an interpreted language). But Visual Basic does not have a database repository, and its database interface is very weak when compared to the DataWindow object in PowerBuilder. Visual Basic has no object-oriented features. Both products have an excellent interface; PowerBuilder is more complex and therefore has a steeper learning curve.

On the other hand, PowerBuilder is data-centric. It assumes from the beginning that you are creating a database application, and at every step it includes a great deal of intelligence about the creation of client/server front-end application. This is the main difference between PowerBuilder and Visual Basic, and the productivity gain for client/server applications is well worth making the switch to PowerBuilder. PowerBuilder's DataWindow object is a high-level construct that encapsulates data access within an intelligent database-aware object. DataWindows are, in many ways, the essence of PowerBuilder's client-server power. Basically the DataWindow stands between your application and the database. You will interact with DataWindows for nearly all of your data access. The DataWindow is unsurpassed by the competition at the moment, and in general your view of DataWindows will also reflect your view of PowerBuilder.

PowerBuilder also creates and maintains its own repository in the target database system. This repository stores information about the tables, columns, indexes, and so forth, that are used by your applications. If you specify a default font for a certain table and define a column heading, such as "Employee ID" for the column EMP_NO from the table EMPLOYEE, that heading and font will be used as the default the next time you add that column to a report (DataWindow) in an application. This will help to implement standards for the database references and the appearance of your screens and reports. You can also define validation rules, foreign keys , and so on.

The PowerBuilder interface is second to none, as far as implementing a graphical point-and-click application development environment. PowerBuilder is clearly the most productive Windows development environment available for client/server development. Your company can get COBOL mainframe programmers (with no Windows experience) up to speed in PowerBuilder development in a very short timeframe,—just a couple of weeks of retraining. They can be productive in a few weeks and at the intermediate level within a few months. There is much more to client/server development than just learning the PowerBuilder tool. You must also understand client/server architecture, SQL, the event-driven paradigm, some object-oriented concepts, and concepts of collaborative programming (including standards, procedures, and methodology).

PowerBuilder takes full advantage of the event-driven Windows environment and provides database-independent development. The PowerBuilder objects that you create can contain program scripts that execute in response to different events. You can develop applications against the local Watcom database engine (provided with PowerBuilder) and then move the application to another DBMS such Sybase or Oracle.

PowerBuilder contains a number of object-oriented features that will greatly increase the productivity of application development by providing reusable objects and code and allowing the use of well-structured applications. This is another area that sets it off from the competition, including Visual Basic.

PowerBuilder has an open architecture, and a number of third-party tools can be integrated into your development environment; these tools include CASE tools, source code control systems, and testing utilities.

USING THIS BOOK

This book is a complete introduction to PowerBuilder 4 and PowerBuilder Desktop. In the text I will usually refer to PowerBuilder, but generally the text and examples all apply to both PowerBuilder and PowerBuilder Desktop.

My approach is very much a hands-on development approach. The examples have been carefully designed to cover all the essential areas of PowerBuilder development. When you have completed the examples, you will have acquired real hands-on experience with the most important details of PowerBuilder.

USING THE SAMPLE PROGRAMS

The program diskette that came with this book contains finished versions of all the exercises used in this book and a number of other objects that you will need to create the example applications (databases, icons, text files, and so on).

Installing the Examples

The diskette that came with this book includes a setup program that will install the example files and database on your system. Run the setup program from Windows and be sure to read the **README** text displayed during the installation. The setup program will create a directory for the examples, such as C:\PB4\CLASS, and will create the ODBC configuration necessary for the Watcom database (all further references assume C:\PB4\CLASS is the directory, so adjust these statements according to the actual location you have chosen). It is highly recommended that you accept the default directory (**C:\PB4\CLASS**). Many of the objects in the applications and the application profile files assume this to be the directory for the example files. If you must install to another directory, you will have to adjust the path references in the example applications.

After installing the example files, you must run the **LIBLIST** example program (found in C:\PB4\CLASS) from within PowerBuilder. This application will update the LibList (the library search path) for the example PowerBuilder applications. When you run this program, you must locate and select the PB.INI file for your system in the directory navigation ListBox. Generally this is located in **C:\PB4**.

All the database examples use a Watcom database C:\PB4\CLASS\IMAGE.DB (and IMAGE.LOG). The install program can set up the ODBC configuration if you accept the default directory. Otherwise, you must configure an ODBC profile before running these examples. Appendix A covers the installation process in much greater detail (but if you accept the default parameters, it is very easy). Chapter 19, on the Database painter, explains how to set up the ODBC configuration and the database profile if you need to do it by hand. Appendix A also includes a table that lists the example applications and will tell you which examples go with which chapters. The example application, CONTROLS, is the same as the HELPDEMO (with the addition of the Help system). If your diskette does not contain CONTROLS, use the HELPDEMO application.

The examples have been carefully designed to cover all the essential areas of PowerBuilder development. You should run each example so that you understand exactly what the application does and how it looks. Next you should attempt to duplicate the example application as precisely as possible. Name your versions of each application library the same as the sample, but append version numbers to the name. You are limited to eight- character names in the DOS file system so you may have to truncate the name by one character. For example, for FIRSTAPP, create a library named **FIRSTAP1.PBL**. Later, if you want to create other versions, you can create a library named **FIRSTAP2.PBL** and so on. You can name all the objects (including windows and application objects) exactly the same as in the exercise text.

You should be able to create each application from the knowledge you have gained by reading the text and using the PowerBuilder Help system. If you cannot complete the exercise in that manner, open the example application and examine the source code. It would be helpful to print out a listing of each application. You can do this in the Library painter.

Throughout this text, we assume that the path to the sample application is **C:\PB4\CLASS**. If that is not the case (perhaps you placed them in directory D:\pbsample), you will have to adjust all references to C:\PB4\CLASS accordingly. The LIBLIST application program will allow you to place the example files in any directory.

Please note:

- **Windows (or MS Windows)**—when capitalized, Windows is a reference to the Microsoft Windows system.
- **window**—when not capitalized, window is a reference to the graphical object, a rectangle that is used as part of the user interface.

Additional Information

Most of the material in this book is based on the PowerBuilder seminars that I have been teaching over the last year and a number of Client/Server and database-related seminars that I have been teaching over the last few years. I teach three one-week seminars on PowerBuilder development (beginning, intermediate, and advanced). The advanced course is usually customized for the client site, and we often begin actual development of an application during that week. Some of the other seminars that I teach are: a one-week introduction to client/server development for Windows, and introductions to SQL, relational database design, Oracle, and Sybase.

Good luck with PowerBuilder. I hope you find this book and the example applications useful.

I can reached on CompuServe at 72517,1124, and through Technalysis Corporation, 4675 Cornell Road, Cincinnati, OH 45241.

CHAPTER ONE

INTRODUCTION TO POWERBUILDER 4

THE DEVELOPMENT ENVIRONMENT

The PowerBuilder (or PowerBuilder Desktop) installation program adds a new program group with the name "Powersoft" to your Windows desktop. In the Powersoft program group, double-click on the icon labeled PowerBuilder 4.0 (or PowerBuilder Desktop), to launch the PowerBuilder application.

After you start the application, the initial PowerBuilder window is displayed. Figure 1.1 shows the initial display format—a window with a menu and a toolbar called the PowerBar. (The PowerBar was added with PowerBuilder version 3.0.) You click on the PowerBar icons to launch the different development environments, each of which works in a certain area of development.

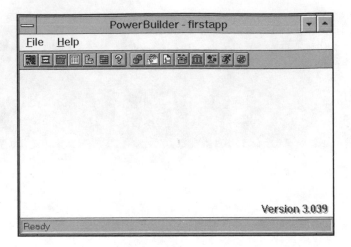

FIGURE 1.1 THE INITIAL POWERBUILDER WINDOW

DISPLAYING TEXT LABELS IN THE TOOLBARS

You can select an option which displays a text label with each icon on the PowerBar and the other toolbars (which will be introduced shortly). These labels are useful as you learn your way around the PowerBuilder environment. The text labels make it easier to identify functions on the toolbars until you know the meaning of each icon. To activate this option, click on the **PowerBar** with the right mouse button. This opens the popup menu (Figure 1.2).

Take note of this popup menu, it is very useful throughout the development process. You will see many references in this book to the "popup menu" or to the RMB (right mouse button) popup menu. This popup is context-sensitive, which means that the contents on the menu change depending on the type of object that you have selected.

Select the **Show Text** menu option to toggle on the display of the descriptive labels for each icon. A checkmark next to the menu option signifies that this option is active. Select it again to toggle off the text display option, this also removes the checkmark. Other options in this popup menu let you set the position for each toolbar (top, bottom, left, right, floating). Figure 1.3 shows the PowerBar icons with the text display option turned on.

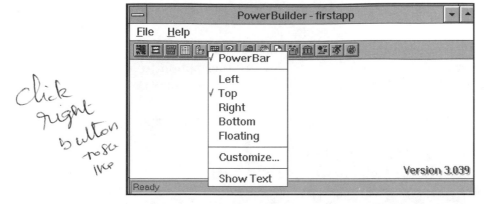

click right button to see like [handwritten note]

FIGURE 1.2 USE THE POPUP MENU TO CONTROL THE DISPLAY OF THE TOOLBARS

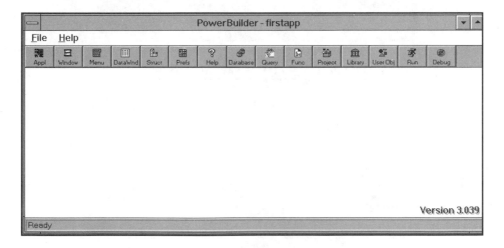

FIGURE 1.3 THE POWERBAR WITH THE DISPLAY TEXT OPTION

CUSTOMIZING THE PRESENTATION STYLE

You can choose not to display the PowerBar (or any other toolbar). To choose this option, click the **PowerBar** with the right mouse button. This opens the popup menu (Figure 1.2). On the popup menu, toggle off the PowerBar option by clicking it. The PowerBar will disappear. This is just one example of how you can customize the details of the PowerBuilder environment.

Even if you don't display the PowerBar, you can still access the various PowerBuilder modules by selecting the **PowerPanel** option from the File menu. This opens the PowerPanel dialog box shown in Figure 1.4.

FIGURE 1.4 THE POWERPANEL DIALOG

This dialog contains dozens of program icons. Clicking on any of these icons will launch one of the painter applications.

If you have hidden the PowerBar and wish to make it visible, select the **Toolbars** option from the File menu in the initial screen. (This option is available in the Window menu of other painters.) This opens the Toolbars dialog shown in Figure 1.5.

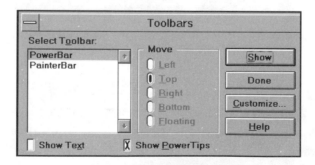

FIGURE 1.5 THE TOOLBARS DIALOG

In this dialog, select the **PowerBar** toolbar, and click on the **Show** command button to display the PowerBar. You can also choose where to display it and whether or not to show text in this dialog.

THE POWERBUILDER PAINTERS

The PowerBar and the PowerPanel give you access to the suite of PowerBuilder painters. Each painter provides a development environment for a specific area of development. For example, the Window painter provides the functions that you need to develop the graphical user interface. It allows you to create new windows and then add controls and other graphical objects to these windows. We will look at each of the painter utilities in detail, but first, we will give you an overview of some of the more important components of PowerBuilder development.

GET TO KNOW THESE FEATURES

In this section, I want to point out some of the most useful features of the PowerBuilder development environment. This is to alert you to the areas of PowerBuilder to which you should pay particular attention as you learn this product. The intent is not to cover these in detail at this point, but to let you know about features that you should take special care to learn well. Being proficient with these features will greatly increase your productivity as you work with PowerBuilder and will accelerate the learning process.

ONLINE HELP!

The Help system in PowerBuilder is excellent, and in the current release it is often more up-to-date than the printed documentation. You can access this extensive help system in several ways. You can click on the **Help** icon (the question mark) on the PowerBar, or choose the **Help Index** option: choose

Help Index from the Help menu (available in all the painters), or simply press **F1** (function key 1). Any of these actions will take you to the table of contents shown in Figure 1.6. In this window you can select a topic such as "Getting Started" to help you find your way through the development environment.

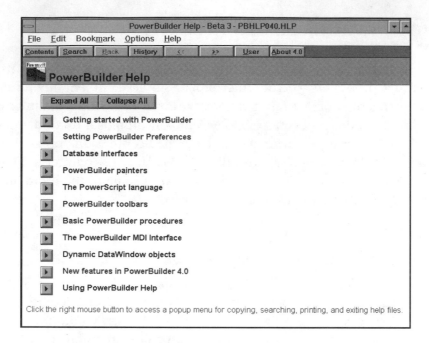

FIGURE 1.6 THE INITIAL POWERBUILDER HELP SCREEN

Help – Search Option

The search option is one of the most useful Help system functions. The search function helps you find a specific topic and locate the related information from the help system. The next paragraphs describe how to use the search function in the help system.

Enter the Search Criteria

From within Help click on the **Search** button, or from within a painter window select the Search menu option **Help|Search**. This opens the Search dialog window (Figure 1.7). Next enter the search criteria into the input field (for this example type **help**). As you type, the upper listbox presents an index of the choices that best match the text that you have entered, see Figure 1.7.

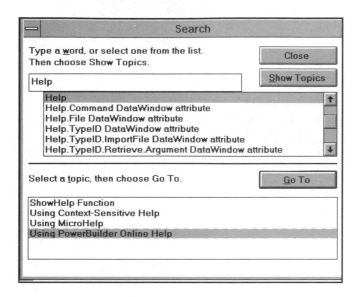

FIGURE 1.7 THE POWERBUILDER HELP SYSTEM SEARCH DIALOG

Select from the Index

To select an entry, tab down to the Show Topics listbox and scroll to an entry, or just use the mouse to click on one. Using one of these techniques, select an item from the list. Then click on the **Show Topics** CommandButton (a shortcut is to double-click on the entry in the list box) to see the list of related help topics that are available. The system displays a selection of help topics in the lower listbox (the **Select a topic** listbox in Figure 1.7).

Select a Topic, Setting Bookmarks

Select one of the listed topics (such as Using PowerBuilder Online Help in this example) and then click on the **Go To** CommandButton. This presents all the information that is available on the topic (Figure 1.8).

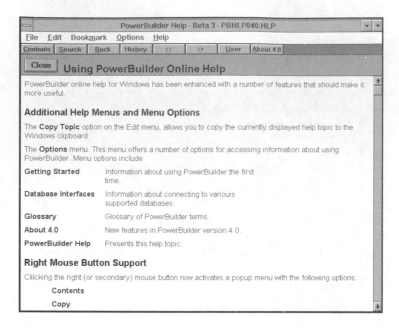

FIGURE 1.8 A HELP TOPIC

Creating Bookmarks

You can place electronic "bookmarks" in the help system so that you can quickly return to a marked entry. After you have found an important entry, create a bookmark by choosing the **Bookmark|Define...** menu option and then enter a name for the bookmark (or accept the default suggested by PowerBuilder). PowerBuilder adds the name that you assign for a bookmark directly to the **Bookmark** menu. After that, you can return to any help entry just by selecting the name from the menu. To delete the bookmark, return to the Bookmark Define dialog by choosing the **Bookmark|Define...** menu option, select the bookmark entry, and then click on the **Delete** button.

Using the Help Button

You can also access the help system by clicking on the **Help** button that appears in many dialog windows. You will find that context-sensitive help is available throughout the development process to explain the choices that you have at each step. When you are performing an action, such as opening an existing application, you will often see the Help CommandButton presented as an option. Click on the **Help** button and the help system displays an entry that is specific for the operation that you are performing, guiding you though the process and explaining what the options are at each step. Context-sensitive help is also available for the commands and functions in the PowerScript programming language. This will be covered in the section on writing code in the PowerScript language.

More Help With Using the Help System

For more information on how to use the Help system, enter the Help system (click on the **Help** icon on the PowerBar), and then hit **F1**. This will give you detailed, step-by-step directions on how to use the Help system. Here's another tip, if you cannot locate an entry that you expected to find in the index, check the glossary. For example, if you were to look for a definition of "events," you will not find that explanation in the help index (try it). However, you will find an entry for "events" in the glossary (Figure 1.9). Events are an essential part of PowerBuilder development, so take a minute to read the glossary definition.

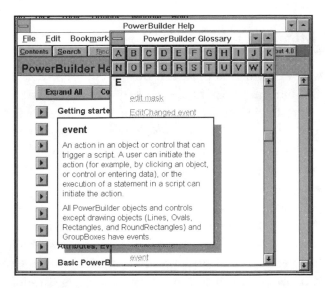

FIGURE 1.9 USING THE GLOSSARY, THIS EXAMPLE SHOWS THE EVENT ENTRY

THE POPUP MENU

In many places throughout the development environment, you can acti-vate a popup menu by placing the pointer on an object and then clicking the right mouse button. In this book, this window is referred to simply as the *popup* or *RMB* (right mouse button) menu. You have already seen the use of the popup menu for positioning the toolbars and toggling the dis-play of text for the toolbar icons. This popup menu is context-sensitive and available throughout the PowerBuilder environment. You often use this menu for setting properties of the various PowerBuilder objects. During the design phase, if you click the right mouse button on an object, such as a window or a control, the popup will present a different set of options that apply specifically to the type of object that you had selected. Using the popup menu is often the fastest way to get around in the devel-opment process because the pointer is often located near the object with which you are currently working, and the right-mouse click is convenient. As you work your way through the various painters, take time to become familiar with the options that are available in different contexts.

THE POWERSCRIPT LANGUAGE

PowerScript is PowerBuilder's programming language. It is a high-level, event-driven programming language, with many object-oriented features. It is modeled after BASIC and C and will be easy to learn for those who already have a solid foundation in one of those languages. Developers who already have some Windows programming experience will do even better. PowerScript (often simply called *script*) provides nearly 500 built-in func-tions with a wide range of functionality such as numeric and string process-ing, and data conversion for your applications. PowerScript allows the direct embedding of SQL statements for database access (this is not always necessary, you will often use DataWindows instead). PowerBuilder provides support for the event-driven Windows environment. PowerScript provides functions that allow communications between objects through messaging (events). More details about events will be found later in this chapter.

PowerScript allows the direct addressing of objects and their attributes by using a "dot" notation. For example, you can disable a CommandButton (cb_close) in the main window (w_main) by assigning a value to one of the control's attributes with the following notation,

```
w_main.cb_close.enabled = FALSE
```

PowerScript includes support for flow control statements (conditional branching and looping), and supports variables with a wide range of data types and a variety of scoping options.

PowerScript is your next programming language, so you must take time to learn its details. From your previous programming experience you will know what types of functions should be available. Often the hardest part of locating a function is just finding the name of the function, the Object Browser (the browser) and help system will assist your search. Make a couple of passes through the list of functions in the help system to become familiar with the types of functions that are available.

Pasting Code Examples Into Your Scripts

You can also copy and paste text from within the Help system using the **Edit|Copy** menu option. This is most useful for copying PowerBuilder function definitions and for copying PowerScript code examples into your scripts when you are writing new code. Context-sensitive help is also available for all the commands and functions in the PowerScript programming language. To access this help while editing a script, just place the cursor on the function or command (in your code) that you need information on, and then press **Shift+F1**.

THE TEXT FILE EDITOR (SHIFT+F6)

If you hold the **Shift** key and press **F6**, PowerBuilder brings up the text file editor. You often find this editor to be useful thoughout the development process. When you first start up the editor, you have the option of opening an existing file (by using the **File Open** dialog box), or you can choose to create and edit a new file (by clicking on **Cancel** in the initial dialog). This editor is similar in functionality to the Windows' Write editor. Menu options will allow you to cut, copy, and paste text within or between windows. Menu options also provide search and replace functionality within the file. You will often use this editor to create, edit, and save text files to the file system.

A similar editor with additional functionality is also used to create and edit the PowerScript code in your PowerBuilder applications (Figure 1.10).

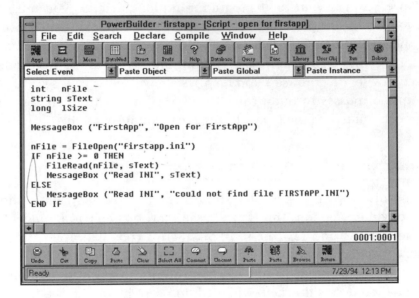

FIGURE 1.10 THE POWERSCRIPT PAINTER (TEXT EDITOR)

One of the differences between the text file editor and the PowerScript editor is that with the PowerScript editor the PowerScript code will be stored automatically within your PowerBuilder application library (as covered later) and not as a separate disk file.

THE OBJECT BROWSER

The Object Browser is a very powerful search utility that is accessible in the PowerScript painter and the Library painter. You can use the browser in several different contexts, and in each you will use it in a slightly different manner. You can use the browser to search for one of the objects in your application. You will, perhaps, find it to be most useful for quickly finding and then pasting object names, attributes, functions, and other values into your PowerScript code. You can access the browser from several places in the PowerBuilder environment. It appears on several menus and also has its own icon on the PainterBar in the Script painter (Figure 1.10). It is used in a slightly different manner in each location. With the browser, you can avoid having to access the PowerBuilder manuals to look up an attribute or function name. When accessed from the Library painter, it is useful for locating and copying code to be pasted into another script.

After you have gained more experience with PowerBuilder and have a good understanding of the development process, using the browser can often be more efficient than using the help system. You will often use it to look up the functions, attributes, and names that relate to a specific class of object (such as a window, or CommandButton) and it quickly narrows the search based on the object type (Figure 1.11). The use of the browser will be covered in detail throughout this book. After you have created one of the larger example applications in this text, use the browser to explore the application, try to locate all the components and related items.

DATAWINDOWS

The DataWindow is the single most powerful feature of PowerBuilder. The DataWindow object is a high-level construct that encapsulates data access within an intelligent, data-centric object. DataWindows are, in many ways, the essence of PowerBuilder's client-server power. Basically the DataWindow stands between your application and the database. You will interact with DataWindows for nearly all of your data access. Understanding and using the DataWindow is a complex topic, and will therefore be the topic of several chapters in this book. I will not go into any further detail here, but I assure you, that an understanding of DataWindows is absolutely essential. You should invest a good percentage of your initial PowerBuilder study into gaining experience with every nuance of DataWindows. While you are learning about DataWindows experiment with them. For example, try using them instead of listboxes. Enough said about that, you have been alerted to their importance!

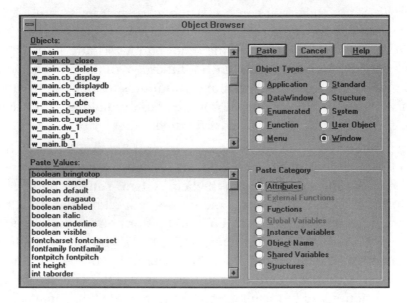

FIGURE 1.11 USING THE OBJECT BROWSER TO
DISPLAY A COMMANDBUTTON'S ATTRIBUTES

OBJECT-ORIENTED FEATURES

PowerBuilder provides some support for each of the major tenets of object-oriented programming: data abstraction, inheritance, and polymorphism. The object-orientation in PowerBuilder is not fully developed, and may not completely satisfy an object-oriented expert; but the object-oriented features are very useful and well worth investigating. The reusability gained from these object-oriented features is one of the main advantages of PowerBuilder over competing products (such as Visual Basic).

Data abstraction is the encapsulation of attributes and functionality within an object. In some ways this is really just a logical extension of structured programming techniques. Data abstraction can help you to build cleaner, easier to extend applications, and will ease the maintenance of those applications. In PowerBuilder development you will define classes and objects. A *class* is a type or category of object. An *object* is an instantiation (instance) of a class. The relationship between a class and an object is similar to the relationship between a data type and a variable. For example, consider the following declaration

```
Integer iCount
```

Integer is a data type, and iCount is a variable, an instance of an integer. You might think of integer as a class of data type, and iCount as an object which is an instantiation of the integer data type.

Initially it may not be clear how PowerBuilder uses classes and objects, the chapter on Inheritance will cover this topic in more detail.

Inheritance allows the developer to derive a new object type from an existing base class. The new class will specialize the more general base class in some way, perhaps by adding attributes, or by restricting the ancestor's behavior in some manner. The pay off is that you gain the reusability of existing objects that may already have some of the features that you need for the new objects, and you gain the reuse of well-tested code, shortening the development process. Sharing a base set of objects can save a great deal of time and effort for a development team, and can also provide a boost to new PowerBuilder developers.

Polymorphism is when a function's behavior varies with the type of the object to which it is applied. For example, three different classes (file, directory, and fileset) may all have a method named *Delete*. The behavior of that method will vary for each of these object types because the rules (the definition) for the delete will need to vary for each.

Spend some time learning about, and utilizing the object-oriented features of PowerBuilder. These features will eventually provide you with reusable objects, and better design modularity, while helping to clarify the functioning and to ease the maintenance of the systems you develop. The object-oriented features of PowerBuilder are optional, and is an advanced topic covered in later chapters.

ATTRIBUTES, EVENTS, FUNCTIONS

PowerBuilder presents almost all of the components that go into creating an application as objects. These objects always have *attributes*, *events*, and *functions.* The help system and the browser are organized around this arrangement.

Attributes

Attributes are the properties that define the characteristics of each object. Attributes are similar to the elements of a structure in other languages such as C. Each object type has a specific set of attributes. You can examine and assign values to these attributes using the dot notation described earlier, or sometimes by calling a function.

Events

Microsoft Windows is an event-driven environment, and an understanding of events and messaging will be essential for the PowerBuilder developer. *Events* are the actions or state changes that apply to an object. Each object type has a different and specific set of events associated with it. You can also define your own events for your PowerBuilder application.

You can create PowerScript code for any event that is available for each object. Events are actually the only way that any of your code can be executed. The developer writes PowerScript code (scripts) to respond to a specific event. An event occurrence will trigger the execution of that code. You can also write functions that are shared between different objects in your applications. These functions are called from within the code that you enter for an event.

For example, a CommandButton contains a hook for the Clicked event (we say that the CommandButton contains a Clicked event). The Clicked event script is where you would place the code for that Clicked event. When the user of your application clicks the left mouse button on that CommandButton, the system triggers the Clicked event for that button and executes the code. In that code you could call functions or even trigger other events. Essentially all code execution is triggered as the result of an event. We will cover events and PowerScript coding in great detail throughout this book.

Functions

The PowerBuilder system provides hundreds of functions (procedures) for the developer. PowerBuilder functions are similar to the functions that are found in developmental libraries that are available for most languages such as C, Pascal, and BASIC. These include functions for data conversion, file access, string manipulation, time, and date manipulation (and much more). As mentioned, you can also write your own functions. We will cover functions in the section on programming.

MICROHELP

In many places throughout the development environment PowerBuilder will display a context-sensitive comment at the bottom of the active window. This text is called *Microhelp*. You see Microhelp text for the first time at the bottom of the initial PowerBuilder screen when it displays the word "Ready" (Figure 1.1).

You can easily add Microhelp to your own PowerBuilder applications. Microhelp is usually preferable to using a message box for displaying informative, but non-critical, context-sensitive comments. Use message boxes for more serious errors and in cases where you need a response from the user.

THE POWERBUILDER PAINTERS

This section presents an overview of the various modules or "painters" that make up the PowerBuilder development environment. You will be working with each of these painters as you develop your PowerBuilder applications. In the PowerBuilder environment you can have multiple painters open at the same time (each in a different window) and you may be working in several painters simultaneously. You can switch from one window to another by pulling down the Window menu, and then by selecting the desired window. There are some restrictions that you will encounter. In a few areas, PowerBuilder appears quite modal, insisting that you complete your work in a specific order. For example, you can only edit the script for one event in a window at any time, and you can not edit a user object while you have a window open that contains one of these objects. We will point out some of these limitations as we step through the development process.

When you open each of these Painter utilities, in addition to the PowerBar you also will see another toolbar called the PainterBar. The icons that appear on the PainterBar vary for each of the Painter utilities. The PainterBar icons are shortcuts for the more important menu options. You can customize the contents of each of the toolbars by adding or deleting icons. You can also control the display of any toolbar, including the PainterBar, by selecting the **Window|Toolbars...** menu option. This opens the Toolbars dialog window (shown in Figure 1.12) where you control the display of each toolbar.

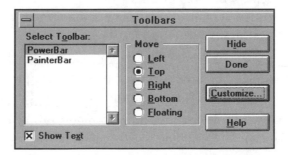

FIGURE 1.12 THE TOOLBAR DIALOG

You can choose to show or hide each toolbar, can set their position on the screen, and can toggle the text display on and off. (You can also use the popup menu to change the display of the toolbars, just right mouse click on a toolbar to bring up the popup menu.) Throughout this book, most of our example screens will show the PainterBar positioned at the bottom of the window. Some developers prefer to place the PainterBar at the left of the screen, you can put it wherever you prefer.

PowerBuilder Painter Overview

The PowerBuilder painters are the set of development environments that you will use to develop PowerBuilder applications. The PowerBuilder initial window (the first screen that opens when you run PowerBuilder) provides a starting point and gives you access to the set of painter utilities. The next section presents a brief overview of each painter. The PowerBar icon (if any) that is associated with each is shown with each description. Briefly they are:

 Application painter—this is where you will define the most general application attributes, and where you will create the application object itself.

 Window painter—this is where you design the windows that make up your application. You will be able to create windows, and add controls to them in a very intuitive, graphical manner.

 Menu painter—this is where you create the menus that will be attached to some of your windows.

 DataWindow painter—the DataWindow is the object that encapsulates data access for your application. DataWindows are at the heart of most PowerBuilder applications. Several chapters will be devoted to DataWindows.

 Structure painter—this is where you create composite variables. A *structure* is a set of data elements grouped together as a unit. The set of variables is then referenced by a single name. You can use a structure as function argument. This will pass the entire structure to the function argument as a unit, reducing the number of arguments necessary in the call. In the structure painter you create and edit structures.

Preferences painter—this is where you set up preferences for applications, windows, menus, DataWindows, database, libraries, debugging, and general environment attributes. This includes setting default fonts, default behaviors of various tools, naming conventions, etc. After you set things the way you prefer, you will only use this painter occasionally.

Help painter—PowerBuilder has an excellent help system. It also provides context-sensitive help through the development process. You should become fluent with this utility.

Database painter—the database painter provides a convenient interface to the database. In this painter, you can create tables, indexes, views, extended attributes, validation criteria, and display formats. You can also create, edit, and activate database connection profiles, and you can export and import database definitions.

Data Manipulation painter—part of the Database painter where you can execute select, update, insert, and delete operations against the database. You can also apply filters and sorting to the select result set, and you export and import data to or from a wide range of formats.

Database Administrator—lets you enter and execute SQL statements manually. You can save these programs as files for later use. The result set is handled as in the Data Manipulation painter.

Query painter—with this painter you can graphically create SQL statements. You can then store these statements in a library where they can be referenced by other objects (such as DataWindows).

PowerScript painter—this is where you create and edit PowerScript code.

Function painter—this is where you declare and code your PowerScript procedures. After declaring a function, you will use the PowerScript editor to enter the code. You will call the functions from event scripts or other functions.

 Project painter—this allows you to create and maintain project objects. A project object contains all the information that is necessary for building application executables.

 Library painter—this is the utility for creating and managing PowerBuilder libraries. Libraries are repositories where the components of the applications reside.

 User Object painter—the developer can create a special type of custom object in this painter. After you create custom objects, you can use them just as if they were any native PowerBuilder control (such as a CommandButton). This is a more advanced topic that is covered later in this book.

 Debug—the PowerBuilder debugger helps you to test your application, and provides the features that are needed to track down and fix programming errors. You can set break points, single-step through the code, examine and change the values of variables, etc.

CHAPTER TWO

THE POWERSCRIPT LANGUAGE

This chapter covers the details of PowerBuilder's programming language, PowerScript (often referred to simply as script). PowerScript is a high-level, event-driven language modeled after BASIC and C and has nearly 500 built-in functions for the developer. PowerScript contains a number of object-oriented features; it allows communications between objects both by directly addressing the object and its attributes, and by sending messages between them.

PowerScript has a wide variety of data types. You can define a local or global scope for variables. You can also create shared variables that provide one value across different instances of an object.

The language contains flow-control constructs for the conditional execution of code and to implement looping. The language has many statements that are very similar to BASIC or C. For example, the flow control statements are IF, DO, FOR, and CASE.

All code execution is triggered by an event or by a message sent from another script. This is a fundamental trait of the event-driven paradigm. This will take some getting used to if you have no programming experience in this type of environment (such as Windows, Macintosh, or X Windows). You can attach PowerScript code to the PowerBuilder objects (such as windows, CommandButtons) by writing code for object events or object-level functions. You can also write functions that are used more generally and are available globally. You will write code for the events in which you are interested. In that code you may trigger other events or call other functions (either system or user-defined).

The PowerScript Language

Identifiers

Identifiers are tags that are used throughout PowerBuilder. Identifiers are used to name variables, controls, functions, labels, and other PowerBuilder objects. In PowerScript, identifiers can be up to 40 characters in length, must begin with a letter, and cannot contain spaces. In addition to the alpha-numeric characters, identifiers may also contain the following special characters:

- – minus (dash)
- _ underscore
- $ dollar sign
- # pound sign
- % percent sign

It is unusual for a programming language to let the minus sign be a character in identifiers and if you are not careful it can cause some unexpected problems. For example:

```
iLen-1
```

is a legal identifier. If you intended this to be an expression where 1 is to be subtracted from the current value of iLen, you are in for a surprise. Consider the following code:

```
iSize = iLen-1
```

When you compile this line of code you may receive an error stating that iLen-1 is an unknown identifier. This is because PowerBuilder has interpreted "iLen-1" to be an identifier and it cannot find a previous declaration for it. Fortunately, you can avoid this type of problem by disallowing the use of the minus sign in identifiers. To do this set the parameter DashesInIdentifiers to zero in the Preferences painter (under the PowerBuilder section). Alternatively you could set it to zero in the PB.INI file as follows:

```
PB.INI
[pb]
DashesInIdentifiers = 0
```

This turns off the option and the previous code example is interpreted in the way that you intended and the script will compile successfully. You should set this constraint as soon as you install PowerBuilder at your site, so that other developers cannot create identifiers with the dash. Otherwise, their code will fail to compile after you make this change.

PowerScript Text

You can enter PowerScript text in a free-form fashion. You can add spaces (but not within an identifier or reserved word) and indent the code as you wish to make the code more readable. Generally, each PowerScript statement should be put on its own separate line. You can put multiple script statements on a single line if you separate them with a semicolon. For example:

```
beep(1) ; MessageBox('Note', 'Hello'); beep(2)
```

Script code is case insensitive so that:

```
bFirstTime =  true
bfirsttime =  True
BFIRSTTIME = TRUE
```

are all the same to PowerBuilder. This applies to all identifiers, including function names. `OpenWithParm()` and `openwithparm()` are the same, but you may find the mixed-case version easier to read. This is the convention that is followed throughout this book.

Many developers use the underscore character to delineate words in their identifiers. For example:

```
b_first_time
```

is a Boolean variable and its value tells us if this is the first time through the code. I prefer to use mixed case to distinguish words instead of using the underscore character to separate them. For the previous example, I would have used:

```
bFirstTime
```

as the identifier for the Boolean, but you can choose whichever style you prefer. In the previous example, the first letter of the identifier is a **b**, which is used to mark the data type as a Boolean. This chapter includes a set of recommended naming conventions that will make the sharing of code and the maintenance of code easier.

Line Continuation

You can continue a code statement on the next line with the use of the ampersand (&) character. Place the **&** at the end of the line you wish to continue. The ampersand must be the last character on the line. This is easy to remember because & means *AND there is more to follow*. An example of line continuation is:

```
MessageBox("Status", "Successfully read " &
                  + string(idx) + " lines of text")
```

You can not break up an identifier by using the continuation character. The following is illegal.

```
iReturn = Message&
    Box('note', 'this message')
```

Comments

PowerScript permits comments to be added in two different forms: in single line and a block (multi-line) form. These forms of comments are the same as the one found in C and C++. A multi-line comment is placed between /* and */. Create a single line comment by using two slashes, //. This can appear anywhere on a line and causes the rest of the line to be interpreted as a comment. For example:

```
/*
    here is a multi-line
    comment
*/


/* it could also be used for a single line */

// or use this for a single line comment
beep(1) // this adds a comment to the end of a line
```

Block comments can be nested as in the next example.

```
int iSum
iSum = 1 + 2 /* add 1,2,and 4
 /* iSum will be equal to 7 at the end of this example */
   + 3 */ +4
```

NOTE You might expect an error in this example because the final "+4" looks like it is dangling on a line by itself. Lines broken up by multi-line comments do not need the continuation character.

Dot Notation

PowerScript allows the direct addressing of objects and their attributes (and functions) by using a "dot" notation syntax. For example, you can disable a CommandButton (cb_close) in the main window (w_main) by setting the button's enabled attribute to false with the following notation:

Command button

```
w_main.cb_close.enabled = FALSE.
```

You can set the focus on the cb_close CommandButton as follows:

```
cb_close.SetFocus()
```

The following alternative notation also works but is not the preferred style:

```
SetFocus(cb_close)
```

Here are a few additional examples:

1. `st_status.text = "OK"`   `// set the text attribute`
   `// of static text object`
   `// st_status`

2. `w_main.sle_count.text = "12"`   `// qualified reference`
   `// made from another window`

3. `w_main.title = "Hello"`   `// set the window caption`
   `// to "Hello"`

4. `dw_1.Retrieve()`   `// execute the retrieve`
   `// function for dw_1`

5. `cb_retrieve.Enable()`   `// enabled a button using`
   `// a user-defined function`

6. `w_main.m_file.m_exit.Disable()` `// qualifies window name,`
   `// menu name, MenuItem`

A control name is known throughout the window, and does not need any further qualification within that window. The window name is required if you are making the reference from outside the window. In example 1, the reference does not require a window name to qualify it if it is made within a script in the window or one of its objects. In example 2, the reference is being made from a window other than w_main, and therefore the qualification is required in order to locate the sle_count object.

A menu name (of a dropdown menu) is known to the MenuItems contained in it.

Data Types

PowerScript offers a wide variety of data types to the developer. This section covers each of the standard data types.

Boolean

The Boolean data type represents a logical condition. A variable of the Boolean data type can only have one of two values: TRUE or FALSE. Since PowerScript is case-insensitive, you could enter the value as true, false, True, False, etc. Boolean identifiers should begin with the letter **b**, such as bFirstTime or b_first_time.

Integer (or Int)

Integers are 16 bit signed whole number values in PowerScript. This means that an integer can hold a value between –32768 and +32767. Integer identifiers should begin with the letter **i** (sometimes **n** is used). For example, iValue or nItems.

UnsignedInteger (or UInt)

The unsigned integer is a 16 bit unsigned whole number value. It can range in value from 0 to 65535. Unsigned integer identifiers should begin with the letters **ui**, such as ui_size or uiSize.

Long

A long integer is a signed 32 bit whole number value. It can hold values between –2,147,483,648 and +2,147,483,647. Long identifiers should begin with the letter **l**, such as lSize or l_size.

Unsigned Long (or ULong)

An unsigned long is a 32 bit unsigned whole number. It can hold values between 0 and 4,294,967,295. Unsigned long identifiers should begin with the letters **ul**, such as ulSize or ul_size.

Decimal (or Dec)

The decimal type is a signed number with a decimal point such as –12.123. It has a maximum of 18 digits. To declare a decimal variable, include the number of post-decimal digits in the declaration. For example, to declare an array of five decimal variables that have 2 post-decimal digits, use the following declaration:

```
dec{2} money[5]
```

Decimal identifiers should begin with the letters **dec**, such as decCost or dec_cost.

Real

The real data type is a signed floating point number, such as 2.2E4. A real has a precision of 6 digits and a range of 1.17E-38 to 3.4E38. Rounding error will effect this type. Real identifiers should begin with the letter **r**, such as rTotals or r_total.

Double

The double is a signed floating point number with 15 digits of precision. It has a range of 2.2E-308 to 1.7E308. Double identifiers should begin with the letter **d**, such as dValue or d_value.

Date

The date data type takes the format YYYY-MM-DD, such as 1994-12-31. Date identifiers should begin with the letters **date**, such as dateStart or date_start.

Time

Time is formatted as HH:MM:SS:mmmmmm, such as 14:30:01:123456. Time identifiers should begin with the letter **t**, such as tStart or t_start.

DateTime

The DateTime data type has a format that combines the date and time into one value. It is most often used to read or write to the database. Use the function DateTime(date, time) to combine a date and time into a DateTime variable. Use Time(datetime), and Date(datetime) to convert a DateTime variable to a time or date data type respectively. DateTime identifiers should begin with the letters **dt**, such as dtDate or dt_timestamp.

Blob

The blob is a binary large object of up to 4,294,967,295 bytes in size. Blob identifiers should begin with the letters **blb**, such as blbImage or blb_image.

You can specify a size for a blob variable when you declare it. If you do not specify a size, then PowerBuilder will decide its size when you assign a value to it.

```
Blob{32000} blbDocument1
Blob blbImage1
```

The first example declares a blob with a length of 32,000 bytes. If you assign longer text to that blob, it will be truncated. The second declaration causes PowerBuilder to define the size when you assign a value to blbImage1. There are functions to manipulate the contents of a blob, which are covered later in this chapter.

The Enumerated Data Type

The enumerated data type is a special type used in the PowerScript language. This data type is used for setting characteristics of objects (or controls) and as arguments for functions with a label that is more meaningful than an integer (i.e. Maximized!). All the enumerated values are predefined by the PowerBuilder system, you cannot add to this predefined set as in other languages. Enumerated values always end with the exclamation character (**!**) to signal their special type.

For example the possible values for the style of arranging windows are Cascade!, Layer!, Tile!, which is far more descriptive than 0, 1, and 2. You could arrange all the currently open windows as follows:

```
w_main_mdi.ArrangeSheets (Cascade!)
```

You can find all the enumerated data type values by using the browser. In the browser, select the **Enumerated Object Type** RadioButton, click on the type in the objects ListBox (such as arrangetypes), and select the **Attributes** RadioButton in the Paste Category group. This lists the enumerated values in the lower listbox. (Figure 2.1)

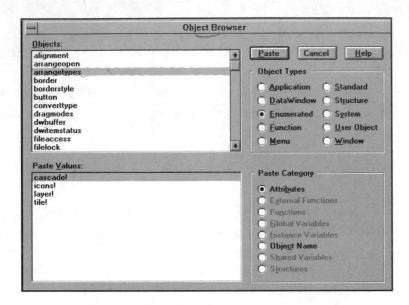

FIGURE 2.1 LISTING THE ARRANGETYPES ENUMERATED VALUES

Char

The char data type is a single ASCII character. You can have an array of type char, but in general you will use the string data type instead. Use the char array when you need to parse the array. Char identifiers should begin with the letter c, such as cChar1 or c_char1.

String

The string data type is an array of ASCII characters (60,000 maximum). String identifiers should begin with the letter s, such as sName or s_name.

String literals can use either single or double quote marks for delimiters. This is useful for including quote marks within the string, i.e. 'She said "Yes", before I asked'. String literals have a limit of 1024 characters. You can assign a string literal to a string variable.

PowerBuilder provides a number of functions for string manipulation. If you assign a string to a char variable, only the first character of the source is assigned to the target. You can assign a string to a char array, and you can assign a char array to a string. If the char array is bounded with a size smaller than the length of the string, the text will be truncated. Several examples follow.

EXAMPLE 1

```
char cChar
string sText
sText = 'hello'
cChar = sText // cChar holds 'h'
```

EXAMPLE 2

```
char cArray[20]
string sText, sHold
sText = 'hello'

 cArray[1] = 'h'
 cArray[2] = 'e'
 cArray[3] = 'l'
 cArray[4] = 'l'
 cArray[5] = 'o'   // cArray[6] is 0
 sHold = 'hello'
```

Strings can be concatenated using the plus sign:

```
string sFullName  = sFirst + ', ' + sLast
```

String comparisons are done directly by using the relational operators:

=   equality

<> not equal

>   greater than

>= greater than or equal

< less than

<= less than or equal

```
IF sText = 'abc' THEN ...
IF sLastName > 'M' THEN ....
```

You can use a character or character array in any function instead of a string. PowerBuilder will promote the char (or char array) to a string in the process.

Using Special ASCII Characters

You can assign special characters, such as the backspace, to a char variable by using the following set of codes (the tilde [~] is used as a marker).

   ~n   newline

   ~t   tab

   ~v   vtab

   ~r   return

   ~f   formfeed

   ~b   backspace

   ~"   quote

   ~'   tick

   ~~   tilde

You can also assign a value by entering the numeric value for any character by using the tilde.

   ~256   decimal

   ~hFF   hex

   ~o377   octal

The NULL Value

Since PowerBuilder is primarily for creating database applications, it is necessary for PowerScript to support the NULL value that is used in all relational database systems. A NULL value is not the same as a zero (for integers), and is not the same as a zero length string (for strings). It is a special marker that signifies an UNKNOWN value for a variable. You assign a NULL value to a variable by using the function SetNull(). You test for a NULL value by using the IsNull() function.

```
SetNull(sCompany)
bTest = IsNull(sCompany)
```

When you read data in from a database it is possible to read in NULL values, you must use the IsNull function to test for that value.

Classes

You can safely skip this section the first time you read this book. It presents some more advanced concepts that are not required reading for new developers.

PowerScript supports the object-oriented concept of classes and objects. When you create a new window (w_main for example), you are actually creating a class (an object type, a new data type).

When you open the window:

```
open (w_main)
```

you are actually opening an instance of that window. PowerBuilder has created an instance of the object type w_main and given it the same name (w_main) as the class. You could declare your own instances of w_main as follows:

```
w_main w_main1, w_main2

open(w_main1)
open(w_main2)
```

Notice how w_main is used as the data type for the w_main1 and w_main2 variables.

You could also create instances of a window by creating an array as follows:

```
w_child w_children[10]
int idx

FOR idx = 1 to 10
      open(w_children[idx])
      w_children[idx].x = idx * 100
      w_children[idx].y = idx * 100
NEXT
```

This example creates ten instances of a w_child window, cascading the child windows across the parent window.

You can also create instances of the predefined object types. These types include: CheckBox, CommandButton, DataWindow, DropDownListBox, EditMask, Graph, ListBox, MultiLineEdit, Oval, Picture, PictureButton, RadioButton, SingleLineEdit, UserObject, Window, Menu.

All of these object types are part of the system object hierarchy defined by PowerBuilder. You can view the object hierarchy in the Class browser as in Figure 2.2. (The Class browser is in the Library painter under the Utilities|Browse Class Hierarchy menu option)

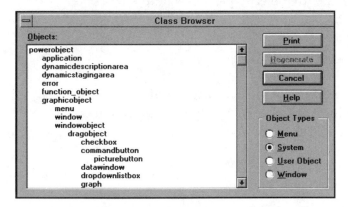

FIGURE 2.2 THE SYSTEM OBJECT HIERARCHY

You could use any of these classes as a data type. For example, you could create a CommandButton variable that could be assigned the name of an existing CommandButton (cb_close in this example). The variable can then be treated like an alias for cb_close.

```
commandbutton cb1
cb1 = cb_close
cb1.text = 'Exit'
cb1.enabled = true
```

All of this becomes more important when using the object-oriented features in PowerBuilder and will be covered in greater detail in the chapter on object-oriented programming, and the chapter on user-defined objects.

DECLARING VARIABLES

A variable is an instance of a data type. Variable declarations are of the form

```
<data type> <variable name>
```

The variable name is an identifier. Examples of several variable declarations follow:

```
int iCount
string sText            ← initialist
double dStart = 12.34
```

You can assign an initial value when you declare a variable. If you do not assign a value when the variable is declared, it will be initialized to a default value; zero for numeric data types, False for Booleans, and to an empty (zero length) string for the string data type.

Data Type	Default Initialization
Numeric	0
Boolean	False
Char	0
String	" "

You can manipulate numeric values with the set of arithmetic operators:

- =   assignment
- +   addition
- –   subtraction
- *   multiplication
- /   division
- ^   exponentiation

```
iValue = iCount * (iIndex - iOffset)
```

PowerScript supports C assignment short-hand in simple assignments *only*.

```
idx += 1 // increments idx
idx++    // also increments idx, but ++idx is not supported
```

Data Type Conversions

PowerBuilder performs implicit type conversion of different data types within an expression or a function argument. For expressions that contain numeric types of differing precision, the value of lower precision will be converted to the higher precision type. The result of an assignment will, of course, end in the precision of the target variable.

```
int      iCount
dec      decValue
int      iTotal
decValue = 2.5
```

```
iCount = 3
iTotal = iCount * decValue // iTotal will be 8
```

In this expression, iCount is converted to a decimal before the multiplication takes place. The result of the multiplication is converted to an integer and assigned to iTotal.

PowerBuilder supplies an entire set of data conversion functions for converting between dissimilar data types, such as strings and integers.

```
string sNumber = '123.45'
int iCount
iCount = Integer(sNumber)
```

TABLE 2.1 TYPE CONVERSION FUNCTIONS

FUNCTION	INPUT	OUTPUT
Char()	Blob, integer, string	Char
Dec()	String	Decimal
Double()	String	Double
Integer()	String	Integer
Long()	String	Long
Real()	String	Real
String()	Date, time, datetime, number	String
String()	String	Formatted String
String()	Blob	String
Time()	Datetime, string	Time
Time()	Integers	Time
Date()	Datetime, string	Date
Date()	Integers	Time
DateTime()	Date	DateTime

Arrays

You can create an array of any of the standard data types. You can also create arrays of other types such as windows, or user objects. Array notation uses square brackets to enclose the array index. Arrays can also be multi-dimensional. Array indexes, by default, begin with the value 1 and are bounded by the size of the array. You can explicitly set the index boundaries by defining them within the brackets.

```
int iBounds[-3 TO 3]
```

Unbounded (variable-length) arrays can be declared by omitting the size from the declaration. This is only permitted with single dimension arrays.

```
int iUnbounded[]
```

There is a performance penalty for expanding the size of unbounded arrays (since new space must be allocated). You can avoid this by setting the highest element in the array to some initial value. This forces the allocation of the array to occur at the time of the assignment, rather than allowing the allocation to occur each time you expand the array.

```
int iUnbounded[]
iUnbounded[999] = 0
```

The UpperBound function returns the upper bound of an array. It accepts an optional second argument. In this second argument, you specify the number of the dimension for which you want to return the upper bound.

```
int iCount[5,10]
string sName[]
int iSize

iSize = UpperBound(iCount,1)    // Returns 5
iSize = UpperBound(iCount, 2)   // Returns 10
iSize = UpperBound(sName)       // Returns 0; nothing assigned
                                // so far
sName[12] = "Kristen"
iSize = UpperBound(sName)       // Returns 12
```

Some other examples of array declarations and assignments follow:

```
int iCount[10]
int iSet[3] = {1,2,3}
int iMulti[3,3,3]
long lBounds[-3 to 3]

iMulti[1,2,3] = 12
lBounds[-2] = 123
iCount[1] = 1
iCount[10] = 5
```

VARIABLE SCOPE OPTIONS

PowerScript variables have several different scoping options that determine the range of visibility. These options are implemented in a manner similar to C language variables in the Windows environment. The variable scopes are local, global, instance, and shared. In general, you should choose the most restrictive scope that is appropriate for each variable.

Global Scope

The global scope is the least restrictive of all the scoping options. A global variable will be known (visible and usable) throughout the entire application. It is good programming practice to limit the use of global variables as much as is possible.

You declare a variable as global by selecting the **Declare|Global** menu option (from within the Window, User Object, or PowerScript painter). This opens the Declare Global Variables dialog shown in Figure 2.3. (This can also be reached from the Menu and Function painters.)

Enter the data type and the name of the variable on a new line in the ListBox and hit the **Enter** key to close the dialog. If you wish to declare multiple variables, use the **Control+Enter** key combination to move to the next line in the ListBox instead of closing it. Use the letter *g* to prefix the name of your global variables, such as int g_iCount.

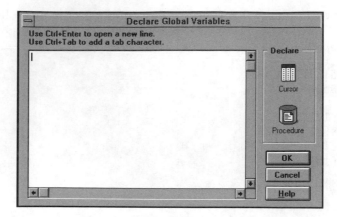

FIGURE 2.3 DECLARING A GLOBAL VARIABLE

Local Scope

The local scope is the most common, and most restrictive option. When you declare a variable within your script (or function) text, it is defined with a local scope. That variable will only be known in the script (or function) in which it was declared. You should declare most of your variables as local variables, unless you definitely need to extend access to the variable beyond the immediate locality where it was declared.

Instance Variables

You declare instance variables within the context of an object. Instance variables have a scope limited to the object level for that occurrence (instance) of the object. The object level can be application, window, menu, or user-object. This means that the variable will be known only within that object (to that object and the objects that it contains). For example, if you declared an instance variable in a menu, it will be known only to the elements of that menu.

You declare instance variables by selecting the Declare|Instance menu option as in Figure 2.4, and by entering the declaration on a new line in the ListBox. Use the letter *i* to prefix the name of your instance variables. In Figure 2.4, the variable was declared at the window level (from a window named w_main) and was given an initial value of 1. Since the instance variable was declared at the window level, it will also be known to all the objects contained in the w_main window (such as CommandButtons, ListBoxes etc.). This variable will not be visible to other windows or the objects in those other windows (except as noted in the next paragraph). One additional note, if you open another instance of w_main, the initial value of i_iCount will always be 1, regardless of any changes of value that had been made to the i_iCount variable in any other previous instance(s) of w_main. In other words, each instantiation of w_main will have its own version of i_iCount to manipulate.

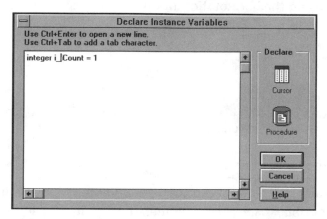

FIGURE 2.4 DECLARING AN INSTANCE VARIABLE

Using Dot Notation with Instance Variables

You can access an instance variable externally by using dot notation to qualify the object and variable name. For example in Figure 2.4, the variable i_iCount was declared as a window level instance variable (in w_main). In the window w_other, access this variable as w_main.i_iCount. In general this is a practice to be limited as much as possible, it will make maintenance difficult if the i_iCount variable is changed. It is even possible to prevent this type of reference by using PowerScript access levels.

Variable Access Levels

Access levels give you another level of control over the scope of instance variables. You can limit, or prevent external references to instance variables by setting the variable's *access level*. The access level is part of the instance variable's declaration and specifies which scripts in the application will have access to the variable. The possible access levels are public, private, and protected.

The Public Access Level

The default access level is public. This means that any script can access the variable by using the dot notation that was demonstrated earlier. The following declaration:

```
integer i_iCount
```

is the same as

```
Public Integer i_iCount
```

The Private Access Level

The Private access level limits variable visibility to the scripts in the object where the variable was declared. If our example integer i_iCount had been declared with a Private access level, it would not be accessible from the w_other window.

```
Private integer i_iCount
```

The Protected Access Level

The third access level is called Protected. Protected access is similar to Private access, but extends it to allow access (to the variable) from scripts in other objects that are inherited from the original object.

This means that window w_other can only access the i_iCount instance variable in w_main if it had been inherited (derived from) the w_main window (either directly or indirectly) when it was created. An example of each type of access level is included in the declarations in the next example. The example also demonstrates group assignment of access levels by creating sections for Private and Protected access levels.

```
Public int i_idx   // the same as int i_idx
Private int i_iCount
Protected int i_iTest
Private:
int i_iPriv1
int i_iPriv2
Protected:
int i_iProtected1
int i_iProtected2
```

The Shared Scope

Shared scope is the last option for a variable scope. A shared scope variable has a scope that is very similar to that of an instance variable in that it is also at the object level (the object can be application, window, menu, or user object). The difference is that the shared scope variable is known and accessible for all instances of that object. Sometimes there are multiple instances of an object (window, menu, or user-object) during the course of the application. There may be values that you would like to maintain and to share between these instances. A shared variable retains its value across instances, and therefore the instances of the object *share* that variable. You could use a shared variable to count the number of times that a window is opened.

You declare variables with shared scope by selecting the **Declare|Shared** menu option, as shown in Figure 2.5. Use the letter *s* as the prefix for your shared variables. In this example, in the first instance of w_main the initial value of s_iCount is 1. If you open another instance of w_main, the initial value of s_iCount is equal to that of the last change of value that had been made to s_iCount in the previous instance(s) of w_main.

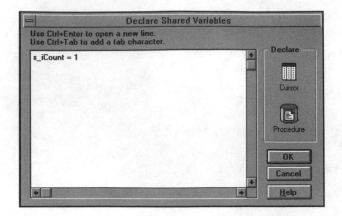

FIGURE 2.5 DECLARING A SHARED VARIABLE

Labeling Scope in Identifiers

It is recommended that your identifier contain a letter that labels the scope of a variable. An underscore is also used to set off the scope.

g_ global

s_ shared

i_ instance

This makes it easy to avoid name collisions. If you use the same name for two different variables it is important that you understand PowerBuilder's order in resolving variables.

Resolving Duplicate Variable Names

It is possible, but not recommended, to use the same identifier to name two or more variables (of different scope). The order in which PowerBuilder searches for variables is:

1. local variables
2. shared variables

3. global variables

4. instance variables

If you had declared a global variable iCount, and also a local variable with the same name, the local variable will be used. This may cause unexpected results if this was unintentional. If the global variable had been named g_iCount, there would be no confusion.

Passing Variables in Function Calls

You can pass variables in function calls either by value or by reference. When passed by value, it is actually a copy of the variable that is made available in the called functions. All changes made to that variable in the called function are limited to the copy, and the changes are not visible back in the calling function.

If the variable has been passed by reference, this works differently. Any change made to the reference variable in the called function will be visible in the calling function. This is because the two functions are actually sharing a reference to a single variable. So all changes are actually made to the original variable in the calling function. This is very similar to how pointers are used in the C language, but the declaration and use is different.

Declaring a Reference Variable

A reference variable is defined when you create the declaration of a function's arguments. When you define a function, you must specify the data type for each argument, and you must specify whether the argument is passed by reference or by value as shown in Figure 2.6.

This declaration is all that is required. Neither the calling function nor the called function use any other notation for the "by reference" variables.

When you are using reference string variables in function calls to Windows DLLs there is one special caveat. You must allocate the space that is needed before making the function call. For example:

```
int rc
```

```
string sReturnName
sReturnName = space(20) // essential statement if calling a DLL
rc = TestCallDLL(sReturnName)
```

In this example, the calling function allocated a space of 20 characters for the string sReturnName. If this statement is left out, you will receive a runtime error (or worse) when the TestCallDLL function assigns a string to the sReturnName string variable. This is an important detail to remember when accessing DLLs.

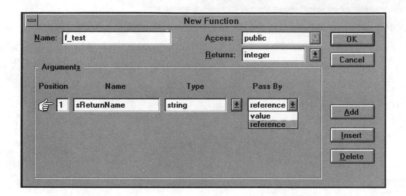

FIGURE 2.6 DECLARING A FUNCTION ARGUMENT

POWERSCRIPT LANGUAGE STATEMENTS

PowerScript has several statements that provide branching. We will look at the IF statement and the CHOOSE CASE statements first.

The IF Statement

The IF statement has several different forms, all of which may be familiar to you if you know BASIC. The first and simplest form is the single line version.

```
IF <condition> THEN action
```

This executes the action if the condition is true. Multiple statements can be combined within the action clause with the use of the semicolon (if there is no ELSE clause).

Examples:

```
IF iCount > 99 THEN iCount = 0; beep(1)
IF iCount > 99 THEN iCount = 0 ELSE iCount = iCount + 1
```

The relational operators that can be used for comparison are:

=   equal

<> not equal

>   greater than

>= greater than or equal

<   less than

<= less than or equal

Operator Precedence

The order of precedence for the mathematical and relational operators is:

MATHEMATICAL OPERATORS

() parenthesis

+,– unary

^

*, /

+, –

the relational operators (including =, <>, >=, etc.)

NOT

AND

OR

More complex conditions can be created by using the logical operators AND, OR, and NOT. Parenthesis are used, in the same manner as other languages, to specify the order of the evaluation. If you nest parenthesis, the inner most set is evaluated first.

```
IF sLastName = 'Smith' AND &
   (sFirstName = 'John' OR sFirstName = 'Mary')
     THEN bValid = false
```

In this example, the condition is true if the last name is Smith and the first name is Mary or John. Without the parenthesis, the condition is true if the last name is Smith and the first name is John, OR if the first name is Mary (regardless of the last name). This is because the AND has higher precedence than the OR operator. It is the same as if the statement had been written as follows:

```
IF (sLastName = 'Smith' AND sFirstName = 'John') &
    OR sFirstName = 'Mary' THEN bValid = false
```

The next form of the IF statement lets multiple statements be grouped together. The ELSE clause is optional.

```
IF <condition> THEN
   <action1>
ELSE
   <action2>
END IF
```

The <action1> and <action2> labels can be replaced by one or more PowerScript statements.

Example:

```
IF sLastName > 'M'   THEN
                     iCount = iCount + 1
                     beep(1)
ELSE
                     iCount = iCount - 1   // or iCount -= 1
                     beep(2)
END IF
```

The last form of the IF statement adds the ELSEIF clause which can occur multiple times. This form is used for checking two or more conditions. The final ELSE clause is optional.

```
IF <condition1> THEN
    <action1>
ELSEIF <condition2> THEN
    <action2>
ELSE
    <action3>
END IF
```

Example:

```
IF x = 1 THEN
    x = y
ELSEIF x = 2 THEN
    BEEP(2)
ELSE
    x = 0
END IF
```

The CHOOSE CASE Statement

The CHOOSE CASE construct is very flexible, and can handle several forms of CASE conditional expressions. It is a better choice, and is much clearer and easier to code, than using multiple ELSEIF clauses in an IF statement. The CHOOSE CASE construct also has better performance (executes faster) than the IF THEN construct.

```
CHOOSE CASE <expression>
    CASE <item>
        <statementblock>
    CASE ELSE
        <statementblock>
END CHOOSE
```

The final CASE ELSE clause is optional. The possible forms of the CASE expression are: a single value, a list of values, a range of values, a relational operator, or combinations of any of these.

A single value is simply listed after the keyword CASE. To create a list, add additional values with a comma (,) between each. For example CASE 1, 3, 5.

A range of values is expressed using the TO keyword. For example, CASE 1 TO 5.

Use the IS keyword with a relational operator, as in CASE IS > 5 or CASE IS <> 'Smith'.

You can combine these forms by using commas, as in CASE 1, 11 TO 15, IS >999.

Example:

```
CHOOSE CASE iCount
    CASE 9, 1 to 5
        iCount += 1
    CASE IS > 5
        iCount = 0
    CASE  -1
        iCount = -iCount
    CASE ELSE
        iCount = -1
END CHOOSE
```

Notice that the "CASE IS > 5" condition never receives iCount with the value 9 because that condition was handled in the previous CASE condition.

LOOPING CONSTRUCTS

PowerScript has several ways to implement looping. The DO...LOOP construct will be covered first. This has four different forms.

```
DO
    <statementblock>
LOOP UNTIL <condition>

DO
    <statementblock>
LOOP WHILE <condition>
```

```
DO UNTIL <condition>
     <statementblock>
LOOP

DO WHILE <condition>
     <statementblock>
LOOP
```

All forms have DO at the beginning and LOOP at the end of the loop. The placement of the WHILE or UNTIL changes the behavior of the loop. The most significant point to notice is that the first two forms will execute the code inside the loop at least once, since the evaluation is not done until the end of the loop. The statements inside the loop for the last two forms may not be executed at all. The WHILE forms execute the loop as long as the condition is true. The UNTIL forms execute the loop as long as the condition is not true.

Examples:

```
rc = 0
DO WHILE rc = 0
     rc = dotest()
LOOP

DO UNTIL rc = 100
     rc = FetchAgain()
LOOP

DO
     rc = FetchAgain()
LOOP UNTIL rc = 100

DO
     rc = FetchAgain()
LOOP WHILE rc = 0
```

The FOR...NEXT Loop

The other looping construct in PowerScript is the FOR...NEXT statement. This is identical to the form that it takes in most versions of the BASIC language.

```
FOR <varname>=<start> TO <end> STEP <increment>
     <statementblock>
NEXT
```

A variable is initialized at the start of the loop and the statements in the statement block are executed. When NEXT is executed, the variable is incremented by the STEP value and the result is then compared against the end value. If the value is still within the start-to-end range, the loop is executed again.

The STEP clause is optional. If the STEP clause is not included, the variable is incremented by 1, if the start value is less than the end value. If the end value is less than the start value, then the loop increments the variable by –1.

Example:

```
FOR iCount = 1 TO 10 STEP 2
     dosomething(iCount)
NEXT
```

This first example initializes the iCount variable to 1. Each time through the loop it is incremented by 2 (1,3,5 etc.). The loop executes as long as iCount is less than or equal to 10. The value of iCount is 11 when it exits the loop.

```
FOR iCount = 10 TO 1
     dosomething(iCount)
NEXT
```

In this example, the STEP value has not been specified. It will default to STEP –1, since the start value is greater than the end value. The value of iCount will be 0 when it exits the FOR loop.

The CONTINUE and EXIT

The CONTINUE and EXIT statements can be used with either a DO or FOR loop. The CONTINUE statement causes the next iteration of the loop to begin immediately skipping any remaining statements in the loop.

This example executes the call to the DoSomething function for the iCount values 1 through 4, and then 6 through 10.

```
iCount = 0
DO
     iCount = iCount + 1
     IF iCount = 5 THEN CONTINUE
     DoSomething(iCount)
LOOP WHILE iCount <= 10
```

The EXIT statement causes an immediate exit from the loop. Execution will then continue with the statement that immediately follows the end of the loop. For example:

```
FOR idx = 1 to 999
     IF iValue[idx] < 0 THEN EXIT
     DoSomething(iValue[idx])
NEXT
```

In this example, the execution of the FOR loop terminates if any value of the iValue array is found to be less than zero.

DO and FOR loops can be nested. In nested loops, CONTINUE and EXIT only apply to the immediate (innermost) loop that they are in. For example:

```
int iArray[10,3]
FOR idx = 1 to 10
    FOR jdx = 1 to 3
        IF idx + jdx = 5 THEN CONTINUE
        iArray[idx,jdx] = idx + jdx
    NEXT
NEXT
```

In this example, the inner FOR loop skips the iArray assignment anytime that idx + jdx is equal to five. The CONTINUE has no affect on the outer loop.

The GOTO Statement

The GOTO statement causes program execution to jump to the referenced label's location. The label must be within the same function or script. The label is any legal identifier terminated with a colon. The identifier must be the first text on its line. In the next example, the GOTO jumps to x2: and skips over the beep(1) statement.

```
GOTO x2
x1:
beep(1)
x2: DoSomething()
```

The HALT Statement

The HALT statement forces the application to terminate. This is most often used to shutdown the application after a serious error has occurred.

HALT CLOSE does the same thing but triggers the application object's CLOSE event before terminating.

The RETURN Statement

The RETURN statement causes the script (or function) to end and returns control to the calling procedure (or to the system). In a function, you can specify a return value with this statement. For example:

```
//Function f_calc
iValue = Calc(iArgument1)
RETURN iValue
```

CREATE and DESTROY

The CREATE statement creates an instance of an object of the specified class. DESTROY deallocates the object. For example:

```
transaction Dbtrans1
Dbtrans1 = CREATE transaction
// use DbTrans1
DESTROY Dbtrans1
```

CALL

The CALL statement is used to call an ancestor object's script from a descendant object. This will be discussed in greater detail in the chapter on inheritance.

To execute a script in an ancestor window use the following:

```
CALL w_sales::open
```

To call a script in an ancestor object in an ancestor window use the following:

```
CALL w_sales`cb_calc::clicked
```

THE SPECIAL RESERVED WORDS

PowerBuilder has 4 special keywords that are used to make a reference to an object without having to specifies its name.

- **This**—used for a reflexive reference to the object itself (window, control, or user object).
- **Parent**—refers to the window that owns or contains the object making the reference.
- **ParentWindow**—this is a reference from a MenuItem referring to the window to which it is attached.
- **Super**—refers to the ancestor script.

This

Use the reserved word This to make a reflexive reference. It is a reference to the object itself (such as a window, control, MenuItem, or user object).

For example, assume that you have a CommandButton labeled "Close Cursor". The purpose of the CommandButton is to close a database cursor after performing a number of fetches against it. In the script for the

Clicked event for this CommandButton, you would close the cursor. You could also disable the Close Cursor CommandButton in this script since the cursor could not be closed again (until it was reopened). This is done in the next example; the Open Cursor CommandButton is also enabled. The Close Cursor CommandButton Clicked event would contain the following lines:

```
//in cb_close_cursor clicked event
Close Cursor1;
This.enabled = False          // cursor is closed so
                              // disable this button
cb_open_cursor.enabled = True // enable that button, so user
                              // could reopen Cursor1
```

The second line (This.enabled = False) is equal to:

```
cb_close_cursor.enabled = False
```

Parent

The reserved word Parent is used most often in the script for an object that is contained in a window. In this case, Parent is a reference to the containing window and is the same as using the name of the window. The object could be a control, such as a CommandButton, a ListBox, or a RadioButton. One of the most common uses is in a CommandButton labeled "Close" placed on a window to close the window. For example:

```
//cb_close Clicked event
Parent.title = "Good-bye"
Close(Parent)
```

The first statement changes the title of the window to "Good-bye" (if only briefly). The second statement closes the window that contains the Close CommandButton. If the window's name was w_main, the statement is the same as the following:

```
w_main.title = 'Good-bye'
Close(w_main)
```

The advantage of using the Parent reserved word is that the same button and code could be used for windows with different names. Another advantage is that it clearly expresses the relationship between the Close button and the unnamed window that it closes.

Using Parent in a MenuItem

If you use the Parent reserved word in a MenuItem script, it has a different meaning. In this case, the word Parent refers to the menu (the next higher MenuItem) that contains the MenuItem. You can use this to enable or disable a menu. The reserved word This can be used to check or uncheck the MenuItem.

```
This.Checked = True
Parent.Disable( )
```

This example checks the current MenuItem and disables the next higher MenuItem.

For a cascading menu, the following disables the next higher MenuItem and also unchecks it:

```
Parent.Checked = False
Parent.Disable()
```

Using Parent in a User Object

In a custom user object, the reference Parent (in one of the controls added to the user object) refers to the user object control. This is not really so surprising, the user object control is really a window on which the custom control is built. In a custom user object, you could use the following statements:

```
Parent.enabled = false
Parent.visible = false
```

The first statement disables the entire custom user object, so that none of the controls that it contains can be used.

The second statement hides the user object. If you include the second statement in a normal CommandButton in a window, it makes the window invisible.

If you experiment, you may find that you can use the reserved word Parent with standard user objects, to some degree. In a standard user object (uo_cb) that is based on a CommandButton, the code:

```
this.text = Parent.ClassName()
close(Parent)
```

changes the CommandButton text to the name of the window and then closes the window. This has limited usefulness. The standard user object is actually parented by a "graphicobject" type, which only has two attributes visible and a tag. So these are the only attributes that you can refer to in the scripts for a standard user object (the standard user object's Parent picks up the attributes of a window at run-time).

ParentWindow

Use the reserved word ParentWindow only in a MenuItem script. In a MenuItem script, ParentWindow is a reference to the window that contains the menu. If window w_main contains menu m_app1, a reference in m_app1 to ParentWindow is like using the name w_main (but with the limitation mentioned in the next paragraph).

In the discussion about the reserved word Parent, an example was given that closed a window with a CommandButton, using the statement Close(Parent). If you want to close a window with a menu option, use the statement:

```
Close(ParentWindow)
```

The ParentWindow reserved word has a limitation. You can not combine it with a control name to access a control's attribute. So the following reference to a CommandButton's enabled attribute is illegal:

```
ParentWindow.cb_test.enabled = False
```

Remember that a MenuItem script is the only place where you can use the ParentWindow reserved word. It is preferred over hard-coding the window name. So instead of the following:

```
w_main_mdi.ArrangeSheets (Cascade!)
```

use:

```
ParentWindow.ArrangeSheets (Cascade!)
```

Super

Super is a reference used in the script of an inherited object to refer to the script in its immediate ancestor. Super will be discussed in more detail in the chapter on inheritance. Use the keyword as in the following:

```
Call Super::Clicked
```

This example calls the clicked event script in the immediate ancestor of the cb_calculate CommandButton. This is equivalent to the following, more verbose call that does the same thing (assuming the name of the ancestor window is w_ancestor):

```
Call w_ancestor`cb_calculate::Clicked
```

POWERSCRIPT STRUCTURES

A structure groups a set of variables together. You can then reference the group with a single name, so that they can be treated as a unit. For example, you could create an employee structure that holds the name, ID, address, and phone number for each employee. The elements of a structure can be PowerScript variables and/or other structures.

Global Structures

Structure definitions also have scope, which can be global or object level. Global structure definitions are visible throughout the entire application.

You create global structures in the Structure painter. Click on the **Struct** icon (on the PowerBar) will open the Select Structure dialog window (Figure 2.7).

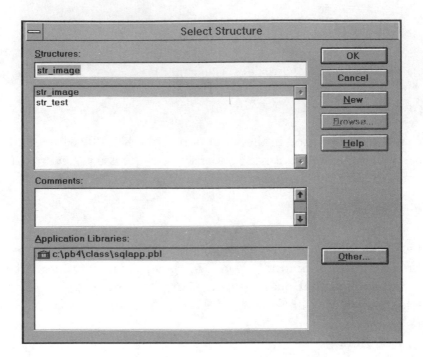

FIGURE 2.7 SELECT STRUCTURE DIALOG

In this panel you can edit an existing structure. To do so, select the directory and library, and then select the structure. This takes you to the Modify Structure dialog window shown in Figure 2.8.

To create a new structure, click on the **New** button in the Select Structure dialog. This takes you to the New Structure dialog which is essentially the same as the Modify Structure dialog shown in Figure 2.8.

In this dialog you can insert new elements to the structure, delete elements from the structure, and save the structure into a PowerBuilder library.

You can locate global structures in the browser by selecting the Structures Object Types RadioButton. If you the select the Attributes

RadioButton in the Paste Category group, the browser enumerates the elements of the selected structure in the Paste Values ListBox.

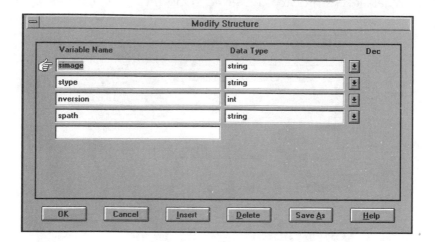

FIGURE 2.8 MODIFY STRUCTURE DIALOG

Object-Level Structures

Object-level structure definitions are scoped just like instance variables. They are visible only within the object where you defined the structure. To create object level structures in the corresponding object painter (such as the Window or Menu painter) by selecting the **Declare|Structure** menu option. Figure 2.9 shows the Select Structure in Window dialog opened when you create a window-level structure.

You can also locate object-level structures in the browser, but in a slightly different manner than locating global structures. First, locate the object where the structure was defined (such as the w_main window), then select the **Structures Paste Category** RadioButton.

Defining versus Declaring Structures

As shown, you can define structures on two levels, but this should not be confused with declaring instances of them. Where you define a structure determines when and how the definition is loaded into memory. The global structure defined in the Structure painter can be declared as a global, instance, shared, or local variable when an instance of the structure is created. The object-level structure is restricted to instance, shared, or local scope.

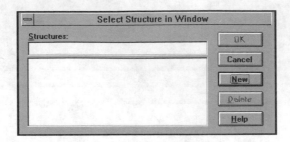

FIGURE 2.9 SELECT STRUCTURE DIALOG

Defining a New Structure

To create a structure, open the **New Structure** dialog, add each of the elements, and then name the structure. Figure 2.8 shows an example of a str_image structure definition. For each element, you must enter a name and the data type for the element.

The str_image structure is defined at the global level. After you have created this structure, you can use it as follows:

(from a script in the window w_embedded_sql)

```
str_image image
image.sImage = sle_image.text
image.sType = sle_type.text
image.nVersion = integer(sle_version.text)
image.sPath = sle_path.text
f_str_image (image)   // the image structure is passed as an
                      // argument to a function
OpenWithParm(w_test, image) // the image structure is passed
                            // to the window open event
```

In the example, the line OpenWithParm(w_test, image) passes the structure as an opening parameter to the w_test window. The w_test window's open event receives the structure on the message object's powerobjectparm attribute. That attribute was assigned to image_str to be able to access the structures attributes.

(in the function f_str_image)

```
MessageBox('Image Structure', x.sImage + '.' + x.sType + &
      string(x.nVersion) + ' ' + x:sPath)
return 0
```

In the line "f_str_image (image)", the structure is passed as an argument to the f_str_image function. In the function f_str_image the argument is declared as a structure as follows:

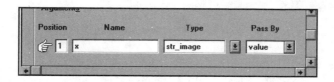

FIGURE 2.10 F_STR_IMAGE ARGUMENT DECLARATION

Within the function f_str_image, the name of the structure is x, and the elements are referred to as x.sImage etc.

(in the window w_test open event)

```
str_image image_str
image_str = message. powerobjectparm
sName = image_str.sImage
```

Object-Level Structures

You could define a structure at the window level. Suppose that the str_customer structure is being defined at the window level (w_embedded_sql). In the window, choose the **Declare|Window Structure** menu option and then define the structure in the same manner as described earlier. This str_customer structure will only be known to the w_embedded_sql window, the objects and controls in this window, and its children.

After you have created this structure, declare an instance variable of the str_customer type. After you have created this variable, use it as follows:

(in the window w_embedded_sql, Declare|Instance Variables...)

```
str_customer i_customer1
```

(Then in one of the w_embedded_sql events.)

```
str_customer customer2
i_customer1.sName = 'David McClanahan'
i_customer1.Id = 123
customer2 = i_customer1
```

(in the window w_test, a child of w_embedded_sql)

```
sName = w_embedded_sql.i_customer1.sName
fw_total_sales(w_embedded_sql.i_customer1)
```

In the last line of this example, a structure is passed as an argument to the fw_total_sales function. This reference must be qualified by including the name of the window. This qualification is required because the i_customer1 variable was declared at the window (w_main) instance level and is not known globally.

It is also possible to define a structure at the global level, and then to create an instance of a structure variable at the object level. You cannot create a global structure variable of a structure type that was defined as the window level. The scope of the structure declaration and the scope of the variable are two different aspects of the process.

POWERBUILDER FUNCTIONS

PowerBuilder has nearly 500 built-in functions providing a wide range of functionality such as numeric and string processing, and data conversion for your applications. You should make a couple of passes through the list of functions in the Help system to become familiar with the types of functions that are available. From your previous programming experience, you will know what kind of functions should be available, and often the hardest part of locating a function is just finding the name of the function. The browser and help system will assist your search.

User-Defined Functions

Even though PowerBuilder provides hundreds of built-in functions, you will need to create functions of your own. You create these *user-defined functions* in the Function painter. After you have created the user-defined functions, you can call them from your other script code just as if they were one of the PowerBuilder built-in functions. User-defined functions are created using the PowerScript language. The process is almost the same as writing code for an event, except that user-defined functions can have arguments (parameters) and a return value, and are not associated with an event.

User-defined functions have scope, either global or object level. Global functions have the same visibility as global variables and can be called from anywhere in your application, just like the built-in PowerBuilder functions that can be used by any object. Define a function with global scope when it provides a general functionality that may be used by various types of objects in your application.

You can define object level user-defined functions at the application, window, menu, or user-object level. This type of user-defined function has a scope like the PowerBuilder functions that are defined for a specific type of object (like menuitem1.Check()). Define a function with an object-level scope when you want to limit the use of that function to a single type of object.

To create or edit a global function you must use the Function painter. Click on the **Func** icon on the PowerBar to create a function. This will open the Select Function dialog window as shown in Figure 2.11.

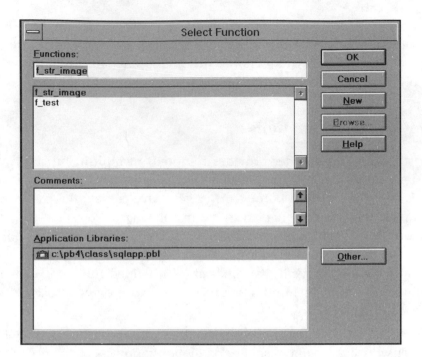

FIGURE 2.11 SELECT FUNCTION DIALOG

In this dialog, you can edit an existing function by selecting the library and the function name. This opens the Function painter and you can edit the code. The Function painter is essentially the PowerScript painter with just a few variations. When you are in the Function painter there are only two list-boxes, the Paste Global listbox and the Paste Argument listbox. The Paste Argument listbox contains the names of the function parameters that you defined when you declared the function (in the New Function dialog); this will let you paste the arguments into your code.

Edit the function declaration by selecting the **Edit|Function Declaration...** menu option. This opens the Function Declaration dialog shown in Figure 2.12.

To create a new function, click on the **New** CommandButton in the Select Function dialog, this will open the New Function dialog window, to essentially the same as the Function Declaration dialog (Figure 2.12).

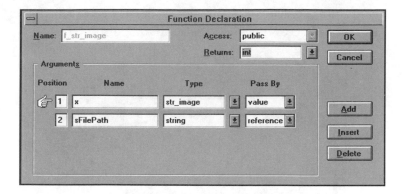

FIGURE 2.12 EDITING A FUNCTION DECLARATION

In this dialog, you define a name for the function, select a return type, and add any arguments that are passed in the function call. The recommended convention is to use f_ as the prefix for global functions, such as f_calc_tax. A set of recommended prefixes for other types of user-defined functions is listed in Table 2.2.

A global function has an access level of public. You can set the access level to public, private, or protected.

Object-Level Functions

To create an object-level function, first open the painter for the object for which you intend to define the function. Then choose the **Declare|Object Functions...** menu selection. The actual text for this menu option will vary according to the type of object that you are editing. For example, for user objects the menu selection is **Declare|User Object Functions...** and for windows it is **Declare|Window Functions...**.

This opens the Select Function dialog window as shown in Figure 2.13. In this dialog window, you can edit an existing function or create a new function.

Clicking on the **New** CommandButton opens the New Function dialog window (similar to Figure 2.12). In the New Function dialog you define a name for the function, select a data type for the return value, and add any arguments that are passed in the function call. For an object-level function you can also set the access level to public, private, or protected.

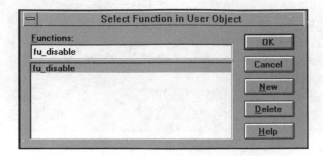

FIGURE 2.13 SELECT FUNCTION DIALOG

The recommendation conventions for function name prefixes is:

TABLE 2.2 RECOMMENDED FUNCTION NAME PREFIXES

PREFIX	OBJECT-LEVEL
f_	global
fa_	application
fw_	window
fm_	menu
fu_	user-object

Function Return Value Type

Most functions return a value, the default data type of the return value is an integer. To choose another data type for the return value, select from the Returns dropdown listbox. You can also decide not to return a value from the function. This is less usual, but specify this by choosing **None** from the Returns dropdown listbox. If you don't need the return value, another technique is to select an integer return type and return a zero. You can also ignore the return value if you wish.

Function Argument List

You can define arguments to be used for the function. To define an argument, you name the argument, specify its data type, and then declare whether the argument is to be passed by value or by reference. Arguments can be used with user object data types or structures. This type of data type does not appear in the Type listbox, but if you enter the data type it will be allowed. In Figure 2.12, the first argument is a str_image structure passed by value. The second argument is a string passed by reference so that it may be assigned a value.

As many arguments as you need can be defined for your function. Just click the **Add** CommandButton to add a new argument. Click on **Insert** to add a new argument at the current position in the list. Click on **Delete** to remove the currently selected argument from the list.

Standard User-Objects and User-Defined Functions

Though you cannot define an object-level function at the control level (such as a CommandButton or listbox), you can define a function for a standard user-object. Since the standard-user object is based on a standard type of control (such as a CommandButton), you can achieve the desired result. This is essentially the same as adding a method to a class in object-oriented languages.

Even though functions are defined at the object-level, you can access these functions from outside the object using dot-notation (described earlier). For example, suppose a user-defined function was created for a standard user-object based on a CommandButton and this function was used to disable the user-object. For this example, assume that the user-object was added to a window and named cb_close. The following code can call this function from another object in the window:

```
cb_close.fu_disable ()
```

or from another window by using:

```
w_main.cb_close.fu_disable()
```

Function Access Level

The access levels for functions are the same as for instance variables. Public access lets the function to be referenced externally using dot notation. The Private access level restricts access to scripts within the object. The Protected access level restricts access to scripts within the object, or within objects that are inherited from this object.

A Sample Function

The next example shows the code for a simple window-level function that displays the current database status information in three fields on the window. The function is named fw_db_status, has three arguments, and returns 1 if there is no error, and a 0 if there is a database error.

Function:	fw_db_status		
Arguments:	SQLCode	long	by value
	SQLDBCode	long	by value
	SQLErrText	string	by value
Returns:	Integer		

```
st_dbcode.text = string(sqldbcode)
st_sqlcode.text = string(sqlcode)
mle_dbtext.text = sqlerrtext
IF sqlcode >= 0 THEN return 1 ELSE return 0
```

After you have created a user-defined function, it is available in the Object Browser for pasting into your code, just like built-in functions. If the function is a global function, select the **Function Object Type** RadioButton. If the function is an object-level function, first locate the object in the Objects listbox, and then click on the **Functions Paste Category** RadioButton. The listing for the function also includes the argument list.

The global function names also appear on the list of user-defined functions, which is available with the **Edit|Paste Function...** menu option in the PowerScript painter (click the **User-define** radio button).

THE POWERSCRIPT DEBUGGER

The PowerScript debugger provides most of the expected features for debugging including:

- **breakpoints**—execution can be stopped at any line of code in your application.

- **single-step code execution**—steps line by line through the code.

- **variable access**—examines and changes the value of any variable.

- **watch points**—defines a list of watch point variables.

The debugger is very good, and provides the basic functions necessary to debug your application. There are a few limitations that you will have to work with in the current version of the debugger. Currently there is no "step-over" function. You can only step into each function. The work around is to set a breakpoint at the line after the function call. You can not usefully set breakpoints within the GetFocus or Activate events, because the debugger would receive the focus and become active. This is a result of the complexity of the event-driven paradigm. You cannot examine variables after the execution of the last line of a script or function. The solution to this is to add an additional line to the code (a return statement will not do).

Start the debugger by selecting the **File|Debug** menu option in the application painter, or by clicking on the **Debug** icon on the PowerBar. Before the debugger starts, it displays the Edit Stops dialog (Figure 2.14). In this dialog you can add or remove breakpoints and then start the debugger.

Adding a Breakpoint

To add a breakpoint click on **Add** to display the Select Script dialog (Figure 2.15). This helps you find the line of code where you want to set the breakpoint. First, make a choice from the Object Type pulldown ListBox. Your choices are Application, Window, Menu, User Object, Function. To set a breakpoint in one of the application events, select **Application**. To set a breakpoint in a window or window object event, select **Window**.

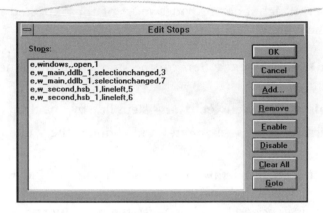

FIGURE 2.14 EDITING BREAKPOINTS

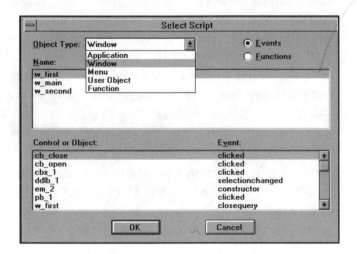

FIGURE 2.15 LOCATING A SCRIPT

Next, select one of the two RadioButtons, either **Events** or **Functions**, depending on whether you are looking for an event script or function code. The top ListBox presents a list of names. When you select one of these names, the lower ListBox lists the related controls or objects (for the events or functions). Make a selection in the lower ListBox and the code is displayed in the Debug window. Double-click on any line of code to set the breakpoint; the display adds a stop sign icon to the line. Remove a breakpoint by double-clicking on the line of code.

You can set additional breakpoints and you can remove, enable, or disable existing breakpoints with the other options in the Edit Stops dialog. The Stops listbox (in the Select Script dialog) lists all the currently defined breakpoints, and the status of each. The status lists the following:

BREAKPOINT STATUS

state—(e,d) for enabled or disabled

object—name of the object

control—name of the control

event—name of the event

lineno—line number

For example:

```
e,w_main,cb_close,clicked,3
```

This first example lists an enabled breakpoint for the third line of the clicked event for the CommandButton cb_close in the window w_main.

```
d,w_main,fw_calculate,,2
```

This status is for a disabled breakpoint in the second line of the function fw_calculate in the w_main window.

Running the Debugger

After you have set your breakpoints, click on the Start icon to start the debugger. The application will run until it hits one of your breakpoints. When you reach any breakpoint you will see the main Debug screen, as in Figure 2.16.

FIGURE 2.16 DEBUGGING A SCRIPT

The options on the Debugger PainterBar are:

- **Continue**—resumes program execution.

- **Step**—single-steps through the next line of code.

- **Select**—adds a new breakpoint (or view the code).

- **Edit Stop**—goes to the Edit Stops dialog (to add or remove break-points).

- **Show Watch**—toggles the display of the Watch window.

- **Add Watch**—adds the selected variable to the Watch window.

- **Remove Watch**—removes the selected variable from the Watch window.

- **Show Variables**—toggles the display of the Variable window.

Displaying and Modifying Variable

When execution stops at any breakpoint, you can display any variable in the application in the Variable window. The Show Variables icon is a toggle to show or hide the Variable window. To display a local variable, double-click on the **Local variable** icon in the Variable window. The icon expands to show a list of the local variables. If there are a large number of local variables, scroll through this window to locate the ones that you are interested in viewing. You can reduce the number of variables that you have to view by adding the important variables to the Watch window as discussed in the next section. To adjust the size of the watch and/or variable windows, drag the Watch or Variable title bar with the mouse to adjust the size.

Locating Window Instance Variables

Instance variables are contained in the definition of the window which is instantiated under the global variables list. To find our instance variable, click on the **Global** icon to expand the list. Scroll down until you find the window. Click on the window's icon to expand the list of objects inside it and scroll until you find the instance variable.

You can modify the current value for any variable. To do this locate the variable, and then double click on its icon. This opens the Modify Variable dialog, which displays data type, name, and current value for the variable. Change the value by entering a new value in the New Value listbox. To assign the NULL value to the variable, click on the **Null** checkbox in this dialog window.

Adding Variables To the Watch Window

To select a set of variables to watch, open the Variable window and click on the type of variable you are interested in watching. You can select from Global, Shared, or Local (instance variables are found under Global). In the Variable window, locate and then click on the variable that you want to add to the Watch window. Next, click on the **Add Watch** icon to add the variable to the Watch window.

You can enter a set of variables by clicking on the type (i.e. "Local"). This adds all the variables in the group to the Watch window. To remove a Watch variable, select it in the Watch window and click on the **Remove Watch** icon.

When you hit a breakpoint, the name of the icon will be grayed out in the Watch window, if it is not in the current scope of the breakpoint.

Using the Debugger

To use the debugger, the next example provides sample code for you to debug. Enter the code in the application open event.

```
// Simple Batch Application (+ Bugs)
// this application just duplicates a text file and adds line
// numbers

int    nFile1, nFile2, nLen, idx
string sBuf, sBuf2
string sInFile = "c:\pb4\class\test.txt" // set this to any
                                         // ASCII DOS file
string sOutFile = "c:\pb4\class\out.txt"
SetPointer(HourGlass!)
nFile1 = FileOpen(sInFile,linemode!,read!,lockread!)
nFile2 = FileOpen(sOutFile,linemode!,write!,lockwrite!)
IF nFile1 < 0 OR nFile2 < 0
       MessageBox("File Error", "could not open file")
       HALT CLOSE
ENDIF
DO
       idx++
       nLen = FileRead(fnum1, sBuf)
       sBuf2 = string(idx) + ' ' + sBuf1
       FileWrite(fnum2, sBuf2)
LOOP WHILE nLen >= 0
FileClose(nFile1)
FileClose(nFile2)
```

The steps that are required to create and run this application are:

1. Create an application ("copyfile", and "copyfile.pbl").

2. Add the script to the open event.

3. Compile the script (fix any code errors).

4. Run and verify the result (notice the two errors in the out.txt file).

5. Debug and fix.

The Debugged Script

```
int     nFile1, nFile2, nLen, idx
string sBuf1, sBuf2
string sInFile = "c:\pb4\class\test.txt" // this could be any
                                         // ASCII DOS file
string sOutFile = "c:\pb4\class\out.txt"
SetPointer(HourGlass!)
nFile1 = FileOpen(sInFile,linemode!,read!,lockread!)
nFile2 = FileOpen(sOutFile,linemode!,write!,lockwrite!,
    Replace!)
IF nFile1 < 0 OR nFile2 < 0 THEN
        MessageBox("File Error", "could not open file")
        HALT CLOSE
END IF
nLen = FileRead(nFile1, sBuf1)
DO
        idx++
        sBuf2 = string(idx) + ' ' + sBuf1
        FileWrite(nFile2, sBuf2)
        nLen = FileRead(nFile1, sBuf1)
LOOP WHILE nLen >= 0

FileClose(nFile1)
FileClose(nFile2)

MessageBox("CopyFile", "Successful")
```

PowerBuilder Naming Conventions

As you learn PowerBuilder, you should take time to adopt good coding standards and use naming conventions for your development process. If you are working in a team situation, this is essential. Powersoft has made a number of recommendations for naming conventions and these are followed with some slight modification, throughout this book.

CHAPTER THREE

THE POWERSCRIPT PAINTER

This chapter introduces the PowerScript painter, the editor that you will use to create and edit most of the PowerScript code that you write (so it is well worth your time to become familiar with the editor). The PowerScript painter is similar in functionality to the Windows' Write editor. Menu options let you cut, copy, and paste text within or between windows, they also provide search and replace functionality from within the file. The PowerScript code that you create will be stored automatically within you PowerBuilder application library.

For this introduction, we will use the code for the FirstApp example that is contained in Chapter 4.

THE POWERSCRIPT PAINTER

You can open the PowerScript painter from within any of the PowerBuilder painters where you may need to create or edit code. This includes the Application, Window, Function, Menu, and User Object painters.

The first opportunity to use the PowerScript painter (after starting PowerBuilder) is in the Application painter. So for this introduction, launch **PowerBuilder** and open the Application painter by clicking on the **Application** icon on the PowerBar.

NOTE

If you are building the FirstApp application, be sure that the current application is set to FirstApp. If not, select the **Open** icon from the PainterBar and select **FIRSTAPP.PBL** in the Libraries listbox. Then click on **OK** to open that application.

When you are in the Application painter, click on the **Script** icon on the PainterBar to open the PowerScript painter (or choose **Edit|Script** menu). Notice that the PowerScript painter title bar displays the name of the object (or control) and the name of event for which you are currently coding (Figure 3.1).

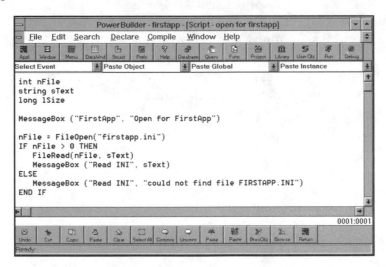

FIGURE 3.1 THE POWERSCRIPT PAINTER

THE DROPDOWN LISTBOXES

There are four dropdown listboxes in the PowerScript painter. They are labeled Select Event, Paste Object, Paste Global, and Paste Instance. You use the Select Event listbox to choose the event for which you are entering code. The other three listboxes are used to paste the names of objects, controls, and variables into your script code. Pasting object names in this manner avoids having to lookup a name, and also avoids typing errors.

When you are in the Function painter there are only two listboxes: Paste Global listbox and Paste Argument. The Paste Argument listbox contains the names of the function parameters that you defined when you declared the function (in the New Function dialog).

Use Ctrl 1, 2, 3, or 4 to drop the list down for any of the dropdown listboxes. Use the up and down arrow keys to move through the list. You can also use the Enter key to select the highlighted item. The Escape key closes the list and cancels the selection.

Select Event Listbox

The Select Event dropdown listbox contains a list of all the events that apply to the current object (the application object in this example). To change to another event, just pull down the listbox list and make your selection. For this example select the open event. The title bar caption should now list the open event ("open for firstapp").

When you pull down the Select Event listbox, the list displays an icon next to the names of any events that already contain code (shaded icons are related to ancestor scripts covered later in the chapter on inheritance).

Paste Object Listbox

The Paste Object listbox lets you paste into your code the name of any objects (or controls) related to the object that you are currently editing. When editing application-level events, this box contains the names of all the windows that have been stored in the related libraries (the library list covered in Chapter 2).

When you are using the PowerBuilder painter in the Window painter, the Paste Object listbox contains the name of the window and all of the controls that have been added the window. This is very convenient for pasting in the names of the controls.

When you are using the PowerBuilder painter in the User Object painter, the Paste Object listbox lists the name of the object and any related controls (as when creating custom controls).

When you are using the PowerBuilder painter in the Menu painter, the Paste Object listbox contains a list of all the menu items that are part of the current menu.

This listbox is not available from the Function painter.

Paste Global Listbox

The Paste Global listbox allows you to paste into your code the name of any global variables known to the application. Again, the main advantage is that it is quick, and avoids having to lookup the name.

Paste Instance Listbox

The Paste Instance listbox is similar to the Paste Global listbox, except that it lists instance variables instead of globals. Instance variables are discussed later in this chapter. This listbox is not available from the Function painter.

Paste Argument Listbox

In the Function painter (only), the Paste Instance listbox is replaced with the Paste Argument listbox. The Paste Argument listbox lists the function arguments, so that you can paste them into your code.

EDIT MENU PASTE OPTIONS

You will find other useful paste options in the PowerScript painter Edit menu. They are grouped together as: Paste Function, Paste SQL, and Paste Statement. The Paste SQL and Paste Statement functions also have icons on the PainterBar.

Paste Function

Selecting the **Edit|Paste Function** menu option opens the Paste Function dialog window (Figure 3.2). This listbox presents an alphabetized list from which you can select and paste function names into your code. You can display either built-in, user-defined, or external functions by selecting the appropriate radio button. You will find this most useful in the first few weeks of your PowerBuilder development as you learn the names of the functions. Later you may find that the Object Browser is a more efficient tool, but it takes a bit more knowledge to use.

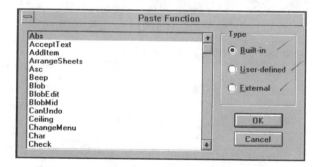

FIGURE 3.2 THE PASTE FUNCTION DIALOG

Paste SQL

To insert a SQL statement into your code, select the **Edit|Paste SQL** menu option. This opens the SQL Statement Type dialog window (Figure 3.3). Choose the type of SQL statement that you want to create. This opens the

SQL painter that assists you in creating the statement. When you have finished, it will paste the SQL statement into your code. This tool is covered in greater detail in the chapter "Embedded SQL."

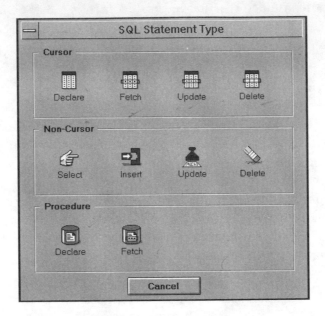

FIGURE 3.3 THE SQL STATEMENT TYPE DIALOG

Paste Statement

To insert one of the logical PowerScript constructs select **Paste Statement** from the Edit menu. This opens the Paste Statement dialog window (Figure 3.4).

This window presents the set of PowerScript branching statements (IF, FOR, DO, and CHOOSE CASE), with multiple forms of each. If you choose one of these statements and then click **OK**, the dialog pastes a prototype of the statement into your code (Figure 3.5). The editor then selects the first entry (<condition> in this example) that you need to complete to use this statement.

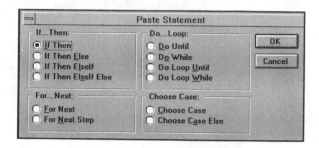

FIGURE 3.4 THE PASTE STATEMENT DIALOG

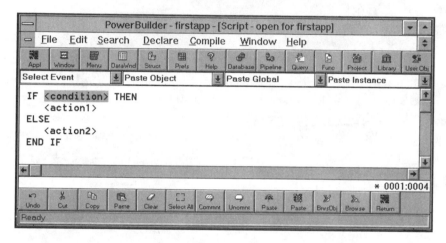

FIGURE 3.5 AFTER PASTING THE IF STATEMENT INTO THE SCRIPT

ENTERING AND EDITING TEXT

Enter a few lines of text into the workspace. If you are working on the FirstApp example enter the following:

```
--------------------------------------------------------------
int    nFile
string sText
long   lSize

beep(3)
```

```
MessageBox ("FirstApp", "Open for FirstApp")
nFile = FileOpen("firstapp.ini")

IF nFile >= 0 THEN
          FileRead(nFile, sText)
          MessageBox ("Read INI", sText)
ELSE
          MessageBox ("Read INI", "could not find file
                    FIRSTAPP.INI")
END IF
```

Selecting Text

The PowerScript painter follows the Windows convention for selecting, cutting, copying, pasting, and deleting text. To select text with the mouse, left-click on the text and drag the pointer to highlight the block of text. You use **Select All** to highlight all the text in the script by clicking on the **SelectAll** icon or by selecting **SelectAll** from the Edit menu. You can also select a word (or string of text) by double-clicking on it. And, you can select text with the keyboard. Place the cursor next to the text that you wish to select, hold the **Shift** key while using the cursor arrows to highlight a word, string, or block of text.

The following key combinations will move the cursor while highlighting (selecting) the text:

- **Left Arrow**—move left one character
- **Right Arrow**—move right one character
- **Up Arrow**—move up one line
- **Down Arrow**—move down one line
- **End Key**—go to the end of the current line
- **Home Key**—go to the beginning of the current line
- **Control+Home**—go to the beginning of the script (or file)
- **Control+End**—go to the end of the script (or file)

To Cut, Copy, Clear, or Replace the Selected Text

After you have selected text, the selected text can be:

- **Cut**—deleted from the script and placed on the Window's clipboard. Use the **Cut** icon or the **Edit|Cut** menu option.
- **Copied**—copied to the clipboard without removing from the script. Use the **Copy** icon or the **Edit|Copy** menu option.
- **Cleared**—deleted from the script, and not placed on the clipboard. Use the **Clear** icon or the **Edit|Clear** menu option.
- **Replaced**—replaced with text copied from the clipboard or typed from the keyboard. To replace the selected text with the contents of the clipboard use the **Paste** icon or the **Edit|Paste** menu option.

Pasting Text

You can paste text from the clipboard in one of two manners depending on whether or not you have a block of text currently selected in the editor:

- **Insert**—if you do not have any text selected, the paste operation just inserts the text at the current cursor position on the screen.
- **Replace**—if you have selected a block of text on the screen, the paste operation will replace the selected text with the text currently on the clipboard. The selected text is not copied to the clipboard.

The replace option also works when you type in new text. If you select a block of text, and then type a character, the entire block will be replaced by the single character.

Keyboard Shortcuts for Cut and Paste Functions

You may already be familiar with the keyboard shortcuts for these functions if you've used other Windows applications. If not, take a minute to memorize them. They are listed in the Edit menu. They are:

- **Control+X**—cut to the clipboard
- **Control+C**—copy to the clipboard
- **Control+V**—paste from the clipboard
- **Delete**—clear, do not copy to the clipboard

Other useful keyboard short-cuts are:

- **Control+Z**—undo the last edit
- **Control+A**—select all
- **Control+F**—find text
- **Control+N**—repeat last find
- **Control+G**—go to line
- **Control+L**—compile script
- **Control+B**—go to the browser
- **Control+S**—select another object

The most often used functions appear on the PainterBar—the first six duplicate functions have already been discussed. These are Undo, Cut, Copy, Paste, Clear, Select All. The other functions that appear on the PainterBar are:

- **Comment**—marks the selected text as comment text. This adds a double-slash ("//") to the beginning of each line.
- **Uncomment**—removes the comment characters from the selected text.
- **Paste SQL**—brings up the SQL Painter to let you paste a SQL statement into your code.
- **Paste Statement**—brings up the Paste Statement dialog window. You can paste the PowerScript IF, FOR, DO, or CHOOSE statements.
- **Browse**—brings up the Browser. This useful utility is covered later in its own section.
- **Return**—compiles the current code (if any) and closes the editor.

THE POWERSCRIPT PAINTER MENU OPTIONS

The PowerScript painter menu bar includes the following pulldown menus:

    File | Edit | Search | Declare | Compile | Window | Help

The options on each menu are:

File Menu

- **Close**—exits the editor. If changes have occurred you will be prompted before changes are saved. If you want to save changes, then compile the code before exiting.

- **Return**—exits the editor and saves any changes without prompting. If changes where made then compile the code.

- **DOS Open**—opens a DOS text file.

- **DOS Save**—saves the code as a DOS file.

- **DOS Save As**—saves the code as a DOS file and prompts for the file name and location.

- **Run**—executes the application.

- **Debug**—runs the application in debug mode. Prompt first for breakpoints.

- **PowerPanel**—changes the display option to PowerPanel style.

- **Print**—prints the code.

- **Printer Setup**—lets the user set print options.

- **Exit**—quits PowerBuilder.

Edit Menu

- **Undo**—returns to the last edit.

- **Cut**—deletes selected text from the script and places it on the Window's clipboard.

- **Copy**—copies selected text to the clipboard without removing it from the script.

- **Paste**—inserts the text current on the clipboard.
- **Clear**—deletes selected text from the script, and it is not placed on the clipboard.
- **Select All**—highlights all of the text in this script.
- **Copy To**—copies the selected text to a DOS file.
- **Paste From**—inserts text from a DOS file.
- **Comment Selection**—marks selected text as comment text. This adds a double-slash ("//") to the beginning of each line.
- **Uncomment Selection**—removes the comment characters from the selected text.
- **Paste Function**—inserts a PowerBuilder or user-defined function (from a listbox selection).
- **Paste SQL**—brings up the SQL Painter, to let you to paste a SQL statement into your code.
- **Paste Statement**—brings up the Paste Statement dialog window. You can paste the PowerScript IF, FOR, DO, or CHOOSE choose statements.
- **Browse Objects**—brings up the Browser. This useful utility is covered in its own section.
- **Select Object**—edits a script for another object.

Search

- **Find Text**—searches for the following text.
- **Find Next Text**—repeats the last search.
- **Replace Text**—finds and replaces.
- **Go to Line**—goes to a specific line number.

Declare

- **Global Variables**—declares or modifies a global variable.
- **Shared Variables**—declares or modifies a shared variable (see below).

- **Instance Variables**—declares or modifies an instance variable (see below).

- **Application Functions**—declares or modifies an application function.

- **Application Structures**—declares or modifies an application structure.

- **Global External Functions**—declares or modifies an external function.

Compile

- **Script**—compiles the current script.

- **Display Compiler Warnings**—shows the compiler messages after a compile.

- **Display Database Warnings**—shows the database warning messages.

IMPORT AND EXPORT

You can import ASCII text from a DOS file into your scripts. You insert a file into your script by using the File|Import menu option. To insert a text file into a script, open the PowerScript editor and select the event that you wish to edit. Position the cursor at the point (in your code) where you want to insert the text. Then select the **File|Import** menu option. This opens the File Import dialog window (Figure 3.6).

Select the correct file and click OK. This will paste the file into you script. The script for the application open event is APPOPEN.TXT. Select the application open event and use the **File|Import** option to copy the file into your application.

You can also choose to replace an entire script with a file by first selecting all of the text in the script (use the **Select All** icon), and then by using the File|Import menu option. This discards all the current code before reading in the DOS file text.

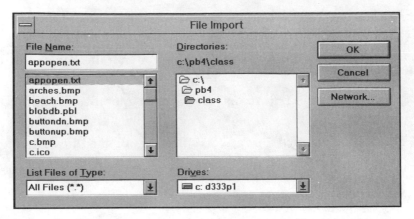

FIGURE 3.6 THE FILE IMPORT DIALOG

Exporting Text

You can also export text from your scripts to a DOS file. To export script text to a DOS file text, open the PowerScript editor and select the event that you wish to save. You can either export the entire script to a file or a block of text. If you wish to export only part of the script, simply select the block of text before doing the export, otherwise the entire script will be exported. Next select the **File|Export** menu option. This opens the Export File dialog window (essentially the same as Figure 3.6). Enter the file name (after setting the directory) and then press **OK**.

COMPILING POWERSCRIPT CODE

The script code can be compiled by using the **Compile|Script** menu option, or simply by closing a script. In most cases, PowerBuilder will insist that the code be compiled successfully before you leave the editor if you want to save your changes to the code.

If the compile fails you have three options:

1. Correct the problems reported by the compiler and recompile successfully.

2. Close the editor (using the **File|Close** menu option) and elect not to save the changes. This will discard all changes that have been made in the current editor session.

3. Comment out the erroneous line(s) of code. The PowerScript editor provides an easy way to quickly comment out all lines of the text. Use the **Edit|Select All** menu option to select all text. The comment option **Edit|Comment Selection** will comment out all of the lines of text that are currently selected. If you choose **Select All** and then select **Comment Selection**, this has the effect of commenting out all the text in the current script. Both of these functions also have icons on the PainterBar for quick access.

In some cases PowerBuilder lets you *Ignore Compiler Warnings*. In this case, you can exit without losing the changes that you have made to the code. Do not confuse this option with the choice you must make in the next example.

It is important that you recognize the message in Figure 3.7, and the effect of answering "No."

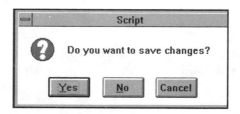

FIGURE 3.7 THE EXIT SCRIPT DIALOG

If you have errors in your code, and you exit the PowerScript painter and see the message *Do you want to save changes?*, PowerBuilder is insisting that you go back to correct the errors or exit without saving the changes. If you click on **No**, all the code changes that you made in the current editing session will be discarded. If you click on **Yes** or **Cancel**, you will be returned to the editor.

If the compile error is a minor problem (and not in the Application Open event), PowerBuilder may give you the option of existing without losing the changes that you have made. In this case you will see the message shown in Figure 3.8.

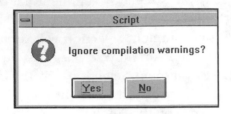

FIGURE 3.8 IN THIS DIALOG, YOU MAY CHOOSE
TO SAVE THE CODE, EVEN WITH ERRORS.

If you see this message, choose **Yes** to exit the editor without losing your code changes. You can return later to fix the code. An example of this would be when you code an open window function call for a window that you have not yet defined.

```
Open(w_next)
```

You may be able to leave the editor. You could then define the window *w_next* and the open statement would work and compile successfully.

CONTEXT-SENSITIVE HELP

You can obtain context-sensitive help for any of the built-in PowerBuilder functions. To access this help first place the cursor on the name of a function in your code. Then press **Shift+F1** for the context-sensitive help about that function. For example, if you place the cursor on MessageBox and press **Shift+F1** you will see the display in Figure 3.9.

This shows the first part of the help system entry for MessageBox (scroll down to read the rest of the text). Each entry typically shows the argument list, explains the use of the function, defines the return value, and provides a short code example. You can copy and paste any of this text into you application by selecting the **Edit|Copy** menu option. This will open the Copy dialog window. In this window you can drag the mouse to select the text you wish to copy. Then hit the **Copy** button to copy the selected text to the clipboard. From there you can paste it into you code.

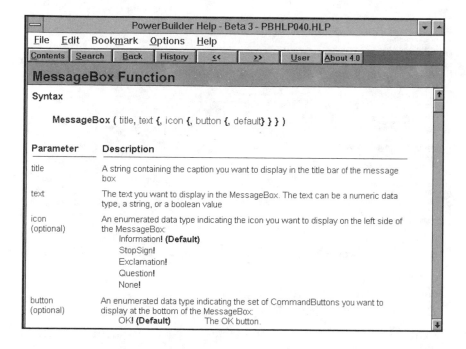

FIGURE 3.9 THE HELP ENTRY FOR MESSAGEBOX

THE OBJECT BROWSER

The object browser is very convenient for pasting a wide range of values into you script. With the browser you can quickly locate the name of a specific attribute, function, enumerated value, variable, or object. You can select the object browser by clicking on the **Browser** icon on the

PowerScript painter's PainterBar or by selecting the **Edit|Browse Objects** menu option. When you select the browser option, the system displays the Object Browser dialog window as shown in Figure 3.10.

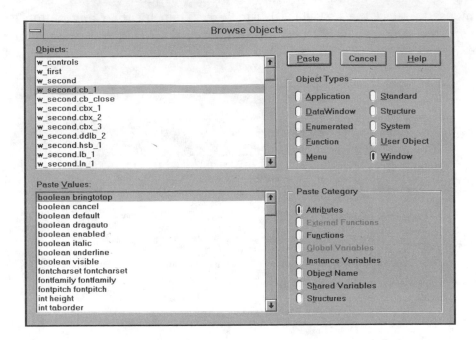

FIGURE 3.10 THE BROWSE OBJECTS DIALOG

This example shows the use of the Object Browser to locate the attribute names for CommandButton *cb_1* in a window named *w_second* (this is from the WINDOW.PBL application). Selecting the **Paste** button would paste "cb_1.bringtotop" into the script.

To locate the value that you wish to paste takes several steps and the steps vary according to the object type that you are using.

Select the **Object Type** from the set of radiobuttons on the top right of the window.

The possible types are:

- **Application**—locates external functions and global variables. It is also used for shared or instance variables that were declared at the application, window or menu level.

- **DataWindow**—information, attributes, functions relating to DataWindow.

- **Enumerated**—locates PowerBuilder enumerated values.

- **Function**—locates user-defined global functions.

- **Menu**—locates menu functions or variables.

- **Standard**—lists the PowerScript data types.

- **Structure**—locates local variables that are part of a structure.

- **System**—locates PowerBuilder system or object level functions.

- **User Objects**—locates the names of controls and functions associated with user objects.

- **Window**—locates a wide range of items: controls, variables, and attributes contained in a window and the objects within a window.

If you want to duplicate the example in Figure 3.10, edit any event in the *w_second* window of the WINDOW application. Select the **Browse** icon, and then select **Window** from the Object Types group box. Then in the objects listbox, double-click on **w_second** to expand the display to include all of the controls that have been added to the *w_second* window.

Select the **Attributes Paste Category** radiobutton found in the lower section of the Object Browser. This lists the attributes for the selected object in the Paste Values listbox. In the Objects listbox, click on different types of objects and notice that the list of attributes changes in the Paste Values list box. Click on the **Functions Paste Category** radiobutton to see the list of functions that apply to the selected object. If you click in the lower listbox (to set the focus), and then type a letter on the keyboard you can jump to the first entry in the listbox that begins with that letter.

For example, select a CommandButton from the Objects listbox and a function from the Paste Category. Click anywhere in the Paste Value listbox and hit the **s** key. The list box will scroll to the "setfocus" function. If you press the **s** key again, the listbox scrolls to the next entry that begins with the letter ("setposition"). You can paste any of these values into your code, just select one of the values and click on **Paste**.

The browser can seem to be difficult to use at first, if only because of the huge amount of information that is available through it. It takes some time to learn where all this information is within the browser. The browser can be a more efficient search tool than the help system or the paste function option on the edit menu. This is because it is only displays the functions and attributes that are associated with the object that you have selected, thus reducing the scope of the search. In general it is easy to use for the following:

- Locating objects, names, attributes, functions, and variables
- Enumerated values
- Standard data types
- DataWindow attributes and functions

Use one of the larger applications (such as Imagedb) in order to explore the browser. Open the main window in the Window Painter and then open the script for an event such as the Window open event. While in the PowerScript painter, select the **Browse** icon. In the Object Browser, select the **Window Object Type** radiobutton. This displays the names of all the windows contained in the application's libraries. Double-click on the name of main window for the application in the Objects listbox. This expands the window and lists the controls and objects that it contains. Find a DataWindow control and examine its attributes and functions.

The object browser is very convenient for pasting a wide range of values into your script. With the browser you can quickly locate the name of a specific attribute, function, enumerated value, variable, or object.

The Browse Object Dialog

To access an attribute or a function for the object that is currently being edited, use the menu option **Browse Object** (on the Edit Menu) and click the **Script** painter Toolbar icon. This opens a dialog that provides access to attributes and function prototypes for the object currently being edited in the script painter. The Browse Object dialog is easier to use than the Object Browser. Figure 3.11 shows the Browse Object dialog, listing the attributes for a CommandButton.

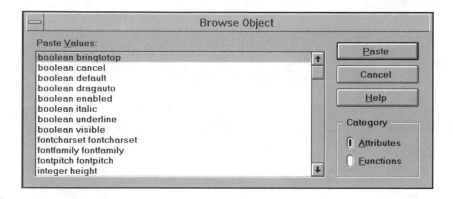

FIGURE 3.11 THE BROWSE OBJECT DIALOG FOR ATTRIBUTES

Figure 3.12 shows the Browse Object dialog, listing the functions for a CommandButton.

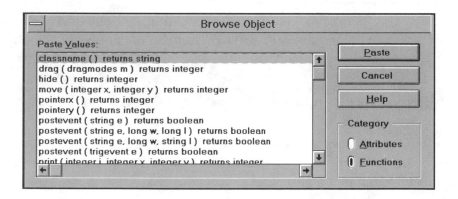

FIGURE 3.12 THE BROWSE OBJECT DIALOG FOR FUNCTIONS

Click on **Paste** to insert the selected item into your script code.

The Browse OLE Classes

Selecting the Browse OLE Classes option from the Edit menu opens the dialog shown in Figure 3.13. This is a list of the OLE classes that are known to PowerBuilder.

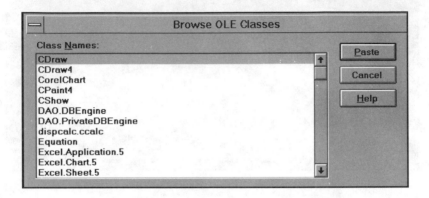

FIGURE 3.13 THE BROWSE OLE CLASSES DIALOG

Selecting Another Object

When you are editing an event for a window or for an object in a window (such as a CommandButton or ListBox), you can switch to another object (or the window) by selecting **Select Object** from the Edit menu as shown in Figure 3.14.

Selecting this menu item opens the Select Object dialog as shown in Figure 3.15.

Choose the object in the list and click on the **Select** CommandButton. This opens an event in the selected object. From there you may choose a different event if necessary.

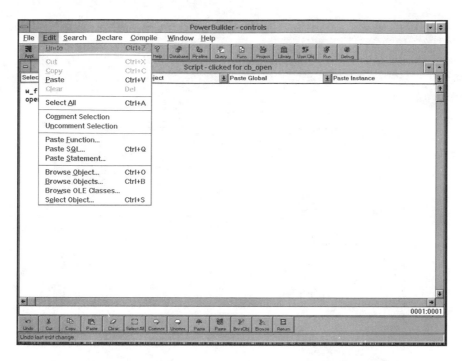

FIGURE 3.14 THE EDIT MENU WITH THE SELECT OBJECT OPTION

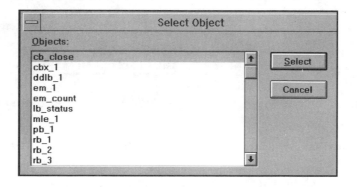

FIGURE 3.15 THE SELECT OBJECT DIALOG

Editing Function Declarations

When you are editing the code for a function, (in the Function painter), the last command on the Edit menu is changed to Function Declaration as shown in Figure 3.16.

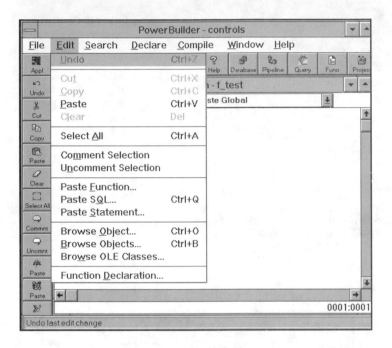

FIGURE 3.16 THE EDIT MENU WITH THE FUNCTION DECLARATION OPTION

Selecting this menu item opens the Function Declaration dialog as shown in Figure 3.17.

The Function Declaration command, added to the Edit menu when you are editing code for a function, lets you make changes to the declaration of the function. (Make a note of this option, this is one of the questions that arises most often in my PowerBuilder classes.)

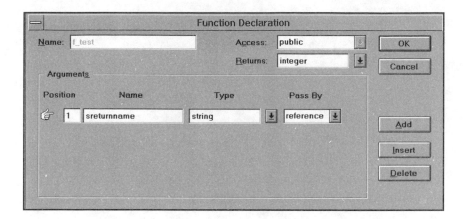

FIGURE 3.17 THE FUNCTION DECLARATION DIALOG

CHAPTER FOUR

CREATING POWERBUILDER APPLICATIONS

A PowerBuilder application consists of many components including windows, controls, functions, and PowerScript code. You will develop each of the components by using the various PowerBuilder painters.

In the Application painter you can create or modify an application object. Every PowerBuilder application has one (and only one) application object. This object is the starting point; the entry point for the entire application.

A typical PowerBuilder application usually contains:

- one application object
- windows
- controls
- menus
- DataWindows

- functions
- structures
- Script language programming code
- external resources (icons, initialization file)
- a project

These components reside mostly in PowerBuilder libraries. When you create a new PowerBuilder object, you save the object in a PowerBuilder library. You can run the application from these libraries in the development environment. Later, when you create an executable, these components may be bound into a single file. More details about libraries will be discussed in the next section. This chapter presents an introduction to the basics of creating executables. For more detail and other options for building executables see the chapter Distributing PowerBuilder Applications.

THE APPLICATION PAINTER

The Application painter is where you define the most general details about each application. In the Application painter you can: create and name the application object, choose an icon to be associated with the application executable, create scripts for application-level events, define the library list, and set the default display characteristics of text (such as the fonts) for the application. The Application painter can also create the application library where the components are stored (you can also create a library with the Library painter). From the Application painter you can also run (execute) or debug the application that you have developed (from within the development environment).

Opening Application Painter

Click on the **Appl** icon (on the PowerBar) to open the Application painter (Figure 4.1). The Application painter title bar displays the current application's name. The painter selects the application that you last worked with by default. The bottom of the window displays other application status, such as the library path and the last modified date.

The main section of the window always contains an icon that represents the application object. You can expand this icon to show the major components of the application (if you have added other components to the application). To do this, double-click the icon, pressing the plus key (+), select the **Tree|Expand Branch** menu option, or use the Expand Branch option on the popup menu. This display contains other components such as windows, menus, DataWindow objects, and user objects. Each type of object has its own icon. You can continue to expand each level by selecting an icon (such as a window icon) and expanding to the next level to get an outline view of your application (Figure 4.1).

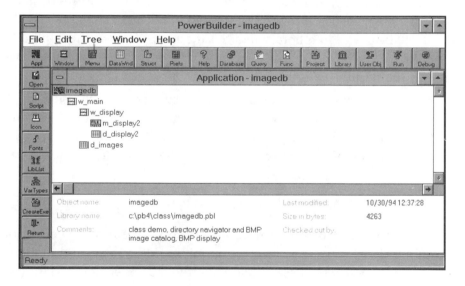

FIGURE 4.1 THE IMAGED APPLICATION TREE

You can edit any object by selecting the object icon and pressing **Enter** or by selecting **Go To Painter** from the popup menu. This launches the painter associated with the type of the object that was selected. (This does not apply to the application object since you are already in the application painter.)

Each of the PowerBuilder painters has its own PainterBar. This Application painter PainterBar contains icons for the most commonly used menu options. In the next section, the functions provided by each of the icons will be outlined. If this is your first introduction to PowerBuilder, then you should follow the explanation through the text and screen figures and try each step yourself. After the available options have been covered, you will learn how to create your first PowerBuilder application.

Application Programs and Application Objects

An *application* is the program that you develop with PowerBuilder; it includes all of the component parts that you have created. Each *application program* must include one *application object*. This application object can reside in any one of the PowerBuilder libraries that contain application components. Most often it will be placed in a library that has the same name as the application object (FIRSTAPP.PBL for the FirstApp object). Creating the application object is usually the starting point for creating a new application program.

The application object holds application-level parameters (such as the default fonts), application-level events, and contains a list of all the libraries (.pbl files) that hold the components for the application program. The application object is sort of a wrapper for the rest of the application components.

PowerBuilder Application Libraries

You store the application components in one or more PowerBuilder libraries. A *library* is a special type of repository file created and managed by PowerBuilder. These files always have the file extension of PBL (pronounced *pibble*). A small application can store all of its components in a single library, but most larger applications will store their components across multiple libraries. Often you will share PowerBuilder components, such as windows or functions, across multiple applications. To do this you will need to place the objects in a shared library. Normally this will be on a network file server where it can be reached by all the developers. The components that are not shared and are only used by a single application (or a single developer) may be placed in other local libraries.

For simplicity, most of the example applications in this book use only a single separate library. For example, the first application, named *FirstApp*, is stored in the library FIRSTAPP.PBL (you will find it on the diskette that is included with this book).

The Application Executable

As you develop your application, you can run it from development environment by clicking the **Run** icon on the PowerBar. Later when you are ready to distribute your application you will create an executable version of your application. When you create the application executable file, PowerBuilder binds the various components into a single file, for example, FIRSTAPP.EXE. Even after creating the executable, additional DLL files will still be required to run the bound executable. You may distribute these required DLLs with your application executable. You may also want to partition the executables for larger applications into multiple files. You can find more information about creating and distributing application in the chapter "Distributing PowerBuilder Applications."

Batch Applications

It is possible to create an application that doesn't contain any windows. Such an application could contain only a block of PowerScript code (in its Application Open event) to do the necessary processing. This type of application is often called a *batch* application. It is more often the case that an application contains at least one window. Without at least one window there is no visible feedback that the program is executing and this can be confusing to the user. In general you will use windows with all of your applications.

OPENING AN APPLICATION

From within the Application painter you can create a new application or open an existing application. The following section contains instructions on opening an existing application. For directions on how to create a new application go to the section Creating a New Application.

Opening an Existing Application

To open an existing application requires that you first select the drive, directory, and the library where the application object resides. Click on the **Open** icon on the PainterBar to reach the Select Application Library dialog window shown in Figure 4.2.

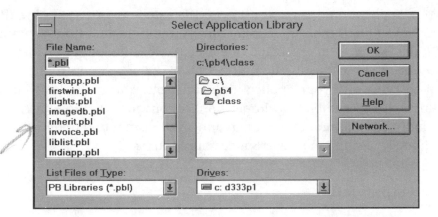

FIGURE 4.2 THE SELECT APPLICATION LIBRARY DIALOG

In this dialog, use the Drives and the Directories listboxes to navigate to the directory that contains the application library (C:\PB4\CLASS for this example). The File Name listbox displays a list of all the PowerBuilder libraries in the selected directory. Select the library that contains the application object for the application that you wish to open. You can select a library by highlighting a selection in the Libraries listbox (i.e. FIRSTAPP.PBL) and then click on **OK** or just double-click on the library in the list box.

Selecting an application library opens the Select Application dialog shown in Figure 4.3.

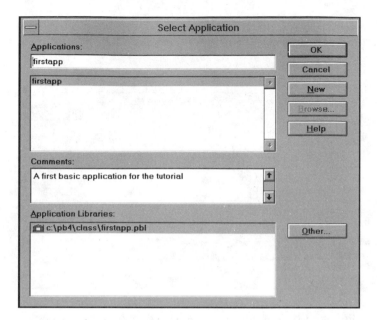

FIGURE 4.3 THE SELECT APPLICATION DIALOG

In this dialog you select the application object from the library. This dialog displays a list of the application objects that are contained in that library. It is possible to have zero, one, or more application objects in a library (for most of the examples in this book there will be one application object in each library). Select the application object and then click **OK** to open that application. At this point you can run, debug, or modify the application as will be covered later in this chapter.

Creating a New Application

To create a new application, click open the Application painter and then select the **File|New** menu option. This opens the Select New Application Library dialog window (Figure 4.4).

If the current directory is not already set correctly, you must tab over to the Directories (or Drives) field and set the correct drive and path (for the examples in this book it will be C:\PB4\CLASS). This will be the directory where the new library file is created.Then enter the library's name in the File Name field. Click on **OK** to open the Save Application dialog (Figure 4.5).

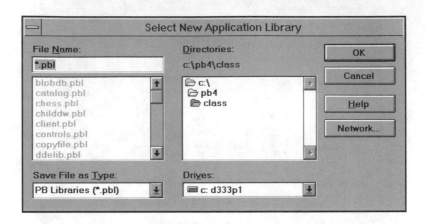

FIGURE 4.4 THE SELECT NEW APPLICATION LIBRARY DIALOG

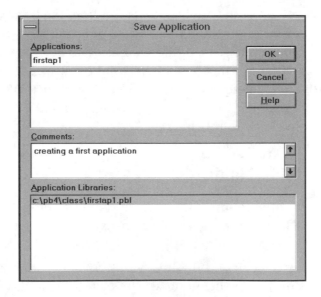

FIGURE 4.5 CREATING A NEW APPLICATION WITH THE SAVE APPLICATION DIALOG

In the first field (under Applications:) enter a name for your new application (such as **myapp**). Tab down to the Comments field and enter a description of the application. You should enter a descriptive comment for every application. PowerBuilder will store this comment in the library with the Application object. Later, you can view these comments in the library painter, and this will help you to find specific objects and code. For example, you could enter the following comment, "This is a temporary application, you may delete it."

Check to see that all the information in the Save Application dialog is correct and then click **OK**. This creates the application object and then returns to the Application painter. If you specified the name of a new library, PowerBuilder also creates the library. The Application painter displays the icon which is associated with this application and other status information about the associated library.

Next, set the other default attributes for the application (icon, font, etc.).

Selecting the Application Icon

To select an icon to be associated with the executable form of your application, click on the PainterBar icon labeled **Icon**. This opens the Select Icon dialog window (Figure 4.6). Use the Directories listbox to navigate to the directory where the icon bitmap file resides. You can use an icon file called FIRSTAPP.ICO, which you will find in the C:\PB4\CLASS directory.

Instead of using an icon file, you could elect to use one of the internal PowerBuilder icons by choosing one from the Stock Icons listbox. PowerBuilder will bind the icon that you select into the executable version of your application.

This icon will be used to represent your application on the Windows desktop. Windows will display this icon if you add the program to one of your Windows groups (such as Powersoft). To add the application icon to one of your existing groups, go to the Windows' Program Manager and select the group, then select the **File|New** menu option. In the New Program Object dialog, select the **Program Item** radio button. Choose **Browse** to locate the file and then click **OK**.

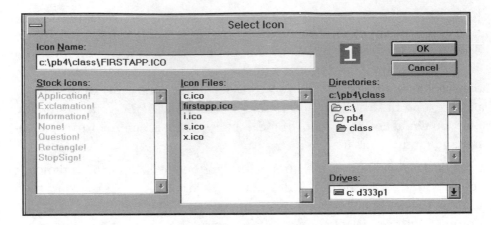

FIGURE 4.6 SELECTING AN APPLICATION ICON

Setting Default Fonts

Click on the PainterBar **Font** icon to set the default fonts that are to be used throughout the application. In the Select Default Fonts dialog (Figure 4.7) you can set the default font for a number of uses including:

- **Text**—refers to the static text fields used in User Objects and Windows.

- **Data**—sets the default font for the data which is displayed in a DataWindow.

- **Headings**—sets the font for the column headings in DataWindows.

- **Labels**—sets the font for the field labels in DataWindows.

You should take time to set these four fonts. Setting the default fonts helps you create more consistent presentations and saves development time if you don't have to specify the fonts each time you add text to your application. You can override any of these default fonts. You will see examples of this when DataWindow objects are created.

You can also define default fonts to be used in other areas of the PowerBuilder environment. The other default fonts are used in the script and DOS editor, and for the Application, Library, and Microhelp painters. The setting of those defaults will be covered later in the preferences/customizing section.

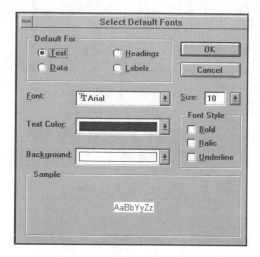

FIGURE 4.7 SELECTING THE DEFAULT FONTS FOR AN APPLICATION

Specifying the Library Search List

Click on the **LibList** icon to open the Select Libraries dialog window (Figure 4.8). In this dialog box you specify the set of libraries that will be used for this application. The application object resides in only one library, but the application itself may use objects from a number of libraries during the execution of the application (in the development environment). When you click on the **LibList** icon you will be presented with the Select Libraries dialog window listing the current set of search libraries (in the Library Search Path listbox). To add libraries to the list, use the Drives and Directories listboxes to navigate to the directory that contains the library, then double-click on the name of the library that you wish to add from the list in the Paste Libraries listbox. To remove an entry from the search list, double-click on the entry in the upper list box, and then hit the **Delete** key (there is no Delete button on this dialog).

117

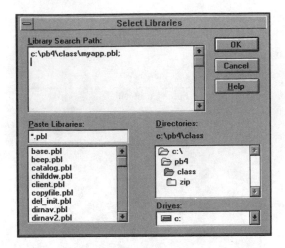

FIGURE 4.8 SETTING THE LIBRARY SEARCH LIST

The Search Order

The order of the entries in the Library Search Path listbox is significant. PowerBuilder will search the libraries in the listed order. This is significant, because the search for an object (such as the main window) ends when the object is located. So, if the application is looking for its main window (i.e. w_main), and there is more than one library that contains a window with that name, the window from the library listed higher in the list will be found first, and then used. You will usually list the development (or test) libraries before the production libraries in order to pick up and test new versions of any objects.

It is possible to have more than one version of an object, but each version must reside in a different library (if the different versions have the same name). This will be useful when testing new (revised) versions of an object. For example, you might check out a window (w_main) from a production library and make some modifications to that window. This new version could be stored in a test library while you are working on the modifications. If you list the test library (with the new version of the object) before the production library in the Library Search Path listbox, your application uses the test version of the object. If you list the production library first, the original version of the object is used. In general, you have a number of shared libraries placed somewhere on the network. There is a test library on the local system and perhaps a test library on the network. When you create a new application you will create a new library. This library can be on the local drive if it is a private application, otherwise it will be on a network drive. The LibList could be as follows:

```
S:\dev1\hr_dept\emp.pbl
C:\PB4\test.pbl
S:\dev1\shared\test.pbl
S:\dev1\shared\shared.pbl
S:\dev1\shared\empdata.pbl
S:\dev1\shared\windows.pbl
```

In this example, emp.pbl contains the emp application. A local test.pbl is used to test any new or revised objects. It is included before the shared libraries so that the object contained in this library is used in this developer's testing.

One final note: The LibList information is not actually stored in the application object. Instead, it is placed in the PowerBuilder initialization file, PB.INI. This file is located in your PowerBuilder directory, usually C:\PB4.

Creating the Application Executable

Choose the **CreateExe** icon to generate an executable version of your application. This opens the Create Executable dialog window (Figure 4.9) where you name the executable, set its directory, and specify any required dynamic libraries. This binds all the application components into a single file. This executable is not a binary file like the .EXE files generated by a 3 GL compiler. The PowerBuilder executable actually contains P-Code (tokenized interpreter code) that is executed by the PowerBuilder interpreter. Though the creation of the executable binds the application into a single file, you must also distribute a number of auxiliary files (DLLs) with the executable in order for it to run successfully. You will find more details about this in the chapter on "Distributing PowerBuilder Applications."

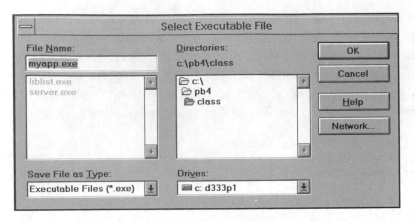

FIGURE 4.9 THE SELECT EXECUTABLE DIALOG

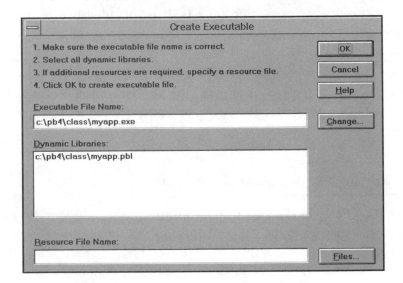

FIGURE 4.10 CREATING AN EXECUTABLE

You can run the new executable from the Windows Program Manager using the File|Run... menu option, or you can add the program icon to the Windows' desktop and just double-click it. To add the application icon to one of your existing groups (perhaps the Powersoft group), go to the Windows' Program Manager and select the group, then select File|New and then select the **Program Item** radio control. Choose **Browse** to locate the file and then click **OK**.

THE PROJECT PAINTER

The Project Manager lets you create and maintain project objects. A *project object* contains all the information that is necessary for building application executables.

Before you create a new project, be sure that the application runs correctly and that you have created any necessary resource files (see the chapter Distributing PowerBuilder Applications for more information). Then, to create a new project, click on the **Project** icon on the PowerBar. This opens the Select Project dialog.

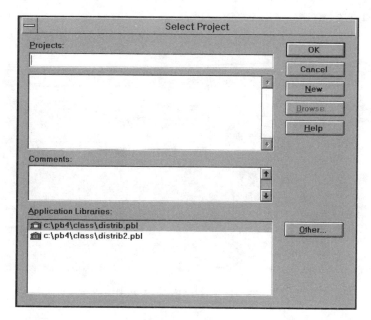

FIGURE 4.11 THE SELECT PROJECT DIALOG

Select the library that is to hold the new project and then click on **New**. This opens the Select Executable File dialog box shown in Figure 4.12.

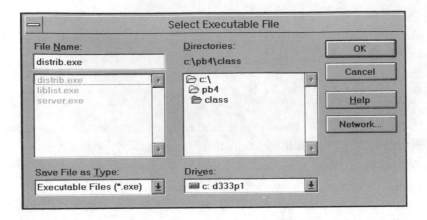

FIGURE 4.12 THE SELECT EXECUTABLE FILE DIALOG

Here, you must specify the File Name of the executable file. This name will be carried over to the next screen.

Figure 4.13 shows the Project painter dialog.

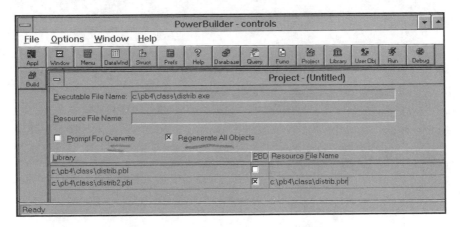

FIGURE 4.13 DEFINING A PROJECT

On this screen you must complete the project painter workspace options. In this dialog you can elect to be prompted before overwrite of .EXE and .PBDs. You can also choose to have all of the objects in the libraries regenerated before the .EXE and .PBDs are built. You may also specify whether each library (in the Application Library path) should be a .PBD and if so, you can choose a Resource File.

Now save the project by selecting **Save** from the File menu.

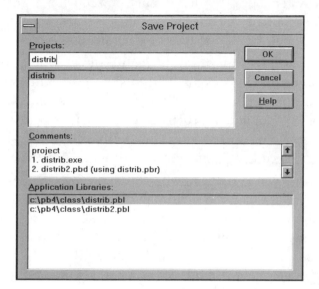

FIGURE 4.14 THE SAVE PROJECT DIALOG

Once the project object has been defined, it is represented by the project object icon in the Library painter.

To execute a project, you select **Execute Project** from the File menu or you can click on the icon on the toolbar. This builds the .EXE and any associated .PBDs.

Closing the Application Painter

Click on the **Return** icon to close and exit from the Application painter. If you made any changes since you last saved the application, PowerBuilder prompts you with an option to save those changes. In most of the PowerBuilder painters, the last icon on the PainterBar provides a way to close the painter and return to the previous work area.

ATTRIBUTES, EVENTS, AND FUNCTIONS

Each object (windows, controls, application objects, menu items) in the PowerBuilder system has attributes, events, and functions. The help system for objects is organized around its attributes, events, and functions—this division will become familiar to the PowerBuilder developers.

Attributes are the properties that define the characteristics of each object. Attributes are data elements that store the characteristics of the object (such as application name). They are variables, like the elements of a structure in other languages. Each object type has a specific set of attributes. You can examine and assign values to these attributes using the dot notation described earlier or sometimes by calling a function.

Events are the triggers that cause the Windows environment to send messages to the various objects in your application. For example, clicking the left mouse button sends a "Clicked" message to the object which is currently under the pointer. If you double-click on the control menu, the system sends a "Close" message to the control menu's window. Each object type has an associated set of events. If you are new to Windows programming, read the chapter on events for a detailed explanation of events and messages.

Functions are the procedures provided by PowerBuilder. PowerBuilder functions are similar to the functions that are found in developmental libraries that are available for most languages such as C, Pascal, and Basic. These include functions for data conversion, file access, string manipulation, time and date manipulation (and much more). You call these functions by embedding a call into your script code. Some functions are related to one (or a few) object types, while other functions are more general and can be used by any object.

APPLICATION OBJECT ATTRIBUTES

The Application Object attributes include:

■ **Appname**—the name of the application object.

- **DDETimeOut**—the maximum time (in seconds) that PowerBuilder waits for a response from a DDE server.

- **dwMessageTitle**—the caption for the DataWindow message boxes that display at run-time.

- **MicroHelpDefault**—the text that is to be displayed in the Microhelp area at the bottom of the application window.

- **ToolbarText**—sets this value to TRUE to display the text labels for the application toolbar (at run-time).

- **ToolBarTips**—a Boolean value. If True, this displays PowerTips for application toolbars.

- **ToolBarUserControl**—a Boolean value. If True, this lets the user use RMB to Hide/Show, ShowText and drag application toolbars.

Dot Notation Addressing

The attributes of PowerBuilder objects can be accessed using the *dot notation* scheme, *ObjectName.Attribute*. For example, to set the application DDE time out factor to 1/2 minute (30 seconds) and to turn on the text display for the application's toolbar you would use the following lines of code:

```
myapp.DDETimeOut = 30
myapp.ToolbarText = TRUE
```

APPLICATION OBJECT EVENTS

There are only four events that apply specifically to the application object. These application-level events are:

- **Open**—triggered when the application is started.

- **Close**—triggered when the application has been closed.

- **Idle**—triggered after a set interval of inactivity (interval set with the idle( ) function).

■ **SystemError**— triggered by a run-time error. In the case of a serious error, you can choose to shut down the application.

You may write code for any of these events. At the least you must provide code for the Open event. If you omit this you will receive an error when you try to run the application. Coding for the other events is optional.

Using the PowerScript Editor, Coding an Event

Clicking the PainterBar **Script** icon opens the PowerScript painter and lets you write code for any of the available events. Figure 4.15 shows you the PowerScript painter. We will give you a very brief (one line) introduction to writing code in this chapter. This is just enough to let you create an application. We will cover PowerScript programming in great detail throughout this book (PowerScript painter is covered in Chapter 3). The events for which you can write code at the application level are Open, Close, Idle, and System Error.

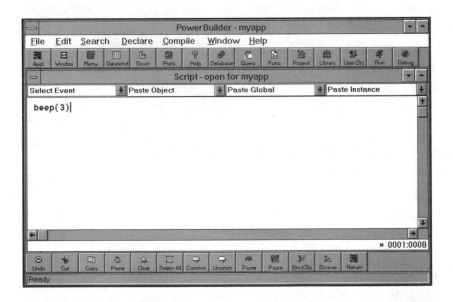

FIGURE 4.15 THE POWERSCRIPT PAINTER (THE SCRIPT EDITOR)

When you want to enter code for a PowerBuilder event, you must first access the object for which you wish to enter code, then open the editor. For application events, enter the Application painter and then the PowerScript painter. For window events (or the events of controls on a window), enter the window painter and then open the PowerScript painter. The exception to this is the Function painter, where you create global code not associated with an single object.

THE APPLICATION-LEVEL EVENTS

The next section discusses the events that occur at the application level. To add PowerScript code to any of these events, you must first open the Application painter. Then click on the **Script** icon on the PainterBar to open the PowerScript editor. Once in the editor, select the event from the Select Event drop down listbox.

The Application Open Event

The system triggers the Application Open event when you begin to execute your application. The Open event is the first chance you have to execute code and is where you begin to direct the application's execution. Depending on your application, the Open event may perform some initialization, connect the application to a database, or makes a call to open the main window (which then takes over). The example applications often read the application initialization file in the open event. PowerBuilder requires that you enter at least one line of code in the application open event, since there would be no point in creating an application that didn't do anything.

The Application Close Event

When the user shuts down the application, the system triggers the Application Close event. The Close event gives you a chance to perform any last processing before the application is terminated. In this event, you can clean up, close files, or save parameters that have been delayed.

The Application Idle Event

The Idle event lets you regain control of the application after the user has been idle for a certain amount of time. You can use the idle event to perform background processing when the user is not using the workstation. You can also use the idle event to trigger other actions. Perhaps it has been decided that no one should have a database connection open (without activity) for more than half an hour. You can set the time parameter to 30 minutes in the application open event,

```
Idle(1800)
```

and then could disconnect the user from the database and close the application. Or perhaps, you could lock the application and display a password dialog window.

The Application SystemError Event

When an error occurs at runtime, PowerBuilder triggers the SystemError event. If you do not write a script for this event, the system displays a window with the error number and an error message. If you write a script for this event, that default behavior will be overridden.

The Application Error Object

The Application Error Object is an object that contains information relating to the occurrence of a system error. You can access the Application Error Object only in the application's SystemError event where you examine the Error object attributes to determine the error information, and then decide how to proceed. The Error Object Attributes are:

- **Number**—PowerBuilder error number (an integer).
- **Text**—error message, a string describing the problem.
- **WindowMenu**—the name of the Window (or Menu) where the error occurred.

- **Object**—the name of the object where the error occurred. This may be the same as WindowMenu.

- **ObjectEvent**—the event in which the error occurred.

- **Line**—line number of the script where the error occurred.

You will often want to display some of the error information on the screen, so that a user can report back to you the information that you need to determine what caused the error. You can display the name of the object, the event, and the line of code where the error occurred.

Table 4.1 shows the PowerBuilder error codes that may occur at run-time.

TABLE 4.1 THE POWERBUILDER ERROR CODES

01	Divide by zero
02	Null object reference
03	Array boundary exceeded
04	Enumerated value is out of range for function
05	Negative value encountered in function
06	Invalid DataWindow row/column specified
07	Unresolvable external when linking reference
08	Reference of array with NULL subscript
09	DLL function not found in current application
10	Unsupported argument type in DLL function
12	DataWindow column type does not match GetItem type
13	Unresolved attribute reference
14	Error opening DLL library for external function
15	Error calling external function
16	Maximum string size exceeded
17	DataWindow referenced in DataWindow object does not exist
50	Application reference could not be resolved
51	Failure loading dynamic library

Application Object Functions

There are only two application level functions:

- **ClassName()**—returns the name of the application object.
- **TriggerEvent()**—initiate a PowerBuilder event, causing the related script (if any) to be executed.

For example, to obtain the name of the application object, you would use the following code:

```
string sClassName
sClassName = myapp.ClassName() //"myapp"
```

or to trigger a Idle event

```
myapp.TriggerEvent(Idle!)
```

THE APPLICATION PAINTER MENUS

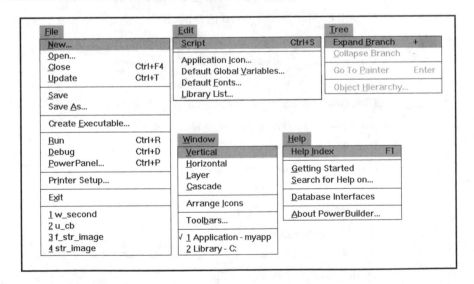

FIGURE 4.16 THE APPLICATION PAINTER MENUS

The Application Painter Menu Options

The PowerScript painter menu bar includes the following dropdown menus:

```
File | Edit | Tree | Window | Help
```

The options on each menu are:

File Menu

- **New**—creates a new application object.
- **Open**—opens another application.
- **Close**—closes this application. If changes have occurred prompt before saving any changes.
- **Update**—saves the changes and close the application.
- **Save**—saves all the changes to the application.
- **Save As**—saves this as a new application object.
- **Create Executable**—generates an executable version of this application.
- **Run**—executes the current application from the development environment.
- **Debug**—runs the application in debug mode. Prompt first for breakpoints.
- **PowerPanel**—changes the presentation style to that of the PowerPanel.
- **Printer Setup**—opens the Printer Setup dialog to specific printer attributes, lets the user set print options.
- **Exit**—quits PowerBuilder.
- **last used**—presents a set of last accessed objects for quick access.

Edit Menu

- **Script**—opens the PowerScript painter to edit code for an application-level event.

- **Application Icon**—associates an icon with this application.

- **Default Global Variable**—opens a dialog which allows you to specify user defined types for SQLCA, SQLDA, SQLSA, ERROR and MESSAGE.

- **Default Fonts**—sets the default application fonts for text, headings, labels, and data.

- **Library List**—modifies the list of libraries that contain application components.

Tree Menu

- **Expand Branch**—explodes the display one level further (from the selected object).

- **Collapse Branch**—closes all the branches below the selected object.

- **Go To Painter**—opens the painter associated with the selected object.

- **Object Hierarchy**—shows the inheritance tree for the selected object, if is an inherited object.

Window Menu

- **Tile**—arranges the currently open windows

- **Layer**—maximizes the current window.

- **Cascade**—arranges the currently open windows in a cascade.

- **Arrange Icons**—arranges the minimized windows' icons.

- **Toolbars**—customizes, hides, displays, or positions a toolbar.

- **window list**—a numbered list of the current windows, selects one to change to that window.

Help Menu

- **Help Index**—opens the help window, and display the index.

- **Getting Starting**—presents an introduction to PowerBuilder.

- **Search**—searches the help system for a topic.
- **Technical Help**—provides help on database connections and customizing toolbars.
- **About PowerBuilder**—the About box; information on version, copyright, and license.

BUILDING AN APPLICATION

In this section, the steps necessary to create a new application will be outlined, going through the minimal steps to explain the basic process. You may follow the directions to create a simple application if you wish. This application has a single line of code, and will only beep the speaker of your PC when it runs. The example application presented in the next chapter, displays a couple of message boxes on the screen when it runs.

You may prefer to read through the next section to get an overview and then build the FirstApp example application. FirstApp will be enough to introduce you to the creation of an application and its executable.

Creating A New Application

The steps involved in creating an a new application are:

1. Define the application object and create the library.
2. Add code to the Open event for the application object.
3. Run the development version of the application to validate it.
4. Create an executable for the application.
5. Run the executable version of the application.

Later, when you are creating larger applications, you will add a step (between steps 2 and 3) which will be the largest amount of the development effort. In that step you will create windows, add controls and/or menus to those windows, and add script code to the events. This example is just to make you familiar with the creation of the application object, and the application executable.

Create the Application and Library

In the initial PowerBuilder window, click on the **Appl** icon on the PowerBar. This opens the Application painter. In the Application painter select the **File|New** menu option to display the Select New Application Library dialog (shown in Figure 4.4). To create the new application fill in the name of the library, such as **myapp.pbl**. Tab over to the directories field and set the drive and path to **C:\PB4\CLASS**. Check that everything looks correct, then click **OK**. This opens the Save Application dialog box (Figure 4.5). In the first field (under Applications:) enter **myapp** for the name of the application. Next tab down to the comments field and add a comment such as "This application just beeps" and then click **OK**. When PowerBuilder asks if you want to generate an application template, click on **No**. This returns you to the Application painter and you can then continue with the next step.

Add Code to the Open Event

The intent of this example is to introduce the process of creating an application, so you will only add a single line of code to the application. The line of code is **beep(3)**. This tells the application to send three tones to the speaker of your PC. This single line of code contains all work that this application will do. To enter the line of code, click the **Script** icon on the Application PainterBar. This opens the Script Painter as shown in Figure 4.17. The script editor should display *Script-open for myapp* on the title bar, if not pull down the SelectEvent drop-down menu and select **Open**.

The title bar shows the event (open) and the object (the myapp application) for which you are entering code. Type **beep(3)** and then click on the **Return** icon or select **File|Return**. This compiles the code, if you mistyped the statement, you will receive an error message.

If for any reason you are unable to complete this step successfully and you wish to exit anyway, you can do one of several things to leave the editor.

1. Double-click on the control menu (or select **File|Close**) and respond "No" when you are prompted "Do You Want to Save Changes", or

2. Click on **Select All** and then the **Comment** icons on the PainterBar to comment out the line of code so that you can exit, or

3. Delete all the code in the Script window and then exit.

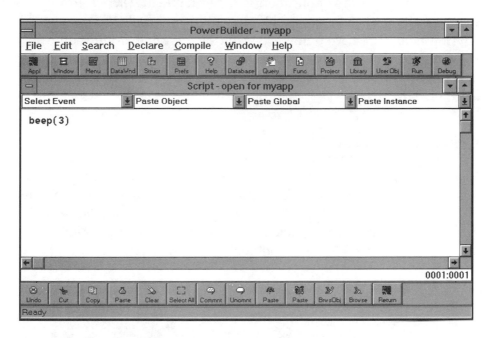

FIGURE 4.17 THE OPEN EVENT FOR THE APPLICATION OBJECT

Run the Application

You must exit the editor before you can run the application. PowerBuilder will not let you execute an application while there are any open PowerScript painter windows. Click on the **Run** icon (or select **File|Run**) to start the application. If you are prompted "Save Changes To...", answer yes (this saves the changes you have made to the application). The application begins to execute and the development environment is minimized showing the Windows desktop (or whatever you were running behind PowerBuilder). The system triggers the Application Open event, executing the code that you placed in that event. If your computer's speaker is active, you should hear the speaker beep three times. The application will then quit and the development environment returns to its previous state.

This version of the application is a development version. In the next step we will develop an executable that will run outside the development environment. The development version of the application requires the PowerBuilder development environment in order to execute. If the application ran successfully (even if you did not hear the three tones), you can go on to the next step.

Create an Executable

This step creates an executable version of the application. The *executable version* is a file (for this example, named MYAPP.EXE) that can be executed directly from the Windows desktop without the use of the PowerBuilder development environment. Check to be sure that you are currently in the Application painter before proceeding on to the next step.

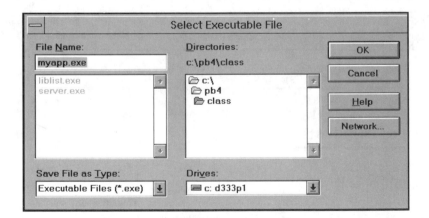

FIGURE 4.18 THE SELECT EXECUTABLE DIALOG

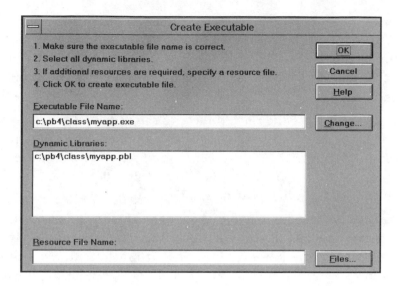

FIGURE 4.19 CREATING AN EXECUTABLE

Click on the **CreateExe** icon or select the **File|CreateExecutable** menu option to create the executable version of your application. (If prompted to save changes, answer *Yes*.) You will see the Create Executable dialog window. It should suggest the name myapp.exe for your executable and select the same directory where the library was created. Check under the Dynamic Libraries listbox to be sure that the correct library (.pbl file) is listed. When everything matches Figure 4.19, click on **OK**. If every goes correctly, you will see the message "Creating Executable File" on the status line and then it will change to "Ready".

Later, if you create a new version of the executable (after undating the application), the system asks if you wish to overwrite the existing myapp.exe; you should answer *Yes*.

Run the Executable from Windows

Next, you will want to see that the executable was created and can be run outside of PowerBuilder. To do this, exit completely out of PowerBuilder (this is not necessary to run the executable; we are doing this to prove that the development environment is not required). Do this by selecting the **File|Exit** menu option. In the Windows Program Manager, select the **File|Run** menu selection and then browse until you find the program (C:\PB4\CLASS\MYAPP.EXE). Run that application and you should hear the three beeps.

You could also use the File Manager to run the application. To do this select the file **MYAPP.EXE** and then the menu option **File|Run** or just double-click on **MYAPP.EXE**. You will want to select an icon to represent the application on the Windows desktop. To do this follow the directions that where given earlier in the Selecting the Application Icon section.

One caveat about running the executable. The executable uses a number of DLLs in the PB4 directory when it runs. The PB4 directory must be on your path (in the autoexec.bat) *or* you must set the PB4 directory (C:\PB4 in our examples) to be the working directory for the application when you define the profile for the MYAPP.EXE. If you do not follow one of these recommendations you may receive a error message. This would be a File Error message box with a message something like the following, *Cannot find PBRTF040.DLL.*

After completing this step you should understand how to create an application, and then how to create and run the executable.

For the next section launch PowerBuilder again and go back to the Application painter. (On the initial PowerBuilder screen, click the **Application** icon.) Notice that the default application is now myapp, since that was the last application that you accessed.

LIBRARY PAINTER

The Library painter manages the PowerBuilder libraries where the application components reside. The Library painter lets you inspect the contents of the libraries, as well as search through them for objects and text. You can move or copy objects from one library to another, delete objects from a library and perform other types of maintenance (covered in detail in the chapter on The Library Painter). PowerBuilder also lets developers check objects out of the libraries for development. When an object has been checked out, it cannot be modified by another developer. This prevents two or more developers from working on the same object at the same time. When the development has been completed, the developer checks the object back into the library.

To open the Library painter, click on the **Library** icon on the PowerBar. This opens a screen which should look similar to Figure 4.20.

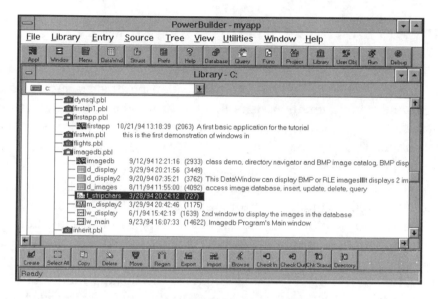

FIGURE 4.20 LIBRARY PAINTER

You can select the desired disk drive from across the top of the painter window. You navigate through the directory structure by double-clicking on a directory. This will expand the directory display (if the directory contains subdirectories). Once expanded, you double-click on a directory to collapse (close) it. Find the library for one of your applications (such as C:\PB4\CLASS\FIRSTAPP.PBL). Double-clicking on the **FIRSTAPP.PBL** icon will expand the library, listing its components. This expansion is somewhat similar to the Application painter, but shows objects by library, not by object. The only component of the FIRSTAPP.PBL library is the FirstApp application object, for that object you should see the modification date, size, and a comment. If you select a larger library, such as IMAGEDB.PBL, you will see a greater number of objects (see Figure 4.20). There is a different icon for each type of object (application objects, windows, DataWindows, menus, user objects, functions). To collapse the library just double-click on it. (If you double-click on one of the application objects, PowerBuilder launches the painter associated with that type of object).

THE APPLICATION INITIALIZATION FILE

Each application should have its own initialization file (sometimes called a profile file). This file will contain application parameters such as database connection information, default values, and other information that is specific to an application but which you do not wish to hard-code into the application. This lets you change parameters at runtime without having to recompile the program.

By convention, the name given to the initialization file is the same as the application, and the initialization file is given the extension INI. The init file should be placed in the same directory as the application executable (or in the \Windows directory). For example, if you create the sample application FirstApp, you will create a init file called FIRSTAPP.INI. You will place this in the same directory as the firstapp library and executable, which is C:\PB4\CLASS. An initialization file is often called the *ini* file, or the *init* file, or sometimes the *dot ini* file (*.INI*).

The format of the profile file is the same as other Windows initialization files and the PowerBuilder PB.INI file. The file is organized in sections which are marked with square brackets (around the section label). In each section a number of entries follow the section label. Each entry has a key (name), equal sign, and a value. An excerpt from IMAGEDB.INI follows. The first section is [sqlca], and the first key is dbms with a value of ODBC. This section specifies the default database connection for the Imagedb application. If a key does not apply or you wish to clear its initial value, the value may be omitted. For example, in the IMAGEDB.INI sample notice, servername=.

```
--------------------------------------------------------
[sqlca]
dbms=ODBC
database=image
userid=
dbpass=
logid=
logpass=
servername=
DbParm=ConnectString='DSN=image;UID=dba;PWD=sql'
firsttime=no

[application]
showtext=no
--------------------------------------------------------
```

PowerBuilder supplies functions for reading and writing to these initialization files. There are three functions:

- **ProfileString** (filename, section name, key, default)—reads an entry from the profile file and returns its value as a string.

- **ProfileInt** (filename, section name, key, default)—reads an entry from the profile file and returns its value as an integer.

- **SetProfileString** (filename, section name, key, value)—writes an entry to a profile file as a string.

For example, you could use the following statement to read the value associated with the DBMS key from the SQLCA section into the string variable sDatabase.

```
sDatabase = ProfileString("IMAGEDB.INI", "sqlca", "dbms", "none")
```

If you do not include the full path for the initialization file the system will look in the current directory first. If it does not find the file there it will search directories in the usual order for Windows applications; first \WINDOWS, \WINDOWS\SYSTEM, and then the directory path from the DOS environment. In this case, you will have set the default directory to C:\PB4\CLASS when you create or run the example applications, and the file will be found in that directory.

The ProfileString() function returns the value associated with a key as a string. ProfileInt() returns the value as an integer. If the file, section, or key is not found then the variable will be set to the default value that you assigned as the last (forth) argument to the function. In the case of an error an empty string will be returned for ProfileString, and a –1 will be returned for ProfileInt.

SetProfileString will set a value in the profile file. There is no SetProfileInt function—since you are writing to an ASCII text file you would still use the SetProfileString function. This function will create an entry (a key and its value) and a section if they do not exist in the profile file. If the key already exists in the profile file, its value will be updated. SetProfileString will not create the profile file if it does not exist. If SetProfileString is successful it returns a 1. If it fails it will return a –1. These return values are typical of a large number of the PowerBuilder functions.

```
SetProfileString("C:\PB4\CLASS\IMAGEDB.INI","SQLCA",
                "firsttime","no")
```

This example would set the value of firsttime to *no*.

A note about security. In our examples we include the database user id and password for simplicity. This would not be suitable for production applications. You should prompt the user for the password or encrypt it.

WHAT'S NEXT

Most applications use one or more windows to provide a interface to the user. The Window Painter is used to create windows and to add controls such as radio buttons to those windows.

Before we get into the creation of windows and the other graphical objects, we will build the FirstApp application.

EXAMPLE: FIRSTAPP

Developing the Exercise Applications

The program diskette that came with this book contains finished versions of all the exercises used in this book. Following the instructions in the introduction of this book, you should have installed the samples on your drive (in C:\PB4\CLASS).

You should run each example so that you understand exactly what the application does and how it looks. Next you should attempt to duplicate the example application as precisely as possible. Name your versions of each application library the same as the sample, but append version numbers to the name. You are limited to eight character names in the DOS file system so you may have to truncate the name by one character. For example, for FIRSTAPP, create a library named FIRSTAP1.PBL. Later if you want to create other versions, you can create a library named FIRSTAP2.PBL (etc.). You can name all the objects (application objects, windows, etc.) exactly the same as in the exercise text.

You may be able to create each application from the knowledge you have gained by reading the text and by using the help system. If you are not able to complete the exercise in that manner, just examine the source code for each application. You should print out a listing for each application for your reference. To do this select the application in the Application painter to set the current application. Then go to the Library painter and select all the objects in the application (click the **Select All** icon). Select the **Entry|Print** menu option.

In the application documentation, you will find an outline section that contains a brief description of each object in the exercise and all of the script code that is required to complete the application. You can also use this outline section as a source of hints as you work on your application.

Exercise 1: FirstApp

FirstApp is a simple application that will demonstrate two of the application events (Open and Close) and the use of an application message box. The message box is an application modal dialog window that displays a message and then waits for the user to respond by clicking on the **OK** button or by pressing the **Enter** key. FirstApp will display a message box in the application Open event. It will also attempt to locate and read the firstapp.ini file. If it is successful then it will display the text of that file in another message box, otherwise it will display an error message. Finally it will display a final message in the application Close event.

Before you build your version of this application, run the sample application from the PowerBuilder environment. To do this, launch PowerBuilder (if necessary), and go to the Application painter (click on the **Appl** icon on the PowerBar). Select the **Open** icon from the Application painter PainterBar. In the Select Application Library dialog window select **C:\PB4\CLASS** in the directories listbox. Then select the **FIRSTAPP.PBL** library in the libraries list box and click the **OK** command button. This should display FIRSTAPP in the Applications field of the Select Application dialog. Select **OK** to return to the Application painter.

In the Application painter check that the window caption is *Application-firstapp*. Click on the **Run** icon or select the **File|Run** menu option to run the application. When the application runs, you will see three different messages on the screen.

Running FirstApp

1. When the application begins, it triggers the application Open event. You will see a message box announcing the occurrence of the Open event. The message *Open for FirstApp* should be displayed as shown in Figure 4.21. Click **OK** to continue.

2. The code in the application Open event then attempts to read the initialization file (FIRSTAPP.INI). If the application successfully locates the file, it displays the message *Found the firstapp.ini file* as shown in Figure 4.22.

    If the application cannot find the file then the message is *Could not find file FIRSTAPP.INI* as in Figure 4.23. In either case, click on **OK** to continue.

FIGURE 4.21 THE FIRST RESPONSE WINDOW

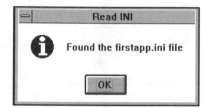

FIGURE 4.22 THIS WINDOW IS DISPLAYED IF THE INI FILE IS FOUND

FIGURE 4.23 WINDOW DISPLAYED IF THE INI FILE IS NOT FOUND

3. When the application has completed the program code in the open event (steps 1 and 2), the application shuts down and finishes. This triggers the application Close event, which displays the message *Closing the FirstApp Application* as shown in Figure 4.24. Click **OK** in this message to allow the application to shutdown.

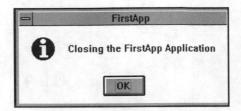

FIGURE 4.24 THE FINAL RESPONSE WINDOW

All the Code You Need

You can complete this application by following the next two steps:

1. Create a new application library and application object. Name them *FirstAp1*.

2. Add the following code to the application Open event:

```
------------------------------------------------
int    nFile
string sText
long   lSize

MessageBox ("FirstApp", "Open for FirstApp")
nFile = FileOpen("firstapp.ini")
IF nFile >= 0 THEN
    FileRead(nFile, sText) // reads file into sText
    MessageBox ("Read INI", sText) // displays sText
ELSE
    MessageBox ("Read INI", "could not find file
                FIRSTAPP.INI")
END IF
------------------------------------------------
```

3. Add the following code to the application Close event:

```
------------------------------------------------
MessageBox ("FirstApp", "Closing the FirstApp Application")
------------------------------------------------
```

FirstApp — Step-by-Step

Create the Application and Library

0. Start PowerBuilder (if necessary).

1. If you are not in the Application painter, click on the **Appl** icon on the PowerBar.

2. In the Application painter select the **File|New** menu option.

3. In the Select New Application Library dialog:

3a. In the File Name field fill in the name firstap1.pbl.

3b. Tab to the directories (or drives) field and set the drive and path to C:\PB4\CLASS.

3c. Be sure that the library name is still firstap1.pbl, if not correct it.

3d. Click on **OK**.

4. In the Save Application dialog:

4a. In the Applications: field enter **firstap1**.

4b. Tab to the comments field and enter **My firstApp version1**.

4c. Be sure that the application name is firstap1, if not correct it.

4d. Click on **OK**.

You have created the firstap1 application object and the firstap1 library.

Add Code to the Open Event

Code will be added to the open event in two stages. Follow the next instructions to add a popup window to your first application to announce the Open event. A later step will add code to read the initialization file. To enter the new code, click on the **Script** icon on the Application PainterBar. This will open the Script Painter as shown in figure 4.25.

Figure 4.25 shows the text of the completed example. In this step we will only add one line of code. The script editor should display *Script-open for firstap1* on the title bar; if not, pull down the SelectEvent drop-down menu and select **Open**. Edit the code until it matches the following exactly.

```
MessageBox ("FirstApp", "Open for the FirstApp Application")
```

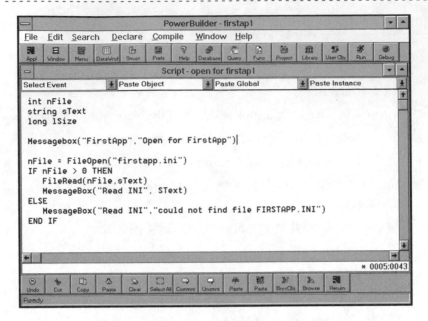

FIGURE 4.25 THE OPEN SCRIPT FOR FIRSTAPP

When it is correct, click on the **Return** icon.

If, for any reason, you are unable to complete this step successfully, and you wish to exit anyway, do the following. Click on the **Select All** and then **Commnt** icons to comment out all lines of code, you can then exit. If you later return to work on this code you can remove the comments by clicking on the **SelectAll** and then **Uncmnt** icons.

Add Code to the Close Event

New code will be entered for the Application Close event. Click on the **Script** icon on the Application PainterBar. This opens the Script Painter. Pull down the SelectEvent dropdown menu and select **Close**. The script editor should then show *Script-close for firstap1* on the title bar. Next you should type the following line of code (be sure that it matches the following exactly):

```
MessageBox ("FirstApp", "Closing the FirstApp Application")
```

When it is correct, click on the **Return** icon. If, for any reason, you are unable to do this step successfully, and you wish to exit anyway, click on **Select All** and then **Comment** to comment out all the line of code, you will then be able to exit.

This line of code was added to show when the application close event occurs. It displays the message *Closing the FirstApp Application* and waits for you to press the **OK** button.

Now you should run the application from the development environment. Nothing should go wrong, but if it does, postpone any work on it until you are familiar with the debugger. If everything runs OK, then create a new executable and run it from the Windows Program Manager as you did before. This will display messages at the open and close events. Now you can proceed to add the code that will read the initialization file and display the result in another response window.

Add More Code to the Open Event

Next add code to read the initialization file. The final result should match the following:

```
int     nFile
string  sText
long    lSize

MessageBox ("FirstApp", "Open for FirstApp")
nFile = FileOpen("firstapp.ini")

IF nFile >= 0 THEN
    FileRead(nFile, sText)
    MessageBox ("Read INI", sText)
ELSE
    MessageBox ("Read INI", "could not find file
                FIRSTAPP.INI")
END IF
```

A few comments on this code are in order. Three variables are declared: an integer, a string, and a long. The next line opens a modal response window, with the title *FirstApp*, and the text *Open for FirstApp*. The window contains an OK command button (this is the default). When you run the application, the Open event causes this code to be executed. The MessageBox statement displays this window and waits until you click on OK.

The next line of code attempts to open the file firstapp.ini. If it is successful, it obtains a file handle (nFile) which is greater than or equal to zero. If the application cannot find the file, a negative number is returned from the FileOpen function. If the file was successfully opened, the next section of code reads the entire contents of the file into the string variable sText, and then displays it in another response window. If the application could not find the profile file, the error message is displayed.

Once again, you can run the application from the development environment. If everything runs OK, you may create a new executable as you did before. If you have any problems, compare your code closely to the code in the firstapp.pbl.

CHAPTER FIVE

CREATING WINDOWS

As a Microsoft Windows user, you are familiar with windows of several types. Windows are used to present information to, and accept input from, the user of the application. Most PowerBuilder applications have one or more windows, and use them extensively for the user-interface. The Window painter provides all the functions that the developer needs to create windows and to add controls (such as CommandButtons and radiobuttons) to those windows. The Window painter works in a graphical and easy-to-use manner. In this chapter we will cover the building of windows. This will include the creation of windows, window attributes, window events, and functions. In the next chapter we cover the addition of controls, such as CommandButtons, to a window.

Window Painter

To open the Window painter, click on the **Window** icon on the PowerBar. This opens the Select Window dialog window (Figure 5.1). In the Select Window dialog you can either open an existing window (in order to modify it), or create a new window. To create a new window, click the **New** CommandButton. (You could also create a new window by using inheritance (by selecting the **Inherit** button), we cover this option later in the chapter on Inheritance).

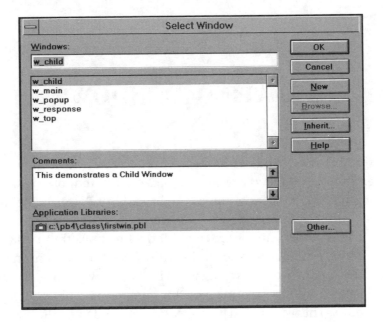

Figure 5.1 The Select Window dialog

The Window Painter Dialog

Clicking the **New** CommandButton on the Select Window dialog opens the Window painter (Figure 5.2) and creates the new window in the process.

The Window painter displays the newly created (and as yet unnamed) window. The new window appears as a rectangle in the upper left of the workspace. If you have the grid display turned on, the window will be covered with dots that will assist in positioning and aligning the objects and controls that you add to the window. (To activate the grid, use the **Design|Grid** menu option and click the **Show Grid** and **Snap to Grid** checkboxes). The workspace is the client area of the Window painter where you design the window and add controls and other objects to the window. While working in this window you are in design mode, you can switch to preview mode to see the current state of the window with the **Design|Preview** menu option. You will spend a great amount of time in the Window painter and it is important that you become familiar with all of its features.

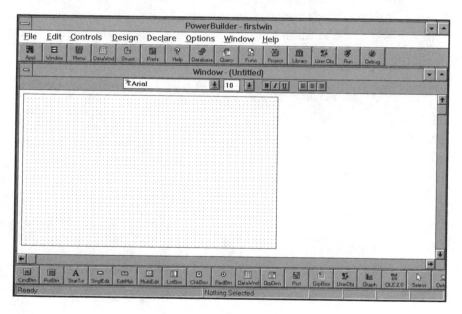

FIGURE 5.2 THE WINDOW PAINTER

The 3D Look

You can (and should) select the 3D look as the default for windows. This creates gray windows with 3D borders, which is the best appearance for most situations, and is standard in many Windows applications. You can select this option in the Window painter **Options|Default to 3D**, or in the Preferences painter under the Window's options. We will cover this option in the appropriate sections.

CREATING WINDOWS

Window Painter Toolbars

Notice that the Window painter has a large number of icons on its PainterBar. Most of these icons represent controls or graphical objects that you can add to the new window. These controls and even more are available under the Control menu. Figure 5.3 shows the Controls menu, and the Window painter toolbar displayed as a floating rectangle.

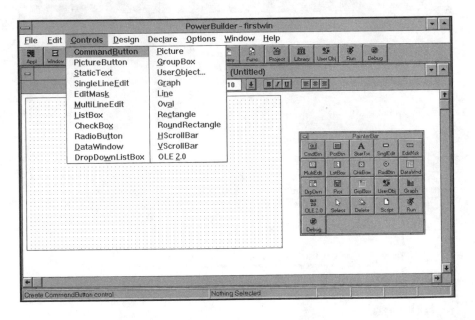

FIGURE 5.3 THE CONTROLS MENU IN THE WINDOW PAINTER

Style Toolbar and Color Bar Toolbars

In the Window painter, you have the option of displaying two additional toolbars, the style toolbar and the color bar. The style toolbar displays and lets you change the attributes of the text on the window such as the font name, and various options such as underlining, italics, bold, and justification. The color bar presents a palette of the color choices for the design process. Figure 5.4 shows the style and color toolbars.

When you choose to add the color bar, you can set the color of any selected objects in the window. First select the object(s) for which you are going to set the color. Then right mouse click on the color (on the color bar) that you want to use for the object's text, and right mouse click on a color to set the object's background color. The left most cell of the color bar will show the current foreground and background colors.

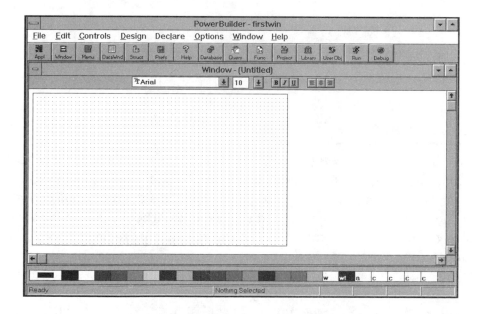

FIGURE 5.4 THE STYLE AND COLOR TOOLBARS

To show (display) these toolbars select the **Window|Toolbars...** menu option. This opens the Toolbars dialog window (Figure 5.5) where you can

155

choose to show, hide, or relocate any of the toolbars, or customize the contents of the PowerBar and PainterBar.

You can position any of the toolbars at the top or bottom of the window. You can also choose to display the PowerBar or PainterBar toolbars at the left or right of the window, or as a floating (repositionable) box. The floating toolbar option is especially appropriate for the PainterBar in the Window painter because of the large number of icons contained within it.

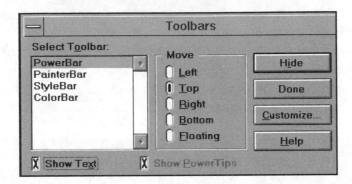

FIGURE 5.5 THE TOOLBARS DIALOG

Resizing the New Window

You can resize and reposition the new window in several ways. First you can use the mouse in the painter workspace. To do this, position the pointer at the outer edge of the rectangle that represents the new window until the pointer's shape changes into a double arrow. Then click and drag the edge of the window to expand or contract it. The top and left edges of the window are fixed and cannot be moved in the workspace. The Window painter itself takes up quite a bit of territory on the screen, so you may have to scroll the workspace (using the vertical and horizontal scrollbars) to allow the window to be fully sized and shaped. You can switch from design mode to preview mode to see what the window will actually look like when it is used in an application. To preview the window's appearance, use the **Shift+Control+W** key combination to toggle on the preview mode. The same key combination will return you to design mode. You can also use the **Design|Preview** menu option to switch to Preview mode, and then double click on the previewed window's control menu to switch back to design mode.

Window Position Dialog Window

There is another, and much easier method for positioning and sizing the new window. In the Window painter's main window, choose the **Design|Window Position...** menu option or activate the popup menu (click the right mouse button while the pointer is positioned on the window) and select the Position menu option. Either action takes you to the Window Position dialog shown in Figure 5.6. This dialog is very easy to use and it gives you a proportional representation of how the window appears on the screen.

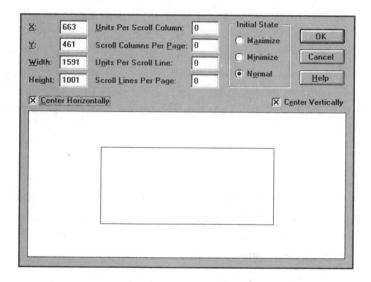

FIGURE 5.6 THE WINDOW POSITION DIALOG

The white rectangular area at the bottom of this dialog window represents the actual display area available on your video screen. In this area you will also see a rectangle that represents the newly created window. That rectangle shows the window's current position and relative size in the display area. You can use the mouse to position and to resize the window. Click and drag any edge of the window to resize it, or click within the window and drag to reposition it.

Automatic Centering

On the Window Position dialog window, you can use the two check boxes to automatically center the window within the display area. Click on the leftmost check box to automatically center the window on the horizontal plane. Click on the rightmost check box to automatically center the window on the vertical plane. If you check these boxes, you will no longer be able to move the window (since its position is fixed at the center), but you can still resize the window in either dimension.

This dialog window also displays the current location and size of the window in PowerBuilder units. You could enter these numbers directly, but that is not very intuitive and there is little reason to do so. The size of a horizontal PowerBuilder unit (PBU) is equal to 1/32 of the width of an average character in the system font. The size of a vertical PBU is equal to 1/64 of the same character. Knowing this you can calculate the size of the standard VGA screen as approximately 2560 horizontal PBUs (80x32) by 1536 (24x64) vertical PBUs. These numbers are only approximate, since they are based on an average size character.

Initial State

You can also set the initial state of the window in this dialog window. This is the state that the window will assume when it is first opened in your application. The choices for the initial state are Maximize, Minimize, and Normal. Normal is the size that is currently displayed in the Window Position work area.

You can also set the scroll rates for the vertical and horizontal scroll bars (if any) for this window by setting the values in the top center of this dialog. If you do not enter values (leave them at zero), the default values will be used. The default scroll rate is 1/100 of the window size for each click on one of the scrollbar arrows. The default paging distance is 10 lines of text vertically and 10 column horizontally. Page scrolling is initiated when you click on one of the scroll bars itself.

Sizing Windows for Different Resolution Monitors

There is an important caveat to consider when sizing the new window. If you are developing your application on a computer that has a different video resolution than the target system for which you are designing the application, you must be careful. When you run your application on the target systems, what you see may not be what you expected and intended. If you have a high resolution monitor (for instance, 800 x 600 or 1024 x 768) and create a window that fills the entire screen, you may be surprised to see that when the application is run on a standard VGA system (640 x 480) the window will be too large to fit on the VGA screen. You should also verify that the font type and size are appropriate for the target system. So plan accordingly, and run a test early in the development process to be sure that the window(s) will fit. You should also consider choosing the centering options to be sure that the window is positioned correctly. The advantage of PowerBuilder units based on an average size character is that the ratio is more accurate on different screen resolution than if you used pixels.

In general, you will find it easier to develop on a lower resolution screen and then deliver to higher resolution screens, rather than the other way around.

DEFINING A WINDOW'S STYLE

A window has a large number of properties that determine its characteristics. These properties define the style of the window and are controlled in the window's style dialog. Select the **Design|Window Style...** menu option from the Window painter menu. This opens the Window Style dialog window, as shown in Figure 5.7.

There is also a shortcut to the window Style dialog window, just double-click within the window. If there are other objects in the window (such as push buttons) you must be sure to actually click on the window area, and avoid the controls.

The first and most important choice in the Window Style dialog, is to choose the Window Type. To do this, select one of the types listed in the group radiobutton section at the bottom of the dialog window. This selection is important because a window's type determines a great deal about the behavior of each window. When you select the type, PowerBuilder will automatically set (and unset) some of the other attributes in this dialog to match the characteristics of the selected type. The type of window determines its relationship with other windows in your application. Some windows may serve as the parent (or owner) of other parented windows.

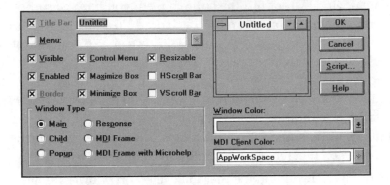

FIGURE 5.7 THE WINDOW STYLE DIALOG

The choices for the window types are:

Main

- This is a standard, independent overlapping window.

- Often used as a base window which holds the application controls and is used to create forms.

- May serve as a parent window for child, popup, and response windows.

- A main window type can also be an MDI sheet (explained below).

Popup

- A parented window, but can appear outside of parent.

- Closed, minimized with parent.

- Closed, minimized separately.

Child

- A parented window, cannot appear outside of parent.
- Can have title.
- Do not have menus.
- Closed, minimized, max within parent.
- Closed with parent.
- Can never be the active window so never fires an activate event.
- Not used as much, now that MDI is standard.

Response

- Is a modal popup window.
- Does not have minimize, maximize buttons.
- The MessageBox that you have already used is actually a PowerBuilder supplied response box.

MDI

- Multiple Document Interface Frame Window.
- Contains sheets (child windows, but may be any type except MDI).
- May also opt for MDI with Microhelp.

Figure 5.8 show an example with one of each type of window (except MDI).

The Main Window

The main window is usually selected for a window that serves as the primary window in an application. A main window stands as a base window, and is not contained in any other window. A main window may be the parent of other windows. These other dependent windows are child, popup, or response. In Figure 5.8 the window with the caption *Double-Click in This Window* is a main window.

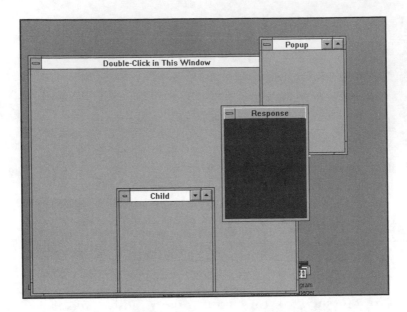

**FIGURE 5.8 THE FIRSTWIN APPLICATION SHOWING
A MAIN, CHILD, POPUP, AND RESPONSE WINDOW**

A main window most often has either a menu or a set of CommandButtons to present different options to the user. This type of window may have a title bar with a caption and usually has a border. It has an overlapping window style for its presentation. A main window can be resized or minimized. When you set its position, its position is set relative to the screen and not in relation to any other window.

The Child Window

A child window is a dependent window. A child window must be associated with a parent window and can only be presented within the bounds of the parent. A child window can be minimized or maximized within the parent window. If you minimize a child window, its icon will appear in the bottom of the parent window. If the parent is minimized, then the child will also be minimized. When you position a child window, all references are made in relation to the top-left corner of the parent window. Child windows cannot have their own menus but may have a control menu. A child window usually has a title bar. In Figure 5.8 you see a child window with the caption "Child". Notice that the bottom of the child window is clipped off by the main (parent) window.

The Popup Window

A popup window has a parent window like a child window but does not have all the limitations of the child window. A popup window's position and display are not limited to the boundary of the parent window. They always appear in front of the parent window and can be minimized separately from the parent (but if the parent is minimized, so is the popup). When minimized, the popup icon appears on Windows' desktop, not inside the parent window. Popups usually have a title bar and may also have their own menus. Popups are often used to provide additional information or greater detail about an object in the parent window. The window with the caption "Popup" in Figure 5.8 is a popup window. Notice that it appears outside but still on top of the parent main window.

The Response Window

A response window is similar in some ways to a popup window, except that it is application modal. A modal window is one that forces a user response before continuing with the application. When your application opens a response window, the user cannot switch to another window (in the same application) until they close the response window. The response window always presents a message and usually one or more CommandButtons to the user. This is often used to present error information or to prompt the user to make a decision that is needed before proceeding. You have already created a response window in the FirstApp example application. The PowerBuilder MessageBox function creates a response window. A response window cannot have a menu, cannot be resized, and is not scrollable. You can move a response window or close it. Figure 5.8 also contains a response type window.

You often see a response window when you attempt to close a Windows program and have not saved some newly created or modified information. For example, if you are using a text editor where you have created a new text file or have perhaps modified an existing file and you attempt to exit the program without having saved those changes, a response window appears. The response window contains a message to warn you that the changed text has not been saved and asks whether you wish to save the changes before closing the program. Figure 5.9 shows a response window from Microsoft Word.

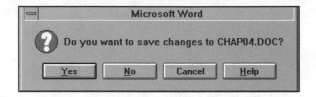

FIGURE 5.9 A FAMILIAR RESPONSE WINDOW

The response window usually utilizes the CloseWithReturn statement to return to the calling statement with the number of the user's choice.

Application Modal versus System Modal

PowerBuilder response windows are application modal—restrictive only within the application. That means that the user cannot switch to another window in the PowerBuilder application until the response window is closed. The user could switch to another Windows application without closing the response window by using the Control+Escape or Alt+Tab key combinations.

A system modal window is totally restrictive and does not let the user switch to another application. This insures that absolutely nothing else can be done until the response window is closed. It is possible to promote a window to make it system modal in your application by making a Windows SDK function call. This can be useful (usually for severe errors), and we give an example of how to implement this in the chapter on extending PowerBuilder in the Windows Environment.

The MDI Frame Window

The MDI Frame window may be the most important of all these types. Most of the larger Windows applications have the MDI (Multiple Document Interface) application style. Microsoft Word for Windows, Microsoft Excel, and PowerBuilder itself are examples of MDI applications. MDI is a presentation style where there is one parent window (called the *MDI frame*) which contains numerous child windows (called *sheets*). In Microsoft Word for Windows, the child windows are the various documents that you are editing and in Excel each child represents a spreadsheet.

MDI frames can also contain toolbars and have the option of including Microhelp.

The sheet windows are similar to child windows described earlier. They always appear within the parent frame window and if you minimize the parent (frame) window, the sheets are also minimized. Sheets can be minimized, maximized, and arranged (tiled, cascaded, or layered) within the frame.

MDI windows are like the main windows discussed earlier, with a number of child windows. The difference is that the MDI style provides greater control in the management of the sheet windows. It automatically provides features, such as scrollbars, as needed.

Sheets and Menus

The MDI sheet does vary a little in style from the child window. For example, sheets can have their own menus (but they are displayed on MDI frame). MDI interaction is accomplished primarily with the use of menus. In general and as a point of style, MDI windows do not have CommandButtons and you should follow that convention unless you have a good reason to do otherwise.

Sometimes the sheets do not have their own menus. In PowerBuilder applications, a sheet without a menu and/or toolbar inherits them from the previous sheet. If there is no previous sheet, they use the frame's menu and/or toolbar.

Recommendation for Sheets and Menus

If any sheet in your application has a menu, then for consistency, every sheet should have its own menu. If your sheets do not have menus, then they should use the menu (and/or toolbar) on the frame. It is highly recommended that you follow this convention, otherwise it can be very confusing to the user.

The drawback to this technique is that there is a severe performance penalty in assigning menus for each sheet. Everytime you assign a menu as an attribute on a window, it will load that entire object into memory (even if it was already used by another window). Windows with large menus can take a long time to open; removing menus will make them open quickly.

Another technique is to use the topmost layer on the menu to represent each sub-application and then enable and disable menu items as sheets are opened or closed. Your application will gain significantly in performance if you have one layer menu with a function to handle the enabling and disabling of menu items.

If your menus are vastly different (as in the PowerBuilder application itself), then you should have one menu on every sheet as described earlier.

MDI Sheet Window Types

You might be wondering if there is a MDI sheet window type. The answer is no. When you create a window that is a sheet in a MDI frame, just create a main window. Actually you could select any type except MDI frame, but you may as well be consistent in you choice.

MDI Frame with Microhelp

The final window type option is the MDI Frame with Microhelp. As you might expect, this is the same as the MDI Frame type except that this adds Microhelp functionality to your application. Microhelp is a brief text message displayed on the status line at the bottom of the active window. This is used to give the user assistance on using menus and icons, or to present status messages and explanatory information. You can add Microhelp to your MDI applications easily and is discussed in menu creation and object tags later. Figure 5.10 shows an example of an MDI application created with PowerBuilder. Notice the Microhelp text in the status line at the bottom of the frame window.

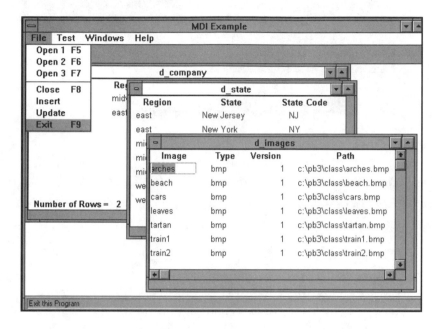

FIGURE 5.10 A MDI APPLICATION

OTHER WINDOW ATTRIBUTES

After defining the type of new window, you can proceed to the setting of the other attributes that determine the window's style. The Window Style dialog (Figure 5.11) presents the attribute options in a series of check boxes, edit fields, and several DropDownListBoxes. When you select a type for the window, PowerBuilder sets the initial state of the check boxes and disables some of them. For example, you cannot add a minimize box to a response window, so that check box is disabled.

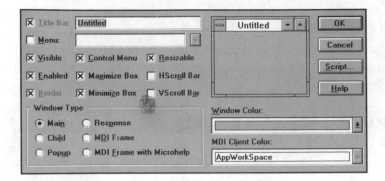

FIGURE 5.11 THE WINDOW STYLE DIALOG

The options that you have are:

- **Title Bar check box**—adds a Title bar to the new window.

- **Title Bar edit field**—the caption that appears in the title bar.

- **Menu check box**—adds a menu to this window.

- **Menu DropDownListBox**—selects the name of the menu from this list.

- **Window Options**—the next section has nine check boxes. These are set to different values depending on the type of window. These attributes are:

  - **Visible**—makes the window visible (which is usual).

  - **Enabled**—makes the window active, able to receive user input (which is usual).

  - **Border**—adds a border to a window. Main window's usually have borders.

  - **Control menu**—adds a control menu to the window. This adds functions to allow the user to move, resize (restore, maximize), minimize, or close the window.

  - **Maximize box**—adds the maximize button to the window.

  - **Minimize box**—adds the minimize button to the window.

- **Resizable**—lets the user resize the window. If selected, this adds a thin frame to the window. The user can resize the window by clicking and dragging this frame.
- **Hscroll bar**—adds a horizontal scroll bar to the window.
- **Vscroll bar**—adds a vertical scroll bar to the window.

The Window Color DropDownListBox lets you set the background color for the window. If you are using the 3D window style as a default, the color will be set to gray.

The MDI Client Color DropDownListBox is enabled only for the MDI window type. It sets the background color for the MDI frame window.

The Model Window

PowerBuilder displays a model window in the upper-right part of the Window Style dialog window. That model reflects the options that you have set for the window. As you make different style selections, such as adding a title bar or a menu, the model changes accordingly. This gives you a good idea of the final appearance of the window. You can preview the exact appearance of the window by selecting the **Design|Preview** menu option when you are in design mode in the Window painter.

WINDOW SCRIPTS

The third CommandButton in the Window Style dialog window is labeled *Script....* Clicking on this button opens the PowerScript painter where you can edit the script for any of the window events.

THE WINDOW PAINTER POPUP MENU

In the Window painter, you can activate the popup menu by clicking on the right mouse button within the window. The popup menu has the following options:

- **Script**—opens the PowerScript painter to edit an event script.
- **Color**—sets the background color.
- **Icon**—chooses the icon to represent the minimized window.
- **Pointer**—sets the type of pointer for this window. PowerBuilder switches to this type when the pointer is over the window.
- **Position**—goes to the Window Position dialog.
- **Style**—presents toggles for the checkboxes in the Window Style dialog (Border, Control Menu, Hscroll Bar, Maximize Box, Minimize Box, Resizeable, Title Bar, Vscroll Bar, Enabled, Visible).
- **Title**—enters the window caption (if it has title bar).
- **Type**—sets the type for the window (main, child, popup, response, MDI).

SAVING THE WINDOW

After you have designed the window, you need to save it. To do this, select the **File|Save As...** menu option. This opens the Save Window dialog. Name the window, usually a window is given the prefix "w_", such as w_main or w_employee. Add a comment that describes the window and set the PowerBuilder library where you want to store the window.

In general, it is a good idea to save the newly created window as soon as you have defined its major characteristics (such as its type and position). To set the style of the window select the **Design|Style...** menu option, or as a shortcut just double-click anywhere within the borders of the window.

Other Window Options

Select the **Options|Default to 3D** menu option to set the Windows 3D style for this window. This style gives a three dimensional characteristic to the controls and sets the default color to gray. Gray works very well with the 3D option and will also usually be the choice for your MDI applications.

WINDOW EVENTS

Windows have over two dozen events. These events include:

- **Activate**—occurs before the window is made the active window. The active window receives the keyboard strokes and is displayed with a highlighted title.

- **Clicked**—when you click in a window, but not within one of the controls (such as a CommandButton or listbox), this event is triggered.

- **Close**—occurs before the window is deactivated and closed.

- **CloseQuery**—queries your window, giving the window a chance to handle any last details such as saving any current changes to a file or table. The event occurs before the Close event and it is possible to refuse to allow the window to close. To do this set the Message.ReturnValue to 1.

- **Deactivate**—triggered before the window is about to become inactive and another window is about to become activated.

- **Double-Clicked**—when you double-click in a window but not within one of the controls (such as a CommandButton or listbox), this event is triggered.

- **DragDrop**—when drag mode is on and the pointer drops an object in the window (not within a control).

- **DragEnter**—when drag mode is on and the dragged object enters the window.

- **DragLeave**—when drag mode is on and the dragged object leaves the window.

- **DragWithin**—when drag mode is on, this event is triggered periodically while an object is dragged within the window.

- **Hide**—the window is about to be made invisible.

- **HotLinkAlarm**—after a DDE connection has been made, a client DDE window may ask for "hot" updates of the data it is interested in. This event notifies the client that such data has been sent from the DDE server.

- **Key**—when a keyboard stroke occurs and the focus is not within a editing control, the window will receive the event.

- **MouseDown**—whenever the left mouse button is pressed and the pointer is within the window (and not within any active controls), this event is triggered.

- **MouseMove**—whenever the mouse pointer is moved within the window (and not within any active controls), this event is triggered.

- **MouseUp**—when the mouse button is released within the window, and the pointer is not located within any active controls.

- **Open**—this event occurs after the open call has been made to open the window, but before the window has been displayed.

- **Other**—all the other Windows' events that have not been mapped to PowerBuilder events are routed to this event. You will rarely use this event; user-defined events are a better choice.

- **RButtonDown**—when the right mouse button is pressed and the pointer is not located within any active controls.

- **RemoteExec**—occurs in a DDE server window, it is a result of an ExecRemote function call in a client window and is used to send a command to the server.

- **RemoteHotLinkStart**—occurs in a DDE server window. It is the result of a StartHotLink function call in the client, used as a request for a live ("hot") update of the source data as it changes.

- **RemoteHotLinkStop**—occurs in a DDE server window. It is the result of a StoptHotLink function call in the client, used to terminate a request for a live ("hot") update of the source data as it changes.

- **RemoteRequest**—occurs in a DDE server window. A result of a GetRemote function call in a DDE client, which is a request for data.

- **RemoteSend**—occurs in a DDE server window. A result of a SetRemote function call in the DDE client used to send data to the server.

- **Resize**—triggered whenever the window is resized, including the initial sizing when the window is opened.

- **Show**—triggered before the window is about to be displayed as result of a Show function call.

- **SystemKey**—triggered when the user presses the ALT key (usually in combination with another key) and the focus is not within an active editing type of control.

- **Timer**—occurs at specified intervals as set by the Timer function. The timer event is only triggered if the Timer( ) function was called.

WINDOW FUNCTIONS

The following PowerBuilder functions apply specifically to window objects.

- **ArrangeSheets**—this a function used for MDI windows. It organizes the sheet windows in a specified style, such as tiled or cascaded.

- **ChangeMenu**—sets the menu associated with a window to a named menu.

- **ClassName**—returns the name of the window.

- **GetActiveSheet**—returns the window which is the currently active sheet window.

- **Hide**—makes the window invisible.

- **Move**—relocates a window to a new position.

- **ParentWindow**—returns the window which is the parent window to a given window.

- **PointerX**—returns the current horizontal location of the pointer, in PBUs from the window's origin.

- **PointerY**—returns the current vertical location of the pointer, in PBUs from the window's origin.

- **PostEvent**—adds an event to an objects message queue (an asynchronous message).

- **Resize**—changes the current size of the window.

- **SetFocus**—sets the focus to a window, making it the currently active window.

- **SetMicroHelp**—assigns the text for the MDI status line and displays it.

- **SetPosition**—moves the window in front, or behind other windows.

- **SetRedraw**—turns on or off the display update for a window.

- **Show**—makes a window visible.

- **TriggerEvent**—sends an event to an objects message queue, (this is a synchronous message).

- **TypeOf**—returns the type of the object.

- **WorkSpaceHeight**—returns the height of the window client area in PBUs.

- **WorkSpaceWidth**—returns the width of the window client area in PBUs.

- **WorkSpaceX**—returns the horizontal position of the window in the video display area (in PBUs).

- **WorkSpaceY**—returns the vertical position of the window in the video display area (in PBUs).

WINDOW ATTRIBUTES

- **BackColor**—a long integer representing the window's background color.

- **Border**—a Boolean value specifies whether a window has a border.

- **BringToTop**—a Boolean value specifies whether a window in front of all other windows.

- **ColumnsPerPage**—the number of columns on a page, used for scrolling.

- **Control[ ]**—an array of the objects that are currently contained in a window.

- **ControlMenu**—a Boolean value specifies whether a window has a control menu.

- **Enabled**—a Boolean value that specifies whether a window is currently enabled (able to receive input).

- **Height**—the vertical size of a window (in PBUs).

- **HScrollBar**—a Boolean value which specifies whether a window has a horizontal scroll bar.

- **Icon**—the name of the icon associated with this window.

- **LinesPerPage**—the number of lines on a page in this window, used for scrolling.

- **MaxBox**—a Boolean value specifies whether a window has a maximize box.

- **MenuID**—the name of the menu associated with this window. This is the value you can manipulate.

- **MenuName**—PowerBuilder's internal name of the menu associated with this window. Do not use this attribute.

- **MinBox**—a Boolean value specifies whether a window has a minimize box.

- **Pointer**—the name of the pointer icon associated with a window.

- **Resizable**—a Boolean value specifies whether a window's size can be changed.

- **Tag**—a string text that is associated with a window.

- **Title**—the caption for the window.

- **TitleBar**—an internal Boolean value, specifies whether the window has a title bar. This can not be changed programatically.

- **ToolbarAlignment**—specifies the positioning used for an MDI toolbar.

- **ToolbarHeight**—the horizontal size of a MDI toolbar when set with the floating style.

- **ToolbarVisible**—a Boolean value, specifies whether a toolbar is visible.

- **ToolbarWidth**—the vertical size of a MDI toolbar when set with the floating style.

- **ToolbarX**—returns the horizontal position of a MDI toolbar when set with the floating style.

- **ToolbarY**—returns the vertical position of a MDI toolbar when set with the floating style.

- **UnitsPerColumn**—a value that sets the number of PBU units used for scrolling horizontally.

- **UnitsPerLine**—a value that sets the number of PBU units used for scrolling vertically.

- **Visible**—a Boolean value which specifies whether or not a window is visible.

- **VScrollBar**—a Boolean value which specifies whether a window has a vertical scroll bar.

- **Width**—the horizontal size (in PBUs) of a window.

- **WindowState**—an enumerated value, returns the current window state.

- **WindowType**—an enumerated value, returns the current window type.

- **X**—the position of the window, in horizontal PBUs.

- **Y**—the position of the window, in vertical PBUs.

WINDOW VARIABLES

A window is a PowerBuilder data type. You can therefore, create variables which are instances of the window data type (class). These variables have scope, just like other variables. Window objects can have the following scope assignments:

- **Local**—known only in the single script containing it.

- **Instance**—shared between objects within window in this instance.
- **Shared**—shared between objects in all instances of the windows.

When you create a new window (w_main for example), you are actually creating a class (an object type, a new data type).

When you open the window:

```
open (w_main)
```

you are actually opening an instance of that window. PowerBuilder has created an instance of the object type w_main and given it the same name (w_main) as the class. You could declare your own instances of w_main as follows:

```
w_main w_main1, w_main2

open(w_main1)
open(w_main2)
open(w_main1)
```

Notice how w_main is used as the data type for the w_main1 and w_main2 variables. The third statement only activates the w_main1 instance (does not fire the open event again). It does not create a third instance of the w_main window type.

You could also create instances of a window by creating an array as follows:

```
w_child w_child[10]
int idx

FOR idx = 1 to 10
    open(w_child[idx])
    w_child[idx].x = idx * 100
    w_child[idx].y = idx * 100
NEXT
```

This example creates ten instances of a w_child window, cascading the child windows across the parent window.

After creating the instances, you can assign attribute values and call window functions as follows:

```
open(w_child[1])
open(w_child[2])
w_child[1].x = 10
w_child[1].y = 10
w_child[2].Move(w_child[2].x+100, w_child[2].y+100)
w_child[2].st_status.text = "2"
```

If you need to create a heterogeneous array of window with mixed types you can use the PowerBuilder window data type.

```
window w_array[2]
string win[2]

win[1] = "w_main"
win[2] = "w_child"
open (w_array[1], win[2])
```

The drawback of this technique is that you are not able to reference any objects using the window arrays. So the following statement:

```
w_array[1].cb_close.enabled = false // illegal
```

would create a compiler error.

WINDOWPAINTER MENUS

The Window Painter Menu Options

The PowerScript painter menu bar includes the following drop-down menus, as shown in Figure 5.12:

```
File | Edit | Control | Design | Declare | Window | Help
```

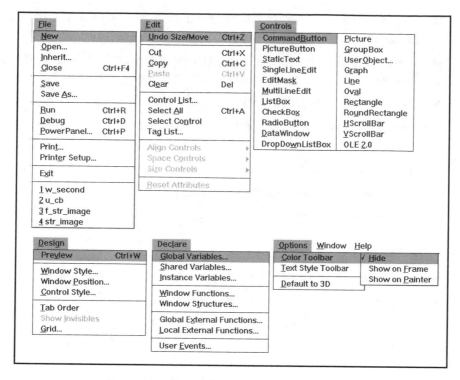

FIGURE 5.12 THE WINDOW PAINTER MENUS

The options on each menu are:

File Menu

- **New**—creates a new window object.

- **Open**—opens another window.

- **Inherit**—creates a new window using inheritance.

- **Close**—closes this window. If changes have occurred prompt before saving any changes.

- **Save**—saves all the changes to the window.

- **Save As**—saves this as a new window object.

- **Run**—executes the current application, preview from the development environment.

- **Debug**—runs the application in debug mode. Prompt first for breakpoints.

- **PowerPanel**—changes the presentation style to that of the PowerPanel.

- **Print**—printouts a description of the current window.

- **Printer Setup**—opens the Printer Setup dialog to specific printer attributes, lets the user set print options.

- **Exit**—quits PowerBuilder.

- **Last used**—the bottom of this menu presents a set of last accessed objects for quick access

Edit Menu

- **Delete**—deletes the currently selected object(s) from the window.

- **Duplicate**—duplicates (make a copy) of the selected object.

- **Control List**—presents a list of the controls on the current window. You can then select one or more controls or you can go to the control's style dialog.

- **Select All**—selects all controls in the window.

- **Select Control**—cancels the selection of a control type that was made from the Controls menu or by clicking a control icon on the PainterBar.

- **Tag List**—presents a list of all the controls in the window and lets you view or edit the tag attribute for each.

- **Bring to Front**—moves the selected control to the top (in the front-to-back order).

- **Send to Back**—moves the selected control to the bottom (of the front-to-back order).

- **Align Controls**—allows easy alignment of selected controls.

- **Space Controls**—automatically adjusts the spacing of selected controls, based on the spacing of the first two controls that were selected.

- **Size Controls**—automatically sizes a set of controls to be the same size as the first selected control in the set.
- **Reset Attributes**—returns the attribute values of an inherited window to the original values of the ancestor window.
- **Script**—opens the PowerScript painter to edit code for an window level event.

Controls Menu

- Lists all the controls that can be added to a window. Selects a type and then clicks in the window to place one of the controls at the position.

Design Menu

- **Preview**—displays the runtime version of the window.
- **Window Style**—opens the style dialog for the window.
- **Window Position**—opens to the Window Position dialog.
- **Control Style**—opens the style dialog for the selected object.
- **Control Status**—toggles the display of the control status window.
- **Tab Order**—sets the tab order for the controls in this window (a toggle).
- **Show Invisibles**—makes all invisible objects visible in the design mode.
- **Grid**—controls the design grid's display, resolution, and the snap-to-grid option.

Declare Menu

- **Global Variables**—defines a variable with global scope.
- **Shared Variables**—defines a variable with shared scope.
- **Instance Variables**—defines a variable with instance scope.
- **Window Functions**—defines a user-defined function at the window level.

- **Window Structures**—defines a structure at the window level.
- **Global External Functions**—declares an external function to be used globally.
- **Local External Functions**—declares an external function with local scope.
- **User Events**—defines a user-defined event for the window.

Options Menu

- **Color Toolbar**—controls the display of the color toolbar.
- **Text Style Toolbar**—controls the display of the text style toolbar.
- **Default to 3D**—a toggle to set the default style to 3D.

Window Menu

- **Tile**—arranges the currently open windows.
- **Layer**—maximizes the current window.
- **Cascade**—arranges the currently open windows in a cascade.
- **Arrange Icons**—arranges the minimized windows' icons.
- **Toolbars**—customizes, hides, displays, or positions a toolbar.
- **Window list**—numbered list of the current windows; select one to change to that window.

Help Menu

- **Help Index**—opens the help window, and display the index.
- **Getting Started**—presents an introduction to PowerBuilder.
- **Search**—searches the help system for a topic.
- **Technical Help**—provides help on database connections and customizing toolbars.
- **About PowerBuilder**—the About box; information on version, copyright, and license.

EXAMPLE: FIRSTWIN

Firstwin is a simple application that demonstrates each of the window types (except MDI windows). The main window (w_main) is shown when Firstwin is launched. If you double-click anywhere within the main window three other windows open as shown in Figure 5.13.

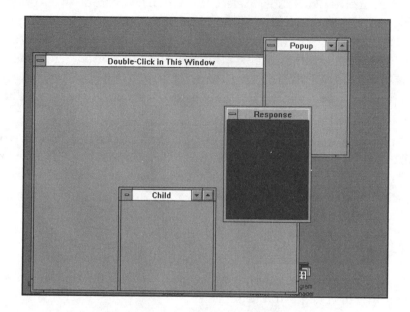

FIGURE 5.13 THE FIRSTWIN APPLICATION

A child window opens inside the parent (w_main), a popup window opens on top (and perhaps outside) the main window, and a modal response window opens in front of all other windows. You must close the response window before you can activate any of the other windows in this application.

Another function demonstrates advanced features that you will not initially implement when you duplicate this example. If you double-click in the child window, a new window, CountDown, appears. The CountDown window displays the number 20. Every second the window beeps and decrements the number by one. When it reaches 0 (zero), it closes the application. How to add the CountDown window to this example is discussed in a later chapter—it uses advanced techniques that have not yet been covered (including access the Windows' API).

Before you build your version of this application, run the sample application from the PowerBuilder environment. To do this, launch PowerBuilder (if necessary), and go to the Application painter (click on the **Appl** icon on the PowerBar). Select the **Open** icon from the Application painter PainterBar. In the Select Application Library dialog select **C:\PB4\CLASS** in the directories listbox. Then select the **FIRSTWIN.PBL** library in the File Name listbox and click the **OK** button. This opens the Select Application dialog and should display "FIRSTWIN" in the Applications field. Select **FirstWin** and click on **OK** to return to the Application painter.

In the Application painter check that the window caption is "Application-firstwin." Click on the **Run** icon or select the **File|Run** menu option to run the application. When the application runs, you will see the main window displayed on the screen.

Running FirstWin

When the application launches, it triggers the application Open event. The only line of code in that event is:

```
open(w_main)
```

This code opens the main window and makes it the active window. If you double-click in the main window, it triggers the double-clicked event. The double-clicked event contains the following code:

```
------------------------------
this.title = 'w_main, Parent'
open(w_popup)
open(w_child, This)
open(w_response)
------------------------------
```

This opens a popup window, a child window, and a response window. The call to open the w_child window makes the w_main window the parent of the w_child using the **This** reserved word. If you left out the keyword **This**, the w_popup window would be the parent of the w_child, since it would be the activate window at the time w_child is opened. So the keyword **This**, is used to insure that the w_main is the parent of w_child.

FirstWin—Step-by-Step

Create the Application and Library

    0. Start PowerBuilder (if necessary).

    1. If you are not in the Application painter, click on the **Appl** icon on the PowerBar.

    2. In the Application painter select the **File|New** menu option.

    3. In the Select New Application Library dialog, set the directory to C:\PB4\CLASS and enter the name **FIRSTWN1.PBL** for the library file name. Click on **OK**.

    4. In the Save Application dialog:

    4a. In the Applications: field enter **firstwn1**.

    4b. Tab to the comments field and enter **My firstwin version1**.

    4c. Be sure that the library name is still firstwn1.pbl, if not select it.

    4d. Click on **OK**.

    5. PowerBuilder asks if you wish to generate an application template. Click on **No** in this dialog as we will create our our application.

This returns you to the Application painter. You have created the firstwn1 application object and the firstwn1 library.

Create the Main Window

Click on the **Window** icon on the PowerBar to open the Window painter. In the Select Window dialog click on the **New** CommandButton to create a new window. In the Window painter double-click on the new window to open the Window Style dialog (or select the **Design|Window Style** menu option).

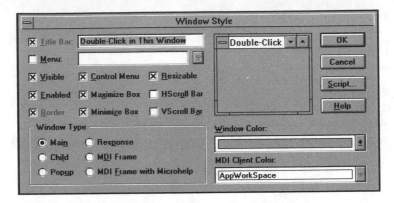

FIGURE 5.14 DEFINING THE W_MAIN STYLE

In this dialog, check **Main** from the Window Type group. This defines the type for the new window. Next check **Title Bar** and enter **Double-Click in This Window** as the text. The other options should match those in Figure 5.14. Close the dialog by clicking **OK**.

In the Window painter, select **Position** from the popup menu (or select the **Design|Window Position** menu option) to open the Window Position dialog.

In this dialog, set the position (and size) of the window as shown in Figure 5.15. The position of a Main window is relative to the display area of your monitor's screen. In this example, the position of the main window is set to the upper left of the screen. Be sure that the options for centering the window are unchecked.

Close the dialog by clicking on **OK**. In the Window painter, select the **File|Save As** menu option. Check to be sure that the library is set to FIRST-WN1.PBL, and then save the window (in the Save Window dialog) with the name *w_main*. Close the Window painter.

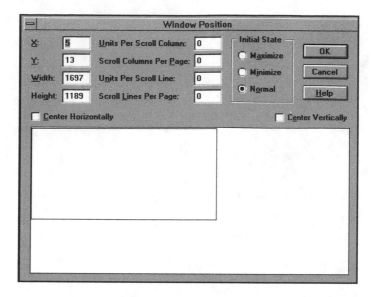

FIGURE 5.15 THE WINDOW POSITION DIALOG

Create the Child Window

Click on the Window icon on the PowerBar to open the Window painter. In the Select Window dialog click on the **New** CommandButton to create a new window. In the Window painter, double-click on the new window to open the Window Style dialog (or select the **Design|Window Style** menu option).

In this dialog check on **Child** in the Window Type RadioButton group. This defines the type for the new window. Next check the **Title Bar** CheckBox, and enter **Child** as the text. The other options should match those in Figure 5.16. Close the dialog by clicking on **OK**.

In the Window painter select the Position option from the popup menu (or select the **Design|Window Position** menu option) to open the Window Position dialog.

FIGURE 5.16 THE WINDOW STYLE DIALOG FOR W_CHILD

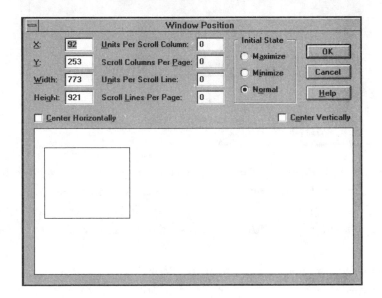

FIGURE 5.17 POSITIONING THE W_CHILD WINDOW

In this dialog, set the position (and size) of the window as shown in Figure 5.17. The position is relative to (and within) the parent window.

Close the dialog by clicking on **OK**. In the Window painter, select the **File|Save As** menu option. Save the window in the FIRSTWN1.PBL with the name *w_child*. Close the Window painter.

Create the Popup Window

Click on the **Window** icon on the PowerBar to open the Window painter. In the Select Window dialog, click on the **New** CommandButton to create a new window. In the Window painter double-click on the new window to open the Window Style dialog (or select the **Design|Window Style** menu option).

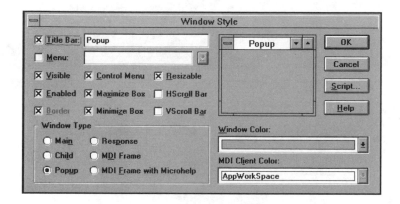

FIGURE 5.18 THE STYLE DIALOG FOR W_POPUP

In this dialog, check on **Popup** in the Window Type RadioButton group. This defines the type for the new window. Next check the **Title Bar** CheckBox, and enter **Popup** as the text. The other options should match those in Figure 5.18. Close the dialog by clicking on **OK**.

In the Window painter select the Position option from the popup menu (or select the **Design|Window Position** menu option) to open the Window Position dialog.

In this dialog, set the position (and size) of the window as shown in Figure 5.19. The position is relative to the display area of your monitor. Position the popup to the right side of the screen.

Close the dialog by clicking on **OK**. In the Window painter, select the **File|Save As** menu option. Save the window in the FIRSTWN1.PBL with the name *w_popup*. Close the Window painter.

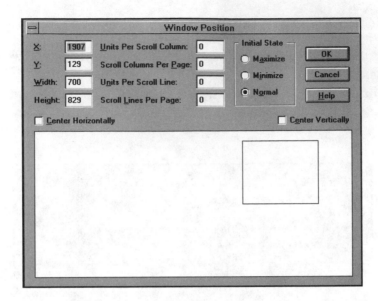

FIGURE 5.19 SETTING THE POSITION OF W_POPUP

Create the Response Window

Click on the **Window** icon on the PowerBar to open the Window painter. In the Select Window dialog, click on the **New** CommandButton to create a new window. In the Window painter double-click on the new window to open the Window Style dialog (or select the **Design|Window Style** menu option).

In this dialog, check on **Response** in the Window Type RadioButton group. This defines the type for the new window. Next check the **Title Bar** CheckBox, and enter **Response** as the text. Select the color **red** from the Window Color DropDownListbox. The other options should match those in Figure 5.20. Close the dialog by clicking on **OK**.

In the Window painter select the Position option from the popup menu (or select the **Design|Window Position** menu option) to open the Window Position dialog.

FIGURE 5.20 DEFINING THE STYLE FOR W_RESPONSE

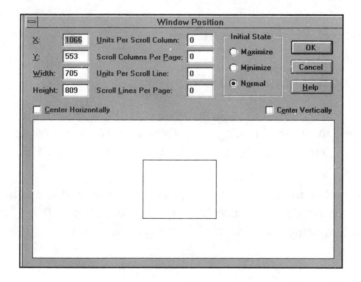

FIGURE 5.21 POSITIONING THE W_RESPONSE WINDOW

In this dialog, set the position (and size) of the window as shown in Figure 5.21. The position is relative to display area of your monitor. Position the Response window in the center of the screen.

Close the dialog by clicking on **OK**. In the Window painter, select the **File|Save As** menu option. Save the window in the FIRSTWN1.PBL with the name *w_response*. Close the Window painter.

Now all four windows have been defined. Now you only need to add the code necessary to open each of the windows.

Add Code to the Application Open Event

To enter the new code, click the **Script** icon on the Application PainterBar. This opens the Script Painter. The script editor should display *Script-open for firstwn1* on the title bar; if not, pull down the SelectEvent drop-down menu and select **Open**. Edit the code until it matches the following exactly.

```
--------------------------------------------
open(w_main)
--------------------------------------------
```

When it is correct, click the **Return** icon.

Add Code to the w_main Window

Next add code to the doubleclicked event in the w_main window. Open the Window painter by clicking the **Window** icon on the PowerBar. Select the w_main window from the list of windows presented in the Select Window dialog.

Select the **Script** option from the popup menu to edit the doubleclicked event for the window. Be sure to select **doubleclicked** from the Events DropDownDataWindow. Add the following code:

```
------------------------------
this.title = 'w_main, Parent'
open(w_popup)
open(w_child, This)
open(w_response)
------------------------------
```

This opens a popup window, a child window, and a response window when the user double-clicks in this window.

Run The Application

Run the application from the development environment. If everything runs OK, create a new executable as you did in the previous chapter. If you have any problems, compare your code closely to the code in the firstwin.pbl.

Use this example to clarify the difference between the types of windows.

CHAPTER SIX

MANIPULATING WINDOW CONTROLS

The window serves as the background or container for the controls that provide the actual interaction with the user. PowerBuilder offers a wide variety of controls that can be added to your windows. You will be familiar with most of these control types from using other Windows applications. Figure 6.1 shows a PowerBuilder application with an example of many of the controls that are covered in this chapter. In these windows are examples of a ListBox, SingleLineEdit, DropDownListBox, StaticText fields, PictureButton, EditMask, RadioButtons, CheckBoxes, CommandButtons, and a scroll bar.

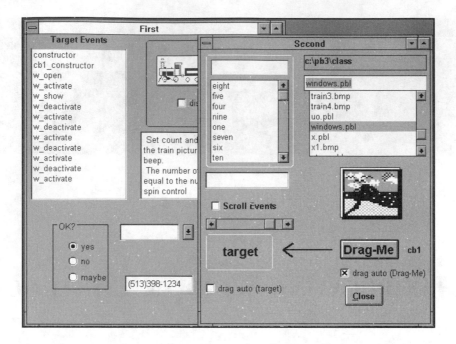

FIGURE 6.1 TWO WINDOWS

Table 6.1 lists the controls (and other objects) that PowerBuilder provides as options for your windows. The first column contains the type of the control, as you would find it listed in the Controls menu. The second column lists the label for the corresponding icon on the PainterBar. Not all the controls have an icon, so you must use the control menu to add them to your windows. The third column shows the default prefix for naming controls of this type. You can set these prefixes in the customization of PowerBuilder. The final column provides a brief summary of the normal use of each type of control.

TABLE 6.1 POWERBUILDER CONTROLS AND OBJECTS

CONTROL	PAINTERBAR LABEL	PREFIX	TYPICAL USE
CommandButton	CmdBtn	cb_	used to trigger some action
PictureButton	PicBtn	pb_	same as a CommandButton
StaticText	StaticTxt	st_	label
SingleLineEdit	SngEdit	sle_	display data, input data
EditMask	EditMask	em_	display data, input data in a specific format
MultiLineEdit	MultiEdit	mle_	display data, input data Input multi-line text data
ListBox	ListBox	lb_	display options for selection
CheckBox	ChkBox	cbx_	input a choice, toggle an option on or off
RadioButton	RadioBtn	rb_	input a choice, or select from mutually exclusive set
DataWindow	DataWnd	dw_	data interface, (usually database), display and input
DropDownListBox	DrpDnLB	ddlb_	display options for selection
Picture	Picture	p_	display
GroupBox	GrpBox	gb_	gather a set of controls
UserObject	UserObj	uo_	varies
Graph	Graph	gr_	display
Rectangle	—	r_	cosmetic
Line	—	ln_	cosmetic
Oval	—	oval_	cosmetic
Rounded Rectangle	—	rr_	cosmetic
HScrollBar	—	hsb_	display/input for a range of values, also to display progress
VScrollBar	—	vsb_	display/input for a range of values

Adding Controls to a Window

This chapter explains how to add controls to your windows. The process is similar for many of the window controls. Before going into the details, here is a brief overview of the process.

The quickest and easiest way to work when building windows is to use the mouse. PowerBuilder is very intuitive and makes excellent use of the mouse and graphical painting of the various objects.

To add a control to a window, start by selecting the object type from the Controls menu or by clicking on the control type in the Window painter's PainterBar. Next click on the location in the window where you want to place the control that you have selected. Controls are easily positioned and sized by dragging the object to position it or by using the sizing handles to resize it.

You then define the attributes of the control. You will assign it a name (or accept a default name); then for some types, such as the CommandButton, you can add text as a label or enter data for the control. After you have added two or more controls to a window you can adjust the relative alignment and size or the controls. You can also define the tab order and accessibility for each.

You will add PowerScript code to some of the control events to define its behavior.

Working with Controls

A number of the procedures for working with controls is common to many different types of controls. The following section applies to all the types of controls that you can add to your windows. If you want to experiment as you read the text, use the CommandButton, it is a control that you will often use.

You add controls to your windows by using the Window painter. Select the **Window** icon from the PowerBar to open the Window painter.

Adding a Control to a Window

To add a control to a window, click on the corresponding icon on the Window painter PainterBar (such as the **CmdBtn** icon for a CommandButton). Not all the controls have icons on the PainterBar, so you may have to select the control type from the Control menu (Figure 6.2).

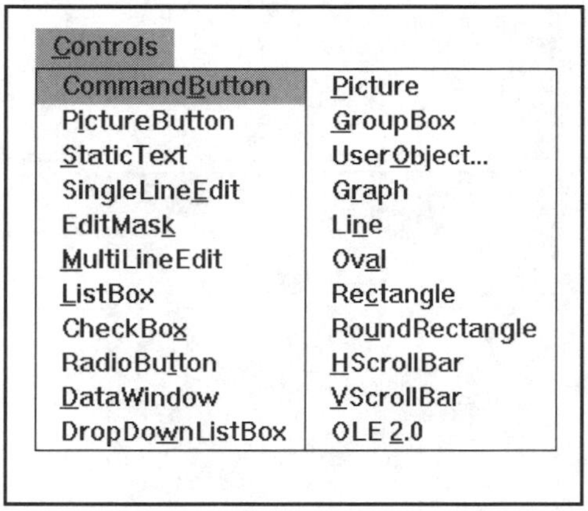

FIGURE 6.2 THE CONTROLS MENU

For the Command Button select the **Controls|CommandButton** menu option. After you have made this choice, click on the point in the window where you want to add the control. The Window painter drops a new control of the selected type (i.e. CommandButton) in the window. The control is given a default name, such as *cb_1*. Figure 6.3 shows the Window painter just after dropping a CommandButton onto the window.

Positioning and Sizing the Control Button

All controls are positioned in basically the same manner, and can be moved by using either the mouse or the keyboard. To move a control with the mouse, click within the control and drag it to its new location. To move a control with the keyboard, use the Tab key to select the control that you wish to move, and then use the four arrow keys to position it. You can also select a control with the **Edit|Control List** menu option. These selection techniques are described in more detail in the next section, *Selecting Controls*. The keyboard method for moving controls is useful for making small adjustments to the position of a control that might be more difficult with the mouse. (The snap-to-grid option must be off to make the most precise adjustments with the keyboard).

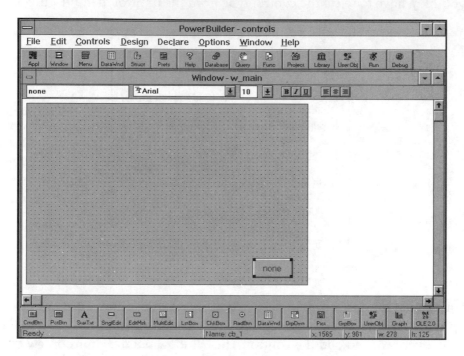

FIGURE 6.3 ADDING A COMMANDBUTTON TO A WINDOW

To resize a control with the mouse, click on the object to select it, and then use the handles that appear around the edges (see Figure 6.3). Drag one of the handles until the control has reached the desired size. The handles on the corners of the control can resize the object simultaneously in two dimensions, while the other handles can only resize in one dimension (either horizontally or vertically) within the window. To use the keyboard for resizing, use the Tab key to select the control that you wish to resize. Then use the four arrow keys while holding the Shift key to resize the control. The movement for resizing with the keyboard is based on the bottom right handle of the control. Therefore, use the right or down arrow to make the control larger and the left or up arrow to make the control smaller.

Selecting Controls

To modify a control you must first select it. Select a single control by clicking it with the mouse. When you select a control, that control is displayed with sizing handles (note the sizing handles on the None button in Figure 6.3). The Tab key can also be used to select a control; each time that you hit the Tab key, the painter selects a different control in the current window. The Tab key will cycle through all the controls and then start over again.

You can also select one or more controls by selecting the **Edit|Control List...** menu option to bring up the Control List dialog window (Figure 6.4). This dialog window lists the names of all the objects in a listbox. In that list, highlight the name of each of the objects that you wish to select, and then click the **Select** button.

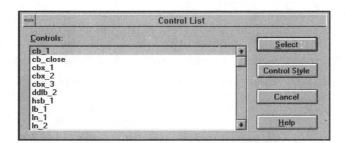

FIGURE 6.4 THE CONTROLS LIST DIALOG

Selecting Multiple Controls

There are also several ways to select a set of controls. You can do this by clicking on the first control of the set, and then Ctrl+click on each of the additional controls. (Ctrl+click is a standard technique for selecting multiple items in Windows applications.)

You can also select multiple controls by lassoing the controls with the mouse. To do this you click the mouse on the window background and then drag the mouse. This creates a "lasso" rectangle that selects all the controls that fall within (even partially) the rectangle's boundaries.

When you select a set of controls using the lasso method, the place-holder control is the bottom right control in the rectangle, regardless of the order in which the controls were selected.

A shortcut for selecting all the controls in a window is the **Edit|Select All** menu option (with the shortcut key combination of **Shift+A**).

Control Status

In the Window painter, you can select an option to display a small status window which shows the name, the current position, and the size of the selected control (in pixels). To display the Selected Control Status window just choose the **Design|Control Status** menu option. This menu option is a toggle switch (choose it again to hide the status window).

Using the Design Grid

The Window painter can display a grid of dots on the window that can help with the alignment and relative sizing of controls. Select this option by choosing the **Design|Grid...** menu option. This opens the Alignment Grid dialog window shown in Figure 6.5.

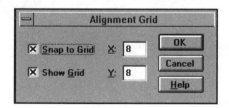

FIGURE 6.5 THE ALIGNMENT GRID DIALOG

In this dialog, display the grid by clicking the **Show Grid CheckBox**. You can also set the distance between the dots (in both the horizontal and vertical planes). The default spacing between dots is 8 pixels, a smaller number (like 4) gives you finer resolution when placing controls.

The Snap to Grid Option

Select **Snap to Grid** by clicking the CheckBox. By activating this option, the Window painter limits the exact placement of controls. Any controls that you resize or move while this option is active will be placed at the dot which is nearest to the place where you release the control. This makes aligning and sizing controls much easier. If you find that you need to have finer resolution in the placement of the controls, decrease the size of the grid cells: just enter smaller values for the X and Y grid options. You do not have to make the grid visible to use the Snap to Grid option. This is something to consider if you want to speed up the display speed, since displaying the grid slows down the environment.

Aligning Controls with the Alignment Function

The Window painter provides a function to automatically align a set of selected controls. To do this, select a set of controls using one of the methods described above. When you select the controls, you must first select the control that you want to use to govern the alignment of the other controls. After you have selected the controls to be aligned, pick the **Edit|Align Controls** menu option. This displays the align controls cascading menu (Figure 6.6).

You have six choices for aligning controls, three in the vertical plane, and three in the horizontal. Controls can be aligned in the following manners (listed in the top down order in which they appear in the cascading menu of Figure 6.6):

Align Vertically

- by the left edge
- centering the controls
- by the right edge

Align Horizontally

- by the top edge

- centering the controls
- by the bottom edge

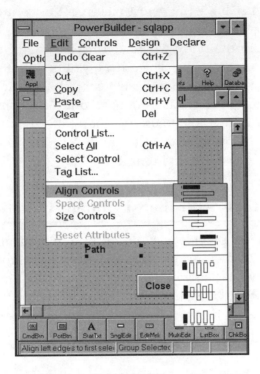

FIGURE 6.6 THE ALIGN CONTROLS MENU

Remember that the order in which you select the controls determines the result. Be sure to first select the control that is already in the correct position. After you use this function to align the controls, the controls still remain selected, so that you can reposition the entire group. Just click and drag any of the selected controls, the entire set will move as you drag the control. To deselect the group click somewhere else in the window, or just hit the Tab key.

Adjusting the Spacing of Controls

The Window painter provides a function to automatically adjust the spacing between a set of selected controls. To do this you first select a set of controls in the same manner as was described under *Aligning Controls*. In this case it is also important to select the controls in a specific order. It is important because the distance between the first two controls that you select will be the spacing that is applied to the other selected controls. So the procedure is to first set up two adjacent controls to have the correct spacing. Then additively select the controls that are to be spaced similarly.

After you have selected the set of controls, select the **Edit|Space Controls** menu option. This displays the cascading menu shown in Figure 6.7. You can set the spacing of the selected controls in either the horizontal or vertical dimension. This option is most useful for aligning a set of RadioButtons, CheckBoxes, or CommandButtons.

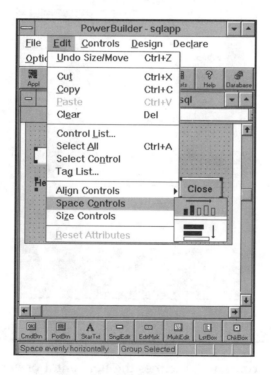

FIGURE 6.7 THE SPACE CONTROLS CASCADING MENU

Automatically Sizing Controls

The Window painter provides a function to automatically adjust the size of a set of selected controls to match that of a model control. To do this you first select the control that has the correct size (in either the horizontal or vertical plane) that you wish applied to the other control(s). Then additively select the rest of the controls that you wish sized.

After you have selected the set of controls, select the **Edit|Size Controls** menu option. This displays the cascading menu shown in Figure 6.8.

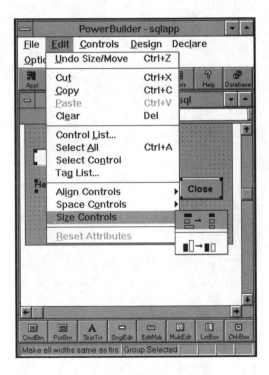

FIGURE 6.8 THE SIZE CONTROLS CASCADING MENU

You can size the control(s) in either the horizontal or vertical dimension. You could, of course, size a control in both dimensions by selecting both these functions, one after the other. You will apply the sizing option most often to a set of CommandButtons.

Undoing Control Movement or Sizing

One of the useful features of PowerBuilder 4.0 is the ability to undo the change caused by aligning, sizing, or spacing controls. When you perform one of these actions, PowerBuilder adds a menu option, Undo Size/Move, to the Edit menu. As long as the items are selected, you can undo the effect of the last operation with Undo Size/Move. After selecting this menu option, you also have the option of redoing the action with Redo Size/Move.

Setting the Tab Order

In the Window painter, you can set the tab order for the controls that have been placed in the window. Select the **Design|Tab Order** menu option to toggle on (or off) the tab order mode. In tab order mode, each control will be displayed with a number that represents its tab order. The tab order determines which control will be selected when the user hits the Tab key. The control that will be selected (receive the focus) will be the control with the next highest tab value. After the highest value control has been selected, the tab order moves down through the series. If you don't want a control to be part of the tab order (such as fields that can not be edited), set the tab order to 0 for that control. Not all objects in the window have a tab order (such as the drawing objects), it only applies to controls that the user can select.

THE CONTROL STYLE DIALOG

This section describes the control style dialog window. An example is shown in Figure 6.9. Notice that the caption is not *Control Style*, but is labeled the same as the type of the control that is currently selected. The exact contents of the Control Style dialog varies from control type to control type. In the Control Style dialog you can name a control, define a keyboard accelerator for the control, set the initial text, and specify a number of attributes (the exact options vary with the type of control).

207

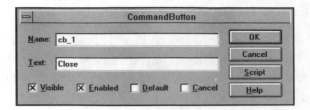

FIGURE 6.9 THE COMMANDBUTTON SYTLE DIALOG

Naming a Control

PowerBuilder assigns a default name to each control when it creates them. You can give the control a more descriptive, easier to remember name. To name a control, open the Control Style dialog window either by double-clicking directly on the control, or by selecting **Name** from the control's popup menu (right mouse click on the control). The actual caption of the Control Style dialog window will vary to match the type of the control. Figure 6.9 shows an example of the Control Style window, in this case it has the caption *Command Button*, the type of control to be renamed. When this window opens, the dialog selects the part of the control's name that immediately follows the control name prefix (**1** in this example). This lets you immediately type in the new name, you don't even have to reposition the cursor. It is recommended that you use a standard set of name prefixes for each type of control. You can specify the prefix for any control type in the customization process if you wish. The recommended naming convention can be found in Table 6.1. Instructions on changing the default name prefixes are in the section on customization.

Setting Text In a Control

Many controls have static text associated with them. For example, CommandButtons, RadioButtons, and CheckBoxes all have text labels. If the control has text associated with it, you can set the default text in the Text field of the Control Style dialog window. The style of the text that you enter is determined by the current settings in the StyleBar. This includes the font type, size, and characteristics (bold, italics, underlined, and alignment). You can also set these defaults when you customize PowerBuilder.

You can enter the text associated with the control in the control style dialog. You can also enter text directly by selecting an object and then typing the text. The text is echoed in an edit box in the top left corner of the window. Figure 6.10 shows a window where the text for the Open CommandButton has just been entered.

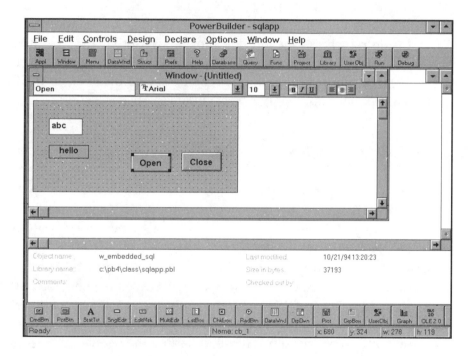

FIGURE 6.10 ENTERED TEXT "OPEN" FOR A COMMANDBUTTON

Notice the edit window in the upper-left hand corner of the Window painter with the text "Open".

Setting Attributes of a Control

The next section of a Control Style dialog varies greatly among the different types of controls. You will always find a set of CheckBoxes in this section.

The set of CheckBoxes lets you define the initial state of the control. These options vary with the different types of controls, the two most common are:

■ **Visible**—sets this CheckBox to make the control visible. Usually controls are visible, but occasionally there are uses for invisible controls.

■ **Enabled**—if enabled, the control is active and able to receive input. If it is disabled the control cannot receive input or events. Disabled controls are grayed in color to mark it as inactive. You can enable and disable controls dynamically; you should disable any control who's function does not apply to the current state of the application. For instance, in the SQLApp example (Figure 6.10), the **Close** CommandButton should be disabled until the **Open** CommandButton has been clicked to open the cursor.

ACCELERATORS FOR CONTROLS

You can assign an accelerator key to most of the controls that you create. An accelerator key is a shortcut that lets the user jump directly to that control by pressing a certain key in combination with the Alt key. You cannot assign an accelerator to the decorative controls, such as lines or rectangles.

You can define an accelerator key for CommandButtons, PictureButtons, StaticTexts, RadioButtons, and CheckBoxes when you enter the Text field (see Figure 6.11). Insert an ampersand (&) immediately before the character that you want to serve as the accelerator key. When you run the application, the display will underline the accelerator character to mark it. In Figure 6.11 the letter C is the accelerator. When the user presses **Alt+C** that CommandButton is selected, receives the focus, and then is sent a Clicked event.

If you use the same accelerator key for more than one control (in the same window), then PowerBuilder ignores that accelerator. So if your accelerator doesn't seem to be working, check to be sure that you have not already assigned that key as an accelerator.

You can define an accelerator for a GroupBox in the same manner. However, when you select the accelerator for the GroupBox, the focus is actually given to the checked RadioButton within the GroupBox (or the first CheckBox).

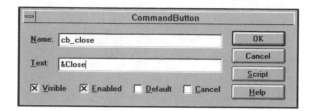

FIGURE 6.11 DEFINING A COMMANDBUTTON ACCELERATOR

The process of defining accelerators is different for SingleLineEdits, Edit Masks, MultiLineEdits, ListBoxes, and DropDownListBoxes. The style dialog window for each of these controls has a field for entering the accelerator key as shown in Figure 6.12. Just enter the letter of the key that you will use as the accelerator for these controls.

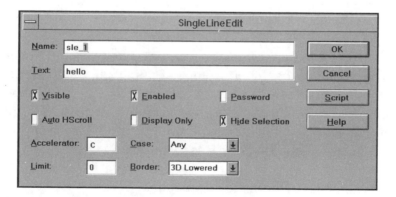

FIGURE 6.12 THE SINGLELINEEDIT STYLE DIALOG

CHANGE AN ATTRIBUTE

The popup menu is especially handy during the window design phase because it allows quick access to many of the attributes that you will access when you first add a control to a window. Clicking the right mouse button on a control brings up the popup menu. Figure 6.13 shows the popup menu for a CommandButton.

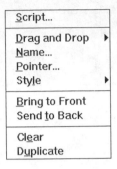

FIGURE 6.13 RMB POPUP FOR A COMMANDBUTTON

DUPLICATING A CONTROL

A shortcut for adding several controls of the same type is to duplicate an existing object. This has the advantage of duplicating the size, text, text style, and other properties of the original object. This is the method to use if you wish to create a number of similar controls. There are several routes that you can use to duplicate a control, but in all cases you must first select the source control. Do one of the following:

- select the **Edit|Duplicate** menu option.
- use the **Ctrl+T** key combination.
- select **Duplicate** from the popup menu.

Duplicating a control does not copy any of the event scripts. You can copy a control from one window to another using the Edit|Copy and Edit|Paste menu options.

POWERBUILDER UNITS (PBUs)

Many of the measurements used in window, controls, and drawing objects are specified in PowerBuilder units. PowerBuilder units are preferable to pixels for setting the size of windows and controls because the number of pixels in a measurement changes with the resolution of the display. PowerBuilder units are calculated on the size of an average character on the screen, which translates better between different resolution displays. The size of a horizontal PowerBuilder unit (PBU) is equal to 1/32 of the width of an average character in the system font. The size of a vertical PBU is equal to 1/64 of the same character. You can calculate the width of 20 characters as approximately 640 horizontal PBUs (20x32). These numbers are only approximate, since they are based on an average size character. But it is correct for 20 characters on a standard VGA display (640x480), or or a higher resolution VGA such as 1024x768. The number of pixels would vary greatly between these displays.

You can usually assume that the unit of measure is PowerBuilder units. There are only a few exceptions. When you set up the Design Grid in the Window (or DataWindow) painter, you define the distance between dots in pixels. When you set the size of the text in your applications, you specify the size as a font point size.

When you create a DataWindow, you can choose the unit of measure. You can select pixels, thousandths of an inch, or thousandths of a centimeter. It is easier to design a report that will be printed if you use the inch or centimeter measurement.

COLORS IN POWERBUILDER APPLICATION

The ColorBar presents a palette of the color choices for the design process.

Color Values

Many of the PowerBuilder objects have attributes that store colors that are used as foreground or background colors for the object. These attributes have a data type of long. They store the color in a RGB representation, the long is partitioned into segments for each color component.

The formula for calculating the long is:

```
65536 * Blue + 256 * Green + Red
```

PowerBuilder provides a function to ease the calculation of this value. The RGB function accepts three input arguments.

```
long lValue
lValue = RGB(iRed, iGreen, iBlue)
```

In this example, you pass in three arguments to specify the color represented by the value iValue:

- **iRed**—the value of the red component of the color.
- **iGreen**—the value of the green component of the color.
- **iBlue**—the value of the blue component of the color.

Each argument is an integer, with a value ranging from 0 to 255. This value represents the amount of that component (red, green, or blue) that is in the color that you are defining. An example of a basic color set using the RGB function follows.

Black	- RGB(0, 0, 0)
White	- RGB(255, 255, 255)
Red	-RGB(255, 0, 0)
Red Dark	- RGB(128, 0, 0)
Green	- RGB(0, 255, 0)
Green Dark	- RGB(0, 128, 0)
Blue	- RGB(0, 0, 255)
Blue Dark	- RGB(0, 0, 128)
Gray	- RGB(192, 192, 192)
Dark Gray	- RGB(128, 128, 128)

Magenta	- RGB(255, 0, 255)
Dark Magenta	- RGB(128, 0, 128)
Cyan	- RGB(0, 255, 255)
Dark Cyan	- RGB(0, 128, 128)
Brown	- RGB(128, 128, 0)

You can set the colors for all controls except CommandButtons. CommandButtons are defined as gray in color and cannot be changed. You could define the RGB values for a custom color by using the Color dialog window to set the value of a color. In general this is not required; the choices that are provided in the ColorBar (and the popup menus) should suffice for most applications.

The 3D Look

You can (and should) select the 3D look as the default for all your windows. This style gives a three dimensional characteristic to the controls and creates windows with 3D borders. This is the best appearance for most situations and is standard in many Windows applications. This option also sets the default color to gray. Gray works very well with the 3D option and will also usually be the choice for your MDI applications.

You can select this option in the Window painter **Options|Default to 3D** or in the Preferences painter under the Window's options. Figure 6.1 shows a window that was created with the 3D option. Notice the 3D effect of the CommandButton and SingleLineEdit.

CHAPTER SEVEN

WINDOW CONTROLS

The previous chapter covered the traits that are common between controls. This chapter covers each of the window controls (and the drawing objects) in detail. An example of each of the controls covered in this chapter is included in the window in Figure 7.1.

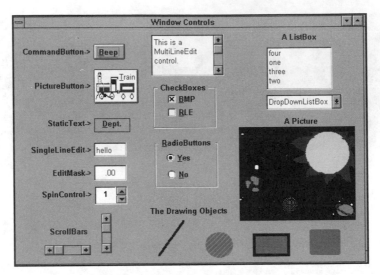

FIGURE 7.1 A CONTROL SAMPLER

DESCRIPTION, ATTRIBUTES, EVENTS, AND FUNCTIONS

The text about each control in this chapter is organized into the following sections:

- **Description**—the first section will show you a picture of the control, and provide a description. In this section, you will find the style dialog window for the control and information about the more important features and attributes of the control.

- **Attributes**—Each type of control has a specific set of attributes or properties that define its exact characteristics. This section lists all of the attributes for the control and provides a brief description of the attribute.

- **Events**—Each control type (except the drawing objects) has a set of events that apply to that type of control. This section lists all of the events that are associated with the control. The events that are most important or unique for each control are marked with bold, underlined text. The last section provides some code examples for some of the events.

- **Functions**—each control has a set of functions that apply to its type. This section lists all of the functions that you will find useful with this type of control and provides a brief description of each function. Many functions can be accessed by more than a single type of control. The most general types of functions are described in Appendix A.

- **Popup Menu Options**—this section provides a list of the options on the popup menu associated with this control.

THE WINDOW CONTROLS

Table 7.1 shows the types of controls that can be added to your windows and that also have events associated with them. This table presents the objects by category. Table 7.2 shows the drawing objects that can be added to your window. These are for decoration only, these objects do not have events.

This chapter covers all the objects listed in these tables, except Graphs, DataWindows, and User Objects. These objects are more complex and the details about each of these will be found in later chapters dedicated to those type of objects.

Some of the information that is common between controls, is repeated in the section for each control. This will group all the information for each group in its own section, making it easier for you to find the information that you need while working with a particular type of control.

The Window Controls Example

The next example is contained in the Controls.pbl. This example contains an example of every control discussed in this chapter. If you complete this exercise you will have created at least one object of each control and will have added code to provide functionality for each of the controls. This example also covers Drag and Drop functionality and provides a detailed demonstration of control and window events. The details on this example are found in Chapter 7.

Controls By Category

TABLE 7.1 CONTROLS THAT HAVE EVENTS

CATEGORY	CONTROL TYPE
Buttons	CommandButton
	PictureButton
Data I/O	SingleLineEdit
	EditMask
	ListBox
	DropDownListBox
	MultiLineEdit
	Picture
	StaticText
	Graph
	DataWindow
Scroll Bars	VScrollBar
	HScrollBar
Option Controls	RadioButton
	CheckBox
	GroupBox
User-Defined	User Object

TABLE 7.2 WINDOW OBJECTS WITHOUT EVENTS

CATEGORY	CONTROL TYPE
Drawing Objects	Line
	Oval
	Rectangle
	RoundRectangle

COMMANDBUTTONS

The CommandButton (or push button) is used to initiate some type of action, or to make a response to a prompt. Each CommandButton displays a caption that describes the function that it represents. You can click on a CommandButton with the mouse or you can select the button (using the Tab key) and then press **Enter**. When you click on a CommandButton it appears to be depressed momentarily.

FIGURE 7.2 A COMMANDBUTTON

Adding a CommandButton to a Window

For this example, the steps required to add two buttons to a new window are discussed. The first button is a Close button; it closes the window when the user clicks on it. The second button sends a beep to the PC's speaker when it is clicked. From the Window painter, click on the PainterBar **CmdBtn** icon or select the **Control|CommandButton** menu selection. This tells the Window painter that you are going to add a CommandButton to the window. Next, click in the window at the location where you want to place the button. This drops a CommandButton into the window.

Open the CommandButton style dialog (Figure 7.3) by double-clicking on the new CommandButton. Name the button **cb_close** and then tab to the Text field and enter a label. If you want to define an accelerator key, place an ampersand before the letter that will be used as the accelerator (&Close). Click on the **Script** button to write a script for the Clicked event.

When the PowerScript painter opens, check to be sure that you are in the Clicked event. If not, pull down the **Select Event** DropDownListBox and choose the clicked event. In the editor add the following line of code:

```
Close(Parent)
```

Close the editor by clicking the **Return** icon on the PainterBar. This returns you to the Window painter design window.

Repeat the process to add the second CommandButton. Give this button the name **cb_beep**. Enter the caption text (and accelerator) **&Beep**. Add the following line of code to its Clicked event:

```
Beep(1)
```

This causes the speaker to beep each time you click on the cb_beep CommandButton and when you click on cb_close, the window closes.

CommandButton Style Dialog

The easiest way to open the CommandButton style dialog is by double-clicking on the **CommandButton** or by selecting the **Name** option from the CommandButton's popup menu. You can also open the dialog by selecting the **Edit|Control List...** menu option. Select the control in the list and then click on the **Control Style** button. In the CommandButton style dialog (Figure 7.3) enter the name and the text caption for the button. You can define one character in the caption to be used as the accelerator by preceding it with an ampersand.

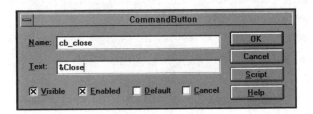

FIGURE 7.3 THE COMMANDBUTTON STYLE DIALOG

The bottom row of checkboxes is used to set some of the most important attributes. The first two attributes are the standard visible and enable options available for most controls:

- **Visible**—set this checkbox to make the control visible.

- **Enabled**—when the CommandButton is enabled, it is active, can be selected, and receive input (clicked). If it is disabled the button cannot receive input or events and will be grayed in color to mark it as inactive.

You can also set the visible and enabled attributes when the program is run. For example:

```
cb_close.enabled = False
cb_open.visible = True
```

The CommandButton dialog also has two checkboxes for two additional properties that apply only to CommandButtons and PictureButtons:

- **Default**—each window can have one default button. When the user runs your application and presses the Enter key, the button that has been defined as the default for the window will receive a Clicked event (if the focus is not on another button). To mark a button as the default, the button will have a unique black outline added around its perimeter. This is one of the features of the Windows style. You have seen this often, such as in response windows where an OK or Continue button can be selected by pressing the Return key.

- **Cancel**—each window can also have one cancel button. When the user runs your application and hits the Esc key when the focus is in this window, the button that has been defined as the cancel button for the window will be clicked just as if the user had clicked on it with the mouse. This button will not be marked in any visible manner (like the Default button), so you should label the button with a caption that suggests its use as a cancel button.

You should set only one button (either a CommandButton or PictureButton) as the default and cancel button on each window. PowerBuilder lets you assign this property to more than one button, it is up to you as the developer to enforce this constraint.

CommandButton Attributes

The attributes of a CommandButton are:

- **BringToTop**—sets this Boolean to True to place the CommandButton on top of other overlapping controls in this window's front-to-back order.

- **Cancel**—if this Boolean value is set to True (and the focus is in this window), the CommandButton is "Clicked" when the user presses the Escape key.

- **Default**—if this Boolean value is set to True, this CommandButton is "Clicked" when the user hits the Enter key (if the focus is not on another button). The button will also be outlined with a dark rectangle to mark it as the default.

- **DragAuto**—if this Boolean is set to True, this CommandButton is automatically set into Drag Mode when the user clicks on it.

- **DragIcon**—a string containing the name of the icon that is displayed when this button is in Drag Mode. If you select **None!**, a ghost outline of the control is used.

- **Enabled**—a Boolean value, set to True to enable the button, making it active and able to be selected or clicked and to receive events.

- **FaceName**—a string value containing the font name for the CommandButton caption.

- **FontCharSet**—an enumerated value that specifies the font character set for the caption.

- **FontFamily**—an enumerated value that specifies the font family for the button caption.

- **FontPitch**—an enumerated value that specifies the font pitch for the button caption.

- **Height**—an integer value that specifies the vertical size of the button in PBUs.

- **Italic**—a Boolean value, set to True if the label font is to be italicized.

- **Pointer**—a string containing the pointer icon to be used when the pointer is over this CommandButton.

- **TabOrder**—an integer that specifies the relative tab order for the controls on the window.

- **Tag**—a text string that is associated with this button and can be used to store the Microhelp text.

- **Text**—the string label (caption) for the CommandButton.

- **TextSize**—an integer that specifies the font size (in points) of the text label (stored as a negative number).

- **Underline**—a Boolean value. True if the text label for this button is to be underlined.

- **Visible**—a Boolean value. True if the button is to be visible (showing).

- **Weight**—an integer that specifies the stroke thickness of the text label font (400 is normal).

- **Width**—an integer value that specifies the horizontal size of the button in PBUs.

- **X**—an integer value that specifies the horizontal position in the window of the button in PBUs.

- **Y**—an integer value that specifies the vertical position in the window of the button in PBUs.

CommandButton Events

The events associated with a CommandButton are:

- **Clicked**—occurs when you click on a button or select the button and press the Enter key, this event is triggered.

- **Constructor**—occurs just before the window is made the active window. The window sends a constructor event to all its objects just before the window Open event occurs. Do not write code that is dependent on the order in which the constructors are triggered within a window. This is an advanced topic and will be discussed in the chapter on user objects.

- **Destructor**—occurs when the window is closing. The window sends a destructor event to all its objects just after the window Close event occurs.

- **DragDrop**—occurs when Drag Mode is on and the pointer drops an object within the CommandButton.

- **DragEnter**—occurs when Drag Mode is on and the dragged object enters the CommandButton. If Drag Mode is off and this button's DragAuto attribute is set, a DragEnter event is triggered (rather than a Clicked event) when the user clicks the button.

- **DragLeave**—occurs when Drag Mode is on, and the dragged object leaves the CommandButton.

- **DragWithin**—occurs when Drag Mode is on, this event is triggered periodically while an object is dragged within the CommandButton.

- **GetFocus**—occurs just before the CommandButton is selected with the Tab key or by clicking.

- **LoseFocus**—occurs just before the CommandButton loses focus (caused by tabbing away or clicking outside of the button).

- **Other**—all the other Windows' events that have not been mapped to PowerBuilder events are routed to this event. You will rarely use this event; user-defined events are a better choice.

- **RButtonDown**—occurs when the right mouse button is pressed, and the pointer is located within the CommandButton.

CommandButton Functions

The following functions apply to CommandButtons:

- **ClassName**—returns the name of the CommandButton.
- **Drag**—begins or ends Drag Mode for this button.
- **Hide**—makes a CommandButton invisible.
- **Move**—relocates the CommandButton in the window.

- **PointerX**—returns the pointer's horizontal position in the button.

- **PointerY**—returns the pointer's vertical position in the button.

- **PostEvent**—places an event on the CommandButton's event queue and continues (asynchronously).

- **Resize**—adjusts the size of the CommandButton.

- **SetFocus**—places the focus on the CommandButton, directs keyboard input to the button.

- **SetPosition**—places the CommandButton in the front-to-back display order (relative to other overlapping controls).

- **SetRedraw**—turns on or off the updating of the control if the caption is changed.

- **Show**—makes the CommandButton visible.

- **TriggerEvent**—triggers a CommandButton event immediately (synchronously).

- **TypeOf**—returns the enumerated type of this control (CommandButton!).

CommandButton Popup Menu Options

FIGURE 7.4 THE COMMANDBUTTON RMB POPUP

The items in the popup menu (right mouse click on the button) for a CommandButton are:

- **Script**—edits a script for a CommandButton event.

- **Drag and Drop**—sets or clears the DragAuto Mode attribute or defines an icon for the Drag Mode.

- **Name**—opens the CommandButton style dialog.

- **Pointer**—selects the pointer icon to be used when the pointer is over this button.

- **Style**—toggles the Cancel, Default, Visible, or Enabled attributes.

- **Bring to Front**—moves this button to the front of other overlapping controls.

- **Send to Back**—moves this button to the back of other overlapping controls.

- **Delete**—removes this button from the window.

- **Duplicate**—makes a copy of this button.

PICTUREBUTTONS

FIGURE 7.5 A PICTUREBUTTON

PictureButtons are essentially the same as CommandButtons, but they display a BMP or RLE image within the button. Choose one image for the enabled state and another for the disabled state of the button. The PictureButton may also contain text that can be aligned horizontally and vertically in the button. The text can also span more than one line in the button.

Figure 7.6 shows the style dialog for a PictureButton. When you first create a PictureButton and attempt to open the style dialog, you will be prompted with the Select Picture dialog, which is described in the next paragraph.

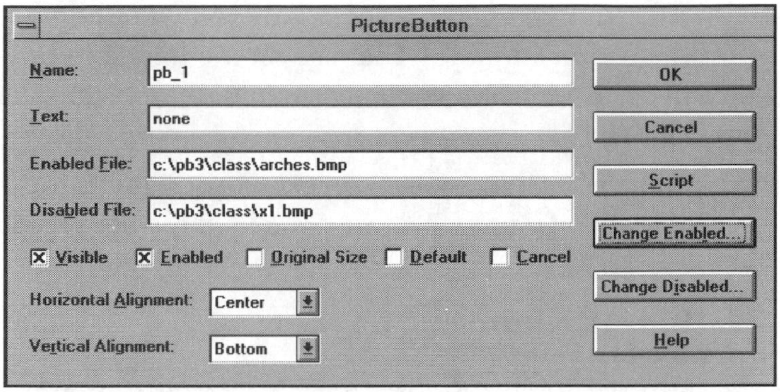

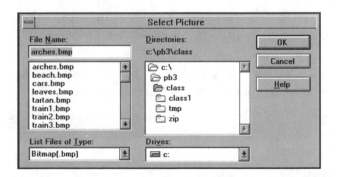

FIGURE 7.6 THE PICTUREBUTTON STYLE DIALOG

In this dialog, you can change the name and enter a text caption for the button. If you add text to the button, you can specify the horizontal alignment as Left, Center, or Right. You can specify the vertical alignment as Bottom, Top, Center, or MultiLine. When you create an icon that will be used for a PictureButton with a text caption, you should create a blank area in the icon to serve as a background for the text.

The next two entries contain the path to the images for the enabled, and optionally for the disabled, modes of the PictureButton. The images are loaded from the disk after you specify a path to the file in the Select Picture dialog window. To change the image, click the **Change Enabled** or **Change Disabled** CommandButton in the style dialog. This opens the Select Picture dialog in Figure 7.7.

FIGURE 7.7 SELECTING A PICTURE FILE FOR A PICTUREBUTTON

In the Select Picture dialog, use the listboxes to specify the path for the file to be used for the button's image. (You can set the image to any BMP or RLE file. You will be able to change it later, so initially you can set it to one of our example BMPs.)

The attributes controlled by the checkboxes at the bottom of the PictureButton style dialog (Figure 7.6) are covered in the next section.

PictureButton Attributes

The attributes of a PictureButton are the same as for CommandButtons with the following additions: DisabledName, HTextAlign, OriginalSize, PictureName, and VTextAlign.

- **DisabledName**—the name (the full path) of the image used for the PictureButton when it is disabled.

- **HTextAlign**—an enumerated value which specifies the horizontal text alignment for the button (Left!, Center!, or Right!).

- **OriginalSize**—a Boolean value, if set to True it automatically sizes the button to the original (unscaled) size of the image.

- **PictureName**—the name (the full path) of the image used for the PictureButton when it is enabled.

- **VTextAlign**—an enumerated value that specifies the vertical text alignment (Top!, VCenter!, Bottom!, MultiLine!).

The other attributes of a PictureButton are the same as a CommandButton, but are repeated here for convenience:

- **BringToTop**—sets this Boolean to True to place the PictureButton on top of other overlapping controls in this window's front-to-back order.

- **Cancel**—if this Boolean value is set to True (and the focus is in this window), this PictureButton is Clicked when the user presses the Escape key.

- **Default**—if this Boolean value is set to True, this PictureButton is Clicked when the user hits the Enter key (if the focus is not on another button). The button will also be outlined with a dark rectangle to mark it as the default.

- **DragAuto**—if this Boolean is set to True, this PictureButton will be automatically set into Drag Mode when the user clicks on it.

- **DragIcon**—a string containing the name of the icon that is displayed when this button is in Drag Mode. If you select **None!**, a ghost outline of the control is used.

- **Enabled**—a Boolean value, set to True to enable the button, making it active and able to be selected or clicked and to receive events.

- **FaceName**—a string value containing the font name for the PictureButton text.

- **FontCharSet**—an enumerated value that specifies the font character set for the text.

- **FontFamily**—an enumerated value that specifies the font family for the button text.

- **FontPitch**—an enumerated value that specifies the font pitch for the button text.

- **Height**—an integer value that specifies the vertical size of the button in PBUs.

- **Italic**—a Boolean value, set to True if the label font is to be italicized.

- **Pointer**—a string containing the pointer icon to be used when the pointer is over this PictureButton.

- **TabOrder**—an integer that specifies the relative tab order for the controls on the window.

- **Tag**—a text string that is associated with this button and can be used to store the Microhelp text.

- **Text**—the string label for the PictureButton.

- **TextSize**—an integer that specifies the font size (in points) of the text label.

- **Underline**—a Boolean value, set to true if the text label for this button is to be underlined.

■ **Visible**—a Boolean value, set to true if the button is to be visible (showing).

■ **Weight**—an integer that specifies the stroke thickness of the text label font (400 is normal).

■ **Width**—an integer value that specifies the horizontal size of the button in PBUs.

■ **X**—an integer value that specifies the horizontal position in the window of the button in PBUs.

■ **Y**—an integer value that specifies the vertical position in the window of the button in PBUs.

PictureButton Events

The events associated with a PictureButton are:

■ **Clicked**—occurs when you click on a button, or select the button and press the Enter key, this event is triggered.

■ **Constructor**—occurs just before the window is made the active window. The window sends a constructor event to all its objects just before the window Open event occurs.

■ **Destructor**—occurs when the window is closing. The window sends a destructor event to all its objects just after the window Close event occurs.

■ **DragDrop**—occurs when Drag Mode is on, and the pointer drops an object within the PictureButton.

■ **DragEnter**—occurs when Drag Mode is on and the dragged object enters the PictureButton. If Drag Mode is off and this button's DragAuto attribute is set, a DragEnter event will be triggered (rather than a Clicked event) when the user clicks the button.

■ **DragLeave**—occurs when Drag Mode is on and the dragged object leaves the PictureButton.

■ **DragWithin**—when Drag Mode is on, this event is triggered periodically while an object is dragged within the PictureButton.

■ **GetFocus**—occurs just before the PictureButton is selected with the Tab key or by clicking.

■ **LoseFocus**—occurs just before the PictureButton loses focus (caused by tabbing away or clicking outside of the button).

■ **Other**—all the other Windows' events that have not been mapped to PowerBuilder events are routed to this event. You will rarely use this event; user-defined events are a better choice.

■ **RButtonDown**—occurs when the right mouse button is pressed and the pointer is located within the PictureButton.

PictureButton Functions

The following functions apply to PictureButtons:

■ **ClassName**—returns the name of the PictureButton.

■ **Drag**—begins or ends Drag Mode for this button.

■ **Hide**—makes a PictureButton invisible.

■ **Move**—relocates the PictureButton in the window.

■ **PointerX**—returns the pointer's horizontal position in the button.

■ **PointerY**—returns the pointer's vertical position in the button.

■ **PostEvent**—places an event on the PictureButton's event queue and continues (asynchronously).

■ **Resize**—used to adjust the size of the PictureButton.

■ **SetFocus**—places the focus on the PictureButton; directs keyboard input to the button.

■ **SetPosition**—places the PictureButton in the front-to-back display order (relative to other overlapping controls).

■ **SetRedraw**—turns on or off the updating of the button (the label).

■ **Show**—makes the PictureButton visible.

■ **TriggerEvent**—triggers a PictureButton event immediately (synchronously).

233

- **TypeOf**—returns the enumerated type of this control (PictureButton!).

PictureButton Popup Menu Options

The items in the popup menu (right mouse click on the button) for a PictureButton are:

- **Change Disabled**—changes the image to be used for the disabled mode.
- **Change Enabled**—changes the image to be used for the enabled mode.

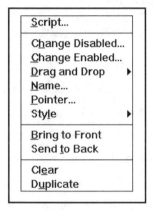

FIGURE 7.8 THE PICTUREBUTTON RMB POPUP

- **Script**—edits a script for a PictureButton event.
- **Drag and Drop**—sets or clears the DragAuto Mode attribute or defines an icon for the Drag Mode.
- **Name**—opens the PictureButton style dialog.
- **Pointer**—selects the pointer icon to be used when the pointer is over this button.
- **Style**—toggles the Cancel, Default, Visible, Enabled, or Original Size attributes. You can also set the horizontal or vertical text alignment here.

- **Bring to Front**—moves this button to the front of other overlapping controls.

- **Send to Back**—moves this button to the back of other overlapping controls.

- **Delete**—removes this button from the window.

- **Duplicate**—makes a copy of this button.

SINGLELINEEDIT CONTROLS

FIGURE 7.9 A SINGLELINEEDIT

A SingleLineEdit control (or edit field) is a rectangular field used for data display and user input. The user can type a single line of text into this field. The text may represent a value with any one of the PowerBuilder data types. Use this for fields that allow input. If the field is display-only you might only need a static text field.

Figure 7.10 shows the style dialog for a SingleLineEdit control.

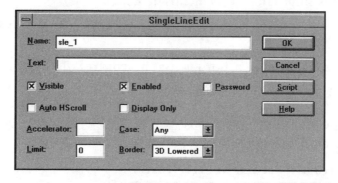

FIGURE 7.10 THE SINGLELINEEDIT STYLE DIALOG

In this dialog, you can rename the control. You can also specify text that will be displayed in the SingleLineEdit field as a default.

The other controls in the dialog are used for setting some of the more important attributes of the SingleLineEdit. The first two attributes are the standard visible and enable options:

- **Visible**—sets this checkbox to make the SingleLineEdit visible.

- **Enabled**—a Boolean value, set to True to enable the control, making it active, able to be selected and to receive events.

- **Password**—this option is useful for accepting passwords and other sensitive information in the SingleLineEdit. Checking this box causes the edit field to echo asterisks (*) as text is typed into the field, instead of displaying the actual text.

- **AutoHScroll**—if True, activates automatic scrolling (horizontally) to let the user enter text wider than the size of the control.

- **Display Only**—check this to use the field for display purposes only. This makes the field read-only, and will not let the user enter or change the text in the field.

- **Accelerator**—defines a keyboard accelerator for the SingleLineEdit in this field. Enter a character (a, b, etc.) that will be used in conjunction with the Alt key to place the focus in this field.

- **Limit**—the maximum number of characters that can be entered in this SingleLineEdit (0 means no limit).

- **Case**—controls the case of the input text. The choices are Any, lower, and UPPER.

- **Border**—selects a border for the control. The choices are 3D Lowered, 3D Raised, Box, None, ShadowBox. Use 3D Lowered borders to show that input is allowed, and use 3D Raised borders or Box borders for display-only fields.

SingleLineEdit Control Attributes

The attributes of a SingleLineEdit control are:

- **Accelerator**—an integer value, the ASCII value of the accelerator.

- **AutoHScroll**—a Boolean value, True sets automatic horizontal scrolling on when data is entered.

- **BackColor**—a long value, representing the color of the background area of the control.

- **Border**—a Boolean value, this is True sets a border around the control.

- **BorderStyle**—an enumerated value containing the border style (StyleBox!, StyleLowered!, StyleRaised!, or StyleShadowBox!).

- **BringToTop**—set this Boolean to True to place the SingleLineEdit on top of other overlapping controls in this window's front-to-back order.

- **DragAuto**—if this Boolean is set to True, the SingleLineEdit control is automatically set into Drag Mode when the user clicks on it.

- **DragIcon**—a string containing the name of the icon that is displayed when this control is in Drag Mode. If you select **None!**, a ghost outline of the control is used.

- **DisplayOnly**—a Boolean value, True sets the text for display only and cannot be changed by the user.

- **Enabled**—a Boolean value, set to True to enable the control, making it active, and able to be selected and to receive events.

- **FaceName**—a string value containing the font name for the SingleLineEdit text.

- **FontCharSet**—an enumerated value that specifies the font character set for the text.

- **FontFamily**—an enumerated value that specifies the font family for the control text.

- **FontPitch**—an enumerated value that specifies the font pitch for the control text.

- **Height**—an integer value that specifies the vertical size of the control in PBUs.

- **Italic**—a Boolean value, set to True if the label font is to be italicized.

- **Limit**—an integer that specifies the maximum number of characters that can be entered for this field, 0 (zero) means no limit.

- **Password**—this option is useful for accepting passwords, setting this Boolean to True causes the SingleLineEdit to echo asterisks (*) as text is typed into the field.

- **Pointer**—a string containing the pointer icon to be used when the pointer is over this SingleLineEdit field.

- **TabOrder**—an integer that specifies the relative tab order for the controls on the window.

- **Tag**—a text string that is associated with this control, can be used to store the Microhelp text.

- **Text**—a string field, containing the initial text to be displayed in the edit field (if any). After the user enters data in the SingleLineEdit, that data will be stored in the Text attribute.

- **TextCase**—an enumerated value that controls the case of the data entered, can be AnyCase!, Lower!, or Upper!.

- **TextColor**—a long value, controls the color of the text in this control.

- **TextSize**—an integer that specifies the font size (in points) of the text label.

- **Underline**—a Boolean value, set to True if the text label is to be underlined.

- **Visible**—a Boolean value, set to True if the control is to be visible (showing).

- **Weight**—an integer that specifies the stroke thickness of the text label font (400 is normal).

- **Width**—an integer value that specifies the horizontal size of the control in PBUs.

- **X**—an integer value that specifies the horizontal position in the window of the control in PBUs.

- **Y**—an integer value that specifies the vertical position in the window of the control in PBUs.

SingleLineEdit Control Events

The events associated with a SingleLineEdit control are:

■ **Constructor**—occurs just before the window is made the active window. The window sends a constructor event to all its objects just before the window Open event occurs.

■ **Destructor**—occurs when the window is closing. The window sends a destructor event to all its objects just after the window Close event occurs.

■ **DragDrop**—occurs when Drag Mode is on. The pointer drops an object within the SingleLineEdit.

■ **DragEnter**—occurs when Drag Mode is on and the dragged object enters the control. If Drag Mode is off and this control's DragAuto attribute is set, a DragEnter event is triggered when the user clicks the control.

■ **DragLeave**—occurs when Drag Mode is on, and the dragged object leaves the SingleLineEdit.

■ **DragWithin**—occurs when Drag Mode is on, this event is triggered periodically while an object is dragged within the SingleLineEdit.

■ **GetFocus**—occurs just before the SingleLineEdit is selected with the Tab key or by clicking. This is a good place to initialize the value in the edit field.

■ **LoseFocus**—occurs just before the SingleLineEdit loses focus (caused by tabbing away or clicking outside of the control).

■ **Modified**—occurs when the text in the field has been changed and the user hits the Enter or Tab key or clicks elsewhere on the window. This event is useful for executing code to validate the data that was entered in the edit field.

■ **Other**—all the other Windows' events that have not been mapped to PowerBuilder events are routed to this event. You will rarely use this event; user-defined events are a better choice.

■ **RButtonDown**—used when the right mouse button is pressed, and the pointer is located within the SingleLineEdit control.

SingleLineEdit Control Functions

The following functions apply to SingleLineEdit controls:

- **CanUndo**—a Boolean value, causes the last edit to be reversed.
- **ClassName**—returns the name of the SingleLineEdit control.
- **Clear**—deletes the selected text from the SingleLineEdit control. Does not place the deleted text in the Windows' clipboard.
- **Copy**—copies the selected text from the SingleLineEdit control to the Windows' clipboard.
- **Cut**—deletes the selected text from the SingleLineEdit control and places the deleted text in the Windows' clipboard.
- **Drag**—begins or ends Drag Mode for this control.
- **Hide**—makes a SingleLineEdit control invisible.
- **LineCount**—returns the number of lines in the control.
- **LineLength**—returns the number of characters in the current line of the control.
- **Move**—relocates the SingleLineEdit control in the window.
- **Paste**—copies the text on the Windows' clipboard into the SingleLineEdit. If text is currently selected in the SingleLineEdit, the clipboard text will replace it.
- **PointerX**—returns the pointer's horizontal position in the control.
- **PointerY**—returns the pointer's vertical position in the control.
- **PostEvent**—places an event on the SingleLineEdit control's event queue and continues (asynchronously).
- **ReplaceText**—replaces the selected text with a new string or inserts text if no text is currently selected.
- **Resize**—adjusts the size of the SingleLineEdit control.
- **SelectedLength**—returns the count of characters that are currently selected (highlighted) in the SingleLineEdit.
- **SelectedStart**—returns the position of the first character that is selected in the control.

- **SelectedText**—returns a string, a copy of the text that is currently selected in the control.

- **SelectText**—selects (highlights) a section of text in the control.

- **SetFocus**—places the focus on the SingleLineEdit control, directs keyboard input to the control.

- **SetPosition**—places the SingleLineEdit control in the front-to-back display order (relative to other overlapping controls).

- **SetRedraw**—turns on or off the updating of the control (the label).

- **Show**—makes the SingleLineEdit control visible.

- **TriggerEvent**—triggers a SingleLineEdit control event immediately (synchronously).

- **TypeOf**—returns the enumerated type of this control (SingleLineEdit!).

- **Undo**—reverses the last edit that was made in this control.

SingleLineEdit Control Popup Menu Options

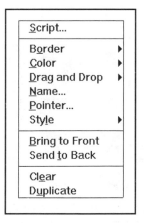

FIGURE 7.11 THE SINGLELINEEDIT RMB POPUP

The items in the popup menu (right mouse click on the control) for a SingleLineEdit control are:

- **Script**—edits a script for a control event.
- **Border**—selects the type of border to be used for this control.
- **Color**—sets the background and text colors for this control.
- **Drag and Drop**—sets or clears the DragAuto Mode attribute or defines an icon for the Drag Mode.
- **Name**—opens the control's style dialog.
- **Pointer**—selects the pointer icon to be used when the pointer is over this control.
- **Style**—toggles the AutoHScroll, DisplayOnly, Password, Visible, or Enabled attributes. You can also set the value for the Case attribute here.
- **Bring to Front**—moves this control to the front of other overlapping controls.
- **Send to Back**—moves this control to the back of other overlapping controls.
- **Delete**—removes this control from the window.
- **Duplicate**—makes a copy of this control.

EDITMASK CONTROL

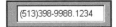

FIGURE 7.12 AN EDITMASK CONTROL

The EditMask control is very similar to a SingleLineEdit, but has a fixed format built into its definition. Examples of common required formats are phone numbers, Social Security numbers, or date and time. This control is similar to a SingleLineEdit, but is used where you wish to format the data that was input into the control.

The actual edit mask consists of a number of special characters that determine what can be entered in the field. The exact characters that are used vary according to the data type of the data being entered.

For a number:

#—the number sign is used to represent a digit.

0— a zero is used to represent a required digit.

For a string:

#—the number sign is used to represent a digit.

!—represents an upper case character.

^—represents a lower case character.

a—represents any alpha-numeric character.

x—allows any character.

Any other characters in the edit mask are taken literally as punctuation characters used for presentation. For example, the edit mask **(###) ###-####** works for phone numbers and **###-##-####** is a Social Security number. **!!##** allows two upper case characters followed by two digits, and **dd/mm/yyyy** is a typical date format.

Figure 7.13 shows the style dialog for an EditMask.

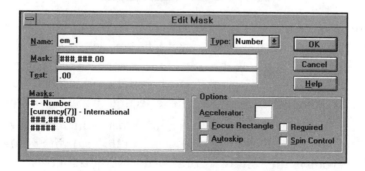

FIGURE 7.13 THE EDITMASK STYLE DIALOG

- **Name**—changes the name of the EditMask.

- **Type**—defines the data type. This can be String, Number, Date, Time, or Datetime.

- **Mask**—enters the actual edit mask. Use the values in the Masks ListBox (the contents will change according to the data type).

This dialog also contains a test box where you can enter test values and see the results of the mask that you have specified.

The final options are:

- **Accelerator**—sets the character that is to be used in conjunction with the Alt key as the keyboard accelerator.

- **AutoSkip**—causes the focus to jump to the next control in the tab order, when the user has enter the maximum number of characters in this field.

- **Spin Control**—creates a spin control style control.

Defining Spin Controls

FIGURE 7.14 A SPIN CONTROL

Checking the spin control option selects the spin control style for this EditMask. The control is displayed as an edit box with two spinners (the up and down arrows). The arrows are used to increment or decrement the value displayed in the control. Figure 7.15 shows the additional options that appear on the EditMask style dialog after selecting the Spin Control option.

You can define a range for the value and the increment value used with the arrows. You can initialize the control to a starting value by placing a line of code in the control's Constructor event as follows:

```
em_2.text = '1'
```

244

Instead of specifying a range, you could enumerate a list of values in a code table. In this case, you must specify each possible value in the list. Click the **Add** CommandButton to add a new item at the bottom of the list, **Delete** to remove the current item, and **Insert** to insert an item at the current position in the list. The data value column is actually not used in this control. It is used in another type of spin control (discussed later) where the data value is read from or written to the database, while the corresponding display values are presented to the user in the control.

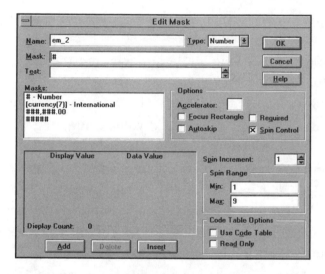

FIGURE 7.15 THE EDITMASK STYLE DIALOG

Spin controls can also be marked as read only, which means that they will only display the defined values, the user cannot enter a value not in the list (or range of values).

(The Focus Rectangle and Required options are not actually used in this dialog.)

EditMask Control Attributes

The attributes of a EditMask control are:

245

- **Accelerator**—an integer, the ASCII value of the accelerator key.

- **Alignment**—an enumerated value that specifies the alignment of the text in the control, either Left!, Center!, or Right!.

- **AutoHScroll**—a Boolean value, True sets automatic horizontal scrolling on for data entry.

- **AutoSkip**—a Boolean value, True causes the focus to jump to the next control in the tab order when the user has entered the maximum number of characters in this field.

- **AutoVScroll**—a Boolean value, True sets automatic vertical scrolling on for data entry.

- **BackColor**—a long value, representing the color of the background area of the control.

- **Border**—a Boolean, True sets a border around the control.

- **BorderStyle**—an enumerated value containing the border style (StyleBox!, StyleLowered!, StyleRaised!, or StyleShadowBox!)

- **BringToTop**—a Boolean, True places the EditMask on top of other overlapping controls in this window's front-to-back order.

- **DisplayData**—the initial text to be display in this control.

- **DisplayOnly**—a Boolean value, False if the EditMask is to be used for input, True if it is limited to display only.

- **DragAuto**—a Boolean value, if True this control is automatically set into Drag Mode when the user clicks on it.

- **DragIcon**—a string containing the name of the icon that is displayed when this control is in Drag Mode. If you select **None!**, a ghost outline of the control is used.

- **Enabled**—a Boolean value, set to True to enable the control, making it active and able to be selected and to receive events.

- **FaceName**—a string value containing the font name for the SingleLineEdit text.

- **FontCharSet**—an enumerated value that specifies the font character set for the text.

- **FontFamily**—an enumerated value that specifies the font family for the control text.

- **FontPitch**—an enumerated value that specifies the font pitch for the control text.

- **Height**—an integer value that specifies the vertical size of the control in PBUs

- **HScrollBar**—a Boolean value, if True a horizontal scroll bar is added to this control as needed.

- **Increment**—this attribute applies only to spin controls. It is a value (with a data type of double) that specifies the increment value for the spin control, used when the user clicks on the up or down arrows.

- **Italic**—a Boolean value, set to True if the text font is to be italicized.

- **Limit**—an integer, the maximum number of characters that can be entered in this control.

- **Mask**—the mask string used to edit the input text.

- **MaskDataType**—an enumerated value, the data type of the data.

- **MinMax**—this attribute only applies to spin controls. It is a string containing the minimum and maximum values for the data (these values are separated by a tab character).

- **Pointer**—a string containing the pointer icon to be used when the pointer is over this EditMask field.

- **Spin**—a Boolean value, True if the EditMask is a spin control.

- **TabOrder**—an integer that specifies the relative tab order for the controls on the window.

- **TabStop**—this is an integer array that stores the positions used for tabbing.

- **Text**—the initial text to be displayed in the edit field.

- **TextCase**—an enumerated value that controls the case of the data entered, can be AnyCase!, Lower!, or Upper!.

- **TextColor**—a long value, controls the color of the text in this control.

- **TextSize**—an integer that specifies the font size (in points) of the text.

- **Underline**—a Boolean value, True if the text for this control is underlined.

- **UseCodeTable**—a Boolean value, True if the user defined a code table for validating the data entered in this control.

- **Visible**—a Boolean value, True if the control is visible (showing).

- **VScrollBar**—a Boolean value, if True a vertical scroll bar is added to this control as needed.

- **Weight**—an integer that specifies the stroke thickness of the text font (400 is normal).

- **Width**—an integer value that specifies the horizontal size of the control in PBUs.

- **X**—an integer value that specifies the horizontal position in the window of the control in PBUs.

- **Y**—an integer value that specifies the vertical position in the window of the control in PBUs.

EditMask Control Events

The events associated with an EditMask control are:

- **Constructor**—occurs before the window is made the active window. The window sends a constructor event to all its objects just before the window Open event occurs. Use this event to initialize the text attribute.

- **Destructor**—occurs when the window is closing. The window sends a destructor event to all its objects just after the window Close event occurs.

- **DragDrop**—occurs when Drag Mode is on, the pointer drops an object within the EditMask.

- **DragEnter**—occurs when Drag Mode is on and the dragged object enters the EditMask. If Drag Mode is off and this control's DragAuto attribute is set, a DragEnter event will be triggered when the user clicks the control.

- **DragLeave**—occurs when Drag Mode is on, and the dragged object leaves the EditMask.

- **DragWithin**—occurs when Drag Mode is on, this event is triggered periodically while an object is dragged within the EditMask.

- **GetFocus**—occurs before the EditMask is selected with the Tab key or by clicking.

- **LoseFocus**—occurs before the EditMask loses focus (caused by tabbing away or clicking outside of the control.

- **Modified**—occurs when the text in the field has been changed and the user hits the Enter or Tab key (or clicks outside the control).

- **Other**—all the other Windows' events that have not been mapped to PowerBuilder events are routed to this event. You will rarely use this event; user-defined events are a better choice.

- **RButtonDown**—occurs when the right mouse button is pressed, and the pointer is located within the EditMask control.

EditMask Control Functions

The following functions apply to EditMask controls:

- **CanUndo**—a Boolean value, causes the last edit be reversed.

- **ClassName**—returns the name of the EditMask control.

- **Clear**—deletes the selected text from the EditMask control, does not place the deleted text in the Windows' clipboard.

- **Copy**—copies the selected text from the EditMask control to the Windows' clipboard.

- **Cut**—deletes the selected text from the EditMask control, places the deleted text in the Windows' clipboard.

- **Drag**—use this function to begin or end Drag Mode for this control.

- **Hide**—makes a EditMask control invisible.

- **LineCount**—returns the number of lines in the control.

- **LineLength**—returns the number of characters in the current line in the control.

- **Move**—relocates the EditMask control in the window.

- **Paste**—copies the text on the Windows' clipboard into the EditMask. If text is currently selected in the EditMask, the clipboard text replaces it.

- **Post**—adds a message to the message queue of a window, asynchronously.

- **PostEvent**—places an event on the EditMask control's event queue and continues (asynchronously).

- **Position**—returns the cursor position in the control.

- **ReplaceText**—replaces selected text with a new string or to insert text into the control if no text is currently selected.

- **Resize**—adjusts the size of the EditMask control.

- **Scroll**—scrolls the control in either direction.

- **SelectedLength**—returns the count of characters that are currently selected (highlighted) in the EditMask.

- **SelectedLine**—returns the line number where the beginning of the current selection is located.

- **SelectedStart**—returns the position of the first character that is selected in the control

- **SelectedText**—returns a string, a copy of the text that is currently selected in the control.

- **SelectText**—selects (highlights) a section of the text in the control.

- **SetFocus**—places the focus on the EditMask control, directs keyboard input to the control.

- **SetMask**—sets the EditMask for the control.

- **SetPosition**—places the EditMask control in the front-to-back display order (relative to other overlapping controls).

- **SetRedraw**—turns on or off the updating of the control (the text).

- **Show**—makes the EditMask control visible.

- **TextLine**—returns a string, containing the text that is on the cursor's current line.

- **TriggerEvent**—triggers a EditMask control event immediately (synchronously).

- **TypeOf**—returns the enumerated type of this control (EditMask!).

- **Undo**—reverses the last edit that was made in this control.

EditMask Control Popup Menu Options

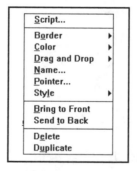

FIGURE 7.16 THE EDITMASK RMB POPUP

The items in the popup menu (right mouse click on the control) for a EditMask control are:

- **Script**—edits a script for a control event.

- **Border**—selects the type of border to be used for this control.

- **Color**—sets the background and text colors for this control.

- **Drag and Drop**—sets or clears the DragAuto Mode attribute or defines an icon for the Drag Mode.

251

- **Name**—opens the control's style dialog.

- **Pointer**—selects the pointer icon to be used when the pointer is over this control.

- **Style**—toggles the DisplayOnly, Visible, or Enabled attributes. You can also assign the Alignment, or Case attributes.

- **Bring to Front**—moves this control to the front of other overlapping controls.

- **Send to Back**—moves this control to the back of other overlapping controls.

- **Delete**—removes this control from the window.

- **Duplicate**—makes a copy of this control.

MultiLineEdit Control

FIGURE 7.17 A MultiLineEdit control

MultiLineEdit controls are similar to SingleLineEdits but, as the name implies, the MultiLineEdit control allows multiple lines of text to be entered and presented within the control. The MultiLineEdit control has a number of functions that lets the control act as a small text editor. Figure 7.18 shows the style dialog window for the MultiLineEdit control.

The control can be renamed. You can also enter the initial text for the control (as in this example). You could also assign this programatically by assigning the string to the text attribute.

You can have automatic scrolling in either the vertical or the horizontal planes during text entry. Check the CheckBox for Auto HScroll or Auto Vscroll. Add scroll bars by checking HScrollBar or VScrollBar. In general you turn off AutoHScroll and turn on AutoVScroll for MultiLineEdits.

Usually, you will also choose to add a VerticalScrollBar to the control and set the alignment as left.

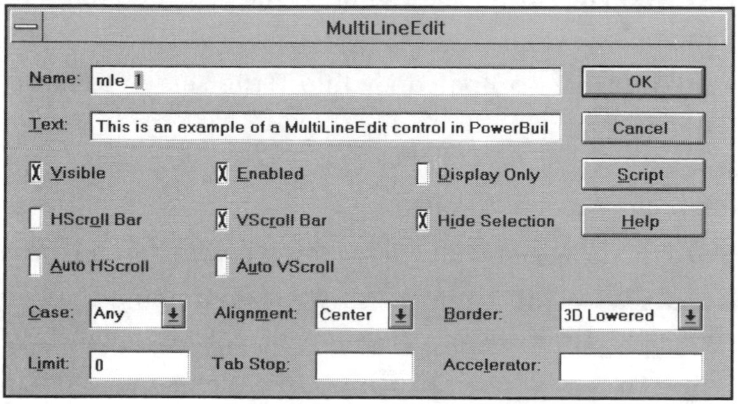

FIGURE 7.18 A MULTILINEEDIT CONTROL STYLE DIALOG

You may set a limit for the maximum number of characters that can be entered (0 means no limit, really 64K).

The Tab Stop edit field lets you specify the character position for each tab stop in the MultiLineEdit for use with importing text from outside the control. Tab stops are normally spaced 8 characters apart (if you do not enter a value for this field). This field holds an array of up to 16 integers. You can specify a single number as a tab stop, which also defines the distance between each tab position. For example, if you enter the number 6 into the Tab Stop field, there will be a tab stop every 6 characters to the right. You can also specify two or more numbers (separated by commas) in the Tab Stop field. This specifies the position for each Tab stop. For example, if you enter 4,8,20 in the Tab Stop field, the first tab stop is at position 4, the second at 8, and the third at 20.

MultiLineEdit Control Attributes

The attributes of a MultiLineEdit control are:

- **Accelerator**—an integer, the ASCII value value of the accelerator.

- **Alignment**—an enumerated value that specifies the alignment of the text in the control, either Left!, Center!, or Right!.

- **AutoHScroll**—a Boolean value, True sets automatic horizontal scrolling on.

- **AutoVScroll**—a Boolean value, True sets automatic vertical scrolling on.

- **BackColor**—a long value, representing the color of the background area of the control.

- **Border**—a Boolean value, True sets a border around the control.

- **BorderStyle**—an enumerated value containing the border style (StyleBox!, StyleLowered!, StyleRaised!, or StyleShadowBox!)

- **BringToTop**—a Boolean value, True places the MultiLineEdit on top of other overlapping controls in this window's front-to-back order.

- **DisplayOnly**—a Boolean value, False if the MultiLineEdit can be used for input, True if it is limited to display only.

- **DragAuto**—a Boolean value, if True, this MultiLineEdit is automatically set into Drag Mode when the user clicks on it.

- **DragIcon**—a string containing the name of the icon that is displayed when this control is in Drag Mode. If you select **None!**, a ghost outline of the control is used.

- **Enabled**—a Boolean value, set to True to enable the control, making it active and able to be selected and to receive events.

- **FaceName**—a string value containing the font name for the MultiLineEdit text .

- **FontCharSet**—an enumerated value that specifies the font character set for the text.

- **FontFamily**—an enumerated value that specifies the font family for the control text.

- **FontPitch**—an enumerated value that specifies the font pitch for the control text.

- **Height**—an integer value that specifies the vertical size of the control in PBUs.

- **HScrollBar**—a Boolean value, True adds a horizontal scroll bar to this control as needed.

- **Italic**—a Boolean value, set to True if the label font is to be italicized.

- **Limit**—an integer, the maximum number of characters that can be entered in this control.

- **Pointer**—a string containing the pointer icon to be used when the pointer is over this MultiLineEdit field.

- **TabOrder**—an integer that specifies the relative tab order for the controls in the window.

- **TabStop**—this is an integer array that stores the positions used for tabbing.

- **Tag**—a text string that is associated with this control, can be used to store the Microhelp text.

- **Text**—the initial text to be displayed in the edit field.

- **TextCase**—an enumerated value that controls the case of the data entered, can be AnyCase!, Lower!, or Upper!.

- **TextColor**—a long value, controls the color of the text in this control.

- **TextSize**—an integer that specifies the font size (in points) of the text label.

- **Underline**—a Boolean value, True if the text label for this control is to be underlined.

- **Visible**—a Boolean value, True if the control is visible (showing).

- **VScrollBar**—a Boolean value, True adds a vertical scroll bar to this control as needed.

- **Weight**—an integer that specifies the stroke thickness of the text label font (400 is normal).

- **Width**—an integer value that specifies the horizontal size of the control in PBUs.

- **X**—an integer value that specifies the horizontal position in the window of the control in PBUs.

- **Y**—an integer value that specifies the vertical position in the window of the control in PBUs.

MultiLineEdit Control Events

The events associated with a MultiLineEdit control are:

- **Constructor**—occurs just before the window is made the active window. The window sends a constructor event to all its objects just before the window Open event occurs.

- **Destructor**—occurs when the window is closing. The window sends a destructor event to all its objects just after the window Close event occurs.

- **DragDrop**—occurs when Drag Mode is on, and the pointer drops an object within the MultiLineEdit.

- **DragEnter**—occurs when Drag Mode is on and the dragged object enters the MultiLineEdit. If Drag Mode is off and this control's DragAuto attribute is set, a DragEnter event is triggered when the user clicks the control.

- **DragLeave**—occurs when Drag Mode is on and the dragged object leaves the MultiLineEdit.

- **DragWithin**—occurs when Drag Mode is on, this event is triggered periodically while an object is dragged within the MultiLineEdit.

- **GetFocus**—occurs just before the MultiLineEdit is selected with the Tab key or by clicking.

- **LoseFocus**—occurs just before the MultiLineEdit loses focus (caused by tabbing away or clicking outside of the control.

- **Modified**—occurs when the text in the field has been changed and the user hits the Enter or Tab key (or clicks outside the control).

- **Other**—all the other Windows' events that have not been mapped to PowerBuilder events are routed to this event. You will rarely use this event, user-defined events are a better choice.

■ **RButtonDown**—occurs when the right mouse button is pressed, and the pointer is located within the MultiLineEdit control.

MultiLineEdit Control Functions

The following functions apply to MultiLineEdit controls:

■ **CanUndo**—a Boolean value, can the effects of the last edit be reversed.

■ **ClassName**—returns the name of the MultiLineEdit control.

■ **Clear**—deletes the selected text from the MultiLineEdit control, does not place the deleted text in the Windows' clipboard.

■ **Copy**—copies the selected text from the MultiLineEdit control to the Windows' clipboard.

■ **Cut**—deletes the selected text from the MultiLineEdit control and places the deleted text in the Windows' clipboard.

■ **Drag**—use this function to begin or end Drag Mode for this control.

■ **DraggedObject**—identifies the object that has been dragged within this control.

■ **Hide**—makes a MultiLineEdit control invisible.

■ **LineCount**—returns the number of lines in the control.

■ **LineLength**—returns the number of characters in the control.

■ **Move**—relocates the MultiLineEdit control in the window.

■ **Paste**—copies the text on the Windows' clipboard into the MultiLineEdit. If text is currently selected in the MultiLineEdit, the clipboard text replaces it.

■ **PointerX**—returns the pointer's horizontal position in the control.

■ **PointerY**—returns the pointer's vertical position in the control.

■ **PostEvent**—places an event on the MultiLineEdit control's event queue and continues (asynchronously).

■ **Position**—returns the cursor position in the control.

- **ReplaceText**—replaces the selected text with a new string, or to insert text if there is no selected text in the control.

- **Resize**—adjusts the size of the MultiLineEdit control.

- **Scroll**—scrolls the control in either direction.

- **SelectedLength**—returns the count of characters that are currently selected (highlighted) in the MultiLineEdit.

- **SelectedLine**—the line number where the beginning of the current selection is located.

- **SelectedStart**—returns the position of the first character that is selected in the control.

- **SelectedText**—returns a string, a copy of the text that is currently selected in the control.

- **SelectText**—selects (highlights) a section of the text in the control.

- **SetFocus**—places the focus on the MultiLineEdit control, directs keyboard input to the control.

- **SetPosition**—places the MultiLineEdit control in the front-to-back display order (relative to other overlapping controls).

- **SetRedraw**—turns on or off the updating of the control (the label).

- **Show**—makes the MultiLineEdit control visible.

- **TextLine**—returns a string, containing the text that is on the cursor's current line

- **TriggerEvent**—triggers a MultiLineEdit control event immediately (synchronously).

- **TypeOf**—returns the enumerated type of this control (MultiLineEdit!).

- **Undo**—reverses the last edit that was made in this control.

MultiLineEdit Control Popup Menu Options

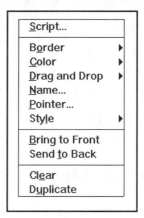

FIGURE 7.19 A MULTILINEEDIT CONTROL RMB POPUP

The items in the popup menu (right mouse click on the control) for a MultiLineEdit control are:

- **Script**—edits a script for a control event.
- **Border**—selects the type of border to be used for this control.
- **Color**—sets the background and text colors for this control.
- **Drag and Drop**—sets or clears the DragAuto Mode attribute or defines an icon for the Drag Mode.
- **Name**—opens the control's style dialog.
- **Pointer**—selects the pointer icon to be used when the pointer is over this control.
- **Style**—toggles the Auto HScroll, Auto VScroll, DisplayOnly, Visible, or Enabled attributes. You can also set the Alignment and Case attributes with this option.
- **Bring to Front**—moves this control to the front of other overlapping controls.
- **Send to Back**—moves this control to the back of other overlapping controls.

- ■ **Delete**—removes this control from the window.
- ■ **Duplicate**—makes a copy of this control.

LISTBOX CONTROLS

FIGURE 7.20 A LISTBOX CONTROL

The ListBox control displays a number of items in a list. The list can be scrollable. The user can select items in the list by single-clicking an item, or by scrolling through the items and then hitting the Enter key. It is possible to allow multiple items to be selected. Often double-clicking a item is used to trigger an event related to that choice.

The items on the list can be hard-coded, or you can add items to the list by using the AddItem and InsertItem functions. The list can be automatically sorted and searched. ListBox controls work well with an associated SingleLineEdit control, where the user enters data into the SingleLineEdit to trigger a search in the ListBox.

In the ListBox style dialog you can change the name of the control. The set of CheckBoxes is used to set some of the most important attributes. The first two attributes are the standard visible and enable options available for most controls:

- ■ **Visible**—set this checkbox to make the control visible.
- ■ **Enabled**—when the listbox is enabled, it is active, able to be selected and to receive input. If it is disabled, the control cannot receive input or events and will be grayed in color to mark it as inactive.
- ■ **Sorted**—check this to alphabetically sort the list.
- ■ **HScroll Bar**—check this to add a horizontal scroll bar to the control.

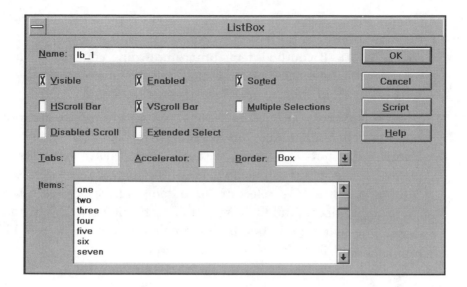

FIGURE 7.21 A LISTBOX STYLE DIALOG

- **VScroll Bar**—check this to add a vertical scroll bar to the control.

- **Multiple Selections**—check this if the user can select more than one item in the list. If this is not checked, the user will only be able to select one item from the list. Selecting a new item will deselect the previous item.

- **Tab Stop**—lets you specify the character position for each tab stop in the ListBox when importing text. Tab stops are normally spaced 8 characters apart (if you do not enter a value for this field). This field holds an array of up to 16 integers. You can specify a single number as a tab stop defines the distance between each tab position. You can also specify two or more number (separated by commas) in the Tab Stop field. This specifies the position for each Tab stop.

- **Accelerator**—to assign an accelerator to this control, enter the character value in this field.

- **Border**—adds a border to the control.

- **Items**—you can add items to the list, or use this listbox to hard-code the items. Enter an item and press the **Control+Enter** key to add additional items in the ListBox. If you only press the Enter key, the dialog closes, since the OK button is the default button for this dialog. NOTE: If you add items programatically, you have to use functions (FindItem, SelectItem, etc.) to see the new ones, they will not appear on the item array (ITEM[]).

- **DisableNoScroll**—a Boolean value, if False, the listbox will not have a scrollbar on it unles it is necessary. The default is False.
- **ExtendedSelect**—a Boolean value, if True, then a scrollbar is always visible, but is disabled when all the items can be accessed without it. When True, select multiple items can be selected using standard Windows' additive selection techniques. This lets you specify the style for selecting multiple items in the listbox. See the MultiSelect attribute for related information.

ListBox Control Attributes

The attributes of a ListBox control are:

- **Accelerator**—an integer, the ASCII value value of the accelerator.
- **BackColor**—a long value, representing the color of the background area of the control.
- **Border**—a Boolean value, True sets a border around the control.
- **BorderStyle**—an enumerated value containing the border style (StyleBox!, StyleLowered!, StyleRaised!, or StyleShadowBox!)
- **BringToTop**—set this Boolean to True to place the ListBox on top of other overlapping controls in this window's front-to-back order.
- **DragAuto**—a Boolean value, True, this ListBox control sets to Drag Mode when the user clicks on it.
- **DragIcon**—a string containing the name of the icon that is used when this control is in Drag Mode.
- **Enabled**—a Boolean value, set to True to enable the control, making it active, and able to be selected or clicked and to receive events.

■ **FaceName**—a string value containing the font name for the ListBox text.

■ **FontCharSet**—an enumerated value that specifies the font character set for the text.

■ **FontFamily**—an enumerated value that specifies the font family for the control text.

■ **FontPitch**—an enumerated value that specifies the font pitch for the control text.

■ **Height**—an integer value that specifies the vertical size of the control in PBUs.

■ **HScrollBar**—a Boolean value, if True a horizontal scroll bar is added to this control as needed.

■ **Italic**—a Boolean value, set to True if the label font is to be italicized.

■ **Item[ ]**—an array of strings, the items in the ListBox.

■ **MultiSelect**—a Boolean value, True if multiple selections are allowed in the ListBox.

■ **Pointer**—a string containing the pointer icon to be used when the pointer is over this ListBox field.

■ **Sorted**—a Boolean value, True if the items should be sorted.

■ **TabOrder**—an integer that specifies the relative tab order for the controls on the window.

■ **TabStop**—an integer array that stores the positions used for tabbing.

■ **Tag**—a text string that is associated with this control, can be used to store the Microhelp text.

■ **TextCase**—an enumerated value that controls the case of the data entered. It can be AnyCase!, Lower!, or Upper!.

■ **TextColor**—a long value, controls the color of the text in this control.

■ **TextSize**—an integer that specifies the font size (in points) of the text label.

■ **Underline**—a Boolean value, True if the text label for this control is underlined.

- **Visible**—a Boolean value, True if the control is visible (showing).

- **VScrollBar**—a Boolean value, if True a vertical scroll bar is added to this control as needed.

- **Weight**—an integer that specifies the stroke thickness of the text label font (400 is normal).

- **Width**—an integer value that specifies the horizontal size of the control in PBUs.

- **X**—an integer value that specifies the horizontal position in the window of the control in PBUs.

- **Y**—an integer value that specifies the vertical position in the window of the control in PBUs.

ListBox Control Events

The events associated with a ListBox control are:

- **Constructor**—occurs just before the window is made the active window. The window sends a constructor event to all its objects just before the window Open event occurs.

- **Destructor**—occurs when the window is closing. The window sends a destructor event to all its objects just after the window Close event occurs.

- **DoubleClicked**—occurs when the user double-clicks on an item in the list. This event is where you will add code that should be triggered for a double-click.

- **DragDrop**—occurs when Drag Mode is on and the pointer drops an object within the ListBox.

- **DragEnter**—occurs when Drag Mode is on and the dragged object enters the ListBox. If Drag Mode is off and this control's DragAuto attribute is set, a DragEnter event is triggered when the user clicks the control.

- **DragLeave**—occurs when Drag Mode is on and the dragged object leaves the ListBox.

- **DragWithin**—occurs when Drag Mode is on, this event is triggered periodically while an object is dragged within the ListBox.

- **GetFocus**—occurs before the ListBox is selected with the Tab key or by clicking.

- **LoseFocus**—occurs before the ListBox loses focus (caused by tabbing away or clicking outside of the control).

- **Other**—all the other Windows' events that have not been mapped to PowerBuilder events are routed to this event. You will rarely use this event, user-defined events are a better choice.

- **RButtonDown**—occurs when the right mouse button is pressed, and the pointer is located within the ListBox control.

- **SelectionChanged**—occurs when the user has selected a different item in the ListBox. This event is where you place the code that you want to execute each time the user selects an item in the list.

ListBox Control Functions

The following functions apply to ListBox controls:

- **AddItem**—inserts a new item into the ListBox at the bottom of the list.

- **ClassName**—returns the name of the ListBox control.

- **DeleteItem**—removes an item (by number) from the list

- **DirList**—reads a directory into the ListBox, you can specify file types and a name mask.

- **DirSelect**—finds the current selection in the ListBox, and use it to set the current directory.

- **Drag**—begins or ends Drag Mode for this control.

- **FindItem**—searches for an item in the ListBox.

- **Hide**—makes a ListBox control invisible.

- **InsertItem**—adds a new item at a specific position in the list.

- **Move**—relocates the ListBox control in the window.

- **PointerX**—returns the pointer's horizontal position in the control.

- **PointerY**—returns the pointer's vertical position in the control.

- **PostEvent**—places an event on the ListBox control's event queue and continues (asynchronously)

- **Reset**—clears the ListBox.

- **Resize**—used to adjust the size of the ListBox control.

- **SelectedIndex**—returns the index (integer) of the selected item.

- **SelectedItem**—returns the text of the selected item.

- **SetFocus**—places the focus on the ListBox control, directs keyboard input to the control.

- **SetPosition**—places the ListBox control in the front-to-back display order (relative to other overlapping controls).

- **SetRedraw**—turns on or off the updating of the control (the label).

- **SetState**—selects or unselects an item in the list (if MultiSelect is True).

- **SetTop**—scrolls so that the specified item is at the top of the ListBox display.

- **Show**—makes the ListBox control visible.

- **State**—returns the state of the ListBox item (1 = selected or 0 = not-selected).

- **Text**—returns a string, containing the text for a specific item in the list.

- **Top**—returns the index of the item at the top of the display area in this control.

- **TotalItems**—returns an integer, a count of items in the ListBox.

- **TotalSelected**—returns an integer, a count of the selected items in the ListBox.

- **TriggerEvent**—triggers a ListBox control event immediately (synchronously).

- **TypeOf**—returns the enumerated type of this control (ListBox!).

ListBox Control Popup Menu Options

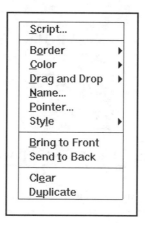

FIGURE 7.22 THE LISTBOX RMB POPUP

The items in the popup menu (right mouse click on the control) for a ListBox control are:

- **Script**—edits a script for a control event.
- **Border**—selects the type of border to be used for this control.
- **Color**—sets the background and text colors for this control.
- **Drag and Drop**—sets or clears the DragAuto Mode attribute or defines an icon for the Drag Mode.
- **Name**—opens the control's style dialog.
- **Pointer**—selects the pointer icon to be used when the pointer is over this control.
- **Style**—used to toggle the HScroll Bar, Multiple Selections, Sorted, VScroll Bar, Visible, or Enabled attributes.
- **Bring to Front**—moves this control to the front of other overlapping controls.
- **Send to Back**—moves this control to the back of other overlapping controls.

- ■ **Delete**—removes this control from the window.
- ■ **Duplicate**—makes a copy of this control.

DropDownListBox Controls

FIGURE 7.23 DropDownListBox controls

A DropDownListBox combines a SingleLineEdit control with a ListBox control. The ListBox portion of the control can be dropped down (displayed) or can be closed. The DropDownListBox can be used to display a read-only list for the user to choose from, or it can be set up to allow the input of new values not in the list. To select an item in the list, you can use the scroll bar to locate and then click on the item. You can also use the up and down arrow keys to scroll through the list, this will select an item as it scrolls.

If the DropDownListBox is set for display only, a search option is provided for items in the list. The ListBox portion will display entries that match the letter that is typed into the SingleLineEdit part of the control. This matches only on the first letter of the items in the list. If there is more than one item beginning with a character, you can cycle through the items that match in the list by repeating the keystroke. You can also use the up and down arrow keys to move through the list while in the edit field.

The editable ListBox displays a space between the edit field and the down arrow to mark it as an editable type ListBox. Compare this ListBox to the previous example (Figure 7.23) which does not have the space and is therefore not editable.

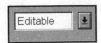

FIGURE 7.24 An Editable listbox

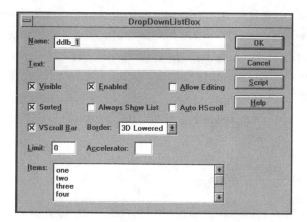

FIGURE 7.25 THE DROPDOWNLISTBOX

The DropDownListBox style dialog is almost the same as the style dialog for the ListBox. In this dialog you can change the name of the control. The set of CheckBoxes is used to set some of the most important attributes. The first two attributes are the standard visible and enable options available for most controls:

- **Visible**—sets this CheckBox to make the control visible.

- **Enabled**—when the DropDownListBox is enabled, it is active, able to be selected, and to receive input. If it is disabled the control cannot receive input or events and will be grayed in color to mark it as inactive.

- **Allow Editing**—makes this an editable DropDownListBox.

- **Sorted**—alphabetically sorts the list.

- **Always Show List**—causes the ListBox portion of the control to always be dropped-down and visible. If this is not checked, the user must click the down arrow to display the list.

- **Auto HScroll**—activates automatic horizontal scrolling, for entering items that are wider than the control.

- **VScroll Bar**—adds a vertical scroll bar to the control.

- **Border**—adds a border to the control.

- **Limit**—specifies the maximum number of characters that can be entered for an new entry (for an editable type control).

- **Accelerator**—assigns an accelerator to this control, enter the character value in this field.

- **Items**—adds items to the list or uses this ListBox to hard-code the items. Enter an item and press the **Control+Enter** key to add additional items in the DropDownListBox. If you only press the Enter key, the dialog will close, since the OK button is the default button for this dialog.

You must size this control (in the window painter) to represent the size that you want for the ListBox portion of this control when it drops down.

DropDownListBox Control Attributes

The attributes of a DropDownListBox control are:

- **Accelerator**—an integer, the ASCII value value of the accelerator.

- **AllowEdit**—this is a Boolean value, if set to True, it lets the user enter a value that is not in the list of items. This also disables the search functionality.

- **AutoHScroll**—a Boolean value, True sets automatic horizontal scrolling on.

- **BackColor**—a long value, representing the color of the background area of the control.

- **Border**—a Boolean, True sets a border around the control.

- **BorderStyle**—an enumerated value containing the border style (StyleBox!, StyleLowered!, StyleRaised!, or StyleShadowBox!).

- **BringToTop**—set this Boolean to True to place the DropDownListBox on top of other overlapping controls in this window's front-to-back order.

- **DragAuto**—if this Boolean is set to True, this control is automatically set into Drag Mode when the user clicks on it.

- **DragIcon**—a string containing the name of the icon that is displayed when this control is in Drag Mode. If you select **None!**, a ghost outline of the control is used.

- **Enabled**—a Boolean value, True makes the control active and able to be selected or clicked and to receive events.

- **FaceName**—a string value containing the font name for the control text.

- **FontCharSet**—an enumerated value that specifies the font character set for the text.

- **FontFamily**—an enumerated value that specifies the font family for the control text.

- **FontPitch**—an enumerated value that specifies the font pitch for the control text.

- **Height**—an integer value that specifies the vertical size of the control in PBUs.

- **HScrollBar**—a Boolean value, if True a horizontal scroll bar is added to this control as needed.

- **Italic**—a Boolean value, set to True if the label font is italicized.

- **Item[ ]**—an array of strings, the items in the DropDownListBox.

- **Pointer**—a string containing the pointer icon to be used when the pointer is over this control.

- **ShowList**—a Boolean value, if True the list always appears opened (dropped down). Otherwise the user must click on the arrow to open the list.

- **Sorted**—a Boolean value, True if the items should be sorted.

- **TabOrder**—an integer that specifies the relative tab order for the controls on the window.

- **TabStop**—an integer array that stores the positions used for tabbing.

- **Tag**—a text string that is associated with this control, can be used to store the Microhelp text.

- **Text**—the text that is displayed in the control.

- **TextColor**—a long value, controls the color of the text in this control.

- **TextSize**—an integer that specifies the font size (in points) of the text label.

- **Underline**—a Boolean value, True if the text label for this control is underlined.

- **Visible**—a Boolean value, True if the control is visible (showing).

- **VScrollBar**—a Boolean value, if True a vertical scroll bar will be added to this control as needed.

- **Weight**—an integer that specifies the stroke thickness of the text label font (400 is normal).

- **Width**—an integer value that specifies the horizontal size of the control in PBUs.

- **X**—an integer value that specifies the horizontal position in the window of the control in PBUs.

- **Y**—an integer value that specifies the vertical position in the window of the control in PBUs.

DropDownListBox Control Events

The events associated with a DropDownListBox control are:

- **Constructor**—occurs before the window is made the active window. The window sends a constructor event to all its objects just before the window Open event occurs.

- **Destructor**—occurs when the window is closing. The window sends a destructor event to all its objects just after the window Close event occurs.

- **DoubleClicked**—occurs when the user double-clicks on an item in the list. You may use this to execute code as the result of the double-click.

- **DragDrop**—occurs when Drag Mode is on, and the pointer drops an object within the control.

- **DragEnter**—occurs when Drag Mode is on and the dragged object enters the control. If Drag Mode is off and this control's DragAuto attribute is set, a DragEnter event will be triggered (rather than a Clicked event) when the user clicks the control.

- **DragLeave**—occurs when Drag Mode is on, and the dragged object leaves the control.

- **DragWithin**—occurs when Drag Mode is on, this event will be triggered periodically while an object is dragged within the control.

- **GetFocus**—occurs before the control is selected with the Tab key or by clicking.

- **LoseFocus**—occurs before the control loses focus (caused by tabbing away or clicking outside of the control.

- **Modified**—triggered when the user has selected a different item in the list. It will also be triggered if AllowEdit is True and if the user entered a new value and has tabbed out of the control.

- **Other**—all the other Windows' events that have not been mapped to PowerBuilder events are routed to this event. You will rarely use this event; user-defined events are a better choice.

- **RButtonDown**—occurs when the right mouse button is pressed, and the pointer is located within the DropDownListBox control.

- **SelectionChanged**—occurs when the user has selected a different item in the list.

DropDownListBox Control Functions

The following functions apply to DropDownListBox controls:

- **AddItem**—inserts a new item into the DropDownListBox at the bottom of the list.

- **ClassName**—returns the name of the DropDownListBox control.

- **Clear**—deletes the selected text from the DropDownListBox control; does not place the deleted text in the Windows' clipboard.

- **Copy**—copies the selected text from the DropDownListBox control to the Windows' clipboard.

■ **Cut**—deletes the selected text from the DropDownListBox control, places the deleted text in the Windows' clipboard.

■ **DeleteItem**—removes an item (by number) from the list.

■ **DirList**—reads a directory into the DropDownListBox. You can specify a file type and name mask.

■ **DirSelect**—finds the current selection in the DropDownListBox, and uses it to set the current directory.

■ **Drag**—begins or ends Drag Mode for this control.

■ **FindItem**—searches for an item in the DropDownListBox.

■ **Hide**—makes a DropDownListBox control invisible.

■ **InsertItem**—adds a new item at a specific position in the list.

■ **Move**—relocates the DropDownListBox control in the window.

■ **Paste**—copies the text on the Windows' clipboard into the DropDownListBox. If text is currently selected in the DropDownListBox, the clipboard text will replace it.

■ **PointerX**—returns the pointer's horizontal position in the control.

■ **PointerY**—returns the pointer's vertical position in the control.

■ **Position**—returns the cursor position in the control.

■ **Post**—adds a message to the message queue of a window, asynchronously.

■ **PostEvent**—places an event on the DropDownListBox control's event queue and continues (asynchronously).

■ **ReplaceText**—replaces a given text with a new string.

■ **Reset**—clears the DropDownListBox.

■ **Resize**—used to adjust the size of the DropDownListBox control.

■ **SelectedLength**—returns the count of characters that are currently selected (highlighted) in the DropDownListBox.

■ **SelectedStart**—returns the position of the first character that is selected in the control.

■ **SelectedText**—returns a string, a copy of the text that is currently selected in the control.

- **SelectItem**—selects an item on the list by position.

- **SelectText**—selects (highlights) a section of the text in the control.

- **SetFocus**—places the focus on the DropDownListBox control, directs keyboard input to the control.

- **SetPosition**—places the DropDownListBox control in the front-to-back display order (relative to other overlapping controls).

- **SetRedraw**—turns on or off the updating of the control (the label).

- **Show**—makes the DropDownListBox control visible.

- **Text**—returns a string, containing the text that is on the cursor's current line

- **TotalItems**—returns an integer, a count of items in the DropDownListBox.

- **TriggerEvent**—triggers a DropDownListBox control event immediately (synchronously).

- **TypeOf**—returns the enumerated type of this control (DropDownListBox!).

DropDownListBox Control Popup Menu Options

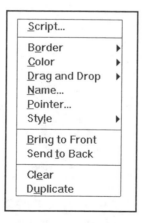

FIGURE 7.26 THE DROPDOWNLISTBOX RMB POPUP

The items in the popup menu (right mouse click on the control) for a DropDownListBox control are:

- **Script**—edits a script for a control event.
- **Border**—selects the type of border to be used for this control.
- **Color**—sets the background and text colors for this control.
- **Drag and Drop**—sets or clears the DragAuto Mode attribute, or define an icon for the Drag Mode.
- **Name**—opens the control's style dialog.
- **Pointer**—selects the pointer icon to be used when the pointer is over this control.
- **Style**—used to toggle the Allow Editing, Always Show List, Auto Hscroll, Sorted, Vscroll Bar, Visible, or Enabled attributes.
- **Bring to Front**—moves this control to the front of other overlapping controls.
- **Send to Back**—moves this control to the back of other overlapping controls.
- **Delete**—removes this control from the window.
- **Duplicate**—makes a copy of this control.

PICTURE CONTROLS

FIGURE 7.27 A PICTURE CONTROL

The Picture control is used to display BMP or RLE images in your PowerBuilder applications. You can resize the image, or invert the image colors. The image is usually on the disk, and the image is displayed by assigning the path to the Picture control. You can also read images in from other sources (like a database), and then display the image in the Picture control (by using Blob objects). (You could also use OLE to display the image in a OLE server, this is covered in a later chapter).

You may use the Picture control as a passive control used only to display images, or you may let the user click on the image or use drag-and-drop functionality with the control.

Figure 7.28 shows the style dialog for a Picture control. When you first create a Picture control and attempt to open the style dialog, you will be prompted with the Select Picture dialog which is described in the next paragraph.

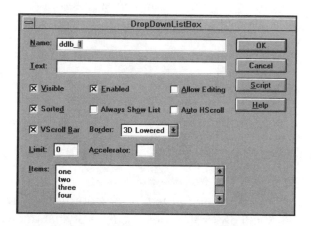

FIGURE 7.28 THE PICTURE CONTROL STYLE DIALOG

In the Picture style dialog you can change the name of the control. The File Name field contains the file name (including the full path) to be used for the image. To change the image click on the **Change...** CommandButton in the style dialog. This opens the Select Picture dialog in Figure 7.29. The image is loaded from the disk after you specify a path to the file in the Select Picture dialog window.

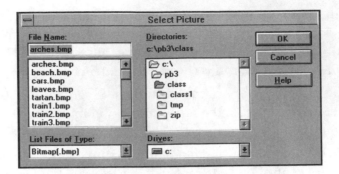

FIGURE 7.29 SELECTING THE PICTURE FILE

In the Select Picture dialog, you use listboxes to specify the path for the file to be used for the control's image. (You can set the image to any BMP or RLE file. You can change it later, so initially you can set it to one of our example BMPs).

Picture Control Attributes

The attributes of a Picture control are:

- **Border**—a Boolean, this is True if there is a border around the control.

- **BorderStyle**—an enumerated value containing the border style (StyleBox!, StyleLowered!, StyleRaised!, or StyleShadowBox!).

- **BringToTop**—set this Boolean to True to place the Picture on top of other overlapping controls in this window's front-to-back order.

- **DragAuto**—if this Boolean is set to True, this control is automatically set into Drag Mode when the user clicks on it.

- **DragIcon**—a string containing the name of the icon that is displayed when this control is in Drag Mode. If you select **None!**, a ghost outline of the control is used.

- **Enabled**—a Boolean value, set to True to enable the control, making it active and able to be selected or clicked, and to receive events.

- **FocusRectangle**—a Boolean value, is True if a focus rectangle is placed around the control when it has the focus.

- **Height**—an integer value that specifies the vertical size of the control in PBUs.

- **Invert**—a Boolean value, if set to True, it reverses the image colors. You can toggle this attribute to make the image flash in response to an event (such as Clicked).

- **OriginalSize**—a Boolean value, if set to True, the image is set back to its original size, otherwise you can resize the image. You cannot change this attribute at run-time.

- **PictureName**—a string containing the filename (full path name) to be displayed in this control.

- **Pointer**—a string containing the pointer icon to be used when the pointer is over this control.

- **TabOrder**—an integer that specifies the relative tab order for the controls on the window.

- **Tag**—a text string that is associated with this control, can be used to store the Microhelp text.

- **Visible**—a Boolean value, True if the control is visible (showing).

- **Width**—an integer value that specifies the horizontal size of the control in PBUs.

- **X**—an integer value that specifies the horizontal position in the window of the control in PBUs.

- **Y**—an integer value that specifies the vertical position in the window of the control in PBUs.

Picture Control Events

The events associated with a Picture control are:

- **Clicked**—occurs when you click on a control, or select the control and press the Enter key, this event is triggered.

- **Constructor**—occurs before the window is made the active window. The window sends a constructor event to all its objects just before the window Open event occurs.

- **Destructor**—occurs when the window is closing. The window sends a destructor event to all its objects just after the window Close event occurs.

- **DoubleClicked**—occurs when the user double-clicks on the control.

- **DragDrop**—occurs when Drag Mode is on, the pointer drops an object within the control.

- **DragEnter**—occurs when Drag Mode is on, the dragged object enters the control. If Drag Mode is off and this control's DragAuto attribute is set, a DragEnter event will be triggered (rather than a Clicked event) when the user clicks the control.

- **DragLeave**—occurs when Drag Mode is on, the dragged object leaves the control.

- **DragWithin**—occurs when Drag Mode is on, this event is triggered periodically while an object is dragged within the control.

- **GetFocus**—occurs just before the control is selected with the Tab key or by clicking.

- **LoseFocus**—occurs just before the control loses focus (caused by tabbing away or clicking outside of the control).

- **Other**—all the other Windows' events that have not been mapped to PowerBuilder events are routed to this event. You will rarely use this event; user-defined events are a better choice.

- **RButtonDown**—occurs when the right mouse button is pressed, and the pointer is located within the Picture Control.

Picture Control Functions

The following functions apply to Picture Controls:

- **ClassName**—returns the name of the Picture Control.

- **Drag**—begins or ends Drag Mode for this control.

- **Draw**—draws the named picture control in the current window at the specified X, Y location. Use to draw pictures in animation.

- **Hide**—makes a Picture Control invisible.

- **Move**—relocates the Picture Control in the window.

- **PointerX**—returns the pointer's horizontal position in the control.

- **PointerY**—returns the pointer's vertical position in the control.

- **PostEvent**—places an event on the Picture Control's event queue and continues (asynchronously)

- **Resize**—adjusts the size of the Picture Control.

- **SetFocus**—place the focus on the Picture Control, directs keyboard input to the control.

- **SetPicture**—creates a new bitmap for the control.

- **SetPosition**—places the Picture Control in the front-to-back display order (relative to other overlapping controls).

- **SetRedraw**—turns on or off the updating of the control (the label).

- **Show**—makes the Picture Control visible.

- **TriggerEvent**—triggers a Picture Control event immediately (synchronously).

- **TypeOf**—returns the enumerated type of this control (Picture!).

Picture Control Popup Menu Options

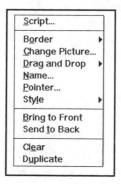

FIGURE 7.30 THE PICTURE CONTROL RMB POPUP

The items in the popup menu (right mouse click on the control) for a Picture Control are:

- **Script**—edits a script for a control event.
- **Border**—selects the type of border to be used for this control.
- **Change Picture**—reassigns the picture to be displayed in this control.
- **Drag and Drop**—sets or clears the DragAuto Mode attribute or defines an icon for the Drag Mode.
- **Name**—opens the control's style dialog.
- **Pointer**—selects the pointer icon to be used when the pointer is over this control.
- **Style**—used to toggle the Focus Rectangle, Invert, Original Size, Visible, or Enabled attributes.
- **Bring to Front**—moves this control to the front of other overlapping controls.
- **Send to Back**—moves this control to the back of other overlapping controls.
- **Delete**—removes this control from the window.
- **Duplicate**—makes a copy of this control.

StaticText Controls

FIGURE 7.31 A STATICTEXT CONTROL

StaticText controls are useful for adding labels to windows. StaticText controls can also be used to display read-only data (data that is not updatable by the user). In this manner, you can use a StaticText control instead of a single-line edit.

StaticText Style Dialog

You can open the StaticText style dialog by double-clicking on the StaticText. In the StaticText style dialog (Figure 7.32) you set the name of the control and the text label. You can also choose a border and set the text alignment.

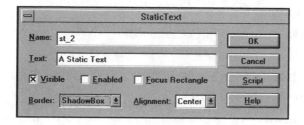

FIGURE 7.32 THE STATICTEXT STYLE DIALOG

StaticText Attributes

The attributes of a StaticText are:

- **Alignment**—an enumerated value that specifies the horizontal text alignment for the text (Left!, Center!, or Right!).

- **BackColor**—a long value, representing the color of the background area of the control.

- **Border**—a Boolean value that specifies whether or not the text has a border.

- **BorderStyle**—an enumerated value containing the border style (StyleBox!, StyleLowered!, StyleRaised!, or StyleShadowBox!).

- **BringToTop**—set this Boolean to True to place the StaticText on top of other overlapping controls in this window's front-to-back order.

- **DragAuto**—if this Boolean is set to True, this StaticText is automatically set into Drag Mode when the user clicks on it.

- **DragIcon**—a string containing the name of the icon that is displayed when this button is in Drag Mode. If you select **None!**, a ghost outline of the control is used.

283

- **Enabled**—a Boolean value, set to True to enable the button, making it active and able to be selected or clicked and to receive events.

- **FaceName**—a string value containing the font name for the StaticText caption.

- **FillPattern**—an enumerated value that specifies the hatch pattern for the StaticText control.

- **FocusRectangle**—a Boolean value, if True, the control will have a dotted rectangle outline when it has the focus.

- **FontCharSet**—an enumerated value that specifies the font character set for the caption.

- **FontFamily**—an enumerated value that specifies the font family for the button caption.

- **FontPitch**—an enumerated value that specifies the font pitch for the button caption.

- **Height**—an integer value that specifies the vertical size of the button in PBUs.

- **Italic**—a Boolean value, set to True if the label font is italicized.

- **Pointer**—a string containing the pointer icon to be used when the pointer is over this StaticText.

- **TabOrder**—an integer that specifies the relative tab order for the controls on the window.

- **Tag**—a text string that is associated with this button, can be used to store the Microhelp text.

- **Text**—the string label (caption) for the StaticText.

- **TextColor**—a long value, that specifies the color of the text.

- **TextSize**—an integer that specifies the font size (in points) of the text.

- **Underline**—a Boolean value, True if the text label for this button is underlined.

- **Visible**—a Boolean value, True if the button is visible (showing).

- **Weight**—an integer that specifies the stroke thickness of the text label font (400 is normal).

- **Width**—an integer value that specifies the horizontal size of the button in PBUs.

- **X**—an integer value that specifies the horizontal position in the window of the button in PBUs.

- **Y**—an integer value that specifies the vertical position in the window of the button in PBUs.

StaticText Events

The events associated with a StaticText are:

- **Clicked**—occurs when you click on a button, or select the button and press the Enter key, this event is triggered.

- **Constructor**—occurs just before the window is made the active window. The window sends a constructor event to all its objects just before the window Open event occurs.

- **Destructor**—occurs when the window is closing. The window sends a destructor event to all its objects just after the window Close event occurs.

- **DoubleClicked**—occurs when the user double-clicks on the control.

- **DragDrop**—occurs when Drag Mode is on, and the pointer drops an object within the StaticText.

- **DragEnter**—occurs when Drag Mode is on and the dragged object enters the StaticText. If Drag Mode is off and this button's DragAuto attribute is set, a DragEnter event is triggered (rather than a Clicked event) when the user clicks the button.

- **DragLeave**—occurs when Drag Mode is on, and the dragged object leaves the StaticText.

- **DragWithin**—occurs when Drag Mode is on, this event is triggered periodically while an object is dragged within the StaticText.

- **GetFocus**—occurs just before the StaticText is selected with the Tab key or by clicking.

■ **LoseFocus**—occurs just before the StaticText loses focus (caused by tabbing away or clicking outside of the button.

■ **Other**—all the other Windows' events that have not been mapped to PowerBuilder events are routed to this event. You will rarely use this event; user-defined events are a better choice.

■ **RButtonDown**—occurs when the right mouse button is pressed and the pointer is located within the StaticText.

StaticText Functions

The following functions apply to StaticTexts:

■ **ClassName**—returns the name of the StaticText.

■ **Drag**—begins or ends Drag Mode for this button.

■ **Hide**—makes a StaticText invisible.

■ **Move**—relocates the StaticText in the window.

■ **PointerX**—returns the pointer's horizontal position in the button.

■ **PointerY**—returns the pointer's vertical position in the button.

■ **PostEvent**—places an event on the StaticText's event queue and continues (asynchronously).

■ **Resize**—adjusts the size of the StaticText.

■ **SetFocus**—places the focus on the StaticText, directs keyboard input to the button.

■ **SetPosition**—places the StaticText in the front-to-back display order (relative to other overlapping controls).

■ **SetRedraw**—turns on or off the updating of the control if the text is changed.

■ **Show**—makes the StaticText visible.

■ **TriggerEvent**—triggers a StaticText event immediately (synchronously).

■ **TypeOf**—returns the enumerated type of this control (StaticText!).

StaticText Popup Menu Options

FIGURE 7.33 THE STATICTEXT RMB POPUP

The items in the popup menu (right mouse click on the button) for a StaticText are:

- **Script**—edits a script for a StaticText event.

- **Drag and Drop**—sets or clears the DragAuto Mode attribute or defines an icon for the Drag Mode.

- **Name**—opens the StaticText style dialog.

- **Pointer**—selects the pointer icon to be used when the pointer is over this button.

- **Style**—toggles the Focus Rectangle, Visible, or Enabled attributes. You can also set the value of the Alignment attribute here.

- **Bring to Front**—moves this button to the front of other overlapping controls.

- **Send to Back**—moves this button to the back of other overlapping controls.

- **Delete**—removes this button from the window

- **Duplicate**—makes a copy of this button.

RadioButton Controls

FIGURE 7.34 RadioButton Control

RadioButton controls are used to select an option. RadioButton controls are usually grouped together in a GroupBox, as in this example. Only one of the RadioButtons in a group can be selected (checked) at a time. RadioButtons in a group can be managed automatically by PowerBuilder. When you select one of the buttons, it will be checked and the others in the group will be unchecked. You must assign a text to label each RadioButton, you place the text on either the left or the right side of the button.

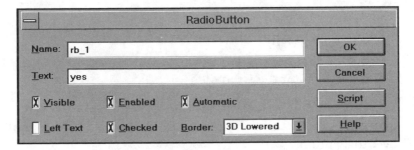

FIGURE 7.35 THE RadioButton Style dialog

RadioButton Attributes

The attributes of a RadioButton are:

- **Automatic**—a Boolean value, if True the checking and unchecking of the RadioButton is managed automatically by PowerBuilder.
- **BackColor**—a long value, representing the color of the background area of the control.

■ **BorderStyle**—an enumerated value containing the border style (StyleBox!, StyleLowered!, StyleRaised!, or StyleShadowBox!)

■ **BringToTop**—set this Boolean to True to place the control on top of other overlapping controls in this window's front-to-back order.

■ **Checked**—a Boolean, True if the button is checked. Use this to set the default choice.

■ **DragAuto**—if this Boolean is set to True, this control is automatically set into Drag Mode when the user clicks on it.

■ **DragIcon**—a string containing the name of the icon that is displayed when this button is in Drag Mode. If you select **None!**, a ghost outline of the control is used.

■ **Enabled**—a Boolean value, set to True to enable the button, making it active and able to be selected or clicked and to receive events.

■ **FaceName**—a string value containing the font name for the control text.

■ **FontCharSet**—an enumerated value that specifies the font character set for the text.

■ **FontFamily**—an enumerated value that specifies the font family for the button text.

■ **FontPitch**—an enumerated value that specifies the font pitch for the button text.

■ **Height**—an integer value that specifies the vertical size of the button in PBUs.

■ **Italic**—a Boolean value, set to True if the label font is to be italicized.

■ **LeftText**—a Boolean, is True if the text appears to the left of the button, otherwise the text appears to the right of the button.

■ **Pointer**—a string containing the pointer icon to be used when the pointer is over this Control.

■ **TabOrder**—an integer that specifies the relative tab order for the controls on the window.

■ **Tag**—a text string that is associated with this button, can be used to store the Microhelp text.

- **Text**—the string label for the RadioButton.

- **TextColor**—a long value, controls the color of the text in this control.

- **TextSize**—an integer that specifies the font size (in points) of the text label.

- **Underline**—a Boolean value, True if the text label for this button is underlined.

- **Visible**—a Boolean value, True if the button is visible (showing).

- **Weight**—an integer that specifies the stroke thickness of the text label font (400 is normal).

- **Width**—an integer value that specifies the horizontal size of the button in PBUs.

- **X**—an integer value that specifies the horizontal position in the window of the button in PBUs.

- **Y**—an integer value that specifies the vertical position in the window of the button in PBUs.

RadioButton Events

The events associated with a RadioButton are:

- **Clicked**—occurs when you click on a button, or select the button and press the Enter key, this event is triggered.

- **Constructor**—occurs just before the window is made the active window. The window sends a constructor event to all its objects just before the window Open event occurs.

- **Destructor**—occurs when the window is closing. The window sends a destructor event to all its objects just after the window Close event occurs.

- **DragDrop**—occurs when Drag Mode is on, the pointer drops an object within the Control.

- **DragEnter**—occurs when Drag Mode is on, the dragged object enters the Control. If Drag Mode is off and this button's DragAuto attribute is set, a DragEnter event is triggered (rather than a Clicked event) when the user clicks the button.

- **DragLeave**—occurs when Drag Mode is on, and the dragged object leaves the Control.

- **DragWithin**—occurs when Drag Mode is on, this event is triggered periodically while an object is dragged within the Control.

- **GetFocus**—occurs just before the Control is selected with the Tab key or by clicking.

- **LoseFocus**—occurs just before the Control loses focus (caused by tabbing away or clicking outside of the button.

- **Other**—all the other Windows' events that have not been mapped to PowerBuilder events are routed to this event. You will rarely use this event; user-defined events are a better choice.

- **RButtonDown**—occurs when the right mouse button is pressed, and the pointer is located within the RadioButton.

RadioButton Functions

The following functions apply to RadioButtons:

- **ClassName**—returns the name of the RadioButton.
- **Drag**—begins or ends Drag Mode for this button.
- **Hide**—makes a RadioButton invisible.
- **Move**—relocates the RadioButton in the window.
- **PointerX**—returns the pointer's horizontal position in the button.
- **PointerY**—returns the pointer's vertical position in the button.
- **PostEvent**—places an event on the RadioButton's event queue and continues (asynchronously).
- **Resize**—adjusts the size of the RadioButton.
- **SetFocus**—places the focus on the RadioButton, directs keyboard input to the button.

- **SetPosition**—places the RadioButton in the front-to-back display order (relative to other overlapping controls).

- **SetRedraw**—turns on or off the updating of the button (the label).

- **Show**—makes the RadioButton visible.

- **TriggerEvent**—triggers a RadioButton event immediately (synchronously).

- **TypeOf**—returns the enumerated type of this control (RadioButton!).

RadioButton Popup Menu Options

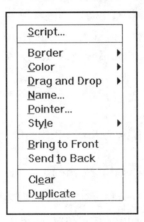

FIGURE 7.36 THE RADIOBUTTON RMB POPUP

The items in the popup menu (right mouse click on the button) for a RadioButton are:

- **Script**—edits a script for a control event.

- **Border**—selects the type of border to be used for this control.

- **Color**—sets the background and text colors for this control.

- **Drag and Drop**—sets or clears the DragAuto Mode attribute or defines an icon for the Drag Mode.

- **Name**—opens the control's style dialog.

- **Pointer**—selects the pointer icon to be used when the pointer is over this control.

- **Style**—used to toggle the Automatic, Checked, Left Text, Visible, or Enabled attributes.

- **Bring to Front**—moves this control to the front of other overlapping controls.

- **Send to Back**—moves this control to the back of other overlapping controls.

- **Delete**—removes this control from the window.

- **Duplicate**—makes a copy of this control.

GroupBox Controls

FIGURE 7.37 GroupBox Controls

GroupBox controls are most often used with RadioButtons. If you enclose a set of RadioButtons within a GroupBox, only one of the RadioButtons in the group can be selected (checked) at a time. PowerBuilder automatically provides this management to the GroupBox control. When you select one of the buttons, it is checked and the others in the group are unchecked. You must label each GroupBox. You place the text on either the left or the right of the button.

You can use GroupBoxes with CheckBoxes and other controls. In the case of controls other than the RadioButton, this is a cosmetic step, and the functionality described in the previous paragraph is not provided.

The GroupBox has attributes and functions, but no events are associated with a GroupBox.

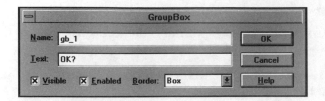

FIGURE 7.38 THE GROUPBOX STYLE DIALOG

The GroupBox style dialog (Figure 7.38) is very simple. Generally you only enter a Text and select the Border style.

GroupBox Attributes

The attributes of a GroupBox are:

- **BackColor**—a long value, representing the color of the background area of the control.

- **BorderStyle**—an enumerated value containing the border style (StyleBox!, StyleLowered!, StyleRaised!, or StyleShadowBox!).

- **BringToTop**—set this Boolean to True to place the control on top of other overlapping controls in this window's front-to-back order.

- **DragAuto**—if this Boolean is set to True this control is automatically set into Drag Mode when the user clicks on it.

- **DragIcon**—a string containing the name of the icon that is displayed when this control is in Drag Mode. If you select **None!**, a ghost outline of the control is used.

- **Enabled**—a Boolean value, True enables the control, making it active and able to be selected or clicked, and to receive events.

- **FaceName**—a string value containing the font name for the control text.

- **FontCharSet**—an enumerated value that specifies the font character set for the text.

- **FontFamily**—an enumerated value that specifies the font family for the control text.

- **FontPitch**—an enumerated value that specifies the font pitch for the control text.

- **Height**—an integer value that specifies the vertical size of the control in PBUs.

- **Italic**—a Boolean value, set to True if the label font is to be italicized.

- **Pointer**—a string containing the pointer icon to be used when the pointer is over this Control.

- **TabOrder**—an integer that specifies the relative tab order for the controls on the window.

- **Tag**—a text string that is associated with this control, can be used to store the Microhelp text.

- **Text**—the string label for the GroupBox.

- **TextColor**—a long value, controls the color of the text in this control.

- **TextSize**—an integer that specifies the font size (in points) of the text label.

- **Underline**—a Boolean value, True if the text label for this control is underlined.

- **Visible**—a Boolean value, True if the control is visible (showing).

- **Weight**—an integer that specifies the stroke thickness of the text label font (400 is normal).

- **Width**—an integer value that specifies the horizontal size of the control in PBUs.

- **X**—an integer value that specifies the horizontal position in the window of the control in PBUs.

- **Y**—an integer value that specifies the vertical position in the window of the control in PBUs.

GroupBox Functions

The following functions apply to GroupBoxes:

- **ClassName**—returns the name of the GroupBox.

- **Drag**—begins or ends Drag Mode for this control.

- **Hide**—makes a GroupBox invisible.

- **Move**—relocates the GroupBox in the window.

- **PointerX**—returns the pointer's horizontal position in the control.

- **PointerY**—returns the pointer's vertical position in the control.

- **PostEvent**—places an event on the GroupBox's event queue and continues (asynchronously).

- **Resize**—adjusts the size of the GroupBox.

- **SetFocus**—places the focus on the GroupBox, directs keyboard input to the control.

- **SetPosition**—places the GroupBox in the front-to-back display order (relative to other overlapping controls).

- **SetRedraw**—turns on or off the updating of the control (the label).

- **Show**—makes the GroupBox visible.

- **TriggerEvent**—triggers a GroupBox event immediately (synchronously).

- **TypeOf**—returns the enumerated type of this control (GroupBox!).

GroupBox Popup Menu Options

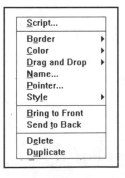

FIGURE 7.39 THE GROUPBOX RMB POPUP

The items in the popup menu (right mouse click on the control) for a GroupBox are:

- **Script**—edits a script for a control event.
- **Border**—selects the type of border to be used for this control.
- **Color**—sets the background and text colors for this control.
- **Drag and Drop**—sets or clears the DragAuto Mode attribute or defines an icon for the Drag Mode.
- **Name**—opens the control's style dialog.
- **Pointer**—selects the pointer icon to be used when the pointer is over this control.
- **Style**—toggles the Visible or Enabled attributes.
- **Bring to Front**—moves this control to the front of other overlapping controls.
- **Send to Back**—moves this control to the back of other overlapping controls.
- **Delete**—removes this control from the window.
- **Duplicate**—makes a copy of this control.

CHECKBOX CONTROLS

FIGURE 7.40 A CHECKBOX CONTROL

A CheckBox control is used most often to toggle an option on and off. When you click the CheckBox an X is toggled on and then off in the square next to the text. You may group a set of related CheckBoxes together, but there is no exclusive relationship between the CheckBoxes as there is when you group radio buttons together.

You can also create a three-state CheckBox which adds a third state to be used to represent a third option (such as "unknown"). The third state is represented in gray color in the CheckBox square.

You can position the text on the left or right of the square, and the display can be automatically updated when the user clicks (or selects the CheckBox with the Tab key and presses the Space Bar).

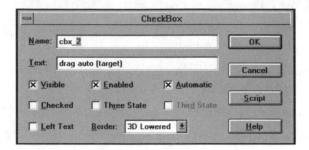

FIGURE 7.41 THE CHECKBOX STYLE DIALOG

CheckBox Attributes

The attributes of a CheckBox are:

- **Automatic**—a Boolean value, if True the checking and unchecking of the CheckBox is managed automatically by PowerBuilder.

- **BackColor**—a long value, representing the color of the background area of the control.

- **BorderStyle**—an enumerated value containing the border style (StyleBox!, StyleLowered!, StyleRaised!, or StyleShadowBox!.

- **BringToTop**—sets this Boolean to True to place the CheckBox on top of other overlapping controls in this window's front-to-back order.

- **Checked**—a Boolean, True if the control is checked.

- **DragAuto**—if this Boolean is set to True this control is automatically set into Drag Mode when the user clicks on it.

- **DragIcon**—a string containing the name of the icon that is displayed when this control is in Drag Mode. If you select **None!**, a ghost outline of the control is used.

- **Enabled**—a Boolean value, set to True to enable the control, making it active and able to be selected or clicked, and to receive events.

- **FaceName**—a string value containing the font name for the Control text.

- **FontCharSet**—an enumerated value that specifies the font character set for the text.

- **FontFamily**—an enumerated value that specifies the font family for the control text.

- **FontPitch**—an enumerated value that specifies the font pitch for the control text.

- **Height**—an integer value that specifies the vertical size of the control in PBUs.

- **Italic**—a Boolean value, set to True if the label font is italicized.

- **LeftText**—a Boolean, is True if the text appears to the left of the control, otherwise the text appears to the right of the control.

- **Pointer**—a string containing the pointer icon to be used when the pointer is over this Control

- **TabOrder**—an integer that specifies the relative tab order for the controls on the window.

- **Tag**—a text string that is associated with this control, can be used to store the Microhelp text.

- **Text**—the string label for the CheckBox.

- **TextColor**—a long value, controls the color of the text in this control.

- **TextSize**—an integer that specifies the font size (in points) of the text label.

- **ThirdState**—a Boolean value, set to True if the CheckBox is currently in the third state.

- **ThreeState**—a Boolean value, set to True if the CheckBox is in three state mode.

■ **Underline**—a Boolean value, True if the text label for this control is underlined.

■ **Visible**—a Boolean value, True if the control is visible (showing).

■ **Weight**—an integer that specifies the stroke thickness of the text label font (400 is normal).

■ **Width**—an integer value that specifies the horizontal size of the control in PBUs.

■ **X**—an integer value that specifies the horizontal position in the window of the control in PBUs.

■ **Y**—an integer value that specifies the vertical position in the window of the control in PBUs.

CheckBox Events

The events associated with a CheckBox are:

■ **Clicked**—occurs when you click on a control, or select the control and press the Space Bar, this event is triggered.

■ **Constructor**—occurs just before the window is made the active window. The window sends a constructor event to all its objects just before the window Open event occurs.

■ **Destructor**—occurs when the window is closing. The window sends a destructor event to all its objects just after the window Close event occurs.

■ **DragDrop**—occurs when Drag Mode is on, the pointer drops an object within the Control.

■ **DragEnter**—occurs when Drag Mode is on, the dragged object enters the Control. If Drag Mode is off and this control's DragAuto attribute is set, a DragEnter event is triggered (rather than a Clicked event) when the user clicks the control.

■ **DragLeave**—occurs when Drag Mode is on, the dragged object leaves the Control.

- **DragWithin**—occurs when Drag Mode is on, this event is triggered periodically while an object is dragged within the Control.

- **GetFocus**—occurs just before the Control is selected with the Tab key or by clicking.

- **LoseFocus**—occurs just before the Control loses focus (caused by tabbing away or clicking outside of the control).

- **Other**—all the other Windows' events that have not been mapped to PowerBuilder events are routed to this event. You will rarely use this event; user-defined events are a better choice.

- **RButtonDown**—occurs when the right mouse button is pressed, and the pointer is located within the CheckBox.

CheckBox Functions

The following functions apply to CheckBoxes:

- **ClassName**—returns the name of the CheckBox.

- **Drag**—begins or ends Drag Mode for this control.

- **Hide**—makes a CheckBox invisible.

- **Move**—relocates the CheckBox in the window.

- **PointerX**—returns the pointer's horizontal position in the control.

- **PointerY**—returns the pointer's vertical position in the control.

- **PostEvent**—places an event on the CheckBox's event queue and continues (asynchronously)

- **Resize**—adjusts the size of the CheckBox.

- **SetFocus**—places the focus on the CheckBox, directs keyboard input to the control.

- **SetPosition**—places the CheckBox in the front-to-back display order (relative to other overlapping controls).

- **SetRedraw**—turns on or off the updating of the control (the label).

- **Show**—makes the CheckBox visible.

- **TriggerEvent**—triggers a CheckBox event immediately (synchronously).

- **TypeOf**—returns the enumerated type of this control (CheckBox!).

CheckBox Popup Menu Options

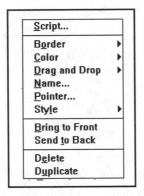

FIGURE 7.42 THE CHECKBOX RMB POPUP

The items in the popup menu (right mouse click on the control) for a CheckBox are:

- **Script**—edits a script for a control event.

- **Border**—selects the type of border to be used for this control.

- **Color**—sets the background and text colors for this control.

- **Drag and Drop**—sets or clears the DragAuto Mode attribute or defines an icon for the Drag Mode.

- **Name**—opens the control's style dialog.

- **Pointer**—selects the pointer icon to be used when the pointer is over this control.

- **Style**—toggles the Automatic, Checked, Left Text, Three State, Third State, Visible, or Enabled attributes.

- **Bring to Front**—moves this control to the front of other overlapping controls.

- **Send to Back**—moves this control to the back of other overlapping controls.

- **Delete**—removes this control from the window.

- **Duplicate**—makes a copy of this control.

HSCROLLBAR

FIGURE 7.43 HSCROLLBAR

The HScrollBar is a control that is often used to graphically show an amount or percentage. For example, you could use the HScrollBar to show the progress as you read in an file, or complete some other task. This control is separate from the scroll bars that are used in other controls such as ListBoxes or MultiLineEdits. You could also use the HScrollBar to allow the user to adjust values, such as shades of colors, or to set limits for computation or number of records to be displayed.

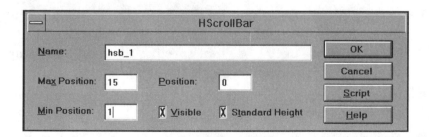

FIGURE 7.44 THE HSCROLLBAR SYTLE DIALOG

Figure 7.44 shows the HScrollBar style dialog window. You can specify three values that affect the positioning of the elevator button in the control. The

Position value, in relation to the Min and Max Position values, will determine the location of the elevator. For example with a Min Position value of 0 and a Max Position value of 100, a Position value of 50 will place the elevator in the center of the bar. A position of 0 places the elevator at the far left of the bar and a position value of 100 places it at the right.

Select the Standard Height CheckBox to set the height of the control to the usual dimension. Size the width to reflect the resolution of the elevator movement that is required.

HScrollBar Attributes

The attributes of a HScrollBar are:

- **BringToTop**—sets this Boolean to True to place the HScrollBar on top of other overlapping controls in this window's front-to-back order.

- **DragAuto**—if this Boolean is set to True, the HScrollBar is automatically set into Drag Mode when the user clicks on it.

- **DragIcon**—a string containing the name of the icon that is displayed when this control is in Drag Mode. If you select "None!", a ghost outline of the control is used.

- **Height**—an integer value that specifies the vertical size of the control in PBUs.

- **MaxPosition**—an integer that specifies the maximum range of values that are represented by the elevator position.

- **MinPosition**—an integer that specifies the minimum range of values that are represented by the elevator position.

- **Pointer**—a string containing the pointer icon to be used when the pointer is over this HScrollBar.

- **Position**—an integer that specifies the current elevator position, relative to the MinPosition and MaxPosition values.

- **StdHeight**—a Boolean value, this is set to True if you specified that the control should be created with the normal height for HScrollBars.

- **TabOrder**—an integer that specifies the relative tab order for the controls on the window.

- **Tag**—a text string that is associated with this control, can be used to store the Microhelp text.

- **Visible**—a Boolean value, True if the control is visible (showing).

- **Weight**—an integer that specifies the stroke thickness of the text label font (400 is normal).

- **Width**—an integer value that specifies the horizontal size of the control in PBUs.

- **X**—an integer value that specifies the horizontal position in the window of the control in PBUs.

- **Y**—an integer value that specifies the vertical position in the window of the control in PBUs.

HScrollBar Events

The events associated with a HScrollBar are:

- **Constructor**—occurs just before the window is made the active window. The window sends a constructor event to all its objects just before the window Open event occurs.

- **Destructor**—occurs when the window is closing. The window sends a destructor event to all its objects just after the window Close event occurs.

- **DragDrop**—occurs when Drag Mode is on, and the pointer drops an object within the HScrollBar.

- **DragEnter**—occurs when Drag Mode is on and the dragged object enters the HScrollBar. If Drag Mode is off and this control's DragAuto attribute is set, a DragEnter event is triggered when the user clicks the control.

- **DragLeave**—occurs when Drag Mode is on, and the dragged object leaves the HScrollBar.

- **DragWithin**—occurs when Drag Mode is on, this event is triggered periodically while an object is dragged within the HScrollBar.

- **GetFocus**—occurs just before the HScrollBar is selected with the Tab key or by clicking.

- **LineLeft**—triggered when the user clicks on the left arrow on the HScrollBar.

- **LineRight**—triggered when the user clicks on the right arrow on the HScrollBar.

- **LoseFocus**—occurs just before the HScrollBar loses focus (caused by tabbing away or clicking outside of the control.

- **Other**—all the other Windows' events that have not been mapped to PowerBuilder events are routed to this event. You will rarely use this event, user-defined events are a better choice.

- **Moved**—triggered when the user drags the elevator in either direction.

- **PageLeft**—triggered when the user clicks on the left side of the bar.

- **PageRight**—triggered when the user clicks on the right side of the bar.

- **RButtonDown**—occurs when the right mouse button is pressed, and the pointer is located within the HScrollBar.

HScrollBar Functions

The following functions apply to HScrollBars:

- **ClassName**—returns the name of the HScrollBar.
- **Drag**—begins or ends Drag Mode for this control.
- **Hide**—makes a HScrollBar invisible.
- **Move**—relocates the HScrollBar in the window.
- **PointerX**—returns the pointer's horizontal position in the control.
- **PointerY**—returns the pointer's vertical position in the control.
- **PostEvent**—places an event on the HScrollBar's event queue and continues (asynchronously).

- **Resize**—used to adjust the size of the HScrollBar.

- **SetFocus**—places the focus on the HScrollBar, directs keyboard input to the control.

- **SetPosition**—places the HScrollBar in the front-to-back display order (relative to other overlapping controls).

- **SetRedraw**—turns on or off the updating of the control if the caption is changed.

- **Show**—makes the HScrollBar visible.

- **TriggerEvent**—triggers a HScrollBar event immediately (synchronously).

- **TypeOf**—returns the enumerated type of this control (HScrollBar!).

HScrollBar Popup Menu Options

FIGURE 7.45 THE HScrollBar RMB POPUP

The items in the popup menu (right mouse click on the control) for a HScrollBar are:

- **Script**—edits a script for a control event

- **Drag and Drop**—sets or clears the DragAuto Mode attribute, or defines an icon for the Drag Mode.

- **Name**—opens the control's style dialog.

- **Pointer**—selects the pointer icon to be used when the pointer is over this control.

- **Style**—toggles the Visible, or Standard Height attributes.

- **Bring to Front**—moves this control to the front of other overlapping controls.

- **Send to Back**—moves this control to the back of other overlapping controls.

- **Delete**—removes this control from the window.

- **Duplicate**—makes a copy of this control.

VScrollBar

FIGURE 7.46 A VSCROLLBAR

The VScrollBar is a control often used to graphically show an amount or percentage. For example, you could use the VScrollBar to show the progress as you read in an file, or complete some other task. This control is separate from the scroll bars that are used in other controls such as ListBoxes or MultiLineEdits. You could also use the VScrollBar to allow the user to adjust values, such as shades of colors, or to set limits for computation or number of records to be displayed.

Figure 7.47 shows the VScrollBar style dialog window. You can specify three values that affect the positioning of the elevator button in the control. The Position value, in relation to the Min and Max Position values, will determine the location of the elevator. For example with a Min Position value of 0 and a Max Position value of 100, a Position value of 50 will place the elevator in the center of the bar. A position of 0 will place the elevator at the bottom of the bar, and a position value of 100 will place it at the top.

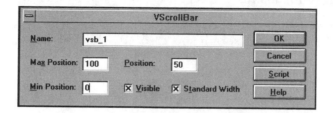

FIGURE 7.47 THE VSCROLLBAR STYLE DIALOG

Select the Standard Width CheckBox to set the width of the control to the usual dimension. You size the height to reflect the resolution of the elevator movement that is required.

VScrollBar Attributes

The attributes of a VScrollBar are:

- **BringToTop**—set this Boolean to True to place the VScrollBar on top of other overlapping controls in this window's front-to-back order.

- **DragAuto**—if this Boolean is set to True, this VScrollBar is automatically set into Drag Mode when the user clicks on it.

- **DragIcon**—a string containing the name of the icon that is displayed when this control is in Drag Mode. If you select "None!", a ghost outline of the control is used.

- **Height**—an integer value that specifies the vertical size of the control in PBUs.

- **MaxPosition**—an integer that specifies the maximum range of values that are represented by the elevator position.

- **MinPosition**—an integer that specifies the minimum range of values that are represented by the elevator position.

■ **Pointer**—a string containing the pointer icon to be used when the pointer is over this VScrollBar.

■ **Position**—an integer that specifies the current elevator position, relative to the MinPosition and MaxPosition values.

■ **StdWidth**—a Boolean value, this is set to True if you specified that the control should be created with the normal width for VScrollBars.

■ **TabOrder**—an integer that specifies the relative tab order for the controls on the window.

■ **Tag**—a text string that is associated with this control, can be used to store the Microhelp text.

■ **Visible**—a Boolean value, True if the control is visible (showing).

■ **Weight**—an integer that specifies the stroke thickness of the text label font (400 is normal).

■ **Width**—an integer value that specifies the horizontal size of the control in PBUs.

■ **X**—an integer value that specifies the horizontal position in the window of the control in PBUs.

■ **Y**—an integer value that specifies the vertical position in the window of the control in PBUs.

VScrollBar Events

The events associated with a VScrollBar are:

■ **Constructor**—occurs just before the window is made the active window. The window sends a constructor event to all its objects just before the window Open event occurs.

■ **Destructor**—occurs when the window is closing. The window sends a destructor event to all its objects just after the window Close event occurs.

■ **DragDrop**—occurs when Drag Mode is on, the pointer drops an object within the VScrollBar.

- **DragEnter**—occurs when Drag Mode is on, the dragged object enters the VScrollBar. If Drag Mode is off and this control's DragAuto attribute is set, a DragEnter event is triggered when the user clicks the control.

- **DragLeave**—occurs when Drag Mode is on, the dragged object leaves the VScrollBar.

- **DragWithin**—occurs when Drag Mode is on, this event is triggered periodically while an object is dragged within the VScrollBar.

- **GetFocus**—occurs just before the VScrollBar is selected with the Tab key or by clicking.

- **LineDown**—triggered when the user clicks on the bottom arrow of the VScrollBar.

- **LineUp**—triggered when the user clicks on the top arrow of the VScrollBar.

- **LoseFocus**—occurs just before the VScrollBar loses focus (caused by tabbing away or clicking outside of the control).

- **Other**—all the other Windows' events that have not been mapped to PowerBuilder events are routed to this event. You will rarely use this event; user-defined events are a better choice.

- **Moved**—triggered when the user drags the elevator in either direction.

- **PageDown**—triggered when the user clicks on the lower section of the bar.

- **PageUp**—triggered when the user clicks on the upper section of the bar.

- **RButtonDown**—occurs when the right mouse button is pressed, and the pointer is located within the VScrollBar.

VScrollBar Functions

The following functions apply to VScrollBars:

- **ClassName**—returns the name of the VScrollBar.

- **Drag**—begins or ends Drag Mode for this control.
- **Hide**—makes a VScrollBar invisible.
- **Move**—relocates the VScrollBar in the window.
- **PointerX**—returns the pointer's horizontal position in the control.
- **PointerY**—returns the pointer's vertical position in the control.
- **PostEvent**—places an event on the VScrollBar's event queue and continues (asynchronously).
- **Resize**—adjusts the size of the VScrollBar.
- **SetFocus**—places the focus on the VScrollBar, directs keyboard input to the control.
- **SetPosition**—places the VScrollBar in the front-to-back display order (relative to other overlapping controls).
- **SetRedraw**—turns on or off the updating of the control if the caption is changed.
- **Show**—makes the VScrollBar visible.
- **TriggerEvent**—triggers a VScrollBar event immediately (synchronously).
- **TypeOf**—returns the enumerated type of this control (VScrollBar!).

VScrollBar Popup Menu Options

FIGURE 7.48 THE VSCROLLBAR RMB POPUP

The items in the popup menu (right mouse click on the control) for a VScrollBar are:

- **Script**—edits a script for a control event.

- **Drag and Drop**—sets or clears the DragAuto Mode attribute or defines an icon for the Drag Mode.

- **Name**—opens the control's style dialog.

- **Pointer**—selects the pointer icon to be used when the pointer is over this control.

- **Style**—toggles the Visible or Standard Width attributes.

- **Bring to Front**—moves this control to the front of other overlapping controls.

- **Send to Back**—moves this control to the back of other overlapping controls.

- **Delete**—removes this control from the window.

- **Duplicate**—makes a copy of this control.

LINE CONTROLS

FIGURE 7.49 A LINE CONTROL

Line objects are one of the drawing objects provided to enhance your screens. The Line object has attributes and functions, but there no events associated with them.

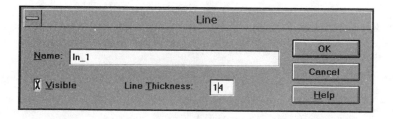

FIGURE 7.50 THE LINE CONTROL STYLE DIALOG

The Line style dialog (Figure 7.50) is very simple. Generally you only enter text and select a border style.

Line Attributes

The attributes of a Line are:

- **BeginX**—an integer value, the horizontal position in the window of the start of the line in PBUs.

- **BeginY**—an integer value, the vertical position in the window of the start of the line in PBUs.

- **EndX**—an integer value, the horizontal position in the window of the end of the line in PBUs.

- **EndY**—an integer value, the vertical position in the position of the end of the line in PBUs.

- **LineColor**—a long value, specifies the color of the line.

- **LineStyle**—an enumerated value, describes the style of the line (continuous!, dash!, dashdot!, dashdotdot!, dot!, or transparent!).

- **LineThickness**—an integer, specifies the thickness in PBUs.

- **Tag**—a text string that is associated with this line.

- **Visible**—a Boolean value, True if the line is visible (usual).

Line Functions

The following functions apply to Lines:

- **ClassName**—returns the name of the Line.

- **Hide**—makes a Line invisible.

- **Move**—relocates the Line in the window.

- **Resize**—used to adjust the size of the Line.

- **Show**—makes the Line visible.

- **TypeOf**—returns the enumerated type of this control (Line!).

Line Popup Menu Options

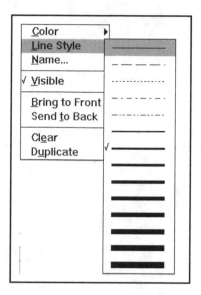

FIGURE 7.51 THE LINE CONTROL RMB POPUP
WITH LINE STYLE CASCADING MENU

The items in the popup menu (right mouse click on the control) for a Line are:

- **Color**—sets the background and text colors for this control.
- **Line Style**—selects the type of line.
- **Name**—opens the Line's style dialog.
- **Bring to Front**—moves this control to the front of other overlapping controls.
- **Send to Back**—moves this control to the back of other overlapping controls.
- **Delete**—removes this control from the window.
- **Duplicate**—makes a copy of this control.

Oval Controls

FIGURE 7.52 THE OVAL CONTROL

Oval objects are one of the drawing objects provided to enhance your screens. The Oval object has attributes and functions, but there are no events associated with them.

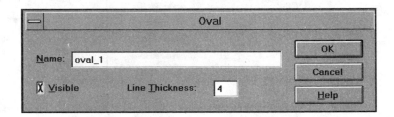

FIGURE 7.53 THE OVAL CONTROL STYLE DIALOG

The Oval style dialog (Figure 7.53) is very simple. Generally you don't even access this dialog.

Oval Attributes

The attributes of a Oval are:

- **FillColor**—a long value that defines the background color of the oval.

- **FillPattern**—an enumerated value that specifies the hatch pattern for the oval.

- **Height**—an integer value that specifies the vertical size in PBUs.

- **LineColor**—a long value that specifies the color of the outline of the oval.

- **LineStyle**—an enumerated value that describes the style of the oval outline (continuous!, dash!, dashdot!, dashdotdot!, dot!, or transparent!).

- **LineThickness**—an integer that specifies the thickness of the oval outline in PBUs.

- **OvalColor**—a long value that specifies the color of the oval.

- **Tag**—a text string that is associated with this oval.

- **Visible**—a Boolean value, True if the oval is visible (usual).

- **Width**—an integer value that specifies the horizontal size in PBUs.

- **X**—an integer that specifies the horizontal position of the oval in the window (PBUs).

- **Y**—an integer that specifies the vertical position of the oval in the window (PBUs).

Oval Functions

The following functions apply to Ovals:

- **ClassName**—returns the name of the Oval.
- **Hide**—makes a Oval invisible.
- **Move**—relocates the Oval in the window.
- **Resize**—adjusts the size of the Oval.
- **Show**—makes the Oval visible.
- **TypeOf**—returns the enumerated type of this control (Oval!).

Oval Popup Menu Options

The items in the popup menu (right mouse click on the control) for a Oval are:

- **Color**—sets the background and text colors for this control.
- **Fill Pattern**—selects the hatch pattern for the object.

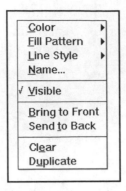

FIGURE 7.54 THE OVAL CONTROL RMB POPUP

■ **Line Style**—selects the type of line for the outline of this object.

■ **Name**—opens the object's style dialog.

■ **Bring to Front**—moves this control to the front of other overlapping controls.

■ **Send to Back**—moves this control to the back of other overlapping controls.

■ **Delete**—removes this control from the window.

■ **Duplicate**—makes a copy of this control.

RECTANGLE CONTROLS

FIGURE 7.55 THE RECTANGLE CONTROL

Rectangle objects are one of the drawing objects provided to enhance your screens. The Rectangle object has attributes and functions, but there are no events associated with them.

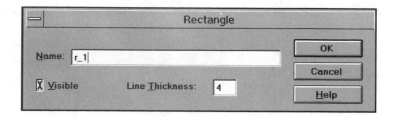

FIGURE 7.56 THE RECTANGLE CONTROL STYLE DIALOG

The Rectangle style dialog (Figure 7.56) is very simple. Generally you don't even access this dialog.

Rectangle Attributes

The attributes of a Rectangle are:

- **FillColor**—a long value, defines the background color of the rectangle.

- **FillPattern**—an enumerated value that specifies the hatch pattern for the rectangle.

- **Height**—an integer value that specifies the vertical size in PBUs.

- **LineColor**—a long value that specifies the color of the outline of the rectangle.

- **LineStyle**—an enumerated value that describes the style of the rectangle outline (continuous!, dash!, dashdot!, dashdotdot!, dot!, or transparent!).

- **LineThickness**—an integer that specifies the thickness of the rectangle outline in PBUs.

- **Tag**—a text string that is associated with this rectangle.

- **Visible**—a Boolean value, True if the rectangle is visible (usual).

- **Width**—an integer value that specifies the horizontal size in PBUs.

- **X**—an integer that specifies the horizontal position of the rectangle in the window (PBUs).

319

- **Y**—an integer that specifies the vertical position of the rectangle in the window (PBUs).

Rectangle Functions

The following functions apply to Rectangles:

- **ClassName**—returns the name of the Rectangle.
- **Hide**—makes a Rectangle invisible.
- **Move**—relocates the Rectangle in the window.
- **Resize**—used to adjust the size of the Rectangle.
- **Show**—makes the Rectangle visible.
- **TypeOf**—returns the enumerated type of this control (Rectangle!).

Rectangle Popup Menu Options

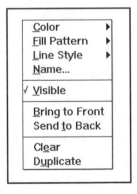

FIGURE 7.57 THE RECTANGLE CONTROL RMB POPUP

The items in the popup menu (right mouse click on the control) for a Rectangle are:

- **Color**—sets the background and text colors for this control.

- **Fill Pattern**—selects the hatch pattern for the object.

- **Line Style**—selects the type of line for the outline of this object.

- **Name**—opens the object's style dialog.

- **Bring to Front**—moves this control to the front of other overlapping controls.

- **Send to Back**—moves this control to the back of other overlapping controls.

- **Delete**—removes this control from the window.

- **Duplicate**—makes a copy of this control.

ROUNDRECTANGLE CONTROLS

FIGURE 7.58 A ROUNDRECTANGLE CONTROL

RoundRectangle objects are one of the drawing objects provided to enhance your screens. The RoundRectangle object has attributes and functions, but there are no events associated with them.

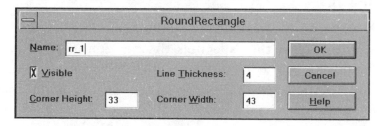

FIGURE 7.59 THE ROUNDRECTANGLE STYLE DIALOG

The RoundRectangle style dialog (Figure 7.59) is very simple. Generally you don't access this dialog.

RoundRectangle Attributes

The attributes of a RoundRectangle are:

- **CornerHeight**—an integer, that specifies the vertical radius of the corner's of the RoundRectangle (in PBUs).

- **CornerWidth**—an integer, that specifies the horizontal radius of the corner's of the RoundRectangle (in PBUs).

- **FillColor**—a long value, that defines the background color of the RoundRectangle.

- **FillPattern**—an enumerated value that specifies the hatch pattern for the RoundRectangle.

- **Height**—an integer value that specifies the vertical size in PBUs.

- **LineColor**—a long value that specifies the color of the outline of the RoundRectangle.

- **LineStyle**—an enumerated value that describes the style of the RoundRectangle outline (continuous!, dash!, dashdot!, dashdot-dot!, dot!, or transparent!).

- **LineThickness**—an integer that specifies the thickness of the RoundRectangle outline in PBUs.

- **Tag**—a text string that is associated with this RoundRectangle.

- **Visible**—a Boolean value, True if the RoundRectangle is visible (usual).

- **Width**—an integer value that specifies the horizontal size in PBUs.

- **X**—an integer that specifies the horizontal position of the RoundRectangle in the window (PBUs).

- **Y**—an integer that specifies the vertical position of the RoundRectangle in the window (PBUs).

RoundRectangle Functions

The following functions apply to RoundRectangles:

- **ClassName**—returns the name of the RoundRectangle.
- **Hide**—makes a RoundRectangle invisible.
- **Move**—relocates the RoundRectangle in the window.
- **Resize**—adjusts the size of the RoundRectangle.
- **Show**—makes the RoundRectangle visible.
- **TypeOf**—returns the enumerated type of this control (RoundRectangle!).

RoundRectangle Popup Menu Options

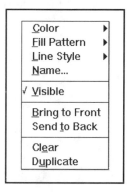

FIGURE 7.60 THE ROUNDRECTANGLE RMB POPUP

The items in the popup menu (right mouse click on the control) for a RoundRectangle are:

- **Color**—sets the background and text colors for this control.
- **Fill Pattern**—selects the hatch pattern for the object.
- **Line Style**—selects the type of line for the outline of this object.
- **Name**—opens the object's style dialog.
- **Bring to Front**—moves this control to the front of other overlapping controls.

- **Send to Back**—moves this control to the back of other overlapping controls.

- **Delete**—removes this control from the window.

- **Duplicate**—makes a copy of this control.

Drag and Drop

The drag and drop function lets the user click on an object and drag an icon representing that object to another location (usually to another object in the application), then release the mouse button to drop the dragged object at that point. This mouse technique is used to trigger some type of action in the application, in a easy, graphical manner. For example, in a file system, you can copy a file's icon to a directory icon in order to copy (or move) that file to that directory. Another familiar example would be to drag a file's icon to a trash bin icon in order to delete the file. Drag and drop is a standard Windows' interface technique and is also used in other systems such as Macintosh and UNIX X Windows system.

Drag and drop is easily implemented in your PowerBuilder applications. Drag and drop always involves two PowerBuilder objects: the dragged object and the target object. The target object is the control to which the object is being dragged. All controls, except for the drawing objects, are draggable controls. When a control is being dragged, the application's Drag Mode is on. Drag Mode is an application wide setting.

Each draggable object has two attributes that are used for the drag and drop function.

- **DragAuto**—if this Boolean is set to True, the control is automatically set into Drag Mode when the user clicks on it. Otherwise, you must turn on Drag Mode programatically.

- **DragIcon**—a string containing the name of the icon that is displayed when the control is in Drag Mode. If you select **None!**, a ghost outline of the control is used.

The icon can be a stock icon or an icon contained in a bitmap file (.ICO). Figure 7.61 shows an example of drag and drop. This is the second window from the CONTROLS.APP example.

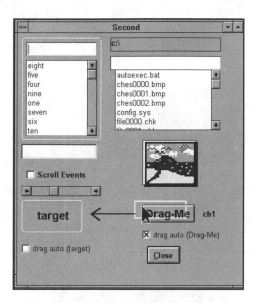

FIGURE 7.61 DRAGGING THE DRAG-ME COMMANDBUTTON

In this example, the user has just clicked on and begun to drag the Drag-Me CommandButton. The default drag icon is displayed here (the ghost outline rectangle). In the next example, the drag has been initiated in the ListBox and the stock Rectangle icon is being used for the display.

If you drag the pointer to a location that can not serve as the target object, the icon changes to the No-Drop icon. Figure 7.63 shows the No-Drop icon as it is displayed, if you drag the pointer to the title bar of the window, which is not a valid target area.

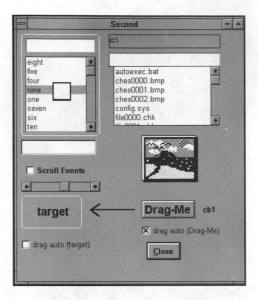

FIGURE 7.62 Dragging an item from the listbox

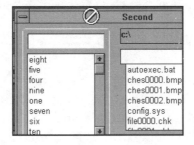

FIGURE 7.63 The Not VAlid icon

The PowerBuilder controls that can serve as target objects have the following events:

- **DragDrop**—occurs when Drag Mode is on, the pointer drops an object within the target control.

- **DragEnter**—occurs when Drag Mode is on, the dragged object enters the target control.

- **DragLeave**—occurs when Drag Mode is on, the dragged object leaves the target control.

- **DragWithin**—occurs when Drag Mode is on, this event is triggered periodically while an object is dragged within the target control.

Scripts in these events determine the effect of the drag and drop function.

The DragEnter event is also triggered for CommandButtons and PictureButtons in another instance. If the button's Drag Mode is off and the button's DragAuto attribute is set, a DragEnter event is triggered (rather than a Clicked event) when the user clicks the button. Because of this action, it is usually better to change the Drag Mode programatically rather than setting the DragAuto attribute.

Drag and Drop Functions

There are two PowerBuilder functions that are used with drop and drop. These are:

- **Drag**—begins or ends Drag Mode for a control.
- **DraggedObject**—returns the type of the dragged object.

In our CONTROLS example, the Drag Mode is controlled for the ListBox. The DragAuto attribute for the ListBox is set to false. A user-defined event to trap the drag movement is created over the ListBox. The following code was added to the we_mousemove event for the the ListBox.

```
IF Message.wordparm = 1 THEN
    This.Drag(begin!)
fw_update_status ('lb_1.clicked')
END IF
```

In this example, check first to see if the left mouse button is down (wordparm = 1). If that is true, then initiate drag mode for this control.

In the target DragDrop event the following code is added (excerpt):

```
ListBox   lb_which
CommandButton      cb_which
string      sText
DragObject      bj_which

obj_which = DraggedObject()
CHOOSE CASE      TypeOf(obj_which)
CASE ListBox!
    lb_which = obj_which
    sText = lb_which.SelectedItem ( )
    This.text = sText
    lb_which.Drag (Cancel!) // if you used end! would be
                            //  recursive!!
END CHOOSE
```

In this code, the DraggedObject function is used. This returns the object that has been dropped on the target. The TypeOf function is used to check if the dragged control is a ListBox. If it was, then we get the text for the selected item in that ListBox and display that text on the target static text.

CHAPTER EIGHT

EMBEDDED SQL

PowerScript allows the direct embedding of SQL statements for database access. This chapter covers everything that you need to know in order to create PowerBuilder applications that access data in a DBMS (Database Management System). This chapter covers the use of embedded SQL in your PowerScript code, explains the use of transaction objects that are required for the database interface, and explains how to set up profile files.

DataWindow Objects: A Preview

Many of your applications will not require the use of embedded SQL, instead you will use DataWindows which provide the ability to query and update the database without writing any SQL code. While this is true, it is still important that the PowerBuilder developer be fluent with SQL and the embedded techniques. When you create a DataWindow object, the SQL painter lets you define the SQL select statement in a graphical manner. The DataWindow can generate the insert, delete, and update statements that are required to provide full database functionality for your application. DataWindow objects should be your primary method for accessing data, but there will be many cases in which you will need to create your own SQL statements. DataWindows are covered in later chapters.

SQL Statements

You can embed SQL statements directly into your PowerScript code. There are several differences between the format of SQL statements and PowerScript statements of which you must be aware.

A SQL statement always requires a semicolon (;) as a delimiter (at the end of each statement). If you need to continue a SQL statement across multiple lines, do not use the PowerScript continuation symbol (the ampersand, **&**). The omission of the semicolon is enough to signal the continuation of the SQL statement.

```
SELECT count(*) INTO :iCount FROM images;
```

or

```
SELECT count(*) INTO :iCount
    FROM images;
```

You should also note that any reference that you make (within embedded SQL statements) to a PowerBuilder host variable (either a script variable or an object attribute) requires that you mark the identifier by adding a colon (:) to the beginning of the identifier. This is a standard SQL requirement for the embedded form of SQL. In the previous example, *:iCount* is required in the SQL statement to make the reference to the script variable iCount. You must always place the colon immediately before the identifier. Two examples follow.

```
int iInv_no
string sCompany
int iCompanyId

iInv_no = 123
SELECT company, id INTO :sCompany, :iCompanyId
    WHERE invno = :iInv_no;
DoSomething(sCompany)

string sImage, sType, sPath
int iVersion
string sImageName = 'pic123'

SELECT image, type, version, path
    INTO :sImage, :sType, :iVersion, :sPath
      WHERE image = :sImageName AND version = 1;
```

You can also select values directly into PowerBuilder controls. In the following example the query places the result in a single line edit control.

```
SELECT company INTO :sle_1.text WHERE invno = :iInv_no;
```

The next example selects an integer directly into a single line edit control. PowerBuilder converts the integer into a string automatically.

```
SELECT Id INTO :sle_1.text WHERE company = 'Best';
```

Cursor operations are also supported in embedded SQL.

```
DECLARE cursor1 CURSOR FOR
    SELECT company, id FROM company;

OPEN cursor1;
```

```
DO
     FETCH cursor1 INTO :sCompany, :iCompanyId;
LOOP WHILE SQLCA.SQLCode = 0 //rc = 100 at end

CLOSE cursor1;
```

Notice the placement of the semicolons in this example. The loop will continue to execute as long as the FETCH is successful (the SQLCode = 0).

Embedded SQL Statements

You will find a complete introduction to the SQL language in the chapter on SQL Basics. For more information on each SQL statement please see that chapter. PowerBuilder supports the following SQL statements in embedded SQL:

Non-Cursor SQL Operations

```
CONNECT, SELECT, INSERT, UPDATE, DELETE, COMMIT, ROLLBACK,
     DISCONNECT
```

Cursor Operations

```
DECLARE, OPEN, FETCH, UPDATE WHERE CURRENT OF, DELETE WHERE
     CURRENT OF, CLOSE
```

Procedure Operations

```
DECLARE, EXECUTE, FETCH, CLOSE
```

CREATING SQL STATEMENTS

PowerBuilder provides utilities to assist in the creation of your SQL statements. These utilities provide a graphical method for selecting the tables and columns in which you are interested. Each utility works interactively with the database, and requires that you are connected to the target database. Each utility is available from within the PowerScript painter for inserting code at the current cursor position. For the following discussion, we assume that you are in the PowerScript painter.

Paste SQL

If you select the **Edit|Paste SQL** menu option or click on the **Paste SQL** icon on the PainterBar, you will open the SQL Statement Type dialog window (Figure 8.1). The SQL Statement Type dialog displays three types of SQL statements cursor, non-cursor, and procedure.

FIGURE 8.1 SQL STATEMENT TYPE DIALOG

The SQL Statement Type Dialog

This dialog window displays the options for creating SQL statements in three groups. The top row presents the options for creating statements that

333

use a cursor, the second row presents the non-cursor version of SQL statements, and the third row lists options that are specific to the DBMS, such as stored procedures.

The cursor statements include:

- **Declare**—creates and names a cursor.
- **Fetch**—retrieves one row from the database.
- **Update**—updates a row.
- **Delete**—deletes a row.

The non-cursor statements are:

- **Select**—this is the singleton select, it may return only 1 row.
- **Insert**—inserts a row into the database.
- **Update**—updates one or more rows in the database.
- **Delete**—deletes one or more rows in the database.

The last section is for stored procedure statements (if your DBMS supports procedures).

- **Declare**—creates a procedure.
- **Fetch**—retrieves the procedure result.

SQL Statement Type

In the SQL Statement Type dialog, you choose the type of SQL statement that you want to create simply by double-clicking on one of the icons. This opens another tool (which varies according to the statement type) that assists you in creating the statement and when you have finished, it pastes the SQL statement into your code.

Cursor SQL Statements

Declare Cursor

Figure 8.2 shows the Declare Cursor painter that opens after double-clicking on the Declare Cursor icon.

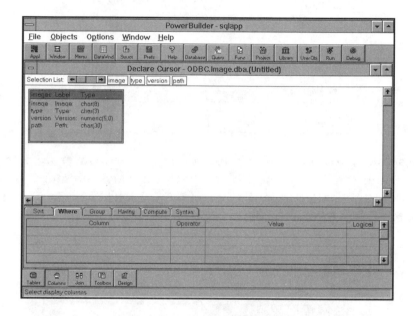

FIGURE 8.2 DECLARING A CURSOR

This is essentially the SQL Painter utility. In this painter, you will open one or more tables for the declare cursor statement. Next you will add columns to the select clause and then specify the join condition (if there are two or more tables): where, group by, having, and order by clauses. These steps are covered in detail in the section on the SQL painter.

Fetch Cursor

Choose the **Fetch cursor** option from the SQL Statement Type dialog and the Select Declared Cursor dialog opens as shown in Figure 8.3.

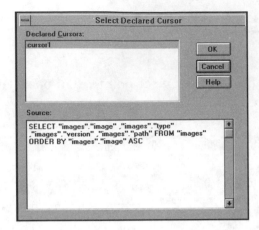

FIGURE 8.3 THE SELECT DECLARED CURSOR DIALOG

In this dialog you must select a previously declared cursor from the list presented in the listbox. The Source edit box displays the source code for the cursor that is selected in the Declared Cursors listbox. Selecting a cursor opens the Into Variables dialog shown in Figure 8.4.

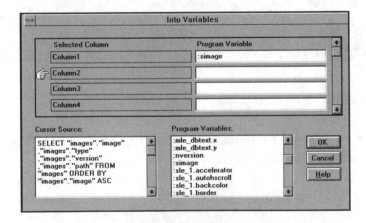

FIGURE 8.4 INTO VARIABLES DIALOG

The Into Variables dialog displays the cursor source code at the bottom left of the window. Each item in the select list is presented in the Selected Column list, in the same order in which they are referenced in the cursor source statement. You must assign a program variable to hold each select list item. The program variable can be a script variable or an object attribute. The Program Variables listbox assists you in locating the name of a variable (or attribute). You can paste the name of the variable into the Program Variable field by clicking on your selection in the Program Variable listbox. Notice that the listbox has already appended a colon to the name of each item in the list.

Update Cursor

Choose the **Update cursor** option from the SQL Statement Type dialog and the Select Declared Cursor dialog opens as shown in Figure 8.3. In this dialog, you must select a previously declared cursor from the list presented in the listbox. The Source edit box displays the source code for the cursor that is selected in the Declared Cursors listbox. Selecting a cursor opens the Update Column Values dialog shown in Figure 8.5.

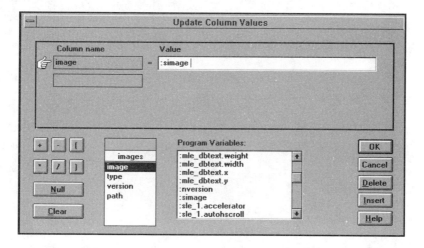

FIGURE 8.5 UPDATE COLUMN VALUES DIALOG

In the Update Column Values dialog, you can add any of the columns from the column listbox to the Column name field. Enter the value for the column in the Value field. This can be an expression or a program variable. You can select the value from the Program variables listbox by scrolling to the correct item and then by clicking it.

Delete Cursor

Choose the **Delete cursor** option from the SQL Statement Type dialog and the Select Declared Cursor dialog opens as shown in Figure 8.3. After you select a previously declared cursor (from the list presented in the listbox) the delete statement is immediately pasted into your code. There is no other dialog associated with this option.

Non-Cursor SQL Statements

Select

Choose the **Non-Cursor Select** option from the SQL Statement Type dialog and the Singleton Select dialog opens as shown in Figure 8.6. This is essentially the SQL Painter utility. In this painter you will open one or more tables for the select statement. Next you will specify the join condition (if there are two or more tables), add columns to the select clause, and then define the where, group by, having, and order by clauses. These steps are covered in detail in the section on the SQL painter.

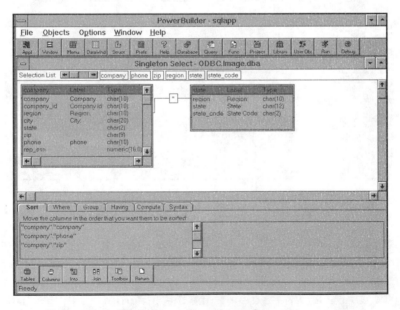

FIGURE 8.6 DEFINING A SINGLETON SELECT STATEMENT

The result set for this SQL select statement can only contain a single row. This is called a *singleton select statement* and the system generates an error if the statement execution results in more than a single row.

Insert

Choose the **Non-Cursor Insert** option from the SQL Statement Type dialog and the Insert Column Values dialog opens as shown in Figure 8.7. In this dialog you must assign a value to each of the columns in the Column Name list. Enter the value for the column in the Value field. This can be an expression or a program variable. Select the value from the Program variables listbox by scrolling to the correct item and then by clicking on it.

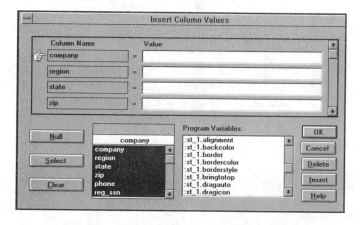

FIGURE 8.7 INSERT COLUMN VALUES DIALOG

Update

Choose the **Non-Cursor Update** cursor option from the SQL Statement Type dialog and the Update Column Values dialog opens as shown in Figure 8.8. In the Update Column Values dialog, you can add each of the columns from the column listbox to the column name field. Enter the value for the column in the Value field. This can be an expression or a program variable. Select the value from the Program variables listbox by scrolling to the correct item and them by clicking on it.

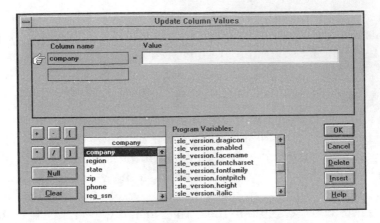

FIGURE 8.8 UPDATE COLUMN VALUES DIALOG

Delete

Choose the **Non-Cursor Delete** option from the SQL Statement Type dialog and the Where Criteria dialog opens as shown in Figure 8.9. In this dialog, you specify the WHERE clause for the delete statement. This determines which rows are deleted from the selected table.

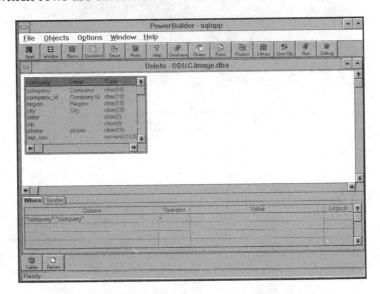

FIGURE 8.9 DEFINING A WHERE CLAUSE

TRANSACTION OBJECTS

A *transaction object* is required for all database access in PowerBuilder applications. The transaction object is like the SQL communications area in systems such as Oracle. It holds the information that is required to connect to the database and it holds the return code and other information that is returned as a result of each database interaction.

When your application begins to execute, PowerBuilder creates a global transaction object called *SQLCA*. This transaction object usually serves as the primary transaction object for your application. It is destroyed automatically when the application closes.

The transaction object contains connection parameters including:

- DBMS
- Database name
- login ID
- Password
- SQLCode

You must initialize a transaction object and use it to make a connection to the database before any interaction with the database. The transaction object represents one connection to a database (to a specific DBMS, database, and user account). You can share a transaction within your application for access to the same DBMS, database, and account.

The attributes of a transaction object are:

TABLE 8.1

ATTRIBUTE	DATA TYPE	DESCRIPTION
DBMS	String	The vendor name (or ODBC). This is a name such as Oracle or Sybase.
Database	String	Database name—the name of the database to which this transaction object will connect.

continued on next page

ATTRIBUTE	DATA TYPE	DESCRIPTION
UserId	String	Database login ID.
DBParm	String	DBMS specific parameters.
DBPass	String	Database password—the password associated with the User ID.
Lock	String	Specifies the isolation level.
LogId	String	The server login ID.
LogPass	String	The server password—the password associated with the LogId.
ServerName	String	The server name—the node name for the DBMS.
AutoCommit	Boolean	Set this flag True to perform automatic commits. If this is False (which is normal) you must explicitly issue commit (or rollback) statement.
SQLCode	Long	Status code—0 if success, –1 failure. +100 means that there were no more rows available as the result of a SELECT.
SQLNRows	Long	The number of rows affected by the last operation.
SQLDBCode	Long	Vendor specific error code. Oracle (and most systems) return 0 for successful operations.
SQLErrText	String	Vendor specific error message. This returns the text associated with SQLDBCode.
SQLReturn Data	String	Vendor specific, but used to return data or return codes.

You can create other transaction objects in your script code as needed for your application. For example, you may access two different databases from within an application. To do this would require that you create another transaction object for the second database. The syntax for doing so is:

```
transaction sqlca2
sqlca2 = create transaction
CONNECT using sqlca2;
//use sqlca2
COMMIT using sqlca2; // or ROLLBACK
DISCONNECT using sqlca2;
destroy sqlca2
```

The SQLCode

The transaction object also reports the status after each SQL statement is executed. You must check the status by examining the SQLCode attribute value in the transaction object. The value will be 0 (zero) if the statement was executed successfully. The value will be –1 if there was an error and 100 in the case of a command that succeeded but did not alter the database (such as a fetch after the last row has already been retrieved).

If there is an error, you can gather additional information from the transaction object by examining the SQLDBCode and SQLErrText attributes. These attributes contain the DBMS-specific error code and error text. For example, if you executed the following fetch statement without first opening the cursor, an error would occur.

```
FETCH Cursor1 INTO :sImage, :sType, :nVersion, :sPath;
IF SQLCA.SQLCode < 0 THEN
     db_err_handler()
END IF
```

After this statement, the SQLCA.SQLCode has a value of –1. (For the Watcom SQL database,this would result in a SQLCA.DBCode of 0, and the SQLCA.DBErrText would be 'Cursor is not open'.)

You must check the SQLCode after each embedded statement. You can also use the SQLNRows attribute to check the number of rows affected by the operation. For example, consider the following statement.

```
UPDATE images SET version = 1 WHERE version = 0
```

After the update you can check the sqlca.SQLNRows attribute (assuming the SQLCA.SQLCode was 0). If the value of SQLNRows is 0 then you will know that no rows where updated as a result of the UPDATE statement.

The Application Initialization File

Each application should have its own initialization file (sometimes called a *profile file*). This file contains application parameters such as database connection information, default value, and other information that is specific to an application, but which you do not wish to hard-code into the application. This lets you change parameters at run-time without having to recompile the program. In the initialization file you can also store state information about the application. In this way your application may "remember" the specific options that the user used in the previous session with the application. This can save time for the user, since they can avoid having to setup preferences each time they use the application.

By convention, the name given to the initialization file is the same as the application and the initialization file is given the extension **INI**. An initialization file is often called the *ini* file, the *init* file, or sometimes the *dot ini* file (**.INI**). The init file should be placed in the same directory as the application executable or in the Windows directory (C:\WINDOWS). For example, if you create the sample application *FirstApp*, you create an init file called **FIRSTAPP.INI**. You place this in the same directory as the firstapp library and executable, which is **C:\PB4\CLASS**.

The initialization file is an ASCII text file and is in the same format as other Window's INI files. The file consists of a number of sections and key entries. Each section is labeled with a statement of the form **[Section label]**; the brackets signify a section label. Each section contains a number of entries that are lines of text with a key label, an equal sign, and a value such as dbms=ODBC. Each entry is in the context of a section. Sections can be in any order, the order has no significance. The same is true of key entries in each section. Key names are unique within each section. For example:

```
IMAGEDB.INI
[sqlca]
dbms=ODBC
database=image
userid=
dbpass=
logid=
logpass=
```

```
servername=
DbParm=ConnectString='DSN=image;UID=dba;PWD=sql'
firsttime=no
;this is a comment

[application]
showtext=no
```

In this example there are two sections, [sqlca] and [application]. The key entries are not ordered in any specific order within the section. The section tile and key names are case insensitive. The values though, may be case sensitive, it is dependent on how the values are used. Comments can be added by beginning the line with a semicolon. This causes all text on that (single) line to be ignored.

You can use the PowerBuilder functions for reading and writing to the initialization file. All access is done by using a section label and a key name. The ProfileString function returns a string value (the key value) from a call where you have specified the fully qualified file name, a section label, and the key name within the section. You can also specify an option default value which will be returned if the entry can not be found.

```
returned_string = &
    ProfileString(file_path,section_label,key_name,default_value)
```

The ProfileInt call is similar to the ProfileSting function, except that it returns the key value as an integer:

```
returned_integer = &
    ProfileInt(file_path,section_label,key_name,default_value)
```

You can write to the ini file with the SetProfileString function:

```
returned_code = &
    SetProfileString(file_path,section_label,key_name,value)
```

An Application Open event could contain the following code:

```
sText = ProfileString(sInitFile,"sqlca", "firsttime","error")
IF sText = 'error' THEN
    MessageBox ("error", "init file not found")
```

```
      HALT CLOSE
END IF
IF Upper(sText) = "YES" THEN
      halt // set up the parameters
ELSE
      sqlca.DBMS        = ProfileString(sInitFile,"sqlca", &
                          "dbms","")
      sqlca.database    = ProfileString(sInitFile,"sqlca", &
                          "database","")
      sqlca.userid      = ProfileString(sInitFile,"sqlca", &
                          "userid","")
      sqlca.dbpass      = ProfileString(sInitFile,"sqlca", &
                          "dbpass","")
      sqlca.logid       = ProfileString(sInitFile,"sqlca", &
                          "logid","")
      sqlca.logpass     = ProfileString(sInitFile,"sqlca", &
                          "logpass","")
      sqlca.servername  = ProfileString(sInitFile,"sqlca", &
                          "servername","")
      sqlca.dbparm      = ProfileString(sInitFile,"sqlca", &
                          "dbparm","")
END IF
CONNECT USING SQLCA;
if sqlca.sqlcode <> 0 then
      MessageBox ("Cannot Connect to Database!", &
                  sqlca.sqlerrtext)
      fw_db_status ( -1,-1, "no database")
      return  // or halt close
end if
fw_db_status ( 0,0, "DB Image")
```

SELECTING AND UPDATING BLOBS

In the SqlApp example, the name of the images was stored in the database, but the actual images were DOS files. It is possible to store binary (or text) data in some DBMSs. The Watcom SQL engine supports the LONG BINARY data type, which can be used to store images such as the BMP files that were used in the SqlApp example. PowerBuilder provides a *Blob* (Binary Large Object) data type that is used in this manner. In the next example, BMP images are stored in the database as LONG BINARY data. The images are then selected into a Blob variable and displayed in a picture control.

You cannot use the normal SQL SELECT and INSERT statements with blob variables. PowerBuilder provides two additional SQL statements specifically for the use with blob variables. The SELECTBLOB statement lets you retrieve data into a blob variable and the UPDATEBLOB statement lets you move the contents of a blob variable to the database (either for an initial insert or a subsequent update).

The format of the SELECTBLOB SQL statement is:

```
SELECTBLOB column_name INTO :blobvariable
     FROM tablename WHERE expression {USING TransactionObject} ;
```

You may also include a host indicator variable (in the INTO list of target parameters) to check for an empty blob.

This statement selects one column with the Blob data type (long binary in Watcom) and only one row from the selected table. You must test the SQLCA.SQLCode after this statement to check for successful execution.

```
blob      blbBmp

SELECTBLOB imagedata INTO :blbBmp FROM imagebmp
        WHERE filepath = :sPath;

IF sqlca.sqlcode <> 0 THEN
     MessageBox('read blob',"Database SelectBlob failure")
ELSE
     p_1.SetPicture (blbBmp)
END IF
```

This example, selects an image into blbBmp. If the sqlcode is 0 (successful); the picture control, p_1, is set to display the image.

UPDATEBLOB SQL Statement

The format of the UPDATEBLOB SQL statement is:

```
UPDATEBLOB table_name SET column_name = :blob_variable
        WHERE expression;
```

This statement updates one column with the Blob data type (long binary in Watcom) in the named table. You must test the SQLCA.SQLCode after this statement to check for successful execution.

For example:

```
UPDATEBLOB Imagebmp SET imagedata = :blbBmp
         WHERE filepath = :sPath;

IF sqlca.sqlcode <> 0 THEN
    messagebox('blob',"database insert failed")
    commit;
ELSE
    rollback;
END IF
```

This example updates (or inserts) the contents of the blbBmp into the ImageBmp table. If the SQLCode is 0 (successful) the following code applies the update to the database and commit the transaction.

To load an image into the blob from a DOS file, you could use:

```
blob blbBmp, blbTmp
string sPath
long lLen, lPos
int nFile, nBytes
sPath = uo_1.fu_get_filepath()
IF len(sPath) < 5 THEN
    return
END IF

lLen = FileLength(sPath)
nFile = FileOpen(sPath,StreamMode!,Read!,LockReadWrite!)
IF nFile > 0 THEN
    nBytes = FileRead(nFile, blbTmp)
    DO WHILE nBytes > 0
        blbBmp = blbBmp + blbTmp
        lPos = lPos + nBytes
        FileSeek(nFile,lPos, FromBeginning!)
        nBytes = FileRead(nFile, blbTmp)
    LOOP
    FileClose(nFile)
ELSE
    return
END IF
```

An example of an application that uses this technique is BlobDb. But this example also uses DataWindow, so read through Chapter 11 before trying to create that application.

CHAPTER NINE

INTRODUCTION TO DATAWINDOWS

The DataWindow is PowerBuilder's high-level construct that encapsulates data access into a powerful, intelligent, data-centric object. You will use DataWindows for nearly all of your data access. Basically the DataWindow stands between your application and the database (or other data source) and retrieves, manipulates, and presents the data as required by your application. Figure 9.1 shows the relation between these objects.

It is essential that every PowerBuilder programmer become fluent with DataWindows. The DataWindow is the topic of several chapters of this book. You should invest a large percentage of your initial PowerBuilder study into gaining experience with every nuance of DataWindows. Experiment with DataWindows. For example, try using DataWindows instead of listboxes in your applications. DataWindows can access data from a number of data sources. In addition to databases, DataWindows can access data in files, through ODBC, through DDE, and other sources. In this chapter the data source will usually be a database, but keep in mind that it could easily be another source.

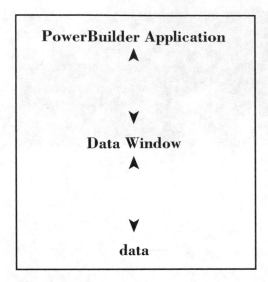

FIGURE 9.1 POWERBUILDER APPLICATIONS USE DATAWINDOWS TO ACCESS DATA

The DataWindow object is at the center of PowerBuilder's power. DataWindows are one of the most powerful objects available today in any class library or toolkit available for any language. If you suspect that something can be done with a DataWindow, then it probably can.

Initially you might think of the DataWindow as sort of a multi-column listbox. The DataWindow is very intelligent, and contains the definitions that it needs to populate itself with data from the database (or another data source as mentioned earlier). Once populated, the DataWindow allows easy manipulation of that data and is great for searching, sorting, filtering, and printing data. PowerBuilder provides functions that let you import and export data between DataWindows and a variety of data sources. These sources include:

- **CSV!**—comma-separated text
- **Clipboard!**—Windows' clipboard
- **dBASE3!**—dBASE-II && III format
- **DIF!**—Data Interchange Format
- **Excel!**—Microsoft Excel format

- **SQLInsert!**—SQL syntax
- **SYLK!**—Microsoft Multiplan format
- **Text!**—tab-separated columns with a return at the end of each row
- **WKS!**—Lotus 1-2-3 format
- **WK1!**—Lotus 1-2-3 format

DataWindow Objects and Controls

Look at the PowerBar and the PainterBar in the Window painter and notice that both have a DataWindow icon (see Figure 9.2). These two icons actually refer to two different constructs. The first icon (contained in the PowerBar) refers to a DataWindow *object*, and the second icon (contained in the PainterBar) refers to a DataWindow *control*.

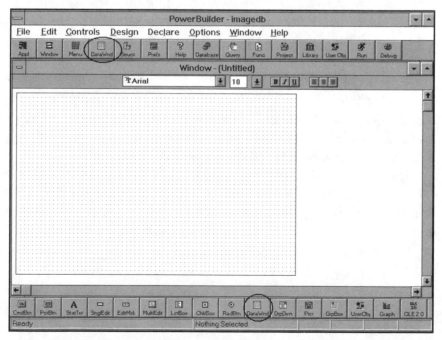

FIGURE 9.2 THE DATAWINDOW PAINTER ICON ON THE POWERBAR, THE DATAWINDOW CONTROL ICON IS ON THE WINDOW PAINTER TOOLBAR

Think of the DataWindow object as the encapsulation of the data source, and the DataWindow control as the connection between a window (and therefore your application) and a DataWindow object. You might think of the DataWindow object as a picture and the DataWindow control as a picture frame. DataWindow objects have attributes. DataWindow controls have attributes, functions, *and* events. There are functions to read or modify DataWindow object attributes; these functions though, are applied to DataWindow controls.

DataWindow Objects

DataWindow objects represent the data source for your application. The DataWindow encapsulates your database access into a high-level object that handles the retrieval and manipulation of data. The DataWindow also offers a wide range of presentation styles for your data, and the presentation can be customized to a large degree. There are other techniques for accessing data in an application (such as embedded SQL, or the file functions), but the DataWindow is the primary means for most data access in PowerBuilder applications. As a general rule, you should use DataWindows for all your data access. If you choose not to use a DataWindow, you should have good, clearly-defined reasons to justify your decision.

Clicking on the **DataWindow** icon on the PowerBar opens the DataWindow painter. The DataWindow painter is where you create and modify DataWindow objects. When created, DataWindows are defined as independent objects: they are not necessarily limited to a particular window, or even to a single application. They are much more tightly bound to the database manager and the table(s) to which they refer. DataWindow objects can be, and often are shared between windows. You will use the same DataWindow objects in different applications that need to access the same tables.

The default prefix for DataWindow object names is **d_**. The name of the DataWindow object should reflect its purpose, or perhaps the name of the table that it accesses. If a DataWindow accesses the employee table, then you could name it d_employee or d_emp_hr_view.

DataWindow Controls

The DataWindow icon on the Window painter PainterBar is a reference to a DataWindow control. You add a DataWindow control to a window just like any other control. You drop it on the window and then position and size it. Then you link (associate) the DataWindow control to a specific DataWindow object. This makes the DataWindow object available to your application. You then code scripts to manipulate the DataWindow control. These scripts control the retrieval, manipulation, and presentation of the data. Often you will add CommandButtons or menu options to the window to trigger the retrieval, updating, and deleting of rows of data from the database. You could also trigger the initial retrieval in the application or window open events. This is covered in great detail in the chapter DataWindow Controls.

DataWindow control names have a default prefix of **dw_**, such as dw_employee. The Window painter assigns a default name, such as dw_1 or dw_2, to the new DataWindow control in the same manner as it names other controls. With most of the other controls, you will probably prefer to give the object a more descriptive name than the one the Window painter assigned. DataWindow controls are a little different in this regard. There are times that you may wish to keep the default DataWindow control names that are assigned by the Window painter. An example would be when you are writing scripts and creating windows that you would like to be available for reuse in other applications. If you name the primary DataWindow for each window dw_1, it makes it easier for code references to be generalized. For example, if you write common functions and scripts that refer to dw_1 and dw_2, those references will be general enough to allow you to reuse the same code for different DataWindow controls. Examples of this will be shown along with some alternative methods for obtaining the same generality.

Figure 9.3 shows the relationship between a window, a DataWindow control, a DataWindow object, and the data source.

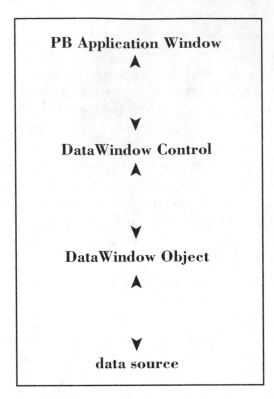

FIGURE 9.3 THE DATAWINDOW CONTROL,
DATAWINDOW OBJECT, AND DATA SOURCE

The DataWindow control is contained in one of your application windows. The DataWindow control is linked to a particular DataWindow object, which has been defined for a specific data source.

CREATING A NEW DATAWINDOW OBJECT

To create a DataWindow object for database access, you must be able to successfully connect to the database. You create DataWindows interactively with the database, so you must be connected to the database and be able to access the target table(s) when you are in the design process. This has the advantage of closely coupling the creation of the DataWindow object with the data source, but also means that you cannot create, or update a DataWindow if you cannot access the database. This can be a hindrance at times, such as when the server is down in a networked development environment. (You can update DataWindows using syntax mode, rather than graphical mode, without accessing the database).

PowerBuilder also creates its own repository in the database for storing the details about the columns and the tables in the database. This includes information such as data validation rules, presentation formats, edit masks, column labels, and field headings. This repository lets you share these definitions between DataWindows and between other developers to help establish standards across your applications.

When you define the attributes of the DataWindow object, you specify everything that the DataWindow object needs to know about accessing, presenting, formatting, validating, and manipulating the data. You may already have defined some of this information in the Database painter. PowerBuilder stored the definitions that you specified for each column in its repository. Later, when you (or another developer) make another reference to one of these columns, the information about that column will be available, without re-entering it. This helps to build more consistent, easier to maintain applications. For example, you can avoid having one report with a column heading of Employee ID, while another report calls the same column an Employee Number by storing and using the column headings in the repository. More details about the repository are in the chapter on the Database painter. You can override many of the repository defaults in the DataWindow painter.

DataWindow Creation

Click on the **DataWnd** icon on the PowerBar to begin the process of creating a DataWindow. Watch the status line and you will see that PowerBuilder first connects to the database before opening the DataWindow painter. By default, the connection is to the database to which you last connected. If the connection is to the wrong database, close the painter, and go into the Database painter and make the correct connection (see the chapter on the Database painter for more details). Then click again on the **DataWnd** icon on the PowerBar.

The Select DataWindow dialog opens as shown in Figure 9.4. To create a new DataWindow, click on the **New** CommandButton.

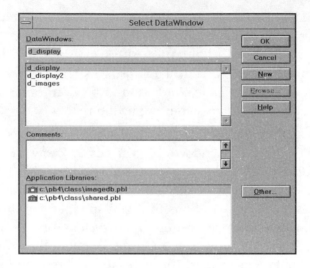

FIGURE 9.4 THE SELECT DATAWINDOW DIALOG

The creation of a new DataWindow is divided into two aspects. The first is the definition of the data source, and the second is the definition of the presentation style. The definition of the data source most often consists of graphically creating a SQL SELECT statement, but there are other possibilities. The definition of the presentation style involves selecting a style and then customizing the appearance of the DataWindow in the DataWindow painter. This painter is somewhat similar to the Window painter; the DataWindow object is presented as a window, to which you add and modify various objects such as columns, computed fields, and labels. The list of available objects is different than the objects that can be added to a window, and the DataWindow object itself is designed to handle data, and is therefore much more complex than a window.

The Data Source and Presentation Style

After clicking the **New** CommandButton in the Select DataWindow dialog (Figure 9.4), the next step involves selecting the data source and presentation style. Make these two choices in the New DataWindow dialog window shown in Figure 9.5

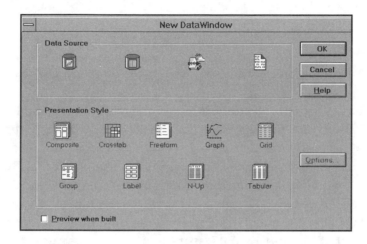

FIGURE 9.5 THE NEW DATAWINDOW DIALOG,
SELECT A DATA SOURCE AND A PRESENTATION STYLE

First you choose a data source. The data source specifies the origin of the data (where PowerBuilder will find the data). In most cases data comes from a database, but other sources are possible.

Next you must specify the presentation style for the new DataWindow object. The presentation style is the format for displaying and accessing the data.

The most common choice is a *SQL Select* data source with a *Tabular* presentation style. Edit the data source in either the Quick Select dialog, the SQL painter, or the Result Set dialog depending on the choice that you make for the data source. Customize the presentation style details in the DataWindow painter.

Data Sources

The choices for the data source fall into two categories, *database* sources and *external* (non-database) sources.

The New DataWindow dialog lists the following *database* data sources:

- Quick Select
- SQL Select
- Query
- Stored Procedure (this is only available with some DBMSs)

The database source can be almost any of the currently available relational DBMSs such as Oracle, Sybase, Informix, SQLBase, or Watcom SQL. Local database managers, such as FoxPro, Paradox, dBase; or other data sources, such as text files, are available through the use of ODBC drivers. The Stored Procedure data source option is only displayed if the DBMS supports stored procedures. If you select a database source, you need only define a SQL SELECT statement. PowerBuilder automatically generates the UPDATE, DELETE, and INSERT statements that are required for the DataWindow.

The *external* data source includes all non-database sources. This includes data sources such as flat files, DDE, PowerScript arrays, and could even be data built by programmatic calculations or user input.

Presentation Style

The DataWindow object has a wide variety of presentation styles to choose from. The most commonly used presentation style is tabular (but you need to become familiar with all of the different styles). The presentation style determines the manner in which data is presented to the user, and it also determines some of the interface options that the user has (such as the ability to resize a column dynamically). Each presentation style has an initial appearance that will be set up by default. The developer can customize the style and can modify many of the presentation details. In

PowerBuilder, there is no other report generator separate from the DataWindow painter. DataWindow objects also serve as the source of all the reports that you generate.

The choices for presentation style are:

- Composite
- Crosstab
- Freeform
- Graph
- Grid
- Group
- Label
- N-Up
- Tabular

DataWindow Data Sources

This section presents information on all the available choices for data sources.

Quick Select

The Quick Select data source is used to create simple queries. This is a fast and easy way to create SQL SELECT statements, but it is limited to queries that have no computed columns, and that have no retrieval arguments (but you may specify fixed selection criteria). Quick Select does allow the option of sorting the result set, but does not support the GROUP BY option. You can use multiple tables only if a foreign key has been defined in the Database painter. The join condition is set automatically.

Choose **Quick Select** on the New DataWindow dialog and click on **OK**. The Quick Select dialog appears (Figure 9.6).

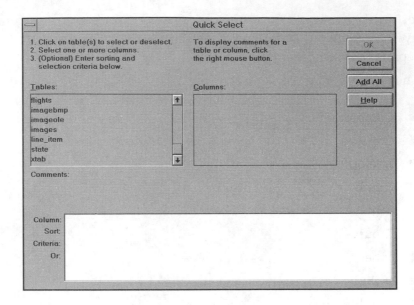

FIGURE 9.6 THE QUICK SELECT DIALOG

It takes only a couple of simple steps in this dialog window to define the SQL statement. The grid (at the bottom of the window) is similar to a QBE (Query By Example) matrix. Though this option is limited to rather simple queries, you should take time to explore the Quick Select dialog window because the QBE format is also available to you as a DataWindow mode. You may find the QBE technique to be a useful function to add to your DataWindows.

The Quick Select Dialog

First, you must select a table from the Tables ListBox. PowerBuilder accesses the database to load the list of columns. Next you select the column(s) that you wish to retrieve from the Columns ListBox. Click on each column to select it or you can click on the **Add All** button if you wish to select every column in the table. To remove a column from the list, click on it and it is deselected. The columns that you select are added to the grid at the bottom of the window (see Figure 9.7).

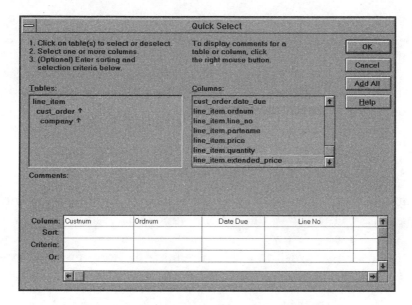

FIGURE 9.7 BUILDING A **SELECT** STATEMENT
FOR THE LINE_ITEM AND CUST_ORDER TABLES

Use this grid to enter the sort order and selection criteria in a QBE fashion. You can reorder the columns in the grid by selecting the column heading (with the mouse) and dragging it to its new position. You may enter selection criteria to restrict the rows that will be selected. It is important to note that any criteria specified on this grid are then hard-coded into the SELECT statement. If you want to defined retrieval arguments (variable arguments) then you must use the SQL painter to define the SELECT statement.

You can also specify a sort order for the result set. If there are no selection criteria (to be added to the WHERE clause), and no requirement to sort the data (to create an ORDER BY clause), then as soon as you choose the table and the columns, you are finished.

Joins

You can select more than one table in the Quick Select dialog only if they share a key relationship. The dialog will help to find related tables. When you select a table, the Columns box and the Tables box will list all tables that have a foreign key that is related to the selected table. If you select a table from the indented list of related tables, the columns in that table are added to the list in the Columns box. The list in the Tables box will be updated to show only the tables that have a foreign key related to the newly selected table. If you want to return to the original table list, just click the first selected table at the top of the list. The join condition will be defined from the primary/foreign key relationship. You can not enter the join condition directly.

Sort Order

Add an ORDER BY clause to the SQL statement by defining a sort order. To do this, click in the grid at the bottom of the Quick Select dialog window. Make entries in the first row of the grid to set the sort order. Click under the column that you wish to use to determine the sort order, this opens a dropdown listbox (Figure 9.8).

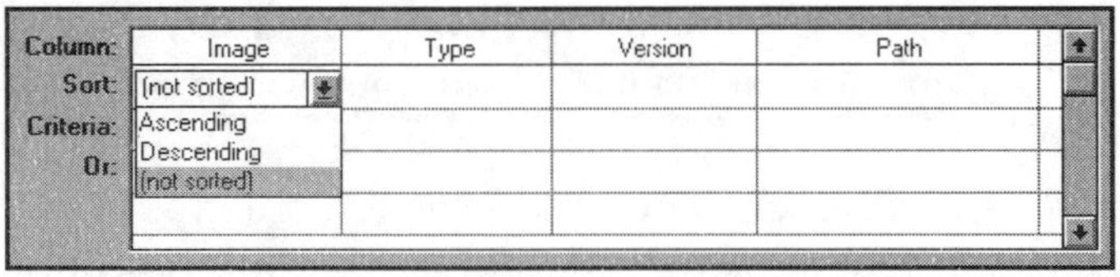

FIGURE 9.8 DEFINING A SORT ORDER FOR THE IMAGE COLUMN

You have the option to select the Ascending or Descending order (or not sorted) from the dropdown listbox. The database sorts the query result rows by any fields that you have specified in this manner. If you use multiple columns in your sort specification, the ORDER BY uses the columns in the order as listed from left to right. You can reorder the columns by clicking on the column heading and dragging it to its new location; this also reorders the columns in the presentation.

Select Criteria

Add selection criteria in the second and succeeding rows to restrict the rows in the result set. The selection criteria are placed in the WHERE clause of the generated SQL statement. The criteria that you are entering here are fixed criteria, always to be applied to the SELECT statement. If you want to add dynamic values, don't try to enter them here. You can do that later by adding Retrieval Arguments after the statement has been created (in the SQL painter). The process is the same as is used for the SQL SELECT option for the data source, covered in the next section.

If the selection criteria is for equality, then just enter the value in the second row of the corresponding column. For example, to select rows from Ohio, enter OHIO under the state column (in the second row of the grid).

For conditions other than equality, you can enter the relational operator to be used for the comparison. For example, enter < OHIO, to list all the states that come before Ohio alphabetically. The legal relational operators are:

```
=, <>, >, >=, <, <=, LIKE, IN
```

Use wildcards to create a search pattern. Use the % (percent sign) to signify any set of characters, and the _ (underscore) to represent any one, single character. For example, %a% selects any entry that contains the letter a. **Th_s**, returns any entry that begins with a **Th** as the first two letters and an **s** as the fourth letter (such as This or Thus). To find all the cities that begin with a **C** you would enter **LIKE C%** in the city column. The search is case sensitive.

The entries in each row (after the first row) are *anded* together to create the criteria. Succeeding rows imply an OR conjunction and let you build more complex queries.

For example, in Figure 9.9 the entry in the second row limits the result to those records with cities that start with the letter C *and* where the state is equal to OHIO. The third row adds an OR conjunction and adds all records which have a city starting with the word **New** (from any state) to the result set.

Column:	Company	City	State	Zip	Ph
Sort:	Ascending				
Criteria:		LIKE C%	OH		
Or:		LIKE NEW%			

FIGURE 9.9 DEFINING SELECT CRITERIA

As a result of this criteria, the Quick Select creates the following SQL statement:

```
SELECT * FROM company
WHERE (city LIKE 'C%' AND state = 'OH') OR city LIKE 'New%'
SORT BY company;
```

You can also override the OR conjunction that is implicit between rows by inserting an AND. Figure 9.10 shows an example where the city must be between Akron and Dayton (alphabetically).

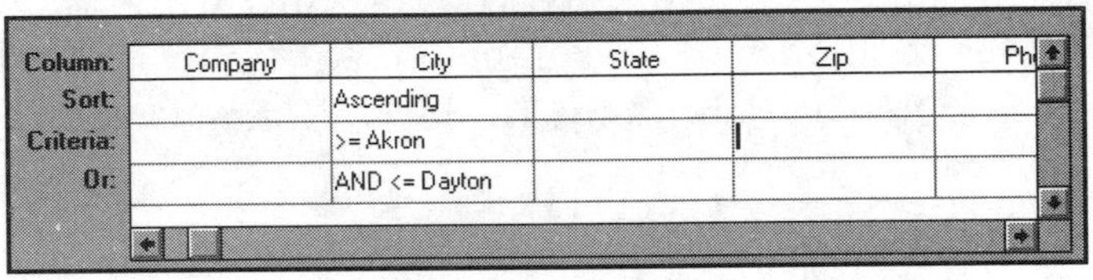

Column:	Company	City	State	Zip	Ph
Sort:		Ascending			
Criteria:		>= Akron			
Or:		AND <= Dayton			

FIGURE 9.10 DEFINING A SELECTION CRITERIA

The Quick Select creates the following SQL statement as a result of this criteria:

```
SELECT * FROM company
WHERE (city >= 'Akron' AND city <= 'Dayton')
SORT BY city;
```

In review, the Quick Select can be used the create queries with the follow limitations:

- simple columns only, no computed fields
- not dynamic retrieval arguments
- no subqueries
- no GROUP BY
- ORDER BY is allowed

The SQL Select Data Source Option

The SQL Select data source option allows the creation of more powerful (and more complex) SELECT statements. Choose the SQL Select option if you need to create queries that use multiple tables, computed columns,

GROUP BY clauses, or if you need to specify retrieval arguments. Many, if not most, of your DataWindow queries will be too complicated to be created in the Quick Select window.

To use this option, choose **SQL Select** on the New DataWindow dialog for the data source. PowerBuilder opens the SQL painter. The first step is to choose one or more tables from the Select Tables dialog window (Figure 9.11).

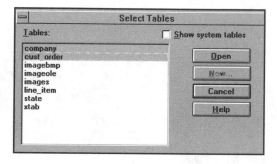

FIGURE 9.11 THE SELECT TABLES DIALOG

This dialog presents a listbox containing all of the tables in the database to which you are connected. Clicking the **Show System Tables** checkbox on that dialog adds the system tables to the listbox. Normally you don't wish to access the system tables and the default is not to include them in the listbox. This list includes both views and tables.

In this dialog, you select the table(s) that will be used in the SQL SELECT statement. After selecting the table(s), click on the **Open** CommandButton to open the table(s) and the SQL Painter (Figure 9.12).

Next, continue with the selection of the columns from these tables, and then define any additional requirements for the SELECT statement. You can also use the SQL painter to modify SQL statements, including those that you created with the Quick Select dialog. If you have selected more than one table you need to specify a join condition for each table.

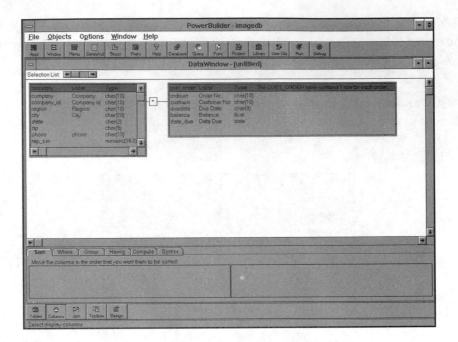

FIGURE 9.12 THE SQL PAINTER UTILITY

Joins

The tables that you have selected are dropped onto the SQL painter's work area. If you have selected two or more tables, PowerBuilder will attempt to determine the join conditions to be used between the tables. The join conditions are presented graphically in the work area as a line drawn between the joining columns; the relational operator is contained in a box on that line. You may have to scroll the column list for each table to see which column(s) is being referenced by the line.

Add a join condition by clicking on the **Join** icon on the Painter bar. Click on the column name in the first table and then click on the column name in the second table. This adds the graphical representation of the join to the display, and also add the join condition to the WHERE clause. The SQL painter assumes that the join condition is equality (which is usual). Change the operator by clicking on the join's relational operator square (|=| in Figure 9.12). This opens the Join dialog window shown in Figure 9.13. In this window you can change the operator, delete the join condition entirely, or specify an outer join. (Outer joins are explained in detail in Chapter 20, SQL Basics.)

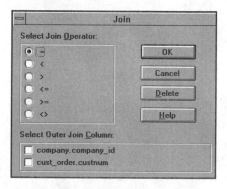

FIGURE 9.13 SELECTING THE JOIN CONDITION

Selecting Columns

Add columns to the select statement by clicking the column name from the table on the SQL painter work area (Figure 9.12). Add all the columns from a table by selecting **Select All** from the control menu (available on each table). The name of each column is highlighted when it is added to the select clause. Remove columns from the list by selecting the column name again. As you add columns, they are added to the selection list area at the top of the SQL painter window as labeled rectangles. Reorder columns by clicking and dragging the column's rectangle to its new location. Figure 9.14 shows an example where two columns have been added from the company table; and the next step is to add all the columns in the cust_order table using **Select All** on the cust_order control menu.

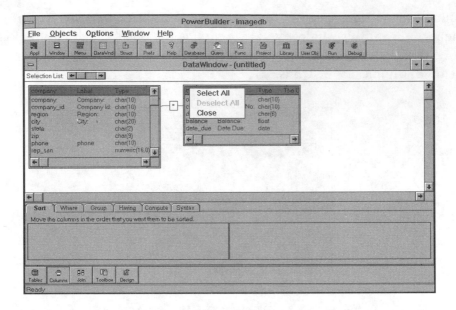

FIGURE 9.14 ADDING COLUMNS TO THE SELECT STATEMENT

Computed Columns

To add a computed column to the SELECT clause, click on the **Compute** icon on the PainterBar. This opens the Create Computed Column dialog window (Figure 9.15).

In this dialog, you can paste column names, SQL functions, and operators into the edit field to build the expression for the computed column. To list the columns in another table, select the table from the listbox.

Click on the **Distinct** button to add the DISTINCT option to the computed column. If you add the DISTINCT option, the result returns only unique values for the column.

When you define a computed column in the SQL painter, you specify a calculation that to be performed by the DBMS. Later (on the presentation side) you have the option to create calculations to be computed in the DataWindow. These calculations are computed by PowerBuilder after the data retrieval.

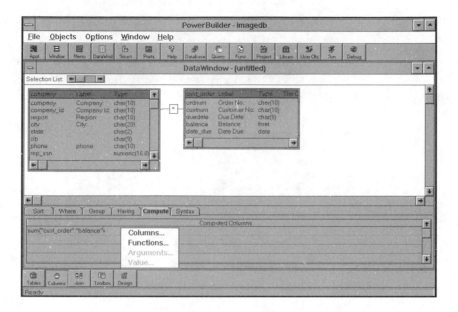

FIGURE 9.15 THE CREATE COMPUTED COLUMN DIALOG

NOTE

If you want to have an additional field on your DataWindow that is accessible in the same way as a column, create a "dummy" column. Then for a numeric field enter **0** (zero), or for a string field enter " (two single quotes). These columns are accessible by any functions that you can use on a regular column (SetItem() or GetItem()), and have the same set of attributes, such as DisplayAsBitmp. Regular calculated columns in the DataWindow do not have this capability.

WHERE Clause Criteria

You can specify any selection criteria to be added to the WHERE clause. This restricts the rows that are selected from the database. You can specify conditions with constants or with variables (called *retrieval arguments*) that will be passed into the DataWindow when the query is actually executed. If you are going to use variables in the WHERE clause, then you must declare retrieval arguments before making a reference to them (in the WHERE clause).

To define retrieval arguments, select the **Objects|Retrieval Arguments...** menu option. This opens the Specify Retrieval Arguments dialog window (Figure 9.16).

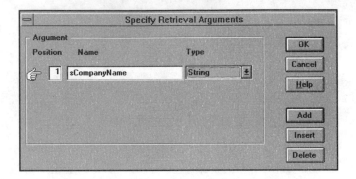

FIGURE 9.16 DEFINING RETRIEVAL ARGUMENTS

In this dialog, you specify a name and data type for each argument. In this example we defined *sCompanyName* as a string.

To add search criteria to the WHERE clause, click on the **Where** icon on the PainterBar or select the **Objects|Where Criteria** menu option. This opens the Where Criteria dialog window.

In this dialog, you build expressions from column names, SQL Functions, operators, and retrieval arguments. At the end of each line you must choose either the AND or the OR conjunction to link to the next line (if any). You can also add parenthesis as necessary to specify the evaluation order of the expression. Use the **Select** button to create subqueries (nested queries).

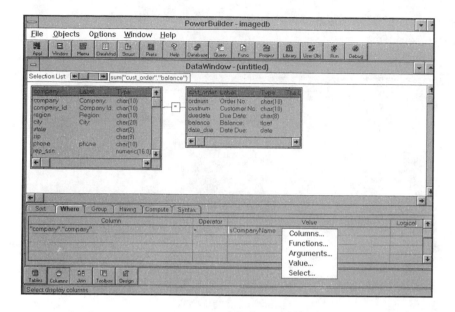

FIGURE 9.17 DEFINING THE **WHERE** CRITERIA

Viewing the SQL Statement

View the SQL statement that the SQL painter has created by selecting the **Options|Show SQL Syntax** menu option. This is actually a toggle menu item. Checking this displays the SQL statement that has been generated as a result of the work you have completed so far in this painter, as in the example in Figure 9.18.

If a join is displayed in the work area, the join condition will be added to the WHERE clause. Edit the SQL statement text if necessary (but you can't do that in the Show SQL window). To edit the SQL statement, select the **Option|Convert to Syntax** menu option. This opens the editor where you can make changes in syntax (text) mode.

When you have finished with the editing, you must select the **Options|Convert to Graphics** menu selection to move the query back to the SQL painter. (I have found this to be one of the rougher sections of the PowerBuilder environment. Often PowerBuilder is unable to convert legal SQL statements to graphics. Hopefully this will improve in future releases.)

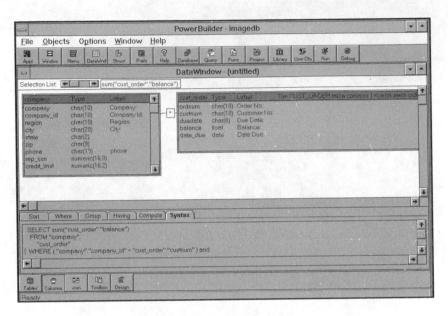

FIGURE 9.18 DISPLAYING THE SELECT STATEMENT

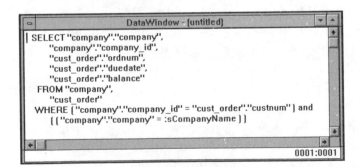

FIGURE 9.19 EDITING A SQL SELECT STATEMENT

Group By

You specify a grouping for the result set by clicking on the **GroupBy** icon on the Painter bar. This opens the Grouping Columns dialog shown in Figure 9.20.

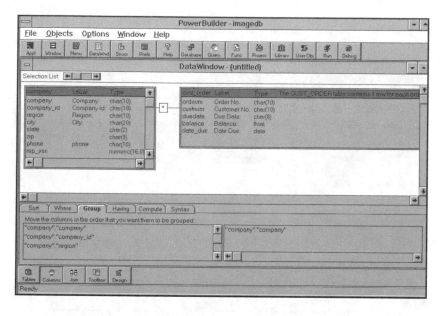

FIGURE 9.20 DEFINING A GROUP BY CLAUSE

Add the column names in the order that you want for the GROUP BY clause. To insert an item into the list, select the point in the list and then click on **Insert**. To remove an item, select it and click on **Delete**.

 Note the following limitations for the SELECT clause when you add a GROUP BY clause. In a SQL statement that has a GROUP BY clause, the items in the select list are limited to the items that are also in the GROUP BY clause, and the aggregate column functions such as MIN, MAX, AVG, SUM, etc. See Chapter 20, SQL Basics for more information.

Having

After you add the GROUP BY condition, you can add a HAVING clause which creates a filter based on the GROUP BY results. Click on the **Having** icon on the Painter bar. This opens the Having Criteria dialog box shown in Figure 9.21.

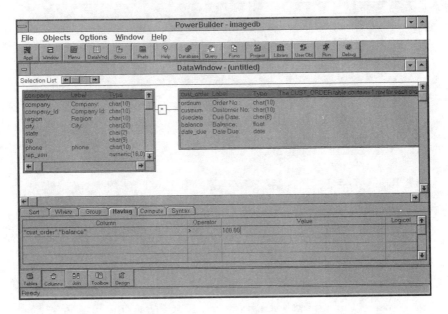

FIGURE 9.21 DEFINING THE HAVING CLAUSE FOR A SELECT STATEMENT

The operation of this dialog is almost the same as the Where Criteria dialog, but is actually a little simpler. In this dialog you can restrict the rows that are added to the result set as a result of a criteria placed on the GROUP BY calculation. In the example shown in Figure 9.21, the result set is limited to companies with a balance greater than $100.00. See Chapter 20, SQL Basics for more information.

Order By

To add an ORDER BY clause to the SQL statement click on the **Sort** icon. This opens the Sort Order dialog window (Figure 9.22). The Selection List ListBox provides the choices that you have for sorting. Select a column from the listbox to add it to the Order Item list. In the list you can select to sort in either Ascending or Descending order (for each column). To insert an item in the list select the point in the list where you want insert an item, then click on **Insert**. This adds a blank entry; you can then select the column from the Selection List listbox. To remove an item, select it and then click on **Delete**. See Chapter 20, SQL Basics for more information.

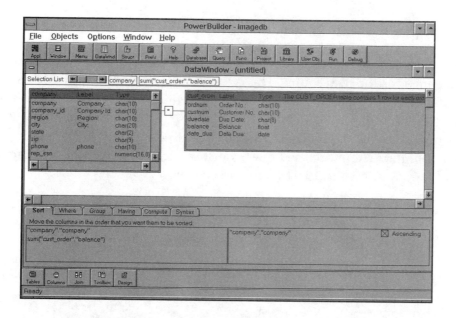

FIGURE 9.22 DEFINING A SORT ORDER

Unions

You can add UNIONs to your SELECT statements. This option is found on the **Objects|Create Union** menu selection. See Chapter 20, SQL Basics for more information on unions.

When you have completed the SQL Statement, click on **Design** to go to the design window.

Saving a Query

If you use the query for other DataWindows, then you can save this query into a PowerBuilder library by selecting the **File|Save As** menu option. You will be prompted to set the library and name the query. By convention, query names use the prefix **q_**, such as q_customer_invoices.

The Query Data Source Option

The Query data source option lets you use a previously defined SELECT statement as the data source. This could be a query that was created as the result of the SQL SELECT data source option that you saved for later reuse. It could also be a SELECT statement that was created in the Query painter, or one that was originally created in a text editor and converted in the SQL painter. The predefined query must reside in a PowerBuilder library. Figure 9.23 shows the Select Query dialog window.

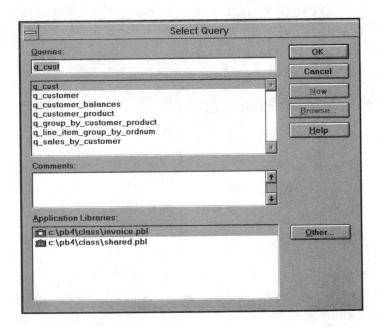

FIGURE 9.23 THE SELECT QUERY DIALOG

Select the library (using the Directories and Libraries listboxes) and then select the query. The DataWindow painter then opens. You can modify the SELECT statement by clicking on the **SQL Select** icon (on the PainterBar) or by selecting the **Design|Edit Data Source** menu option.

The External Data Source Option

The External data source option lets you use a non-database source for a DataWindow. This can be from a variety of sources including files, the clipboard, DDE, and even hard-coded values. When you select the external data source option, PowerBuilder opens the Result Set Description dialog.

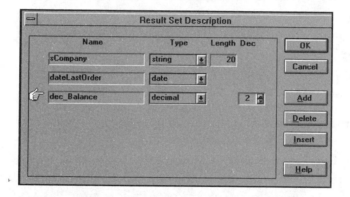

FIGURE 9.24 DEFINING A RESULT SET

In this window, you define the name, data type, length, and the number of decimal places (only for numerics) for each column of the DataWindow. This window provides buttons to let you **Add** a new column to the end of the result set, **Insert** a new column at the current location, **Delete** the currently selected column, or to receive **Help** on using this dialog. When you have defined all of the columns, click on **OK**; this opens the DataWindow painter.

The Stored Procedure Data Source Option

The Stored Procedure data source option is only available if your DBMS supports stored procedures. If so, you can select a stored procedure as a database source for a DataWindow. The DataWindow executes the stored procedure and display: the result set based on that procedure. After you choose the Stored Procedure data source option, PowerBuilder opens the Select Stored Procedure dialog window. In this dialog, pick one procedure from the listbox. You can view the source code for the stored procedure in the Source edit box at the bottom of the dialog window. After you select a stored procedure, define the result set in the Result Set dialog window as described in the previous section on external data sources. If a stored procedure computes more than one result set, you may specify which result set you want to populate the DataWindow. When you finish defining the result set and click on **OK**, the DataWindow painter opens and you can continue with the editing of the presentation style.

PRESENTATION STYLES

After defining the new DataWindow's data source, your next task is to specify the details of the presentation style. The presentation style determines the layout of the data and specifies the general manner in which the user interacts with that data. You can modify the presentation style to a large, almost unlimited degree. PowerBuilder provides you with eight presentation styles to choose from, each is different in the way that it presents the data.

The choices for presentation style are:

- **Composite**—combines DataWindow reports.
- **Crosstab**—presents the data in a cross tabulation format. This is most useful for calculating totals by groups. Crosstab presents data in a manner similar to spreadsheet programs.
- **Freeform**—this is the "forms"-like presentation. Generally, you use the freeform presentation style to enter, update, delete, and display individual records. The DataWindow presents all of the fields (column values) of a single record with a field label.

■ **Graph**—PowerBuilder has an excellent selection of graphs, similar to the graphs available in Microsoft Excel.

■ **Grid**—the grid style is similar to the tabular presentation style. The user can reorder and resize the columns in the DataWindow. This provides the advantages of the tabular presentation style, and also allows the user to adjust the display. The disadvantage of the grid style is that while the user can rearrange columns, the developer is not able to modify the layout in the flexible manner available in the tabular style. This style is most often used for display only purposes.

■ **Group**—the group presentation style makes it very easy to create reports with group summations. The format is attractive and immediately useful if it matches your requirements. The display is divided into groups with headings and summation rows predefined. The report includes page header, time, and page count.

■ **Label**—presents data in a simple mailing label format.

■ **N-Up**—presents data in columns across the screen like a newspaper. When a column reaches the bottom of the screen the data continues in the next column (left to right). The exception to this is that sorted data is presented across the columns in rows.

■ **Tabular**—the most important, and most often used presentation style. Data is presented in columns under column headings. Each row is presented in a separate line initially. This presentation allows a great deal of flexibility. You can take a tabular presentation and create a form presentation, or a group presentation very easily. You can create summary bands.

Most commonly used is *Select/Tabular*, so be sure that you are fluent with this combination before you spend a great deal of time exploring the other options.

The next section presents a sample of each presentation style. The next chapter has details on how to create DataWindows with each of these presentation styles.

Crosstab

The Crosstab presentation style presents the data in a cross tabulation format, this is most useful for calculating totals by groups. The Crosstab DataWindow uses the data from the SQL SELECT statement that you specify and analyzes the data and displays it in a tabular format.

Invoice					
Crosstab DataWindow					
	Sum For 111	Sum For 222	Sum For 333	Sum For 444	Product Totals
consulting	$2,752.75	$7,507.50	$8,758.75	$2,752.75	$21,771.75
hardware	$4,400.00	$4,800.00	$10,400.00	$1,200.00	$20,800.00
software	$2,964.00	$6,916.00	$8,892.00	$864.50	$19,636.50
Page 1 of 1				9/3/94	

FIGURE 9.25 A CROSSTAB REPORT

This DataWindow displays the total sales made to each company broken out by product. The total sale to each company is computed in the summary band, and the total sales for each product is totaled in the computed column (Product Totals).

Freeform

This is the "forms"-like presentation. Generally, you use the freeform presentation style to enter, update, delete, and display individual records. The DataWindow presents each of the fields (column values) of a single record with a field label. This format can be customized to a large degree.

Figure 9.26 presents a row from the company table. This form would probably be used to input new records. It could also be used to update, delete, and view records.

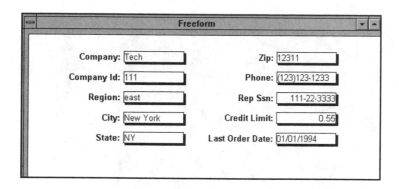

FIGURE 9.26 A FREEFORM REPORT

Graph

PowerBuilder has an excellent selection of graphs, similar to the graphs available in Microsoft Excel. A later chapter is devoted entirely to the process of creating graphs. You can actually create graphs in three different manners. The graph presentation style will present the result of the SQL query (or other data source) only as a graph.

You can also add graphs (in the DataWindow painter) to DataWindows that have been defined with other presentation styles (other than graph). In this case, the graph is an object that is added to the DataWindow in a manner similar to how a control is added to a window.

It is also possible to add a graph control to a window in the Window painter. However, you must develop a routine to calculate and display the graph. For this discussion we are considering graphs that are created as a result of defining a DataWindow with the graph presentation style. Figure 9.27 shows the selection of graphs that are available when you choose a graph presentation style.

Figure 9.28 shows an example of a 3D pie chart that displays total sales divided by customer. The legend presents the customer ID (111,222, etc.).

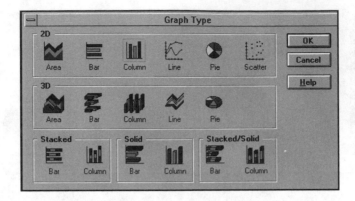

FIGURE 9.27 THE GRAPH TYPE DIALOG

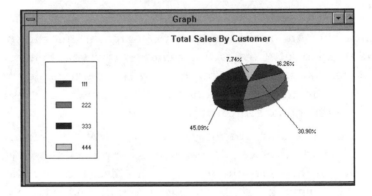

FIGURE 9.28 A GRAPH REPORT

Grid

The grid style is similar to the tabular presentation style. Data is presented in rows and columns like the tabular style, but grid lines are added to the display. The user can reorder and resize the columns in the DataWindow by dragging the column headings and by using the grid lines. This provides the advantages of the tabular presentation style, and also lets the user adjust the display. The disadvantage of the grid style is that while the user can rearrange the columns, the developer is not able to modify the layout in the flexible manner available in the tabular style.

An example of a grid is shown in Figure 9.29. In this DataWindow the user can resize and reorder the columns easily with the mouse.

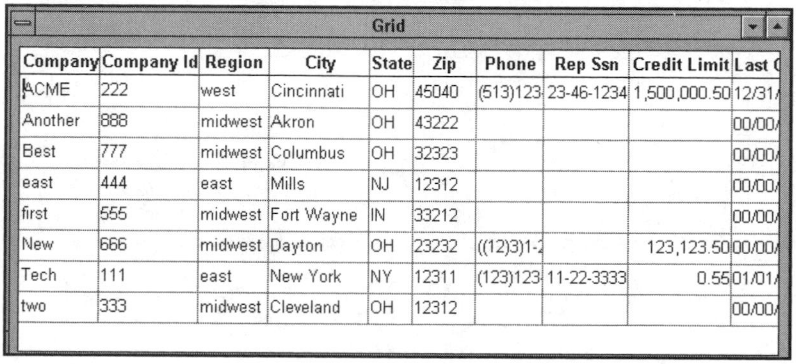

Company	Company Id	Region	City	State	Zip	Phone	Rep Ssn	Credit Limit	Last (
ACME	222	west	Cincinnati	OH	45040	(513)123-	23-46-1234	1,500,000.50	12/31/
Another	888	midwest	Akron	OH	43222				00/00/
Best	777	midwest	Columbus	OH	32323				00/00/
east	444	east	Mills	NJ	12312				00/00/
first	555	midwest	Fort Wayne	IN	33212				00/00/
New	666	midwest	Dayton	OH	23232	((12)3)1-2		123,123.50	00/00/
Tech	111	east	New York	NY	12311	(123)123-	11-22-3333	0.55	01/01/
two	333	midwest	Cleveland	OH	12312				00/00/

FIGURE 9.29 A GRID REPORT

Group

The group presentation style makes it very easy to create reports with group summations. The format is attractive and useful. The display is divided into groups with headings and summation rows predefined. The report includes page header, time, and page count.

It doesn't take very much work to make a great looking presentation with the group presentation style. An example of the group presentation style is shown in Figure 9.30.

This DataWindow groups the line items for each customer (company), and also calculates the total amount for all the invoices for that customer. A final summation has been added to calculate the total of all sales.

Group					

Current Customer Orders Report

9/4/94

Order Number	Line No	Partname	Price	Quantity	Extended Price
Customer Number 444					
7777	1	hardware	400.00	1	400.00
8892	1	hardware	400.00	1	400.00
8892	2	consulting	250.25	1	250.25
99001	1	hardware	400.00	1	400.00
99001	2	consulting	250.25	10	2,502.50
99001	3	software	123.50	7	864.50
				Customer Total =	**4,817.25**
				Total of All Sales =	**62,208.25**

Page 6 of 6

FIGURE 9.30 A GROUP REPORT

Label

Presents data in a simple mailing label format. For this example, a SQL SELECT statement was created that returns the list of addresses from the company table.

An example of the label presentation style is shown in Figure 9.31.

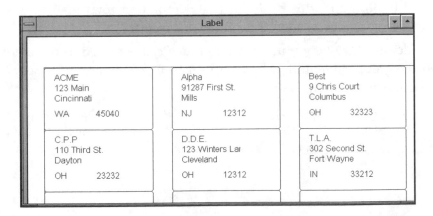

FIGURE 9.31 THE LABEL STYLE

N-Up

Presents data in columns across the screen like a newspaper. When a column reaches the bottom of the screen the data continues in the next column (left to right). The exception to this is that sorted data is presented across the columns in rows.

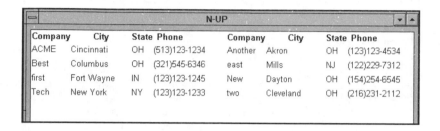

FIGURE 9.32 THE N-UP STYLE

Tabular

The tabular style is the most important and most often used presentation style. Data is presented in columns under column headings. Each row is presented initially as a separate line. This presentation allows a great deal of flexibility. You can take a tabular presentation and create a form presentation, or a group presentation very easily.

Figure 9.33 shows an example of a tabular DataWindow. In this example, invoice line items are displayed and grouped together by order number and customer number. The DataWindow also totals the amount of each order.

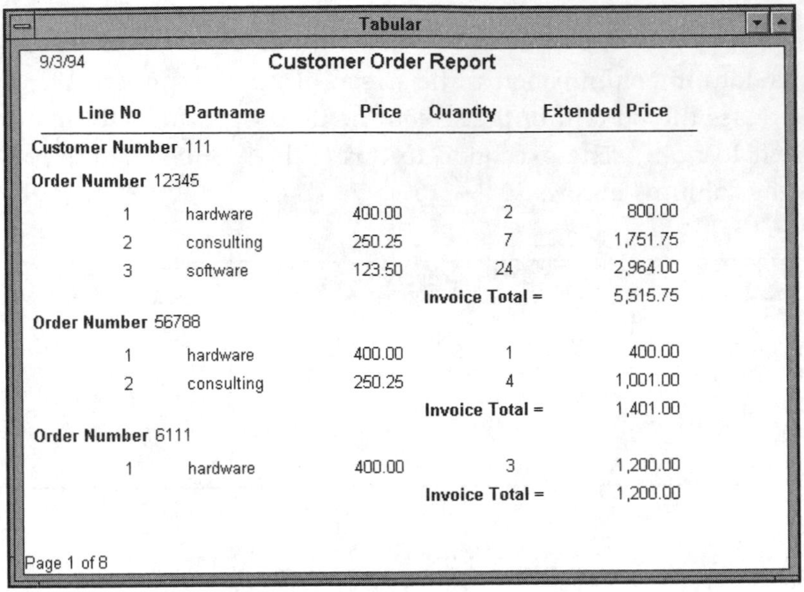

FIGURE 9.33 THE TABULAR STYLE

The Composite Presentation Style

The composite presentation lets you combine DataWindows into one report. The composite report is a container for other reports, but does not allow a database relationship to be defined between the reports.

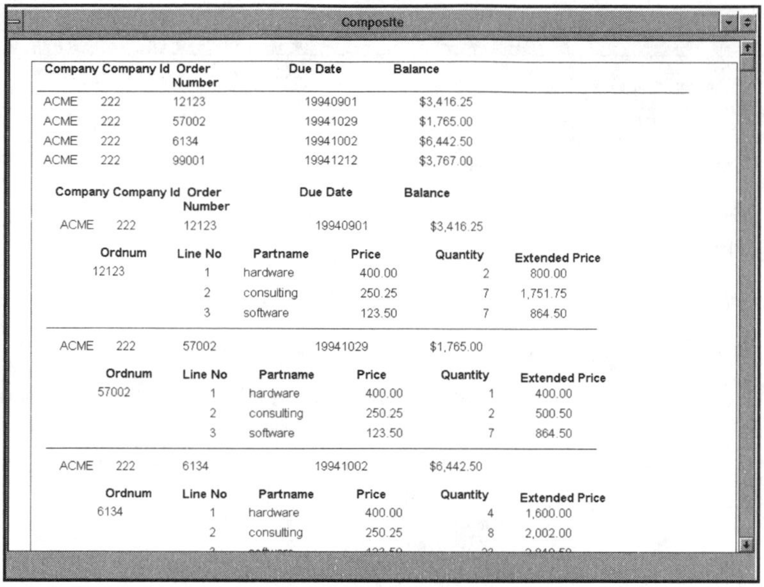

FIGURE 9.34 A COMPOSITE DATAWINDOW

Nested Reports

Nested reports can be created for any of the presentation styles except Crosstab. A nested report places one or more reports (read only DataWindow objects) into another report. Figure 9.35 shows an example of a nested report. This is an example of a master-detail relationship between two DataWindow objects.

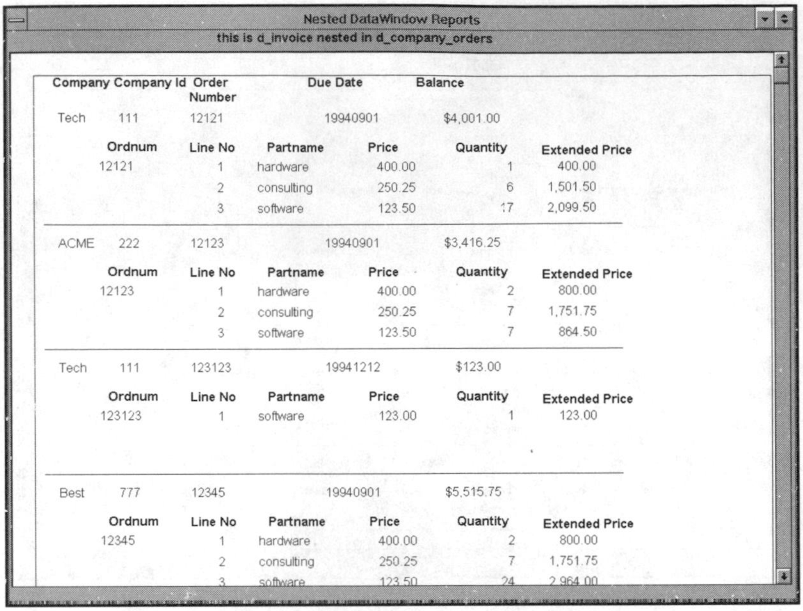

FIGURE 9.35 A NESTED-REPORT IN A TABULAR STYLE DATAWINDOW

CHAPTER TEN

THE DATAWINDOW PAINTER

ENHANCING DATAWINDOW OBJECTS

After you have completed the definition of the data source, the DataWindow painter creates a DataWindow object. For a tabular presentation style, the DataWindow painter positions the labels, columns, and summation fields (if any) in a default layout. The DataWindow presentation is essentially a report, and its format looks similar to many reports that you have seen before. In the PowerBuilder system there is no report generator other than the DataWindow painter. DataWindows can be used to display information on the screen and/or for printing hardcopy reports. For this reason, the DataWindow object will often be referred to as a report.

This chapter discusses the customization of DataWindow objects. Most of this discussion assumes that a DataWindow object was defined with the tabular presentation style, but a great deal of this discussion also applies to the other presentation styles. The tabular presentation is the most often used style, and it has the widest range of customizing abilities.The other presentation styles are covered in the last section of this chapter.

In the tabular presentation style, data is presented in columns under column headings. Each row is presented initially in a separate line. This allows a great deal of flexibility. You can take a tabular presentation and create a form presentation, or a group presentation very easily.

Customizing the DataWindow Presentation

The DataWindow painter is actually the DataWindow object design editor. You can customize the DataWindow presentation by rearranging fields, changing font styles, adding labels, date, time, and page numbers. You can add graphs and other graphical objects (including pictures), and change the font, colors, and the style of presentation for each of the columns. You can also divide the rows into sets of records grouped by the value of one or more columns, and you can add summarizations for those groups.

Figure 10.1 shows a DataWindow report.

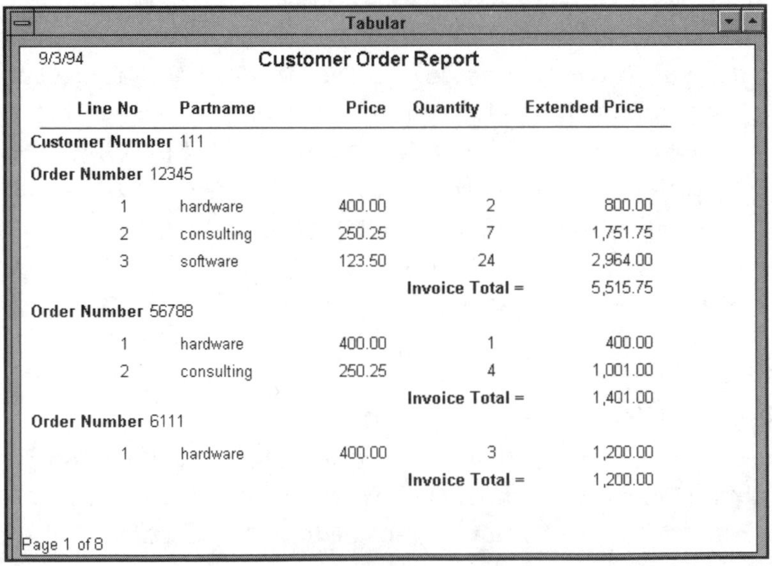

Tabular				
9/3/94	**Customer Order Report**			
Line No	**Partname**	**Price**	**Quantity**	**Extended Price**
Customer Number 111				
Order Number 12345				
1	hardware	400.00	2	800.00
2	consulting	250.25	7	1,751.75
3	software	123.50	24	2,964.00
			Invoice Total =	5,515.75
Order Number 56788				
1	hardware	400.00	1	400.00
2	consulting	250.25	4	1,001.00
			Invoice Total =	1,401.00
Order Number 6111				
1	hardware	400.00	3	1,200.00
			Invoice Total =	1,200.00
Page 1 of 8				

FIGURE 10.1 A DataWindow report

In the DataWindow in Figure 10.1, notice that the report is divided into sections. At the top of the report (above the horizontal line) there is a heading that contains a label for the report (*Customer Order Report*) and the date of the report. The heading also contains column headings for the rows of data that appear in the main body (the detail band) of the report. The invoice line items are grouped by customer number and then by order number.

The detail section contains the actual data from the SQL query. This is the main section of the report that presents the details for each of the lines in the invoice.

A single line immediately follows each detail section to display the total balance for the invoice. This is a calculated value, computed in the DataWindow. A summary line presents the total balance due from the customer and follows after the last order for each customer.

Finally, at the very bottom of the report window, appears footer information. In this case, it only includes the page number of the report in a format that tells you how many total pages there are in this report.

This example uses the tabular presentation style, but has been customized to have an appearance somewhat like a group presentation style.

Figure 10.2 shows the design screen version of the same DataWindow. This is in the DataWindow painter. In the DataWindow painter you can customize the report to make it exactly what you want.

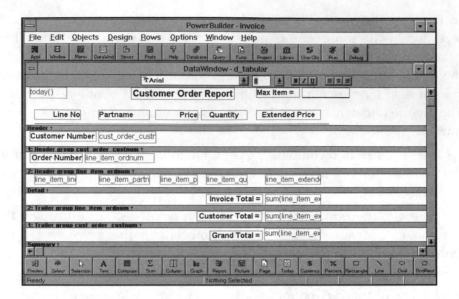

FIGURE 10.2 DESIGNING A DATAWINDOW OBJECT

BANDS

The design screen for the DataWindow painter is divided into a number of sections called *bands*. You may recognize the design format, it is presented in a manner similar to that used by a number of database report generators. The tabular display format always has at least four bands: *header*, *detail*, *summary*, and *footer* bands. Each band represents a section of the final DataWindow report.

Each band has a different function in building the DataWindow presentation. The header band contains column heading, report labels, and other information that is to be displayed at the top of the report. The detail band contains the selection result set (the actual rows from the database), usually presented in rows across the DataWindows. The summary band is used to display summation totals, like the invoice total in Figure 10.1. The footer band is used to present page numbers and other information that is to appear at the bottom of each page. If you create groups in the DataWindow, two additional bands are added for each group. In the example (Figures 10.1 and 10.2) a group for customer number and order numbers were created.

The Header Band

The header band contains the information that appears at the top the DataWindow and at the top of each page of the report (the printout). This band usually includes a report title, the date, and column headings for the rows of data that appear in the detail band. The header band may also show the report parameters such as the value of the retrieval arguments, or the date range for the data. Anything placed in the header band is automatically defined for display only.

FIGURE 10.3 THE HEADER BAND

In this example, the header contains the report label (Customer Order Report), the date (today()), a label, and static text field for the maximum item in any invoice, and the five column headings for the detail band.

The Detail Band

The detail band presents the actual data that is the result of the Select statement (or other data source). The detail band displays the result set columns in rows of data across the DataWindow. The DataWindow painter initially adds one SingleLineEdit field for each column in the select list of the Select statement. You can add computed fields to any band, including the detail band. If you add a computed field in the DataWindow painter, the calculation is done by PowerBuilder after the data retrieval has taken place.

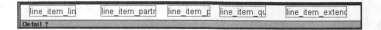

FIGURE 10.4 THE DETAIL BAND

In this example, the detail band contains five columns for the line_item table. These are the line_no, partname, price, quantity, and extended_price columns.

The Summary Band

The summary band contains information that is presented at the end of the report (or DataWindow), after the display of all the detail records. The summary band is used to present final totals, usually summations, but it could be averages, counts, minimums, or maximums.

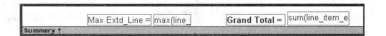

FIGURE 10.5 THE SUMMARY BAND

In this example, the summary band contains the sum of all the extended_price columns, and also the maximum value found in any extended_line field.

The Footer Band

The footer band holds data that appears at the bottom of each page (on the screen or printout) of the report. The footer usually includes a page number (usually of the form "page 1 of 20"), and sometimes the date of the report. You might also consider adding the name of the DataWindow object to the footer (perhaps using a smaller font size). This label will be useful later when a user shows you a report and asks for some enhancements.

This example footer contains the page number (with the format Page 1 of 20), and the name of the DataWindow object.

FIGURE 10.6 THE FOOTER BAND

Group Bands

You may choose to subdivide (*group*) the result set either as part of the presentation or for use in creating aggregate functions such as presenting summations in groups. You define a group by selecting the **Rows|Create Group** menu option and then by defining **Group Item Expressions** in the Specify Group dialog (this is covered in the next section). For each group that you define, the DataWindow painter adds a pair of group bands to your DataWindow.

Group Header Band

Each grouping that you define adds a corresponding group header band and a group trailer band to the design window. The group header band is where you place the information that you want presented at the start of each new group in the report. Here you usually list the values for the group criteria, and sometimes you may place computed fields for the group in this area.

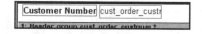

FIGURE 10.7 THE GROUP HEADER BAND

This example is the group header for group 1 in Figure 10.2 (and Figure 10.1). This header contains the field label and the custnum column. This will appear once for each customer number in the report.

Group Trailer Band

The group trailer band is where you place information that you want to follow each group in the report. This is most often used to present a calculation, usually a summation based on the subdivision of the detail records. The information in the group trailer immediately follows the set of detail records on which it is based.

There could be multiple pairs of the group bands, remember that there is one pair for each of the groups that you defined for the detail records.

FIGURE 10.8 THE GROUP TRAILER

This example is the group trailer for group 1 in Figure 10.2 (and Figure 10.1). This trailer contains a label and the sum of the extended_line columns in the detail band for one customer (custnum). This will appear once for each customer number in the report.

CHANGING THE DESIGN

You can move objects from one band to another simply by dragging the object to its new location. In Figure 10.2, the Customer Number column heading was moved from the Header band to the Group header for cust_order_custnum. The custnum column was moved from the detail band to the Group header for cust_order_custnum. You can also remove (some) bands or resize any of them. To resize a band just click on the band and drag it. Right click on the band to open the popup menu. The popup menu will let you set the color and the pointer for the band. The detail band popup menu also has a toggle called Autosize height. If you select this, it will dynamically adjust the size of the band to allow for variable height columns in the band.

The design window presents the bands and data in a manner that assist in the customization process. The bands are only used in the design mode and will not be visible in the final object. You can preview the DataWindow, to see what the actual presentation will look like. To do this select the **Design|Preview** menu option.

SAVING THE DATAWINDOW OBJECT

Choose the **File|Save** or **File|Save As** menu option to save the DataWindow object. The default prefix for DataWindow object names is **d_**. The name of the DataWindow object should reflect its purpose, or perhaps the name of the table that it accesses. If a DataWindow accesses the employee table, then you could name it d_employee or d_emp_hr_view. Be sure to first select the PowerBuilder library where you want to place the DataWindow object.

CREATING GROUPS

You can create groups in the DataWindow painter during the design process. This grouping is fundamentally different than GROUP BY (which is available in the SQL statement); and it is important to understand the difference. The grouping created in the DataWindow painter partitions the detail records into groups determined by the group expression that you define in the Specify Group dialog. This grouping does not reduce the number of rows in the display in any way. It just divides the result set into groups. Each group that you define will have a group header and a group trailer.

If you specified the grouping in the SQL GROUP BY clause, the number of rows returned in the result set will be limited to one row for each group (see the chapter on SQL Basics for a more detailed explanation).

To create a new group, choose the **Rows|Create Group** menu option. This opens the Specify Group dialog window shown in Figure 10.9.

Specify the column(s) that create the group in the Group Item Expressions field. To add additional fields, click on **Add**. You may insert a grouping column into the current list by clicking on **Insert**. This opens a new entry at the current position. To delete the current entry click on **Delete**.

At the bottom of the dialog window, you can select an option to force a new page for each group break. For example, if the grouping is by customer number and you have selected this option, the information for each customer will begin on a new page. You can also select an option to reset the page number for each group. The example in Figure 10.9 shows the criteria that were used for creating the first group for the DataWindow in Figures 10.1 and 10.2. Another group was created for the invoice number column. To create the second group, choose the **Rows|Create Group** menu option again and specify the invoice number grouping as another grouping. If you want to delete or edit a grouping, pick the number of the grouping from a cascading menu as shown in Figure 10.10.

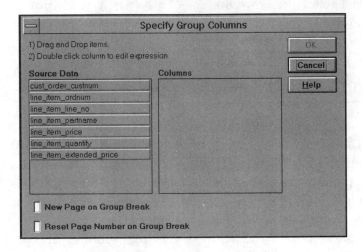

FIGURE 10.9 THE SPECIFY GROUP DIALOG

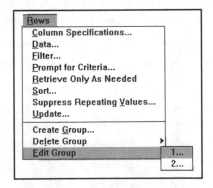

FIGURE 10.10 THE EDIT GROUP CASCADING MENU

In this case, two groups have been defined for the DataWindow. You can select either 1 or 2 in the cascading menu to edit the group definition. If you delete a group, its group header and group trailer bands will be removed from the DataWindow.

MODIFYING THE DATAWINDOW

You can modify many of the details of the DataWindow presentation including:

- object names
- fonts, field size, field location, field alignment
- set on Autosize Height for a band
- object borders
- color
- background
- add text
- change field edit styles
- format
- pointer
- query criteria
- validation
- bring to front
- send to back
- layer
- delete

Selecting DataWindow Objects

Selecting, moving, and aligning objects in the DataWindow painter is similar to how you manipulate objects in the Window painter.

You select a single control by clicking on it with the mouse. When you select a control, that control is displayed with sizing handles. When you click on another control, the previously selected control(s) is deselected. The Tab key can also be used to select a control. Each time that you hit the Tab key, the painter selects a different control in the DataWindow. The Tab key cycles through all the controls and then starts over again.

Selecting Multiple Controls

There are several ways to select a set of controls. You can do this by clicking on the first control of the set, and then Ctrl+click on each of the additional controls. Ctrl+click is a standard way to select multiple objects in Windows applications.

You can also select multiple controls by lassoing the controls with the mouse. To do this, click the mouse on the DataWindow background and then drag the mouse. This creates a "lasso" rectangle that selects all the controls that fall within (even partially) the rectangle's boundaries when you release the button. Beware of using this technique for the functions that depend on the order in which the objects are selected, since it may be difficult to determine which objects were selected first (the first selected is the bottom right object).

Selecting Objects with the Menu Option

The **Edit|Select** menu option provides another technique for selecting an object during the design process. Figure 10.11 shows the cascading menu that opens when you select this menu option.

With the following options, you can select all objects, all of the columns, or all of the text:

- **Select All**—selects all objects in the DataWindow.
- **Select Columns**—selects all of the DataWindow columns.
- **Select Text**—selects all of the labels in the DataWindow.

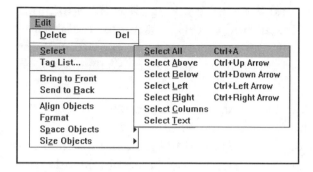

FIGURE 10.11 SELECTING A SET OF OBJECTS

The other options on this menu (Figure 10.11) select a set of objects in rela-tion to the position of the currently selected object(s). To use these options, select an object, and then select the **Edit|Select** menu option. On the cas-cading menu you can choose:

- **Select Above**—selects all objects that are located above the select-ed object.

- **Select Below**—selects all objects that are located below the select-ed object.

- **Select Left**—selects all objects located to the left of the selected object.

- **Select Right**—selects all objects located to the right of the selected object.

You can also use these functions one after another. For example, you can select all of the objects to the left and below a selected object (or objects).

Positioning and Sizing Objects

All DataWindow objects are positioned in basically the same manner, and can be moved by using either the mouse or the keyboard. To move an object with the mouse, just click within the object and drag it to its new location. To move an object with the keyboard, select the object that you wish to move, and then use the four arrow keys to position it. The keyboard method for moving objects is useful for making small adjustments to the position of a object that might be more difficult with the mouse. (The snap-to-grid option must be off to make the most precise adjustments with the keyboard).

To resize an object with the mouse, click on the object (to select it) and then use the handles that appear around the edges. Drag one of the handles until the object has reached the desired size. The handles on the corners of the object can resize the object simultaneously in two dimensions, while the other handles can only resize in one dimension (either horizontally or vertically). To use the keyboard for resizing, first select the object that you wish to resize. Then use the four arrow keys while holding the Shift key to resize the object. The movement for resizing with the keyboard is based on the bottom right handle of the object. Therefore, use the right or down arrow to make the object larger and the left or up arrow to make the object smaller.

Using the Design Grid

The DataWindow painter can display a grid of dots on the window that can help with the alignment and relative sizing of objects in the same way that the grid is used in the Window painter. You select this option by choosing the **Design|Grid...** menu option. This opens the Alignment Grid dialog window shown in Figure 10.12.

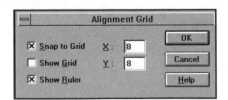

FIGURE 10.12 THE ALIGNMENT GRID DIALOG

In this dialog, you can display the grid by checking **Show Grid**. You can also set the distance between the dots (in both the horizontal and vertical planes). The default spacing between dots is eight pixels, a smaller number (like four) will give you finer resolution when placing controls.

The Snap to Grid Option

Select Snap to Grid by checking its checkbox. With Snap to Grid, the DataWindow painter creates a grid for the exact placement of objects. Any objects that you resize or move while this option is active will be placed at the dot which is nearest to the place where you release the object. This makes aligning and relatively sizing objects much easier. If you find that you need to have finer resolution in the placement of the objects, you can decrease the size of the grid cells, just enter smaller values for the X and Y grid options.

SHORTCUT

You do not have to make the grid visible to use the snap to grid option. This is something to consider if you want to speed up the display speed, since displaying the grid slows down the environment.

The Show Ruler Option

Select Show Ruler by checking its checkbox. Show Ruler displays a ruler along the top and left edges of the DataWindow painter. This ruler makes it easier to place objects during the design process, and to predict the final presentation when the report is displayed or printed. This is most useful when designing reports that will be printed on a certain size paper. The unit of measure used on this ruler is set with the DataWindow Style dialog. Open this dialog by choosing the **Design|DataWindow Style** menu option. In this dialog, you set the unit of measure to be thousands of an inch or thousands of a centimeter. This dialog is covered in more detail in the section Defining a DataWindow's Style, later in this chapter.

Using the Zoom Option

You may want to change the viewing size of the DataWindow object which you are creating. PowerBuilder lets you increase or decrease the size of the display of the DataWindow object during the design process. Selecting the **Design|Zoom** menu option opens the Zoom dialog window (Figure 10.13).

FIGURE 10.13 THE ZOOM DIALOG

In this dialog, you can set the Magnification to one of the preset percentages (200%, 100%, 65%, 30%), or you can enter a custom value in the edit field.

Using the Preview Option

Selecting the **Design|Preview** menu option, or clicking the **Preview** icon on the PainterBar presents a preview of the DataWindow's appearance at run-time (Figure 10.14). You may also toggle this option with the Control+W key combination.

   If you have defined retrieval criteria in the SELECT statement, you will be prompted for these values when you enter preview mode. When you are in preview mode, the DataWindow painter removes the **Preview** icon and adds a **Design** icon to the PainterBar. Clicking on this icon returns you to design mode.

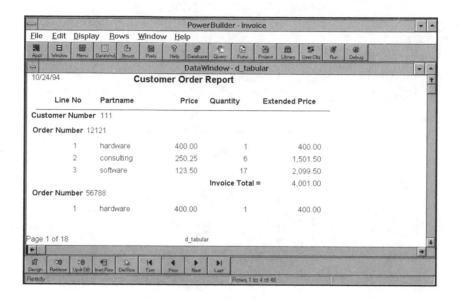

FIGURE 10.14 PREVIEWING A DATAWINDOW OBJECT

Aligning Objects with the Alignment Function

The DataWindow painter provides a function to automatically align a set of selected objects. To do this, select a set of objects using one of the methods described above. When you select the objects, you must first select the object that you want to use to govern the alignment of the other objects. After you have selected the objects to be aligned, choose the **Edit|Align Objects** menu option. This displays the align objects cascading menu (Figure 10.15).

You have six choices for aligning objects, three in the vertical plane, and three in the horizontal. You can choose to align the objects in the following manners (listed in the top down order in which they appear in the cascading menu of Figure 10.15):

Align Vertically

- by the left edge
- centering the objects
- by the right edge

Align Horizontally

- by the top edge
- centering the objects
- by the bottom edge

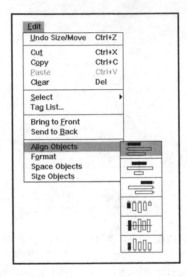

FIGURE 10.15 THE ALIGN OBJECTS CASCADING MENU

Remember that the order in which you select the objects determines the result. Be sure to first select the object that is already in the correct position. After you use this function to align the objects, the objects still remain selected, so that you can reposition the entire group. To do this, just click and drag any one of the selected objects, the entire set will move as you drag that object. To deselect the group, click somewhere else in the DataWindow or just press **Tab**.

Adjusting the Spacing of Objects

The DataWindow painter can automatically adjust the spacing between a set of selected objects. To do this, first select a set of objects in the same manner as was described earlier in this chapter. In this case, it is also important to select the objects in a specific order because the distance between the first two objects that you select will be the spacing that is applied to the other selected objects. So the procedure is to first set up two adjacent objects with the correct spacing. Then Ctrl+click select the objects that are to be spaced similarly.

After you have selected the set of objects, select the **Edit|Space Objects** menu option to display the cascading menu shown in Figure 10.16. You can set the spacing of the selected objects in either the horizontal or vertical dimension.

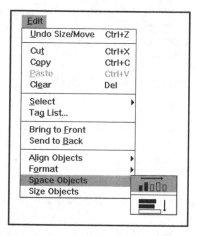

FIGURE 10.16 THE SPACE OBJECTS CASCADING MENU

The top option in the cascading menu spaces the objects horizontally, based on the distance between the first two objects selected. The second option spaces objects vertically.

Automatically Sizing of Objects

The DataWindow painter can automatically adjust the size of a set of selected objects to match that of a model object. To do this, first select the object that has the correct size (in either the horizontal or vertical plane) that you wish applied to the other object(s). Then Ctrl+click the rest of the objects that you want to size.

After you have selected the set of objects, select the **Edit|Size Objects** menu option. This displays the cascading menu shown in Figure 10.17.

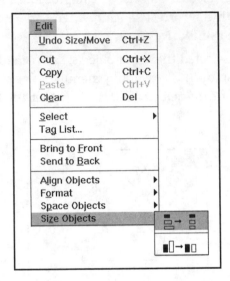

FIGURE 10.17 SIZING OBJECTS

You can size the object(s) in either the horizontal or vertical dimension. Select the first option on the cascading menu to size the selected objects to the horizontal size of the first object that was selected. Select the second option to vertically size the objects. You could, of course, size the object(s) in both dimensions by selecting both these functions, one after the other. You will apply the sizing option most often to a set of fields or labels.

The Style Toolbar and Color Bar

In the DataWindow painter, you can display two additional toolbars: the style toolbar and the color bar. The style toolbar displays and lets you change the attributes of the text used on the DataWindow. This include attributes such as the font name, and various options such as underlining, italics, bold, and justification. The color bar presents a palette of the color choices for the design process. Figure 10.18 shows all four toolbars.

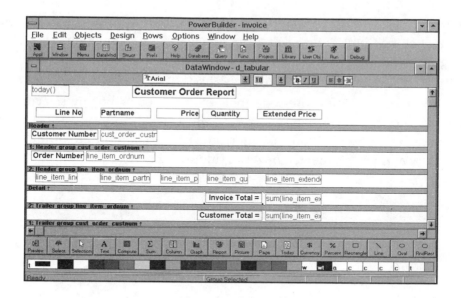

FIGURE 10.18 THE STYLE TOOLBAR AND COLOR BAR

To show (display) these toolbars select the **Window|Toolbars...** menu option. This opens the Toolbars dialog window (Figure 10.19) where you can choose to show, hide, or relocate any of the toolbars, or customize the contents of the PowerBar and PainterBar.

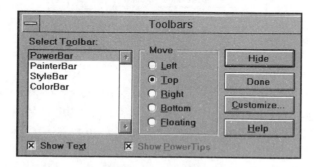

FIGURE 10.19 THE TOOLBARS DIALOG

You can display the PowerBar or PainterBar toolbars at the top, bottom, left, or right of the DataWindow painter, or as a floating (repositionable) box. The floating toolbar option is helpful for the PainterBar in the DataWindow painter because of the large number of icons contained within it.

You can reposition the style toolbar or the color bar by selecting a menu option. To reposition the style toolbar, select the **Options|Text Style Toolbar** menu option. You can attach the style toolbar to the frame or to the DataWindow painter as shown in Figure 10.20

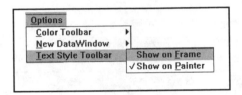

FIGURE 10.20 THE TEXT STYLE TOOLBAR MENU OPTION

To reposition the color bar, select the **Options|Color Toolbar** menu option (Figure 10.21).

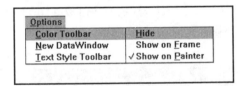

FIGURE 10.21 THE COLOR TOOLBAR MENU OPTION

You can attach the color toolbar to the frame or to the DataWindow painter. When you add the color bar, you can set the color of any selected objects in the DataWindow. First select the object(s) for which you are going to set the color. Then right mouse click on the color (on the color bar) that you want to use for the object's text, and right mouse click on a color to set the object's background color. The left most cell of the color bar will show the current foreground and background colors.

Setting the Tab Order

In the DataWindow painter, you can set the tab order for the objects in the same way that you set the tab order for the controls in a window in the Window painter. Select the **Design|Tab Order** menu option to toggle on (or off) the tab order mode. In tab order mode, each object is displayed with an integer value that represents its tab order. Figure 10.22 shows the DataWindow in tab order mode.

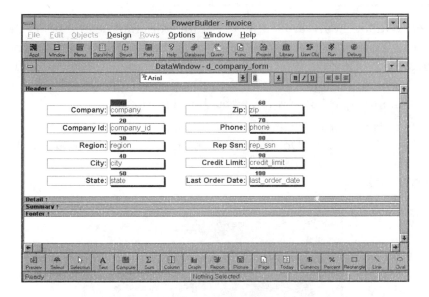

FIGURE 10.22 SETTING THE TAB ORDER

The tab order determines which object is selected when the user presses the Tab key at run-time. The object that is selected (receives the focus) is the object with the next highest tab value. After the highest value object has been selected, the selection cycles through the series again. If you don't wish an object to have the focus (such as fields that cannot be edited), set the tab order to 0 for that object. Not all objects in the DataWindow have a tab order, it only applies to objects that the user may need to select.

When you enter tab order mode, the values are initially presented with an increment of 10 between each value. This lets you enter values between

411

existing values to change the tab order. If you exit and then reenter tab order mode, you will notice that the values have been renumbered with a increment of ten. You can set the tab order of objects with the SetTabOrder function (or with the dwModify function for Tabsequence, though this is an advanced technique).

DEFINING A DATAWINDOW'S STYLE

A DataWindow has a large number of properties that determine its characteristics. These properties define the style of the DataWindow and are controlled in the DataWindow's style dialog. Select the **Design|DataWindow Style...** menu option from the Window painter menu. This opens the DataWindow Style dialog window, as shown in Figure 10.23.

There is also a shortcut to the DataWindow Style dialog window: just double-click within the DataWindow. You must be sure to actually click on the window area and avoid the objects that have been placed in the DataWindow.

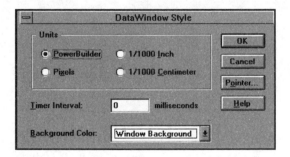

FIGURE 10.23 THE DATAWINDOW STYLE DIALOG

In this dialog, you can set the unit of measure to PowerBuilder Units (PBUs), pixels, thousandths of an inch, or thousandths of a centimeter. You can also set the timer interval in milliseconds. This attribute controls how often the time is updated in this DataWindow. This applies to objects that use time in a DataWindow. The default (if left at 0) is 1 minute

(60,000 milliseconds). You can set the background color of the DataWindow by using the listbox at the bottom of the style dialog.

If you click on the **Pointer** CommandButton, the DataWindow painter opens the Select Pointer dialog window. In this dialog (Figure 10.24), you can select the icon that will be used when the pointer is over the DataWindow.

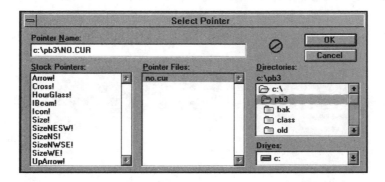

FIGURE 10.24 THE SELECT POINTER DIALOG

In this dialog, you can choose to use a stock pointer, or you can use a cursor bitmap file (.CUR file). The dialog shows you the currently selected icon in the area just to the left of the OK button.

ADDING COMPUTED FIELDS

One of the powerful features of DataWindows is the ability to add computed fields. Computed fields perform a computation within the DataWindow. The calculation is updated as the data in the DataWindow changes. When you add a computed field to your DataWindow, you must define an expression that specifies the computation that is to take place to determine the field's value. In this expression, you can use functions, constants, other columns, and the set of arithmetic operators. The functions that are used here are the PowerScript functions (not SQL functions), since the calculations are done in the DataWindow not on the database server. You can also use user-defined global functions in these computed fields.

Computed fields are useful for calculating values such as the minimum, maximum, average, or a count for a group or the entire result set. They can also be used to concatenate two or more fields into one field.

To add a computed column to a DataWindow, click on the **Compute** icon on the PainterBar or select the **Objects|Computed Field** menu option to add a computed field to the DataWindow. Next click on the DataWindow at the point where you want to place the computed field. This opens the Computed Field Definition dialog window (Figure 10.25).

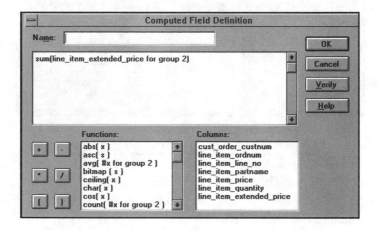

FIGURE 10.25 DEFINING A COMPUTED FIELD

In this dialog, you must enter the expression for the computed column. You can paste functions, columns, or operators into the expression using the controls at the bottom of the dialog. You can refer to a column value in a specific row by using an integer argument with the column name. The integer gives the position of the required row, relative to the current position in the DataWindow. For example, line_item_quantity[–2] is a reference to the value of line_item_quantity in the row which is two rows prior to the current position. line_item_quantity[0] is a reference to the same column in the current row. Line_item_quantity[+3] is a reference to the column in the row which is three rows after the current row.

You can also enter a name for the computed column in this dialog. If you name the column, you can reference the column in your PowerScript code. There are many examples of where this is useful. See the INVOICE example program for such a reference.

After you have defined the expression, you can have PowerBuilder validate the expression. Click on **Verify** and you will receive a message that the *Expression is OK* or that the *Expression is not valid*. When you are finished, click on **OK**; this closes the dialog.

DBMS Computations versus DataWindow Computations

As with grouping, you must understand the difference between computations that are performed in the DataWindow and computations that are performed by the DBMS. Assume that you need to create a report that listed each customer and the total dollar amount of all invoices associated with each customer. You could do this in at least two ways. First you could create a DataWindow with the following SQL SELECT statement as its data source.

```
SELECT "cust_order"."custnum",
       "line_item"."extended_price"
    FROM "cust_order",
       "line_item"
   WHERE ( "cust_order"."ordnum" = "line_item"."ordnum" )
ORDER BY "cust_order"."custnum" ASC;
```

You then create a group in the DataWindow painter on the custnum column. In the group trailer band for custnum you add a computed field with the expression:

```
sum(line_item_extended_price for group 1)
```

This is similar to a calculation in the DataWindow shown in Figure 10.1. What occurs in this example, is that the rows of the invoices are returned sorted by custnum. Each time custnum changes, it creates a new group in the DataWindow. The DataWindow totals the amount off the extended_price fields for each group and displays it following the group. Two points are important: first, all of the invoice line_item rows are returned in the result set, and second, the actual calculation is done in the DataWindow (on the client machine).

The other alternative would be to create a DataWindow using the following SQL SELECT statement:

```
SELECT "cust_order"."custnum",
       sum("line_item"."extended_price")
    FROM "cust_order",
         "line_item"
  WHERE ( "cust_order"."ordnum" = "line_item"."ordnum" )
GROUP BY "cust_order"."custnum" ASC;
```

In this case, the DBMS returns only one row for each custnum. Each row contains two fields, custnum and the total for the extended_price column for all the invoices associated with that custnum. Note the difference in the number of records returned to this DataWindow, and that the computations have taken place on the database server instead of on the client.

Which method you choose depends on several considerations. If the requirement is only to return the customer number and the total invoice sums for each, then you should choose the second method. This could reduce the number of records that have to be retrieved and avoid the expense of performing the computations on the client.

If, on the other hand, you have a requirement to display each of the invoice totals in addition to the customer totals, or if you must be able to add or modify rows to the DataWindow and then recalculate the totals, then the first method is required.

Predefined Calculated Fields

PowerBuilder provides several objects that you can add to your DataWindows that are actually calculated fields of various types. These include the following:

- **Average**—calculates the average value for a given set.
- **Count**—counts the number of items.
- **Sum**—calculates the total amount.
- **Page**—displays the current page number.
- **Today**—displays today's date.

To add an average, count, or sum object, click on one of the columns in the DataWindow, then select the function that you want from the Objects menu. The Sum object is also available as an icon on the PainterBar.

The Computed Field Definition dialog opens as shown in Figure 10.25. The expression used to calculate the average of the extended_price column in each group is:

```
avg(line_item_extended_price for group 1)
    // or group 2 if there are 2 groups
```

The Sum computed field is very handy, and is actually a shortcut for creating a computed column to do the same calculation. If you click on a column in a detail band, and then click on the **Sum** icon, a Sum computed field is added to the summary band (or the group trailer band if a group has been defined).

The Page and Today objects are easier to use. Just select them from the Objects menu, or click on the **Page** or **Today** icon on the PainterBar, then click at the point in the DataWindow where you want to insert the object. These objects are generally placed in the header or footer bands of a report.

FILTERING AND SORTING

You can filter and sort data in the SQL SELECT statement using the WHERE clause and the ORDER BY clause. However, there may be times when you want to filter and sort data that is already in the DataWindow. As a matter of fact, the filtering and sorting functions in DataWindows are often reason enough to use DataWindows for the presentation of data that doesn't even come from a database. These functions are probably more useful at run-time, when you can dynamically restrict the rows displayed in the DataWindow and/or sort the DataWindow in one or more of its columns. The dynamic uses of these functions is covered in the next chapter on DataWindow controls. The next sections discuss how to use these functions in the DataWindow painter at design time.

Filtering DataWindow Rows

To set the filter criteria for the DataWindow, select the **Rows|Filter** menu option in the DataWindow painter. This opens the Specify Filter dialog window (Figure 10.26).

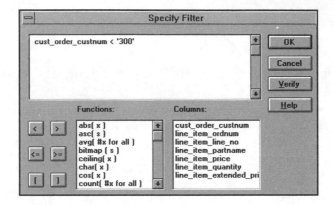

Figure 10.26 Defining a DataWindow filter

In this dialog, you must enter the expression for the filter condition. You can paste functions, columns, or operators into the expression using the controls at the bottom of the dialog. When you have completed the expression click on **Verify** to validate the expression.

Sorting DataWindow Rows

To set the sort criteria for the DataWindow, select the **Rows|Sort** menu option in the DataWindow painter. This opens the Specify Sort Columns dialog window (Figure 10.27).

In this dialog, you specify the columns that determine the sort order. You can add columns to the criteria by clicking on **Add**. To insert an item within the current list, select the position and then click on **Insert**. You can select the column name from the listbox which contains the names of all the columns in the DataWindow.

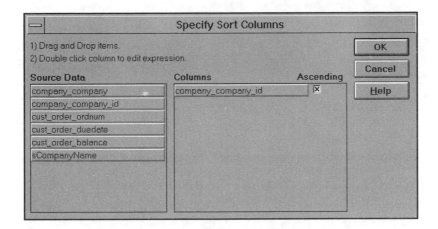

FIGURE 10.27 SETTING A SORT ORDER

To remove an item, select it and then click on **Delete**. Click on **Delete All** to remove all items from the list.

Suppressing Repeating Values

You can suppress repeating values in one or more DataWindow columns to improve the appearance and the readability of a report. For example, look at the DataWindow in Figure 10.28. This is a list of the invoice line items by company and order number. The next example, Figure 10.29, is exactly the same information but repeating values in the company, company ID, and order number fields have been suppressed. The improvement in appearance should be obvious, and that result is easily achieved. One note, if the fields that are suppressed have a tab order value greater than zero, the values will be displayed on the screen when the user tabs to the field even though the values are suppressed.

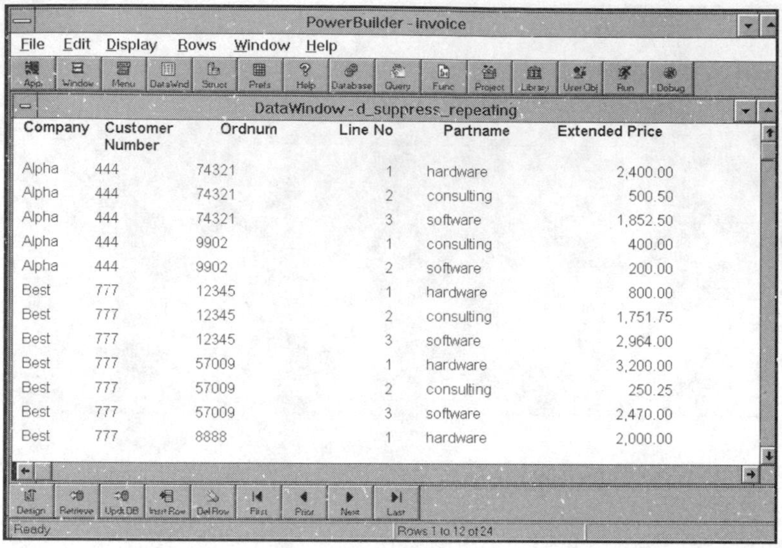

FIGURE 10.28 A SAMPLE DATAWINDOW

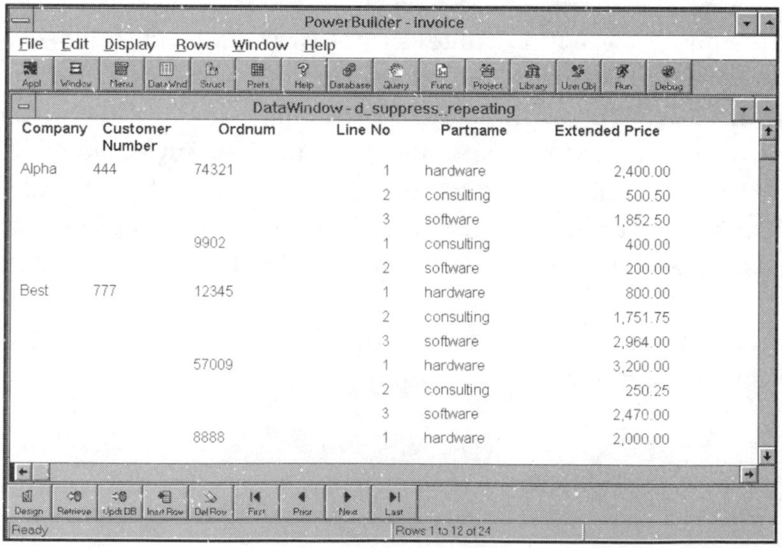

FIGURE 10.29 SUPPRESSING REPEATED VALUES

When you choose to suppress a repeating value, the value displays at the start of each new page and, if you are using group levels, each time a value changes in a higher group level.

To suppress repeating values in a DataWindow select the **Rows|Suppress Repeating Values** menu option. That opens the Specify Repeating Value Suppression List dialog box (Figure 10.30).

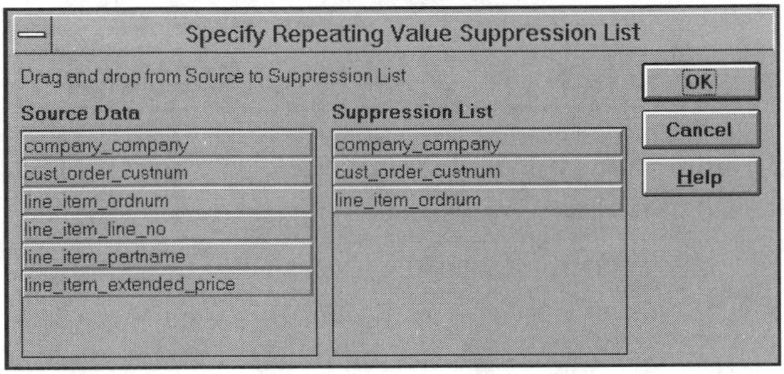

FIGURE 10.30 SUPPRESSING REPEATING VALUES

In this dialog, select the columns (or objects) for which you want to suppress repeating values. Each time you click on an item in the lower listbox, the item is added to the list. To deselect an item from the list, just click the name of the column (or graphic object) in the lower listbox. When you have completed the list, click on **OK** to return to the DataWindow painter. Use the preview mode to see the result of your specification. To cancel the suppression completely click on **Clear All**; this deselects all columns that are currently in the list.

Adding Database Columns

To add another column to the DataWindow, click on the **Column** icon on the PainterBar or select the **Objects|Column** menu option. Then click in the DataWindow at the position where you want to place the column. This opens the Select Column dialog (Figure 10.31).

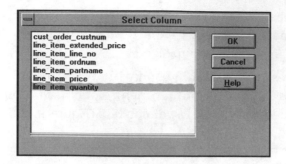

FIGURE 10.31 ADDING A COLUMN TO A DATAWINDOW

Select the column from this dialog, and then click on **OK** to add the column to the DataWindow.

Update Characteristics

You may have noticed that when you define a DataWindow you are only required to define a SQL SELECT statement. But as you have seen, besides retrieving rows from the database, a DataWindow can also insert, update, and delete rows against the database. The INSERT, UPDATE, and DELETE statements are generated automatically by the DataWindow Update() function that will be covered in detail in the next chapter on DataWindow controls. The details that are necessary for creating these additional SQL statement are called Update Characteristics. These details are usually handled automatically by PowerBuilder, and often you will not have to deal with these details. There will be times when you will need to change the default behavior that has been defined by the DataWindow. How to specify those update characteristics is the topic of this section.

Select the **Rows|Specify Update Characteristics** menu option and PowerBuilder opens the Specify Update Characteristics dialog window (Figure 10.32).

This dialog determines whether or not a table can be updated and if it can, it determines how that update is handled. If you do not want to allow the DataWindow to perform updates to the database, you can uncheck the Allow Update option. Normally, for single table queries, the Allow Update option is checked by default—if a unique key is chosen or if the table had a primary key and you selected all the columns that make up that key. For multiple table queries the Allow Update option is unchecked.

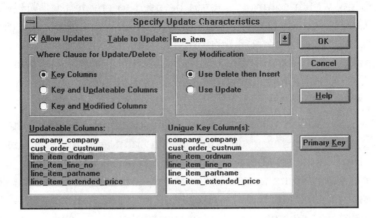

FIGURE 10.32 SETTING UPDATE CHARACTERISTICS

The SELECT statement for this example (Figure 10.32) uses a join between two tables (Company and Line_item); Allow Update was initially unchecked when this dialog was opened. To allow updates, click on the **Allow Update** checkbox. This is required before any of the Update Characteristics in this dialog can be changed. The next step is to select the line_item table from the Table to Update listbox.

In this dialog, only one table can be selected for update, you can programatically allow the update of multiple tables.

N O T E

In the Updateable Columns ListBox, you can select the columns that may be updated and deselect the columns which may not be updated. Initially, all the column names are highlighted (for single table queries). You should also change the tab value to 0 for the columns for which you are not allowing updates.

In the Unique Key Columns listbox, you can change the unique key column selections for the DataWindow object or select another unique key.

If you click on the **Primary Key**, all changes are canceled and the fields in the Primary key are selected.

In the Where Clause for Update/Delete groupbox, you tell the DataWindow which columns should be used to create the WHERE clause for the SQL Update or Delete statements that are automatically generated when you call the Update() function. The choices here are to use just the Key Columns, the Key, and Updateable Columns, or the Key and Modified Columns. Generally Key and Updateable will provide the most stringent data integrity.

In the Key Modification groupbox, you specify the method that is used to update rows when the update involves a change to one (or more) of the columns that make up the primary key. Some DBMSs will not allow you update a column value that belongs to the primary key. In that case you should select the **Use Delete then Insert** radiobutton. In this case, PowerBuilder first deletes the original row that you are changing and then inserts the new version of the row. This may not be acceptable in all cases; if you have a DBMS that supports cascading deletes, it is possible to lose records when you delete a row.

COLUMN ATTRIBUTES

This section discusses attributes that are common between column styles.

The Column Popup Menu

If you right click on a column (in the DataWindow painter), the popup menu will display a list of options, some of which will be new to you.

The items in the popup menu are:

- **Autosize Height**—if you have an object that varies in size (such as a variable length string), you can select this option to automatically resize the column's height as necessary. For this to work you must also check the Autosize Height option on the detail band,

and turn off the Auto H Scroll option and the AutoVScroll on in the edit style for the column.

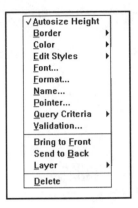

FIGURE 10.33 THE COLUMN POPUP MENU

- **Border**—selects the type of border to be used for this column.

- **Color**—sets the background and text colors for this column.

- **Edit Styles**—selects a column edit style as covered below in the section Column Edit Styles.

- **Font**—opens the Font dialog, where you can specify the font characteristics for the text in this column.

- **Name**—opens the Column Name dialog, where you can specify a DataWindow name for the column. All columns should be referenced by name, not by number since the number could change as you modify the DataWindow object. If you later add a column to your SELECT statement, you will need to name using this option.

- **Pointer**—selects the pointer icon to be used when the pointer is over this column.

- **Query Criteria**—lets you control two details when you are using the DataWindow query mode (described in the next chapter). If you select Equality Required the user can only user equality in the query specification. If you select Override Edit, the user will not be limited the the length of the database column in the QBE cell.

425

- **Validation**—opens the Column Validation dialog, where you can specify a PowerScript expression to be used for validation.

- **Bring to Front**—moves this object to the front of other overlapping objects.

- **Send to Back**—moves this object to the back of other overlapping objects.

- **Delete**—removes this object from the window.

Using Autosize Height

If you have a column that varies in size (such as a variable length string), select this option to automatically resize the column's height as necessary. For this to work you must also check the **Autosize Height** option on the detail band and turn off the **AutoHScroll** option and turn on the **AutoVScroll** option in the edit style for the column. If you do not select the Autosize Height option for detail band the results will be truncated as shown in Figure 10.34.

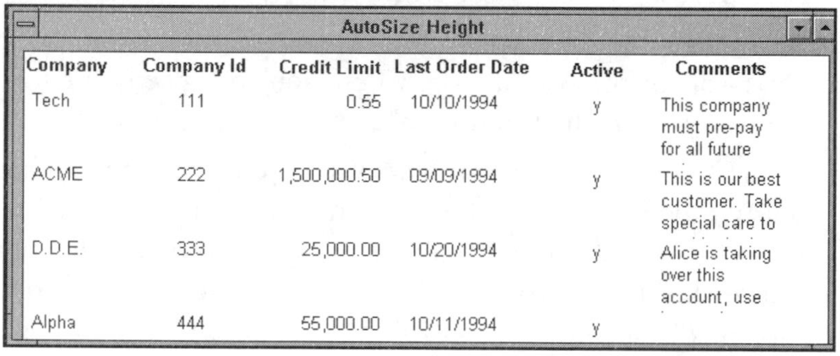

Company	Company Id	Credit Limit	Last Order Date	Active	Comments
Tech	111	0.55	10/10/1994	y	This company must pre-pay for all future
ACME	222	1,500,000.50	09/09/1994	y	This is our best customer. Take special care to
D.D.E.	333	25,000.00	10/20/1994	y	Alice is taking over this account, use
Alpha	444	55,000.00	10/11/1994	y	

FIGURE 10.34 THE COMMENTS HAVE BEEN TRUNCATED

Notice that the comments fields has been sized to be three lines in height. If the text is too large to fit in three lines, it will be truncated as in this example. If you set the Autosize Height option for the detail band, the size of the band adjusts automatically as shown in Figure 10.35.

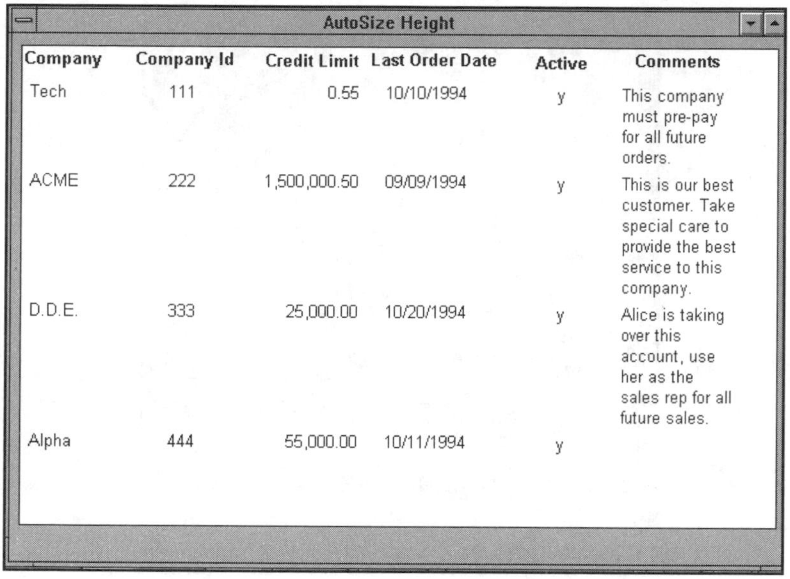

FIGURE 10.35 USING A VARIABLE HEIGHT FIELD

Notice that the complete text for each comment is now visible. The first comment has five lines, the next two have six lines. The band is expanded to allow the correct amount of space for this field.

Using Column Validation

Most often you define validation criteria in the Database painter (see the chapter on the Database painter for details). You may however, choose to define validation criteria for a column in the DataWindow painter. To do so, select the **Validation** option from the popup menu to open the Column Validation Definition dialog (Figure 10.36).

In this dialog, you enter a Boolean PowerScript expression for the column validation. You can paste functions, columns, or operators into the expression using the controls at the bottom of the dialog. You can refer to columns outside of the column that is being validated. In this example, the value in the active column must be either *y* or *n*.

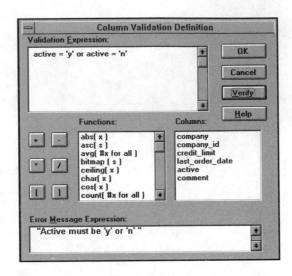

FIGURE 10.36 DEFINING COLUMN VALIDATION

COLUMN EDIT STYLES

As a default, each column is given an edit style of Edit when it is added to a DataWindow. This works well for most columns, and is certainly the most common choice, but DataWindows provide a wide range of edit style choices for the columns. The column edit style controls the display of data and the manner in which the user interacts with the data. Select the **Edit Style** option from the popup menu (click the right mouse button on a column) to see the choices for column edit styles (Figure 10.37).

The column edit styles are CheckBox, DropDownDataWindow, DropDownListBox, Edit, EditMask, and RadioButton. There is also an option called Display As Bitmap. The first five of these are familiar to you as control types in the Window painter (Edit is essentially a SingleLineEdit). The two others are specific to DataWindows. The DropDownDataWindow is a powerful control that is used to present a list of values for one column of a DataWindow that is derived from the data in another DataWindow. The Display As Bitmap option lets you display images in the DataWindow, similar to how a picture control works. Currently you can only display images that have a file type of BMP and RLE. This last option is only available for certain data types, it will be disabled for data types that can not be used.

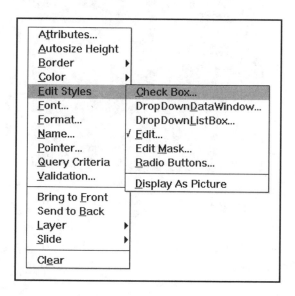

FIGURE 10.37 SETTING THE COLUMN EDIT STYLE

You can also define code tables when using DropDownListBox, CheckBoxes, RadioButtons, or Edit. You don't have to define a code table for a DropDownDataWindow, by default it works like one.

The Default Edit Style

The default edit style (Edit) for a column is basically a SingleLineEdit. If you select the Edit option from the cascading menu in Figure 10.37, the Edit Style dialog will open (Figure 10.38).

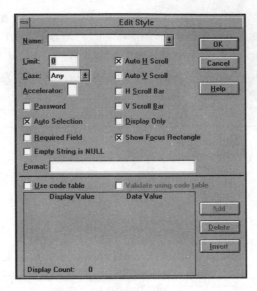

FIGURE 10.38 THE EDIT STYLE DIALOG

In the dialog, you can set the most important attributes for the style. The attributes of the Edit style that you can set in this dialog are:

- **Name**—assigns a previously-defined edit style to this object by selecting it from the dropdown listbox.

- **Limit**—the maximum number of characters that can be entered in this SingleLineEdit (0 means no limit).

- **Case**—controls the case of the input text. The choices are Any, lower, and UPPER.

- **Accelerator**—defines a keyboard accelerator for the SingleLineEdit in this field. Enter a character (a, b, etc.) that will be used in conjunction with the Alt key to place the focus in this field.

- **Password**—this option is useful for accepting passwords and other sensitive information in the SingleLineEdit. Checking this box causes the edit field to echo asterisks (*) as text is typed into the field, instead of displaying the actual text.

- **Required Field**—check this if the user must make an entry in this field. If this is checked, the user will not be able to tab away from this field without making an entry.

- **Empty String is NULL**—if this is checked, the DataWindow interprets an empty string in this field to represent a NULL value.

- **AutoHScroll**—if True, this activates automatic scrolling (horizontally) to let the user enter text that is wider than the size of the control.

- **AutoVScroll**—if True, this activates automatic scrolling (vertically) to let the user enter multiple lines of text.

- **H Scroll Bar**—check this option to add a horizontal scroll bar to this object (as needed).

- **V Scroll Bar**—check this option to add a vertical scroll bar to this object (as needed).

- **Display Only**—check this to use the field for display purposes only. This makes the field read-only, and will not let the user enter or change the text in the field, but the text can still be selected (highlighted) to cut or copy to the clipboard.

- **Show Focus Rectangle**—check this to display a rectangle around the object when it has the focus.

- **Format**—in this field you can add a format string to be used with the GetText() function. The GetText() function is covered in the next chapter.

You could use a code table to map column data values to display values by selecting the **Use Code Table** option. With this option, you enumerate a list of values in a code table. You must specify each possible value in the list. Click **Add** to add a new item at the bottom of the list, **Delete** to remove the current item, and **Insert** to insert an item at the current position in the list. The data value is the value actually read from or written to the database, while the corresponding display values are presented to the user in the object. The Data Value is optional, if you do not make an entry in that column, the Data Value will be the same as the Display Value.

With a code table, you can also use the **Validate using Code Table** option. With this option selected, the user can only enter values that are in the Code Table. If the user makes an entry that is not in the table and then tries to tab away from the field, the user receives an error message, and focus returns to the field.

EditMask Style

The EditMask style is very similar to the SingleLineEdit style, but it has a fixed format built into its definition. Examples of common required formats are phone numbers, Social Security numbers, or date and time. This control is used like a SingleLineEdit, but to format data that is displayed by, and input into, the field.

The actual edit mask consists of a number of special characters that determine what can be entered in the field. The exact characters that are used vary according to the data type of the data being entered.

For a number:

> **#**—represents a digit.
>
> **0**—represents a required digit.

For a string:

> **#**—represents a digit.
>
> **!**—represents an upper case character.
>
> **^**—represents a lower case character.
>
> **a**—represents any alpha-numeric character.
>
> **x**—allows any character.

Any other characters in the edit mask will be taken literally as punctuation characters used for presentation. For example, the edit mask (###) ###-#### works for phone numbers, and ###-##-#### is a Social Security number. !!## allows two upper case characters followed by two digits, and **dd/mm/yyyy** is a typical date format.

The Edit Mask style dialog is shown in Figure 10.39. In this case, the predefined EditMask company_phone was selected from the Name listbox. This mask was defined in the Database painter (see the chapter on the Database painter for more details).

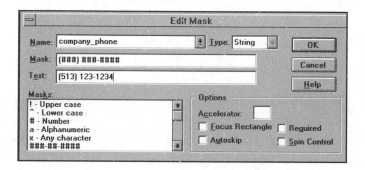

FIGURE 10.39 DEFINING AN EDIT MASK

- **Name**—assigns a previously-defined edit style to this object by selecting it from the dropdown listbox.
- **Type**—specifies the data type. This can be String, Number, Date, Time, or Datetime, the type is determined by the datatype of the column.
- **Mask**—enters the actual edit mask in this field. Use the values in the Masks ListBox (the contents will change according to the data type).

This dialog also contains a test box where you can enter test values and see the results of the mask that you have specified.

The final options are:

- **Accelerator**—sets the character that is to be used in conjunction with the Alt key as the keyboard accelerator.
- **Focus Rectangle**—click on this to display the focus rectangle on this field when it has the focus.

- **AutoSkip**—causes the focus to jump to the next control in the tab order, when the user has entered the maximum number of characters in this field.

- **Required**—if you check this, this will be a required field. The user will not be able to leave this field (once entered it) without making an entry.

- **Spin Control**—creates a spin control style control.

RadioButton

Use the RadioButton edit style to select an option from a small set of choices. RadioButtons are grouped together in a groupbox. Only one of the RadioButtons in a group can be selected (checked) at a time. RadioButtons in a group are managed automatically: when you click one of the buttons it will be checked and the others in the group will be unchecked. You must assign a text (Display Value) to label each RadioButton; you place the text on either the left or the right of the button.

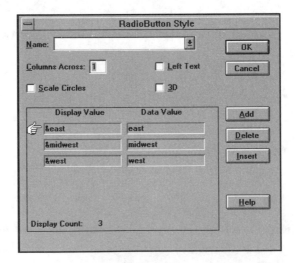

FIGURE 10.40 THE RADIOBUTTON STYLE

The attributes of the RadioButton style are:

- **Name**—assigns a previously-defined edit style to this object by selecting it from the dropdown listbox.

- **Columns Across**—an integer, this is the number of columns used to present the RadioButtons. The default is 1.

- **LeftText**—a Boolean, is True if the text appears to the left of the button, otherwise the text appears to the right of the button.

- **Scale Circles**—scales the size of the radio buttons to the size of the text.

- **3D**—gives radio buttons a three-dimensional appearance.

The label for each RadioButton is entered in the Display Value column. The actual database value for each RadioButton is entered in the Data Value column.

Click on **OK** and the style is changed to the RadioButton style. You then have to resize the control to display the buttons.

DropDownListBox Style

A DropDownListBox combines a SingleLineEdit with a listbox. The listbox portion of the control can be dropped down (displayed) or can be closed. The DropDownListBox can be used to display a read-only list for the user to choose from, or it can be setup to allow the input of new values not in the list. To select an item in the list, use the scroll bar to locate and then click on the item. Use the up and down arrow keys to scroll through the list, this will select an item as it scrolls.

If the DropDownListBox is set for display-only, a search option is provided for items in the list. The listbox portion displays entries that match the letter that is typed into the SingleLineEdit part of the control. This matches only on the first letter of the items in the list, if there is more than one item beginning with a character, you can cycle through the items that match in the list by repeating the keystroke. You can also use the up and down arrow keys to move through the list while in the edit field.

If you select the DropDownListBox style the following dialog opens:

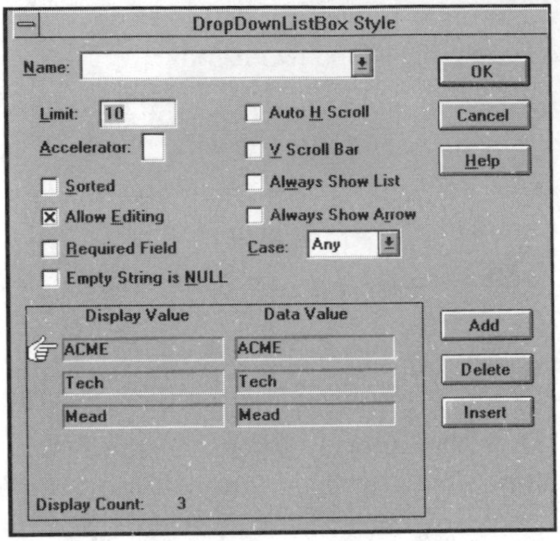

FIGURE 10.41 THE DROPDOWNLISTBOX STYLE

The DropDownListBox style dialog is almost the same as the style dialog for the listbox. In this dialog you can change the name of the control. The set of checkboxes is used to set some of the most important attributes.

DropDownListBox Attributes

The attributes of a DropDownListBox style are:

- **Name**—assigns a previously-defined edit style to this object by selecting it from the dropdown listbox. Use an existing edit style as a starting point by selecting its name from this list. After you make a modification to the style, the link to the source style is broken and the Name field is blank.

- **Limit**—specifies the maximum number of characters that can be entered for an new entry (for an editable type control).

- **Accelerator**—to assign an accelerator to this control, enter the character value in this field.

- **Sorted**—checking this attribute alphabetically sorts the list.

- **Allow Editing**—check this to make this an editable dropdown listbox.

- **Required Field**—check this if the user must make an entry in this field. If this is checked, the user will not be able to tab away from this field without making an entry.

- **Empty String is NULL**—if this is checked, the DataWindow will interpret an empty string in this field to represent a NULL value.

- **Always Show List**—causes the listbox portion of the control to always be dropped-down and visible *when that column has focus*. If this is not checked the user must click the down arrow to display the list.

- **Always Show Arrow**—causes the listbox to display the down arrow at all times. If this is not checked, the arrow only appears whenever the field has the focus.

You use a code table to map column data values. You enumerate a list of values in a code table and must specify each possible value in the list. Click **Add** to add a new item at the bottom of the list, **Delete** to remove the current item, and **Insert** to insert an item at the current position in the list. The data value is the value actually read from, or written to, the database, while the corresponding display values are presented to the user in the object.

When you click on **OK** the DropDownListBox style is applied to the field. You must size this object (in the DataWindow painter) to represent the size that you want for the ListBox portion of this control when it drops down. If you size this larger than the number of entries in the drop-down portion, it will default to the size needed for the entries.

DropDownDataWindow Style

The DropDownDataWindow style is a very powerful and useful style. It connects a column in the DataWindow with a pair of columns in another DataWindow object. The other DataWindow object is called a

DropDownDataWindow object. Pay careful attention to the terms used here. The DataWindow under-construction is referred to as the local DataWindow to clarify this discussion. One of the columns in the local DataWindow has the DropDownDataWindow style, and refers to another source DataWindow object called the DropDownDataWindow object.

A column with a DropDownDataWindow style, is similar to one with the DropDownListBox style, but the display and data values originate in the database via the DropDownDataWindow object. This is most useful in the case where you want to limit the user's choices for a column's input values, but the list changes from time to time, or is too large to be embedded in a DropDownListBox. For example, the employee table has a column called *Department*. The list of departments can be stored in another table (the Department table) and the DropDownDataWindow style provides a current list of departments to the user when they need to enter the department for an employee. In an example included with this book, we use a DropDownDataWindow style to provide a list of the states in the Company table. In that case we also do some filtering based on the region where the company is located, to limit the list of states to those that are in that region.

Previously (prior to PowerBuilder 3.0), this type of relationship had to be implemented through a separate routine and took a great deal of work to create this type of object. Now it is available as a column style, and is dramatically easier to implement.

In order to use this style for a column, you must have previously-defined the DropDownDataWindow object that will be used as the source for the column. Usually that DataWindow object has to be defined with two columns, the first (left-most) column should be the display values for the column in the local DataWindow. The second column usually serves as the data values for the local DataWindow. The column used for the data value must match the datatype of the local DataWindow object column.

You must create the presentation of the source DataWindow as you want it to be displayed in the dropdown listbox portion of the object. You can control the width of the DropDownDataWindow to control the display of the list. The height is determined automatically. The display column should be the first (left-most) column in the DropDownDataWindow object, because this is what is displayed in the dropdown portion of the column. Regardless of the column that you enter in the Display Column field of the DropDownDataWindow Edit Style dialog, the first column will be displayed.

To define the attributes of this style, open the DropDownDataWindow Edit Style dialog (Figure 10.42).

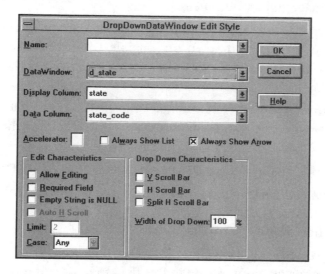

FIGURE 10.42 DEFINING A DROPDOWNDATAWINDOW

The attributes of a DropDownDataWindow are:

- **Name**—assigns a previously-defined edit style to this object by selecting it from the dropdown listbox. Use an existing edit style as a starting point by selecting its name from this list. After you make a modification to the style, the link to the source style is broken and the Name field will be blank.

- **DataWindow**—this is the name of the source DataWindow object. Select the name from the dropdown listbox.

- **Display Column**—the column in the source DataWindow that is to be used for the display. This column's values are displayed in the line edit portion of the DropDownDataWindow when you select a row in the DropDownDataWindow.

- **Data Column**—the column in the source DataWindow that is to be used for the data values. This column's values will be used as the data value that is actually stored in the database for the column when you update the data source for the local DataWindow.

- **Accelerator**—to assign an accelerator to this control, enter the character value in this field.

- **Always Show List**—causes the listbox portion of the control to always be dropped-down and visible when the column has the focus. If this is not checked, the user must click the down arrow to display the list.

- **Always Show Arrow**—causes the listbox to display the down arrow whenever it has the focus. This also displays when it doesn't have focus unless you also choose Always Show List.

- **Allow Editing**—check this to make an editable DropDownListBox.

- **Required Field**—check this if the user must make an entry in this field. If this is checked, the user will not be able to tab away from this field without making an entry.

- **Empty String is NULL**—if this is checked, the DataWindow interprets an empty string in this field to represent a NULL value.

- **AutoHScroll**—if True, this activated automatic scrolling (horizontally) to let the user enter text that is wider than the size of the control.

- **Limit**—the maximum number of characters that can be entered in this SingleLineEdit (0 means no limit).

- **Case**—you can control the case of the input text. The choices are Any, lower, and UPPER.

- **V Scroll Bar**—check this option to add a vertical scroll bar to this object (as needed).

- **H Scroll Bar**—check this option to add a horizontal scroll bar to this object (as needed).

- **Split H Scroll Bar**—check this to display the split bar in the DataWindow object, this lets the user divide the DataWindow into two windows.

■ **Width of Drop Down**—specifies the width of the drop-down portion of the DropDownListBox. This is a percent of the width of the column.

The Display as Bitmap Option

The Display as Bitmap menu selection is a toggle. It is an option that is applied to an object with a compatible edit style that lets you display images in the DataWindow. The images can be either BMP or RLE images that originate as files whose path is stored in the database. When a row is retrieved from the database, the image is loaded and displayed in this column. The data type of this column must be suitable for storing the name of the image.

It is important to understand, that in this case the images are stored as files on a disk drive, and it is the name that is stored in the database. You can also store images in the application executable file, this is discussed in the chapter on distributing applications.

Database Images

You can also store the image itself in the database (if your DBMS provides a binary data type such as blob). You can display it by using a Picture control in the window (outside of the DataWindow). But you cannot display the image directly in the DataWindow. See Chapter 8, Embedded SQL for an example which stores images in the database.

That is all there is to the Display as Bitmap option. Just size the object. Note, if you update the image through OLE, you can not use the SetPicture with it.

PRESENTATION STYLES

The previous discussion was centered on the Tabular presentation style. While this is the most often used style, there are seven other styles from which to choose. The presentation style determines the layout of the data and specifies the general manner in which the user interacts with that data. This section covers the other presentation styles. PowerBuilder provides you with seven other presentation styles to choose from, each is different in the way that it presents the data.

The other choices for presentation style are:

- **Composite**—combines two or more DataWindow reports.

- **Crosstab**—presents the data in a cross tabulation format. This is most useful for calculating totals by groups. This can present data in a manner similar to spreadsheet programs.

- **Freeform**—this is the "forms"-like presentation. Generally, you use the freeform presentation style to allow individual records to enter, update, delete, and display individual records. The DataWindow presents all of the fields (column values) of a single record with a field label.

- **Graph**—PowerBuilder has an excellent selection of graphs, similar to the graphs available with Microsoft Excel.

- **Grid**—the grid style is similar to the tabular presentation style. The user can reorder and resize the columns in the DataWindow. This has the advantages of the tabular presentation style and also lets the user adjust the display. The disadvantage of the grid style is that while the user can rearrange the columns, the developer is not able to modify the layout in the flexible manner available in the tabular style

- **Group**—the group presentation style makes it very easy to create reports with group summations. The format is attractive and useful. The display is divided into groups with headings and summation rows predefined. The report includes page header, time, and page count.

- **Label**—presents data in a simple mailing label format.

- **N-Up**—presents data in columns across the screen like a newspaper. When a column reaches the bottom of the screen the data continues in the next column (left to right). The exception to this is that sorted data is presented across the columns in rows.

The next section presents the details about each of these presentation styles. Included in the discussion is an example of each of the presentation styles.

Crosstab

The Crosstab presentation style presents the data in a cross tabulation format, this is most useful for calculating totals by groups. The Crosstab DataWindow uses data from the SQL SELECT statement that you specify and analyzes the data and displays it in a tabular format. When you choose the Crosstab presentation style PowerBuilder opens the Crosstab Definition dialog window shown in Figure 10.43.

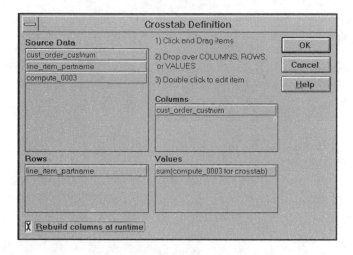

FIGURE 10.43 CROSSTAB DEFINITION

In this dialog you must specify the source for the columns, rows, and values in the tabulation. The dialog displays a model of the cross-tabulation in the bottom on the window with labels to show you where each element is displayed in the resulting table. The column that you specify as the source for the Crosstab column, creates a new Crosstab column for each value found in the result set. One row is generated for each distinct value in the column which you specify as the source for the Crosstab rows. The actual values in the Crosstab are calculated with a function such as COUNT or SUM.

For example, in Figure 10.44, the following SQL SELECT statement is used as the source for the DataWindow.

```
SELECT "cust_order"."custnum",
        "cust_order"."ordnum",
        "line_item"."partname",
        "line_item"."extended_price"
    FROM "cust_order"
        "line_item"
    WHERE ( "cust_order"."ordnum" = "line_item"."ordnum" )
```

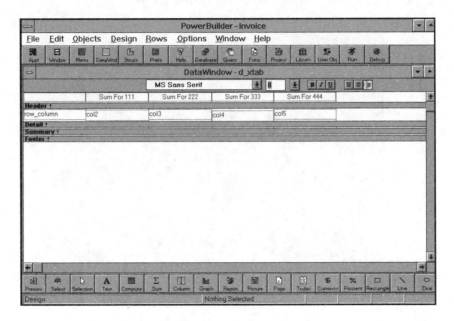

FIGURE 10.44 THE DATAWINDOW PAINTER

This statement joins the cust_order table to the line_item table. The cust_order table supplies the custnum (customer ID) field, and the line_item table supplies the partname and extended_price fields for the result set.

Figure 10.44 shows the definitions that are required to create this Crosstab showing the total sales to each customer, broken down by the category of the product (partname). The Columns field is specified as the custnum column. This creates a new column in the Crosstab result for each distinct value found in the custnum column in the result set. The Rows field is specified as the partname column. This creates a new row for each distinct value found in the partname column for each custnum. Finally the source for the values in the Crosstab is specified. The sum (extended_price for Crosstab) is selected from the list of options in the dropdown listbox. This will sum the line_item extended_price column for each custnum and partname, and display that as the value for the field in the Crosstab.

After completing these entries, click on **OK** to close the dialog. This opens the DataWindow painter shown in Figure 10.44.

The DataWindow painter executes the SQL SELECT statement and found four companies (customers) in the result set. The DataWindow painter created a Crosstab with a column for each company and added a label for each column.

You could add summations for the columns and rows if you need to display the totals for the each company and/or for each product. To add the column summations click on the column in the detail band and then click on the **Sum** icon on the PainterBar. This adds the summation field to the summary band. Repeat this for each column.

To add a row summation requires a little more effort. Add a computed column to Crosstab by clicking on the **Compute** icon on the PainterBar and then by clicking to the far right in the detail band. This adds a computed column to the Crosstab and prompts you for the formula for the computation. Enter **crosstabsum(1)** as shown in Figure 10.45.

There are a series of special functions available for Crosstab style DataWindows. These functions can produce the average, count, maximum, minimum, or sum of the columns in each row of the Crosstab. The crosstabsum(1) function was used to generate a summation for each row. Figure 10.46 shows the result of the additions to the design of the DataWindow.

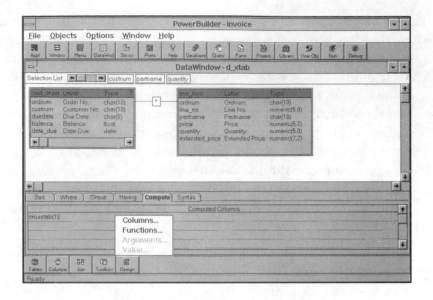

FIGURE 10.45 COMPUTED FIELD DEFINITION

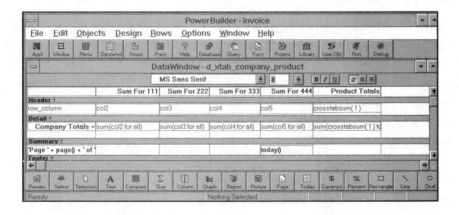

FIGURE 10.46 AFTER ADDING REPORT LABELS.

A column heading was added for the computed table and a label for the summary band. A page number and date were added to the summary band of the DataWindow. The DataWindow as it appears at run-time is shown in Figure 10.47.

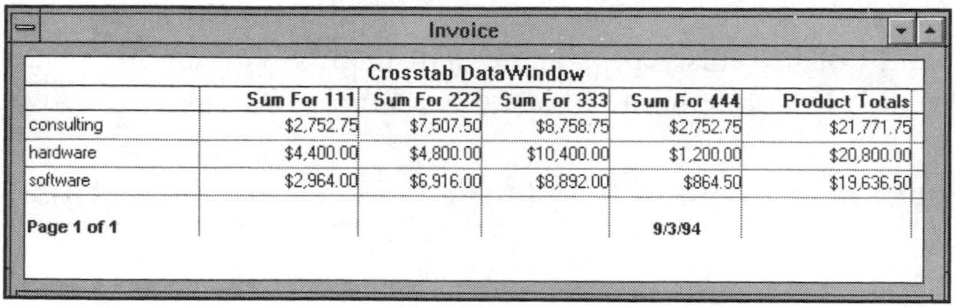

Invoice					
Crosstab DataWindow					
	Sum For 111	Sum For 222	Sum For 333	Sum For 444	Product Totals
consulting	$2,752.75	$7,507.50	$8,758.75	$2,752.75	$21,771.75
hardware	$4,400.00	$4,800.00	$10,400.00	$1,200.00	$20,800.00
software	$2,964.00	$6,916.00	$8,892.00	$864.50	$19,636.50
Page 1 of 1				9/3/94	

FIGURE 10.47 THE FINAL RESULT

This DataWindow displays the total sales made to each company broken down by product. The total sale to each company is computed in the summary band, and the total sales for each product is totaled in the computed column (Product Totals). Examine the SQL SELECT statement that was used to create the Crosstab.

```
SELECT "cust_order"."custnum",
       "cust_order"."ordnum",
       "line_item"."partname",
       "line_item"."extended_price"
  FROM "cust_order",
       "line_item"
 WHERE ( "cust_order"."ordnum" = "line_item"."ordnum" )
```

Look closely at the result in Figure 10.47, and notice how the DataWindow processed the result set of the SELECT statement to produce the cross-tabulation.

This data can also be generated by creating a SQL SELECT statement with a GROUP BY clause that uses the custnum and partname columns. That statement would be:

```
SELECT "cust_order"."custnum",
       "line_item"."partname",
       sum("line_item"."extended_price" )
  FROM "cust_order",
       "line_item"
 WHERE ( "cust_order"."ordnum" = "line_item"."ordnum" )
GROUP BY "cust_order"."custnum",
       "line_item"."partname"
```

This statement is presented in order to explain the Crosstab processing, you would not use this type of statement in this type of DataWindow. If you executed this statement against the database, the result is:

COMPANY	PRODUCT	TOTAL
111	consulting	2752.75
111	hardware	4400.00
111	software	2964.00
222	consulting	7507.50
222	hardware	4800.00
222	software	6916.00
333	consulting	8758.75
333	hardware	10400.00
333	software	8892.00
444	consulting	2752.75
444	hardware	1200.00
444	software	864.50

Freeform

This is the "forms"-like presentation. Generally, you use the freeform presentation style to enter, update, delete, and display individual records. The DataWindow presents each of the fields (column values) of a single record with a field label. This format can be customized to a large degree.

For this example, a SQL SELECT statement is created in the SQL Painter.

```
SELECT "company"."company",
       "company"."company_id",
       "company"."region",
       "company"."city",
       "company"."state",
```

```
            "company"."zip",
            "company"."phone",
            "company"."rep_ssn",
            "company"."credit_limit",
            "company"."last_order_date"
      FROM "company"
  ORDER BY "company"."company_id" ASC
```

After defining the SELECT statement the DataWindow painter opens with the display in Figure 10.48.

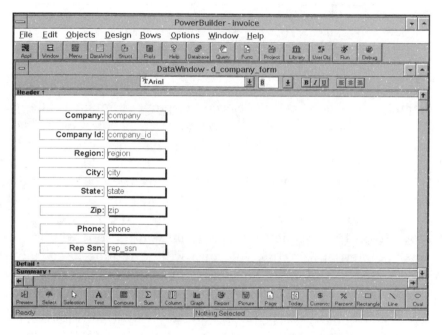

FIGURE 10.48 THE DATAWINDOW PAINTER

The DataWindow painter initially arranges all the fields in a single column. In this example, there are too many fields to be presented on the screen at one time in this manner. Therefore we moved five of the fields to the right half of the screen. Figure 10.49 shows the rearranged DataWindow as it will display at run-time.

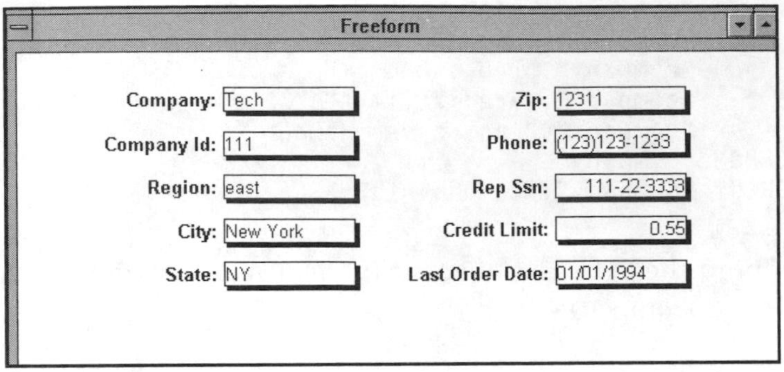

FIGURE 10.49 A FREE FORM DATAWINDOW

Graph

PowerBuilder has an excellent selection of graphs, similar to the graphs available in Microsoft Excel. A later chapter is devoted entirely to the process of creating graphs. The graph presentation style presents the result of the SQL query or other data source. You can add graphs in the DataWindow painter to DataWindows that have been defined with other presentation styles (other than graph). In this case, the graph is an object that is added to the DataWindow similar to how a control is added to a window. It is also possible to add a graph control to a window in the Window painter. In this case, you must write a routine to calculate the graph. For this discussion, we are considering graphs that are created as a result of defining a DataWindow with the graph presentation style.

For this example, a SQL SELECT statement is created that returns the summation of the sales to each customer (company). The SQL statement is:

```
SELECT "cust_order"."custnum",
       sum("line_item"."extended_price" )
   FROM "cust_order",
        "line_item"
  WHERE ( "cust_order"."ordnum" = "line_item"."ordnum" )
GROUP BY "cust_order"."custnum"
```

After defining the SQL SELECT statement, the DataWindow painter opens the Graph Data dialog shown in Figure 10.50.

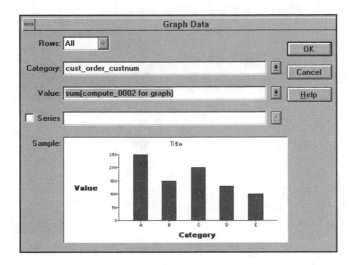

FIGURE 10.50 DEFINING GRAPH DATA

In this dialog, you must define the source for the Category and Value axis. In this example the custnum column serves to define the category. The summation of the extended_price serves for the value. There is no series in this example. After defining these parameters of the graph the DataWindow painter opens. Select **Type** from the popup menu to open the Graph Type dialog window. In this window the 3D Pie was selected as the type for our graph.

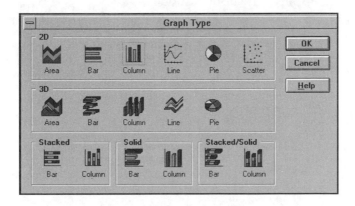

FIGURE 10.51 THE GRAPH TYPE DIALOG

We added a title to the graph, and the final result is shown in Figure 10.52.

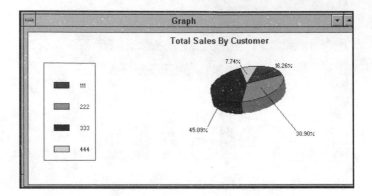

Total Sales By Customer

7.74%
16.26%
111
222
333
444
45.09%
30.90%

FIGURE 10.52 A GRAPH

Grid

The grid style is similar to the tabular presentation style. Data is presented in rows and columns like the tabular style, but grid lines are added to the display. The user can reorder and resize the columns in the DataWindow by dragging the column headings and by using the grid lines. This provides the advantages of the tabular presentation style, and also lets the user adjust the display. The disadvantage of the grid style is that while the user can rearrange the columns, the developer is not able to modify the layout in the flexible manner available in the tabular style.

For this example, an SQL SELECT statement is created that returns all of the rows in the company table. The SELECT statement is:

```
SELECT "company"."company",
       "company"."company_id",
       "company"."region",
       "company"."city",
       "company"."state",
       "company"."zip",
       "company"."phone",
       "company"."rep_ssn",
       "company"."credit_limit",
```

```
        "company"."last_order_date"
   FROM "company"
ORDER BY "company"."company" ASC
```

After defining the SQL statement the DataWindow opens with the columns presented in grid style as shown in Figure 10.53.

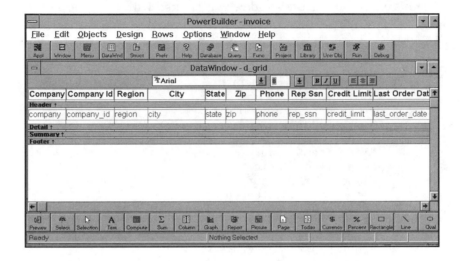

FIGURE 10.53 A GRID STYLE

The resulting DataWindow is shown in Figure 10.54. In this window the user can resize and reorder the columns easily with the mouse.

Company	Company Id	Region	City	State	Zip	Phone	Rep Ssn	Credit Limit	Last C
ACME	222	west	Cincinnati	OH	45040	(513)123	23-46-1234	1,500,000.50	12/31/
Another	888	midwest	Akron	OH	43222				00/00/
Best	777	midwest	Columbus	OH	32323				00/00/
east	444	east	Mills	NJ	12312				00/00/
first	555	midwest	Fort Wayne	IN	33212				00/00/
New	666	midwest	Dayton	OH	23232	((12)3)1-2		123,123.50	00/00/
Tech	111	east	New York	NY	12311	(123)123	11-22-3333	0.55	01/01/
two	333	midwest	Cleveland	OH	12312				00/00/

FIGURE 10.54 THE RESULTING DATAWINDOW

Group

The group presentation style makes it easy to create reports with group summations. The format is attractive and useful. The display is divided into groups with headings and summation rows predefined. The report includes page header, time, and page count.

For this example, a DataWindow was created with the group presentation style. The SQL SELECT statement joins the cust_order and the invoice_line tables, ordering by custnum, ordnum, and line_no. Sort the result set by the field (or fields) by which you intend to group the rows in the DataWindow. The SELECT statement is:

```
SELECT "cust_order"."custnum",
        "cust_order"."ordnum",
        "line_item"."line_no",
        "line_item"."partname",
        "line_item"."price",
        "line_item"."quantity",
        "line_item"."extended_price"
    FROM "cust_order",
        "line_item"
    WHERE ( "cust_order"."ordnum" = "line_item"."ordnum" )
ORDER BY "cust_order"."custnum" ASC,
        "cust_order"."ordnum" ASC,
        "line_item"."line_no" ASC
```

After creating the SQL statement, you are prompted to define the page header for the DataWindow with the Specify Page Header dialog (shown in Figure 10.55).

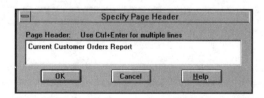

FIGURE 10.55 THE SPECIFY PAGE HEADER DIALOG

Click on **OK** to open the Specify Group dialog window. In this dialog, you must specify the column or columns that determine the grouping of the rows in the DataWindow.

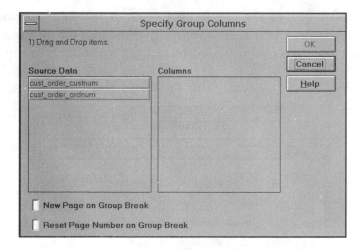

FIGURE 10.56 DEFINING A GROUP

Next the DataWindow painter opens. Some minor adjustments were made in the display of Figure 10.57. It doesn't take very much work to make a great looking presentation with the group presentation style.

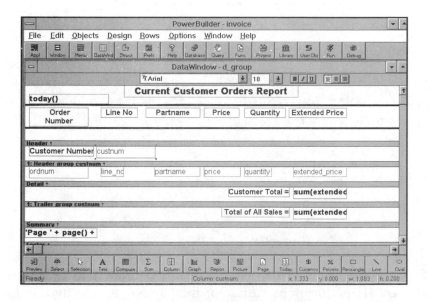

FIGURE 10.57 A GROUP REPORT

The final result groups the line items for each customer (company), and also calculates the total amount for all the invoices for that customer. A final summation has been added to calculate the total of all sales as shown in Figure 10.58.

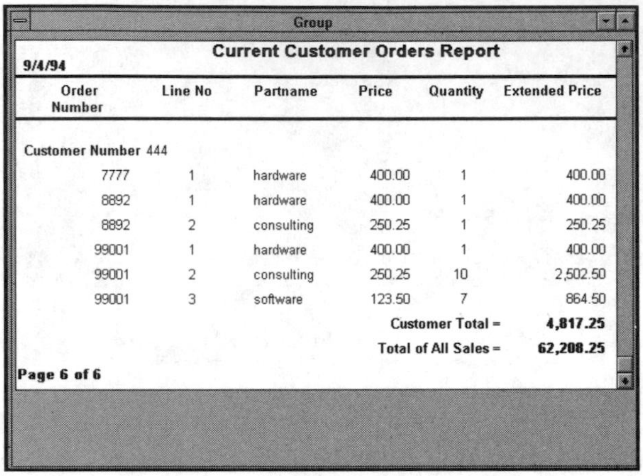

Current Customer Orders Report

9/4/94

Order Number	Line No	Partname	Price	Quantity	Extended Price
Customer Number 444					
7777	1	hardware	400.00	1	400.00
8892	1	hardware	400.00	1	400.00
8892	2	consulting	250.25	1	250.25
99001	1	hardware	400.00	1	400.00
99001	2	consulting	250.25	10	2,502.50
99001	3	software	123.50	7	864.50
				Customer Total =	4,817.25
				Total of All Sales =	62,208.25

Page 6 of 6

FIGURE 10.58 WITH SUMMATIONS

Label

Label presents data in a simple mailing label format. For this example, an SQL SELECT statement is created that returns the list of addresses from the company table. The SELECT statement is:

```
SELECT "company"."company",
       "company"."address",
       "company"."city",
       "company"."state",
       "company"."zip"
    FROM "company"
ORDER BY "company"."company" ASC
```

After defining the SQL statement, the DataWindow painter opens the Specify Label Specifications dialog. In this dialog you specify the dimensions, layout, and type of label.

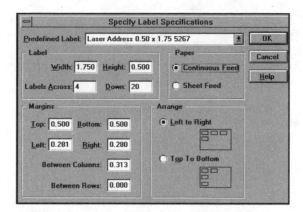

FIGURE 10.59 DEFINING LABEL DETAILS

After completing these details, the DataWindow painter opens. In the painter, a single label is presented with the columns that were in the select list in the SQL SELECT statement. Figure 10.60 shows a sample label.

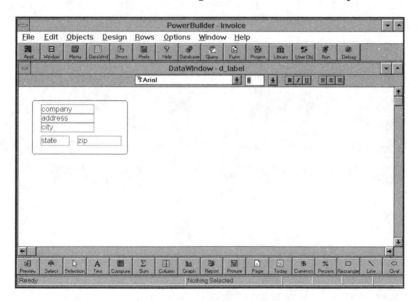

FIGURE 10.60 A SAMPLE LABEL

After adjusting the position of the fields on the label, the DataWindow is placed into a window. The result is shown in Figure 10.61.

457

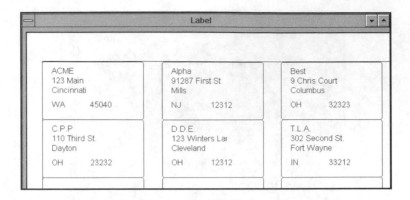

FIGURE 10.61 A LABEL STYLE DATAWINDOW

N-Up

Presents data in columns across the screen like a newspaper. When a column reaches the bottom of the screen the data continues in the next column (left to right). The exception to this is that sorted data is presented across the columns in rows. Figure 10.62 shows the DataWindow painter.

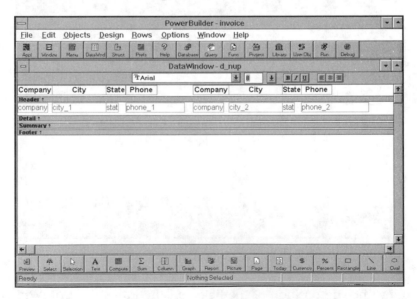

FIGURE 10.62 THE N-UP STYLE

Figure 10.63 shows the final result of the DataWindow using the N-Up presentation style.

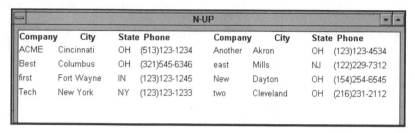

FIGURE 10.63 A N-UP REPORT

Tabular

Tabular is the most often used presentation style. Data is presented in columns under column headings. Each row is initially presented in a separate line. This presentation allows a great deal of flexibility. You can take a tabular presentation and create a form presentation, or a group presentation very easily.

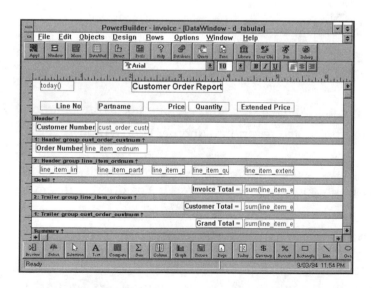

FIGURE 10.64 THE TABULAR PRESENTATION STYLE

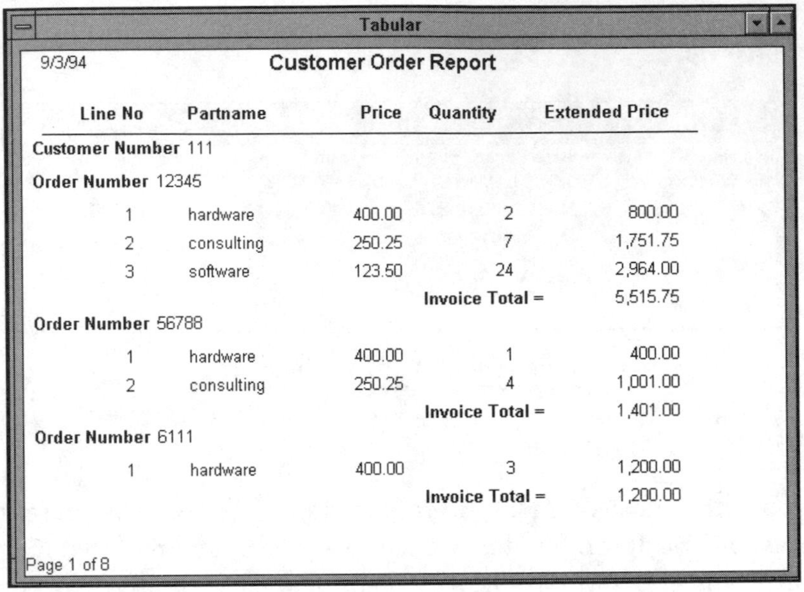

Tabular				

9/3/94   **Customer Order Report**

Line No	Partname	Price	Quantity	Extended Price
Customer Number 111				
Order Number 12345				
1	hardware	400.00	2	800.00
2	consulting	250.25	7	1,751.75
3	software	123.50	24	2,964.00
			Invoice Total =	5,515.75
Order Number 56788				
1	hardware	400.00	1	400.00
2	consulting	250.25	4	1,001.00
			Invoice Total =	1,401.00
Order Number 6111				
1	hardware	400.00	3	1,200.00
			Invoice Total =	1,200.00

Page 1 of 8

FIGURE 10.65 THE FINAL TABULAR REPORT

Creating Nested Reports

Nested reports combine two or more DataWindow objects into one report. There are two techniques for creating nested reports:

1. Create a DataWindow with the Composite presentation style.
2. Insert a nested report into another DataWindow.

I find the 2nd technique to be the more useful one, it can be used to create master-detail reports. First we will cover the creation of a composite report.

The Composite Report Presentation Style

To create a composite report, begin the process of creating a new DataWindow as you have in the previous examples. Choose the **Composite** presentation style. This immediately opens the DataWindow painter, by passing the SQL painter. A DataWindow witht the Composite presentation style does not have its own SQL statement. Instead, this type of DataWindow provides a container to hold other reports. This can be useful for printing more than one report on a page.

To add a report (DataWindow) to the new DataWindow, just click the **Report** icon PainterBar. This opens the Select Reports dialog box. (The list contains all DataWindows in the libraries that are in the current application's library search path.) Select a DataWindow object from the list and click **OK**. The DataWindow painter drops a rectangle representing the selected report onto the painter work area. You can position and size the rectangle as necessary. Repeat this process for each report that you want to add the the composite report.

Save the new DataWindow by selecting the **Save** option from the File menu.

Now you can preview the composite report. PowerBuilder retrieves all the rows for one nested report, then for another nested report, and so on until all retrieval is complete.

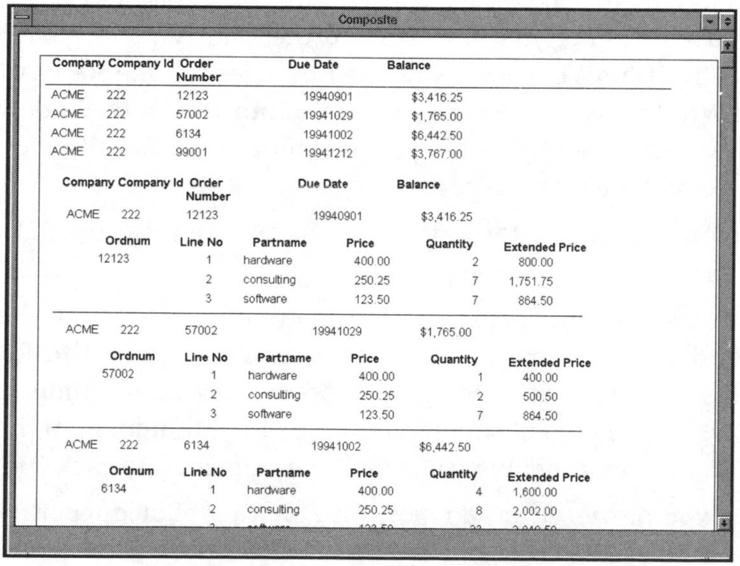

FIGURE 10.66 A COMPOSITE REPORT

Nesting Reports to Create Master-Detail Relationships

The second technique requires that you first create the DataWindow (report) that is to be nested into another DataWindow. This will usually be (but is not required to be) the detail part of a master-detail relation. For example, you may wish to display the invoice records from one table, followed by the line_items for each invoice from another table. In this example, the nested report is the line_item report, which will be nested in the invoice report.

Define a retrieval argument for the nested report, this will be used to create the relationship between the base and nested reports. To do this select the **Retrieval Arguments** option from the Objects menu in the Select painter. Define a retrieval argument in the **Specify Retrieval Arguments** dialog box. In the example, i_invoice_no could be the name assigned to the retrieval argument. Use this for the retrieval argument in a WHERE clause for the SELECT statement. Finish the creation of the DataWindow and save it.

Next you will create a DataWindow, called the *base report*, the invoice DataWindow in this example. This can be any type presentation style except CrossTab. After you have defined the DataWindow, you can add other exisitng DataWindows (as reports) by selecting the **Report** icon on the DataWindow Painter PainterBar, selecting the DataWindow object from the list, and then by clicking at the point in the DataWindow where you wish to add the nested report.

You can create master-detail reports by creating a relationship between the base and nested reports.

To do this, open the popup menu (right-mouse button) for the nested report and select **Retrieval Arguments**. This opens the Retrieval Arguments dialog. In this dialog you specify how information from the base report will be used to supply the value of the argument to the nested report. Enter the source of the value for the argument and click **OK**.

When you preview (run) a report with another related report nested in it, PowerBuilder retrieves all the rows in the base report first. Then PowerBuilder retrieves the data for all nested reports related to the first row. Next, PowerBuilder retrieves data for nested reports related to the second row, and so on, until all retrieval is complete for all rows in the base report.

You can preview the report and then make whatever adjustments you require. Save the report and add to it a window by associating it with a DataWindow control.

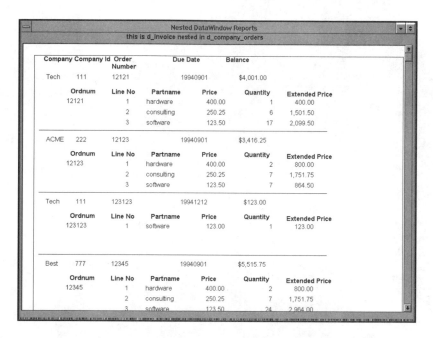

FIGURE 10.67 A NESTED REPORT

CHAPTER ELEVEN

DATAWINDOW CONTROLS: ADDING DATAWINDOWS TO YOUR APPLICATIONS

Chapters 9 and 10 have covered the creation and customization of DataWindow objects. In order to use a DataWindow *object* in your application, you must first add a DataWindow *control* to a window. This chapter covers the use of DataWindow controls. We assume that the DataWindows are working with a database data source; they can also be used for data from sources other than databases.

Figure 11.1 shows the relationship between a window, a DataWindow control, a DataWindow object, and the data source.

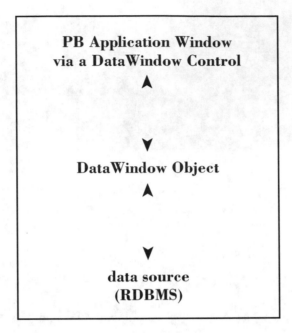

**FIGURE 11.1 RELATIONSHIP BETWEEN A WINDOW,
A DATAWINDOW CONTROL, A DATAWINDOW OBJECT, AND THE DATA SOURCE.**

You will use a set of PowerScript functions with most of the DataWindow controls that you create. These functions include:

- SetTransObject ()
- Retrieve()
- Update()
- InsertRow()
- DeleteRow()

The Retrieve and Update functions automatically generate the necessary SQL statements including:

- SELECT
- UPDATE

- INSERT
- DELETE

You will still use the following embedded SQL Statements in your script code:

- connect;
- commit;
- rollback;
- disconnect;

OVERVIEW: USING DATAWINDOW CONTROLS

You add a DataWindow control to a window and then position and size it like any other control in the Window painter. The next step is unique to DataWindow controls: you must link (associate) the DataWindow control to a specific DataWindow object, each DataWindow control has an attribute that specifies the name of the related DataWindow object. This will make the DataWindow object available to your application.

To use the DataWindow control you must initialize a transaction object (such as SQLCA) and then connect to the database. This part of the process is the same as the process for embedded SQL. After the connection is made to the database, you must assign the transaction object to a DataWindow control before it can access the database. From this point on, you use DataWindow control functions to retrieve and manipulate the data, instead of using embedded SQL. Use the Retrieve() function to issue the SELECT statement against the database and populate the DataWindow. You can then insert and delete rows in the DataWindow using the InsertRow() and DeleteRow() functions. You can also allow the update of fields in the DataWindow. These changes are made to rows of data in the DataWindow, not to the database. It is very important that you understand that the InsertRow and DeleteRow functions only affect the DataWindow control and *not* the database. When you want to apply the DataWindow changes to the database, use the Update() function. The

Update function issues the necessary INSERT, UPDATE, or DELETE SQL statements to the database. At this point you can issue a COMMIT statement to make the changes to the database permanent; otherwise you can issue a ROLLBACK statement to cancel them. Your application is interacting with the DataWindow object through the DataWindow control.

The association between a DataWindow control and a DataWindow object is nonexclusive. That is, you can associate more than one control with a particular DataWindow object.

ADDING A DATAWINDOW CONTROL TO A WINDOW

In the Window painter, click on the **DataWnd** icon or select the **Control|DataWindow** menu selection. This tells the Window painter that you are going to add a DataWindow control to the window that you are editing. Then click at the position in the window where you wish to add the DataWindow control. You can then position and size the control as you would any other window control (Figure 11.2).

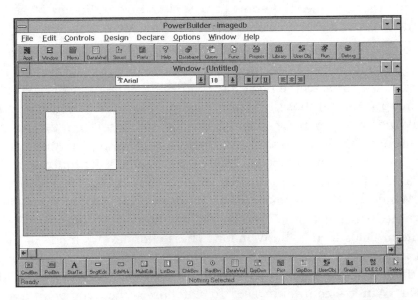

FIGURE 11.2 AFTER ADDING A DATAWINDOW CONTROL TO A WINDOW

Select a DataWindow Object

Each DataWindow control must be associated with a specific DataWindow object. To do this, open the DataWindow's popup menu (right mouse-click on the DataWindow control) and select the **Change DataWindow** menu option (Figure 11.3). This opens the Select DataWindow dialog window (Figure 11.4).

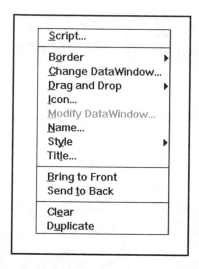

FIGURE 11.3 THE DATAWINDOW CONTROL POPUP MENU

Select the Application library (in the bottom ListBox) that holds the DataWindow object. Then select the DataWindow object from the list in the DataWindows ListBox at the top of the dialog window, and then click the **OK** CommandButton. This links the DataWindow control to the selected DataWindow object. If you need help locating a DataWindow object, you can click on **Browse** (Figure 11.4) to open the Browse DataWindows dialog window (Figure 11.5). In this dialog box, first select the libraries (.PBL files) that you want to search, then enter the search criteria in the Search For field. Click on **Search** and the Matches Found ListBox displays all DataWindow objects matching your search criteria. You can make the search case-sensitive by checking the CheckBox that is located just below the criteria field.

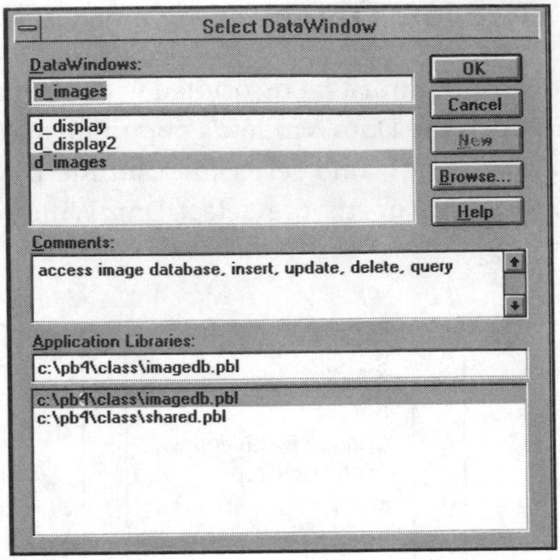

FIGURE 11.4 SELECT A DATAWINDOW OBJECT FOR THE DATAWINDOW CONTROL

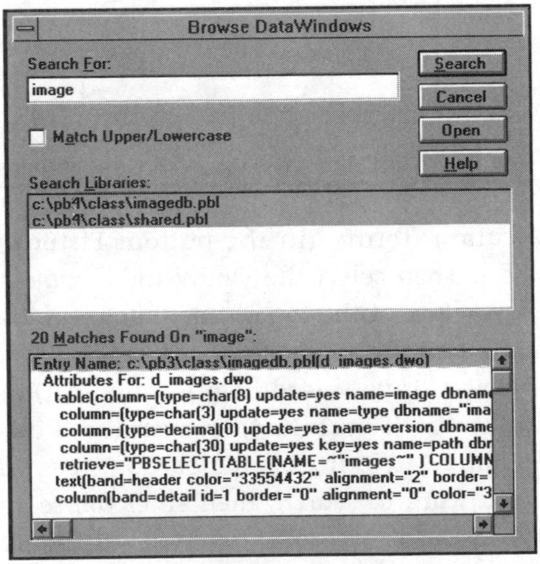

FIGURE 11.5 USING THE BROWSE FUNCTION IN THE LIBRARY PAINTER

You can also change the associated DataWindow object for the DataWindow control at run time. To do this, assign the name of the DataWindow object to the DataWindow control attribute named DataObject:

```
dw_1.DataObject = 'd_company'
rc = dw_1.SetTransObject(SQLCA)
```

The first line of this example assigns the d_company DataWindow object to the dw_1 DataWindow control. The second line reassigns the transaction object for the control as described below (the reassignment of the transaction object must be done after changing the DataWindow object). Using this technique, you could offer the user a selection of reports (DataWindow objects) to choose from in one of your windows. Then you would dynamically assign the DataWindow object to the DataWindow control on that window, instead of creating separate windows for each report. The DataWindow objects must be stored in libraries on the application search path so that PowerBuilder can find them at run time; see Chapter 18 "Distributing Your Applications" for more details.

Set the DataWindow Attributes

Double-click on the DataWindow control to open the DataWindow Style dialog box. You will notice that the Style dialog box's title bar contains the name of the DataWindow object that you associated with the control (Figure 11.6).

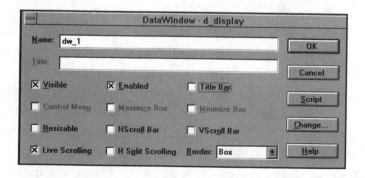

FIGURE 11.6 THE DATAWINDOW CONTROL STYLE DIALOG BOX

The attributes of a DataWindow that you can change in this dialog box are:

- **Name**—changes the name of the DataWindow control. PowerBuilder uses the prefix **dw_** for DataWindow controls (you should stick with this convention; use the prefix **d_** for DataWindow objects).

- **Title**—adds a title to the DataWindow. This has the unfortunate side effect of making the DataWindow movable, which is not usually desirable. Usually you add a static text control to the window instead.

- **Visible**—sets this CheckBox to make the control visible.

- **Enabled**—when the control is enabled, it is active and can be selected and receive input. If it is disabled the control cannot receive input or events and the user cannot tab to the fields within the control.

- **Title Bar**—adds a title bar to the DataWindow, then add the caption in the Title field.

- **Control menu**—adds a control menu to the DataWindow. This menu adds functions to let the user move, resize (restore, maximize), minimize, or close the DataWindow. This option is only available if you have added a title bar to the DataWindow.

- **Maximize box**—adds the maximize button to the DataWindow. This option is available only if you have added a title bar to the DataWindow.

- **Minimize box**—adds the minimize button to the DataWindow. This option is available only if you have added a title bar to the DataWindow.

- **Resizable**—lets the user resize the DataWindow. If selected, this adds a thin frame to the window. The user can resize the window by clicking and dragging this frame. This is available only if you have added a title bar to the DataWindow.

- **H scroll bar**—adds a horizontal scroll bar to this control (this appears as needed).

- **V scroll bar**—check this option to add a vertical scroll bar to this control (this will appear as needed).

- **Live scrolling**—lets the user move through the rows in the DataWindow using the scroll bar.

- **H split scrolling**—check this to display the split bar in the DataWindow object, this will allow the user to divide the DataWindow into two vertical windows that can be scrolled separately.

- **Border**—selects a border for the control (an enumerated value). The choices are 3D Lowered, 3D Raised, Box, None, and ShadowBox.

If you do not make the DataWindow control resizable, you must size this control (in the Window painter) to be large enough to display what you intended when you created the DataWindow object. You may have to run the application several times to fine-tune the adjustment of the DataWindow size.

DataWindow Control

Your PowerScript programming deals with the DataWindow control. Your code scripts for the DataWindow control events. These scripts control the retrieval, manipulation, and presentation of the data. Some of the more important DataWindow functions that you use for data manipulation are:

- **Retrieve**—issues the SQL Select statement for this DataWindow and populates the DataWindow with rows from the database.

- **InsertRow**—adds a new row to the DataWindow at a specified location. This function also initializes any of the columns in the new row with values that you specified as default (initial) values in the Database painter.

- **DeleteRow**—this function removes a specific row from the DataWindow.

■ **Update**—applies all the changes (additions, deletions, modifications) made to the rows in the DataWindow back to the database.

NOTE

These are DataWindow PowerScript functions, not embedded SQL statements. For example, you could place the following code in a window Open event to populate dw_1 (on this window):

```
lRows = dw_1.Retrieve()
```

or

```
lRows = dw_1.Retrieve('OHIO')
```

The second example passes a retrieval argument to the SQL Select statement. Notice that the functions are applied to the DataWindow control, not to the DataWindow object. The Retrieve function returns a long value, which is the number of rows returned to the DataWindow.

Often you will add CommandButtons or menu options to the window to trigger the retrieval, updating, and deleting of rows of data from the database. You could also trigger the initial retrieval in the application or Window Open events, but you must populate the DataWindow explicitly. During the design process the population of the DataWindow object was automatic when you selected the **Design|Preview** menu option in the DataWindow painter. To access the database each DataWindow needs a transaction object.

TRANSACTION OBJECTS

A transaction object is required for all database access in PowerBuilder applications. The transaction object was discussed in Chapter 8, but now we will discuss some additional details that relate to DataWindows. The transaction object holds the information that is required to connect to the database and it holds the return code and other information that is returned as a result of each database interaction.

SetTransObject

You can set a transaction object for each DataWindow control using the SetTransObject function (do not confuse this with the SetTrans function). The transaction object represents one connection to a database (to a specific DBMS, database, and user account). You can share a transaction object between DataWindows (and embedded SQL) in your application, if they access the same DBMS, database, and account. The syntax for associating the transaction object for a DataWindow control is:

```
rc = dw_1.SetTransObject ( SQLCA )
```

This statement will assign the SQLCA transaction object to the dw_1 DataWindow control. This function returns an integer; a value of 1 signals success. When you use SetTransObject, you must take responsibility for managing database transactions. You must issue COMMIT (or ROLL-BACK) statements to the database (using embedded SQL). You will often issue a COMMIT statement immediately after calling the DataWindow Update() function (if the Update was successful).

SetTrans

It is possible to set the transaction object with another (seldom used) function, SetTrans(). In addition to setting the transaction object, this function takes over the transaction management by issuing COMMIT statements after each database operation. The SetTrans function also connects before each database operation and disconnects after each operation. This is not usually desirable, so use the SetTransObject function. The only time to consider using the SetTrans function to specify the transaction object is when you are running short on connections to the database. Since

SetTransObject commits and disconnects after each operation, the connects are closed more often. This also means that each database operation must open a new connection (with SetTrans), and the application will suffer a rather large performance penalty.

If you use SetTrans, you do not need to issue the CONNECT, DISCONNECT, COMMIT, or ROLLBACK statements or call the Update function since this is handled internally. We will not use the SetTrans function in our examples, and for the rest of this book you can assume that we are using SetTransObject.

DATABASE ACCESS WITH A DATAWINDOW AND TRANSACTION OBJECT

Using the Transaction Object

You must have assigned the transaction object parameters that are required to connect to your DBMS before you can use the transaction object to connect to the database. You must also be connected to the database with a transaction object before using that object with the SetTransObject function.

The following code is from the Application Open event script for the Imagedb application. The code in this script reads the database parameters (for the Watcom database) from the IMAGEDB.INI file into the SQLCA transaction object. If the file is read successfully, the code connects to the database, sets the transaction object for dw_1 (in w_main), and then performs a retrieval for that DataWindow. You could move some (or all) of this code to the w_main Window Open event. The advantage of placing the code here is that the main window will open and display the status messages in the st_status field.

```
string sText
int rc
```

```
long lRowsRetrieved
string sInitFile

sInitFile = "c:\pb4\class\imagedb.ini"
Open (w_main)
sText = ProfileString(sInitFile,"sqlca","firsttime","error")
IF sText = 'error' THEN
    MessageBox ("error", "init file not found")
    halt close
END IF
IF Upper(sText) = "YES" THEN
    OpenWithParm (w_db_login,sInitFile)
ELSE
    SetPointer (HourGlass!)
    sqlca.DBMS = ProfileString(sInitFile,"sqlca","dbms","err")
    sqlca.database = ProfileString(sInitFile,"sqlca", &
                     "database","")
    sqlca.userid =
   ProfileString(sInitFile,"sqlca","userid","")
    sqlca.dbpass = ProfileString(sInitFile,"sqlca", &
                     "dbpass","")
    sqlca.logid = ProfileString(sInitFile,"sqlca","logid","")
    sqlca.logpass = ProfileString(sInitFile,"sqlca", &
                     "logpass","")
    sqlca.servername = ProfileString(sInitFile,"sqlca", &
                     "servername","")
    sqlca.dbparm = ProfileString(sInitFile,"sqlca", &
                     "dbparm","")
END IF

IF sqlca.DBMS <> 'err' THEN
   connect;
ELSE
    sqlca.sqlcode = 1
END IF
IF sqlca.sqlcode <> 0 THEN
    MessageBox ("Cannot Connect to Database!", &
        sqlca.sqlerrtext)
    w_main.st_status.text = "no database"
    return  // or halt close
END IF

w_main.st_status.text = "connected"
rc = w_main.dw_1.SetTransObject ( sqlca )
IF rc = 1 THEN
    lRows = w_main.dw_1.Retrieve ( )
    // did the retrieve succeed?
```

```
        IF RowsRetrieved < 0 THEN
            w_main.st_status.text = "retrieve failed"
        END IF
    ELSE
        w_main.st_status.text = "SetTransObject failed"
    END IF
    return
```

The first executable statement opens the w_main window. This window contains a StaticText field name st_status, which is used to report the database status:

```
    Open (w_main)
```

The next line of code checks for the existence of the imagedb.ini profile file. If it is not found, the application will display an error message (in a MessageBox) and then shutdown.

```
    sText = ProfileString(sInitFile,"sqlca","firsttime","error")
    IF sText = 'error' THEN
        MessageBox ("error", "init file not found")
        HALT CLOSE
    END IF
```

The next section of code checks the profile file to see if this is the first time the user has run this application. If so, it opens a window (w_db_login) and prompts the user for the database login information. This window also writes that information back out to the profile file and changes the **firsttime** value to **no**.

```
    IF Upper(sText) = "YES" THEN
        OpenWithParm (w_db_login,sInitFile)
    END IF
```

If this was not the first time the user has run this application, we assume that the connection information is in the profile file. The next section of code (following the ELSE), reads each of the database parameters from the file and assigns them to the attributes of the SQLCA transaction object. Notice that the default for the sqlca.DBMS attribute has been set to **err**, so that we can determine if these parameters are not in the file:

```
ELSE
  SetPointer (HourGlass!)
  sqlca.DBMS = ProfileString(sInitFile,"sqlca","dbms","err")
  sqlca.database = ProfileString(sInitFile,"sqlca", &
                  "database","")
  sqlca.userid = ProfileString(sInitFile,"sqlca","userid","")
  sqlca.dbpass = ProfileString(sInitFile,"sqlca","dbpass","")
  sqlca.logid = ProfileString(sInitFile,"sqlca","logid","")
  sqlca.logpass = ProfileString(sInitFile,"sqlca", &
                  "logpass","")
  sqlca.servername = ProfileString(sInitFile,"sqlca", &
                  "servername","")
  sqlca.dbparm = ProfileString(sInitFile,"sqlca","dbparm","")
END IF
```

If the database parameters were read successfully, the code issues an embedded SQL statement to connect to the database. Otherwise, we set the sqlcode to 1:

```
IF sqlca.DBMS <> 'err' THEN
        connect;
ELSE
    sqlca.sqlcode = 1
END IF
```

After the connection attempt, you must check the transaction object's sqlcode attribute for success. It will be 0 (zero) if it was successful. If it failed, we display an error message and exit:

```
IF sqlca.sqlcode <> 0 THEN
    MessageBox ("Cannot Connect to Database!", &
              sqlca.sqlerrtext)
    w_main.st_status.text = "no database"
    return  // or halt close
END IF
```

If the connection to the database was successful, then we display a **connected** message in the status field and set the transaction object for the dw_1 DataWindow object in the w_main window. If that is successful, then we use the DataWindow **Retrieve** function to populate the DataWindow. The Retrieve function returns a 1 if it is successful. We check this return value and display an error message if it failed. The final statement executes a RETURN from the application open event, and if everything was successful, the w_main window takes control:

```
w_main.st_status.text = "connected"
rc = w_main.dw_1.SetTransObject ( sqlca )
IF rc = 1 THEN
    lRowsRetrieved = w_main.dw_1.Retrieve ( )
    // did the retrieve succeed?
    IF RowsRetrieved < 0 THEN
        w_main.st_status.text = "retrieve failed"
    END IF
ELSE
    w_main.st_status.text = "SetTransObject failed"
END IF
return
```

DATABASE ERROR HANDLING IN DATAWINDOWS

Chapter 8, "Embedded SQL" covered error handling using the SQLCA.SQLCode attribute. This applies only to embedded SQL and not to the DataWindow database functions. There is a different technique for handling database errors in DataWindows.

When a database error occurs as a result of a DataWindow database function (such as Retrieve or Update), the DBError event will be triggered in the DataWindow control. In that event, you must use the DBErrorCode and DBErrorText functions instead of accessing the transaction object's attributes. The DBErrorCode function will return the number of the database error (from the DBMS), and DBErrorText will return the text message associated with the error code.

For example, if you placed the following statement in the Clicked event for a CommandButton (cb_retrieve):

```
lRows = dw_1.Retrieve(start_date, end_date)
```

and a database error occurred, the DBError event in dw_1 would be triggered. In that event you could place the following code:

```
long lErrorCode
string sErrorText
int rc

lErrorCode = This.DBErrorCode()
sErrorText = This.DBErrorMessage()
st_status.text = "DB Error:" + string(lErrorCode) + ' '&
    + sErrorText,StopSign!)
rc = this.SetActionCode(1)
// this will override the default error behavior
```

THE MAJOR DATAWINDOW FUNCTIONS

This section covers the major functions that you use with DataWindow controls. This includes retrieving data, inserting and deleting rows, and applying updates to the database. Additional functions will provide print, query, import, and export functionality. For this discussion, we assume that the code is being placed in a CommandButton, but you can use the code in menu item scripts, object events, or script functions.

Retrieve()

In the script for the Clicked event for a CommandButton (cb_retrieve), you could place the following code, to retrieve data into the DataWindow using the SQL SELECT statement that is associated with the DataWindow object. You may also place this code in a window's Open event if you want the DataWindow to be populated as soon as the window opens:

```
long lRowsRetrieved
lRowsRetrieved = dw_1.Retrieve ( )
// lRowsRetrieved will be >= 0 if successful
```

In this script, the Retrieve function populates the DataWindow and returns the count (a long value) of rows retrieved if successful or a –1 in the case of an error.

If you had declared arguments for the DataWindow's SELECT statement (in the select or SQL painter), then you may include arguments for the Retrieve function:

```
long lRowsRetrieved
lRowsRetrieved = dw_1.Retrieve ('OH', 1 )
// lRowsRetrieved will be >= 0 if successful
```

or

```
long lRowsRetrieved
string sState
int iActiveAccount

sState = 'OH'
iActiveAccount = 1
lRowsRetrieved = dw_1.Retrieve (sState, iActiveAccount )
// lRowsRetrieved will be > 0 if successful
```

If you use a CommandButton to perform the Retrieve, the focus will be set on the button after the retrieval is executed. In that case, you may wish to add the following line of code to set the focus to the DataWindow control:

```
dw_1.SetFocus ( )
```

InsertRow()

In the script for the Clicked event for a CommandButton (cb_insert), you could place the following code to insert a new row in the DataWindow:

```
long lRow
lRow = dw_1.InsertRow (0)
// insert a new row after the last row
IF lRow > 0 THEN
    dw_1.SetItem ( lRow, 'version', 1)// initialization
    dw_1.SetColumn ('version') // set focus
    dw_1.ScrollToRow ( lRow )
        // also does a dw_1.SetRow ( lRow)
END IF
dw_1.SetFocus ( )
```

In this script, the InsertRow function adds a new row to the DataWindow (but not to the database). The argument for the InsertRow function specifies the number of the row where you wish to add the new row. For example, a 5 will insert a row at the fifth position, the row that is currently fifth will become sixth and so on. A 0 (zero) tells the function to add the row at the bottom of the DataWindow. The InsertRow function returns the number of the new row or a –1 if an error occurred. In this code example, if the return value was greater than zero, we initialize the value of the version column to 1 using the SetItem function. This could have been done in the Database painter by setting an initial value for the column, but we use the SetItem function for the example.

In the next lines, we set the current row to be the new row and the current column to be the version column so that the user may edit the assigned value if necessary.

The next lines of code scroll the window to the new row since it may have been added out of the range of rows currently displayed in the DataWindow.

Clicking the **cb_insert** CommandButton sets the focus onto the CommandButton, so the dw_1.SetFocus() line sets the focus back on the DataWindow control. This is not necessary for any of this code to work correctly; it is added so the user can begin typing a new entry in the DataWindow without having to tab to (or click on) the DataWindow.

DeleteRow()

In the script for the Clicked event for a CommandButton (cb_delete), you could place the following code to delete the current row from the DataWindow:

```
rc = dw_1.DeleteRow (0 )
```

The argument for DeleteRow is the row number (a long) that you want to delete. The 0 (zero) means that the current row should be deleted. This function returns an integer 1 if it is successful.

Update()

In the script for the Clicked event for a CommandButton (cb_update), you could use the following code to apply the changes against the database:

```
rc = dw_1.Update()
// if rc <> 1 then the DBError event will be triggered
IF rc = 1 THEN
    Commit;
ELSE
    Rollback;
END IF
IF sqlca.sqlcode <> 0 THEN
    MessageBox ("Transaction Failure", sqlca.sqlerrtext)
    w_main.st_status.text = "Trans Failed"
    return  // or halt close
END IF
```

If the return code is 1 (successful), then we commit the changes to the database, otherwise we cancel the transaction. The COMMIT (or ROLLBACK) is an embedded SQL statement that requires checking the SQLCode value.

COMMIT

The COMMIT statement is an embedded SQL statement, not a DataWindow function. This means that this statement requires a semicolon, and you check the success of the COMMIT by checking the SQLCode value. The COMMIT statement makes all changes applied to the database by the Update function in the current transaction permanent. It also ends the current transaction and begins a new one.

ROLLBACK

The ROLLBACK statement is an embedded SQL statement, not a DataWindow function. This statement requires a semicolon, and you check the success of the ROLLBACK by checking the SQLCode value. The ROLLBACK statement cancels all changes applied to the database by the Update function in the current transaction permanent. It also ends the transaction and begins a new one.

Adding QBE to a DataWindow

You can use a DataWindow to provide a QBE (query-by-example) interface for your applications. This is basically the same as the Quick Select
interface and is referred to as the Query Mode for a DataWindow. To use a
DataWindow to define a query, use the following line of code:

```
dw_1.Modify("datawindow.querymode = yes")
```

With PowerBuilder 3, that function was dwModify and it would have been:

```
dw_1.dwModify("datawindow.querymode - yes")
```

(See the comments below on function name changes.)

This will initiate query mode for dw_1. The user can then enter the
search criteria.

To turn off query mode and perform the database retrieval, use the following code:

```
dw_1.Modify("datawindow.querymode = no")
lRows = dw_1.Retrieve()
```

This would be a good time to use the SetRedraw function to turn off the
updating of the display until the retrieval is complete. To do that use the
following code:

```
rc = dw_1.SetRedraw (False)
dw_1.Modify("datawindow.querymode = no")
lRows = dw_1.Retrieve()
rc = dw_1.SetRedraw (True)
```

Turning query mode off adds the QBE criteria entered in the window by
the user, to the WHERE clause of the DataWindow's SELECT statement.
SetRedraw returns an integer, which is 1 if successful.

After the user has entered the query criteria, you can display the resulting SQL SELECT statement using the following:

```
mle_1.Text = dw_1.GetSQLSelect ()
```

485

To clear the QBE display, use the following code:

```
dw_1.DataObject=dw_1.DataObject
rc = dw_1.SetTransObject(SQLCA)
```

This resets the dw_1 DataWindow to its initial state (without the search criteria). See the FirstDW example for a QBE example.

DataWindow query mode doesn't work with SetTrans. You *must* use SetTransObject.

NOTE

This function uses the DataWindow Modify function (dwModify in PowerBuilder 3). This function is a powerful—and rather complex—function used for advanced programming techniques in PowerBuilder. This function allows dynamic modification of the DataWindow. Modify returns a string value. This value will be an empty string (" ") if it is successful and will contain text if an error occurs. The error text will describe the line and column where the syntax error occurred.

NOTE

UPDATING DATA IN A DATAWINDOW

It is important to understand how the DataWindow works to display and update rows in the database. The DataWindow has four buffers:

1. **primary**—the currently available data in the DataWindow
2. **filter**—rows that have been filtered out
3. **delete**—rows that have been deleted
4. **original**—contains the original retrieval set

After the initial SELECT (resulting from the Retrieve function call) all data is held in the primary buffer. When you apply a filter condition, some rows may be moved to the filter buffer. When you delete a row, it is moved to the delete buffer.

486

It is important to note that changing the data in the DataWindow does not change the database! To apply DataWindow changes to the database, you must call the Update function to update the database from the DataWindow and then commit the transaction.

Use the following code to apply changes to the database:

```
rc = dw_1.Update()
IF rc = 1 THEN
    COMMIT;
ELSE
    ROLLBACK;
END IF
```

When you execute the Update function PowerBuilder examines the DataWindow buffers to decide what changes need to be applied to the database. PowerBuilder then generates the necessary SQL INSERT, DELETE, and UPDATE statements and sends them to the database.

You can allow the user to update the data on a column-by-column basis. To allow the update of a field, set a tab value greater than 0 for that column (in the DataWindow painter) to make it accessible.

THE DATAWINDOWS EDIT CONTROL

The DataWindow fields are generally displayed (for input and output) as text in an edit control. Remember that changing the text in the field of a DataWindow does not change the database! Those changes are only made in the DataWindow.

As the user tabs through the DataWindow fields, an edit control (which is more like a multiline edit control) is placed over the field that has the focus. Only one field may have the focus in a DataWindow at any given moment. The field data is moved into the edit control when the field receives the focus. Then the user can enter or modify data in the selected field. When the user types into the edit control, that text is held in the edit control. The text in the edit control is not in any of the DataWindow buffers (as long as it is being edited).

When the cursor leaves the field (such as when the user presses the **Tab** key), the text in the edit control will either be moved into the primary buffer or rejected, retaining the initial value. The data will be moved into the primary buffer only if the entry is of the correct data type and if it passes the validation rules (if any).

The following functions work with the edit control located at the current row and column in the DataWindow:

dw_1.GetText() This returns a string containing the text currently in the edit control.

dw_1.SetText("hello") This function assigns a string to the edit control.

dw_1.AcceptText() This function moves the text from the edit control into the current buffer cell. Generally, this action is performed automatically by the DataWindow; it is not usually necessary to use this function.

The data type of the data in the edit control is *string*, regardless of the column data type. The text will be converted to the appropriate data type when it is moved into the DataWindow buffer. If you are accessing the edit control text, you will have to do the conversion (if required). For example:

```
iSize = Integer(dw_1.GetText())
```

This would convert the edit control text to an integer.

You can also use other MultiLineEdit functions:

- Clear, Copy, Cut, Paste, SelectText, Undo
- CanUndo, LineCount, Position, ReplaceText
- Scroll, Selection
- Undo

DataWindow Items

Each field in a DataWindow buffer is called an *item*. Each item can be referenced with functions such as:

```
dw_1.GetItemDate(row, "start_date");
GetItemDatetime(row, 2);
GetItemDecimal(row, "cost", Delete!, True);
GetItemNumber(row, "age", Filter!, False);
GetItemString(row, 2);
GetItemTime(GetRow(), 4);
```

The GetItem functions take the row and column (either as a number or a column name) as required arguments. You may also specify the buffer (Primary is the default), and you may add an argument to obtain the original value that was retrieved from the database.

Status Codes

As mentioned, each row has a buffer:

- **Primary!**
- **Delete!**
- **Filter!**

Each item (in each buffer) also has a status code. The values are enumerated as:

- **NotModified!**   Unchanged
- **DataModified!**   Updated by the user
- **New!**   Newly inserted item
- **NewModified!**   A new item that has been modified

Rows also have a status: The enumerated values are:

- **New!**   Added
- **NewModified!**   A newly added row has also been modified
- **DataModified!**   Contains a modified field
- **notModified!**   Unchanged since retrieval

You can determine the status of an item using the GetItemStatus (dwGetItemStatus in PowerBuilder 3) function.

When rows are initially retrieved into a DataWindow, all rows and columns are initially marked with a status of NotModified!. When you update an item's value the column and row status will change to DataModified!.

When you insert a new row into a DataWindow, the row's status will be initialized to New!. Its columns will be initialized to NotModified! if there is no default value or to DataModified! if there is a default value. If a column status is set to DataModified! then the row's status will follow.

A new row's status will change to NewModified! when you update any item in that row, the column will be DataModified!.

Use the GetItemStatus function to read a column or row status. For example:

```
dwItemStatus    ItemStatus, RowStatus

ItemStatus = dw_1.GetItemStatus(dw_1.GetRow(), "name", PRIMARY!)
RowStatus = dw_1.GetItemStatus(dw_1.GetRow(), 0, PRIMARY!)
```

You can use the SetItemStatus function to change the status for a DataWindow's row or column. If you change a row's status to NotModified! or New!, the status of all the columns will change to NotModified! You can use the SetItemStatus after you copy a row from one DataWindow to another.

UPDATING A ROW IN A DATAWINDOW

In this section, we will present the sequence of steps required to update a row in a database using a DataWindow.

First you must populate a transaction object (SQLCA in this example) and connect to the database. Then assign the transaction object to the DataWindow and retrieve rows into the DataWindow:

```
connect using SQLCA;
dw_1.SetTransObject(SQLCA)
dw_1.Retrieve()
```

At this point, data is displayed in DataWindow. The focus is set to a field on the DataWindow. Item data is moved to text in the edit control. The user updates the edit control text and attempts to move to another field (by tabbing or clicking elsewhere on the screen).

The edit control text is converted to data and validated. If the data conversion or validation fails, PowerBuilder triggers the DataWindow ItemError event. Otherwise, the DataWindow performs an implicit AcceptText (unless you write a ItemChanged event), and the buffer item is set to the new value.

PowerBuilder triggers at least two DataWindow events during this process. They are:

- **ItemChanged**—triggered when the user moves the focus away from the field after making a change.
- **ItemFocusChanged**—triggered when the focus changes.

PowerBuilder allows the focus to change if everything was successful.

The user may continue to update other fields in the DataWindow. At some point, the user finally clicks your **Apply Update** CommandButton. In response to this, you issue the following statements:

```
rc = dw_1.Update()
IF rc = 1 THEN commit;
```

The Update function performs an AcceptText by default. The Update applies the changes to the database, and the COMMIT makes the changes permanent.

DataWindow Event Details

There are two other DataWindow events that may be triggered during the process of entering or editing a field's value. The events are:

- **ItemChanged**
- **ItemError**

The ItemChanged event occurs when the user changes the text in the edit control and then moves away from the field. You may write your own code to handle this event, or you may use the default processing, which is usual. If you use the default processing (do not write your own script), the ItemChanged event will issue an AcceptText function.

You may want to write your own script so that you can test the data. If you want to reject the data that has been entered, you issue a SetActionCode(1) function to override the default processing, reject the entry, keep the focus on the edit control, and trigger the ItemError event. For example:

```
int     nInvoice

nInvoice = Integer(dw_Invoice.GetText( ))
IF nInvoice < nLastInvoice THEN dw_Invoice.SetActionCode(1)
```

The ItemError event is triggered when the data conversion fails or if the validation fails. The default behavior is to display a message box with an error message and hold focus on the same field. You can write a script to this event also.

THE OBJECT BROWSER

You can use the Object Browser to display DataWindows and attributes. Selecting a DataWindow in the top ListBox lists the DataWindow attributes in the lower window. Another option is to double-click on the DataWindow in the top window. This expands the DataWindow, listing the attributes. You can then click on the attribute in the top window and list the element attributes in the lower window.

DATAWINDOW CONTROL ATTRIBUTES

- **Border**—a Boolean, this is True if there is a border around the control.

- **BorderStyle**—an enumerated value containing the border style (StyleBox!, StyleLowered!, StyleRaised!, or StyleShadowBox!).

- **BringToTop**—sets this Boolean to True to place the DataWindow on top of other overlapping controls in this window's front-to-back order.

- **ControlMenu**—adds a control menu to the DataWindow. This will add functions to allow the user to move, resize (restore, maximize), minimize, or close the DataWindow. This is available only if you have added a title bar to the DataWindow.

- **DataObject**—changes the DataWindow object that is associated with this control.

- **DragAuto**—if this Boolean is set to True this control will be automatically set into Drag Mode when the user clicks on it.

- **DragIcon**—a string containing the name of the icon that will be displayed when this control is in Drag Mode. If you select **None!**, a ghost outline of the control will be used.

- **Enabled**—a Boolean value, set to True to enable the control, making it active and able to be selected or clicked and to receive events.

- **Height**—an integer value that specifies the vertical size of the control in PBUs.

- **HScrollBar**—a Boolean value, True if a horizontal scroll bar will be added to this control as needed.

- **HSplitScroll**—displays the split bar in the DataWindow object, this lets the user divide the DataWindow into two windows.

- **Icon**—specifies the icon that should be used when the DataWindow is minimized.

- **LiveScroll**—set this to True to allow the user to move through the rows in the DataWindow using the scroll bar.

- **MaxBox**—adds the maximize button to the DataWindow. This is available only if you have added a title bar to the DataWindow.

- **MinBox**—adds the minimize button to the DataWindow. This is available only if you have added a title bar to the DataWindow.

- **Resizable**—lets the user resize the DataWindow. If selected, this adds a thin frame to the window. The user can resize the window by clicking and dragging this frame. This is available only if you have added a title bar to the DataWindow.

- **TabOrder**—an integer that specifies the relative tab order for the controls on the window.

- **Tag**—a text string associated with this control can be used to store the Microhelp text.

- **Title**—adds a title to the DataWindow. This attribute is the caption for the title.

- **TitleBar**—a Boolean, True to add a title bar to the DataWindow.

- **Visible**—a Boolean value, True if the control is visible (showing).

- **VScrollBar**—a Boolean value, if True a vertical scroll bar will be added to this control as needed.

- **Width**—an integer value that specifies the horizontal size of the control in PBUs.

- **X**—an integer value that specifies the horizontal position in the window of the control in PBUs.

- **Y**—an integer value that specifies the vertical position in the window of the control in PBUs.

DataWindow Control Events

- **Clicked**—occurs when the user clicks within the DataWindow.

- **Constructor**—occurs just before the window is made the active window. The window sends a constructor event to all its objects just before the window Open event occurs.

- **DBError**—triggered when a database error occurs as a result of a DataWindow operation.

- **Destructor**—occurs when the window is closing. The window sends a destructor event to all its objects just after the window Close event occurs.

- **DoubleClicked**—occurs when the user double-clicks on an item in the list. You may use this to execute code as the result of the double-click.

- **DragDrop**—occurs when Drag mode is on and the pointer drops an object within the control.

- **DragEnter**—occurs when Drag mode is on and the dragged object enters the control. If Drag mode is off and this control's DragAuto attribute is set, a DragEnter event will be triggered (rather than a Clicked event) when the user clicks the control.

- **DragLeave**—occurs when Drag Mode is on and the dragged object leaves the control.

- **DragWithin**—occurs when Drag Mode is on, this event is triggered periodically while an object is dragged within the control.

- **EditChanged**—occurs when the entry in the DataWindow edit control is changed.

- **GetFocus**—occurs just before the control is selected with the Tab key or by clicking.

- **ItemChanged**—occurs when the text in the edit control has been changed and the user presses the **Enter** or **Tab** key or clicks elsewhere on the window.

■ **ItemError**—triggered after an ItemChanged event if the validation fails for that field.

■ **ItemFocusChanged**—triggered when the user changes the focus to another item in the DataWindow.

■ **LoseFocus**—occurs before the control loses focus (caused by tabbing away or clicking outside of the control.

■ **Other**—all the other Windows events that have not been mapped to PowerBuilder events are routed to this event. You will rarely use this event; user-defined events are a better choice.

■ **PrintEnd**—triggered when a DataWindow print ends.

■ **PrintPage**—triggered just before each page (of a DataWindow) is printed. You can use this event to skip the printing of each page.

■ **PrintStart**—triggered when a DataWindow print begins.

■ **RButtonDown**—occurs when the right mouse button is pressed and the pointer is located within the DataWindow control.

■ **Resize**—triggered when the DataWindow is resized.

■ **RetrieveEnd**—triggered when a DataWindow completes a retrieve operation.

■ **RetrieveStart**—triggered when a DataWindow begins a retrieve operation.

■ **RowFocusChanged**—triggered each time a different row is selected in the DataWindow.

■ **ScrollHorizontal**—triggered when the user scrolls the DataWindow left or right.

■ **ScrollVertical**—triggered when the user scrolls the DataWindow up or down.

■ **SQLPreview**—triggered just before the SQL statement is issued as a result of a DataWindow data manipulation function including Retrieve, Update, and ReselectRow.

■ **UpdateEnd**—triggered after the updates have been completed against the database.

■ **UpdateStar**t—triggered when an update is about to be issued against the database.

DataWindow Control Functions

■ **AcceptText**—moves the edit control text into the current item buffer cell.

■ **CanUndo**—a Boolean value, the effects of the last edit can be reversed.

■ **ClassName**—returns the name of the DataWindow control.

■ **Clear**—deletes the selected text from the DataWindow control, does not place the deleted text in the Windows clipboard.

■ **ClearValues**—deletes all the values from the value list for the column of a DataWindow.

■ **Copy**—copies the selected text from the DataWindow control to the Windows clipboard.

■ **Cut**—deletes the selected text from the DataWindow control, places the deleted text in the Windows clipboard.

■ **DBCancel**—cancels the current database retrieval.

■ **DBErrorCode**—returns the DBMS specific error code for the last database operation.

■ **DBErrorMessage**—returns the DBMS specific error text for the last database operation.

■ **DBHandle**—returns the database connection handle.

■ **DeletedCount**—returns the number (count) of rows that have been deleted from the primary DataWindow buffer (that have not yet been deleted from the database).

■ **DeleteRow**—removes a row from the DataWindow.

■ **Drag**—begins or ends Drag Mode for this control.

■ **Filter**—applies the current filter to the DataWindow.

- **FilteredCount**—returns the number (count) of rows that are in the filtered DataWindow buffer (that have been removed from the primary buffer as a result of the current filter).

- **GetBorderStyle**—returns the enumerated value describing the type of border on the DataWindow column.

- **GetClickedColumn**—returns an integer, the number of the column that was clicked.

- **GetClickedRow**—returns a long, the number of the row that was clicked.

- **GetColumn**—returns the number of the current column.

- **GetColumnName**—returns the name (a string) of the current column.

- **GetData**—retrieves data from a control, used for graphs and EditMasks.

- **GetFormat**—returns the data format (a string) of the current column.

- **GetItemDate**—returns the value in a specific DataWindow item (row and column) as a date.

- **GetItemDateTime**—returns the value in a specific DataWindow item (row and column) as a datetime data type.

- **GetItemDecimal**—returns the value in a specific DataWindow item (row and column) as a decimal.

- **getItemNumber**—returns the value in a specific DataWindow item (row and column) as a number.

- **GetItemString**—returns the value in a specific DataWindow item (row and column) as a string.

- **GetItemTime**—returns the value in a specific DataWindow item (row and column) as a time.

- **GetRow**—returns the number (a long) of the current row in the DataWindow.

- **GetSelectedRow**—returns the number (a long) of the first selected row in the DataWindow.

- **GetSQLSelect**—returns a string containing the SQL SELECT statement currently associated with this DataWindow.

- **GetText**—returns a string, the text in the edit control.

- **GetTrans**—returns the values that have been assigned to the transaction object that has been assigned to this DataWindow.

- **GetValidate**—returns the validation rule (a string) for a specific column in the DataWindow.

- **GetValue**—returns the value of a specific value list item for a column.

- **Hide**—makes a DataWindow control invisible.

- **ImportChipboard**—copies data from the Windows clipboard into a DataWindow.

- **ImportFile**—copies data from a DOS file into a DataWindow.

- **ImportString**—copies data (in a string) into a DataWindow.

- **InsertRow**—adds a new row to the DataWindow at a specified location, may initialize some of the column values.

- **IsSelected**—returns a Boolean, True if the specified row is currently selected.

- **LineCount**—returns the number (the count) of lines that are in the current field.

- **ModifiedCount**—returns the number (count) of rows that have been changed in the primary DataWindow buffer (that have not yet been updated in the database).

- **Move**—relocates the DataWindow control in the window.

- **Paste**—copies the text on the Windows clipboard into the DataWindow. If text is currently selected in the DataWindow, the clipboard text will replace it.

- **PointerX**—returns the pointer's horizontal position in the control.

- **PointerY**—returns the pointer's vertical position in the control.

- **Position**—returns the cursor position in the control's current field.

- **Post**—adds a message to the message queue of a window asynchronously.

- **PostEvent**—places an event on the DataWindow control's event queue and continues (asynchronously).

- **Print**—prints a copy of the DataWindow.

- **PrintCancel**—cancels the current print job.

- **ReplaceText**—replaces given text with a new string.

- **ReselectRow**—reissues the SQL SELECT statement for the DataWindow and then reselects the current row.

- **Reset**—clears the DataWindow.

- **ResetTransObject**—resets the DataWindow to use the internal transaction objects, disassociating the connection to the previously assigned transaction object.

- **Resize**—adjusts the size of the DataWindow control.

- **Retrieve**—issues the SQL SELECT statement for this DataWindow.

- **RowCount**—returns the current number of rows in this DataWindow's primary buffer.

- **RowsCopy**—copies a set of rows from one DataWindow control to another, or from buffer to buffer within one DataWindow.

- **RowsDiscard**—removes a set of rows from a DataWindow control.

- **RowsMove**—moves a set of rows from one DataWindow control to another, or from buffer to buffer within one DataWindow.

- **SaveAs**—writes the rows in this DataWindow out to another format, such as dBase or Lotus.

- **Scroll**—scrolls (moves) to a specific relative row in the DataWindow.

- **ScrollNextPage**—scrolls forward one page (a page is the number of rows that display in the DataWindow).

- **ScrollNextRow**—scrolls forward one row in the DataWindow.

- **ScrollPriorPage**—scrolls backward one page in the DataWindow.

- **ScrollPriorRow**—scrolls backward one row in the DataWindow.

- **ScrollToRow**—scrolls (moves) to a specific row number in the DataWindow.

- **SelectedLength**—returns the count of characters currently selected (highlighted) in the DataWindow

- **SelectedLine**—returns a string, a copy of the text that is currently selected in the control.

- **SelectedStart**—returns the position of the first character selected in the control.

- **SelectedText**—returns the text selected in the control.

- **SelectRow**—selects (highlights) an item on the list by position.

- **SelectText**—selects (highlights) a section of the text in the control.

- **SetActionCode**—specifies the behavior of the DataWindow after an event (such as RetrieveRow).

- **SetBorderStyle**—assigns an enumerated value to determine the border style.

- **SetColumn**—sets the current column.

- **SetDataPieExplode**—lets you explode a pie slice in a pie graph.

- **SetDetailHeight**—sets the height of each row to a specific height.

- **SetFilter**—defines the PowerScript expression used for the Filter function associated with this DataWindow.

- **SetFocus**—places the focus on the DataWindow control, directs keyboard input to the control.

- **SetFormat**—sets the column display format (a string) for the column.

- **SetItem**—sets the value of an item in the DataWindow.

- **SetPosition**—places the DataWindow in the front-to-back display order (relative to other overlapping controls).

- **SetRedraw**—turns on or off the updating of the control if the data is changed.

- **SetRow**—sets the current row to be the specified row.

- **SetRowFocusIndicator**—assigns an icon to be used as the row focus indicator.

- **SetSort**—specifies the criteria to be used for the Sort() function to order the rows in this DataWindow.

- **SetSQLSelect**—assigns an SQL SELECT statement to the DataWindow.

- **SetTabOrder**—sets the relative tab order value for a column in the DataWindow.

- **SetText**—assigns a string to the edit control.

- **SetTrans**—assigns a transaction object to the DataWindow, also manages transactions.

- **SetTransObject**—assigns a transaction object to the DataWindow; you must control the transactions. Use this instead of SetTrans.

- **SetValidate**—assigns a validation rule (a string) to a column in the DataWindow.

- **SetValue**—assigns a value to a value list associated with a column in the DataWindow.

- **Show**—makes the DataWindow control visible.

- **Sort**—orders the rows in the DataWindow according to the sort criteria defined for the DataWindow (may be set by SetSort).

- **TextLine**—returns a string containing the text on the cursor's current line.

- **TriggerEvent**—triggers a DataWindow control event immediately (synchronously).

- **TypeOf**—returns the enumerated type of this control (DataWindow!).

- **Undo**—reverses the last edit made in this control.

- **Update**—applies all the changes made to the DataWindow to the database.

ADVANCED FUNCTIONS FOR
A DATAWINDOW CONTROL

- **Create**—creates a DataWindow.

- **Describe**—returns information about the DataWindow components.

- **Find**—searches for the first row that matches the search criteria.

- **FindRequired**—finds the next column that has been marked as a required column in the DataWindow and that currently contains a NULL value. You may also check only newly added or modified rows.

- **FindGroupChange**—returns the row number of the first row in the next group.

- **GetBandAtPointer**—returns the name of the band currently under the pointer.

- **GetChild**—returns the name of the child DataWindow for a specific column. Used with DropDownDataWindows.

- **GetItemStatus**—returns the DataWindow buffer status for a specific item.

- **GetNextModified**—returns the row number of the next modified item.

- **GetObjectAtPointer**—returns the name of the column or object under the pointer.

- **GetSQLPreview**—returns the current SQL SELECT statement (a string) for the DataWindow.

- **GetUpdateStatus**—returns the row number and buffer for a row that will be updated.

- **GroupCalc**—triggers a recalculation for the groups in a DataWindow.

- **Modify**—changes a DataWindow object using the specified string.

- **OLEActivat**—turns on the OLE function for an OLE object.
- **ResetUpdate**—clears the update flags for the rows in a DataWindow.
- **SetItemStatus**—specifies the update status for an item in the DataWindow.
- **SetPosition**—sets the front-to-back order for the DataWindow object.
- **SetSQLPreview**—assigns a new SQL SELECT statement (a string) to the DataWindow.
- **ShareData**—activates the sharing of a DataWindow buffer between DataWindows.
- **ShareDataOff**—terminates the sharing of data between DataWindow controls.
- **SyntaxFromSQL**—returns a string containing the DataWindow syntax (source code) related to the specified SQL statement.

GRAPH FUNCTIONS FOR A DATAWINDOW CONTROL

- **CategoryCount**—returns the number of categories in the graph.
- **CategoryName**—returns the name for a specfic category.
- **Clipboard**—copies the graph to the Windows clipboard.
- **DataCount**—returns the number of data points in a specific graph category.
- **DataStyle**—returns the style.
- **FindCategory**—returns the number of a specific category.
- **FindSeries**—returns the number of a specific series.
- **GetData**—returns a data value for a series in the graph.
- **ObjectAtPointer**—returns the object type, the series and data point under the pointer.

- **ResetDataColors**—resets the colors to the default values.
- **SaveAs**—saves the data associated with the graph to a file.
- **SeriesCount**—returns the number of series in the graph.
- **SeriesName**—returns the name of a specific series.
- **SeriesStyle**—returns the FillPattern or the color for a specific series.
- **SetDataStyle**—sets the FillPattern or the color for a specific data point.
- **SetSeriesStyle**—sets the FillPattern or the color for a specific series.

Function Name Changes in PowerBuilder 4

PowerBuilder 4 changed the names of the two sets of functions that have just been discussed. The first set, the Advanced functions, have been renamed to drop the dw prefix for each fuction's name. The second set have dropped the gr prefix for the graph functions. For example, **dwCreate** is now **Create**. The old names are still supported in PowerBuilder 4 for backward compatibility, but we recommend that you use the new names. Tables 11.1 and 11.2 list the function name changes.

TABLE 11.1   DW FUNCTION NAME CHAGES

POWERBUILDER 3	POWERBUILDER 4
dwCreate	Create
dwDescribe	Describe
dwFind	Find
dwFindGroupChange	FindGroupChange
dwFindRequired	FindRequired
dwGetBandAtPointer	GetBandAtPointer

continued on next page

POWERBUILDER 3	**POWERBUILDER 4**
dwGetChild	GetChild
dwGetItemStatus	GetItemStatus
dwGetNextModified	GetNextModified
dwGetObjectAtPointer	GetObjectAtPointer
dwGetSQLPreview	GetSQLPreview
dwGetUpdateStatus	GetUpdateStatus
dwGroupCalc	GroupCalc
dwModify	Modify
dwOLEActivate	OLEActivate
dwResetUpdate	ResetUpdate
SetItemStatus	SetItemStatus
dwSetPosition	SetPosition
dwSctSQLPreview	SetSQLPreview
dwShareData	ShareData
dwShareDataOff	ShareDataOff
dwSyntaxFromSQL	SyntaxFromSQL

TABLE 11.2 gr FUNCTION NAME CHANGES

POWERBUILDER 3	**POWERBUILDER 4**
grAddCategory	AddCategory
grAddData	AddData
grAddSeries	AddSeries
grCategoryCount	CategoryCount
grCategoryName	CategoryName
grClipboard	Clipboard

continued on next page

POWERBUILDER 3	POWERBUILDER 4
grDataCount	DataCount
grDataStyle	GetDataStyle
grDeleteCategory	DeleteCategory
grDeleteData	DeleteData
grDeleteSeries	DeleteSeries
grFindCategory	FindCategory
grFindSeries	FindSeries
grGetData	GetData
grImportClipboard	ImportClipboard
grImportFile	ImportFile
grImportString	ImportString
grInsertCategory	InsertCategory
grInsertData	InsertData
grInsertSeries	InsertSeries
grModifyData	ModifyData
grObjectAtPointer	ObjectAtPointer
grReset	Reset
grResetDataColors	ResetDataColors
grSaveAs	SaveAs
grSeriesCount	SeriesCount
grSeriesName	SeriesName
grSeriesStyle	GetSeriesStyle
grSetDataStyle	SetDataStyle
grSetSeriesStyle	SetSeriesStyle

DATAWINDOW CONTROL POPUP MENU OPTIONS

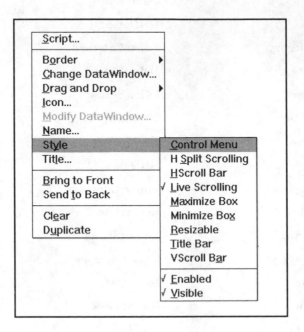

FIGURE 11.7 THE DATAWINDOW POPUP MENU

The items in the popup menu (right mouse click on the control) for a SingleLineEdit control are:

- **Script**—edits a script for a control event.

- **Border**—selects the type of border to be used for this control.

- **Change DataWindow**—opens the Select DataWindow dialog box so that you can assign (or reassign) a DataWindow object to this DataWindow control.

- **Drag and Drop**—sets or clears the DragAuto Mode attribute or defines an icon for the Drag Mode.

- **Icon**—selects an icon for when the DataWindow control is minimized (if you allowed the user that option).

- **Modify DataWindow**—opens the DataWindow painter so that you may edit the DataWindow object associated with this control.

- **Name**—opens the control's Style dialog box.

- **Style**—toggles Control menu, Hsplit Scrolling, Hscroll Bar, Live Scrolling, Maximize Box, Minimize Box, Resizable, Title Bar, Vscroll Bar, Visible, or Enabled attributes.

- **Title**—sets the title for the DataWindow.

- **Bring to Front**—moves this control to the front of other overlapping controls.

- **Send to Back**—moves this control to the back of other overlapping controls.

- **Delete**—removes this control from the window.

- **Duplicate**—makes a copy of this control.

You can change the control's name from the default that was assigned by the Window painter. All references that you make in script code will be to the DataWindow control (i.e., dw_1) rather than to the DataWindow object.

You can add a title bar to the DataWindow, but this has the unfortunate side effect of making the DataWindow movable (by dragging the title bar) in the window at run time. This would seldom be desirable, so rather than use a title bar, it is better to add a static text field to the window.

CREATING A DATAWINDOW

The example programs include several applications for this chapter:

- **FirstDw**—creates the first DataWindow application. The second version of this application will add a second DataWindow and create a master-detail relationship with the first.

- **ImageDb**—creates a version of SQLApp (the embedded SQL example from Chapter 8) using a DataWindow. This application then adds directory navigation and a window to display the images.

- **ChildDw**—creates a DataWindow that uses the other edit styles for DataWindow columns. This includes Check Box, DropDownDataWindow, DropDownListBox, EditMask, and Radio Button styles.

- **BlobDb**—an embedded SQL example that stores blobs (images in this case) in the database. This was introduced in Chapter 8.

- **DwStyles**—demonstrates each of the DataWindow presentation styles.

The first version of the FirstDw example will be the minimum amount of code to populate and undate a DataWindow. Create a new application object and library to begin this application. Create a window (w_main) and save it it the new application library.

Create a DataWindow object. Use the cust_order table to create the following SQL SELECT statment:

```
SELECT "company"."company",
       "cust_order"."ordnum",
       "cust_order"."duedate",
       "cust_order"."balance",
       "cust_order"."custnum"
   FROM "company",
       "cust_order"
ORDER BY "company"."company" ASC,
       "cust_order"."ordnum" DESC
```

Accept the default field layout, and save this DataWindow object as d_customer_orders. Add a DataWindow control (dw_1) to the w_main window. Assign the d_customer_orders DataWindow object to dw_1 (use the RMB popup menu on dw_1 and select **Change DataWindow**). Be sure to add a vertical scroll bar to the DataWindow. To do this, open the popup menu (right-mouse click on the DataWindow), select the **Style** option, and toggle on the **VScroll Bar** option in the cascading menu. Also check that the **Live Scrolling** option is turned on in the same menu.

Add a static text field to w_main to serve as a status field. Name the static text control st_status, assign it the default text of **Connecting to DB...**, and position it at the bottom of the window. You may also add a **Close** command button. Name the button **cb_close** and add the following line to its Clicked event:

```
Close(Parent)
```

Now you can add the code to the application Open event. Open the Application painter and click on the **Script** icon. In the PowerScript editor select the **Open** event. You can use the APPOPEN.TXT file for the script. You will find the APPOPEN.TXT file in the examples for this book (the default directory is C:\PB4\CLASS). This will use the IMAGEDB.INI file as the initialization (profile) file. This provide the information necessary to connect to the Image database that is used for all the example programs.

The Open script opens the w_main window, reads the INI file, populates the SQLCA transaction object, and connects to the database. The st_status field is updated to reflect the success or failure of the database connection.

Next, add the code required to set the transaction object for dw_1 and then populate the DataWindow using the **Retrieve** function. Go back to the application Open event and add the following two lines of code to set the transaction object and retrieve the data:

```
w_main.dw_1.SetTransObject ( sqlca )
w_main.dw_1.Retrieve ( )
```

In the Application Open event add the above two lines as shown (at the bottom of the script).

Change this code:

```
connect;
IF sqlca.sqlcode = 0 THEN
    w_main.st_status.text = "connected"
ELSE
    w_main.st_status.text = "db connect failed"
END IF
```

to this:

```
connect;
IF sqlca.sqlcode = 0 THEN
    w_main.st_status.text = "connected"
    w_main.dw_1.SetTransObject ( sqlca )
    w_main.dw_1.Retrieve ( )
ELSE
    w_main.st_status.text = "db connect failed"
END IF
```

Now run the application and check that the database connection is successful. The DataWindow should be populated with rows from the cust_order table. If you added the vertical scroll bar to the DataWindow, you will be able to scroll through the rows in the DataWindow.

So far the application only retrieves and displays the rows from the cust_order table. Next we will add buttons that allow you to add rows to or delete rows from the DataWindow, and to apply the changes in the DataWindow to the database.

Insert

Add a CommandButton, **cb_insert1**, to the window. Add the following code to that button's Clicked event:

```
long lRow
lRow = dw_1.InsertRow(0)
IF lRow > 0 THEN
    dw_1.SetColumn(1)
    dw_1.ScrollToRow(lRow)
    dw_1.SetRow(lRow) //implicit
    dw_1.SetFocus()
END IF
```

This example inserts the new row at the bottom of the DataWindow. The next lines of code scroll to the new row and set the focus on the first column. You could also insert the new row at the top or somewhere else in the DataWindow by specifying the row number.

Delete

Add a CommandButton, **cb_delete1**, to the window. Add the following code to that button's Clicked event:

```
dw_1.DeleteRow(0)
dw_1.SetFocus()
```

This code will delete the current row from the DataWindow. To use this select a row and then click the **Delete** button.

Update

Add a CommandButton, **cb_update**, to the window. Add the following code to that button's Clicked event:

```
int rc
rc = dw_1.Update()
IF rc = 1 THEN
    commit;
ELSE
    rollback;
END IF
```

This code will apply all changes to the database. If the Update is successful the changes are committed to the database, otherwise the transaction is rolled back.

Test the application. At this point you should be able to insert, update, and delete rows against the cust_order table. You should also go back and check the status code for each fuction. Most of these checks where left out to simplify this example.

Other DataWindow Enhancements

SaveAs

Next we will add a **SaveAs** button to the window. Clicking this will allow the user to export the contents of the DataWindow. The user will be presented with a list of export file types, such as dBase3 or Excel.

Next we will add a button to print the contents of the DataWindow. Create a button, **cb_saveas**, and add the following line of code to its Clicked event:

```
dw_1.SaveAs ( )
```

Print

Finally, we will add a button to print the contents of the DataWindow. The simplest solution is to add the single line:

```
dw_1.Print()
```

This will print the entire contents of DataWindow dw_1. You can also open a print job. That involves a few more lines of code as follows:

```
int nJob
nJob = PrintOpen("Report")
PrintDataWindow(nJob, dw_1)
PrintClose(nJob)
```

The format of the printout is determined in the DataWindow painter. In the painter you would select the **Design.Print Specifications** menu option. This opens the Print Specifications dialog box, where you can specify margins, paper orientation, and so on. If you click the **Prompt before printing** check box, the user will be prompted for this information when the print is triggered.

514

In the DataWindow painter you can set the print units of measure to inches or centimeters. Set this parameter under the Design.DataWindow Style menu option.

Query Mode

Add two more CommandButtons to the window. Name the first **cb_qbe** and assign it the text **SetQuery**. Name the second **cb_reset** and assign it the text **Reset**. The cb_qbe button serves two purposes. Initially it will be used to initiate query mode. Then the label will switch to Execute and the button will be used to execute the query. Add the following code to the clicked event for cb_qbe:

```
IF cb_qbe.Text = "Execute" THEN
    dw_1.SetRedraw (FALSE)
    dw_1.Modify ("datawindow.querymode=no")
    dw_1.Retrieve ()
    dw_1.SetRedraw (TRUE)
    cb_qbe.Text = "SetQuery"
    st_status.text  = " "
ELSE
    dw_1.Modify ("datawindow.querymode=yes")
    dw_1.SetFocus ()
    cb_qbe.Text = "Execute"
    st_status.text  = "Enter Query Criteria & Click Execute"
End If
```

Clicking the **cb_reset** button resets the DataWindow and initiates a new query. Add the following code to the clicked event for cb_reset:

```
dw_1.DataObject = dw_1.DataObject
dw_1.SetTransObject (sqlca)
cb_qbe.Text = 'SetQuery'
cb_qbe.PostEvent(Clicked!)
```

At this point you may wish to make some slight modifications to the d_customer_orders DataWindow object. In order to allow enough space for query expressions you should widen each column. Also, while in the DataWindow painter you should set the Query Criteria Override Edit option. This lets the user enter expressions for the query criteria (otherwise the comparison is only for equality). To do this, select the **Edit** option from each column's popup menu. Then select **Query Criteria** and **Override Edit** from the cascading menu. Do this for each column.

CREATING A MASTER-DETAIL RELATIONSHIP

The next version of FirstDW will add a second DataWindow to the w_main window and establish a master-detail relationship with the first DataWindow. In this example, when you click on a row in dw_1 (the customer order), dw_2 will display the invoice line items for the clicked row. This requires that you define the second DataWindow with a retrieval argument for the invoice number (ordnum). When the user clicks in the first DataWindow you must determine the clicked row and retrieve the order number of the invoice in that row. Using this value as the retrieval argument, you then trigger the retrieval for the second DataWindow. Essentially the code to perform this function would look something like the following:

```
1Row = dw_1.GetClickedRow()
sInvno = dw_1.GetItemNumber(1Row, 2)
dw_2.Retrieve(sInvno)
```

The code that we use is a little more complicated that this sample, but this is essentially how our example functions.

Create a second DataWindow object. Use the line_item table as the source. Create a retrieval argument as follows:

```
string sOrderNumber.
```

Then create the following SQL SELECT statment:

```
SELECT "line_item"."ordnum",
       "line_item"."line_no",
       "line_item"."partname",
       "line_item"."price",
       "line_item"."quantity",
```

```
        "line_item"."extended_price"
    FROM "line_item"
   WHERE "line_item"."ordnum" = :sOrderNumber
ORDER BY "line_item"."line_no" ASC
```

Accept the default field layout and save this DataWindow object as d_invoice. Add a DataWindow control (dw_2) to the w_main window. Assign the d_invoice DataWindow object to dw_2 (use the RMB popup menu on dw_1 and select **Change DataWindow**). Be sure to add a vertical scroll bar to the DataWindow. To do this open the popup menu (right-mouse click on the DataWindow), select the **Style** menu option and then toggle on the **VScroll Bar** option in the cascading menu. Also check that the **Live Scrolling** option is turned on in the same menu.

Add the following line to the end of the Application Open event:

```
w_main.dw_2.SetTransObject ( sqlca )
```

This will assign the SQLCA transaction object to dw_2.

To implement the master-detail relationship declare the following as instance variables:

```
string i_sInvoice
long i_lRow = 0
```

Then add the following code to the Clicked event for dw_1:

```
long lRow

IF cb_qbe.Text <> 'Execute' THEN // needed only for cb_qbe
    IF i_lRow = 0 THEN
        lRow = dw_1.GetClickedRow ()
    ELSE
        lRow = i_lRow
    END IF
    IF lRow > 0 THEN
        i_sInvoice = dw_1.GetItemString ( lRow, 'cust_order_ordnum' )
        dw_2.Retrieve (i_sInvoice )
    END IF
    i_lRow = 0
END IF // needed on for cb_qbe
```

The two commented lines should be included only if you added the cb_qbe CommandButton in the previous section. If you did not add that CommandButton, leave these two lines out.

Now clicking on a row (an invoice) in dw_1 will trigger a retrieval of the corresponding line items in dw_2.

Add a set of buttons to insert, delete, and update dw_2. Now it is possible to add invoice line items. If you add line items, you will need to update the balance in the invoice table (dw_1). To do this add a button labeled **Update Totals** and add the following code to its clicked event:

```
long idx, jdx
decimal{2} decBalance, decOld
FOR idx = 1 to dw_1.RowCount()
    dw_1.SetRow(idx)
    i_lRow = idx
    dw_1.TriggerEvent(Clicked!)
    decBalance = 0
    FOR jdx = 1 to dw_2.RowCount()
        decBalance += dw_2.GetItemDecimal(jdx, 'extended_price')
    NEXT
    decOld = dw_1.GetItemDecimal(idx, 'cust_order_balance')
    IF decOld <> decBalance THEN
        dw_1.SetItem(idx, 'cust_order_balance', decBalance)
    END IF
NEXT
```

NESTED REPORT EXAMPLE

The same master-detail relationship can be created by nesting the detail DataWindow object (d_invoice) directly into the customer order DataWindow. To do this, create a new window for the nested report. You can use the d_customer_orders DataWindow object for a starting point. Open this object and save a new version of it named d_customer_orders_base_report. Create a space at the bottom of the DataWindow for the nested report.

To add the nested DataWindow, click on the **Report** icon on the PainterBar or select **Report** from the Object menu. Next, click at the point where you wish to add the nested DataWindow. This opens the Select Report dialog box (Figure 11.8).

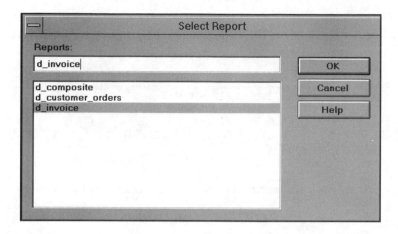

FIGURE 11.8 SELECT THE DATAWINDOW IN THIS DIALOG BOX

Select the **d_invoice** report and then click **OK**. This drops the nested report into the DataWindow. Position and size the nesting report (the rectangle) as shown in Figure 11.9.

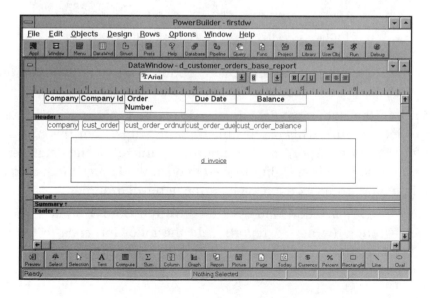

FIGURE 11.9 A NESTED DATAWINDOW

Next, we need to create the association between the DataWindows. Click the right mouse button on the nested report to open the RMB popup menu as shown in Figure 11.10.

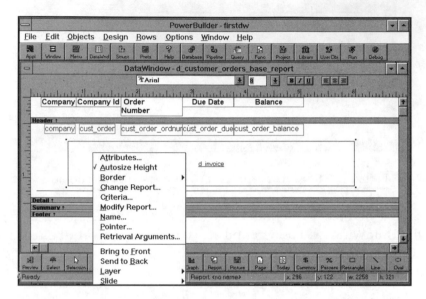

FIGURE 11.10 SELECT RETRIEVAL ARGUMENTS

Select the **Retrieval Arguments** menu option. This opens the Retrieval Arguments dialog box shown in Figure 11.11.

Click in the right-most field to drop down the ListBox and then select **cust_order_ordnum**. This assigns the ordnum value from the cust_order field (in the master report) as the retrieval argument for the detail report. You could also double-click in this field to open the Expression dialog box to build a more complex expression for the retrieval argument.

Save the DataWindow and associate it with a DataWindow control in the new window (w_nested_report). Add the following code to the window's Open event:

```
int rc

rc = dw_1.setTransObject ( sqlca )
IF rc = 1 THEN dw_1.Retrieve ( )
```

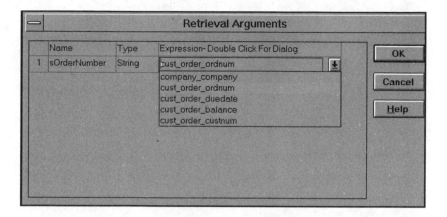

FIGURE 11.11 SPECIFY THE RETRIEVAL ARGUMENT FOR D_INVOICE

You may also add a vertical scroll bar to the DataWindow. The final result appears as in Figure 11.12.

Company	Company Id	Order Number	Due Date	Balance			
ACME	222	99001	19941212	$3,767.00			

	Ordnum	Line No	Partname	Price	Quantity	Extended Price
	99001	1	hardware	400.00	2	800.00
		2	consulting	250.25	10	2,502.50
		3	software	123.50	7	864.50

ACME	222	6134	19941002	$6,442.50		

	Ordnum	Line No	Partname	Price	Quantity	Extended Price
	6134	1	hardware	400.00	4	1,600.00
		2	consulting	250.25	8	2,002.00
		3	software	123.50	23	2,840.50

ACME	222	57002	19941029	$1,765.00		

	Ordnum	Line No	Partname	Price	Quantity	Extended Price
	57002	1	hardware	400.00	1	400.00
		2	consulting	250.25	2	500.50
		3	software	123.50	7	864.50

ACME	222	12123	19940901	$3,416.25		

FIGURE 11.12 A NESTED DataWindow REPORT

CHAPTER TWELVE

MENUS

INTRODUCTION TO THE MENU PAINTER

Most Windows applications use menus rather than CommandButtons. Menus use commands and other options in the place of CommandButtons and checkboxes. CommandButtons are okay to use in simple applications, but for most of your applications, you will prefer to use menus. MDI applications, as a characteristic of their style, use menus and not CommandButtons. As an exercise, convert the example applications to use menus instead of buttons. To do this involves these steps: create the menu, move the scripts from the CommandButton Clicked event to the Clicked event for the menu item, and change any script references from Parent to ParentWindow (or add the name of the window).

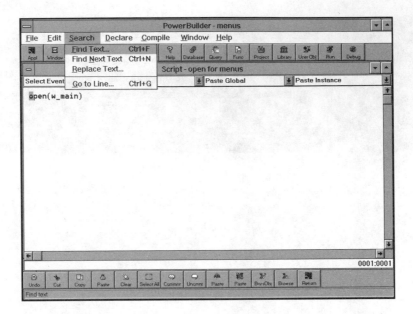

FIGURE 12.1 THE POWERSCRIPT PAINTER SEARCH MENU

Figure 12.1 shows the menu in the PowerScript painter. The menu bar contains one entry for each dropdown menu. In this example, the menu bar contains the items: File, Edit, Window, and Help (among others). When you select one of the menus (Edit in this example), the dropdown menu opens, displaying the menu options. Most of these options will perform some immediate action. It is possible that a menu option will open another window (usually a dialog window) or a cascading menu. The menu items that open other windows are marked with an ellipsis. For example, in Figure 12.1, the item Find Text... opens a dialog window to accept the search criteria.

If the menu item opens another cascading menu, a right triangle symbol is displayed next to the menu item to mark it. Cascading menus are not often used, but can be useful.

Popup menus are another type of menu that you can create for your applications. These are menus that appear in the window, not related to a menu bar. By now, you are very familiar with the PowerBuilder popup menu which is opened by clicking the right mouse button.

CREATING MENUS

PowerBuilder makes the creation of menus easy. To create a new menu, click on the PowerBar **Menu** icon to open the Select Menu dialog window (Figure 12.2).

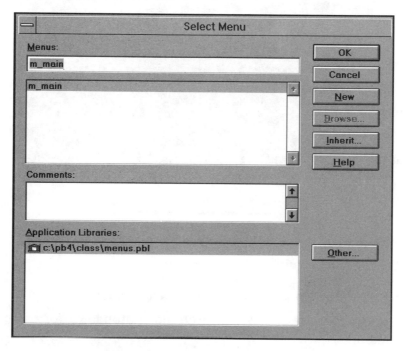

FIGURE 12.2 THE SELECT MENU DIALOG

Click on the **New** CommandButton to open the Menu painter (Figure 12.3).

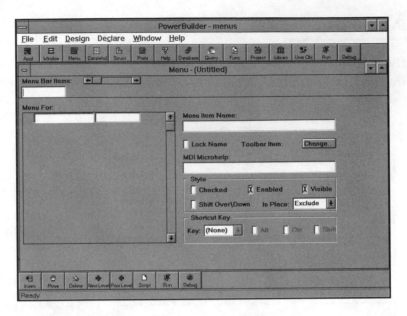

FIGURE 12.3 THE MENU PAINTER

The menu painter is one of the simpler painters to use. It contains three sections (see Figure 12.3):

1. **Menu Bar Items**—an area to create a menu bar.
2. **Menu For item**—an area to build a dropdown (or cascading) menu.
3. **Attributes**—an area to specify attributes such as menu item name, enabled, or checked.

The Menu painter calls each component of the menu bar and the dropdown (or cascading) menu a menu item. In this chapter, the menu items that are on the menu bar will be referred to as *menu bar items*.

To create a menu, add an item to the menu bar and then add the items to the dropdown menu. You must then add PowerScript code to implement the commands and menu options. This code will be added to the Clicked event for each dropdown menu item. You have several other options, such as accelerators, that are also covered in this chapter.

ADDING MENU BAR ITEMS

When you add a menu to one of your windows, the menu bar items appear in the menu bar across the top of the window (just below the Title bar). The exact design for each menu varies from application to application, but the menu bar for most Windows applications typically includes the entries File, Edit, Window, and Help, as shown in Figure 12.1. Your first task in creating a menu, is to add the first menu bar item. Your menu bar must, of course, contain at least one item. Click in the menu bar definition area to open a SingleLineEdit box where you can enter the text for the menu bar item. The Menu painter will suggest a name for the menu bar item, such as m_file.

Add additional menu bar items by clicking just to the right of the last menu bar entry. This opens the SingleLineEdit box where you can enter the label for the new menu bar item.

You can add a separation line to a menu by entering a single dash (–) for the MenuItem label.

Adding Dropdown (or Cascading) Menu Items

Add items to the menu in the second area of the Menu painter window under the label *Menu For: Test* in this example.

Menu PainterBar Icons

The most common menu operations are available on the Menu painter PainterBar. The insert, move, delete, and script icons work for both menu items and menu bar items.

The PainterBar icons are:

- **Insert**—adds a new menu item at the current location. This shifts all entries (if any) from this point down one row.
- **Move**—relocates a menu item.
- **Delete**—removes a menu item.
- **New level**—steps down into the next lower level of a cascading menu.

- **Prev level**—steps up to the next higher level in a cascading menu.
- **Script**—edits the code for a menu item event.
- **Run**—runs the application.
- **Debug**—debugs the application.

Script

There are only two events for MenuItems.

- **Selected**—triggered when the user highlights the menu item, either with the mouse or with a keyboard combination. You will not usually code for this event. If you do, it will probably be to present some additional information to the user.
- **Clicked**—triggered when the user clicks on a menu item, or selects a menu item with the mouse and then releases the mouse button. Every menu item (except those that trigger a cascading menu) will have PowerScript code associated with it. This is where the command is executed or the menu option is set.

The Clicked event for the menu bar items can be used to set the options (enabled, disabled) for the menu items on the dropdown menu.

Creating Cascading Menus

To create a cascading menu, do the following: add the menu item which triggers the cascading menu (*Show Many* in our example Figure 12.4).

While that menu item is selected, click on the **NextLvl** icon or select the **Edit|Next Level** menu option. The second area (*Menu for*) of the Menu painter changes to display a new dropdown menu. Enter the menu items in this menu just as you did for the first level. You can add additional levels in the same manner. In general, you should avoid multiple-level cascaded menus, as they can be difficult to navigate. To return to the next higher level in the cascading menu just click on the **Prior Lvl** icon or selected the **Edit|Prior Level** menu selection.

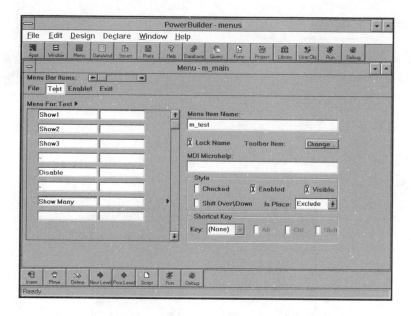

FIGURE 12.4 CREATING A MENU

Figure 12.5 shows the final result.

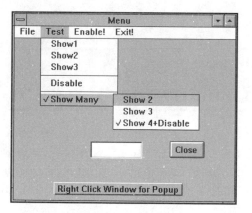

FIGURE 12.5 THE MENU EXAMPLE APPLICATION

Creating Popup Menus

To make a previously-defined menu serve as a popup menu, use the **Popup**() function. In the example, the following line of code is added to the window's RButtonDown event.

```
m_main.M_test.PopMenu(PointerX( ), PointerY( ))
```

This opens the m_test menu (from the m_main menu) at the current pointer position in the window. Figure 12.6 shows the popup menu.

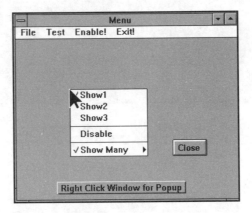

FIGURE 12.6 A POPUP MENU

DEFINING ATTRIBUTES FOR MENUITEMS

Each MenuItem must be named as you add them to a menu. This name lets you reference the menu item from within your PowerScript code. This is most useful for enabling and disabling menu items as a result of another selection. The Menu painter will create a default name for each MenuItem. The name for the MenuItem is a PowerScript identifier and must follow the constraints that were outlined in Chapter 2 (such as a limit of 40 characters).

The Lock Name option tells the Menu painter to keep the name of the MenuItem even if the text associated with that MenuItem is changed.

When you assign a label to a MenuItem the name of the MenuItem was created. Later you may need to change the text that is displayed for that menu item, but you may already have coded references to that MenuItem name in one or more of the events (or in a function). In this case, you would not want to rename the MenuItem based on the modification that you just made to the label. The Lock Name option prevents any change to the MenuItem name. If you have not coded any references to the MenuItem, you can change the name by deselecting the Lock Name checkbox and entering the new name.

ADDING MDI MICROHELP

When creating a menu for an MDI style application, you can add Microhelp text to be displayed when the MenuItem is selected. Just add the text to the edit box that has the label *MDI Microhelp*. In the MDI example, the Images text was added for Microhelp (Figure 12.7).

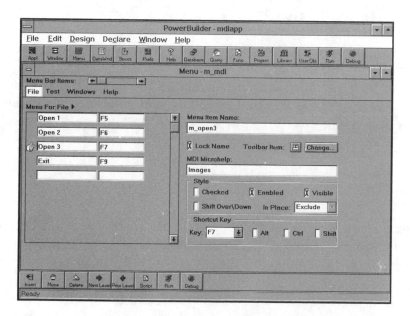

FIGURE 12.7 ADDING MICROHELP TEXT

Adding Icons to the MDI Toolbar

You can add an icon for any menu item to your application's toolbar by clicking **Change...** to open the Select Icon dialog window. Select a predefined icon or an icon file. In Figure 12.7, an icon for the Open3 MenuItem was added.

Other Attributes

You can set other characteristics for the style of a MenuItem in the attributes section of the Menu painter. In the attributes section, you can define the initial state for the MenuItem and define a shortcut key to the item.

- **Checked**—specifies that the item is checked or unchecked.
- **Enabled**—sets the initial state, to enable or disable the menu item.
- **Visible**—sets the initial state as either visible or invisible.

Adding Icons to the MDI Toolbar

You can define a shortcut key for each MenuItem. Select the key from the **Key** dropdown listbox. You may optionally add the Alt, Ctrl, or Shift key to the shortcut by clicking the corresponding checkbox. Generally, you use shortcut keys for a few frequent selections, and you define an accelerator key for every item.

ADDING SCRIPTS

The scripts that you write will be similar to the scripts that you have written for the clicked event of CommandButtons (such as cb_close). The most important difference is that you cannot use the reserved word Parent to refer to the window that contains the menu. To make this type of reference from within a menu, requires the ParentWindow reserved word. In the MenuItem script, use ParentWindow to refer to the window that the menu is in.

You can refer to the attributes of the parent window using the ParentWindow reserved word as follows:

```
ParentWindow.X = 1
```

The major drawback to menus is that the MenuItem event scripts cannot make a reference to the controls on the parent window using the ParentWindow reserved word. You might expect that the following statement:

```
ParentWindow.cb_close.TriggerEvent('Clicked')
```

would trigger the clicked event for the cb_close CommandButton on the w_main window. It would be very useful if this worked, but it does not. It does not work because PowerBuilder cannot resolve the ParentWindow reference at design time. Therefore:

```
w_main.cb_close.TriggerEvent('Clicked')
```

is required to make this work as expected, but it has the disadvantage of requiring the explicit naming of the window.

PREVIEWING THE MENU

Preview the final presentation form for the menu by selecting the **Design|Preview** menu option. You can select menu bar items to: drop down the menu, select menu options, and pull down cascading menus. The preview mode only presents the menu; however, it does not execute any of the script code. To actually test the menu, you need to save it, attach it to a window, and then run (or debug) the application.

SAVING THE MENU

Select the **File|SaveAs** menu option to save the menu. Select the PowerBuilder library in which you wish to save the menu. Give the menu a name (such as m_main) and click on **OK**.

ATTACHING THE MENU TO A WINDOW

To add a menu to a window, go to the Window painter where you have the option of adding a menu to the window. Select the **Design|Style** menu option to open the Window Style dialog. In this dialog, check the Menu CheckBox, then use the dropdown listbox to select the name of the menu. This will add the menu to the window. Run the application to test the newly created menu.

MENUITEM ATTRIBUTES

MenuItems have the following attributes:

- **Checked**
- **Enabled**
- **Item[]**
- **MicroHelp**
- **ShortCut**
- **ParentWindow**
- **Tag**
- **Text**
- **ToolbarItemDown**
- **ToolbarItemDownName**
- **ToolbarItemName**
- **ToolbarItemOrder**
- **ToolbarItemSpace**
- **ToolbarItemText**
- **ToolbarItemVisible**
- **Visible**

MenuItem Functions

The following functions apply to MenuItem:

- **Check**—adds a check mark next to the MenuItem.
- **ClassName**—returns the name of the MenuItem.
- **Disable**—disables the MenuItem.
- **Enable**—enables the MenuItem.
- **Hide**—makes a CommandButton invisible.
- **PopMenu**—opens a menu as a popup window.
- **PostEvent**—places an event on the MenuItem's event queue and continues (asynchronously).
- **Show**—makes the MenuItem visible.
- **TriggerEvent**—triggers an event immediately (synchronously).
- **TypeOf**—returns the enumerated type of this control (MenuItem!).
- **Uncheck**—removes the check mark next to the MenuItem.

CHAPTER THIRTEEN

MULTIPLE DOCUMENT INTERFACE

This chapter presents an example of a Multiple Document Interface (MDI) application. By now you should be familiar with at least one MDI application, PowerBuilder. MDI is a style of application that has become the standard for most larger Windows applications. Microsoft Word and Excel are other familiar examples of MDI applications. The main feature of the MDI style is the use of multiple child windows (called *sheets*) within a parent window (called the *frame*). The components of an MDI application always include a frame window, two or more sheet windows, and one or more menus. MDI applications use menus rather than CommandButtons. This is a style that you should follow as far as possible.

The MDIAPP Example

Run the sample MDI application found in the Class directory. To do this, open the **mdiapp** application in the MDIAPP.PBL. Figure 13.1 shows the mdiapp application's MDI frame window. The status line displays *Connecting to DB…* and then *Ready* if the connection was made successfully.

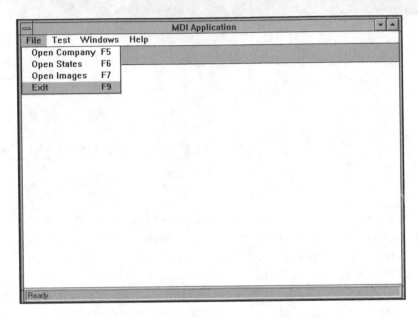

FIGURE 13.1 THE EXAMPLE MDI APPLICATION

In this example, the frame window, the menu bar, the client area where the sheets will be opened, and the MicroHelp status line are shown.

Look first at the menu options. Under the File menu, there are options to open three different types of sheets: one for the COMPANY table, one for the STATES table, and one for the IMAGES table. Selecting any one of these will open a sheet and add the name of the sheet to the Window menu. You can also open multiple instances of each type of sheet. Figure 13.2 shows an example where the user has opened two of each type of sheet.

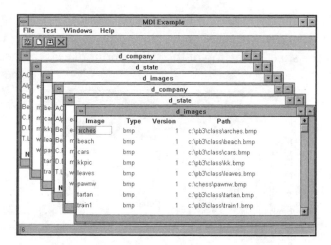

FIGURE 13.2 AFTER OPENING SHEETS IN THE MDI APPLICATION

After you have opened the first sheet, look at the File menu. There, you will find options that have been added to insert or update rows in the table (in the active sheet), to close the current sheet, or close all sheets (see Figure 13.3). It is possible for sheets to have their own menus but in this example the frame menu provides the functions for all the sheets.

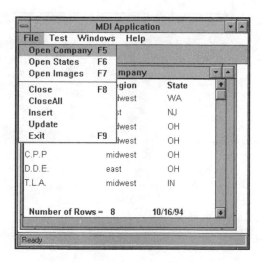

FIGURE 13.3 THE FILE MENU

Pull down the Windows menu to find a set of options to arrange the sheets, and a list of the open sheets. Choose the name of one of the open sheets and it raises the sheet to the top of the stack and makes it the active sheet.

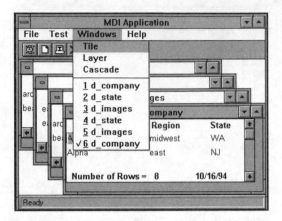

FIGURE 13.4 THE WINDOWS MENU LISTING OPEN SHEETS

The arrangement options are provided to let the user cascade, tile, or layer the sheets. Clicking the tile option arranges the sheets as shown in Figure 13.5.

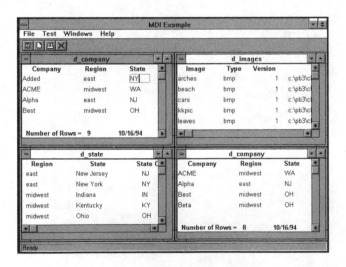

FIGURE 13.5 TILED WINDOWS

In this example, there are four open sheets. Two sheets are opened for the Company table. Notice that in the first sheet, an additional row has been added. This added row does not show up in the other d_company sheet.

CREATING A MDI FRAME

To create the frame window for this example, create a new application and name it **FIRSTMDI**. Create a window. Open the Window Style dialog and under the Window type and select the MDI Frame with MicroHelp option. You can create MDI frames with or without MicroHelp. For this example, select the option for MicroHelp. Save the window with the name **w_main_mdi**.

The MDI frame *must* have a menu. Menus are part of the MDI style. In general, you do not use buttons in MDI applications. There are exceptions of course, but to follow the recommended style, always attempt to place the functions in menu options if possible. (Menus will be created in a later step in this chapter.) After you create the m_mdi menu, add the menu to this window by opening the Window Style dialog. Check the **Menu** CheckBox and select the menu from the dropdown listbox as shown in Figure 13.6.

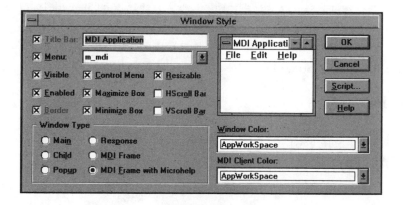

FIGURE 13.6 ADDING A MENU TO A WINDOW

CREATING THE SHEET WINDOW

Next, create a window to serve as the MDI sheet. Create a new window and click the **Main** radio button under Type. Actually the type of the sheet can be any type other than a MDI frame, but the convention is to select Main as the type. The sheets are opened by using menu options (under the File menu). All of the sheets will be instances of the same window type.

Add a DataWindow control to the window. The DataWindow object will be assigned dynamically, so do not assign the object at this time. The DataWindow control will be sized dynamically at run-time, so the size is not important, but do position the DataWindow in the top left corner of the window.

Add the following script to the window's Open event (be sure you are in the window's events, not the DataWindow control's events.)

```
//w_ma_sheet  Open script
dw_1.dataobject = message.stringparm
this.title = message.stringparm
dw_1.SetTransObject(sqlca)
dw_1.Retrieve()
```

Add the following statement to the window's Resize event:

```
dw_1.Resize(this.WorkSpaceWidth( ) - 55, this.WorkSpaceHeight( ) - 55)
```

Declare two user events for the window as shown in Figure 13.7.

Add the following code to the ue_dw1_insert event:

```
long lRow
int rc

SetPointer(HourGlass!)
lRow = dw_1.insertrow (1)
rc = dw_1.setfocus ( )
rc = dw_1.scrolltorow ( lRow ) // also does a dw_1.setrow
                               // ( lRow)
rc = dw_1.setcolumn(1)
rc = 0
```

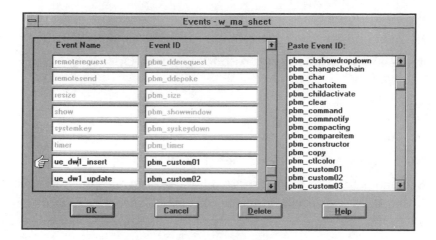

FIGURE 13.7 DECLARING USER EVENTS

Add the following code to the ue_dw1_update event:

```
IF dw_1.update ( ) = 1 THEN
    commit;
ELSE
    rollback;
END IF
```

Save this window with the name **w_ma_sheet**.

The sheet window is opened by menu options. To open a sheet, use the function OpenSheet, rather than the Open function that you have used to open non-MDI windows. PowerBuilder provides windows opened with the OpenSheet function with more automatic management, such as adjustment of size.

For example:

```
OpenSheet(w_inv, "Invoice", "w_main", nListPosition, Cascade!)
```

The OpenSheet function has the following arguments:

- type of window
- name of the sheet (optional)

- name of the frame window
- menu pad number (for listing open windows) default is next-to-last
- opening arrangement (Cascade!, Layered!, Original!)

Note the following:

- often sheets do not have their own menus.
- if any sheet has a menu, then they all should.
- menus (and/or toolbars) are inherited from the previous sheet if a menu is not provided for a newly opened sheet.
- set the toolbar Alignment, Height, Visible, Width, X, Y in the Window Painter.

CREATING THE MENUS

Next, create two menus for the MDI application. The first menu is used when the application opens. It provides the options to open a sheet or the exit the application. The first window is attached to the w_main_mdi in the Window Style dialog as shown earlier in Figure 13.6.

The second menu is an extension of the first menu; it will be displayed as long as one or more of the sheets are open. This menu adds options to Insert rows into the DataWindow, Update changes to the database, and to close the current or all sheets. This menu belongs to the w_ma_sheet window and is placed on the frame whenever a sheet window is open. Figure 13.8 shows the m_mdi menu.

In the MDI MicroHelp field, add the line of text to be displayed in the MicroHelp status area for each menu option.

To add an icon to the MDI frame's toolbar, click on the **Change** CommandButton for the Toolbar Item to open the dialog shown in Figure 13.9. For this example, select any of the stock icons for each open option. You could also create and use your own BMP file as an icon.

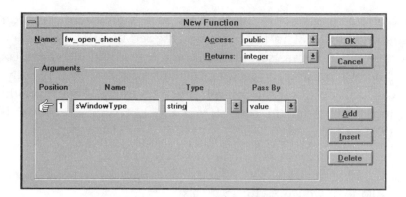

FIGURE 13.8 CREATING THE M_MDI MENU

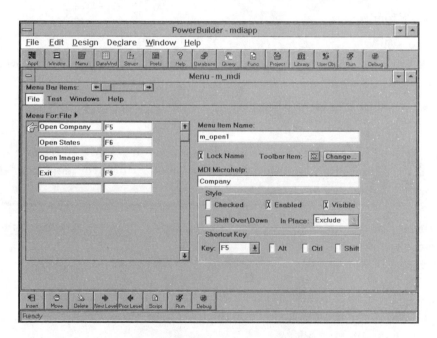

FIGURE 13.9 SELECTING AN ICON

In this example, a menu item is provided to open each window. A Window menu bar item is also provided; this dropdown menu lists the open windows.

MicroHelp text was also inserted for each menu item. You can also dynamically set the MicroHelp text using the SetMicroHelp() function. The application Open event uses this technique. You could also have controls set the MicroHelp using the SetMicroHelp() function. This is usually done in the GetFocus event for the control. If you do this you can store the text in the tag attribute for the control; you should then clear the Microhelp text in the LoseFocus event.

To create a toolbar in MenuPainter you can set:

- up and down icons (16x15 pixels)
- text (display controlled in app)
- spacing (if no text)
- order on bar
- visible
- display down (stick, until you set MenuItem1.ToolbarItemDown = FALSE)
- toolbar Item details

 The toolbar icons must be dimmed with program code. PowerBuilder will not do this for you when you enable or disable a menu option.

NOTE

In the script for the Clicked event for the Open Company menu option, add the following line of code:

```
w_main_mdi.fw_open_sheet("d_company")
```

In the script for the Clicked event for the Open States menu option, add the following line of code:

```
w_main_mdi.fw_open_sheet("d_state")
```

In the script for the Clicked event for the Open Images menu option, add the following line of code:

```
w_main_mdi.fw_open_sheet("d_images")
```

Under the Windows menu, add the options as shown in Figure 13.10.

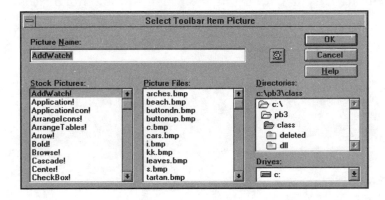

FIGURE 13.10 ADDING OPTIONS TO THE WINDOW MENU

In the script for the Clicked event for the Tile menu option, add the following line of code:

```
ParentWindow.ArrangeSheets (tile!)
```

In the script for the Clicked event for the Layer menu option, add the following line of code:

```
ParentWindow.ArrangeSheets (layer!)
```

In the script for the Clicked event for the Cascade menu option, add the following line of code:

```
ParentWindow.ArrangeSheets (cascade!)
```

Creating the m_mdi2 Menu

Open the Menu painter and select the m_mdi menu. Immediately save the menu as **m_mdi2**. After saving the menu, any changes that you make will now be to the m_mdi2 menu. Insert the new options in the File menu as shown in Figure 13.11. (Notice that the top MenuItem has been scrolled off the display in order to show the items that are to be added.) The separator is created by adding only a dash as the menu item. You will have to name that menu item as **m_s**, for example since **m_–** would not be legal.

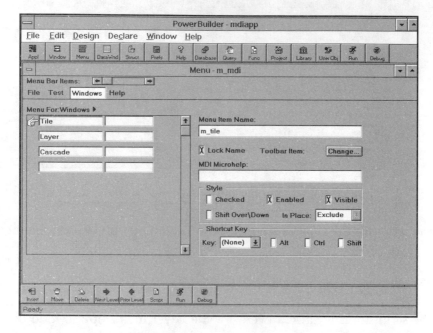

FIGURE 13.11 THE M_MDI2 MENU

In the script for the Clicked event for the Close menu option, add the following line of code:

```
Close(ParentWindow) // this will close the active sheet
```

In the script for the Clicked event for the CloseAll menu option, add the following line of code:

```
w_main_mdi.fw_close_all_sheets()
```

In the script for the Clicked event for the Insert menu option, add the following line of code:

```
ParentWindow.TriggerEvent ( "dw1_insert" )
```

In the script for the Clicked event for the Update menu option, add the following line of code:

```
ParentWindow.TriggerEvent ( "dw1_update")
```

In the script for the Clicked event for the Exit menu option, add the following line of code:

```
close(w_main_mdi) // exit the application
```

Save this menu and then add this menu to the w_ma_sheet window.

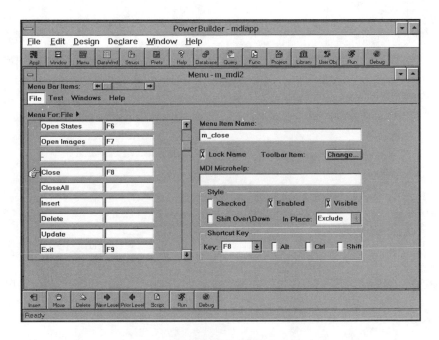

FIGURE 13.12 THE FILE MENU

w_main_mdi Instance Variable

Now that you have created the w_ma_sheet window, you must return to the Window painter to add an instance variable array of this type to the w_main_mdi window. To do this open the Window painter, select the **m_main_mdi** window, and then select the **Declare|Instance Variables...** menu option. Declare an instance variable array, i_wsheet, of type w_ma_sheet (w_ma_sheet i_wsheet[ ]) as shown in Figure 13.13.

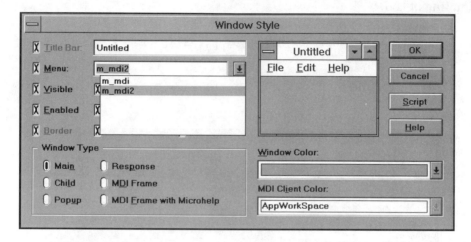

FIGURE 13.13 DECLARING THE INSTANCE VARIABLES

w_main_mdi Window-level Functions

Go back to the Window painter and add two functions to the w_main_mdi. To do this open the Window painter, select the **m_main_mdi** window and then select the **Declare|Window Functions...** menu option. Add a function named **fw_open_sheet**, Figure 13.14 shows the declaration for that function.

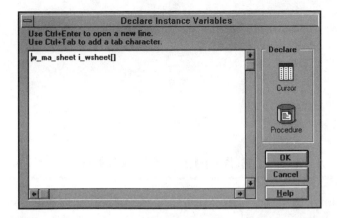

FIGURE 13.14 DECLARING THE FW_OPEN_SHEET FUNCTION

Add the following code to the fw_open_sheet function:

```
//fw_open_sheet
//instance declaration :::  w_ma_sheet i_wsheet[]
int idx, nCount, nMax

nMax = UpperBound(i_wsheet)
FOR nCount = 1 to nMax
    IF NOT IsValid(i_wsheet[nCount]) THEN
        idx = nCount
        exit
    END IF
NEXT
IF nCount > nMax THEN idx = nCount
OpenSheetWithParm(i_wsheet[idx], sWindowType, this)
this.SetMicrohelp(string(idx))
return 0
```

Next declare another window function, fw_close_all_sheets. This function takes no arguments. Add the following code to that function:

```
//fw_close_all_sheets
//instance declaration :::  w_ma_sheet i_wsheet[]
int idx, jdx, nMax

nMax = UpperBound(i_wsheet)
FOR idx = 1 to nMax
```

```
        IF IsValid(i_wsheet[idx]) THEN
            Close(i_wsheet[idx])
            FOR jdx = 1 to 1000
            NEXT
        END IF
NEXT
return 0
```

Add Code to the Application Open Event

. Add the following code to the Application Open event. This code will open the main window, make the connection to the database, and dynamically update the MicroHelp status line.

```
// application open event script
string sText

Open (w_main_mdi)
sText =
    ProfileString("imagedb.ini","sqlca","firsttime","error")
IF sText = 'error' THEN
    w_main_mdi.setmicrohelp ( "Could Not Locate INI File")
END IF
IF Upper(sText) = "YES" THEN
    OpenWithParm (w_set_sqlca,"imagedb.ini")
ELSE
    SetPointer (HourGlass!)
    w_main_mdi.setmicrohelp ( "Connecting to DB...")

    sqlca.DBMS       = ProfileString("imagedb.ini","sqlca", &
                                    "dbms","")
    sqlca.database   = ProfileString("imagedb.ini","sqlca", &
                                    "database","")
    sqlca.userid     = ProfileString("imagedb.ini","sqlca", &
                                    "userid","")
    sqlca.dbpass     = ProfileString("imagedb.ini","sqlca", &
                                    "dbpass","")
    sqlca.logid      = ProfileString("imagedb.ini","sqlca", &
                                    "logid","")
    sqlca.logpass    = ProfileString("imagedb.ini","sqlca", &
                                    "logpass","")
    sqlca.servername = ProfileString("imagedb.ini","sqlca", &
                                    "servername","")
```

```
        sqlca.dbparm    = ProfileString("imagedb.ini","sqlca", &
                                        "dbparm","")
END IF
IF sqlca.DBMS <> 'err' THEN
    connect;
ELSE
    sqlca.sqlcode = 1
END IF
IF sqlca.sqlcode <> 0 THEN
    w_main_mdi.setmicrohelp ( "DB Connect Failed")
ELSE
    w_main_mdi.setmicrohelp ( "Ready")
END IF

//// end of application open event script///////
```

CREATING AN MDI TEMPLATE

When you create a new application, PowerBuilder 4.0 can create an MDI application template. This creates an application with frame and sheet windows, a menu for the frame, and an about box. To use this option, open the Application painter and select the **File|New** menu option. This opens the Select New Application Library dialog (Figure 13.15).

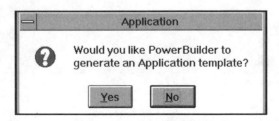

FIGURE 13.15 SELECT THE NEW APPLICATION LIBRARY

For this example, enter the name **mdiapp2.pbl** for the library and choose **C:\PB4\CLASS** as the directory. Click on **OK** to open the Save Application dialog.

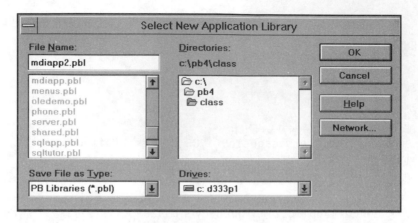

FIGURE 13.16 THE SAVE APPLICATION DIALOG

Enter the name of the application and a comment in this dialog. Click on **OK** and PowerBuilder gives you the option of creating an MDI application template (Figure 13.17).

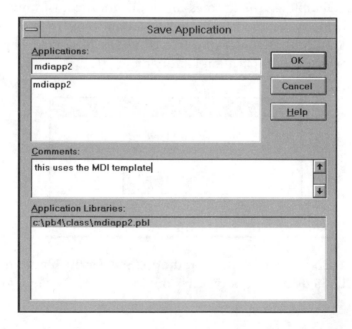

FIGURE 13.17 CLICK ON OK TO CREATE AN MDI APPLICATION

Click on **OK** to create an MDI application template. The application painter shows the components that were added to your application (see Figure 13.18).

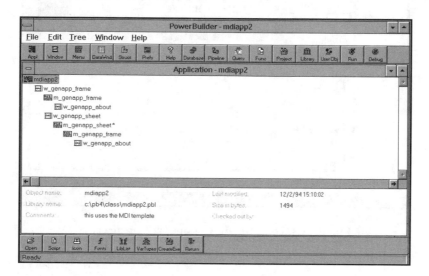

FIGURE 13.18 THE MDI TEMPLATE OBJECTS IN THE APPLICATION PAINTER

Figure 13.19 shows the resulting application. You can expand this application as required.

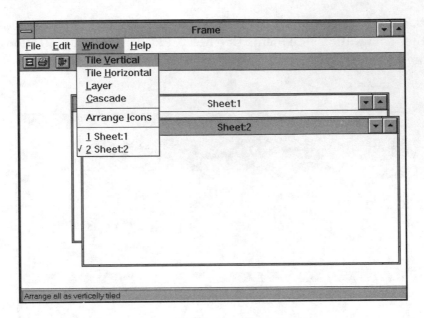

FIGURE 13.19 THE MDI TEMPLATE APPLICATION

CHAPTER FOURTEEN

EVENT-DRIVEN PROGRAMMING

TRADITIONAL PROCEDURAL PROGRAMMING

I n earlier systems implemented without an event-driven paradigm, an application was launched and then was "in control." A typical application would start up (with the Main procedure in C programs), perform some initialization, and then call various functions provided by the compiler, the operating system, or libraries (commercial or developed) in addition to its own subroutines.

Generally users only ran one application at a time. The application assumed that it had control of the CPU and determined the execution path that it would follow. The application determined in what order the functions were executed. Users often were presented with menus of selections, but overall, everything was tightly controlled.

In some systems, applications accessed computer hardware directly. Manipulating the video display was a basic technique for DOS programmers and was essential for reasonable performance on the first PCs.

Windows Event-Driven Programming

In the late 1980s, MS Windows began gathering momentum, and in the 1990s, it became the primary GUI for PC applications. MS Windows prior to version 4.0 (Windows 95), was not actually an operating system, but was an application that ran on top of MS-DOS. Windows provides an event-driven environment that is similar to the Unix X-Window system and the Apple Macintosh system for the user and developer.

For the user, the system is more intuitive, and easier to use. It also provides a common interface across the applications that follow the style guides and conventions created for Windows applications. Users are in control, the user decides the order of execution. The user often runs several applications at a time. The user can switch between applications and expects to be able to integrate the applications, at least to be able to share data between them.

While this is good news for the user, the challenge of developing applications under MS Windows was much greater than developing MS-DOS applications. Many of us spent days or even weeks developing our first simple applications for the Windows environment in the C language.

Windows provides over 1,000 API calls for the application developer. Becoming familiar with a base set of these functions could take a couple of weeks research and experimentation. The event-driven paradigm seemed to turn the programming process inside-out. Instead of creating an application where you called the system as you needed it, we found that we had to design applications where we waited for the system to call us. When the system did call, the application had to be able to respond to a wide variety of message (events) in a less predictable order. The designers and developers also had to take time to learn the Windows interface in order to know how to present and receive data to the user in the Windows style.

All hardware is accessed through Windows. So just reading the keyboard or updating the video display required calls to the MS Windows system; the developer could no longer directly access the hardware. The application must also be a "good citizen" in the environment and cooperate with the other applications by giving up the CPU after completing the response to the event that triggered the instance of code execution.

In pre-preemptive systems, the application may lose the CPU at any time (when its time slice is over). However, Windows 3.1 is non-preemptive, applications give up the CPU voluntarily and wait for the next message. The application must be designed and built to handle these messages.

After the Window application starts and completes its initialization, it enters a wait state. The application is triggered by events that control the execution of its code. Events are conveyed to the application by Windows as message types.

EVENTS

The Windows system receives all the events, both hardware and software events. These events include a keyboard stroke, a mouse movement, or a system timer event. The Windows system converts each event into a message. Each message has a message type that represents the type of event that has occurred. The message also carries along with it, other information about the nature of the event.

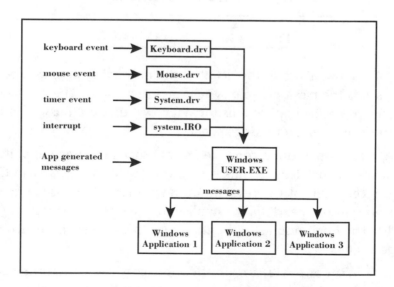

FIGURE 14.1 WINDOWS EVENTS

Figure 14.1 shows that each event is funneled into the USER.EXE component of Windows. Windows then creates a message for the event and dispatches it to one of the applications currently running in the environment.
The decision as to which application is selected is based on several criteria
including the type of event and the current state of each application.

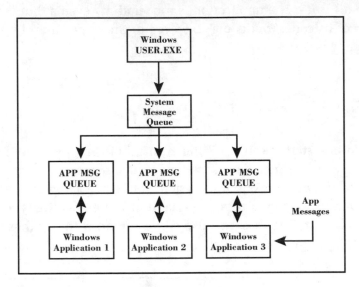

FIGURE 14.2 WINDOWS EVENTS

Figure 14.2 shows more of the detail of the messaging process. The USER
module sends the messages to a system message queue. The messages are
addressed to specific applications (or Windows) and are passed on to the
appropriate application message queue.

A Windows application can take one message at a time out of its message queue. The application makes GetMessage calls to the system (Figure
14.3) to receive one of the pending messages from its message queue. If
there is no message pending, the application goes into a wait state (yields
the CPU). The application sleeps until a new message is dispatched to the
message queue.

In the Windows API, an application can use functions such as
PostMessage and PostAppMessage to send application message to an
application message queue.

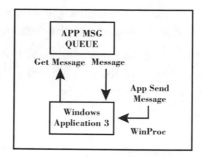

FIGURE 14.3 THE APPLICATION MESSAGE LOOP

The WinProc entry on the right of Figure 14.3 represents an alternative path that is possible for message delivery. Some messages are dispatched directly to an application, bypassing the application message queue. The Windows API function, SendMessage, passes a message directly to an applications WinProc procedure.

In the Windows system, messages that are sent directly to an application, are sent to the application's WinProc function. This is a special function that is designed to handle the various types of messages that the application can handle. Details of this follow in the next section.

DISPATCHING MESSAGES

The step involved in how the Windows system dispatches message are:

1. Get Next Message From the System Message Queue.

2. Dispatch it to the appropriate window message queue.

3. Do any required system functions (i.e., switch to another application).

Any system functions performed in the third step are the result of the type of event that generated the message. For instance, if your application has two open windows, only one can be the active window, which means it is receiving the current keyboard input. If you move the mouse and click in the other application window, Windows generates a mouse click message (after the mouse move events). This mouse click causes the system to activate the second window, and to deactivate the first window.

The system must make a number of decisions based on the type of the message and the current status of the applications that are currently running and the windows that are on the screen.

For a keyboard event:

■ Where is the current focus?

■ Send WM_CHAR message to that window

For example, consider the message associated with a keyboard stoke. Keyboard events belong to the currently active window (the window that currently has the focus). The system determines which window is the active window and sends the WM_CHAR message (among others) to that window.

For a mouse event:

■ What is the location of the pointer?

■ Send WM_xxx message to the window under the pointer

Mouse events are resolved differently. The mouse event belongs to the window that is under the mouse pointer, regardless of whether or not it is the active window. Mouse-move messages are sent out a number of times per second, while the pointer is moving. This message contains the X and Y position of the pointer, and other details of interest (like which mouse buttons are down).

For an application message:

■ What window is the message addressed to?

■ Send WM_USER message to that window

Application messages are addressed to a specific application, and have a message type of WM_USER. The message is sent to the application along with a couple of optional parameters.

WinApp: A Windows Application

This section examines a typical Windows application, named WinApp and provides an overview of the program logic that is required for every Windows application, along with code from a typical application. The code is in C, but the comments should make its operation clear even if you don't know the C language.

WinApp Outline

Startup/Initialize

- Registers the Application. Tells Windows that a new application has been launched.

- Windows gives the application a unique ID (handle).

- Windows allocates a message buffer and attaches the application to it.

- The application can perform any required initialization, and then goes into the next program loop to wait for messages.

```
TOP: Get Next Message() // the message loop
     Do I handle this type of message?
     · If NOT
          · send Message back to Windows
          · (pass to DefWindowProc, back to USER.EXE for
            default handling)
     · If YES
          · dispatch to WinApp's internal functions
          · those functions may generate more messages
     · If Message says QUIT
          · then shutdown
GOTO TOP
```

The application calls GetNextMessage(), if there is no message pending, the application yields the CPU and waits for a message. In this case, the other applications may capture the CPU and will execute until the application yields the CPU (usually with a GetNextMessage() function).

Winapp Sample Application Code

This is a sample of a minimal main function (WinMain) from a Windows application.

```
WinMain(HANDLE hInstance,
        HANDLE hPrevInstance,
        LPSTR  sCmdLine,
        int    nCmdShow)
{
    static char pAppName = "WinApp";
    HWND hMainWnd = NULL;
    WNDCLASS wndClass;
    MSG msg;
    int rc = 0;

    rc = SetupClass(&wndClass, pAppName, WinProc);
    if (rc == OKAY && !hPrevInstance)
        rc = RegisterClass(&wndClass);
    if (rc != OKAY)
    {
        hMainWnd = CreateWindow(pAppName, "Hello World",
                                  x, y, size);
        ShowWindow(hMainWnd);
        Update(hMainWnd);
    }
    if (RC == 0)
    while (GetMessage(&msg)) // loop while NOT WM_QUIT
    {
        if (msg.hwnd)
        {
            TranslateMessage(&msg);
            DispatchMessage(&msg); //to WinProc
        }
        else
            ProcessPostAppMessages(&msg); //receive PostAppMessage
    }
    if (rc)
        return (msg.wParam);
    else
        return (FALSE);
}
```

The WinProc function receives all messages addressed to this application. The WinProc function dispatches the message (according to the message type) to the appropriate functions in the application.

```
WinProc (HWND hWnd,
         UINT iMessage,
         WORD wParm,
         LONG lParm)
{
   switch (iMessage)
   {
       case WM_DESTROY: // user chose "Close"
           PostQuitMessage(0); //sends WM_QUIT (==0)
           break;
       case WM_PAINT:
           PaintWindow();
           break;

       case WM_USER:
         if (wParm == 1)
         {
             PostMessage(hWnd, WM_USER, 2, GetHandle("hello"));
             DoSomeThing1(hWnd); //first
             SendMessage(hWnd, WM_USER, 3, GetHandle("hello"));
             DoSomeThing3(hWnd);//third
         }
         else if (wParm == 2)
             DoSomeThing4(hWnd);//forth
         else if (wParm == 3)
             DoSomeThing2(hWnd);//second
         break;
       default:
           DefWindowProc(hWnd, iMessage, wParm, lParm);
   }
}
```

Comments on WinApp Code

RegisterClass() //Class level

- ■ tells Windows about this class of application
- ■ shared among instances of this application

CreateWindow() //Instance level

- ■ create (but does not display) the main window
- ■ returns a HANDLE, by which it is referenced for the rest of its life

565

USER EVENTS

You have seen a number of event types in the examples presented thus far. Application objects have 4 events (Open, Close, Idle, SystemError), Windows have 29 events (Open, Activate, CloseQuery etc.), command buttons have 11 events (Clicked, GetFocus etc.). Many of these events are mapped by PowerBuilder from the Windows system. PowerBuilder has also added its own events. There are many events in the Windows system that are not initially available in your PowerBuilder objects. The Other event, found in most objects, is a PowerBuilder event that receives a number of different types of Windows events that have not been explicitly mapped.

You can create your own events (User Events) of two different types. First you can create new, custom events, these are similar to the WM_USER message in the WinApp example. You can also create user events that are mapped to some of the Windows events that are not handled by PowerBuilder. The Windows system will trigger the events that you map from the Windows system. You must trigger your custom events in script code using the TriggerEvent or PostEvent PowerScript functions.

This is a basic, essential technique for PowerBuilder development, in this section will we create both types of user events to demonstrate their use and power.

Creating a User Event

You create a user event by selecting the **Declare|User Event...** menu option that is available from within a number of the painters such as the Window painter and the PowerScript editor. The event will be created at the object level where you select this menu option. If you create a user event in the Window painter, the event will be attached to that window object. If you create a user event in the PowerScript editor for a command button event, the user event will be attached to that command button. This creates the scope of the user event.

When you select this menu option, the Events dialog opens (as shown in Figure 14.4).

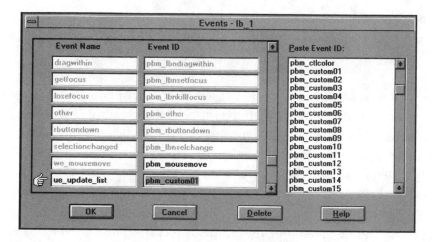

FIGURE 14.4 DEFINING A USER EVENT

This dialog displays the events that have already been defined for the current object and the event ID associated with each predefined event. The Paste Event ID list box lists all the available event Ids. This includes all the Windows events and 75 custom event Ids for your use.

There are two types of events that you can create. The first, is to create a custom event, the second is to map an existing Windows events. You should use the **ue_** prefix for the name of a the custom event that you create and use the **we_** prefix for events that you create that map to existing Windows' events. We will give an example of each type of user event.

Creating a Custom Event

The steps to create a custom event are:

- Select the object for which the event is to be defined.
- Open the Events Dialog Box. For window controls you must do this from within the script editor. For windows and user objects you do this in the object painter. You will find the User Event option on the Declare menu.
- Assign a name to the event.

- Assign a custom event ID to the event
- Close the Declare Events dialog box and write the script for the event.

Figure 14.4 shows the creation of a user event, **ue_update_list**. This example event is being created as an event for a listbox, **lb_1**. Notice that the predefined PowerBuilder events for this control are listed in this dialog. The event Ids for the predefined events are grayed out so that you can not change them. All the User Event event Ids are darkened, so you can select and change or delete these events.

To create the custom event, you must first specify a name for the new event. Use the **ue_** prefix for the name of a custom events. For this example (in Figure 14.4) we named the event **ue_update_list**.

You must then assign an event ID to your new event. For the custom type of event you must select one of the values reserved for custom user events. You will find these IDs in the Paste Event ID list box. They range from pbm_custom01 through pbm_custom75. You should start with pbm_custom01 for the first user event you create and use successive custom Ids for the next events that you create. PowerBuilder uses these custom IDs to identify user-defined events internally. You can select any custom ID that has not already been assigned in the object.

After you name the event and assign the event Id click on **OK**. This closes the dialog window.

When you return to the script editor, pull down the **Select Event** dropdown list box and scroll to the very last entries. You will find that the ue_update_list event has been added to the events for the listbox. Next you would enter the code for the event. For this event, you would select **ue_update_list** from the Select Event dropdown listbox and then add then following code.

Remember that Windows will not trigger custom event, you must do this in your script code. You can trigger this event by using the TriggerEvent function as follows:

```
lb_1.TriggerEvent('ue_update_list')
```

or the PostEvent function as:

```
lb_1.PostEvent('ue_update_list')
```

From outside this window you would have to qualify the window as:

```
w_second.lb_1.TriggerEvent('ue_update_list')
```

Mapping a Windows' Event

The second type of user event is used to access exisiting events in the Windows' system. These events will be triggered by Windows and not pro-gramatically as the custom user event in the previous example.

The steps to map a Windows' event are:

- Select the object for which the event is to be defined.
- Open the Events Dialog Box. For window controls you must do this from within the script editor. For windows and user objects you do this in the object painter. You will find the User Event option on the Declare menu.
- Assign a name to the event.
- Locate the event ID for the desired event. If you can not find the ID for an event that you know exists in the Windows system, you could trap this event in the Other event of the object rather than here.
- Close the Declare Events dialog box and write the script for the event.

Figure 14.5 shows an example of the second type of event, where we map an existing Windows events. In this case we are mapping the pbm_mouse-move event as we_mousemove (for this example, assume it is for lb_1). This event will be triggered by the Windows system when the mouse is moved over the object (list box) that has this event.

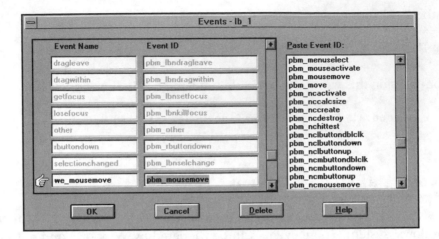

FIGURE 14.5 MAPPING THE WINDOWS WM_MOUSEMOVE EVENT

First you must name the event. We use the **we_** prefix for the name this type of event. For this example (in Figure 14.5) we named the event **we_mousemove**.

You must then locate the Windows' event ID for the existing event. You will find these IDs in the Paste Event ID list box. You can find more information on these events in the Windows Software Development Kit.

After you name the event and assign the event Id click on the **OK** command button. This closes the dialog window.

When you return to the script editor, pull down the Select Event dropdown list box and scroll to the very last entries. You will find that the we_mousemove event has been added to the events for the object. Next you would enter the code for the event.

This event will be triggered by the Windows system. You do not usually trigger this event by using the TriggerEvent function, but you could for testing as follows:

```
lb_1.TriggerEvent('we_mousemove')
```

The Other Event

PowerBuilder doesn't trap every Microsoft Windows event that is available. The events for each object that are not mapped to PowerBuilder events (listed in the Paste Event ID list box in the previous examples) are routed to the Other event for that object. If you want to access one of these events you must place code in that event to identify the event that you are interested in trapping. The information that you need to identify the event is located in the PowerBuilder message object.

The Message Object

When a Microsoft Windows event occurs that is not a PowerBuilder-defined event, PowerBuilder populates the global PowerBuilder Message object with information about the event. The Message object contains the event information for MS Windows events. The first four attributes correspond to the first four attributes of the MS Windows message structure.

The Message object attributes:

TABLE 14.1 MESSAGE OBJECT ATTRIBUTES

ATTRIBUTE	DATA TYPE	USE
Handle	Unsigned Integer	The event handle.
Number	Unsigned Integer	Windows event ID.
WordParm	Unsigned Integer	Event word parameter (from Windows).
LongParm	Long	Event long parameter (from Windows).
Processed	Boolean	Set this to True in the Other event if you processed the event, otherwise it is sent on the DefWindowProc
ReturnValue	Long	If you process the event, this is the return value you send to the Windows system.
StringParm	String	A string

continued on next page

ATTRIBUTE	DATA TYPE	USE
DoubleParm	Double	A numeric
PowerObjectParm	PowerObject	Any PowerBuilder object

In the Other event you must example the value of the Number parameter to see if it is the event that you wish to handle. For example, to trap a click of the middle mouse button (for a three-button mouse):

```
int iEvent
int iParm
long lParm

iEvent = Message.Number
IF iEvent =  519 THEN
    iParm = Message.WordParm
    lParm = Message.LongParm
    // do whatever
END
```

How do I arrive at the 519 value for the middle mouse button click? First I found the WM_MBUTTONDOWN event (message) in the Windows Programmer's Reference. Then I search for that message in the WINDOWS.H file (used to develop Windows applications, and included with the Windows SDK). There I found the line

```
#define WM_MBUTTONDOWN      0x0207
```

Hex 207 is equal to 519 as a decimal value. So that is the number for which the code must check. The WordParm for that event contains information about what other keys are down. For this example the possible values are:

```
0x0001    MK_LBUTTON - left mouse button
0x0002    MK_RBUTTON - right mouse button
0x0004    MK_SHIFT - the SHIFT key
0x0008    MK_CONTROL - the CONTROL key
```

These are bit values, so if the Shift and Control keys are both down then the value will be 12.

Note that the value for the middle button will also be included in this WordParm value. That value is:

```
0x0010    MK_MBUTTON
```

We're not interested in that information, so you can subtract 16 (0x0010) from the iParm value before examing its value.

The LongParm value returns the X and Y position of the pointer over the object. The X position is in the low word position, the Y position is in the high word. You can use the IntLow and IntHigh functions to extract the integers from the LongParm.

```
x = IntLow (Message.LongParm)
y = IntHigh (Message.LongParm)
```

The information about the WordParm and LongParm values was obtained from the Windows Programmer's Reference.

Warning: For the Other Event

The major drawback to using the Other event, is that performance can be impacted significantly. This is because a number of event will trigger the Other event, and the IF statement must be executed for each event. This can result in significant over-head for trapping the event in which you are interested. So you should only use this technique when absolutely necessary.

CHAPTER FIFTEEN

USER OBJECTS

PowerBuilder gives you the ability to create a special type of control called a *user object*. User objects are one of the most powerful resources in PowerBuilder. You will find these most useful when you identify a functionality (or object) that has a usefulness that you would like to share between applications or that you would like to standardize.

A user object is a reusable object (a class or a control) that you create to encapsulate functionality you would like to use in various places in your applications. You could use a user object to input or display information to users, respond to mouse or keyboard actions, or to encapsulate data processing, and much more. After you build a user object you can use it almost as if it were one of the original PowerBuilder controls. The most basic user objects are derived from one of the standard PowerBuilder objects (such as a CommandButton). Another type of user object may include multiple objects within a user object, building more a complex functionality. User objects take advantage of the object-oriented features of PowerBuilder. You will design the user object to be reusable by generalizing its behavior when you write the script code for its events and internal functions.

User objects have characteristics that are similar to the controls that we have already seen. User objects have:

- **Attributes**—variables, the values of which determine the characteristic of the user object.
- **Events**— which may contain script code.
- **Functions**—procedures that serve several purposes.

A user object's style is defined by its attributes. The events are used to trigger the execution of your scripts just as in the standard controls. Functions implement the behavior of the user object or provide an interface to the user object (often used to set or obtain the values of user object attributes). Functions are part of the definition of the user object and may be used in scripts to change the style or behavior of the user object.

User objects may also contain variables and structures.

TYPES OF USER OBJECTS

There are six types of user objects divided into two general categories. Each type has a different manner of construction and use. The two categories are:

1. **Class**—a nonvisual object, created without any PowerBuilder controls. The class user objects are implemented entirely by using user object attributes and functions (PowerScript code that may reference external objects such as DLLs).

2. **Visual**—an object based on PowerBuilder controls, including other user objects. Script code will work with these controls.

The types of user objects are:

Class Category

■ **Standard**—a nonvisual user object that is based on one of the built-in nonvisual PowerBuilder objects such as the Message or Error object.

■ **Custom**—a nonvisual user object not based on any of the built-in PowerBuilder objects, but may be inherited from another custom class user object.

Visual Category

■ **Standard**—based on a single standard PowerBuilder control.

■ **Custom**—an object (like a window) than can contain multiple standard PowerBuilder controls.

■ **External**—used to access externally (to PowerBuilder) defined controls.

■ **VBX**—accesses Visual Basic controls.

We often refer to the types of user objects in the following manner: standard class user object, standard visual user object, custom class user object, or custom visual user object. The external and VBX types don't really need any further qualification.

You will use the User Object painter to create any of these types of objects. You can use inheritance to derive a new user object from an existing one. Since one of the main advantages of user objects is reusability, you will most often place user objects in a shared library on the network, where they can be accessed for multiple applications. Sometimes you create application-specific user objects; these are better placed in one of that application's libraries.

After you create a visual user object, you can add it to any of your windows in the Window painter. User Object is an option on the Controls menu and there is a User Object icon on the Window painter PainterBar. When you select one of these, a ListBox presents the list of user objects in the selected PowerBuilder library. You select a type of user object and place it in a window like any other control. You can then position or size it on the window. You can perform other developmental activities, such as adding script code to its events and communicating between the user object and other PowerBuilder objects.

After you create a class user object, you implement an instance of that user object by declaring a variable of that type and using the CREATE statement to instantiate the object. This object will be scoped like any other variable. When you are finished with the instance, deallocate the object using the DESTROY statement.

The Standard User Object

The first and simplest type of user object is called the standard user object. The standard user object is limited to, and is based on, a single standard PowerBuilder control as its source. It simply packages a standard PowerBuilder control as a reusable control and extends the control's normal behavior.

If you find that you frequently define a similar PowerBuilder control for a certain use in different windows (or across different applications), you should create a standard visual user object control to avoid having to redefine that type of control and to recode the script(s) and to ensure that this type of control will always have the same appearance and behavior. It is also easier to maintain and make global changes throughout a user object.

A common example would be the cb_close CommandButton that we have used in many of the windows in our example applications. Each time that we needed to use a button to close a window, we had to define it, set the label, and add the code to the clicked event to close the parent window. If this button had been defined as a standard user object, we could just add the button (user object) to any window.

The steps necessary to build a standard user object are:

- Click on the **User Object** icon on the PowerBar to open the User Object painter. In the Select User Object dialog box, click on the **New** CommandButton.

- In the New User Object dialog, select the Standard Visual user object type (click on **Standard** under the Visual category), then click **OK**.

- The Select Standard Visual Type dialog lists the standard controls that can be used as the basis for the new object. Select the standard PowerBuilder control on which you wish to build your standard user object. Click on the **OK** CommandButton. Your new user object inherits the attributes and events associated with that control.

- The User Object painter opens. The screen displays the object in the painter's workspace. In this painter you can modify the control just as you worked with controls in the Window painter. Size and shape the user object using the sizing handles. Open the object's Style dialog to change those settings. You can add functions, events, structures, or variables for the user object. This is the main value of a standard visual user object over a PowerBuilder control. You cannot attach functions, structures, or variables to a standard PowerBuilder control but you can define any of these for user objects.

- Save the user object to a library. Select **Save** (or **Save As**) from the File menu. Use the prefix **u_** for user objects.

- Add the user object to one of your windows. In the Window painter select the **Controls|User Object** menu selection (or click the **User Obj** icon on the painter bar). This opens the Select User Object dialog. Select the user object in this dialog and then click in the window to add the object to that window.

A standard user object has the same events as the PowerBuilder control on which it is based. The events inherited from each standard PowerBuilder control will vary but may include events such as:

- Constructor
- Destructor
- DragDrop
- DragEnter
- DragLeave
- DragWithin
- Other
- RButtonDown

An Example Standard Visual User Object

For the first example, a CommandButton that displays a popup window to serve as an About Box (information about the application) will be created. The purpose is to let you place a copyright notice and author's credit in each of your applications. Once you create the About user object, you can add it to the main window of any of your applications without having to redefine the button or the Message box function call.

A couple of other features to the About user object will be added. The title (caption) for this MessageBox will be the name that the developer gave to the control when it added the user object to the window. We will also add an object-level function that will return this name when it is called.

To create the About user object start by clicking on the **User Object** icon on the PowerBar. This displays the Select User Object dialog window shown in Figure 15.1.

Click on the **New** CommandButton. This opens the New User Object dialog (Figure 15.2).

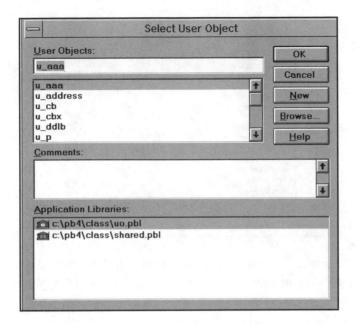

FIGURE 15.1 THE SELECT USER OBJECT DIALOG

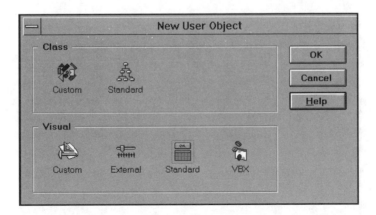

FIGURE 15.2 NEW USER OBJECT DIALOG

When this dialog opens, select the **Standard user object type** icon in the Visual category. This opens the Select Standard Visual Type dialog (see Figure 15.3).

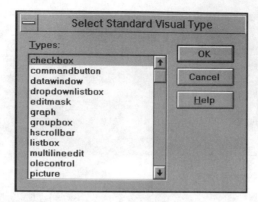

FIGURE 15.3 SELECT STANDARD VISUAL TYPE DIALOG

This determines the type of the control that is to be the basis for your new object. For this example, select **CommandButton** as the standard type and then click on **OK**.

The User Object painter opens with an instance of a CommandButton in the work area (similar to Figure 15.4, except it will have "none" for the label).

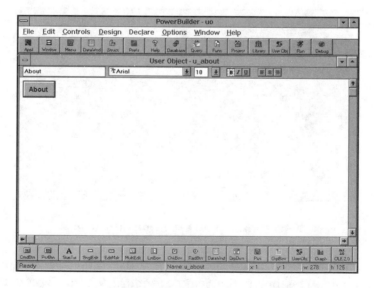

FIGURE 15.4 THE USER OBJECT PAINTER

Now build your user object in a manner similar to how you worked in the Window painter after you added a CommandButton to a window. However, in the case of standard user objects, you are limited to working with a single control. You can now modify the CommandButton, add variables, events, object-level functions, and so forth.

Use the **File|Save** menu option to save and name the object (**u_about**). Double-click on the user object (the CommandButton) to open the Style dialog (Figure 15.5).

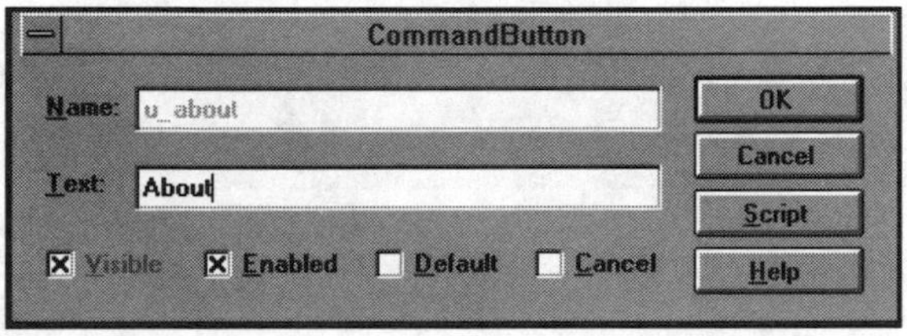

FIGURE 15.5 THE STYLE DIALOG

In the text box, enter **About**. The name of the object is **u_about**. Notice that the name is grayed and cannot be changed in the Style dialog. Next click on the **Script** button (in the Style dialog window) to add the script code for the user object. You will enter scripts for the Constructor and the Clicked events.

Declare an instance variable, string **i_sClass**, from the **Declare|Instance Variables...** menu option. Then add the following code to the user object Constructor script:

```
i_sClass =This.ClassName ( )
```

This code is executed when the object is created. The i_sClass variable receives the name of the control for display as the caption for the MessageBox.

Add the following code to the Clicked event (substitute your own name for this example):

```
MessageBox(i_sClass, 'This Application by David McClanahan
            (c)1994-1995')
```

583

This is executed when the user object is clicked. It displays the user object's name on its title bar and displays the text as the information message.

Create an Object-Level Function

Next, create an object-level public function (fu_query) by selecting the **Declare|User Object Functions...** menu selection.

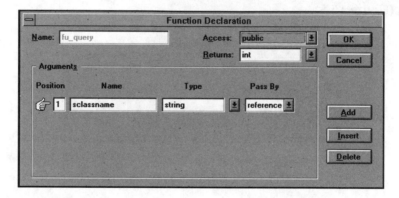

FIGURE 15.6 DECLARING THE USER OBJECT FUNCTION

Figure 15.6 shows how to declare the single argument sClassName with the string data type. Declare this with the Pass By reference argument type, so that sClassName is used to pass back the object name. The function returns an integer. Then add the following code to the function:

```
sClassName = i_sClass
return len(i_sClass)
```

Close the script editor, then close the User Object painter (saving the object) and go back to the Window painter.

Adding a User Object to a Window

Now you can add an instance of your new user object to the window. To do this, select the **Controls|User Objects...** menu option (or click the **User Obj** icon on the PainterBar). This displays the Select User Object dialog window (see Figure 15.7).

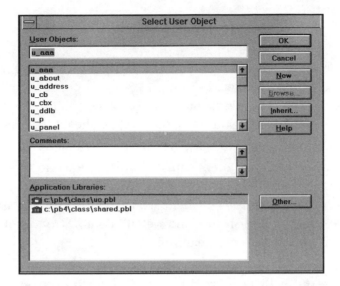

FIGURE 15.7 THE SELECT USER OBJECT DIALOG

In this dialog select the name of the library where you saved the object in the Application Libraries ListBox and then select **u_about** in the User Objects ListBox.

Next you will click in the window to drop the control as you have done for the standard PowerBuilder controls. PowerBuilder will name the user object **cb_1** by default. Add a single-line edit control (**sle_1**) and a CommandButton (named **cb_query**) to the window. Figure 15.8 shows the three controls in a new window.

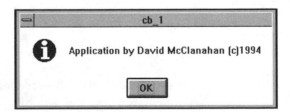

FIGURE 15.8 THE USER OBJECT'S MESSAGE BOX

Add the following code to cb_query's clicked event:

```
int rc
rc = cb_1.fu_query(sle_1.text)
```

Now run the application. When you click on the user object, you should see the MessageBox, as shown in Figure 15.8.

Add another instance of the About user object. When you run the application, click on each **About** object. Notice that the name in the title bar changes.

This example also shows how to use a user-object-level function to communicate from the cb_query control in the window to the user object. When you click on the **cb_query** button, the name of the control will be inserted into the single-line-edit field. You could also have used a user-defined event to accomplish this and we will demonstrate that technique in the custom visual user object example.

Communicating from the user object to other controls in the window is also possible but a little more difficult. The custom visual user object example will also show an example of an object that manipulates a DataWindow control in the window.

Dynamic User Objects

You can also create user objects at run time. This is most appropriate when you need to create a number of user objects in response to the actions and choices of the user at run time. PowerBuilder provides a number of functions that create user objects dynamically. These functions are:

- OpenUserObject
- OpenUserObjectWithParm
- CloseUserObject

Figure 15.9 shows the example application that creates user objects dynamically. (This is application uo_cbs in the UO.PBL library.)

In this example we create an array of five dynamic user objects. Each user object is a CommandButton standard visual user object, labeled from 1 to 5. Each button beeps the number of times on the label on the object.

FIGURE 15.9 DYNAMIC CREATION OF USER OBJECTS

In the lower part of the window, we create a single user object dynamically: the type is selected from the list in the DropDownListBox. The choices are CommandButton, CheckBox, RadioButton, DropDownListBox and Picture. One user object has been created for each of these types; they will be found in the SHARED.PBL library. Use these or create one of each for your application.

At the window level, declare the following instance variables:

```
u_cb i_cb[10]
DragObject i_dragobject
```

In the Clicked event for the cb_make CommandButton (labeled Make Cbs) add the following code:

```
int idx
FOR idx = 1 TO 5
    i_cb[idx] = create u_cb
    i_cb[idx].text = string(idx)
    OpenUserObjectWithParm (i_cb[idx], idx, 100, 150 * idx)
NEXT
this.enabled = false
```

This example uses the OpenUserObjectWithParm function to open five user objects. Each user object receives the parameter (idx in this example) in its constructor event as an attribute of the message object (DoubleParm in this case).

In the constructor event, the parameter is assigned to the instance variable i_nBeeps.

```
i_nBeeps = message.DoubleParm
```

The i_nBeeps variable is used in the Clicked event to control the number of times the beep is issued. As a result, the first object beeps once, the second twice, and so on. The following code was added to the Clicked event:

```
int idx, idx2

FOR idx = 1 TO i_nBeeps
    beep(1)
    FOR idx2 = 1 to 1000 //delay loop
    NEXT
NEXT
```

To create the single dynamic user objects at the bottom of the window, first add a rectangle (r_1) to serve as a background for the bottom area of the window, then add the following code to the SelectionChanged event of the DropDownListBox. This event closes the set of five CommandButton user objects using the CloseUserObject function.

```
------------------------------------------
string sObject
int idx

sObject = ddlb_1.text

IF IsValid(i_DragObject) THEN CloseUserObject(i_DragObject)

OpenUserObjectWithParm(i_DragObject, 2, sObject, r_1.x+64,
    r_1.y+64)

IF NOT cb_make.enabled THEN
    FOR idx = 1 TO 5
        CloseUserObject(i_cb[idx])
```

```
    NEXT
    cb_make.enabled = true
END IF

return
```

In this code, the selected text is assigned to the sObject string. In this example, since the type of user object varies, another variation of the OpenUserObjectWithParm function is used.

```
OpenUserObjectWithParm(i_dragobject, 2, sObject, r_1.x+64, &
                       r_1.y+64)
```

The first parameter is i_dragobject. This must be a variable of the data type dragobject and this holds the reference to the object that is opened. The second parameter is the argument that you want to pass to the user object. This will be assigned to an attribute of the message object. The third argument is a string, which contains the name of the user object to be opened. You must have created a standard user object for each possible value of sObject. As mentioned, you can create a set of user objects with the names listed in the DropDownListBox in Figure 15.9 or you can use the objects in SHARED.PBL. The final parameters are the X and Y position of the user object.

The OpenUserObjectWithParm function opens an instance of the type contained in sObject. It then places a reference to the user object in i_dragobject. This function returns an integer; it will return 1 if successful and –1 in the case of an error.

The CloseUserObject function is used to close the object.

```
CloseUserObject(i_dragobject)
```

CUSTOM VISUAL USER OBJECTS

The second type of user object is called a custom visual user object. It lets you package two or more standard PowerBuilder controls together as a new reusable control. Creating a custom control is almost an identical process to creating a new window with multiple controls. The custom control is represented by using a window as the form in the User Object painter. After creating this window, the new object combines multiple controls into a unit, a new type of control.

The following steps necessary to build a custom user object are:

- Click on the **User Obj** icon on the PowerBar to open the User Object painter. In the Select User Object dialog window, click on the **New** CommandButton.

- In the New User Object dialog, select the Custom user object type in the Visual category, and click on **OK**.

- The User Object painter opens in the workspace, the user object is displayed as a window. In this painter you can add and modify controls just as you did in the Window painter. You can add functions, events, structures, or variables for the user object.

- Save the user object to a library. Select **Save** (or **Save As**) from the File menu.

Custom user objects have a fixed number of events. The events include:

- Constructor
- Destructor
- DragDrop
- DragEnter
- DragLeave
- DragWithin
- Other
- RButtonDown

The controls within the user object are not individually addressable from outside the user object. However, you can trigger the user object events (including user defined events), and you can call object-level functions. Examples of user object events and functions.

For the Custom type user object, several examples will be created that you may find useful. The first example custom object is named U_DW_NAV. A control (a button bar) will be created that can navigate through the rows in a table using a DataWindow. This user object will take the form of a button bar (see Figure 15.10), with buttons for FIRST, PRIOR, NEXT, and LAST record access. The purpose of creating this as a user object is to create a generalized control for reuse. The goal is to allow you to place this custom user object into any window that has a DataWindow and to gain navigation functionality without any additional effort (you will need one line of code to tie the user object control to the DataWindow). In many cases, this control will provide all that is necessary, without needing any other controls for navigation. You can easily expand this user object. For example, you could easily add buttons for QBE functionality.

The second example combines a SingleLineEdit box with a ListBox. This is done to provide an incremental search functionality between the text as it is entered in the SingleLineEdit box and the items in the listbox. This is similar to two controls that you created in the second window (W_SECOND) of the CONTROLS.PBL example. In that window, a single-line edit was paired with a listbox to provide an incremental search in the ListBox for the first item that began with the letters entered in the edit box. This is useful enough to be packaged together as a user object.

The U_DW_NAV User Object

Start creating the U_DW_NAV object by clicking the **User Object** icon on the PowerBar. This displays the Select User Object dialog window shown in Figure 15.1. Click on the **New** CommandButton to open the New User Object dialog window (Figure 15.2). In that dialog, click on the **Custom** icon in the Visual category and then click **OK**. This opens the Custom User Object painter.

In this painter, you will build the user object in a manner similar to how you add controls to a window in the Window painter. The window in this painter represents the custom user object. Click on the **PainterBar** to select the type of control that you want to add to the user object, drop the control on the window, and then proceed as you would expect. The size of the window in this painter determines the size of the custom object.

For this example, add four CommandButtons to the window. Arrange and label the buttons as shown in Figure 15.10.

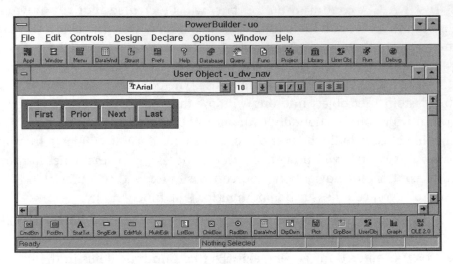

FIGURE 15.10 ARRANGING THE COMMANDBUTTONS

Declare an instance variable (using the **Declare|Instance Variables...** menu selection) as:

```
datawindow dw1
```

Add the following lines of code to the First Clicked script:

```
dw1.ScrollToRow(1)
dw1.SetFocus () // do you see why this line is required
```

Add the following line of code to the Prior Clicked script:

```
dw1.ScrollPriorRow()
dw1.SetFocus ()
```

Add the following line of code to the Next Clicked script:

```
dw1.ScrollNextRow()
dw1.SetFocus ()
```

Add the following line of code to the Last Clicked script:

592

```
dw1.ScrollToRow(dw1.RowCount())
dw1.SetFocus ()
```

Assigning the dw1 DataWindow Value

We declared an instance variable as:

```
datawindow dw1
```

All the code that you just added to the CommandButtons makes references to this variable. At the moment, dw1 is acting as a placeholder for the actual DataWindow that will be controlled by this user object. When you add this user object to a window (containing a DataWindow), it will be necessary to assign the DataWindow control, which is to be controlled with this navigation object, to the dw1 instance variable. This is necessary to allow the user object to make references to the DataWindow control. When you define the user object, the name of the DataWindow control is not known and we wish to allow the use of this user object with a DataWindow of any name, so it must be assigned at run time.

There are several ways to accomplish this assignment. The first technique is *not* the recommended technique but is included here for completeness. The first method is to add code to the user object's constructor that will make the assignment.

Add the following to the constructor for u_dw_nav (just as you would enter a window event script):

```
//complete and add the third line
//to activate this user object
//this.dw1 = dw_1

// NOTE!! the dw_1 control must
//        be constructed before the uo_x or this reference
//        will be unresolved .. use Send To Back to set
//        construct order
```

This code is all comments to document the initialization required to use this user object. This code assumes that most of your DataWindows are named dw_1 (see the third line of code). If this is true, you would not need to modify the DataWindow name when you add this user object to a window. Just add the line (uncommented, of course) to the constructor of the user object. (Do this when you add it to a window in the Window painter.)

In the case where the DataWindow is named something other than dw_1, you will have to modify the code when you add it to the user object's constructor. For example, if the DataWindow control was named **dw_2**, you would change the line to **this.dw1 = dw_2**. (In other cases, you would substitute the actual name of the DataWindow control for the dw_2 reference.) You should also select the **Compile|Override Ancestor Script** (a toggle) menu option to make this script override the ancestor script rather than extend it, though it will work either way. (This actually involves inheritance which is covered in the next chapter and won't be discussed further here.)

The drawback to this method (assignment in the constructor) is mentioned in the comments included in the constructor code. Each of the controls in a window is constructed (sent a constructor event) just before the window actually opens (just before the window open event is triggered; the PB 3 user manual is incorrect in this regard). The order in which PowerBuilder triggers the control constructor events can be controlled by the developer. But this is difficult (and clumsy) to do. This is also extremely prone to error because the order could easily be accidentally changed by another developer (because they didn't notice the dependency). If the user object constructor is triggered before the DataWindow constructor, you will receive the run-time error shown in Figure 15.11.

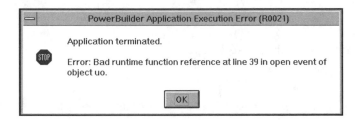

FIGURE 15.11 RUN-TIME ERROR CAUSED BY A WRONG CONSTRUCTOR SEQUENCE

To use this technique would require that the DataWindow object be constructed before the user object (because the user object makes a reference to the

DataWindow). If that DataWindow had not yet been constructed, then this reference would not be possible and would cause an error. This is an important concept; if it is new to you take time to be sure that you understand it.

To change the order for the constructors in a window, just use the **Send To Back** option on the popup menu (in the Window painter). As you send to back and then send to front, the constructor order is set in last-modified–first-constructed order. So if you do this for the user object and then the DataWindow control, the constructors will fire in the correct sequence. But this is too risky to depend on for team development projects.

Using a Registration Function (or Event)

Because of these difficulties, the next method is the technique we recommend. It is to add a registration function to the user object. This registration function can be called in the window's open event to initialize the DataWindow control reference variable. The window's Open event is triggered only after all the control constructors have been executed, so the reference (to DataWindow, dw_1, or whatever it is named) must be valid. You could also use a user-defined event added to this user object for the same result.

To use the object-level registration function, choose the **Declare|User Object Functions** menu selection. Declare the function as shown in Figure 15.12. Be sure to add the function argument dw_control, and that its data type is DataWindow.

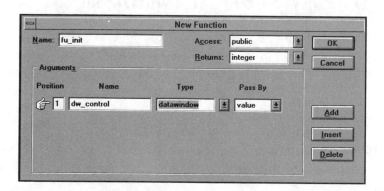

FIGURE 15.12 THE REGISTRATION FUNCTION DECLARATION

After creating the fu_init user object function, add the following line of code to that function:

```
This.dw1 = dw_control
```

Now you can close the function and the User Object painter.

To use this registration function, you must add a line of code, like the following, to your window's open event:

```
uo_1.fu_init(dw_1)
```

Substitute the name of the DataWindow control (if not dw_1) for the dw_1 argument (and the name of the user object control if not uo_1).

Use either of the techniques (the constructor or the object-level function), but you only need to implement one of them. (If you use the second technique, be sure to remove the code provided in the previous example from the constructor event for the user object).

Save the object as **U_DW_NAV** by selecting the **File|SaveAs** menu option.

Consider how you would implement this registration as a user-defined event (in the user object). You can look at the U_DW_NAV user object for an example solution.

The U_DW_NAV_VERTICAL User Object

Figure 15.13 shows a variation of U_DW_NAV where the CommandButtons are arranged vertically instead of horizontally. Create this user object if you may have windows where this design would be preferable. An easy way to create this version is to open the User Object painter and select **U_DW_NAV** as the object. Resize the user object and then rearrange the buttons in a vertical stack. Then choose the **File|Save As...** menu option to save the object as **U_DW_NAV_VER-TICAL**. (In the next chapter a better technique for doing this, inheritance, is discussed.)

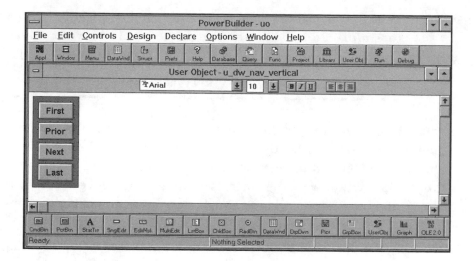

FIGURE 15.13 U_DW_NAV_VERTICAL

The U_DW_NAV_WITH_CLOSE User Object

This version of U_DW_NAV adds a Close CommandButton that closes the parent window. Again, the simplest technique would be to open the U_DW_NAV object, make these changes, and then save the user object with the new name. Consider for a moment, how you would implement the Close button on this user object.

Here is the first technique for closing the parent window from a CommandButton in the user object. Add a user-object-level function by selecting the **Declare|User Object Functions** menu selection. Declare the function as fu_close_parent without any arguments. Add the following code to the function:

```
Close(Parent)
return 0
```

To the Clicked event for the Close button add the following line of code:

```
fu_close_parent()
```

597

NOTE

Your first thought on how to close the window might have been to simply add the following line of code to your Close CommandButton's Clicked event:

```
Close(Parent) // this will not work
```

This will not work and it is very important to understand why. The parent of the Close button is actually the U_DW_NAV_WITH_CLOSE user object. If this is confusing, consider that the user object itself is a window (of sorts), much like any other window with controls added to it. If you added a CommandButton to a normal window, that button's parent would be the window. In the same manner, the parent of the Close button is the user object.

However, the parent of the user object itself (represented by the window in the User Object painter) is the window to which you add an instance of the user object. The function implemented was declared at the user object level. So the Parent reference in that code is containing window. It is essential that you understand this and the previous paragraphs, so please reread them.

The U_DW_NAV_WITH_CLOSE_TRIGGER User Object

The purpose of the next example is to demonstrate communication between a button on the user object and an object on the window (the window's cb_close button). This is a variation on the U_DW_NAV_WITH_CLOSE object. This version also uses a Close CommandButton that will close the parent window, but a TriggerEvent function call implements that function. In the user object's Close button we will add a TriggerEvent('Clicked') command to trigger the Clicked event for the window's Close button (this version requires that you have a Close button on the w_main window in the example).

The first problem we encounter when we are designing the user object is that we don't know the name of the Close button on the window. So how can we address the trigger from within the user object? The answer is to use an object-level instance variable to hold a reference to the window's Close button; this variable will be assigned the value of the window's CommandButton at run time. Create the instance variable by selecting the

Declare|Instance Variable menu option (in the User Object painter). Add the following declarations:

```
datawindow dw1
CommandButton cb1
```

The user object constructor must assign these values in the w_main window or you must use the registration function technique. Either technique works.

Continue working in the User Object painter. Add the following code to the user object's Close CommandButton:

```
IF IsValid(cb1) THEN cb1.TriggerEvent("Clicked")
```

This code first checks to see that the cb1 instance variable has been assigned (use the IsValid function to check to see if objects have valid values). If the reference is valid, the TriggerEvent function is used to trigger the Clicked event for the window's CommandButton.

N O T E We are using IsValid here just to demonstrate its use. In this case, this error would have been caught during development, so it is not really necessary. It could be useful, though, to remind the developer to hook up this user object.

To add object level functions to "register" the controls (the window's close CommandButton and a DataWindow) with the user object, do the following. Choose the **Declare|User Object Functions** menu selection. Declare fu_register_cb as shown in Figure 15.14.

Declare function fu_register_dw as shown in Figure 15.15.

Add the following code to the fu_register_cb function:

```
This.cb1 = cb
return 0
```

Add the following code to the fu_register_dw function:

```
this.dw1 = dw
return 0
```

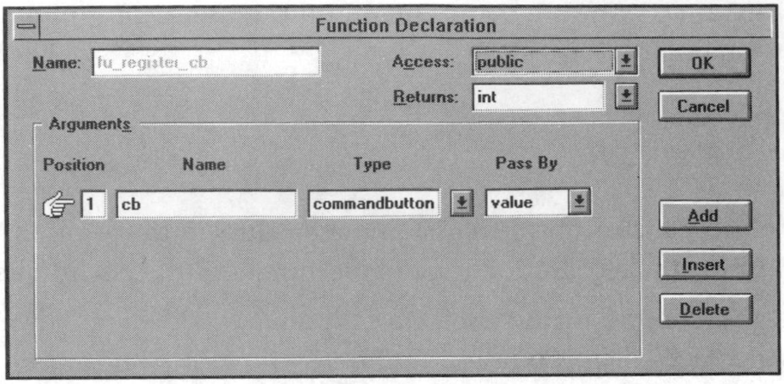

FIGURE 15.14 FU_REGISTER_CB FUNCTION DECLARATION

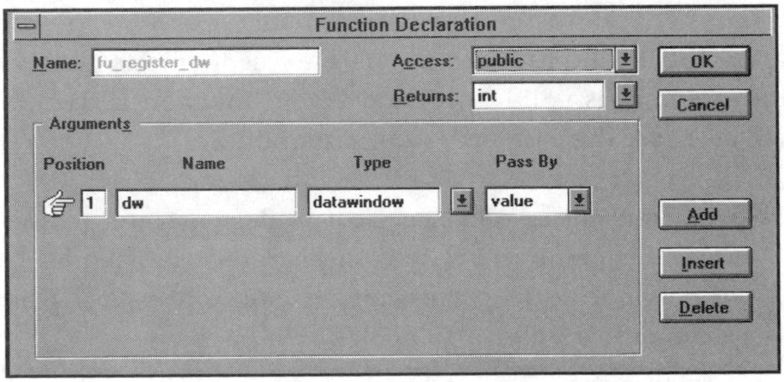

FIGURE 15.15 FU_REGISTER_DW FUNCTION DECLARATION

Of course, these functions could have been also implemented as a single function. When you add this user object control to a window you can add the following code to the window Open event:

```
uo_3.fu_register_cb ( cb_close)
uo_3.fu_register_dw ( dw_1 )
```

Or, if you want to use the other technique, add the following code to the uo_1 constructor:

```
this.dw1 = dw_1
this.cb1 = cb_close
```

Next, we will add a function to this user object that will allow any of the CommandButtons to be enabled or disabled (we will also implement this as a user-defined event in the user object). Create a user object-level-function named **fu_change_state**. It has two arguments:

```
sButton          string          value
bEnabled     boolean         value
```

Add the following code to the function:

```
int rc = 1

CHOOSE CASE sButton
    CASE 'first'
        cb_first.Enabled = bEnabled
    CASE 'prior'
        cb_prior.Enabled = bEnabled
    CASE 'next'
        cb_next.Enabled = bEnabled
    CASE 'last'
        cb_last.Enabled = bEnabled
    CASE 'close'
        cb_closex.Enabled = bEnabled
    CASE ELSE
        rc = 0
END CHOOSE

return rc
```

Now add a CheckBox to the window and name it **cbx_first**. Add the following code to the cbx_first Clicked event:

```
uo_3.fu_change_state("first", This.Checked)
```

Now, this CheckBox will enable or disable the cb_first CommandButton.

Next we will add a user-defined event to do the same. Create a user-defined event with the label **ue_change_state** and the value pbm_custom01. Add the following code to that script:

```
string sButton
boolean bEnabled

sButton = Message.StringParm
```

```
bEnabled = Message.WordParm = 1

CHOOSE CASE sButton
    CASE 'first'
        cb_first.Enabled = bEnabled
    CASE 'prior'
        cb_prior.Enabled = bEnabled
    CASE 'next'
        cb_next.Enabled = bEnabled
    CASE 'last'
        cb_last.Enabled = bEnabled
    CASE 'close'
        cb_closex.Enabled = bEnabled
    CASE ELSE
END CHOOSE
```

Now add a CheckBox to the window and name it **cbx_last**. Add the following code to the cbx_first Clicked event:

```
Message.StringParm = 'last'
IF This.Checked THEN
    Message.WordParm = 1
ELSE
    Message.WordParm = 0
END IF
uo_3.TriggerEvent("ue_change_state")
```

Now this CheckBox enables or disables the cb_last CommandButton.

The U_LB_WITH_SEARCH User Object

The next example of a custom visual user object combines a SingleLineEdit control with a listbox to perform the incremental type of search in the listbox that was implemented in the second window of the CONTROLS application. As you enter text in the SingleLineEdit field the listbox selects the first entry that best matches the entire text (in the edit field).

To create the U_LB_WITH_SEARCH object start by clicking on the **User Object** icon on the PowerBar. This will display the Select User Object dialog window shown in Figure 15.1. Click on the New button to open the New User Object dialog window. In that dialog click on the **Custom** icon in the Visual category and click **OK**. This opens the Custom User Object painter.

For this example, add a SingleLineEdit control to the window and then a ListBox control. Arrange the controls as shown in Figure 15.16.

Add a user event, we_keyup, to the SingleLineEdit box. Do this by opening the script editor using the popup menu (over the sle). Select the **Declare|User Events** menu option. Name the event **we_keyup** and assign it the **pbm_keyup** event ID.

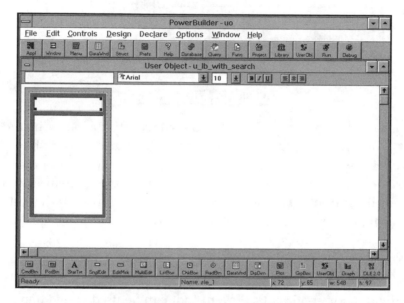

FIGURE 15.16 U_LB_WITH_SEARCH

This adds a new event to the SingleLineEdit control which maps one of the Window events to the SingleLineEdit control. In the PowerScript editor, select that event (at the bottom of the list), and add the following text to that script:

```
int index
Index = lb_1.SelectItem(this.text, 0)
```

This event is triggered as each keystroke ends (when the focus is in the SingleLineEdit). The script code searches the items in the ListBox (lb_1) for a match to the sle_1.text value.

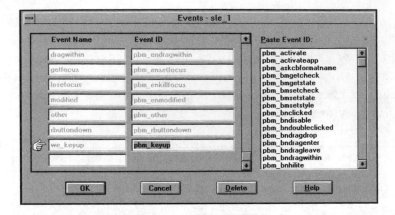

FIGURE 15.17 WE_KEYUP

Next, add a user event at the user object level (the window in the User Object painter). To do this, first open the editor at the user object level. Right-click the mouse on the user object (the window area) and select **Script** from the popup menu. Add a user event **ue_add_item** and give it the event ID of **pbm_custom01**. Select the new event from the Select Event DropDown ListBox and add the following code:

```
int idx
idx = lb_1.AddItem ( Message.StringParm )
```

This provides a user-object-level event that can be used to add items to the listbox. Another way to do this would be with a user-object-level function, we will also implement that method for this example. To add that, declare a function at the user object level (use the **Declare|User Object Functions** menu selection). Declare a function as shown in Figure 15.18.

The function name is fu_add_item, with a single string argument, sItem. Add the following code for that function:

```
int idx
idx = lb_1.AddItem ( sItem )
return idx
```

This works the same as the ue_add_item event. Save the object as U_LB_WITH_SEARCH by selecting the **File|SaveAs** menu option.

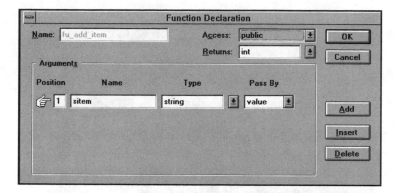

FIGURE 15.18 FU_ADD_ITEM FUNCTION DECLARATION

Add one of these new user objects to a window. Name the user object **uo_isearch**. To demonstrate both methods of adding items to the listbox you will also need to add two SingleLineEdit controls to the window.

For the first of the SingleLineEdits, add the following code to the modified event:

```
uo_isearch.fu_add_item(This.text)
This.text = ''
```

For the second of the SingleLineEdits add the following code to the modified event:

```
Message.StringParm = This.text
uo_isearch.TriggerEvent('ue_add_item')
This.text = ''
```

Create a window with all these objects, as shown in Figure 15.19. This example also includes user objects explained in the next section.

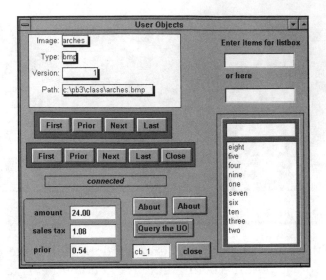

FIGURE 15.19 THE EXAMPLE WINDOW IN THE UO APPLICATION

CUSTOM CLASS USER OBJECTS

The next type of user object is a *nonvisual user object*. It lets you encapsulate a behavior (or functionality) very much like creating a class in the C++ language. You cannot use any of the standard PowerBuilder controls in this type of user object. Instead the user object is comprised of PowerScript code, variables, functions, structures, and events. This type of control is used mostly for data processing functions. For example, you might have a customer object that contains functions to handle customer transactions.

The class user object is not added to one of your applications in the Window painter as were the other types of user objects that we have seen. Instead, you must instantiate an instance of the class type by using the CREATE command.

For example, in a script you would declare a variable of the type u_calc_sales_tax. Then use the CREATE statement to instantiate the uo_tax object.

```
u_calc_sales_tax  uo_tax

uo_tax = CREATE u_calc_sales_tax
// use the object
// for a while
DESTROY uo_tax
```

For the example, a class user object is created that calculates the sales tax for a given purchase amount. This object is used in the lower left section of Figure 15.19. In the section, you enter a sales amount in the field labeled **amount**. The sales tax will be calculated by a user object and displayed in the **sales tax** field. The previously calculated tax is displayed in the **prior** field.

To create the U_CALC_SALES_TAX user object start by clicking on the **User Object** icon on the PowerBar. This displays the Select User Object dialog window shown in Figure 15.1. Click on the **New** button. This opens the New User Object dialog (Figure 15.2). Click the custom icon in the Class category and click **OK**. This choice specifies that you are creating a nonvisual user object.

The Custom Class object only has only two events:

■ constructor
■ destructor

The User Object painter opens with a window that represents the user object. You will not be able to add any controls to the window. For this example, declare a shared variable by selecting the **Declare|Shared Variables** menu option. Add the following declaration to the dialog:

```
decimal {2} s_decLast
```

Now, create a structure at the object level. Choose the **Declare|User Object Structures** menu option and create a new structure named **str_tax**. This structure has two member elements, in and out, which have the decimal data type.

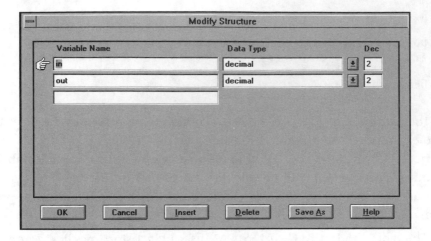

FIGURE 15.20 STR_TAX

Add an instance variable of the str_tax type (chose the **Declare|Instance Variables** menu option):

```
str_tax i_tax
```

Create an object level function by selecting the **Declare|User Object Function** menu option.

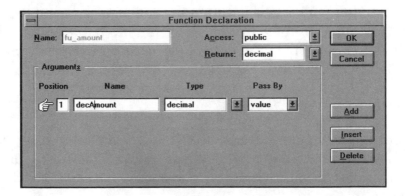

FIGURE 15.21 FU_AMOUNT

Name the function **fu_amount** and add the decimal argument decAmount. Add the following code to the function:

```
decimal{2} decOut

decOut = decAmount * .045
i_tax.in = decAmount
i_tax.out = decOut
s_decLast = decOut
return decOut
```

This function calculates and returns the sales tax. It also assigns the value to the i_tax structure. Add another object-level function.

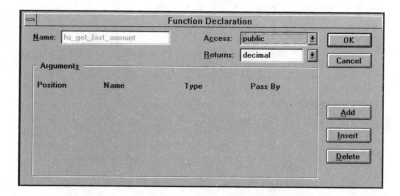

FIGURE 15.22 FU_GET_LAST_AMOUNT

Name the function **fu_get_last_amount**. It has no arguments, but it does return a decimal value. Add the following line of code to the function:

```
return (s_decLast)
```

Save the object as **U_CALC_SALES_TAX** by selecting the **File|SaveAs** menu option.

Next, the new class user object will be used in an application. To demonstrate this object you will need to add an edit mask and two SingleLineEdit controls to the window. See Figure 15.19 for an example.

Name the SingleLineEdit box **sle_out**. Name the SingleLineEdit controls **sle_out** and **sle_last**.

Define the edit mask (em_1) with the data type number and use the following mask:

"####,####.00"

Add the following script to the Modified event for the EditMask:

```
decimal {2} decValue, rc, decIn, decOut
u_calc_sales_tax uo_tax

sle_out.text = 'calculating'
uo_tax = create u_calc_sales_tax
sle_last.text = string(uo_tax.fu_get_last_amount())

decValue = dec(em_1.text)
rc = uo_tax.fu_amount(decValue)
sle_out.text = string(rc)
decIn = uo_tax.i_tax.in
decOut = uo_tax.i_tax.out
destroy uo_tax
```

Cross-Window References

To demonstrate a cross-window reference to a user object, a second window (w_second) is created. We would like to place an EditMask in this window that can accept a sales amount and then display the tax in a SingleLineEdit (or StaticText) field. Rather than create a new instance of the u_sales_tax user object, we wish to use the instance uo_tax in the w_main window. Clearly some code will be added to the Modified event of the SingleLineEdit to access uo_tax. Consider for a moment how you might implement this. Complete the following step while you consider this.

Create w_second and place an EditMask control on the window (em_1) and a SingleLineEdit (sle_1). Add an instance variable to w_second:

```
Window i_Parent_Window
```

Add the following line of code to w_second's open event:

```
i_parent_window = Message.PowerObjectParm
```

Place a CommandButton (cb_open) in the first window and add the following line of code to its Clicked event:

```
OpenWithParm(w_second, Parent)
```

This function opens the w_second window and passes a parameter in the Message object. In this case the parameter is the Parent window, so it will be placed in the PowerObjectParm attribute of the Message object.

Okay, back to the problem; it isn't very difficult. The simplest solution is as follows:

```
decTax = w_main.i_uo_tax.fu_amount(decValue)
```

But suppose we would like to avoid having to hard-code the w_main window name. If we can do that, then any window could share this i_uo_tax object. Can you find a solution for that problem? Remember, we have an instance variable (i_parent_window) in w_second that was assigned the Parent window in the Open event (you must have suspected that we would find a way to use that). So considering that, the first idea that probably occurs to you is something like the following:

```
decTax = i_parent_window.i_uo_tax.fu_amount(decValue)
```

Unfortunately, this won't work. PowerBuilder refuses to compile this or to allow you to save this line in the script because the window class that is used for the instance variable, does not contain the user object i_uo_tax, so it is a bad reference. For the same reason, the following will also fail (in the w_second Open event):

```
u_sales_tax uo_tax
uo_tax = i_parent_window.i_uo_tax
// etc.
```

However, there *is* a solution that does work. It is a variation on our registration function (as an event this time) used throughout this chapter. That may be enough of a hint to get you going. If so, try to create a solution before reading further.

In w_main, we created an instance variable:

```
uo_tax i_uo_tax
```

In the Open event for w_main, we instantiated that object:

```
i_uo_tax = CREATE uo_tax
```

Now you must add an event to w_main. Create a window level user-defined event **ue_get_i_uo_tax**. It has no arguments and returns a u_calc_sales_tax object. It has only one line of code:

```
Message.PowerObjectParm = i_uo_tax
```

It simply assigns the instance to the Message object as a parameter.

Now add the following code to the Modified event for the em_1 in w_second:

```
u_calc_sales_tax uo_tax2
decimal{2} decTax

i_parent_window.TriggerEvent('ue_get_i_uo_tax')
uo_tax2 = Message.PowerObjectParm
uo_tax2.fu_set_rate(.055)
decTax = uo_tax2.fu_amount (dec(em_1.text))
sle_1.text = String(round(decTax,2))
```

The interesting lines of code are:

```
u_calc_sales_tax uo_tax2

i_parent_window.TriggerEvent('ue_get_i_uo_tax')
uo_tax2 = Message.PowerObjectParm
```

The first line declares a variable uo_tax2 of type u_calc_sales_tax. The next line triggers the event in the w_main window that will return the instance i_uo_tax in the Message object. The third line assigns that Message parameter to uo_tax2. From this point on, any reference to uo_tax2 is a reference to w_main.i_uo_tax. So the following line:

```
decTax = uo_tax2.fu_amount (dec(em_1.text))
```

calls the fu_amount function in w_main.i_uo_tax.

STANDARD CLASS USER OBJECTS

The next type of user object is another nonvisual one. It lets you base the class on one of the PowerBuilder objects such as Message, Error, or Transaction. This user object is built from PowerScript code, variables, functions, structures, and events.

The Standard class object is not added to one of your applications in the Window painter as the visual types of user objects were. You must instantiate an instance of the class type by using the CREATE command as you did for the Custom class user object.

For example, in a script you would declare a variable of the type u_my_message:

```
u_my_message   uo_message

uo_message = CREATE u_my_message
// use the object
// for a while
DESTROY uo_message
```

For our example, we will create a Standard class user object based on the message object. We will add two functions to the user object and an instance variable.

To create the U_MY_MESSAGE user object, start by clicking on the **User Object** icon on the PowerBar. This displays the Select User Object dialog window shown in Figure 15.1. Click on the **New** button. This opens the New User Object dialog (Figure 15.2). Click the **Standard** icon in the Class category and click **OK**. This choice specifies that you are creating a class (non-visual) user object based on one of the PowerBuilder objects.

The Standard Class object has only two events:

■ constructor
■ destructor

The User Object painter opens with a window that represents the user object. You will not be able to add any controls to the window. For this example, declare an instance variable by selecting the **Declare|Instance Variables...** menu option. Add the following declaration to the dialog:

```
int i_iLen
```

Create an object-level function by picking the **Declare|User Object Function** menu option. Name the function **fu_set_stringparm** and add a string argument sText passed by value. Add the following code to the function:

```
This.StringParm = sText
This.i_iLen = len(sText)
return 0
```

This function stores the sText and the length of the text in the user object.

Add another object-level function and name it **fu_get_stringparm**. It has one string argument, sText, which is passed by reference. This function should return a decimal value. Add the following lines of code to the function:

```
sText = This.StringParm
return (This.i_iLen)
```

Save the object as **U_MY_MESSAGE** by selecting the **File|SaveAs** menu option.

Next, we will use the new standard class user object in an application. Open a window and add a CommandButton and a SingleLineEdit control (sle_1) to the window.

Add the following code to the button's Clicked event:

```
u_my_message uo_message
int rc
string sText, sText2

sText = 'Testing'
uo_message = create u_my_message
rc = uo_message.fu_set_stringparm('test')

rc = uo_message.fu_get_stringparm(sText2)
sle_1.text = sText2
destroy uo_message
```

Run the application. When you click the CommandButton, the sle_1 displays the *Testing* message.

EXTERNAL USER OBJECTS

The next type of user object is called an *external user object*. It lets you access a DLL (dynamic link library). This DLL will be a control that has been created in C or C++. The external control provides a registered class, a window procedure, and a DLL as part of the package.

The events for an external user object are:

- Constructor
- Destructor
- DragDrop
- DragEnter
- DragLeave
- DragWithin
- Other
- RButtonDown

To create the external user object start by clicking on the **User Object** icon on the PowerBar. This displays the Select User Object dialog window shown in Figure 15.1. Click on the **New** CommandButton. This opens the New User Object dialog (Figure 15.2). When this dialog opens, select the **External** icon and click **OK**. You then must select a custom control DLL from the Select Custom Control DLL dropdown list.

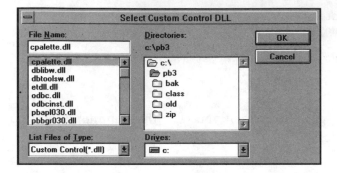

FIGURE 15.23 SELECT CUSTOM CONTROL DLL

In the External User Object Style dialog, fill in the class name and set other important attributes.

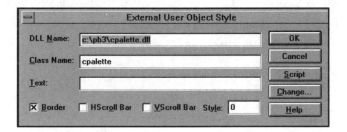

FIGURE 15.24 THE EXTERNAL USER OBJECT

The External User Object has the following style options:

- **Name**—enters the name of the user object.
- **DLL Name**—selects a DLL file for the user object.
- **Class Name**—enters the class of the custom control supported by the DLL.

- **Text**—text for the object.
- **Visible**—visible if True.
- **Border**—with Border if True.
- **Style**—holds any additional style bits that control the display of the custom control.
- **Enabled**—active if True.
- **HScroll Bar**—added if True.
- **VScroll Bar**—added if True.

At this point, you would complete the development of the user object. Select the **File** |**Save As** menu option to save it to a library.

VBX USER OBJECTS

The final type of user object, called a *VBX user object*. It lets you access Visual Basic controls. It is similar to an external control.

The events for a VBX user object are:

- Constructor
- Destructor
- DragDrop
- DragEnter
- DragLeave
- DragWithin
- Other
- Plus events unique to VBX

To create the VBX user object, start by clicking on the **User Object** icon on the PowerBar. This displays the Select User Object dialog window shown in Figure 15.1. Click on the **New** CommandButton. This opens the New User Object dialog (Figure 15.2). When this dialog opens, select the **VBX** icon.

You must then select a VBX from the Select VBX Control dialog as shown in Figure 15.25.

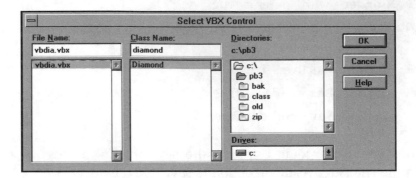

FIGURE 15.25 SELECTING THE VBX CONTROL

Figure 15.26 shows the example VBX control that is included with PowerBuilder.

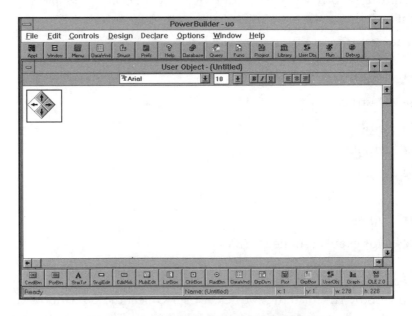

FIGURE 15.26 THE SAMPLE VBX CONTROL

ADVANCED TECHNIQUES

In the UO.PBL you will find several applications. The next one to look at is UO_CBS. This application demonstrates the dynamic creation of user objects. Open this application and run it. If you click on the **Make Cbs** CommandButton, the application created five versions of a standard user object based on a CommandButton. Each of these are labeled with a number, which is the number of times the PC speaker beeps when you click the button.

If you pull down the DropDownListBox, you will see a list of types from which to choose. Selecting one of these types creates a Standard user object of that type dynamically.

FIGURE 15.27 THE DYNAMIC USER OBJECT EXAMPLE

To create this you may use the Standard user objects already created and stored in UO.PBL. First create the following instance variables (at the window level):

```
u_cb i_cb[10]
dragobject i_dragobject
```

i_cb is an array of standard visual user objects based on the CommandButton. The i_dragobject is used to create a variety of types of standard visual user objects. It can be used to create a CheckBox, RadioButton, DropDownListBox, and so on. It is the direct ancestor for most of the Window controls with which you are now familiar. So it can be used with any of them.

The code for the Make Cbs CommandButton Clicked event is:

```
int idx
FOR idx = 1 TO 5
    i_cb[idx] = CREATE u_cb
    i_cb[idx].text = String(idx)
    OpenUserObjectWithParm (i_cb[idx], idx, 100, 150 * idx)
NEXT
this.enabled = false
```

This code creates five u_cb user objects. To make the objects visible the OpenUserObjectWithParm function is called. That function's second argument is the parameter that is passed to the user object's Constructor event. You can pass any one argument to the user object. The user object will pull the value off the Message object. The third and fourth arguments determine the X and Y positions of the user object on the window. The parameter that is passed to the u_cb object is the FOR loop index. This is used as a caption for the user object and it controls the number of beeps that the user object triggers when it is clicked. The Y position is incremented by 150 PBUs for each object; to space them down the window vertically.

The code for the u_cb constructor is:

```
i_nBeeps = message.DoubleParm
```

The value is stored in an instance variable, i_nBeeps, at the user object level. The Clicked event of the u_cb object contains the following:

```
int idx, idx2

FOR idx = 1 TO i_nBeeps
    beep(1)
    FOR idx2 = 1 to 1000 // 10000 for faster machines
```

```
      NEXT
NEXT
```

This is a simple loop, which will beep once and then pause temporarily (to separate the beeps). The number of beeps is equal to the index value of the Make Cbs FOR loop.

The DropDownListBox, ddlb_1, has been initialized with a list of user object types. This includes:

- **u_ddlb**—a DropDownListBox

- **u_cb**—CommandButton

- **u_cbx**—CheckBox

- **u_p**—Picture control

- **u_rb**—RadioButton

The code for the Modified event of the DropDownListBox, ddlb_1, follows:

```
string sObject
int idx

sObject = ddlb_1.text
IF IsValid(i_DragObject) THEN CloseUserObject(i_DragObject)
OpenUserObjectWithParm(i_DragObject, 2, sObject, r_1.x+64,
    r_1.y+64)
IF NOT cb_make.Enabled THEN
    FOR idx = 1 TO 5
        CloseUserObject(i_cb[idx])
    NEXT
    cb_make.Enabled = true
END IF
return
```

In this script, sObject is assigned the value that was selected by the user. The IsValid function is used to see if a user object has already been created (in this script). If so, then the CloseUserObject function is called. Another form of the OpenUserObjectWithParm function is called on the next line to create the new object. Since this user object may have a variety of types, this function will allow the type to be specified as the third argument (a string). The first argument is a variable that will receive the initialization (reference) to the new object. The second argument is the parameter that is passed as in the earlier example. The last two arguments are the X and Y positions, placed relative to the top left of the rectangle drawing object. The r_1.x and r_1.y attributes are the top-left corner of the rectangle.

The next section closes the five u_cb user objects (if they have been opened). Select the various types, and notice that they work (to some degree) even with no programming. You could, of course, access the attributes, events, and functions of these user objects to more fully implement the behaviors you wish to establish.

UO_BUTTON_LIST

The UO_BUTTON_LIST application is also in the UO.PBL library. This implements a custom visual user object. This is a dynamically created list of buttons (picture controls). Each button can open a child window when clicked. These child windows may also contain other Button lists.

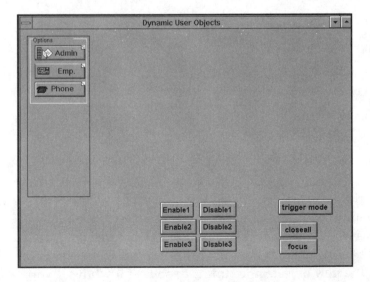

FIGURE 15.28 THE BUTTON LIST EXAMPLE

Run this example and consider how you would have implemented this functionality. There are several ways to do this. What are the major advantages of using a user object for the button list? Give this some thought and then examine the source code for more details.

The opening screen has three buttons. Pressing one "lights" up the button and open a child window. The child window may also contain a button list. Pressing that opens a smaller child window as shown in Figure 15.29.

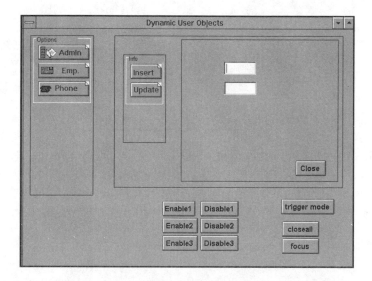

FIGURE 15.29 THE BUTTON LIST EXAMPLE

The U_BUTTON_LIST is a custom visual user object. To add one of these user objects to a window requires that you provide three BMP images for each button. A version is needed for the enabled, disabled, and pressed states. You may also specify an accelerator key for each button and the name of the child window that should be opened when the button is pressed. There are several functions that are used to initialize the button list.

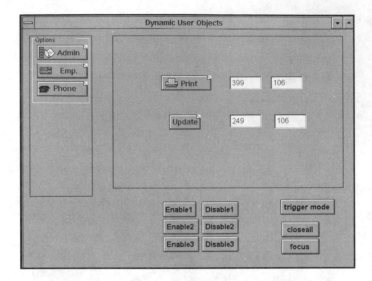

FIGURE 15.30 THE BUTTON LIST EXAMPLE

First, you must call the fu_init function to register the number of buttons that will be on the user object, the Parent window for the object, and the type of button. The type is an integer, which represents large (1) or smaller (2) buttons. An example would be:

```
uo_1.fu_init(3, 'Options', This, 1)
```

Next, you must initialize each button in the button list. You supply the index number, the name of the BMP images, the accelerator key (if any), and the window to be opened when the key is pressed. The last argument is used to set a mode, where windows are only hidden rather than closed. This is a performance enhancement.

```
uo_1.fu_init_button_wxy(1, 'c:\pb4\class\w_admin.bmp', &
                        asc("A"), 'wc_first', True)
uo_1.fu_init_button_wxy(2, 'c:\pb4\class\w_emp.bmp', 50, &
                        'wc_second', True)
uo_1.fu_init_button_wxy(3, 'c:\pb4\class\w_phone.bmp', 51, &
                        'wc_third', False)
```

U_BUTTON_LIST contains a set of U_P_FOR_LIST user objects.

U_P_FOR_LIST is a standard visual user object based on the picture control. This user object is very simple. It only knows about its accelerator key assignment, its name (stored in the tag attribute), and when it has been clicked. Most of the processing is encapsulated within the button list user object.

UO_TOGGLE

The UO_TOGGLE application is also in the UO.PBL library. This implements a custom visual user object that combines several controls at the same location on the screen. The user can click on a small square box to flip the control to show the other set of controls associated with an instance. Since this is a nonstandard type of control, we do not recommend its use, but it does demonstrate some interesting techniques for hiding and showing controls.

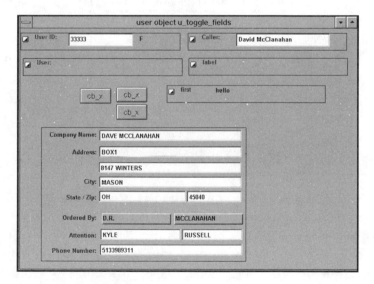

FIGURE 15.31 THE TOGGLE EXAMPLE

Figure 15.31 shows a window with five U_TOGGLE user objects. The customer information at the bottom of the screen is a Custom class user object that encapsulates customer information and functions.

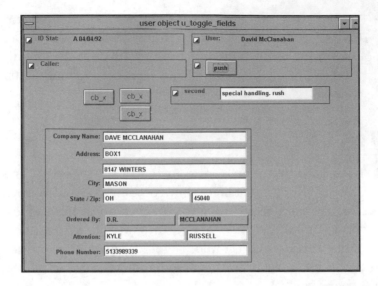

FIGURE 15.32 THE TOGGLE EXAMPLE

Figure 15.32 shows the same window after the toggles have been flipped for each of the objects. Notice the appearance of the CommandButton (labeled push). Pressing this populates the customer user object based on the information in one of these fields.

UO_WITH_STRUCTURES

The UO_WITH_STRUCTURES application is also in the UO.PBL library. This implements a Custom visual user object that encapsulates a structure within a user object. This is a very useful object that has been used in a number of real-world applications. Often you have an entity, with an associated structure, that may need to span a number of windows. This provides a way to package the structure and pass it around as required, and it avoids having to create a global structure (avoiding globals as we recommend). The technique used for passing this user object to other windows is somewhat similar to the registration function technique that we used throughout this chapter.

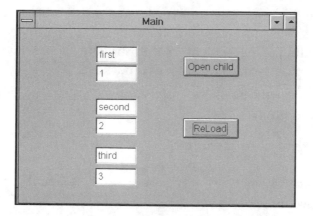

FIGURE 15.33 THE STRUCTURE EXAMPLE

Figure 15.33 shows a simple structure of six elements (three pairs). Pressing **Open child** opens the second window and passes the object to the second window.

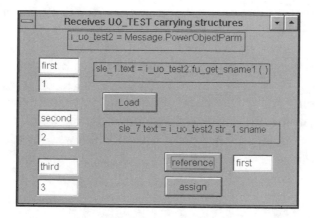

FIGURE 15.34 THE STRUCTURE EXAMPLE

The second window *aliases* the user object (as i_uo_test2) by assigning its own instance variable to the Message.PowerObjectParm. Functions and attributes are then accessible in the object's instance in the first window. sle_1 calls a function, sle_7 references an attribute.

To create this example, we first defined a user object, u_carry_structures. It contains a structure and accessor functions to provide for the reading and updating of the elements of that structure. So we have encapsulated attributes and functions together as a package.

In the main window of this application (w_structure_test), we create an instance of our user object:

```
u_carry_structures i_uo_test
```

When the second window, w_structure_test2, is opened, the i_uo_test object is passed as a parameter:

```
OpenWithParm(w_structure_test2, i_uo_test)
```

In the second window we declared an instance of our user object as:

```
u_carry_structures i_uo_test2
```

The Open event of the second window assigns the PowerObjectParm to that instance variable:

```
i_uo_test2 = Message.PowerObjectParm
```

From that point on, all references to the i_uo_test object are references to the i_uo_test in the first window. So we have created an alias for i_uo_test. We could have named it the same in both windows, but we changed the name for clarity.

CHAPTER SIXTEEN

INHERITANCE

owerBuilder provides some degree of support for each of the major tenets of object-oriented programming: data abstraction, inheritance, and polymorphism. This chapter provides an introduction to object-oriented programming concepts followed by a detailed explanation of the use of inheritance in PowerBuilder. The object-oriented features in PowerBuilder are very useful and worth investigating. The reusability gained from these object-oriented features is one of the main advantages of PowerBuilder over competing products (such as Visual Basic).

OBJECT-ORIENTED CONCEPTS

In an object-oriented system, the object is the basic element that is used to build the system. Object-oriented programming encompasses the creation and use of objects as a fundamental part of the development process. Objects are embedded with a number of operations that can be used to access and manipulate these objects. What is an object? That will become clearer in the next section, but essentially an *object* is a bundle of variables and functions that act as a unit.

It is essential to understand the aspects of object-orientation before proceeding with the PowerBuilder examples.

DATA ABSTRACTION

Data abstraction is the encapsulation of attributes and functionality within an object. Once defined, the object becomes an abstract data type. In many ways, this is really just a logical extension of structured programming techniques. For example, most languages let the programmer define structures. A *structure* is a set of variables that are treated as a unit (the beginnings of our object). Data abstraction takes this a step further by adding functions and scoping (of functions and variables) to the object. These functions perform operations on the structure elements. The data elements and functions are internal to the object, and therefore encapsulated in the object. In the chapter on user objects, you learned how to package a set of controls into an object and how to add functions to user objects.

The definition of a type of object is called a *class*. In effect, a class creates an object definition and defines the interface that is used to access that class of object. The code (external to the object) that uses this interface becomes the client of the object. It makes requests, for retrieving and for setting values to the interface, not by directly manipulating the object's attributes. The object, in essence, handles the manipulation of its own attributes. If another object, external to it, wishes to modify it, that external object would make a request (via a function call or triggered event) to the object to handle it. A class is similar to a data type in that it allows the creation of variables of its type, and provides a number of operations and/or operators to manipulate the objects. This encapsulation make the object a standalone object, independent of things that may affect it, making its reuse easier.

Data abstraction helps you build cleaner, easier to extend applications, and simplifies the maintenance of those applications. In PowerBuilder development, you define classes and objects. In the early stages of PowerBuilder development this process is somewhat hidden from the developer. This was mentioned in Chapter 2, The PowerScript Language, and is covered again in this chapter.

As we have seen, a class is a type or category of object. An object is an instantiation (instance) of a class. The relationship between a class and an object is similar to the relationship between a structure definition (typedef in the C language) and the declaration of a variable of that type of structure. Classes have elements (*member variables*) somewhat like structures, but classes also contains functions (called *methods* in some languages) that manipulate the member variables and perform other processing.

For example, consider the following declaration (this example is similar to C++ and is used as a general example):

```
class Person
{
        char first_name[12];
        char last_name[20];
        char phone[20];
    public:
        Person (); // a constructor function with the same
                   // name as the class
        GetFirstName();
        SetFirstName();
};
```

In this example, a class has been defined with three data elements (first_name, last_name, phone). The class also contains three functions (methods). The first is the constructor used to create an instance of this class (an object). The other two functions are used to access the first_name element (the code for these methods would be defined somewhere else). You could implement this function as a non-visual user object in

PowerBuilder. The variables are instance variables and the methods are object-level functions.

Continuing with the Person example, consider the following code:

```
Person emp1;
emp1.SetFirstName("David")
```

In these two lines of code, an instance of this class was created (emp1), and the first_name was assigned to David. The class is used just like a data type in the declaration. The dot notation is used to specify that the SetFirstName() function (a method in the Person class), is to be called with the argument David and applied to the variables in the emp1 object.

The emp1 object encapsulates variables and functions to capture the meaning (behavior) of a Person. Each object that is instantiated for this class, represents an individual, one unique person. Notice that instead of directly manipulating the values of the object's data members, the object's SetFirstName function was used to update the value. This is an essential part of object-oriented programming. You must (in most cases) access the member variables only through the defined interface (the methods). That encapsulation is essential for the concept of data abstraction.

INHERITANCE

Inheritance lets the developer derive a new class (object type) from an existing base class. The descendant class inherits all the attributes (variables) and functions of the ancestor class. The new class will specialize the more general base class in some way, perhaps by adding attributes, or by restricting the ancestor's behavior in some manner. The payoff is that you gain the reusability of existing objects that may already have some of the features that you need for the new objects, and you gain the reuse of well-tested code, shortening the development process. Sharing a base set of objects can save a great deal of time and effort for a development team, and can also provide a boost to new PowerBuilder developers.

For example, a Customer class based on the Person class can be created. It is clear that a customer has all the attributes of a person, but is a
person that has special kind of relationship with our company. To capture
that relationship, a customer ID (cust_id) is added to the person class and
one or more methods to handle customer processing. The next example,
defines the Customer class, and creates an instance of that class (we continue to use C++ as the example language for this discussion.)

```
Class Customer : public Person
{
        int cust_id;
    public:
        Customer();
        SetCustId();
}

Customer cust1;
cust1.SetFirstName("David")
```

The first line (of the Customer class declaration) defines the customer class
as derived from class Person (the colon means *is derived (inherited) from*).
The new customer class inherits all the member data elements and member functions from the person class. The Customer class is a *descendent* of
the Person class and Person is an *ancestor* of the Customer class.

The Customer class could have been created without using inheritance
with the following definition:

```
class Customer
{
        char first_name[12];
        char last_name[20];
        char phone[20];
        int cust_id;
    public:
        Customer ();
        Person();
        GetFirstName();
        SetFirstName();
        SetCustId();
};
```

The advantage of using inheritance is the reusability of the parts that are in common with Person and Customer. Another benefit is, that if later, other fields are added to the Person class, such as address, city, state, and zip, then the Customer class automatically gains these attributes. If the length of the first_name attribute in the Person class is changed, it is changed in the Customer class. If methods are added to the Person class, the Customer class also gains these functions. If corrections or extensions are made to the Person functions, these changes are also inherited in the Customer class.

You can add elements to the descendent class (you can also override behavior). You cannot delete members (either data or functions) from the ancestor when you define a descendent class. This is a fundamental concept for inheritance. It is important that only the elements that are truly in common with all the descendants are placed in the base class.

It is possible to create a new class that is derived from Customer or from Person creating an inheritance hierarchy for the classes.

```
Person
      — Customer
            — Government Customer
      — Sales Rep
            — Sales Rep Manager
```

A class may serve as the source for multiple descendants. In some object-oriented languages it is possible to create a descendant class that is derived from more that one base (ancestor) class. This is called *multiple inheritance*. Multiple inheritance is not supported in PowerBuilder. You may only derive a class from one ancestor class. This avoids the complexity that is introduced by multiple inheritance. Single inheritance is suitable for most cases.

POLYMORPHISM

Polymorphism is another characteristic of object-oriented programming. This features allows a function's behavior to vary with the type of the object to which it is applied. For example, three different classes (file, directory, and fileset) may all have a method named *Delete*. The behavior of that method varies for each of these object types because the rules (the definition) for the delete will need to vary for each.

An example of polymorphism in PowerBuilder is provided later in this chapter.

OBJECT-ORIENTED POWERBUILDER

To become a proficient PowerBuilder developer you must spend some time learning about and utilizing the object-oriented features of PowerBuilder. These features provide you with reusable objects and better design modularity, while helping to clarify the functioning and to ease the maintenance of the systems you develop.

PowerBuilder provides some support for each of the major tenets of object-oriented programming. PowerBuilder provides classes (and objects), inheritance, and polymorphism.

When you create a new window (w_main for example), you are actually creating a class (an object type, a new data type).

When you open the window:

```
open (w_main)
```

you are actually opening an instance of that window. PowerBuilder has created an instance of the object type w_main and given it the same name (w_main) as the class. In effect, PowerBuilder has generated the following statement:

```
w_main w_main
```

The first reference in this statement is to the w_main class, the window that you defined. The second w_main reference declares a window object of type w_main. Reconsider the open(w_main) statement in the following context:

```
w_main w_main
open(w_main)
```

Here, the w_main reference in your open function is a reference to the object (variable), not to the class (data type). PowerBuilder hides this declaration to allow beginning PowerBuilder developers to use the system without having to understand object-oriented details. However, this does confuse the terminology (specifically the use of the word object), in the PowerBuilder system.

Now that you understand that w_main is a class, you could declare your own instances of w_main as follows:

```
w_main w_main1, w_main2

open(w_main1)
open(w_main2)
```

Notice that w_main is used as the data type for the w_main1 and w_main2 variables.

You could also create instances of a window by creating an array as follows:

```
w_child w_children[10]
int idx

FOR idx = 1 to 10
    open(w_children[idx])
    w_children[idx].x = idx * 100
    w_children[idx].y = idx * 100
NEXT
```

This example creates ten instances of a w_child window, cascading the child windows across the parent window.

In the same manner, you can also create instances of any of the predefined object types. These types include: CheckBox, CommandButton, DataWindow, DropDownListBox, EditMask, Graph, ListBox, MenuItem, MultiLineEdit, Oval, Picture, PictureButton, RadioButton, SingleLineEdit, UserObject, and Window. All of these object types are part of the system object hierarchy defined by PowerBuilder. You can view the object hierarchy in the Class browser shown in Figure 16.1. The Class browser is in the Library painter under the **Utilities|Browse Class Hierarchy** menu option.

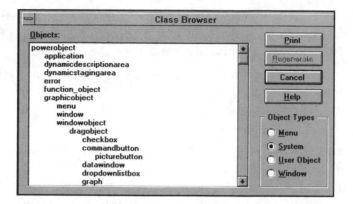

FIGURE 16.1 THE CLASS BROWSER

Use any of these classes as a data type. For example, create a CommandButton variable that is assigned the name of an existing CommandButton (cb_close in this example). The variable can then be treated as an *alias* for cb_close. This is a fundamental technique. You will use this often, such as when you make references from user objects to other controls in the window (outside the user object).

```
commandbutton cb1
cb1 = cb_close
cb1.text = 'Exit'  // cb_close.text
cb1.enabled = true // cb_close.enabled
```

All of this becomes more important when using the object-oriented features in PowerBuilder.

WINDOW INHERITANCE

Inheritance lets the developer derive a new window, menu, or user object from an already existing object. The ancestor must be of the same type; that is, you can only derive a window from a window, a menu from a menu, and a user object from a user object. The descendent object inherits all of the components of the ancestor object. This includes attributes, variables, structures, functions, events, and script code. The new class will specialize the more general base class in some way, usually by adding new items to the object, but it could be limited to modifying the ancestor in some way (such as repositioning the controls).

Most companies involved with sizable PowerBuilder projects have a team of developers that specialize in the design and development of libraries of reusable objects to be provided to the application developers. Sharing a base set of objects can save a great deal of time and effort for a development team and can help to implement standards for PowerBuilder coding and presentation of information. Most often it is better to review the current requirements of various projects, and then to generalize the requirements into a set of base objects. Sometimes it is possible to create a set of base objects for the most obvious requirements, but it is usually better to create these objects as a direct result of a requirement. Otherwise, you may find that you spend time developing a set of objects that never get used.

Inheritance is one of the features that makes PowerBuilder the leading front-end development tool for developing client-server applications for Windows. You can only use inheritance with windows, menus, and user objects. Any time that you create one of these objects, you have the option of using inheritance to derive the object from an existing object rather than starting a new one with the creation of the new object. This provides you with a jump-start, since the base (ancestor) object provides a starting point for your new object. Another benefit of inheritance is that it lets you create and promote standards for labels and the presentation of data.

Window inheritance is probably the most useful in this regard. For example, you may create a main window for every application that has the same size, and contains some basic controls such as a command-button to close the application. Instead of re-creating this each time, you can create a base window to serve as the ancestor for the descendant windows derived from it. The advantages of this is that you get a window with the attributes, controls, and script code already implemented. To create a new window using inheritance, open the window painter, and select the **Inherit** CommandButton option when you create a new window. When you derive a new window (which I'll call the descendant window) from a base window (the parent or ancestor), your new window inherits the attributes, controls, events, and scripts of the base window. Detailed examples are provided throughout this chapter.

The INHERIT.PBL example shows examples of inheritance for a window, a user object, and a menu. Create a new application, and call it **INHERIT1** (and name the library **INHERIT1.PBL**). Next, create the w_ancestor window shown in Figure 16.2. Be sure to set the Snap to Grid option on. This is essential for windows that are used as base windows. This is recommended for the following reason: if you move any of the controls on a descendent window, the link between the control in the ancestor and in the descendent will be lost for the position attributes. This means that if the control is moved in the ancestor, its new location will not be passed on to the descendent window. Other attributes of that control, such as the label text or size, will be intact. The connection is lost only for the attributes that you change in the descendent. If you have set Snap to Grid off, it is very easy to accidentally move a control in the descendent window.

You can reestablish the inheritance connection with the original object by selecting the object(s) and selecting the **Edit|Reset Attributes** menu option. To reset the attributes for a descendant window, click on the window and then select the **Edit|Reset Attributes** menu option.

In this window add the controls, mle_1, st_status, cb_beep, and cb_close. Add the following code to the Clicked event for cb_beep.

```
beep(1)
MessageBox('w_ancestor', 'That beep was from w_ancestor')
```

For cb_close add the following to the Clicked event:

```
Close(Parent)
```

Add a window function to the w_ancestor window (choose the **Declare|Window Function** menu option). The function declaration is shown in Figure 16.3.

The only argument is a string containing the text for the st_status field. The argument is passed by value. The function should be named fw_update_status, and return an integer.

The code for the fw_update_status is:

```
st_status.text = sText
return 0
```

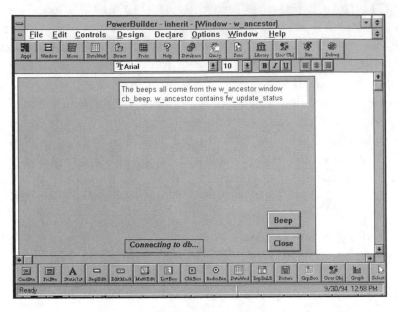

FIGURE 16.2 CREATE A WINDOW INHERITED FROM W_ANCESTOR

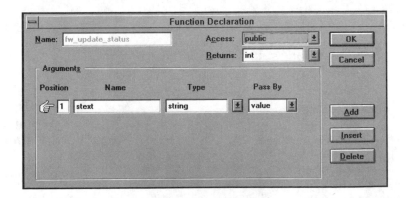

FIGURE 16.3 FW_UPDATE_STATUS

Save the w_ancestor window in your new library (INHERIT1.PBL) and close the Window painter.

w_main

Next, create a new window (w_main) that will be inherited from the w_ancestor window that you just created. Click on the **Window** icon on the PowerBar to open the Window painter. This opens the Select Window dialog shown in Figure 16.4.

To create a new window using inheritance click on the **Inherit** CommandButton (Figure 16.4). This opens the Inherit From Window dialog in Figure 16.5.

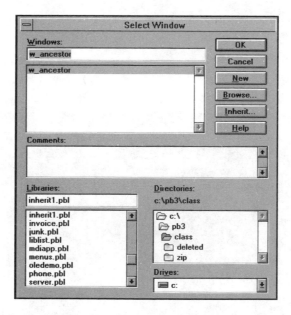

FIGURE 16.4 CLICK ON INHERIT TO CREATE A NEW WINDOW USING INHERITANCE

In this dialog, you can select any window that is included in any of the libraries that is in the Library list for this application. First, select the application library in the lower listbox, then select the base window and click **OK**. This opens the Window painter as shown in Figure 16.6. Notice that the title is *Untitled*, inherited from w_ancestor.

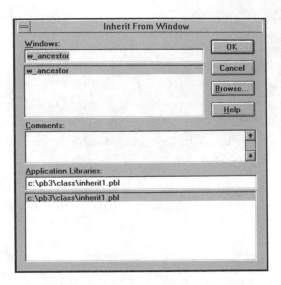

FIGURE 16.5 THE INHERIT FROM WINDOW DIALOG

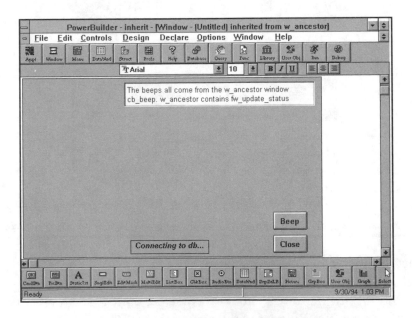

FIGURE 16.6 THE DESCENDANT WINDOW

In the Window painter, make the modifications that you wish to be in the descendent (but not in the ancestor window) and then save the window with a new name. In this window, for this example, add one more commandbutton. Place it directly to the left of cb_beep, name it **cb_push**, and give it the label **Push**. For that button, add the following line of code to its Clicked script:

```
This.text = Parent.title
```

This assigns the title of the parent window to the label for the command-button when it is clicked. Also add the MultiLineEdit control, as shown in Figure 16.7.

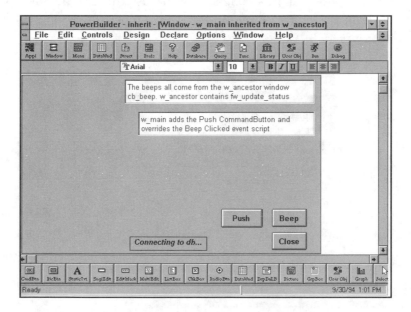

FIGURE 16.7 W_MAIN

Next, add program code to the cb_beep CommandButton. Remember that a couple of lines of code were written in the w_ancestor window for this button. Those lines called the beep function and then displayed a MessageBox. Now add several lines of code to the cb_beep button in the Clicked event in the w_main window. To do this, select **Script** from the popup menu. In the script editor, check that you are editing the script for the clicked event (if not select the event from the dropdown listbox).

Add the follow code to the cb_beep Clicked event:

```
MessageBox('w_main', 'From the Clicked event (overrides
          ancestor)')
MessageBox('w_main', 'Will "Call Super::Clicked" and then
          change title')
Call Super::Clicked
parent.title = 'w_main'
```

When you enter code in a descendant, you must tell PowerBuilder whether this code should be used as a replacement for the ancestors code in the same event, or whether this code should be used to extend the ancestor script. Click on the **Compile** menu bar item to open the dropdown menu shown in Figure 16.8.

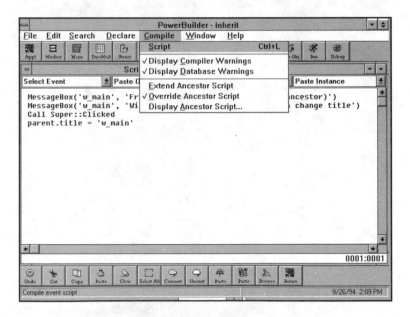

FIGURE 16.8 THE COMPILE MENU

On this menu, you must choose either *Extend Ancestor Script* or *Override Ancestor Script*. If you extend the ancestor script, your script will be executed after the ancestor script. If you choose override, your script will be executed instead of the ancestor. Suppose you want to execute your script and then the ancestor script? To do that, choose the override option and then call the ancestor script from within your new script. This example shows you how to call the ancestor script:

```
Call Super::Clicked
```

This uses one of the PowerScript reserved words, *Super*. This example calls the Clicked event in the ancestor object. Since the Clicked script is being edited for the cb_beep CommandButton, the reference Super is a reference to the ancestor cb_beep CommandButton. The word Super is used because ancestor classes are sometimes called *super-classes* and descendants are called *sub-classes*. In this example script, two MessageBoxes show that this is the w_main descendant. The cb_beep Clicked event is then called in the ancestor. Finally, change the caption for the window to *w_main* (it had been set to *w_ancestor* before this).

w_main2

To demonstrate multiple levels of inheritance, a new window (w_main2) is created that will be inherited from the w_main window. Follow the same procedure as before to create the new window, but select w_main as the ancestor.

In the Window painter, make the modifications that you see in Figure 16.9. First, declare a window function (use the **Declare|Window Function** menu option). Declare the function fw_status as shown in Figure 16.9.

The function is named fw_status. It has only one argument, a string passed by value, called *sText*. In this case (None) was chosen as the return value. Now, add the following code the fw_status function:

```
w_ancestor::fw_update_status ( "Hey, I'm OK" )
```

This line of code demonstrates a technique for accessing ancestor scripts. The code calls fw_update_status function in the w_ancestor window. The two colons (::) set the scope for the fw_update_status function.

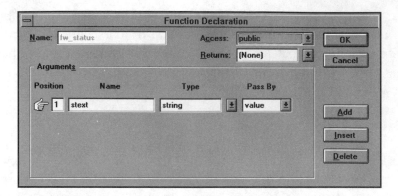

FIGURE 16.9 FUNCTION FW_STATUS DECLARATION

In this window add one more CommandButton. Place it directly to the left of cb_close, name it **cb_status** and give it the label **Status**. For that button, add the following lines of code to its Clicked script:

```
//we want to update the st_status
//
// but not the following!!
// w_ancestor.fw_update_status ( "Hey, I'm OK")
//
//the next would be legal from a window event or window function
//
//w_ancestor::fw_update_status ( "Hey, I'm OK" )
//
// so create fw_status and therein call w_ancestor::fw_update_status

fw_status ( "Hey, I'm OK" )
```

In the w_main2 window, add the third MultiLineEdit control, as shown in Figure 16.10. (Do not add the user object at this time).

Add the following code to the cb_beep CommandButton Clicked event:

```
MessageBox('w_main2', &
     "Clicked event Extends ancestor script, will call w_ancestor")
Call w_ancestor`cb_beep::Clicked
parent.title = 'w_main2'
```

In this event, choose the option to have this code override the code in the w_ancestor Clicked event. To do this, select the **Compile|Extend Ancestor Script** menu option (this is a toggle).

The second line demonstrates another technique for accessing ancestor scripts. This line calls the Clicked event for the cb_beep CommandButton in the w_ancestor. Be sure to include the back tick between the window name and the control name.

This assigns the title of the parent window to the label for the CommandButton when it is clicked. From the Compile menu, choose the **Extend Ancestor Script** option. This code will be executed after the script in the w_main cb_beep CommandButton. Now we have code in all three levels of the cb_beep button. The MessageBoxes lets you know which level is currently being executed.

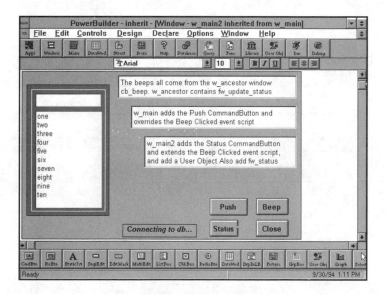

FIGURE 16.10 W_MAIN2

Save the window as w_main2. Add it to you application (remember to add the open function to your application open event). Run the application, click the CommandButtons, and think about the levels at which the code is executed.

Go to the Application painter and examine the application icon. Notice that the objects that were created with inheritance are marked with an asterisk in the display (see Figure 16.11).

Click the right mouse button on the w_main2 icon; you will see that the popup menu has a new option, Object Hierarchy.

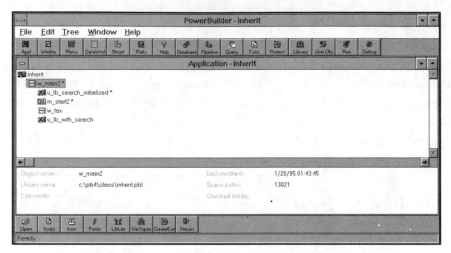

FIGURE 16.11 W_MAIN2 IS MARKED WITH AN ASTERISK

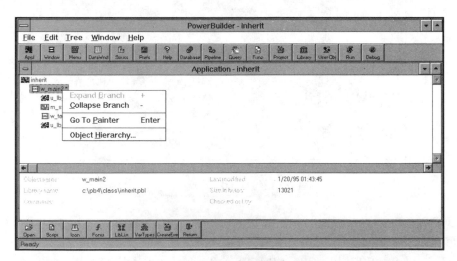

FIGURE 16.12 THE OBJECT HIERARCHY POPUP MENU OPTION

Clicking this option opens the Object Hierarchy dialog. It shows the inheritance hierarchy for the selected object. In Figure 16.13, w_main2 is inherited from w_main, which is inherited from w_ancestor.

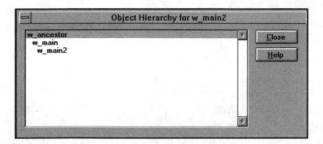

FIGURE 16.13 THE OBJECT HIERARCHY FOR W_MAIN2

Updating the Ancestor

You can only update one level (one ancestor) at a time. You can open an object in a painter if you are editing one of its ancestors (or descendents) in another window. To demonstrate the effect of updating the w_ancestor window, do the following exercise. In the w_main2 window move the Close CommandButton slightly down and to the right. Save the window. Next open the Window painter for the w_ancestor window and move both buttons up an inch or so. Change the label for cb_close to **CloseIt**. Close the window and run the application. You will see the new label and the cb_beep button will be positioned higher in the window. The position of cb_close is determined by the change you made in w_main2.

Next, add another control, such as another CommandButton, to the w_ancestor window. The w_main2 window will be updated with any changes that you make to the w_ancestor or w_main windows. This update occurs when you run the application, edit the w_main2 window, or build the next application executable.

MENU INHERITANCE

You can use inheritance with menus, but this feature is rather limited in PowerBuilder. You can only make additions to the end of the menu bar, add new MenuItems at the end of each dropdown menu, or insert one item into an existing menu. You can override items on a menu, but in general, inheritance is more limited for menus than windows.

For this example, a simple menu is created. The items for the menu bar are: File, Test, and Help. For the Test dropdown menu add the menu items shown in Figure 16.14.

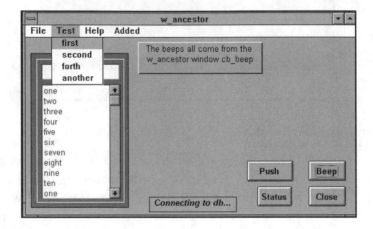

FIGURE 16.14 MENU M_START

Save the menu as **m_start** and close the Menu painter.

Next, create a new menu, m_start2, as a descendant of the m_start menu. Click on the **Inherit** CommandButton shown in Figure 16.15. Select the m_start menu in the dropdown listbox.

In the Menu painter, disable and make the "third" MenuItem invisible. Add a statement to the "third' MenuItem script to beep when it is clicked.

```
beep(1)
```

Add a MenuItem at the bottom of the menu and label it **another**. Now save the menu as **m_start2**. Add it to your window and run the application. Select the **Test** menu bar option to pulldown the menu. Notice the missing third item (see Figure 16.16).

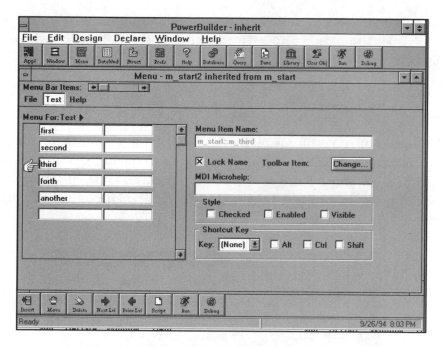

FIGURE 16.15 MENU M_START2

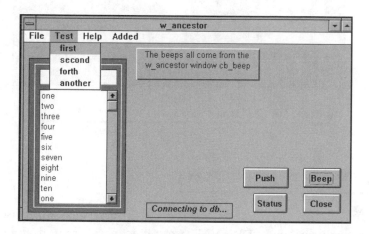

FIGURE 16.16 OUR EXAMPLE MENU

Close the application and add a CommandButton to the w_main2 window. Label the button **Show Third** and add the following code to the Clicked event for the button:

```
m_start2.m_test.m_third.show ( )
m_start2.m_test.m_third.enable ( )
```

These lines of code will make the third item visible, and then enable it. Now run the application again. Check the test menu as you did before. Now click on **Show Third** and check the menu again. The third menu item appears. Using this technique, you can then control the menu dynamically at run-time.

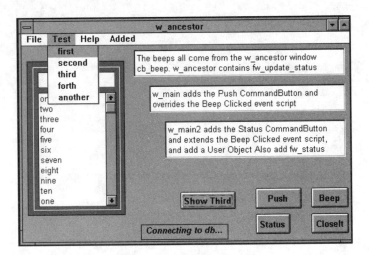

FIGURE 16.17 DYNAMICALLY CHANGING THE TEST MENU

USER OBJECT INHERITANCE

Inheritance is very useful with user objects. In the chapter on user objects, several versions of the U_DW_NAV user object were created. It would have been better to have used inheritance to create the successive versions since the variations used most of the components of U_DW_NAV.

For the first example of user object inheritance, the user object which appears in Figure 16.10 will be added. For this example, use the U_LB_WITH_SEARCH user object that was developed in the previous chapter as the ancestor. (This user object can also be found in the SHARED.PBL library). The only changes made to the descendant user object are the addition of ten items to the listbox. To create the new user object, click on **User Obj** icon on the PowerBar. This opens the Select User Object dialog (Figure 16.18). In this dialog, click on the **Inherit** CommandButton.

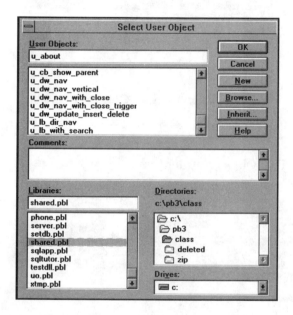

FIGURE 16.18 CREATE A NEW USER OBJECT WITH INHERITANCE

In the Inherit From User Object dialog, select the library and the U_LB_WITH_SEARCH user object as the ancestor.

FIGURE 16.19 THE INHERIT FROM USER OBJECT DIALOG

This opens the User Object painter.

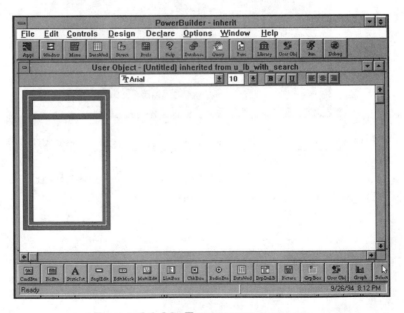

FIGURE 16.20 THE NEW USER OBJECT

In this painter, double-click on the ListBox control to open the Style dialog.

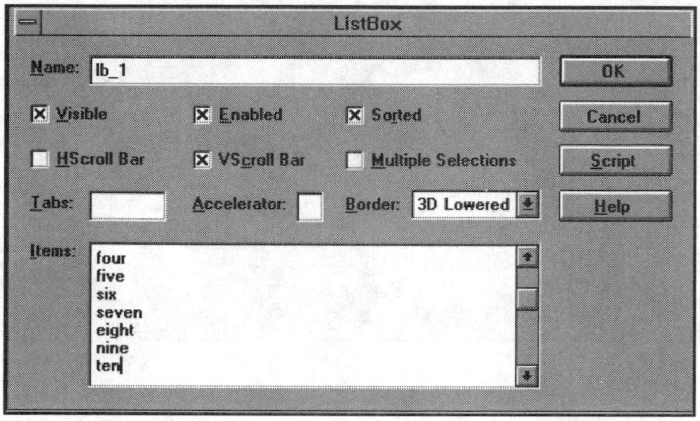

FIGURE 16.21 THE LISTBOX STYLE DIALOG

In the items ListBox, add the numbers from one through ten (as shown in Figure 16.21). Use the Control-Enter key combination between each item otherwise the **OK** CommandButton would be clicked by default. Be sure that the Sorted CheckBox is marked. Save this user object as **U_LB_WITH_SEARCH_INITIALIZED**. Then add it to your main application window.

If you would like to work further with user object inheritance, go back to the U_DW_NAV user object and build user objects U_DW_NAV_VERTI-CAL, U_DW_NAV_WITH_CLOSE, and U_DW_NAV_WITH_CLOSE_TRIG-GER user objects based on inheritance.

MORE ON USER OBJECTS

In the previous chapter, a non-visual user object was created that calculated the sales tax at a 4.4 percent rate. Create a new window for the inherit1.pbl application and name the window **w_tax**. In this window, add an EditMask and two SingleLineEdit controls as shown in the next Figure 16.22.

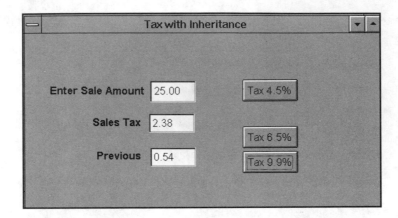

FIGURE 16.22 THE TAX WITH INHERITANCE WINDOW

Create a new user object U_CALC_TAX_4_4 to calculate the tax at the 4.4 percent rate. Then create a new object, U_CALC_TAX_5_5 to calculate the tax at a 5.5 percent rate. Use inheritance to create the second object.

Add two CommandButtons to the w_tax window. The first will calculate the tax at the 4.4 percent rate for the entry in the Enter Sales Amount field. The second button will calculate at the 5.5 percent rate. This may take some experimenting, and thinking to complete this implementation.

Add a button to the main window (w_main) to open the w_tax window.

Inheritance is one of the most powerful features in PowerBuilder and it will pay to invest the time necessary to implement it in your development process.

CHAPTER SEVENTEEN

EXTENDING POWERBUILDER

This chapter covers three advanced techniques for extending the power of your applications. These are Dynamic Data Exchange (DDE), Dynamic Link Libraries (DLLs), and Object Linking and Embedding (OLE).

DDE

The first method that we will cover is *Dynamic Data Exchange* (DDE). DDE provides a method for interprocess communications within the Windows system. DDE, which takes place at the window level, is a communication between windows using messages. One process establishes itself as a DDE server, which means that it advertises itself as a provider of data and/or other services. Another process, the DDE client, establishes contact with the server (note that the client initiates the communication), a channel is opened for communications between the server and client, then a conversation takes place through messages passed back and forth over the opened channel. The conversation consists of a number of requests and responses. A server could also be a client of another server. For this discussion we will consider one PowerBuilder application to be a server and another to be a client.

A server is usually documented with a number of services and the syntax of the messages that it will use. Any client that uses those definitions can receive services from the server. The server has a name, and the server has one or more topics for which it provides services. Within each topic there are data items.

Most data is received from the server by a series of requests from a client. This is called a *cold link* and it means that there is one request for each data item sent from the server.

It is also possible for the client to request a *hot link* with the server. In this case, when there is new information about a topic, the server automatically sends the new data to the client without waiting for a request from the client. This continues until the client requests an end to the hot link.

A third possibility is called a *warm link*. A warm link is when the client tells the server that it wishes to be notified only that data has changed, but not to have the changed data actually sent. If the client wants the changed data, it will make a normal request to receive that data.

The DDE Process

The following steps outline the process of establishing a DDE communication, sending data between server and client, and the termination of the communications.

Initiate

The client initially sends out an INITIATE message. This message is a broadcast message sent to all the currently running programs. The initiate call conveys the type of service that the client is requesting. Any servers that meet the requirements of the client can respond to set up the conversation. The client request will be for an application and a topic in that application, for example, SERVER.EXE, for an application and "System" for the topic.

Opening a Channel

If a server that can meet these requirements is running, it responds to the client with an acknowledge message, establishing the communications channel.

Client Request

Once the client has made contact with a server, it sends DDE requests for data to the server. This is a request for certain data, specified in the server's documented format.

Server Ships Data

The server then sends the requested data (if possible) to the client. This process continues until the client is finished using the server.

Terminate Conversation

When the client has all that it requires, it sends a termination message to the server. This closes the DDE communications channel.

THE SAMPLE DDE APPLICATIONS

Before proceeding with the details of DDE programming, you should take time to run the DDE example applications. The example programs include two applications, CLIENT (in CLIENT.PBL) and SERVER (in SERVER.PBL). There is also a DDELIB.PBL, which is required for both of these applications.

First you must build an executable for the SERVER program; name this executable **SERVER.EXE**. Be sure to place it in the C:\PB4\CLASS directory, otherwise you must adjust the path reference in the client application. The client application can launch the server application, so it does not need to be running at this point.

Next, open the client application in CLIENT.PBL. Run this application. It opens with the window shown in Figure 17.1.

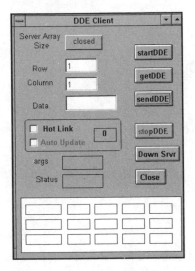

FIGURE 17.1 THE DDE CLIENT

The DDE client contains a static text field labeled Server Array Size. When the DDE communications channel is open, this field displays the size of the data array in the server. This displays the number of columns and rows in the DataWindow in the server's window. When communications are not active, this field displays *closed*.

The startDDE CommandButton opens a communications channel with the server. If the server is not currently running, the MessageBox (Figure 17.2) gives you the option to start up the server.

If the server startup is successful, the Server Array Size field displays a value such as "R3C5," representing 3 rows of 5 columns.

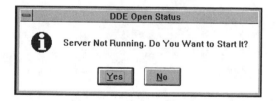

FIGURE 17.2 SELECT YES TO LAUNCH THE DDE SERVER

The getDDE CommandButton makes a request to the server. The request is for the data in the cell (a field in the server's DataWindow) that is in the row and column specified in the SingleLineEdit fields (labeled Row and Column). The Data field displays the result of the request. The status field displays the status code for the last DDE operation.

The sendDDE CommandButton sends the value in the Data field to the server. The server inserts the value in its DataWindow at the row and column location specified by the client.

The stopDDE CommandButton terminates communications with the server.

The DownSrvr CommandButton tells the server to shut it down and then terminates the communications with the server.

The Close CommandButton terminates the DDE communications and close the application.

The Hot Link CommandButton initiates a hot link with the server. Data is sent from the server automatically, without a specific request from the client.

If you check the Auto Update CheckBox, the data sent as a result of the hot link will automatically be inserted into the client's DataWindow.

The DataWindow at the bottom of the client application accepts data from the server application. Figure 17.3 shows the server application.

The DataWindow holds the data that will be sent to the client. The client can also send data to the server to replace values in the DataWindow. If the hot link has been established with the client, you can push data over to the client by clicking any field in the DataWindow. To do this you must first select the field, then click the item. This sends that item to the client.

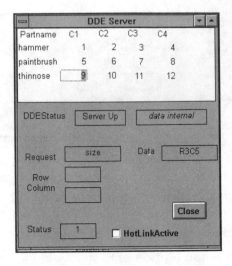

FIGURE 17.3 THE DDE SERVER

The DDEStatus field reflects the status of the server. The next field displays "data internal" if the DataWindow data has been populated with the Retain Data option.

The Request field displays the last request from the client. The initial request will be for the "size" of the data array. The Data field displays the value that was sent back.

The Row and column fields display the current DataWindow row and column.

The Status field displays the status code from the last DDE operation.

The HotLinkActive CheckBox will be checked if a hot link is currently in effect with the client.

The Close Command Button shuts down the server.

Run the application, trying each of the functions. When the client establishes communications with the server, the server array size will be displayed, such as "R3C5," representing 3 rows of 5 columns (see Figure 17.4).

Figure 17.4 shows the result of a client request for the data in row 1 column 1. If you type into the Data field and assign a value to the row and to the column, the server will be updated. If you establish a hot link with the server and then click on row 3 column 5 in the server window, that cell will be sent across to the client. The server side of this process is shown in Figure 17.5.

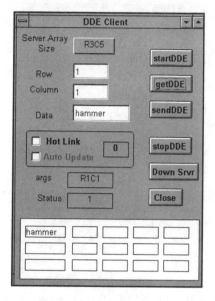

FIGURE 17.4 AFTER ESTABLISHING A DDE CONVERSATION

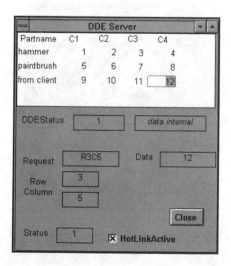

FIGURE 17.5 THE DDE SERVER RECEIVES
A REQUEST FOR AN ITEM AT ROW 3 COLUMN 5

Figure 17.6 shows the client side of the same operation.

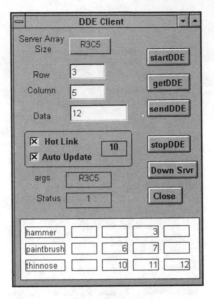

FIGURE 17.6   THE DDE SERVER RECEIVING THE ROW 3, COLUMN 5 DATA ITEM

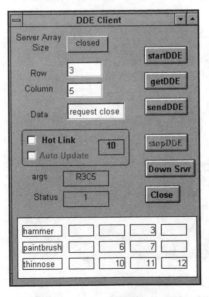

FIGURE 17.7   CLOSING THE DDE CONVERSATION

When you close the application, the server array size displays "closed" in that field (see Figure 17.7).

The next section explains the DDE window events that you will find in PowerBuilder.

DDE WINDOW EVENTS

Windows have a number of events used only for DDE communications. These events include:

- **HotLinkAlarm**—after a DDE connection has been made, a client DDE window may ask for "hot" updates of the data it is interested in. This event notifies the client that such data has been sent from the DDE server.

- **RemoteExec**—occurs in a DDE server window; it is a result of an ExecRemote function call in a client window used to send a command to the server.

- **RemoteHotLinkStart**—occurs in a DDE server window. It is the result of a StartHotLink function call in the client, used as a request for a live ("hot") update of the source data as it changes.

- **RemoteHotLinkStop**—occurs in a DDE server window. It is the result of a StopHotLink function call in the client, used to terminate a request for a live ("hot") update of the source data as it changes.

- **RemoteRequest**—occurs in a DDE server window, as a result of a GetRemote function call in a DDE client, which is a request for data.

- **RemoteSend**—occurs in a DDE server window as a result of a SetRemote function call in the DDE client used to send data to the server.

THE DDE CLIENT

All DDE communications are handled at the window event level. This section discusses the code that is required to implement a DDE client application. The window in this discussion is w_main.

At the w_main window level, the following instance variables are declared:

```
int i_nHandle = -123
boolean i_bFirstTry = true
```

The handle is initialized to an easily recognized negative value.

The following code initiates the initial client request.

```
string sItem, sHeader2, sHeader3
string sCust1, sInv, sTotal
int nInv, rc, iUsage
dec dTotal
long lHandle

SetPointer (hourglass!)
i_nHandle = OpenChannel("DDESource", "System") //, handle(Parent))
st_status.text = string(i_nHandle)

IF i_nHandle >= 0 THEN
    cb_stopdde.enabled = true
    rc = GetRemote ("0", sItem, i_nHandle)
    st_status.text = string(rc)
    IF rc = 1 THEN
        st_size.text = sItem
    END IF
ELSE
    st_status.text = 'open fail'
    lHandle = GetModuleHandle("c:\PB4\class\server.exe")
    IF lHandle <= 0 OR NOT i_bFirstTry THEN
        MessageBox('DDE Open Status', &
        'Server Not Running, and Can Not Find SERVER.EXE')
    ELSE
        iUsage = GetModuleUsage(lHandle)
        IF (iUsage = 0) THEN
            IF MessageBox('DDE Open Status',&
                    'Server Not Running. Do You Want to Start &
                    It?',
                    Information!, YesNo!, 1) = 1 THEN
                rc = Run ("c:\PB4\class\server.exe")
```

```
                    i_bFirstTry = false
                    IF rc <> 1 THEN
                        MessageBox('DDE Open Status','Can Not Run &
                        SERVER.EXE')
                    ELSE
                        st_status.text = 'launched'
                        cb_start.PostEvent('Clicked') //retry
                    END IF
                END IF
            END IF
        END IF
END IF
SetPointer (arrow!)
```

To send a DDE message from the client to a server, use the following code:

```
int rc
string sRowColumn
sRowColumn = f_dde_pack_row_column (integer(sle_row.text), &
             integer(sle_column.text))
st_arg.text = sRowColumn
rc = SetRemote (sRowColumn, sle_data.text, i_nHandle)


F_DDE_PACK_ROW_COLUMN
string sText
sText = 'R' + trim(string(nRow))
sText = sText + 'C'+trim(string(nColumn))
return sText
```

To receive a DDE message, place the following code:

```
string sItem, sHeader2, sHeader3
string sCust1, sInv, sTotal
int nInv, rc
dec dTotal
string sRowColumn

sRowColumn = f_dde_pack_row_column (integer(sle_row.text), &
    integer(sle_column.text))
st_arg.text = sRowColumn
rc = GetRemote (sRowColumn, sItem, i_nHandle)
st_status.text = string(rc)
sle_data.text = sItem

if rc = 1 THEN fw_dw1_insert(sRowColumn, sItem)
```

To stop the DDE communications, use the following:

```
int rc
SetPointer (hourglass!)
this.enabled = false
sle_data.text = 'request close'
if i_nHandle >= 0 then
    IF cbx_1.checked THEN
        cbx_1.TriggerEvent('Clicked')
    END IF
    CloseChannel (i_nHandle)
    i_nHandle = -123
    st_size.text = 'closed'
end if
SetPointer (arrow!)
```

To tell the DDE server to shut itself down, use the following:

```
int rc
if i_nHandle >= 0 then
    rc = ExecRemote("[quit()]", i_nHandle)
    CloseChannel (i_nHandle)
    i_nHandle = -123
    sle_data.text = 'closed'
end if
```

To close the client application, use the following code:

```
int rc
this.enabled = false
SetPointer (hourglass!)
//don't shutdown with a channel open
if i_nHandle >= 0 then
    CloseChannel (i_nHandle)
    i_nHandle = -123
end if
close(parent)
```

To create a DDE hot link, use the following code:

```
int rc = -999
IF i_nhandle < 0 THEN return
IF cbx_1.checked THEN
    rc = StopHotLink("Any", "DDESource", "System")
    cbx_1.checked = false
    cbx_2.checked = false
    cbx_2.enabled = false
ELSE
    rc = StartHotLink("Any", "DDESource", "System")
```

```
    cbx_1.checked = true
    cbx_2.enabled = true
END IF
st_status.text = string(rc)
```

Then, in the w_main hotlinkalarm event, use the following:

```
int rc, idx, jdx
string sRowColumn

rc = GetDataDDE(sRowColumn)
st_status.text = string(rc)
sle_data.text = sRowColumn
st_arg.text = 'alarm'
IF    cbx_2.checked THEN
    f_dde_row_column (sRowColumn, idx, jdx)
    sle_row.text = string(idx)
    sle_column.text = string(jdx)
    st_incount.text = string(integer(st_incount.text)+1)
    cb_get.PostEvent('Clicked')
END IF


F_DDE_ROW_COLUMN

int nPos, nPos2 = -1
string sTmp

nPos = pos(sString, "R", 1)
if nPos > 0 then
    nPos2 = pos(sString, "C", 1)
    if nPos2 > 0 then
        nPos += 1
        sTmp = mid(sString, nPos, nPos2 - nPos)
        nRow = integer(sTmp)
        nColumn = integer(mid(sString, nPos2+1))
    end if
end if
return
```

To stop a DDE hot link, use the following code:.

```
int rc = -999
IF i_nhandle < 0 THEN return
IF cbx_1.checked THEN
    rc = StopHotLink("Any", "DDESource", "System")
    cbx_1.checked = false
```

669

```
    cbx_2.checked = false
    cbx_2.enabled = false
ELSE
    rc = StartHotLink("Any", "DDESource", "System")
    cbx_1.checked = true
    cbx_2.enabled = true
END IF
st_status.text = string(rc)
```

DDE Server

This section presents the code that is necessary to implement a DDE server. In this case the application window is w_main. In the server application, w_main has the following instance variables:

```
int i_bShutDown
int i_nRows
int i_nColumns
```

In the open event for the server application, use the following code:

```
int rc
rc = StartServerDDE(w_main,"DDESource", "System")
if rc <> 1 then
    st_dde_status.text = 'DDE err'
    i_bShutDown = 1
else
    st_dde_status.text = 'Server Up'
    i_bShutDown = 0
end if
st_status.text = string(rc)
```

In the w_main remoterequest event, use the following code:

```
int rc,idx,jdx, nPos
string sColType, sDataType, sText, sFormat, sFieldName
string sApp, sTopic, sItem

GetDataDDEOrigin(sApp, sTopic, sItem)
st_request.text = sItem

i_nRows = dw_1.RowCount()
i_nColumns = integer(dw_1.dwDescribe("DataWindow.Column.Count"))

IF sItem ='0' THEN
```

```
                st_request.text = 'size'
                sText = f_dde_pack_row_column (i_nRows, i_nColumns)
                rc = SetDataDDE(sText)
                st_data.text = sText
                return
         END IF
         f_dde_row_column(sItem, idx, jdx)
         fw_dde_server_send(idx,jdx)
```

In the w_main remotesend, use the following code:

```
         string sData
         string sApp, sTopic, sItem
         int rc, nRow, nColumn

         GetDataDDE(sData)
         st_data.text = sData
         rc = GetDataDDEOrigin(sApp, sTopic, sItem)
         st_request.text = sItem

         f_dde_row_column (sItem, nRow, nColumn)
         IF nRow > 0 AND nRow <= i_nRows AND nColumn > 0 &
                 AND nColumn <= i_nColumns THEN
             IF nColumn = 1 THEN
                 dw_1.SetItem ( nRow, nColumn, sData )
             ELSE
                 dw_1.SetItem ( nRow, nColumn, integer(sData))
             END IF
         END IF
```

In the w_main remoteexec, use the following code:

```
         string sAppName
         string sRequest
         int i
         st_request.text = 'exec'
         GetCommandDDEOrigin(sAppName)
         GetCommandDDE(sRequest)
         IF sRequest = '[quit()]' AND i_bShutDown = 0 THEN
             st_dde_status.text = 'down'
             i_bShutDown = 1
             beep(1)
             cb_close.PostEvent('Clicked')
         ELSE
             messagebox('dde exec', srequest)
         END IF
```

In the w_main remotehotlinkstart, use the following code:

```
st_request.text = 'hot link start'
cbx_1.checked = true
```

In the w_main remotehotlinkstop, use the following code:

```
st_request.text = 'hot link stop'
cbx_1.checked = false
```

When the w_main shuts down, use the following code:

```
int rc
if i_bShutDown = 0 then
    st_dde_status.text = 'down'
    i_bShutDown = 1
//    rc = StopServerDDE(w_main,"DDESource", "System")
end if
close(parent)
```

In dw_1 doubleclicked event, use the following code:

```
IF cbx_1.checked THEN
    fw_dde_server_send_alarm ( dw_1.getrow ( ), dw_1.getcolumn ( ))
END IF

In dw_1 itemchanged event:

IF cbx_1.checked THEN
    fw_dde_server_send_alarm ( dw_1.getrow ( ), dw_1.getcolumn ( ))
END IF
```

DLLs

The next method that we will cover is Dynamic Link Libraries (DLLs). DLL are Windows libraries created most often in C or C++ (also Pascal or COBOL). PowerBuilder provides easy access to DLL functions; just declare the function as an external function and call it in your PowerScript code just as you call other PowerScript functions. Included in the examples with this book, you will find a DLL that was created with Microsoft's Visual C++. The DLL is called TESTDLL.DLL. A sample function follows:

```
// testdll.cpp : excerpt
static char szTest[20] = "TestDLL";
extern "C"
int FAR PASCAL _export Test(char FAR * pString)
{
    char FAR *p;
        p = szTest;
        _fstrcpy(pString, p );
        return (0);
}
```

The declaration for that function is:

```
// testdll.h This interface can be included by C or C++ code
int FAR PASCAL _export Test(char FAR *p);
```

In the PowerBuilder application you woudl declare the following global external function:

```
FUNCTION int Test(ref string p) library "testdll.dll"
```

This declaration allows you to call any functions in that DLL so long as you place the testdll.dll in a directory where it can be found by the Windows system. This would include the current working directory, the WINDOWS or WINDOWS\SYSTEM directory, or a directory on the DOS path. Otherwise, you would have to include the full path to the DLL in the declaration.

To call the DLL test function from a PowerBuilder application use the following code (perhaps in the application open script):

```
string sValue
int rc

sValue = space(20)
rc = Test(sValue)
IF sValue <> " TestDLL " THEN
    MessageBox ('ERROR', 'DLL Error')
    halt close
ELSE
    w.main.st_status.text = 'Found DLL'
END IF
```

N O T E

If you are returning strings using reference parameters, you must allocate the space for the string before making the DLL function call. In this example, sValue = space(20) is required, otherwise you may (probably) crash the application.

Window SDK calls are made in exactly the same manner. For example, you can't make a window system modal in a PowerBuilder application with any PowerScript functions. But the Windows system provides a function that will make a window system modal. This function is SetSysModalWindow; it is found in the USER.EXE DLL in the Windows directory. You can call this from your PowerBuilder application by declaring the function as external

```
Function int SetSysModalWindow(int hWnd) Library "USER.EXE"
```

and then calling it from your application. The example application, FIRSTWIN.PBL, has a window, w_top, that is made system modal using this function. Place the following code into the window open event to make a window system modal:

```
int rc
rc = SetSysModalWindow(Handle(This))
```

PowerScript provides a set of functions that can be useful when calling Windows functions.

- **Handle()**—returns Windows handle of an object.
- **IntHigh()**—extracts uint from long Windows param (the upper word).
- **IntLow()**—extracts uint from long Windows param (the lower word).
- **Long(uiLow, uiHigh)**—packs two uints into a long for use as a Windows param.

TestDLL Application

The TESTDLL application demonstrates the use of the TESTDLL.DLL. When the application opens, the status field (bottom left) displays *wait... looking for DLL*. If the TESTDLL.DLL is found the status field will display *ok*. This example application can send and return a value of each PowerBuilder data type that can be used in DLL calls. The application also sends and returns a simple structure. Click on the **get** CommandButton to get the data from the DLL. Figure 17.8 shows the initial values for each data type.

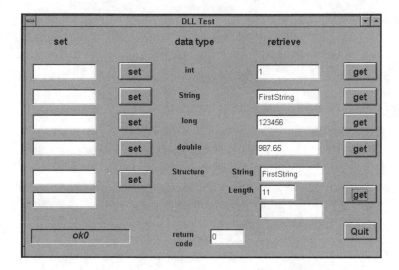

FIGURE 17.8 THE DLL TEST APPLICATION

You can set any of the values by entering the value in a SingleLineEdit and clicking on the **set** CommandButton. The return code from each operation is displayed in the return code field.

The next section presents the code for the application.

```
//Get Int CommandButton

int nValue
int rc

nValue = GetInt()
```

```
sle_int.text = String (nValue)
rc = nValue
sle_rc.text = string(rc)
Get String

string sValue
int rc
sValue = space(20)
rc = GetString(sValue)
sle_string.text = sValue
sle_rc.text = string(rc)

//The Get Long CommandButton

long nValue
int rc = 0

nValue = GetLong()
sle_long.text = String (nValue)
sle_rc.text = string(rc)

//TheGet Double CommandButton

double nValue
int rc = 0

rc = GetDouble(nValue)
sle_double.text = String (nValue)
sle_rc.text = string(rc)

//The Get Structure CommandButton

str_test x
int rc

x.text = space(20)
x.text2 = space(20)
rc = GetStructure(x)
sle_sptr.text = x.text
sle_sptrlen.text = string(x.len)
sle_sptr2.text = x.text2
sle_rc.text = string(rc)


// The Set Int CommandButton

int nValue
int rc
nValue = integer(sle_setint.text)
rc = SetInt(nValue)
```

```
sle_rc.text = string(rc)

// The Set String CommandButton

string sValue
int rc
sValue = sle_setstring.text
rc = SetString(sValue)
sle_rc.text = string(rc)

// TheSet Long CommandButton

long x
int rc
x = long(sle_setlong.text)
rc = SetLong(x)
sle_rc.text = string(rc)

// The Set Double CommandButton

double dValue
int rc
dValue = double(sle_setdouble.text)
rc = SetDouble(dValue)
sle_rc.text = string(rc)

// The Set Structure CommandButton

str_test x
int rc

x.text = space(20)
x.text2 = space(20)
x.len = 12
x.text = sle_text1.text
x.text2 = sle_text2.text
rc = SetStructure(x)
sle_rc.text = string(rc)
```

The DLL functions are declared as global external functions (under the Declare menu):

```
FUNCTION int GetInt() library "testdll.dll"
FUNCTION int SetInt(int n) library "testdll.dll"
FUNCTION int SetString(string p) library "testdll.dll"
FUNCTION int GetString(ref string p) library "testdll.dll"
FUNCTION int SetFloat(double p) library "testdll.dll"
FUNCTION int SetDouble(double p) library "testdll.dll"
```

```
FUNCTION int GetFloat(ref real p) library "testdll.dll"
FUNCTION int GetDouble(ref double p) library "testdll.dll"
FUNCTION long GetLong() library "testdll.dll"
FUNCTION int SetLong(long x) library "testdll.dll"
FUNCTION int Test(ref string p) library "testdll.dll"
FUNCTION int SetStructure(ref str_test x) library "testdll.dll"
FUNCTION int GetStructure(ref str_test x) library "testdll.dll"
```

The script for the application open event makes a call (Test) to test the communications with the DLL.

```
--------------------------------------------------------
string sValue
int rc

open(testdll_main)

sValue = space(20)
rc = Test(sValue)
IF sValue = "TestDLL" THEN
    testdll_main.st_status.text = 'ok' + string(rc)
ELSE
    testdll_main.st_status.text = 'DLL ERR'
    MessageBox ('ERROR', 'DLL Error')
    halt close
END IF
--------------------------------------------------------
```

The DLL C++ Code

This section contains the C++ code for the TESTDLL.DLL.

```
//TESTDLL.H

struct testdllData
{
    BOOL  bEnabled;
    UINT  flags;
};

typedef struct s_array{
    int nInt;
    char *szString;
    char *szString2;
} SARRAY, FAR *S_PTR;

extern "C"
```

678

```
{
int FAR PASCAL __export WEP (int );

int FAR PASCAL _export SetInt(int nIn);
int FAR PASCAL _export GetInt();
int FAR PASCAL _export SetString(char FAR *p);
int FAR PASCAL _export GetString(char FAR *p);
int FAR PASCAL _export Test(char FAR *p);
int FAR PASCAL _export SetFloat(float nIn);
int FAR PASCAL _export GetFloat(float FAR *p);
int FAR PASCAL _export GetDouble(double FAR *p);
int FAR PASCAL _export SetDouble(double p);
int FAR PASCAL _export SetLong(long nIn);
long FAR PASCAL _export GetLong();

int FAR PASCAL _export GetStructure(S_PTR p);
int FAR PASCAL _export SetStructure(S_PTR p);
}


// TESTDLL.CPP : TESTDLL.DLL implementation and initialization
//        code.
// TESTDLL.CPP
// created with MSVC++ 1.51
// to create the project, copy file to C:\msvc\testdll
// then select Project|New and set the following:
//      project name = C:\msvc\testdll\testdll
//      project type = DLL
//      Use MFC = NO
//      then add testdll.cpp, testdll.def to the project
//      (*.h are automatic)
//      set large memory model under Options|Project..
//      memory model

#include <windows.h>
#include <string.h>
#include "testdll.h"

static char szValue[20] = "FirstString";
static char szValue2[20] = "";
static int nValue =1;
static float fValue = 123.45;
static double dValue = 987.65;
static long lValue = 123456;
static char cValue;

// initialization exectued when DLL loaded
int FAR PASCAL LibMain(HANDLE hModule, WORD wDataSeg, WORD
    wHeapSize, LPSTR lpszCmdLine )
{
```

```
if (wHeapSize)
    UnlockData(0);
return 1;
}

// Windows Exit Procedure
extern "C"
int FAR PASCAL __export WEP (int bSystemExit)
{
    return 1;
}


// the following are the test functions
// they store and retieve one of each data type
extern "C"
int FAR PASCAL _export GetFloat(float FAR *p)
{
        *p = fValue;
        return (0);
}

static char szTest[20] = "TestDLL";
extern "C"
int FAR PASCAL _export Test(char FAR * pString)
{
    char FAR *p;
        p = szTest;
        _fstrcpy(pString, p );
        return (0);
}

extern "C"
int FAR PASCAL _export SetFloat(float nIn)
{
        fValue = nIn;
        return (0);
}

extern "C"
int FAR PASCAL _export GetInt()
{
        return (nValue);
}
extern "C"
int FAR PASCAL _export SetInt(int nIn)
{
        nValue = nIn;
        return (0);
}
```

```
long FAR PASCAL _export GetLong()
{
        return (lValue);
}
extern "C"
int FAR PASCAL _export SetLong(long nIn)
{
        lValue = nIn;
        return (0);
}

extern "C"
int FAR PASCAL _export GetString(char FAR * pString)
{
    char FAR *p;
        p = szValue;
        _fstrcpy(pString, p );
        return (0);
}

extern "C"
int FAR PASCAL _export SetString(char FAR *p)
{
         if (p)
          {
           strcpy(szValue2, szValue);
           _fstrcpy(szValue, p);
             return (0);
          }
         else
             return -3;
}

extern "C"
int FAR PASCAL _export GetDouble(double FAR *p)
{
        *p = dValue;
        return (0);
}

extern "C"
int FAR PASCAL _export SetDouble(double nIn)
{
        dValue = nIn;
        return (0);
}

extern "C"
int FAR PASCAL _export GetStructure(S_PTR pString)
{
```

```
        char FAR *p, *p2;
            p = szValue;
            p2 = szValue2;
            pString->nInt = strlen(szValue);
            _fstrcpy(pString->szString, p );
            _fstrcpy(pString->szString2, p2 );
            return (0);
    }

    extern "C"
    int FAR PASCAL _export SetStructure(S_PTR pString)
    {
        char FAR *p, *p2;
            p = szValue;
            p2 = szValue2;
            _fstrcpy(p, pString->szString);
            _fstrcpy(p2, pString->szString2);
            return (0);
    }
```

OLE

OLE support is provided in PowerBuilder. To implement OLE, you create a DataWindow and add a special type of control, an OLE Database Blob, to the DataWindow. When you add this blob to the window, The Database Binary/Text Large Object dialog box opens. In this dialog box you must enter the information that describes the OLE server.

Add a DataWindow control, and associate it with the DataWindow object. The example OLE application appears as in Figure 17.10. Clicking the **Display** CommandButton launches the PaintBrush application as an OLE server.

Paintbrush opens and the image can be edited, as in Figure 17.11.

The code required to activate the OLE function is:

```
long lRow
int rc

lRow = dw_1.GetRow()
IF lRow > 0 THEN
    rc = dw_1.dwOleActivate ( lRow, 2, 0 )
END IF

long lRow
```

```
string sPath
int rc

SetPointer(HourGlass!)
sPath = uo_1.fu_get_filepath()
if len(sPath) < 5 THEN
    return
END IF
lRow = dw_1.insertrow (0 )
rc = -1
IF lRow > 0 THEN
    rc = dw_1.setitem ( lRow, 1, sPath)
    IF rc = 1 THEN
        dw_1.setfocus ( )
        dw_1.setrow ( lRow)
        dw_1.scrolltorow ( lRow )
        rc = dw_1.dwOleActivate ( lRow, 2, 0 )
    END IF
END IF
IF rc <> 1 THEN
    MessageBox('ole', 'Error Inserting FilePath')
    return
END IF
```

Run the OLEDEMO application and examine the code for further details.

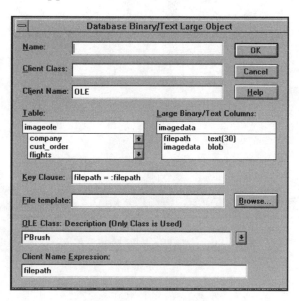

FIGURE 17.9 THE OLE DIALOG

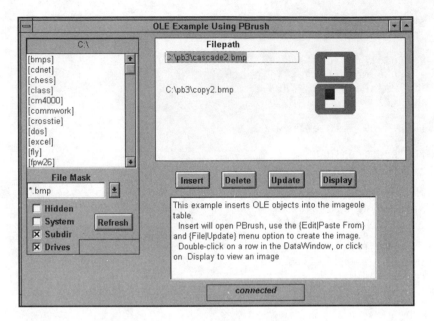

FIGURE 17.10 THE OLE EXAMPLE APPLICATION

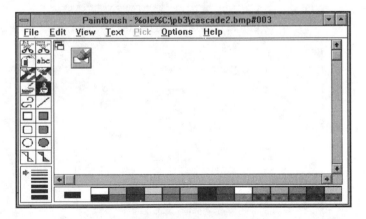

FIGURE 17.11 THE PAINTBRUSH OLE SERVER APPLICATION

CHAPTER EIGHTEEN

DEVELOPING AND DISTRIBUTING POWERBUILDER APPLICATIONS

This chapter covers important details about distributing you applications. It also has information on how to most effectively and efficiently develop PowerBuilder applications. The first and easiest steps that you can take to ensure your success is to purchase a number of tools that provide a great deal of help for your development. I have worked extensively with all of the tools that I recommend and I am confident that you will find them as useful as I have in the projects that I have directed using PowerBuilder.

Powersoft Infobase CD-ROM

My first recommendation is that you subscribe to the Powersoft Infobase CD-ROM, which is issued quarterly. This CD-ROM is included in the Enterprise edition of PowerBuilder and is a gold-mine of information. It includes a collection of information acquired from the Powersoft support hotline. The subscription is $95 per year and it may pay for itself the first time you use it. It is also very interesting just to browse through; you will come across a number of tips and undocumented techniques that you will find useful. This CD-ROM also includes all the FaxLine documents, product information, and other useful information. This is essential!

CompuServe's Powersoft Forum

You should also have a CompuServe account so that you can access the Powersoft forum. In this forum you can post questions to the PowerBuilder experts and download files that contain example code, topics of interest, and software updates. This is another invaluable resource.

Blue Sky Software's RoboHELP

Don't even consider trying to create a Help system for your applications without using this great Help authoring system. I provide more detail on this system later in this chapter, but this modestly priced product more than pays for itself in the time that it saves as you create your Help system. For more information see the section on adding online-help to your applications in this chapter.

Logic Work's ERwin/ERX for PowerBuilder

Logic Work's ERwin/ERX is a database design tool for client-server system development. It is a Windows CASE tool for creating and generating ERDs (entity-relationship diagrams). Erwin can also create the logical and physical objects for your database. ERwin/ERX is capable of creating or re-engineering relation databases from a wide variety of vendors including

Oracle, Sybase, SQL Server, and Watcom. Erwin can reverse-engineer logical data models from existing SQL database applications. With ERwin you will create a data model for your system. Erwin uses the standard IDEF1X diagramming method to create entity-relationship diagrams to capture the data and business requirements (rules) for your business.

Logic Works make a version of ERWin/ERX specifically for PowerBuilder. This is easily the best choice for a PowerBuilder project CASE tool in its price range. It can work directly with PowerBuilder and it integrates Erwin data modeling with PowerBuilder's development system. You can access the PowerBuilder repository from within ERWin. This is a two-way link that allows you to import, view, or modify a PowerBuilder application's repository attributes while you are still in the Erwin environment.

There is an entire section in Chapter 19 (Database Painter) devoted to ERwin; it is an essential tool if you do not already have a CASE system. We discuss the use of ERWin as a tool used to move tables (including the PowerBuilder repository information) from one database to another. This will prove very useful, for example, if you need to move a system from a test to a production system.

LBMS' Systems Engineer

If you want to step up (way up) to the next level of CASE tools, then I can recommend Systems Engineer from LBMS. Systems Engineer is a complete CASE system that can manage the entire software engineering process. This system can also interface to PowerBuilder. The LBMS system is much more powerful (and more expensive) than Erwin. This is the system that I use in the larger developments. Another system from LBMS, Process Engineer, is also highly recommended.

PVCS Version Manager

Intersolv's PVCS Version Manager is the standard source-code control system for many developers. PVCS interfaces very well with PowerBuilder 4; it is another essential product for successful PowerBuilder development in a team environment. PVCS will control the check out and check in of each of the PowerBuilder objects at the object level. This means that you can check out one (or more) objects (such as a window, user object, or DataWindow) from a PowerBuilder library (PBL). PVCS will track the changes and assist in creating different releases of your application. This works from within the PowerBuilder environment, it works *much* better than in PowerBuilder 3, and it is much better than the native management provided by PowerBuilder.

PowerBuilder Applications Developer Magazine

Of the several PowerBuilder magazines available, I have found this one to be most interesting.

DISTRIBUTING YOUR POWERBUILDER APPLICATIONS

You have several options for distributing your PowerBuilder applications. The simplest solution is to generate a single EXE file that contains the entire application. This is suitable for the smaller applications that you create. Additional resources that are required by your application, such as bitmaps and icons, can be stored in the EXE file, or you can distribute each of these files individually with your application.You are familiar with the process of building a single executable, as you have used this technique for the examples in this book.

The EXE file contains several components:

- code that is required to launch and run a Windows application.
- a compiled version of the objects that make up your application.
- other resources such as bitmaps and icons that are used in your application.

Dynamic Libraries

You can also choose to partition your application into separate modules; the first is an EXE file, the others are PowerBuilder Dynamic libraries, or PBD files. For larger applications this is the better choice. This results in improved performance and the PBD libraries have the advantage that they can be shared between applications. Powersoft recommends that you limit the size of the EXE file to 1.5 megabytes and it is a good idea to limit them to 1.2 megabytes or less in size. If your application is approaching that size you should use PBDs.

A PBD is a dynamic library that supplies objects for the application at run time. You create PBDs in the Library painter. An example will be given.

PBR Files

When your PowerBuilder application executes, the run-time environment looks for each referenced object in a specific order.

1. First it looks in the current EXE file.
2. Next it looks in the PBDs that have been specified for the application (when you built the EXE).
3. Next it looks in the current directory.
4. Next it looks in the directories on the Windows search path.

A PBR file is a text file in which you can list a number of components, such as bitmap files, icon files, and DataWindow objects, that are to be compiled into a PBD or EXE file. This is required for objects that are assigned dynamically, such as DataWindow objects. Create the PBR file with the text editor. A PBR file could contain the following statements:

```
KK.BMP
C:\BMPS\W_ADMIN.BMP
c:\pb4\class\company.pbl (d_customer)
```

In this example, there are two bmp files and one DataWindow object. You must specify which PBL holds the DataWindow object. If the PBL is not in the current directory or in the search path (when the EXE is built), then you must specify the full path to the PBL.

To use a PBR file you include the resource file in the Additional Resources File Name box in the Create Executable dialog box window or when you define a project (examples will be found later in this chapter). This will tell PowerBuilder to include all the listed objects in the EXE file. You may also use resource files when you create a PowerBuilder dynamic library, in order to add objects to the PBD file.

DISTRIB.PBL

The DISTRIB.PBL and DISTRIB2.PBL demonstrate the process of creating a PBD file and then creating an EXE that uses the PBD. This example partitions the CONTROLS example into two components. The application and first window are in the executable (DISTRIB.EXE). The second window and the KK.BMP file are in the DISTRIB2.PBD file. The DISTRIB2.PBR file contains a single line, listing the KK.BMP so that it will be inserted into the PBD library.

```
//DISTRIB2.PBR
C:\PB4\CLASS\KK.BMP
```

Creating a PBD

We covered the process of creating executables and projects in Chapter 4. Creating a PBD file is similar to creating an EXE file. You create PBDs in the Library painter. Select the **Utilities|Build Dynamic Library** menu option. This opens the Build Dynamic Runtime Library dialog box (Figure 18.1).

Select the DISTRIB2.PBL in the Library Name ListBox. Next, click the **Files** CommandButton and select the **DISTRIB2.PB**R file in the Additional Resources File Name list box. The resource file lists the objects to be included in the PBD. Clicking on the **OK** CommandButton creates the PBD.

The text of the DISTRIB2.PBR file is **C:\PB4\CLASS\KK.BMP**. If you have installed the examples to a different directory, then you must change the path of this statement to match.

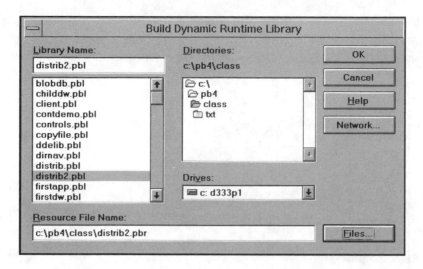

FIGURE 18.1 BUILDING A DYNAMIC RUNTIME LIBRARY (PBD)

Building an Executable that Uses PBD Files

Next you will create the executable for the DISTRIB.PBL. Go to the Application painter and click on the **CreateExe** icon. This opens the Select Executable dialog box (Figure 18.2).

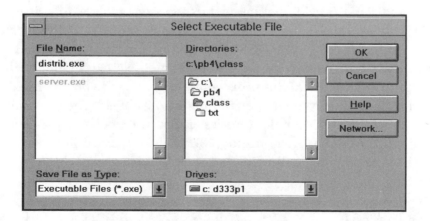

FIGURE 18.2 THE SELECT EXECUTABLE DIALOG

Check that the path is set to the directory where you want to create the executable. Enter **DISTRIB.EXE** for the executable name and click **OK**. This opens the Create Executable dialog box (Figure 18.3).

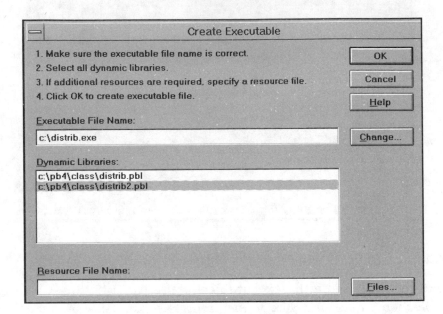

FIGURE 18.3 THE CREATE EXECUTABLE DIALOG

Verify that DISTRIB.EXE is displayed as the Executable Name; if it's not click on the **Cancel** button and set the name correctly. In the Dynamic Libraries list box, select **DISTRIB2.PBL** (only), unselecting DISTRIB.PBL (if necessary). The PBLs that are listed here but not selected (highlighted) will be used to create the EXE file. This will also include the objects listed in a resource (PBR) file if you enter one in the Resource field. The objects in the PBLs selected in the Dynamic Libraries ListBox will not be inserted into the EXE file. Instead, a reference to the PBDs for the selected libraries will be added to the executable file. Create the executable file by clicking on the **OK** CommandButton.

Now this application would be distributed as DISTRIB.EXE and DISTRIB2.PBD (along with the run-time PowerBuilder DLLs). The KK.BMP image is imbedded into the DISTRIB2.PBD through the PBR reference. The w_second window is in the DISTRIB2.PBD file and will be found at run time.

Creating a Project

We could also create the DISTRIB application using a project. A project object contains all the information that is necessary for building application executables and would make the process a bit easier. Once you create a project definition, you can build or rebuild the executable, and you will not have to reenter any of the information. The Project Manager allows you to create and maintain project objects.

Before you create a new project, be sure that the application runs correctly, and that you have created any necessary resource files. Then, to create a new project, click on the **Project** icon on the PowerBar. This opens the Select Project dialog box.

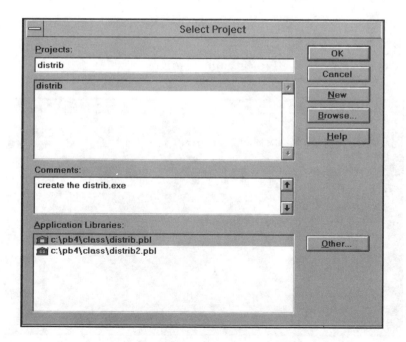

FIGURE 18.4 THE SELECT PROJECT DIALOG

Click on the **New** command button. This opens the Select Executable File dialog box shown in Figure 18.5.

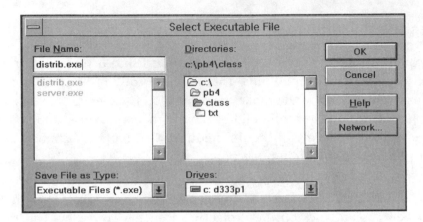

FIGURE 18.5 THE SELECT EXECUTABLE FILE DIALOG

Here, you must specify the file name of the executable file. This name will be carried over to the next screen.

Figure 18.6 shows the Project painter dialog box.

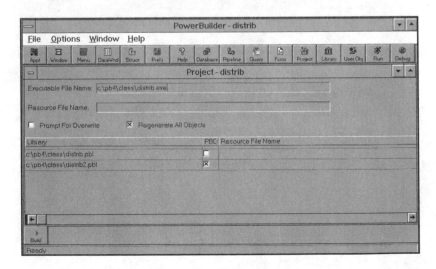

FIGURE 18.6 DEFINING A PROJECT

On this screen you must complete the project painter workspace options. In this dialog box you can elect to be prompted before overwrite of .EXE and .PBDs. You can also choose to have all of the objects in the libraries regenerated before the .EXE and .PBDs are built. You may also specify whether each library (in the Application Library path) should be a .PBD and if so, you can choose a Resource File. Set the information up as shown in Figure 18.6. Then save the project by selecting **Save** from the File menu (Figure 18.7). You can build the project executable by clicking the **Build** icon or by choosing the **Build Project** option from the Options menu.

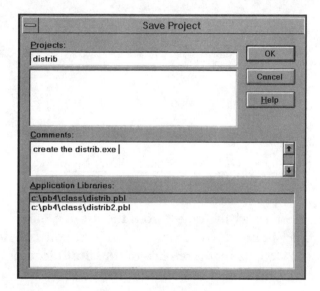

FIGURE 18.7 THE SAVE PROJECT DIALOG

Using Projects

Once the project object has been defined, it is represented by the project object icon in the Library painter. Now to rebuild the executable, you only need to open the project and click on the **Build** icon. Click on the **Project** icon on the PowerBar to open the Select Project dialog box (Figure 18.8).

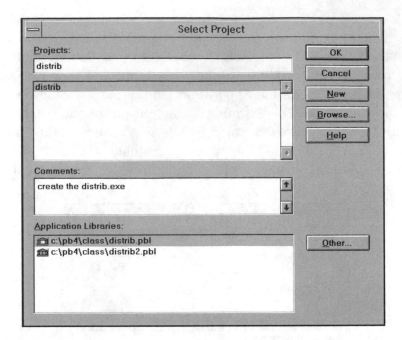

FIGURE 18.8 THE SELECT PROJECT DIALOG

In this dialog box you must select the directory and library that hold the project object. Then select the object from the list box and click **OK**. This opens the Project painter. To execute a project, you can select **Build Project** from the Options menu or click on the **Build** icon on the Painter toolbar. This builds the executable.

In the Project painter you also have options to restore PowerBuilder libraries. To do this just specify a new library name for each Old Library Name listed in the dialog. The New Library Name is where the new libraries will be placed. PowerBuilder restores the libraries to the state they were in when you built the application executable file.

Another option is to list the objects in the application. You can sort the objects in any way you wish, and you may print a list of objects from this same dialog box. Figure 18.9 shows the List Objects dialog box.

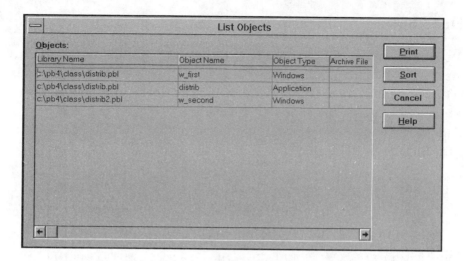

FIGURE 18.9 THE LIST OBJECTS DIALOG

Managing Libraries

You should break your PBLs into separate libraries to limit the size and number of objects in each. You should limit the size of a PBL to 800K and a maximum of 50 to 80 objects.

In the Library painter you can regenerate objects and optimize libraries. This will compile the source code for the selected objects and replace the compiled versions of each object. It is necessary to regenerate objects from time to time. If an object begins to behave incorrectly, try regenerating the object. This is most often required when you are using inheritance. After changing an object you may have to regenerate the related objects in the inheritance hierarchy.

Optimizing libraries compresses the library by removing deleted objects. Select the **Optimize** option under the Library menu. You should do this regularly to reduce the size of your PBL files.

Distributing Applications

An important fact that you may not be aware of is that you must distribute a set of PowerBuilder run-time DLLs with your EXE file. This is required because the EXE is not a true Windows binary file and additional files are required to execute the code that is stored in your EXE file. You have the right to distribute the DLLs that are necessary for your application; those DLLs include the following:

PBBGR040.DLL	PBECT040.DLL	PBRTE040.DLL
PBCMP040.DLL	PBIDBF40.DLL	PBRTF040.DLL
PBDBI040.DLL	PBITXT40.DLL	PBSHR040.DLL
PBDEC040.DLL	PBLMI040.DLL	PBTYP040.DLL
PBDWE040.DLL	PBOUI040.DLL	PBVBX040.DLL
PBDWO040.DLL	PBPRT040.DLL	

In addition to these DLLs, you will also need to distribute any DLLs that are required by the database system that you are using for the application. All these are included in the Database Development and Deployment Kit, which is included in the Enterprise edition. You need this kit to distribute your applications; there is no additional run-time fee or distribution charge. This also allows you to distribute a single-user version of the Watcom DBMS with your application. The Watcom SQL run time engine requires files such as:

```
DB32W.EXE
DBL40W.DLL
WL40EN.DLL
```

and the driver

```
WOD40W.DLL
```

If your application uses the ODBC drivers, you will need the PowerBuilder ODBC files:

- **ODBC.DLL**—this ODBC DLL is placed in the WINDOWS\SYSTEM directory.

- **PBODB040.DLL**—PowerBuilder's ODBC driver.

- **PBODB040.INI**—the INI file.

and you must create or update two ODBC.INI files (in the Windows directory):

```
ODBCINST.INI
ODBC.INI
```

The Advanced Developer Toolkit makes the distribution of applications much simpler. It includes an application, Install Disk Builder, that will create the installation diskettes for your application. It will add files to your diskettes, including a setup program that will install your application for the user. The Install Disk Builder utility will create the ODBC configuration if required. Without this utility you (or the user) must set up the data source definition in the ODBC.INI file.

For example, for our image example application, the ODBC.INI will contain:

```
[ODBC Data Sources]
image=WATCOM SQL 4.0

[WATCOM SQL 4.0]
driver=c:\windows\system\WOD40W.DLL

[image]
Driver=c:\windows\system\wod40w.dll
UID=dba
PWD=sql
Database=C:\PB4\CLASS\IMAGE.DB
Start=db32w
DatabaseFile=C:\PB4\CLASS\IMAGE.DB
DatabaseName=Image
AutoStop=yes
```

ONLINE HELP

Windows applications often provide context-sensitive help to the user, often through the use of the F1 function key, a Help CommandButton, or menu option. The Windows Help system is a hypertext-like system that allows you to find information about how to use an application, how to perform tasks, and explanations and definitions. The information is organized into a number of Help topics.

Often, the information in the Help system contains one or more jumps, which are links to other Help topics or additional information on the current topic. The Help system makes it easy to find the related information that you need to perform a task in the application. The Help system is a hypertext system; this means that you can click on certain words or graphics to bring up additional information or move to another area of the Help system. Those areas where you can click on text or graphics to initiate one of these actions are called *hot spots*. You can recognize hotspots because they are underlined (if they are text) or marked with a dotted rectangle (if they are graphics).

Your Help system is organized into subject areas called topics. Linking these topics together, and allowing the user to navigate through the topics, is the main work of the Windows Help system. Topics are subject areas that are described with text and/or graphics. The first topic is "Contents," which is a list of the available information; it provides an entry point into the Help system.

The Help system in the application is actually a separate application provided by Microsoft. Microsoft Windows includes a program, WINHELP.EXE, that helps you locate help topics and then lets you navigate through the Help system. WINHELP.EXE is launched when the user selects the **Help** menu option, clicks on a **Help** CommandButton, or presses the **F1** function key. The HELPDEMO application uses a HLP file (CONTROLS.HLP) that was created with the help compiler. The HELPDEMO application is a version of the CONTROLS application to which I have added a Help system. When you run this application you can click on the **Help** CommandButtons or press **F1** to see the help topics.

When you access help information in a Windows application, you are launching the WINHELP application. WINHELP runs as a separate application but uses a file provided by the application that contains the Help information for that application. You can use the WINHELP application for any of your Windows applications. All that is required is that you create a help file in the format required by WINHELP. These files always have the file extension HLP, such as CONTROLS.HLP. Microsoft provides a program, called a *help compiler* that creates a HLP file from a set of files that you create in a specific format.

Before we describe the process of creating these files, you can view our example help file. To do this, start PowerBuilder (any application will do), and press **F1** or select the **Index** option from the Help menu as shown in Figure 18.10.

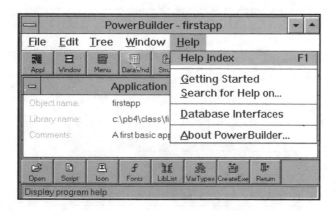

FIGURE 18.10 SELECT THE HELP | INDEX MENU OPTION

This launches the WINHELP application. When WINHELP is launched it is given the name of the PowerBuilder help file, PBHLP040.HLP. Select the **Open** option from the File menu, as shown in Figure 18.11, to open the sample help file.

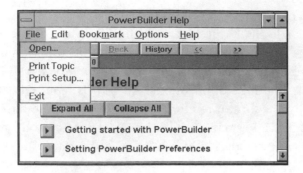

FIGURE 18.11 SELECT THE FILE|OPEN MENU OPTION

This opens the Open dialog box, (see Figure 18.12), where you select the **CONTROLS.HLP** file in the C:\PB4\CLASS directory.

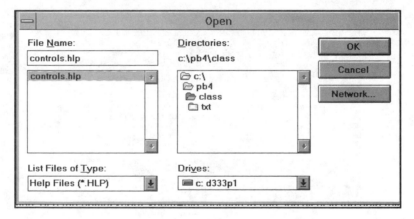

FIGURE 18.12 SELECT THE **CONTROLS.HLP** HELP FILE

Click **OK** to display the contents screen for this example. Figure 18.13 shows the contents screen of our sample help file.

Notice that some of the text is green and underlined. This is to alert you to the fact that there exists other related information for those words. Click on **Help Topics** to display additional information on the term Help Topics. Clicking on any of the topics listed in green jumps to the text for that topic. For example, click on **First Window Overview** to open the help topic that explains the various objects on the First window (see Figure 18.14).

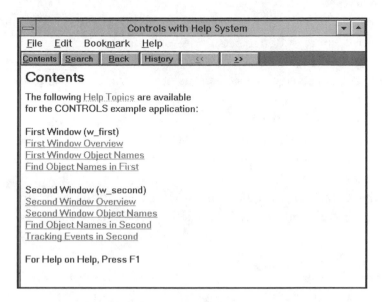

FIGURE 18.13 THE CONTENTS SCREEN OF OUR SAMPLE HLP FILE

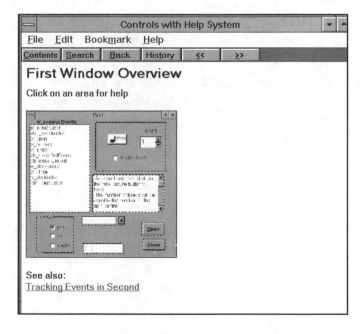

FIGURE 18.14 FIRST WINDOW OVERVIEW

This screen displays a graphic, a snapshot of the First window. Notice that there are a number of dotted rectangles on this screen. If you click within one of these rectangles, a description of the controls in that part of the window will be displayed. Select various options and become familiar with the contents of this HLP file.

Note that the WINHELP application provides all of the display and navigation that you see in this example. You can also programmatically open and navigate through the CONTROLS.HLP file from within a PowerBuilder application. In our examples directory, you will find a version of the CONTROLS application to which Help has been added. This application is called HELPDEMO and is in the HELPDEMO.PBL file.

Creating Your Help Text

You can add online help to your applications by using the Windows Help compiler. To do this you must create a Help text file and a help project file. Using the Microsoft Help compiler you then create the HLP file, which is used by your application. You use the PowerScript ShowHelp function to find and display the help text throughout your application. We will give several examples that show how to use this function.

The Help text file must be a document in RTF (rich text format). You can create the RTF file in most word processors, such as Microsoft Word for Windows. Figure 18.15 shows part of the RTF file that was used to create the example help file.

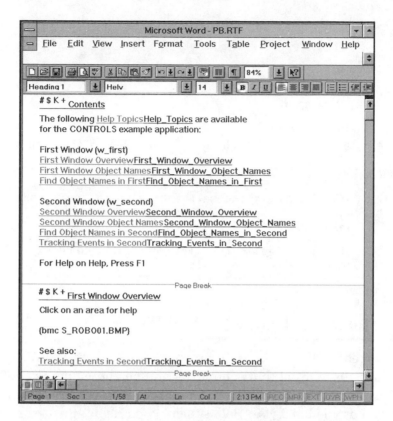

FIGURE 18.15 THE SAMPLE RTF FILE

The help project file is a control file that tells the help compiler how to create the HLP file and describes the help text file(s). Listing 18.1 shows the beginning of the example project file, controls.hpj.

Listing 18.1

```
;* * * * * * * * * * * * * * * * * * * * * * * * * * * * * *
; Help Project File for Controls
;
;  You may edit this file.
;
;  It's probably best not to change the CONTENTS= value
;  unless you rename the IDH_CONTENTS context string in
```

```
;   the PB.DOC file.
;

[OPTIONS]
; The optional ROOT= entry sets the working directory for the
; Help Compiler
; ROOT=C:\PROJECT

; The optional BMROOT= entry sets forth the directories which the
; help compiler will search for bitmaps used in the Help system.
;
;BMROOT=C:\ROBOHELP

; The CONTENTS= tells the help Engine which topic contains
; the contents
CONTENTS=IDH_CONTENTS

; Title is Displayed in the Title Bar of WINHELP.EXE
TITLE=Controls with Help System
;*************************************************************
```

Robo Help: The Better Method

You can create HLP files by creating your own RTF and HPJ files, but the best solution is to avoid that complexity and purchase Blue Sky Software's Robo Help system. This is a Help authoring tool, which is a utility that assists you as you build your Help system. Robo Help is the best product of its type and it greatly simplifies the process of creating your Help system. It provides such a productive environment that it easily pays for itself with the time you save when creating your Help system.

Robo Help currently works only with Word for Windows; versions for other word processors may be available in the future. Robo Help automates the entire process and takes it to a higher level, where you do not have to be concerned with the exacting details of the files and the file formats required by the help compiler. Robo Help also includes the Microsoft help compiler and uses it to create the final target HLP file.

As you have seen, the details of the RTF and project files are quite complex. Robo Help simplifies this process and allows you to create the Help system at a higher more conceptual level, since it handles the lower-level details automatically. It provides a number of tools for creating the hypertext links, creating and working with images, and it manages all the details necessary for the project. It creates the RTF document and the project file that are required by the Help compiler. It also runs the Help compiler and builds the HLP file that you distribute with your application.

Adding Help to a PowerBuilder Application

After creating the HLP file, you access the topics from within your PowerBuilder application by using the ShowHelp function. The format of the ShowHelp function is:

```
ShowHelp ( Helpfile, Command {, TypeId } )
```

Helpfile is a string containing the name of the compiled Help file (such as CONTROLS.HLP). The Command argument is an enumerated type, of the HelpCommand type. The legal values are **Index!**, **Keyword!**, and **Topic!**. Index! displays the contents topic for your Help file. Keyword! searches for the topic identified by the keyword found in the third argument of the function (TypeId). Topic! displays the topic identified by the TypeId argument, which is a number. The TypeId argument is optional. If used, it will be a number identifying the topic or a string that is a keyword of a help topic. This function returns an integers, it returns a 1 if it is successful, otherwise it returns a –1.

To display the index for your Help system, you would make the following call:

```
ShowHelp("CONTROLS.HLP", Index!)
```

By using a topic with the ShowHelp function, you can implement context-sensitive help throughout your PowerBuilder application. You would add ShowHelp function calls to scripts throughout your applications. By using specific topic IDs or keywords as the arguments to the ShowHelp function, the appropriate Help topic displays in the Help window. You decide the number of topics and a name for each, and you must give some thought to the organization of your help system.

For example, when the user presses **F1** in one of your windows, you can locate the help topic that is specific to that window by inserting the following code in the Key event for that window:

```
IF KeyDown(keyF1!) THEN
    ShowHelp("controls.hlp", Keyword!, "First Window Overview")
END IF
```

In this case the ShowHelp function locates the entry for the keyword *First Window Overview* and displays that topic. In this case, the keyword *First Window Overview* is one of the topics that you defined when you created the help entries. This code is just the beginning for implementing your Help system. In more complex Help systems you may have to determine where the focus is or what operation the user is doing before issuing the ShowHelp call.

For example, on a data-entry screen, you can provide help for each field on the screen. If you are using a DataWindow, you will have to use the GetColumn or GetColumnName() function to determine which topic should be used for help. For example, in the DataWindow control you would create a user-defined event to capture the Windows wm_keydwn event. We would name this event we_keydwn. Then the following code would provide context-sensitive help for each field (column) when **F1** is pressed.

```
// in the DataWindow's we_keydwn event
string sColumn, sTable
sTable = 'image_'
IF KeyDown(keyF1!) THEN
    sColumn = This.GetColumnName()
    ShowHelp("CONTROLS.HLP", Keyword!, sTable+sColumn)
END IF
```

For this to work correctly, you must have named the topic for each column by concatenating the table and column names. You could also hard-code the Context Ids using the ShowHelp function as follows:

```
ShowHelp("CONTROLS.HLP", Topic!, 123)
```

This would require a case (CHOOSE CASE) statement for each topic in order to display the related topic.

CHAPTER NINETEEN

USING THE DATABASE PAINTER

T his chapter contains information on the Database painter. It also contains directions on how to set up the ODBC configuration that is required to connect to and use the example database that came with this book. The example files included with this book include two files, IMAGE.DB and IMAGE.LOG. These files form the example database. Check to be sure that you can locate these files; they should be in the directory where you installed the examples, i.e. C:\PB4\CLASS. You must also have successfully installed the Watcom SQL 4.0 database engine that was included with your copy of PowerBuilder 4.0. If you can access the PowerBuilder demo database, then you can be sure that the Watcom DBMS is installed and working correctly.

The last section covers Logic Work's ERwin/ERX. ERwin is a database design tool used for creating and generating ERDs (entity-relationship diagrams). Logic Works makes a version of ERWin/ERX specifically for PowerBuilder.

DATABASE PAINTER

In the Database painter PowerBuilder provides facilities for creating and maintaining tables, views, and indexes; retrieving and manipulating data; graphically painting SQL statements and switching between multiple data sources.

When you create or update a table definition, PowerBuilder will either apply the changes immediately to the database or you may choose to have PowerBuilder only generate the SQL statements that would be required to either create or update a table (depending on the actions that you have just performed). In cases where you want to execute specific SQL statements, optimize existing SQL, or test SQL statements, the database administration painter provides the means to create the SQL and execute it immediately.

For each table (or view) in the database, you may also use the Database painter to specify PowerBuilder extended attributes including column headings, display formats, validation rules, and other characteristics for each column. These display formats and validation rules then become the default standards for each column when it is referenced in DataWindows. You can override these definitions in the DataWindow painter if you wish, but in general, it is best to define these attributes here in order to establish company standards and provide consistency between applications.

You can also use the Database painter to maintain data in your databases. In the painter you can view and manipulate the data using the validation rules discussed in the previous paragraph. You may also import data into, or export data from, a database in the Database painter to (or from) a variety of sources.

THE DATABASE PAINTERBAR

Click on the PowerBar's **Database** icon to open the Database painter. To work in the Database painter, you must connect successfully to a database. The default database is stored in your PB.INI file in the Database section. The default database is set in the PB.INI file each time you explicitly connect to a database using the Database painter; these details will be covered in this chapter. When you open the Database painter, PowerBuilder may display the Select Tables dialog box as shown in Figure 19.1. This dialog box is described later in this chapter. For now, if that dialog box opens just click on the **Cancel** button to close it. You can suppress the display of the Select Tables dialog box when the painter opens by setting the TableDir attribute to **0** in the preferences painter. Figure 19.1 shows the Database painter (with the Select Tables dialog box).

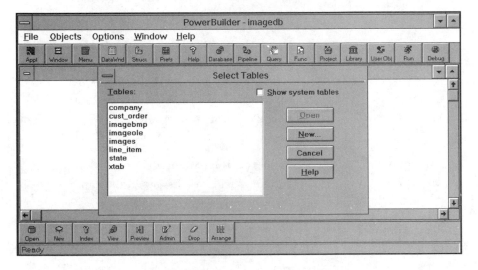

FIGURE 19.1 THE DATABASE PAINTER

The PainterBar for the Database painter contains eight icons that perform the same functions as some of the most commonly used menu options (which will be discussed in detail later). The following table briefly describes each of these icons and their menu equivalents.

TABLE 19.1 THE DATABASE PAINTERBAR ICONS

Select Tables	**Objects	Tables...** Display the Table Select dialog box.
Create Table	**Objects	New	Table** Opens the Create Table dialog box.
Create Index	**Objects	New	Index** Opens the Create Index dialog box for the selected table and allows you to select which columns to create an index on and in what sort order.
Create View	**Objects	New	View** Opens the View Painter which allows you graphically select the tables and columns and selection criteria to be included in the view. Once the SQL is saved as a query you are presented with a screen that allows you to set comments and default fonts for the view.
Data Manipulation	**Objects	Data Manipulation** Display a grid style listings of the data records in the currently selected table.
Database Administration	**Objects	Database Administration** Opens the Database Administration painter where you can enter SQL statements directly. This can be useful for testing SQL before implementation or for general database administration tasks.
Drop	**Objects	Drop Table/View/ Key** Deletes the currently selected table from the database along with all of its associated data.
Arrange Tables	Rearranges all of the tables on the table window. This function is similar to the arrange icons option found in Windows.

Now that you have a basic feel for the Database painterbar, we will take a look at each of the menus in the Database painter. We will look at what each option lets you do and how to accomplish the various tasks. We will start at the very beginning, connecting to and/or creating a database.

CONNECTING TO A DATABASE

PowerBuilder lets you connect to a wide range of database systems. PowerBuilder provides a set of native drivers for DBMSs such as Oracle, Sybase, SQL Server, and Informix. PowerBuilder and PowerBuilder Desktop also use ODBC drivers. This lets you connect to any ODBC compliant database. In order to establish this connection you must first enter the database as an ODBC data source, then create a PowerBuilder database profile for that data source. Once you complete these two steps, you need only select the **Connect** option from the File menu in the Database painter (see Figure 19.2).

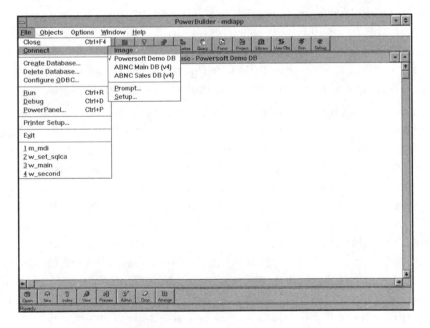

FIGURE 19.2 CONNECTING TO A DATABASE

Configuring ODBC

Microsoft has defined a database interface standard for Windows, the *Open Database Connectivity* (ODBC) interface. The purpose of ODBC is to provide transparent access to data sources for Windows applications so that, in a manner similar to printer drivers, an application written to the ODBC interface can access many different types of database systems and other data sources simply by adding a driver for that source. Microsoft has been incredibly successful in getting database and tools vendors to provide drivers for ODBC; they are widely available and in use today. The Watcom database, used for the PowerBuilder example and the examples that came with this book, uses the ODBC interface so that it is essential that you understand how to configure the system and what is required to be able distribute applications using ODBC and the Watcom database. This section will step through the process of setting up the ODBC data source. ODBC is covered in greater detail in a later section of this chapter.

If you already have a database you wish to use but do not have a profile set up or do not have it configured in the ODBC data sources, you must complete the following steps. For this example, we will step through the process of defining the data source that is required for the example database for this book. First, select the **Configure ODBC...** option from the File menus. This opens the Configure OBC dialog box shown in Figure 19.3.

In this dialog box you must select the appropriate driver for your database. These drivers have been installed by the PowerBuilder installation program or may be added by the installation program of another vendor. Select the appropriate driver for the data source that you wish to set up and click on the **Create** button. This establishes the database as an ODBC data source. (ODBC can also use some nondatabase objects, such as text files, as data sources. But for this discussion we assume that we are connecting to a database system.) Our sample database used the WATCOM SQL 4.0 driver, so select that entry in the **Installed Drivers** ListBox and then click the **Create** button. After clicking the Create button, you will be prompted to define a PowerBuilder database profile for your data source. Depending on the type of data source you selected (Watcom, text, etc.) the next dialog box displays a set of options for that particular type.

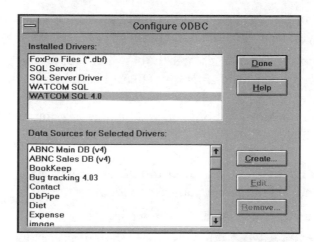

FIGURE 19.3 THE CONFIGURE ODBC DIALOG

In the Database Profile Setup Window you must enter the information that will be required to access the database. In a corporate environment you may have to contact the network or database administrator for the information that is required. The exact data that is required varies between vendors, but in general it includes the following:

- **Profile Name**—a label for the profile; this is used when you make the connection.

- **DBMS**—this is the name of the DBMS. You may type in the entry or make a selection from the dropdown listbox.

- **UserID**—your database user ID.

- **Password**—the password for your userID. This displays in protected mode, echoing only asterisks on the screen, but the password is stored in the PB.INI file in ASCII format (unencripted). Therefore, in most cases you will not want to enter a password in this dialog box. You may also choose to have the user prompted for his or her password each time he or she connects to the database. If you specify the password in the dialog box that appears to prompt you for additional connection information, the password will not be stored in the PB.INI file. For our example database, we store the password in the PB.INI file so that you will not be promoted each time you login into the database.

- **DBParm**—this varies greatly between DBMS vendors. If this is required, you would enter any PBParm variables here.

If you click on the **More** button, you will be able to enter additional information. This includes:

- **Server Name**—if you are running on a network, you may enter the name of the server you wish to login to.
- **Login ID**—your userID for the server.
- **Login Password**—the password for your server login.

Configuring the Example Database

For this example we will define the options necessary for the sample Watcom database, as shown in Figure 19.4.

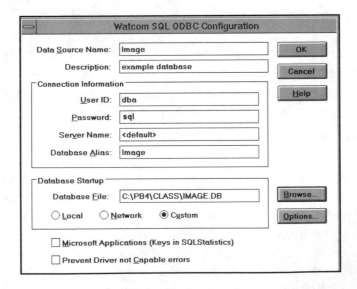

FIGURE 19.4 CONFIGURATION FOR THE EXAMPLE WATCOM DATABASE

In this dialog box, you must supply the file name of the database, the file path, the user ID, and your password for the database. If you are unsure of the exact file name or path you can click the **Browse** button, which provides a directory listing of applicable files, and fill in the appropriate fields when you select a file. For this example, enter the information exactly as it appears in Figure 19.4. You may have to adjust the path to the IMAGE.DB file if you have installed the example applications in a location other than C:\PB4\CLASS. Also note that when you enter the Password **sql** your screen will only echo three asterisks.

Check that everything is correct, then click on **OK**. This returns you to the Configure ODBC dialog box that was shown in Figure 19.3. In this dialog box click on the **Done** button. At this point, PowerBuilder saves the profile in the PB.INI file and adds the name of the profile to the list in the cascading menu that opens when you select the **Connect** option from the File menu.

Connecting to an Existing Database

From the initial File|Connect menu option (in the Database painter) you may select a data source for the connection or choose either the **Prompt** or **Setup** options to connect to a database. The Prompt option presents you with a list of all current ODBC data sources and lets you select one from the list. The Setup option lets you create and edit any database profile for any ODBC data source you have defined. For this example, select the **Image** database entry in the list to connect to the Image database. First, you will see a status message that says *Connecting to database...*, then you will see either the Select Table dialog box or just a Ready status. This is customizable and you will only see the Select Table dialog box if the preference TableDir is set to 1 (set it to 0 to suppress this dialog box). If you get this far, that means that the connection was successful.

If the connection to the Image database is not successful, then connect to the PowerBuilder demo database (or any other data source). This is necessary because you cannot edit the data source that is currently active. Then go back to the File|Configure ODBC... menu option and choose to edit the Image data source for the Watcom SQL 4.0 driver. Be sure that your configuration matches that shown in Figure 19.3 and use the **Browse** CommandButton to be sure that you have the correct location of the image database.

OPENING TABLES

Now that you have successfully defined the example ODBC data source, database profile, and have connected to the database, it is time to explore table navigation and maintenance. If you are not connected to the database, do so now by choosing the **Connect** option from the File menu. Any time you enter the Database painter or connect to a database the first response from PowerBuilder is to open the Table Select dialog box (if the TableDir preference is set to 1). If that dialog box does not display, then you can click on the PainterBar's **Open** icon to open the dialog box shown in Figure 19.5.

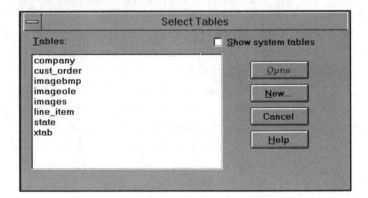

FIGURE 19.5 THE TABLE SELECT DIALOG

In this dialog box, you are selecting the tables that you wish to work with in the Database painter. If you are only connecting to a database so that you can work in the DataWindow painter, then you do not need to select any tables. In that case, if the Table Select dialog box has opened, then you can just click on **Cancel** to close the dialog box.

If you wish to work with one or more tables in the Database painter you must select each table to add it to the Database painter work area. To select a table, simply click on the table name. You may select as many tables as you wish. Once you have selected all the tables you wish to view, click on the **Open** button. You may deselect a table name by clicking on the table name once more or you can open tables immediately by double-clicking on the table name. If you wish to view the system tables from your database, you may do so by checking the **Show system tables box** in the upper-right corner.

If you are only interested in completing the steps that are necessary for setting up the ODBC configuration for the example database (image.db) then you are finished. And you may browse through the tables or exit and close the Database painter. The connection remains in effect and has become the default database connection.

Once you have opened the appropriate tables you will see the graphic representation of the tables in the work area. PowerBuilder displays each table as a list box containing a list of the columns in the table (or view). PowerBuilder also displays any indexes and key fields are alongside the table at this point. Figure 19.6 shows the display for the line_item table.

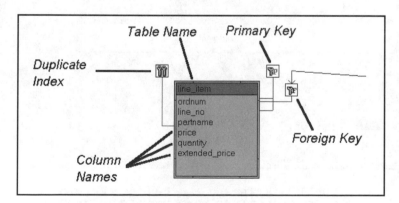

FIGURE 19.6   THE LINE_ITEM TABLE IN THE DATABASE PAINTER

If you double-click on the **Index** icon, a dialog box opens to display the key details. If you double-click on the **Primary Key** icon in Figure 19.6, you will see the dialog box in Figure 19.7.

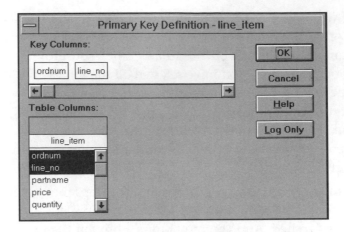

FIGURE 19.7 THE LINE_ITEM PRIMARY KEY INDEX

If you click on the **Foreign Key** icon in Figure 19.6 you will see the dialog box shown in Figure 19.8.

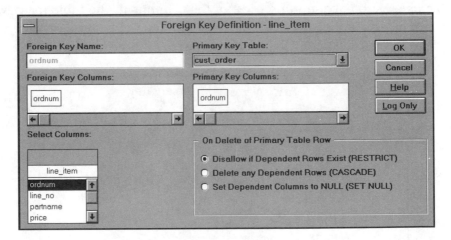

FIGURE 19.8 THE LINE_ITEM FOREIGN KEY INDEX

Table Creation and Maintenance

You may also add a new table to the current database while you are in the Database painter. To create a new table, simply click on the **New Table** icon in the painterbar or select **Objects|New|Table** from the menu. This opens the dialog box shown in Figure 19.9.

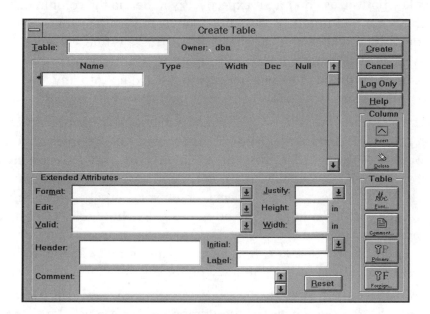

FIGURE 19.9 CREATING A NEW TABLE

On a field-by-field basis you enter the name, data type, width, and null option for each field that is included in the table from this screen. Each of these field options are only restricted by the database manager that is in use. You should be careful when defining these attributes. Once you have created the table, PowerBuilder may not let you change the data type, reduce the width of a field, change the null option, or insert a field anywhere except at the end of a table. You can drop (delete) tables from the database and you may need to drop and then re-create a table if you later decide on changes that are not allowed by the database system.

This screen lets you set default values for both the entire table and the individual columns in the table. The default characteristics that you can set for the table include fonts, comments, primary key, and foreign keys. By clicking the font button you can establish a different default font, style, and size for headers, labels, and data when the columns are used in

DataWindows. The comments button allows you to add descriptive information to further define the contents and/or usage of the table. The primary key button, as you might expect, lets you define the column or set of columns that will uniquely identify a row in the selected table. Clicking this opens the dialog box shown in Figure 19.7. While you can create tables in most relational databases without a primary key (control tables, for example), PowerBuilder will not let you insert data into any table without a primary key.

The foreign key button is used to define relationships between fields in the current table and primary keys in other tables. An example of a foreign key would be having two tables, one containing an entry for each invoice (cust_order) and another having an entry from each item on the invoice (line_item) of item a customer ordered. The Invoice number (ordnum) column in the cust_order table is the primary key for that table. The primary key for the line_item table is formed from the ordnum and lineno columns. The ordnum is a foreign key that references the primary key (ordnum) of the cust_order table. Figure 19.8 shows the Foreign Key dialog box.

If you open tables that are related by foreign keys, the Database painter will draw lines between the Primary key and any related foreign keys. Figure 19.10 shows the relationship between three tables.

As you are defining each column you should also define the extended attributes at the bottom of the screen (see Figure 19.9). PowerBuilder uses these extended attributes whenever you access the data. This means that when you create a Data Window or just want to browse the data from the Database painter, PowerBuilder applies these default formats. You should set each of these extended attributes in the Database painter to their most commonly used format. This greatly reduces the time required later to build data windows because most of the formatting will already be in place. It also provides for consistency between your applications and the reports that you create. The extended attributes and their uses are as follows:

- **Format**—selects the default display format for the data in the column.

- **Edit**—selects the default edit mask for the data in the column.

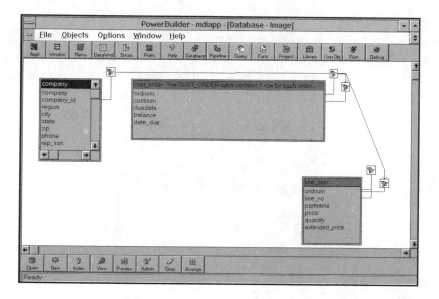

FIGURE 19.10 COMPANY, CUST_ORDER, AND LINE_ITEM

- **Valid**—selects the default validation rule for the data in the column.

- **Header**—enters the heading to be used for the column in all reports/data windows.

- **Comment**—enters comments to further the columns content. Any comments entered for a column automatically generates a tag value for that column. This tag value is used in application development for items such as microhelp.

- **Justify**—selects the justification for the column (left, right, centered).

- **Height**—enters a default height (in inches) for the column.

- **Width**—enters a default width (in inches) for the column.

- **Initial**—enters an initial value for this column to be set to for new records.

- **Label**—enters the label to be used for the column in all reports/data windows.

You may also modify each of these extended attributes without opening the table definition for an existing table. A right mouse click on any individual column in the table will activate the extended attribute popup menu. Figure 19.11 shows the popup menu that resulted from a right-mouse click on one of the columns in the line_item table.

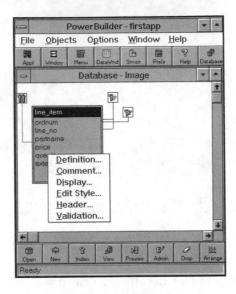

FIGURE 19.11 THE RMB POPUP MENU

The remaining two buttons on this screen (Figure 19.9) are the Create and Log Only buttons. As you might expect, the Create button actually generates and executes the SQL statements that are necessary to create the new table. The Log Only button only generates the SQL statements necessary to create this table, however, it will not send the SQL statements to the DBMS. The Log Only button pops up the activity log and pastes the SQL statements into it. You may then save the log as a text file or copy the log into the Database Administration painter and execute it manually.

Maintaining Tables

To view the actual composition of the fields in a table, double-click on any field in the table or on the table name in the Database painter work area

(Figure 19.10). The only notable difference between the screens for creating and maintaining a table is that the word **Alter** is substituted for the word **Create**. All other functions and icons act the same. There are a few distinctions to note, however, when you are modifying an existing table. Various DBMS' have different constraints as to how you may alter a table. In many systems the following constraints apply:

■ You cannot decrease the length of a field, you may only increase it.

■ You cannot change the data type for a column.

■ You cannot change the null option for a column.

When maintaining a table, a screen such as the one shown in Figure 9.12 will open.

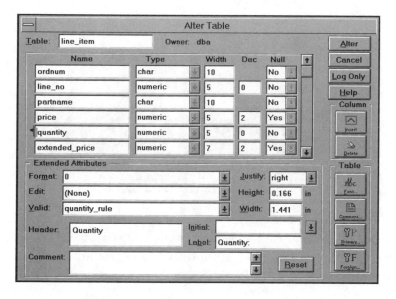

FIGURE 19.12 THE LINE_ITEM TABLE

After making your changes to the table you can choose to apply the changes or just to create the SQL statements that would implement the changes. The Alter button generates and actually executes the SQL necessary to alter this table. The Log Only button only generates the SQL statements necessary to alter this table. This all works the same as if you were creating a table. The Log Only button pops up the activity log and pastes the SQL statement into it. The Activity Log is displayed on the Database painter work area as shown in Figure 19.13.

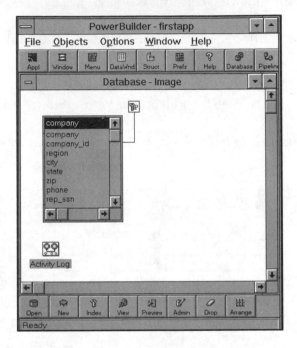

FIGURE 19.13 THE ACTIVITY LOG

You may then save the log as a text file or copy the log into the Database Administration painter and execute it manually. To save the log to a file, select the **Save Log As...** option from the Options menu. This prompts you for a file name, such as COMPANY.SQL.

Exporting Table Syntax

You may also export table definitions to SQL statements. Do this by first selecting the table in the work area and then by selecting the **Export**

Table/View Syntax To Log... option from the Objects menu in the Database painter. When you choose this option you will be prompted for a destination data source (see Figure 19.14).

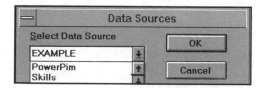

FIGURE 19.14 SELECT A DATA SOURCE

PowerBuilder creates the syntax in the dialect that is suitable for the destination data source. This can be very useful for re-creating tables or moving tables to another database. The data pipeline function also helps in this regard.

DISPLAY FORMAT MAINTENANCE

Continuing with the Objects menu and extended attributes, we come to the Display Format Maintenance option. When you select this option the Display Formats dialog box opens and displays all of the current display formats defined for your database. You may delete an existing format by clicking on the format name and then clicking on the **Delete** button, modify one of the existing formats by clicking on the **Edit** button, or create a new display format by clicking on the **New** button.

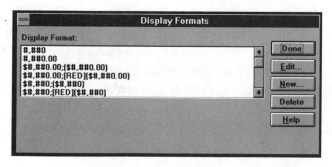

FIGURE 19.15 DISPLAY FORMATS

If you choose to create a new display format, you must first name this new format and select the data type for the format. Finally you must enter the display mask (see Figure 19.16).

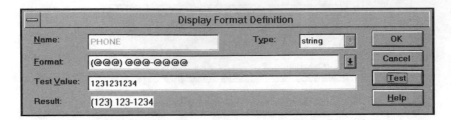

FIGURE 19.16 DEFINING A DISPLAY FORMAT

The mask may consist of specific characters for each data type, as described in the following examples. A complete list of display mask characters can be found in the PowerBuilder User's Guide.

DISPLAY MASK	DISPLAYS AS
###-##-####	555-55-5555
##,###.00	12,555.90
$##,##0.00	$12,555.90
@@@-@@@@	555-BOOK
mm/dd/yy	12/25/94
mmm dd, yyyy	December 25, 1994

After entering your display mask enter some data in the test value box and click on the **Test** button. This applies your display mask to the data and display the result. If the result matches your intent, then click on the **OK** button to save the display format and make it available for future use.

EDIT MASK STYLE MAINTENANCE

Display formats are excellent tools for displaying data to a user, but sometimes you will have more specialized needs for data entry. You can best handle these cases through the use of edit styles. To create or modify an edit style select the **Edit Style Maintenance** option from the Objects menu or select the **Edit Style** option from the RMB popup menu. This opens the Edit Styles dialog box, shown in Figure 19.17.

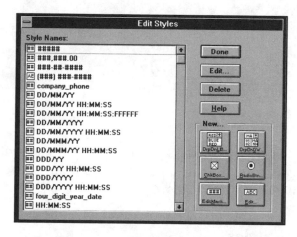

FIGURE 19.17 THE EDIT STYLES DIALOG

To edit an existing edit mask, select the mask from the list box and then click on **Edit.** You can also delete a mask by clicking **Delete.** To create a new edit mask click on the **Edit Mask** button in the New group. (We will discuss the other options in the New group in the next section.)

This opens the Edit Mask dialog box shown in Figure 19.18.

In this dialog box you must enter the name for the new edit mask. Next you must enter the data type in the Type box. If this is not the correct type for the column, select the correct type from the list of valid types in the Type dropdown listbox. Next you must define a new edit mask or modify an existing mask (which would be displayed in the Mask box). Use the characters displayed in the Mask Characters box at the bottom of the dialog box. You can enter a character or click the icon representing the character to paste it into the mask. You can also enter literal characters in the mask such as a hyphen, slashes, or parenthesis. To use one of the special mask characters in the mask as a literal you must precede it with a tilde (~).

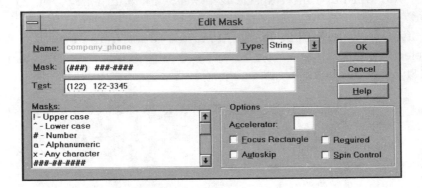

FIGURE 19.18 THE EDIT MASK DIALOG

After defining the edit mask you can test it by entering a value in the test area. This works exactly as the edit mask operates when the user is inputting data into your application.

The Six Edit Styles

The six basic edit styles that PowerBuilder provides for you to work with are:

- **Single Line Edit**—Use this style if you want a standard line edit and with limited standard choices for the user. This style lets the user enter a data value and have the display value show on the screen.

- **Edit Mask**—This operates in the same manner as the display formats in its creation and character selection. The primary difference between the two is that the edit mask is for data entry and limits the user to entering only a specific type of character, whereas the display format is strictly to determine how the data displays on the screen.

■ **Radio Buttons**—This style displays a list of selections from which the user may choose one. This style displays a text value to identify the selection but stores the data value when the user makes selection.

■ **Check Box**—A check box lets the user describe a field in terms of its being on, off, or in a third state. This edit style lets you store a separate data value for each condition.

■ **Drop-Down List Box**—Similar to the other edit styles, the drop-down list box allows you to store a different value than what displays to the user. This style also offers the option of sorting the list, allowing the user to edit the list, requiring the user to select from the list and scrolling options.

■ **Drop-Down DataWindow**—This is perhaps the most powerful of all the edit styles because it affords you all the benefits of a drop-down list box combined with a dynamic source for the list. You should use a drop-down data window to store a code in the database but display the meaning of the code to the user.

For most of the edit styles, defining new styles is self-explanatory from their respective dialog boxes. However, the drop down DataWindow requires a little extra attention. Before defining an edit style of this type, you must first create a DataWindow from the base table containing both the code and description of the field being used. For example, if you are creating an edit style for a list of annual quarters you would first create a DataWindow containing quarter code and a description of the quarter. You could then define a drop-down DataWindow edit style where the displayed values to the user would be quarter descriptions, but the data value stored in the database would be the quarter codes (see the following example).

Once you have created an edit style of any type, choosing **Edit Style Maintenance** from the Objects menu displays all available edit styles. Once you have selected one, the appropriate editor opens based on the type you selected.

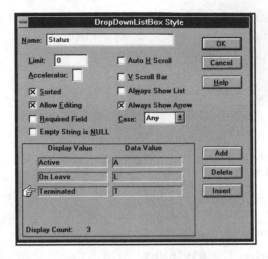

FIGURE 19.19 CREATING A DROP-DOWN DATAWINDOW

VALIDATION MAINTENANCE

The final section of the user input maintenance is validation rules. Validation rules describe in detail what values are legal for a field (column). In a validation rule you can limit the number of characters, type of characters, beginning of strings, ending of strings, or ranges of acceptable characters. To open the input validation window select the **Validation Maintenance** option from the objects menu or select the **Validation** option from the RMB popup menu. This opens the Column Validation dialog box shown in Figure 19.20.

In this dialog box you can choose to edit an existing rule or to create a new one. If you click on **New**, the Input Validation dialog box opens (see Figure 19.21).

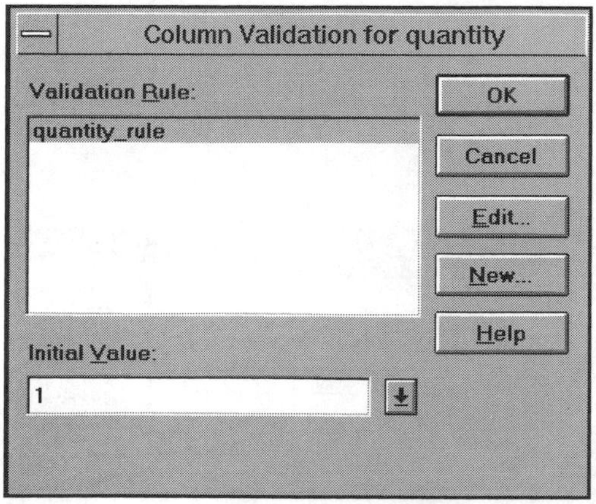

FIGURE 19.20 THE COLUMN VALIDATION DIALOG

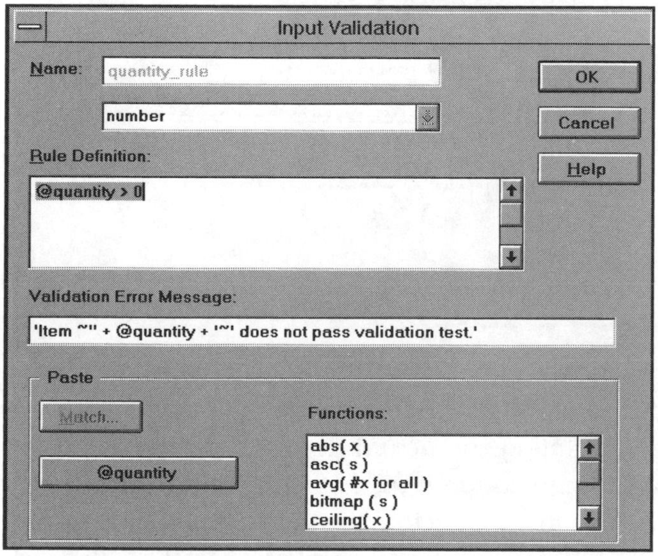

FIGURE 19.21 INPUT VALIDATION DIALOG

Once the input validation window is open you must enter a name for the rule, the data type for which the rule is being defined, the validation expression, and a text message to display when a user enters invalid data. All validation rules must have at least one column name. The column

733

name is represented by a variable beginning with the **@** sign. In the next example, Figure 19.22, the validation rule ensures the data entered into this column is exactly five characters long and the first three are letters and the last two are numbers.

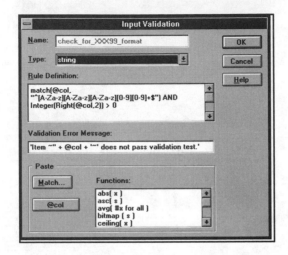

FIGURE 19.22 A MORE COMPLEX VALIDATION RULE

DATA MANIPULATION

Now that you have created your tables, edit styles, and validation rules and defined the extended attributes using the those edit styles, it is time to examine manipulating the actual data. After selecting a table you can start the data manipulation screen ether by clicking on the **Preview** icon in the painterbar or by selecting **Data Manipulation** from the Objects menu. If you select from the menu you will also be able to choose which display style you prefer: tabular, grid, or freeform. If you choose the painterbar icon, the default display style is grid. From this painter you can add, delete, update, and navigate through the rows in the table using the icon buttons.

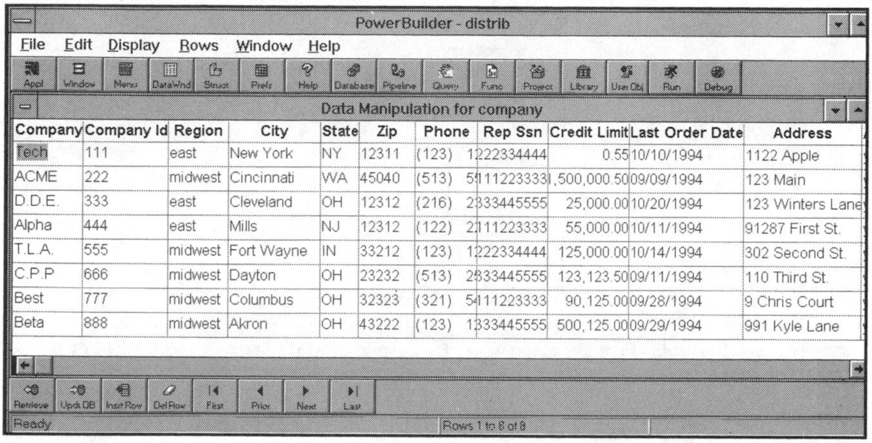

FIGURE 19.23 THE DATA MANIPULATION GRID

When you enter the data manipulation painter notice that the menu and Painterbars change. You may insert, update, and delete rows. However, from this menu you will notice that you may also filter the data, whereby you can set select criteria and limit the amount of data displayed. Another option from the Rows menu is Import. Using this option you can import data directly from a text file. When you select the Retrieve option, as you would expect, the data for the selected table is retrieved. You must be careful when retrieving the data because if you have made changes to the data, you will lose them unless you specifically choose the update button prior to retrieving. The remaining two options on this menu are Described, which simply displays information on the current set of retrieved data, and Sort which lets you sort the data into any sequence you would like.

You will also notice that in the File menu you now have the option to save the rows that are currently active, those rows that meet all filtering criteria, into a file. When you select this option, PowerBuilder prompts you for the file format you wish to save the data as. You can save the data in a number of formats, including comma-separated text, tab-separated text, SQL syntax, and many other popular file formats.

FIGURE 19.24 THE ROWS MENU IN THE DATA MANIPULATION PAINTER

DATABASE ADMINISTRATION

The database administrator painter is similar to the data manipulation painter in that you can only access it through the Database painter. The main function of this painter is to let you create SQL statements, manually or via the SQL painter, and submit them directly to the database for immediate execution. You will primarily use this painter to perform DBA-type functions or to test SQL before implementing it in an application.

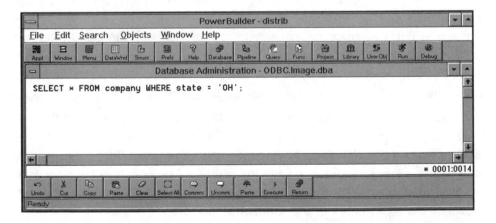

FIGURE 19.25 THE DATABASE ADMINISTRATION PAINTER

Two points of significant interest in the database administration painter is that you have the ability to save and retrieve any SQL syntax to or from a DOS file at any time and that you can use the SQL painter to graphically generate the SQL syntax. To execute the SQL painter you need only click on the **SQL** icon in the Painterbar where you will then be prompted for the type of SQL statement desired: insert, update, delete, or cursor. From this point the SQL painter functions exactly the same as that found in the Query painter, with the exception of the final step. The final step when entering from the database administration painter is to return to the painter and paste the SQL onto the current screen. Once your SQL is in place on the screen, you may click the **Execute** button to have the database process the SQL immediately.

ACTIVITY LOGS

This section will touch on the Database painter activity logs. An activity log is simply a listing of all SQL statements that PowerBuilder generates and submits to your database. From the Options menu of the Database painter you have the option of starting or stopping a log file at any point in time. Once you have started a log file, you have the ability to clear or save the log file as you see fit. You can find each of the options on the Options menu, and each is straightforward in its operation (Figure 19.26).

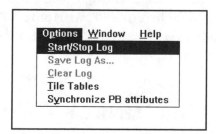

FIGURE 19.26 ACTIVITY LOG MENU OPTIONS

Any time you start the activity log you will notice a new icon in the bottom of the Database painter. This icon not only lets you know the log is active, but by double-clicking on it you can view the contents of the log at any time. This can be proven to be very useful when trying to trace back through your steps after issuing a series of SQL statements to the database.

You will find another use of the activity log in the last menu option from the Objects section of the Database painter menu, Export Table/View Syntax to Log.... After you have opened a table or set of tables or views you can select this option and PowerBuilder automatically generates all of the SQL syntax necessary to create each of the opened tables with all of their extended attributes. This technique can be extremely useful to generate the SQL syntax for your database tables that have been created graphically in PowerBuilder. By having this SQL syntax available you will be able to port your databases from one back-end DBMS to another using SQL syntax in text files, which you can edit to account for changes between the two databases such as differences in data type names. After you have exported to the activity log you must still save the log. Once you have saved any log file you may choose the **File|DOS Open** menu option and resubmit the SQL at any time.

You probably noticed that there is another selection available from the Options menu, Synchronize PB Attributes. This option serves only one purpose. Its sole purpose is to delete orphaned table information such as extended attribute information. Since PowerBuilder builds and maintains all of the extended attribute data in its own set of tables it is possible for a table to be dropped outside of PowerBuilder and the extended attributes to remain. This menu option is specifically designed to clean up this situation. When you select **Synchronize PB Attributes**, PowerBuilder asks if you are sure. If you answer **Yes**, then PowerBuilder drops all orphaned table information from the database.

CREATING A WATCOM DATABASE

You can create a local Watcom database easily from within the Database painter. To do so, first select the **File|Create Database...** menu option (this applies only to Watcom databases). This opens the Create Database dialog box as shown in Figure 19.27.

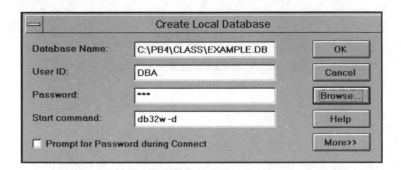

FIGURE 19.27 THE CREATE DATABASE DIALOG

If you would like to create a database, fill in the information in Figure 19.27. We can use this EXAMPLE database in the next section on the data pipeline. This action creates two files, EXAMPLE.DB and EXAMPLE.LOG, for the Watcom system. It also automatically creates an ODBC data source and PowerBuilder database profile.

The Data Pipeline

The Data Pipeline is one of the new features of PowerBuilder 4.0. You can use the Data Pipeline to copy tables and data from one database, even across different DBMSs. You could copy a database table in an Oracle database to a Watcom database. This is useful when you want to copy data to a local database so you can work on it without needing access to the network.

To use the Data Pipeline click on the PowerBar's **Data Pipeline** icon. This opens the Select Data Pipeline dialog box (Figure 19.28).

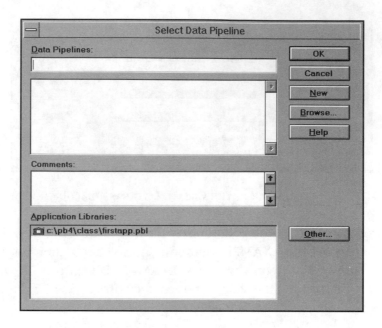

FIGURE 19.28 THE SELECT DATA PIPELINE DIALOG

To create a new pipeline click the **New** command button. This opens the Choose Database Profiles dialog box (Figure 19.29).

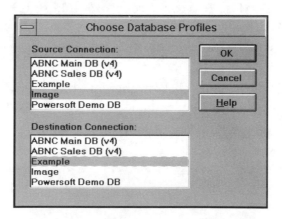

FIGURE 19.29 THE CHOOSE DATABASE PROFILES DIALOG

In this dialog box you must select the profile for the source database and the destination database to which you wish to copy tables. For this example, use the IMAGE database as the source and use the new Watcom database, EXAMPLE (which was created in the section on Creating Watcom Databases) and the destination database. PowerBuilder then connects to the source database and displays the Select Tables dialog box.

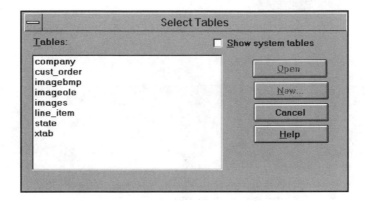

FIGURE 19.30 THE SELECT TABLES DIALOG

This dialog box lists the tables in the source database. Select the table(s) that you want to use and then click on the **Open** command button. The Select painter opens with the selected tables displayed.

You may use a join between two or more tables as the source. If you do this, the name of the first table that you selected will be the name for the destination table. Create the SQL SELECT statement you want to use to select the columns and data you want to add to the destination database. Use the same technique that you use to paint the SQL SELECT statement for a DataWindow when the data source is SQL SELECT. When you have completed the SQL statement, click on the **Design** icon to move to the Data Pipeline workspace.

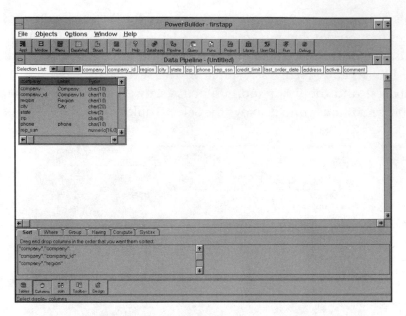

FIGURE 19.31 THE SELECT PAINTER

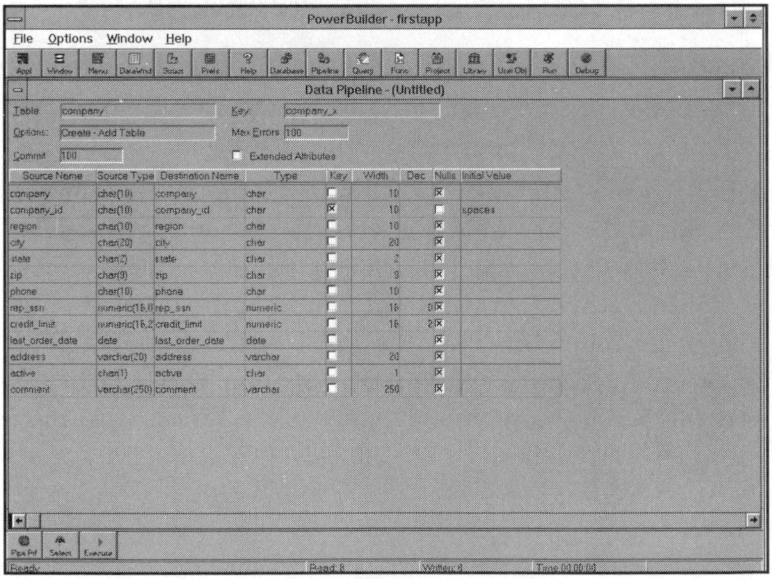

FIGURE 19.32 THE DATA PIPELINE PAINTER

You can edit the entries in the edit fields at the top of this screen.

- **Table**—names the destination table.

- **Option**—you can choose the options from a drop-down list box. You can choose to create, replace, refresh, append or update the table in the destination database.

- **Commit**—lets you determine the frequency at which commits are issued as data is moved to the destination database. The default is to commit after every 100 rows are written to the database. If you set Commit to 0, PowerBuilder only issues a COMMIT after all rows have been written. If the value of Commit is less than 100, PowerBuilder uses it as the blocking factor. For example, if commit is 10, 10 rows will be read and then written at once.

- **Key**—you may change the primary key (for destination table). You can only change the key if the option is Create or Replace.

- **Max Errors**—sets the maximum number of errors that you will allow (the default is 100). When the number of errors exceeds this number, PowerBuilder stops the pipeline.

- **Extended Attributes**—check this option to copy extended attributes to the new database. This will only work for validation rules, display formats, or edit masks if they have been defined in the new database.

When everything is set, you may save the Data Pipeline using the File|Save menu option.

The PainterBar only has three icons:

- **Pipe Prf**—selects the destination database profile.

- **SQL Select**—goes back to edit the SQL Select statement for the current pipeline.

- **Execute**—executes the pipeline that you have defined.

More on ODBC

If you are working with Windows, then at some point you will work with Microsoft's new database interface standard, the Open Database Connectivity (ODBC) interface. ODBC is an application-level programming interface used to access database systems. The purpose of ODBC is to provide transparent access to data sources for Windows applications. This means that, in a manner similar to printer drivers, an application written to the ODBC interface can access many different types of database systems and other data sources simply by adding a driver for that source. Microsoft has been very successful in getting database and tools vendors to provide drivers for ODBC; they are widely available and in use today. The Watcom database uses the ODBC interface, so it is essential that you understand how to configure the system and what is required to distribute applications using ODBC and the Watcom database.

ODBC is an application-level interface (API) that is defined basically to be a superset of the SQL Access Group's call-level interface (CLI) standard. ODBC takes a somewhat least-common-denominator approach and defines the API as a subset of the SQL language. ODBC defines the API only; it is left to the vendors to implement the drivers. The advantage is that the application developer can write to this one API and have connectivity to any database for which there is an ODBC driver. Because of the power of Microsoft endorsement, it has become a widely accepted standard.

A Brief Look at the ODBC Architecture

Single-tier is used for DBMS sources that do not support SQL. This includes dBase, FoxPro, Excel, Paradox, Btrieve, and text files. ODBC translates the SQL requests into the lower-level calls necessary for each system.

Multiple-tier is used for true client/server relational DBMSes; this includes ORACLE, SQL Server, Watcom, Informix, and many others. For the Watcom database, your PowerBuilder application talks to the ODBC manager. The WOD40W.DLL is the ODBC driver for the Watcom 4.0 engine (db32w.exe). You can see the layers as follows:

Windows Application	(PowerBuilder)
The ODBC manager	(ODBC.DLL)
ODBC driver	(WOD40W.DLL)
DBMS	(db32w.exe)
database	(Image.db)

ODBC Installation

The PowerBuilder installation will have installed the ODBC administrator files and the ODBC driver manager files on your system. After this step, you will add ODBC drivers for each of the DBMSes that you access (Oracle, Watcom, dBase), and define data source names for each connection. (ODBC can even connect to sources such as Excel files or text files as if they were database systems. Even though these are not really DBMSes, we will not distinguish from this type of access throughout this discussion.)

ODBC Administration

You use the ODBC Administrator to install drivers and set up connections to the data source. You can access the ODBC Administrator by choosing **Configure ODBC** in the Database painter. When you run the administrator from within PowerBuilder you are using the ODBC administrator, which the PowerBuilder installation will usually place in the C:\WINDOWS\SYSTEM directory. If you have installed the stand-alone ODBC Administrator on your system (from another application such as Access), you may find it on your Windows Control Panel; in this case you will execute the stand-alone version ODBCINST.EXE.

ODBC Drivers

An ODBC driver is a Windows DLL library that is used to provide database access to a Windows application. You must install an ODBC driver for each type of data that you wish to access. For example, Watcom, Oracle, Sybase, and Informix databases all require separate drivers. There are some drivers that can actually access more than one database type (generally because they are closely related, such as dBase and FoxPro). Normally, to install a new driver (which will be on a floppy diskette), you will run a setup program that copies one or two DLLs onto your hard drive. Sometimes there are two: one handles the installation, updating, removal of data sources, and the other is the actual ODBC driver used to access the data. Table 19.1 shows a number of sample drivers; these drivers are usually found in the C:\WINDOWS\SYSTEM directory.

TABLE 19.1 ODBC DRIVERS

DATABASE	DRIVER	SETUP
Watcom SQL	WOD40W.DLL	WOD40W.DLL
Oracle7 DBMS	ORA7WIN.DLL	ORA7WIN.DLL
FoxPro Files (MS Driver)	SIMBA.DLL	SIMADMIN.DLL
dBase Files (MS Driver)	SIMBA.DLL	SIMADMIN.DLL
dBase Files (Q+E Driver)	QEDBF02.DLL	QEDBF02.DLL

Microsoft's SIMBA.DLL handles all the single-tier requests.

ODBC abstracts the source of the data into an object called a *data source*. The data source is specific to a particular DBMS, network, and operating system. This means that it requires two different data sources to access an Oracle7 database on a Novell server and an Oracle7 on a UNIX server. When you run the ODBC Administrator the first List Box in the ODBC Administrator dialog window will display a list of all the data sources that have been created. The lower List Box shows the ODBC drivers that are currently installed on your system. You can run the ODBC Administrator from PowerBuilder's Database painter by selecting **Configure ODBC** from the File menu.

To add a new data source, select the appropriate driver (such as WATCOM SQL 4.0), from the ListBox (the upper one). Then click **Create** to define a new data source, or select a data source and click **Edit** to modify a definition, or click **Remove** to delete a data source definition.

Another dialog window (ODBC Configuration) will appear to accept the details of the data source. Figure 19.33 shows the configuration details that were used for our example database and are used by many of our example applications (such as imagedb).

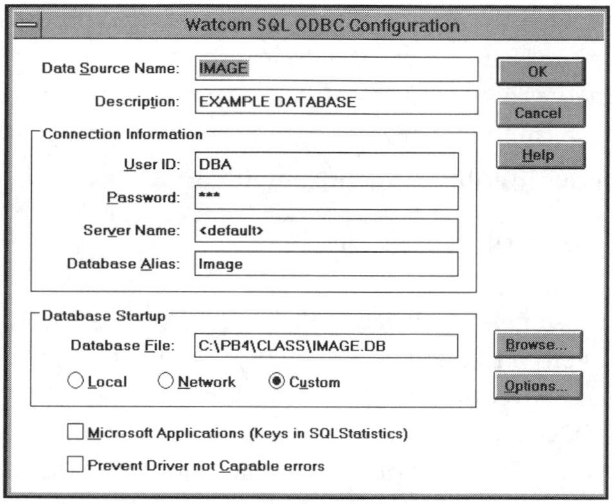

FIGURE 19.33 THE ODBC CONFIGURATION
FOR THE EXAMPLE DATABASE (IMAGE.DB)

Clicking on the **Options** CommandButton in Figure 19.33 opens the Startup Options dialog box shown in Figure 19.34.

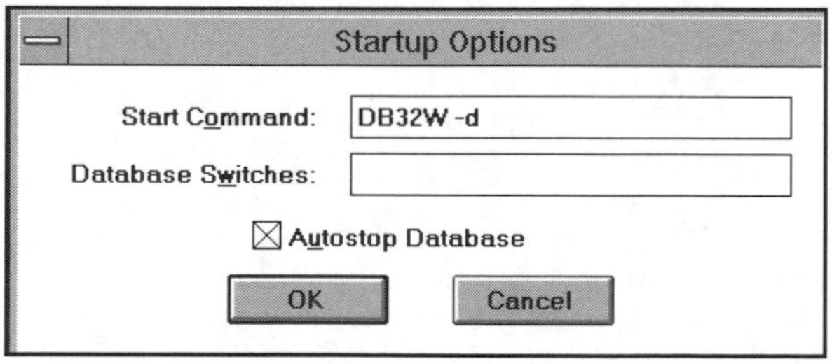

FIGURE 19.34 THE ODBC CONFIGURATION
FOR THE EXAMPLE DATABASE (IMAGE.DB)

Figure 19.34 shows the startup options for the example database. The **Autostop Database** option is checked. This tells the system to close the example Watcom database when you exit PowerBuilder.

There will be times when you are required to edit an existing data source. For example, if you move a database file to a different directory, you will have to tell the driver. To edit an existing data source select the driver from the top ListBox, and then select the data source name that you wish to edit in the lower ListBox. Click on **Edit** and you will be able to make the changes in the ODBC Configuration dialog window.

You must have installed the Watcom driver.

```
C:\WINDOWS\SYSTEM\ WOD40W.DLL
```

Listing 1 shows a sample ODBCINST.INI file. This file keeps a list of the ODBC drivers that have been installed on your system in the first section (ODBC Drivers). For each driver, there will be a section (such as WATCOM SQL 4.0), that tells the ODBC manager the location of the DLLs for each system; it will list a driver path and a setup path. The driver path is the DLL that is used for the actual data access; the setup path is the DLL used for the ODBC Configuration by the ODBC Administrator when you edit a data source. This is the list of drivers in the ODBC Driver ListBox in the ODBC Administrator.

Listing 1   C:\WINDOWS\ODBCINST.INI

```
[ODBC Drivers]
SQL Server Driver=Installed
WATCOM SQL 4.0=Installed
Access Data (*.mdb)=Installed
Excel Files (*.xls)=Installed
ODS Gateway=Installed
SQL Server=Installed

 [SQL Server Driver]
Driver=C:\WINDOWS\SYSTEM\sqlsrvr.dll
Setup=C:\WINDOWS\SYSTEM\sqlsrvr.dll

 [WATCOM SQL 4.0]
Driver=c:\windows\system\wod40w.dll
Setup=c:\windows\system\wod40w.dll
```

```
[Access Data (*.mdb)]
Driver=C:\WINDOWS\SYSTEM\simba.dll
Setup=C:\WINDOWS\SYSTEM\simadmin.dll
FileUsage=2
FileExtns=*.mdb
DirectConnect=0

[ODS Gateway]
Driver=c:\windows\system\odsgate.dll
Setup=c:\windows\system\odsgate.dll
```

The ODS gateway is the Open Data Services driver, which uses the Micro Decisionware gateway to access IBM's DB/2 database on a mainframe or an AS/400 minicomputer. The SQL Server driver can access both the Sybase and the Microsoft versions of SQL Server.

Listing 2 shows an example ODBC.INI file; this file is used to track the data source definitions.

The first section, ODBC Data Sources, shows each data source name that has been defined and links it with a driver, in this case the image data source name is linked to the WATCOM SQL driver:

```
[ODBC Data Sources]
image=WATCOM SQL 4.0
```

The next part of this file contains a list of the drivers that have been installed.

```
[WATCOM SQL 4.0]
DRIVER=c:\windows\system\wsqlodbc.dll
```

shows the driver for the WATCOM SQL system.

The next section contains the details of the data source that you defined in the ODBC Configuration dialog box:

```
[image]
Driver=c:\windows\system\wod40w.dll
UID=dba
PWD=sql
Description=example database
```

749

```
Database=C:\PB4\CLASS\IMAGE.DB
Start=db32w -d
DatabaseFile=C:\PB4\CLASS\IMAGE.DB
DatabaseName=Image
AutoStop=yes
```

The previous code shows the details for the image data source. The line Start=db32w -d tells the ODBC manager to run the program **db32w.exe** and pass it the database name as an argument; db32w.exe is the version of the Watcom SQL database manager for Windows.

The warning at the top of the file should not be taken lightly, but there will be times that you find it necessary to edit this file. If you do so, be sure to make copies of this and any other file that you are going to modify in case you are forced to put things back the way they were.

Listing 2   C:\WINDOWS\ODBC.INI

```
;------------------------------------------------------------
; WARNING:   Do not make changes to this file without using
;            the ODBC Control panel device or other utilities
;            provided for maintaining data sources.
;
;            Incorrect changes to this file could prevent ODBC
;            from operating or operating correctly.
;------------------------------------------------------------

[ODBC Data Sources]
Powersoft Demo DB=Watcom SQL 4.0
Image=WATCOM SQL 4.0
EXAMPLE=WATCOM SQL 4.0

[Powersoft Demo DB]
Database=c:\pb4\psdemodb.db
UID=dba
PWD=sql
Driver=c:\windows\system\WOD40W.DLL
Description=Powersoft Demo Database
Start=db32w -d -c512
DatabaseFile=c:\pb4\examples\PSDEMODB.DB
DatabaseName=PSDEMODB

[WATCOM SQL 4.0]
driver=c:\windows\system\WOD40W.DLL
```

```
 [Image]
Driver=c:\windows\system\wod40w.dll
UID=dba
PWD=sql
Description=example database
Database=C:\PB4\CLASS\IMAGE.DB
Start=db32w -d
DatabaseFile=C:\PB4\CLASS\IMAGE.DB
DatabaseName=Image
AutoStop=yes
```

Listing 3 shows an excerpt from the PowerBuilder initialization file, PB.INI. We have excepted the sections that relate to the Image database (our example database). Near the top of the file, you will find a section labeled *database*. This section holds the current default values for the database connection in the PowerBuilder development environment. This is the data source that will be used to connect to the database when you attempt to perform an operation, such as opening the DataWindow painter, that requires database access. This data is reset each time you connect to a database in the Database painter.

Further down in the file you will find a series of one or more sections labeled PROFILE *xxxx*, where *xxxx* is the name of a database profile. There will be a section for every database profile that that you have defined. If the profile uses an ODBC driver, then the DBMS will be "ODBC," and the database will be the data source name. For example:

```
[PROFILE Image]
DBMS=ODBC
Database=
UserId=dba
DatabasePassword=
LogPassword=
ServerName=
LogId=
Lock=
DbParm=Connectstring='DSN=image'
Prompt=0
```

If the driver is not an ODBC driver, the DBMS name will be part of the name of the DLL driver name. For example, the profile for connecting to

the Oracle7 NLM on a Novell network has a DBMS named OR7. This uses
the PBOR7030.DLL driver and does not involve ODBC.

```
[PROFILE Oracle7]
DBMS=OR7
Database=dev1
UserId=
DatabasePassword=
LogPassword=
ServerName=
LogId=
Lock=
DbParm=Connectstring='DSN=@t:orasrv:dev1'
Prompt=0
```

Listing 3   C:\PB4\PB.INI

```
[Database]
Vendors=ODBC
DBMS=ODBC
ServerName=
Database=Image
UserID=dba
DatabasePassword=
LogId=
LogPassword=
; DBParm=DelimitIdentifier can be added to DbParm
; to control whether quotes are placed around
; table and column names in SQL
; DbParm=DelimitIdentifier='YES'
DbParm=Connectstring='DSN=Image'
;

[DBMS_PROFILES]
CURRENT=Image
PROFILES='Image','Example','Powersoft Demo DB','ABNC Main DB
    (v4)','ABNC Sales DB (v4)'
History='Image','Example','Powersoft Demo DB','ABNC Main DB
    (v4)','ABNC Sales DB (v4)'

[PROFILE Image]
DBMS=ODBC
Database=
```

```
UserId=
DatabasePassword=
LogPassword=
ServerName=
LogId=
Lock=
DbParm=Connectstring='DSN=Image'
Prompt=0

[Profile Powersoft Demo DB]
DBMS=ODBC
Database=Powersoft Demo DB
UserId=
DatabasePassword=
LogPassword=
ServerName=
LogId=
Lock=
DbParm=ConnectString='DSN=Powersoft Demo DB;UID=dba;PWD=sql'
Prompt=0
```

LOGIC WORK'S ERWIN/ERX FOR POWERBUILDER

Logic Work's ERwin/ERX is a database design tool for client-server system development. It is a Windows CASE tool for creating and generating ERDs (entity-relationship diagrams). ERwin makes it easy to define new application data requirements and to document both new and existing application data requirements through its point-and-click user interface. It can be used to forward-and-reverse engineer an application's data requirements. This can be accomplished through the use of ASCII DDL scripts or ERwin's active interface to supported physical database systems. ERwin uses the standard IDEF1X diagramming method to create entity-relationship diagrams to capture the data and business requirements (rules) for your business.

Logic Works makes a version of ERWin/ERX specifically for PowerBuilder. This is the best choice for a PowerBuilder project CASE tool in its price range. It can work directly with PowerBuilder, and it integrates ERwin data modeling with PowerBuilder's development system. ERwin for PowerBuilder has been extended to include support for the client/server paradigm. Additionally, ERwin for PowerBuilder provides the PowerBuilder extended attribute editor. You can access the PowerBuilder repository from within ERWin. This is a two-way link that allows you to import, view, or modify a PowerBuilder application's repository attributes while you are still in the ERwin environment.

The system requirements for ERwin for PowerBuilder version 2.0 are: IBM-compatible 386, 486, or Pentium; a minimum of 1.5 megabytes of free disk space; a mouse; a VGA monitor; a minimum of 2 megabytes of RAM; DOS 3.1 or higher; and Windows 3.0 or higher. Supported relational database systems include DB 2.3, Ingres, Informix, Oracle, Rdb, SQLServer, Sybase, and Watcom.

Benefits of Using ERwin

Some of the benefits of using ERwin are:

- Generation of a consistent system documentation set that can be used by database and application designers and developers as well as the end-user community to translate business requirements into a consistent and implementable data model;
- Definition and generation of referential integrity data constraints
- Translation of logical data relationships into physical schema relationships
- Reverse-engineering of existing physical database schema.

The ERwin Data Model

An ERwin data model consists of entities, attributes, and relationships between entities. An *entity* is a set of like objects or instances. *Attributes* are facts about the entity. A correlation of the ERwin data model, English language sentences, and relational database representation is shown in Table 19.2.

TABLE 19.2

TABLE 19.2

ERWIN	ENGLISH LANGUAGE	RELATIONAL
Entity	Noun	Table
Attribute	Adjective	Table column
Relationship	Verb	Table key

If one considers entities to be the data elements and relationships to be the rules used to support a business, then the ERwin model represents the information requirements of a business. This model is referred to as a business information model.

ERwin itself does not have direct support for any particular process modeling style. it does, however, use a relational entity relationship model in the sense that it uses shared keys to represent the relationships between logical data model entities. This causes ERwin to be more closely aligned with relational database management systems than with network or hierarchical database systems. However, it can be used to represent the logical structure of data for network and hierarchical systems as well as relational database systems. ERwin supports the IDEF1X standard.

It is recommended that readers new to the concepts of data modeling refer to the ERwin methods guide prior to developing either a logical or a physical data model.

ERwin and Normalization

ERwin supports normalization to the extent that each object (entity or attribute) must have a unique name. There is an option to allow multiple attributes having the same name. The second use of an entity name is flagged. For attributes, unless a rolename is specified, the second use of an attribute name is flagged. Multiple occurrences of a foreign key name are flagged unless it is given a rolename. Thus, ERwin supports first normal form and second and third to the extent described above. ERwin itself has no formal normalization algorithm. Therefore normalization is the responsibility of the data designer and application development team.

Client/Server Support

As stated above, ERwin for PowerBuilder supports the client/server paradigm. This implies that ERwin for PowerBuilder provides support for server domains, client domains, and client/server domains. Server domain support includes user defined datatypes, column-level server values, validation rules, defaults, and NULL/NOT NULL. Client domain support gives PowerBuilder extended-attribute support for edit styles, display formats, validation rules, initial values, labels, headings, comments and client inheritance. Client/server domain support implies that there is an association between the client domain and the server domain. This can be accomplished with the ERwin PowerBuilder extended-attribute editor by choosing **Pb sync** at the entity level or choosing the **Pb Synchronization** option on the Client menu. This synchronizes the PowerBuilder extended attributes entered in ERwin for PowerBuilder with the PowerBuilder data dictionary system tables and lets the user ignore or export ERwin-entered attributes into the PowerBuilder data dictionary tables in the physical RDBMS. Similarly, extended attributes entered into the PowerBuilder data dictionary tables using PowerBuilder itself can either be ignored or imported into the ERwin for PowerBuilder model's client domain.

If you switch between the target server, you may need to remap RDBMS datatypes.

NOTE

ERwin and the Application Design Process

It is typical in new application design that the logical database-independent model is designed prior to the physical platform-dependent, data model. With ERwin, this is done by creating entities and defining each entity's attributes and the relationships between entities using the ERwin toolbox and editors. In the ERwin toolbox, shown in Figure 19.35, entities are represented by rectangles and relationships by lines. This is used to draw the logical data model. The model is managed through the series of editors shown in Figure 19.36.

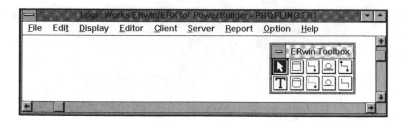

FIGURE 19.35 ERWIN TOOLBOX

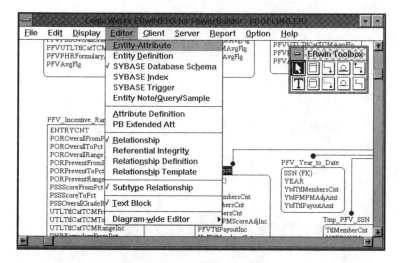

FIGURE 19.36 EDITOR SELECTIONS

The Entity Attribute Editor, shown in Figure 19.37, is used to define each attribute associated an entity as either a key on non-key attribute. The Entity Definition Editor, shown in Figure 19.38, defines the entity's name and allows you to enter a description of the entity into the definition window.

The physical model is defined using the database system Database Schema editor shown in Figure 19.39, the database system Index Editor shown in Figure 19.40, and the database system Trigger Editor shown in Figure 19.41.

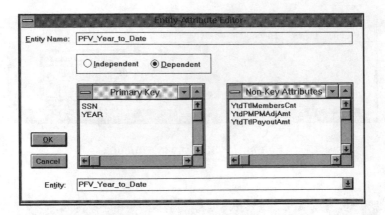

FIGURE 19.37 THE ENTITY-ATTRIBUTE EDITOR

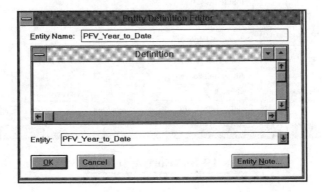

FIGURE 19.38 THE ENTITY DEFINITION EDITOR

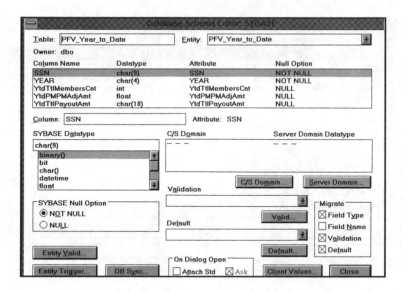

FIGURE 19.39 THE DATABASE SCHEMA EDITOR

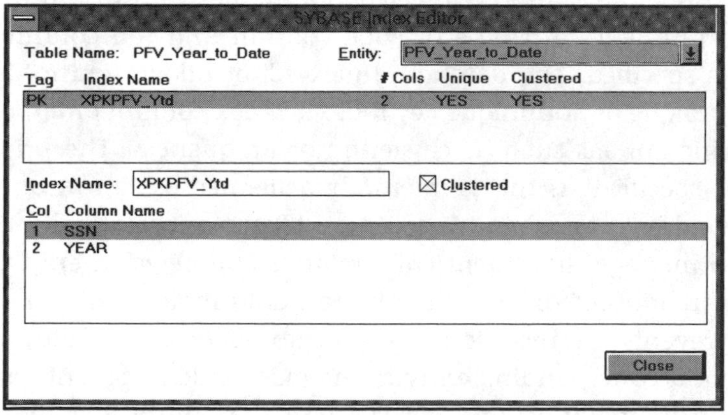

FIGURE 19.40 THE DATABASE SYSTEM INDEX EDITOR

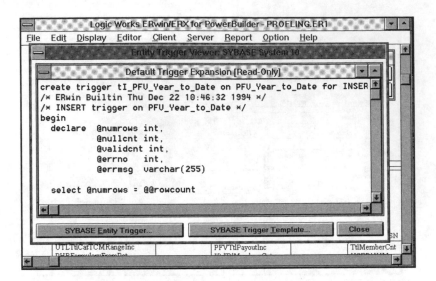

FIGURE 19.41 THE DATABASE SYSTEM TRIGGER EDITOR

The Database Schema editor associates a database system table name with the entity and database table column names with the entity's attributes. The physical data type of each column and the column's NULL option are specified. The database Index editor allows you to define the alternate unique or nonunique key indices, index column order, and database-specific options such as clustering or uniqueness. The primary key cannot be specified, as this is internally generated by ERwin once a relationship is drawn between two entities. ERwin automatically generates triggers to manage the parent/child relationship between entities and to ensure referential integrity in the physical data model. The generation of triggers prevents the insertion of data into dependent (child) entities if there is not a corresponding entry in the independent (parent) entity. The trigger can be modified and viewed with the database Trigger editor. Additionally, trigger action types and referential integrity options can be viewed and modified using the Referential Integrity editor shown in Figure 19.42.

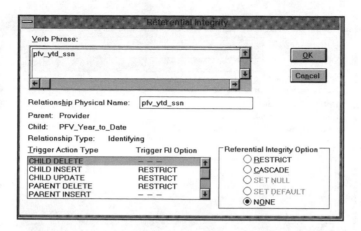

FIGURE 19.42 THE REFERENTIAL INTEGRITY EDITOR

The relationship between entities is drawn using the ERwin tool. It can also be specified—and the cardinality defined—with the Relationship editor, shown in Figure 19.43, and a description of the relationship can be specified in the Relationship Definition window of the Relationship Definition Editor, which is shown in Figure 19.44.

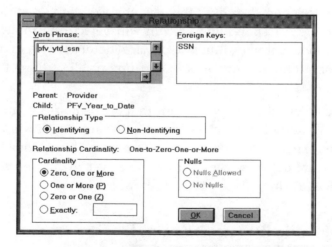

FIGURE 19.43 THE RELATIONSHIP EDITOR

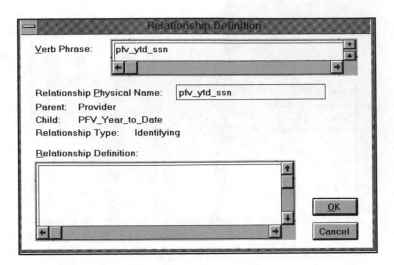

FIGURE 19.44 THE RELATIONSHIP DEFINITION WINDOW

Once the physical model has been determined, ERwin can synchronize with supported relational database systems. This can be done through either native API or ODBC DLLs. During the synchronization process, ERwin will detect any new physical database tables and give the user the opportunity to ignore or import the new physical database tables into the ERwin model. Correspondingly, ERwin will detect any tables that exist within the model but not within the physical database system and give the user the opportunity to ignore or export any or all of these tables to the physical RDBMS.

In the case of existing applications that are being redesigned or reengineered, particularly for the client/server environment, ERwin can reverse-engineer an existing physical database schema. This is done by selecting the appropriate database server from the Server menu and selecting the **Synchronize ERwin with server** from the Server menu.

An ERwin Client/Server Example

In the following example, we need to update a reverse-engineered ERwin model due to changes that have occurred in the physical database system.

The physical database changes were made using the PowerBuilder Database painter. The name of the table shown in Figure 19.45 was changed from PFV_Hist to PFV_History. Additionally, the table's extended attributes were defined using the PowerBuilder Database painter. The table PFV_Hist was already synchronized between the physical database and ERwin. Since some column names in the table—and the table name—were changed in the table, the easiest approach is to drop the ERwin entity PFV_Hist and resynchronize the ERwin model and the physical database. An ERwin entity is dropped by selecting the entity, pressing the **Delete** key and responding **OK** when ERwin asks if you really want to delete the entity. Since PFV_Hist is dropped, we will proceed to synchronize the model with the physical database system by selecting the **Sync ERwin with SYBASE...** option from the Server menu, as shown in Figure 19.46.

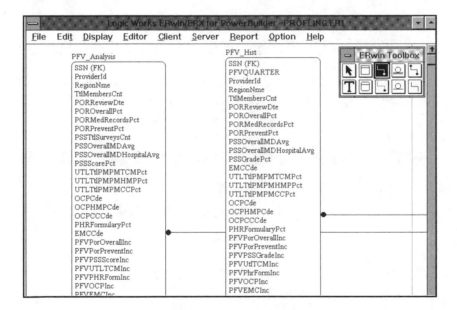

FIGURE 19.45 PFV_HIST

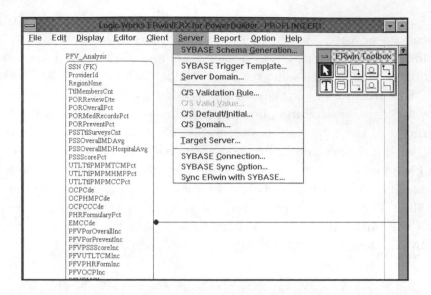

FIGURE 19.46 SELECT SYNC ERWIN WITH SYBASE FROM THE SERVER MENU

The synchronization process allows ERwin to actively connect to the physical database system, Sybase in this case, and generates a list of unsynchronized ERwin and Sybase tables, as shown in Figure 19.47.

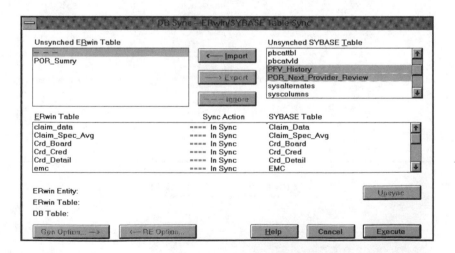

FIGURE 19.47 LIST OF UNSYNCHRONIZED ERWIN AND SYBASE TABLES

Scroll through the Unsynched Sybase table window and click on the **PFV_History** table and the **Import** button. This moves PFV_History from the Unsynched Sybase table window to the Sync Action ListBox with Rev Eng indicated, as in Figure 19.48.

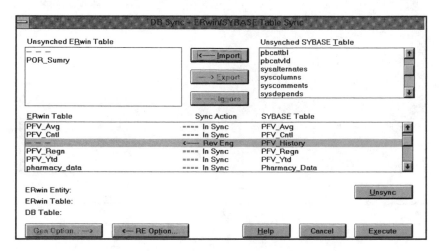

FIGURE 19.48 SYNC ACTION LISTBOX WITH REVERSE ENGINEER CHOSEN

Clicking on the **Execute** button causes ERwin to reverse-engineer PFV_History into the model. During the synchronization process ERwin asks if you want to have ERwin lay out the model. Choose **NO**, as the synchronization process may cause tables to be overlayed as shown in Figure 19.49.

Once ERwin puts the table into the model, move the table to an appropriate place, choose the **PB Extended Att Editor** from the Editor menu, and open the table by double-clicking on its name. The PowerBuilder Extended Attribute editor opens as shown in Figure 19.50.

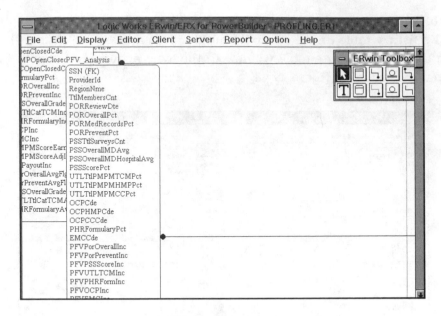

FIGURE 19.49 OVERLAYED TABLES

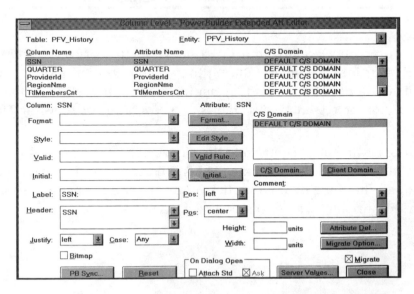

FIGURE 19.50 THE POWERBUILDER EXTENDED ATTRIBUTE EDITOR

Click the **PB Sync...** button to synchronize the model's PFV_History table with the PowerBuilder extended attributes stored in PowerBuilder's data dictionary tables within the Sybase physical database. The extended-attribute synchronization process will check the ERwin column-level extended attributes against PowerBuilder's and display the unsynchronized column's extended attributes in a ListBox, as shown in Figure 19.51.

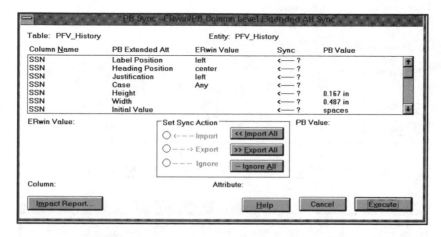

FIGURE 19.51 THE UNSYNCHRONIZED COLUMN'S EXTENDED ATTRIBUTES

At this point, an impact report can be viewed or printed or an appropriate sync action can be selected for any or all attributes. Click the **Import All** button since we want all the extended attributes for PFV_History to be imported into the model. Then click the **Execute** button to begin the import. During the extended-attribute import process ERwin may find that some columns use an edit mask that was not imported into the model. If this is the case, it is necessary to click the **Edit Style** button in the PowerBuilder Extended Attribute editor and open the **Edit Style Editor** shown in Figure 19.52 to import the edit masks.

This is done by clicking the **PB Sync...** button in the Edit Style editor, which will begin the edit style synchronization and open the ERwin/PB Edit Style Sync window as shown in Figure 19.53.

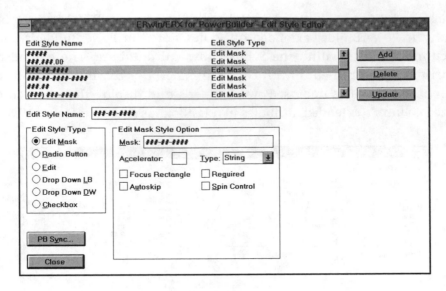

FIGURE 19.52 EDIT STYLE EDITOR

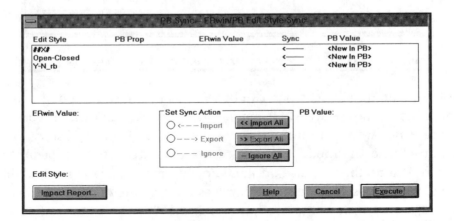

FIGURE 19.53 ERWIN/PB EDIT STYLE SYNC WINDOW

Click on **Import All** and **Execute** to import all the edit styles from the physical database PowerBuilder data dictionary table into the ERwin model. Once the edit style synchronization is complete, we need to resynchronize the extended-column attributes because they were not all imported due to not having all the edit masks in the model. This is done by clicking the **PB Sync...** button in the PowerBuilder Extended Attribute editor. The ERwin/PB Column Level Extended Att Sync window opens, as shown in Figure 19.54

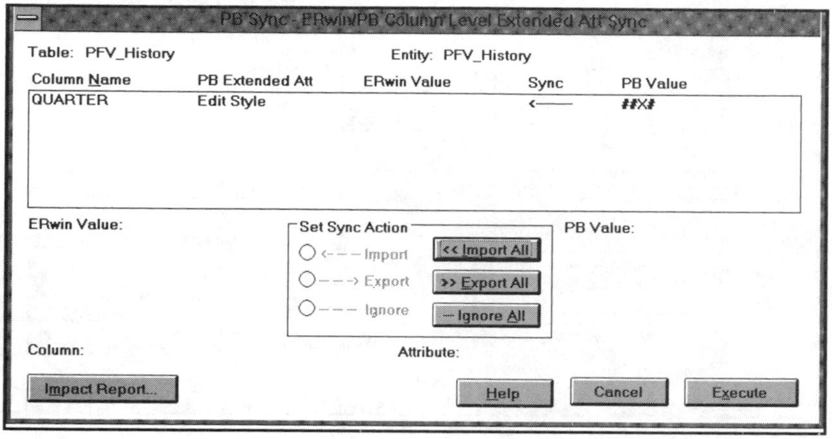

FIGURE 19.54 THE ERWIN/PB COLUMN LEVEL EXTENDED ATT SYNC WINDOW

This indicates that QUARTER column's edit style needs to be imported into the model. Click the **Import All** and **Execute** buttons. The table definition and PowerBuilder extended attributes are now stored in the ERwin model, as shown in Figure 19.55.

Now that PFV_History is in the model, we discover that we need to add three columns—CCMemberCnt, HMPMemberCnt, and PSSTtlSurveyCnt—to the table. This is done with the Entity Attribute Editor, shown in Figure 19.56, which we select from the Editor menu. Double-click on the **PFV_History** entity.

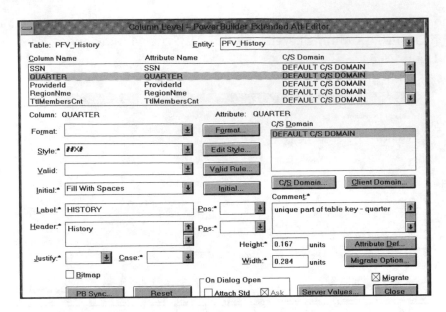

FIGURE 19.55 PFV_HISTORY

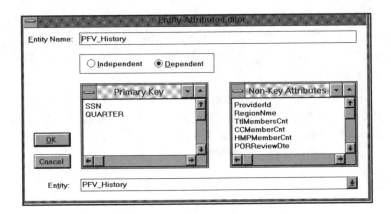

FIGURE 19.56 THE ENTITY ATTRIBUTE EDITOR

The three attributes to be added are not key attributes. We scroll the Non-Key Attribute ListBox to the location where we want to add the attributes, position the cursor at the end of the previous attribute (TtlMembersCnt), press **Enter** on the keyboard and add the two attributes, find the appropri-

ate location for PSSTtlSurveyCnt, and then add it. Now that the attributes
are added, select the **Database Schema Editor**, shown in Figure 19.57,
from the Editor menu.

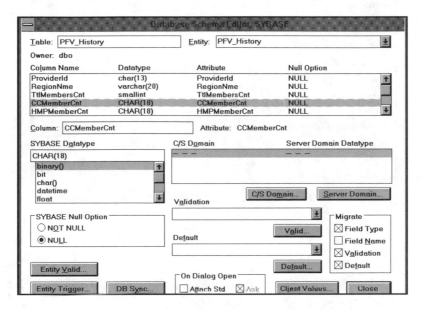

FIGURE 19.57 THE DATABASE SCHEMA EDITOR

Make sure that the physical column data types are correct. The default
data type when an attribute is added is **CHAR(18)**, which is not the correct
data type for the attributes just added. Verify that the column's NULL
option is set to **NULL**. Once this is done and the data types are correct, as
shown in Figure 19.58, choose the **PB Extended Att Editor** from the Editor
menu and reopen the table. Note that the label and header for the new
columns shown in Figure 19.59 are the same as the names of the columns.

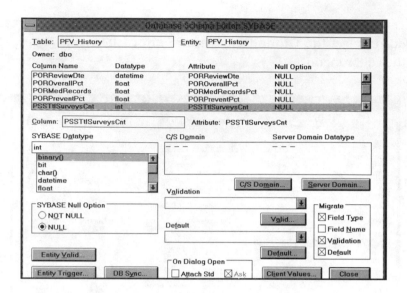

FIGURE 19.58 THE CORRECT DATATYPES

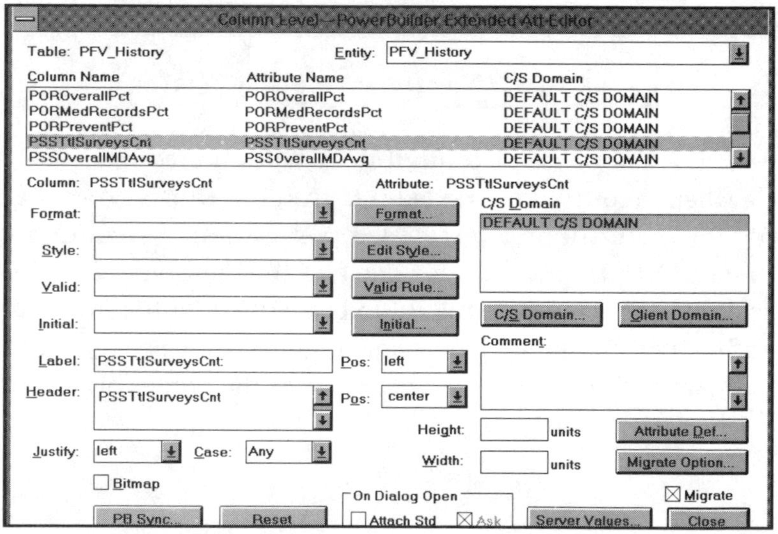

FIGURE 19.59 THE NEW COLUMNS

Enter the extended attributes for the columns just added, as shown in Figure 19.60 and resynchronize with the physical database system by clicking the **PB Sync...** button. This time ERwin detects that there are three columns in the ERwin PFV_History entity that are not in the Sybase table, as shown in Figure 19.61.

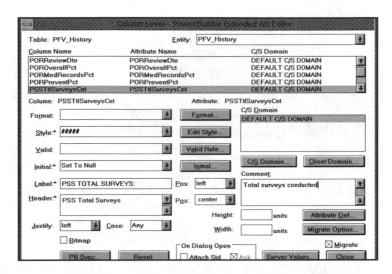

FIGURE 19.60 THE EXTENDED ATTRIBUTES

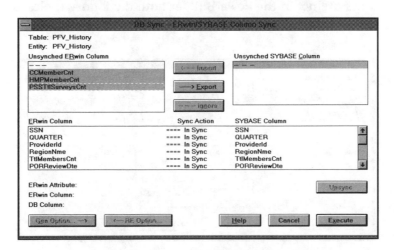

FIGURE 19.61 ERWIN DETECTS UNSYNCHED COLUMNS

Since we want these new columns in the Sybase table, press the **Export** button. This moves the unsynched columns from the Unsynched ERwin Column window to the Sync Action ListBox, as shown in Figure 19.62.

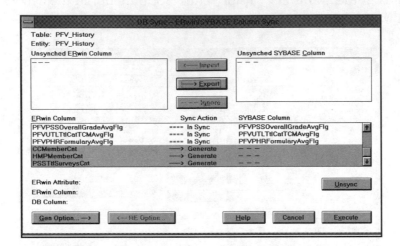

FIGURE 19.62 THE SYNC ACTION LISTBOX

Click the **Execute** button to export the new columns to the Sybase PFV_History table. ERwin then detects that the extended attributes for the new columns are not in the PowerBuilder data dictionary tables, as shown in Figure 19.63.

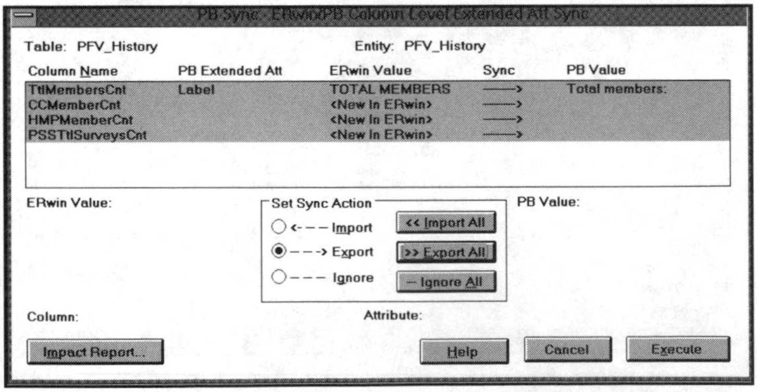

FIGURE 19.63 ERWIN DETECTS OUT-OF-SYNC ATTRIBUTES

Since we want the ERwin extended attributes to be placed into PowerBuilder's data dictionary, click the **Export All** and **Execute** buttons to export these attributes to the appropriate Sybase database tables.

Now that the table is updated in Sybase and the extended attributes are exported, let's use the PowerBuilder Database painter to view the table. This is shown in Figure 19.64.

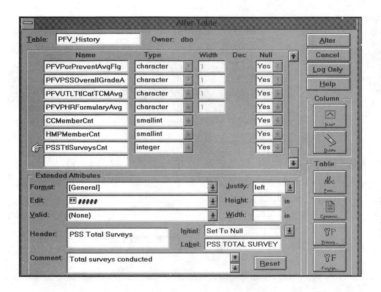

FIGURE 19.64 THE PFV_HISTORY TABLE

We notice that the columns we added are at the bottom of the table and not where we want them! This is due to the fact that when a physical database table is altered and new columns are added, the new columns are always added after the last column currently in the table. Since this is not where we want the columns, we will drop the physical database table using the PowerBuilder Database painter, return to the ERwin data model, and resync the physical database system with ERwin. This will allow ERwin to re-create the table with the columns in the correct order. We do this with the ERwin PowerBuilder Extended Attribute editor by pressing the **PB Sync...** button. During the synchronization process, ERwin detects the fact that there is no longer a Sybase table to sync with PFV_History and, as shown in Figure 19.65, asks us what table sync option to use. We want to re-create the PFV_History table so we click the **Generate New Sybase Table** option and click **OK**. ERwin then generates SQL to actively create the new PFV_History table in the Sybase database and add the extended attributes to the Sybase PowerBuilder data dictionary tables. Figure 19.66 shows the order of the ERwin entity.

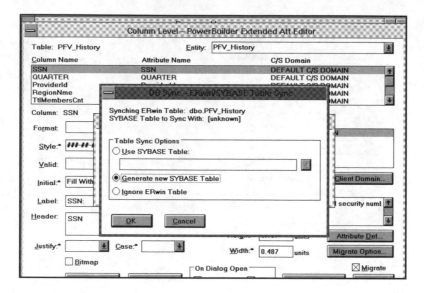

FIGURE 19.65 ERWIN DETECTS A MISSING TABLE

We see in Figure 19.67 that the column order of the ERwin entity and the Sybase table are the same.

In addition, the Sybase table, viewed with the PowerBuilder Database painter, has the extended attributes that were exported from the ERwin model. In Figure 19.68, we see that the foreign and primary key definitions for the table were also exported from ERwin. The new PFV_History table is created, all PowerBuilder extended attributes have been placed into the physical database system, and referential integrity constraints are in place.

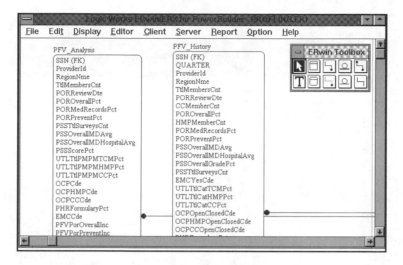

FIGURE 19.66 THE ERwin PFV_HISTORY ENTITY

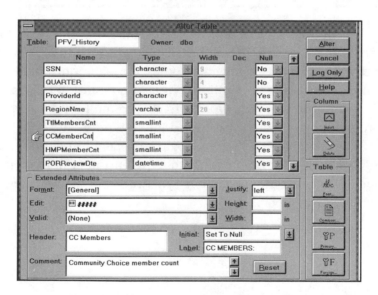

FIGURE 19.67 NOTICE THE COLUMN ORDER

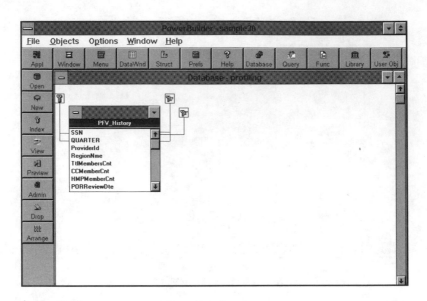

FIGURE 19.68 THE FOREIGN AND PRIMARY KEY DEFINITIONS WERE EXPORTED

In a similar manner, ERwin can be used to move a physical database schema from one platform to another or to make a copy of a production physical database for development purposes. One caution should be noted when you use ERwin across multiple physical database platforms. ERwin does not always translate data types correctly; a small int data type in one server target database may be translated into a binary data type in another server target database. If the ERwin model is small, it is best to use the Database Schema editor after changing between target databases and to review each column's data type before synchronizing the new target database with the ERwin model.

CHAPTER TWENTY

SQL BASICS

This chapter presents a basic introduction to SQL for the application programmer. The SQL statements covered in this chapter include the following:

NONCURSOR SQL

CONNECT	Create a session with a specified database
SELECT	Retrieve specific rows from the specified tables
INSERT	Insert a row in the specified table
UPDATE	Update the rows of a table
DELETE	Delete rows from a tables
COMMIT	Make all changes in the current transaction to the database permanent
ROLLBACK	Back-out all changes to the database made in the current transaction
DISCONNECT	End the database session

Cursor Operations

DECLARE Cursor	Define a cursor and its associated SELECT statement
OPEN	Execute the SELECT cursor's statement
FETCH	Retrieve one row of the cursor's result set
UPDATE WHERE CURRENT OF Cursor	Update rows touched by this cursor
DELETE WHERE CURRENT OF Cursor	Delete rows touched by this cursor
CLOSE Cursor	Shut down the cursor

Our primary focus here will be on the SELECT statement.

The SQL Language

One of the fundamental requirements of the relational data model is a high-level language that expresses relational operations on tabular structured data stored in relational database management systems (RDBMS). The most popular relational language currently is Structured Query Language (SQL, often pronounced as *sequel*). The SQL language is based on relational algebra constructs.

SQL has been standardized by several organizations, including ANSI. This accounts for part of its popularity. Other factors accounting for the popularity of SQL include its ease of use, English-language-like constructs, and SQL application portability across a number of vendor database systems. The ANSI committee has finalized a second version of SQL, SQL2, which greatly extends the previous SQL standard. SQL2 includes data integrity constraints.

The intent of SQL (or any relational language, for that matter) is to provide a method of performing operations from the conceptual view of the database. The access is set-oriented and is implemented through the content and structure (schema) of the database system, not by using a record number or the address of a record.

SQL is a sublanguage that can be placed into a programming language, such as C or COBOL, that has no direct method to express relational database operations. In these host languages, SQL statements are embedded and then precompiled into database library calls. In 4GL systems, such as PowerBuilder, SQL statements are also embedded into PowerScript code but require no additional processing (such as a precompiling). Host variables are used to move data values to and from the SQL statements that are being executed. This technique is referred to as *dynamic SQL*.

For simpler applications, SQL can be hidden from PowerBuilder developers to a large degree. SQL queries can be created through a graphical interface called a painter, and PowerViewer handles all the programmatic functions.

Though PowerBuilder and other 4GL tools greatly ease the creation and use of SQL statements for the developer, that will only be suitable for the initial stages of development. A successful client-server developer must be fluent with at least a subset of the SQL language. A good deal of the SQL language is involved with Database Administrator (DBA) level functions. Client-server developers, on the other hand, are interested in the SQL statements necessary for data access from their application's view.

The most important SQL statements for the applications developer are:

- **SELECT**—a statement that gets data from database tables.
- **INSERT**—places new rows into a table.
- **UPDATE**—modifies values in a table.
- **DELETE**—removes rows from a table.
- **COMMIT**—makes all changes in the current transaction to the database permanent.
- **ROLLBACK**—back-out all changes to the database made in the current transaction.
- **CONNECT**—start a session with the RDBMS.
- **DISCONNECT**—terminate a session with the RDBMS.

Applications may occasionally create or drop tables or use a few of the other SQL statements. However, more than 90% of applications will limit their use of SQL to these statements.

Connecting to the Database

Before any operations can occur between an application and the database, you must establish a database session, which is also referred to as a *database connection*. The SQL connect statement establishes this session. A connection is to a particular RDBMS, a specific database, and a specific account associated with the database. Each database session has an SQL Communications Area (SQLCA) that is used to communicate information between the application and the RDBMS. One of the items of special interest to an application is the SQLCode, which communicates the success or failure of an SQL statement execution from the RDBMS to the application. A successful SQL statement execution is indicated by a zero (0) SQLCode. The SQLCode should be checked by the application after each SQL statement to verify that the statement completed successfully.

```
connect;
IF SQLCA.SQLCode < 0 THEN
    MessageBox('DB Error', 'Connect Failed')
END IF
```

If the connect was successful, then you can execute the other SQL statements. The connection will remain intact until a disconnect statement is executed. All statements between a connect and the disconnect are said to be executed in the context of this connection. When you are ready to close the application, you should end the database session with the disconnect statement.

```
disconnect;
IF SQLCA.SQLCode < 0 THEN
    MessageBox('DB Error', 'Disconnect Failed')
END IF
```

If you do not end the session with a disconnect, the RDBMS will issue a disconnect when the program terminates.

TRANSACTIONS

A set of one or more SQL statements taken together as an atomic unit of work is called a *transaction*. A transaction will ensure either that all the statements in the set are applied to the database or that all the statements are canceled. The first transaction begins immediately after a successful connection to the database. As you apply changes (inserts, updates, deletions) to tables during a transaction, the changes are only applied temporarily to the database. To make the changes permanent, you must issue a COMMIT statement to the RDBMS. If an error has occurred and you do not wish to commit the changes, you can back-out the changes by issuing a ROLLBACK statement to the RDBMS. This transaction ends when either a COMMIT or a ROLLBACK statement is issued. At this point, a new transaction begins. If you disconnect from the database without issuing a final commit (or rollback), the RDBMS will usually implicitly issue the commit for you.

Consider the following statements:

```
UPDATE cust_order SET balance = balance - 100
   WHERE ordnum = 12345;
UPDATE line_item SET extended_price = extended_price - 100
   WHERE ordnum = 12345 and partname = 'consulting';
```

In this example, we are deducting $100.00 from the customer order number 12345 and a corresponding part in the line-item table. It is essential that either both these statements succeed or neither should be applied to the database, otherwise the credit will not take place as intended. In order to ensure this result, these two statements are issued within the same transaction. If both statement execute correctly, we will commit the transaction, otherwise we will rollback the transaction.

```
commit; // end the previous transaction.
    //Not necessary if there where no previous updates to the
    //database
```

```
UPDATE cust_order SET balance = balance - 100
    WHERE ordnum = 12345;
IF SQLCA.SQLCode = 0 THEN
    UPDATE line_item SET extended_price =
    extended_price - 100
        WHERE ordnum = 12345 and partname = 'consulting';
    IF SQLCA.SQLCode = 0 THEN
        commit;
    ELSE
        rollback;
    END IF
ELSE
    rollback;
END IF
```

SELECT Statement

The SQL SELECT statement performs the relational algebra operations of selection, projection, and theta-join. In a selection, either all or some of the rows from a table are returned based on the conditions you specify. A projection returns all or some of the columns in a table. A join is the relationship between two tables that is based on the values in specified table fields. A select statement consists of three distinct parts: the select list, the FROM clause, and, the WHERE clause. The select list tells the RDBMS which table columns or expressions you want returned. The FROM clause specifies the tables you want rows returned from. The WHERE clause restricts what table rows will be returned to you. The SELECT statement, therefore, finds the set of tuples from one or more tables that meet the value restrictions specified in the WHERE clause. The result of the SELECT is a set of tuples that create a report. The columns that appear in the resulting set may be a subset of the attributes of the select tables.

An example of a SELECT statement is:

```
SELECT * FROM cust_order WHERE ordnum = 12345 ;
```

The result of this select is shown in Table 20.1.

Table 20.1 Result of Select Statement

ORDNUM	CUSTNUM	DUEDATE	BALANCE	DATE_DUE
12345	777	1994-09-01	5515.75	9/1/94

When formulating a SELECT statement, the best starting point is usually the FROM clause.

The FROM clause lists the tables, such as CUST_ORDER and LINE_ITEM, involved in the query and determines the other choices for values specified in the remaining clauses. Next, consider which columns, functions, and/or constants you wish to retrieve from the tables in the FROM clause. These are listed in the SELECT clause. If you wish to retrieve all columns then the asterisk (*) can be used as short-hand notation rather than explicitly listing all the columns. This is equivalent to using the SELECT ALL option in the PowerBuilder SQL Painter.

The simplest selection is an unconditional single table reference that retrieves all the columns in the table. This is a SELECT statement where the select clause is represented by * and there is no WHERE clause.

So the query:

```
SELECT * FROM cust_order ;
```

will list the entire customer order table on the screen. The results of this select are shown in Table 20.2.

Table 20.2 Results of Select

ORDNUM	CUSTNUM	DUEDATE	BALANCE	DATE_DUE
12121	111	1994-09-01	4001	9/1/94
12123	222	1994-09-01	3416.25	9/1/94
12345	777	1994-09-01	5515.75	9/1/94
54322	888	1994-10-29	2802	10/29/94

continued on next page

ORDNUM	CUSTNUM	DUEDATE	BALANCE	DATE_DUE
56788	111	1994-10-29	1401	10/29/94
57002	222	1994-10-29	1765	10/29/94
57009	777	1994-10-29	5920.25	10/29/94
58990	888	1994-10-29	5788.75	10/29/94
6111	111	1994-10-02	1200	10/2/94
6134	222	1994-10-02	6442.5	10/2/94
6167	333	1994-10-02	5363.75	10/2/94
74321	444	1994-10-22	4753	10/22/94
76901	555	1994-10-22	7021.75	10/22/94
7777	666	1994-10-22	400	10/22/94
8888	777	1994-11-23	2000	11/23/94
8892	777	1994-11-23	650.25	11/23/94
9900	111	1994-12-12	400	12/12/94
99001	222	1994-12-12	3767	12/12/94
9901	333	1994-12-12	627.38	12/12/94
9902	444	1994-12-12	600	12/12/94
9903	555	1994-12-12	600	12/12/94
123123	111	1994-12-12	123	12/12/94

The SELECT *clause* of the SELECT statement contains the select-list. The select-list consists of columns, constants, or expressions that you want returned. Each column reference must be to a column contained in one of the tables listed in the FROM clause. If we wish to see only the company names and the company identification number contained in the company table, the following SELECT clause would stipulate that projection.

```
SELECT company, company_id FROM company ;
```

This statement will list all the companies and their company_id from the entire company table to the screen as shown in Table 20.3.

TABLE 20.3 LIST OF COMPANIES AND COMPANY IDS

COMPANY	COMPANY_ID
ACME	222
Tech	111
D.D.E.	333
Alpha	444
T.L.A.	555
C.P.P	666
Best	777
Beta	888

The following statement would list all the regions found in the state table. It would list a region once for each state in that region:

```
SELECT region FROM state ;
```

or

```
SELECT ALL region FROM state ;
```

This is shown in the following list:

REGION
midwest
midwest
midwest
east
east
west
west

ALL tells the SELECT statement to list every occurrence of each region. This is the default, so ALL is not required if that is the desired effect. The SELECT statement will not remove duplicate tuples from the result unless you explicitly specify it. In order to eliminate the duplicate listings, place DISTINCT at the beginning of the select-list:

```
SELECT DISTINCT region FROM state ;
```

This will list each region only once.

The WHERE clause of the SELECT statement lists the criteria that are applied in the selection of the output tuples. This is referred to as a search condition.

Each criteria in the search condition is of the form:

```
[NOT] <expression> <comparison operator> <expression or value>
```

where an expression can be a table column name, a constant or function, or another SELECT statement. An example of a search condition is shown by the WHERE clause in the following SQL statement:

```
SELECT * FROM cust_order WHERE ordnum = 12345 ;
```

This will select only the tuple(s) that have a value of 12345 for ordnum. The following code:

```
SELECT * FROM cust_order WHERE NOT ordnum = 12345 ;
```

or

```
SELECT * FROM cust_order WHERE ordnum <> 12345 ;
```

will select only the tuple(s) that do not have a value of 12345 for ordnum.

In the case of Boolean expressions the format of the restrictions is:

```
[NOT] <expression>
```

as in

```
SELECT * FROM company WHERE NOT state = 'OH';
```

This will list all the customer companies that are in any state except Ohio.

If there is more than one table in the FROM clause, then the WHERE clause will almost always contain a join expression for each table. The tables being joined do not require the joining columns to be indexed, but joins on indexed columns will be much faster.

An example of a SELECT statement with a join condition and a WHERE clause is:

```
SELECT co.company, co.company_id, ord.ordnum, ord.balance,
    ord.date_due
    FROM company co, cust_order ord
        WHERE     co.company_id IN (111, 777) AND
                    co.company_id = ord.custnum;
```

This statement shows the three main clauses in a SELECT statement. The join condition is discussed in more detail later. The result of this select is shown in Table 20.4.

TABLE 20.4 RESULT OF SELECT

ORDNUM	CUSTNUM	DUEDATE	BALANCE	DATE_DUE
Tech	111	12121	4001	9/1/94
Best	777	12345	5515.75	9/1/94
Tech	111	56788	1401	10/29/94
Best	777	57009	5920.25	10/29/94
Tech	111	6111	1200	10/2/94
Best	777	8888	2000	11/23/94
Best	777	8892	650.25	11/23/94
Tech	111	9900	400	12/12/94
Tech	111	123123	123	

A table may be assigned a correlation name in the FROM clause by following the table name with the desired correlation name. The correlation name is an alias for a table that is used to reference the table in the rest of the SELECT statement. This is most useful for assigning shorter names to tables and for establishing correlated references in subqueries. Correlated subqueries are discussed later in this chapter.

The term *alias* is used to mean a synonym for a table name.

```
SELECT co.company, co.company_id, ord.ordnum, ord.balance,
    ord.date_due
    FROM company co, cust_order ord
        WHERE    co.company_id IN (111, 777) AND
                    co.company_id = ord.custnum;
```

In this statement the alias 'co' is established in the FROM clause to refer to the COMPANY table and the alias 'ord' is established to refer to the CUST_ORDER table. The establishment of table alias name occurs in the FROM clause. The alias names are used in the SELECT list and WHERE clause to refer to the COMPANY and CUST_ORDER tables and to qualify column references.

The 'LIKE' predicate is very useful for selection based on a character string pattern that is to be matched in a particular column. It allows the use of wildcards in the pattern being selected. It is of the following form:

```
<column> [NOT] LIKE <string-pattern-to-be-matched>
```

In Table 20.5, we have assigned a number to each name for reference in the following examples. We will be referencing the table only through the NAME column, which is a character string field, and referring to the tuples selected by the value of NUMBER in each tuple.

TABLE 20.5 THE TEST TABLE

TEST	NAME	NUMBER
	Kristen McKay	1
	Kyle Russell	2
	Nicole Russell	3
	Christine McKay	4
	Chris Russell	5
	Kris McKey	6

To select the tuple for NUMBER = 1 we could use:

```
SELECT * FROM test WHERE name = 'Kristen McKay';
```

or

```
SELECT * FROM test WHERE name LIKE 'Kristen McKay';
```

The LIKE predicate is most useful when used with the wildcard characters:

% means to match any set of characters

_ means to match any single character

If we wish to select all the tuples with the last name 'McKay' we would use the following query:

```
SELECT * FROM test WHERE name LIKE '%McKay';
```

This says to select all tuples that end with 'McKay,' with anything preceding the 'McKay' and would return tuples number 1 and 4.

To select all the tuples that have a first name beginning with a 'K,' we would use the following query:

```
SELECT * FROM test WHERE name LIKE 'K%' ;
```

This would return tuples 1,2, and 6.

To select all tuples that have 'Mc' in them, use the following:

```
SELECT * FROM test WHERE name LIKE '%Mc%' ;
```

This would return tuples 1, 4, and 6.

Suppose that we wanted to find the tuple for someone whose last name is "McKey," but we are not sure of the spelling of her first name: it could be "Chris," "Christine," or "Kris." How can we find the correct tuple (assuming there are many tuples with the last name "McKey")?

```
SELECT * FROM test WHERE name LIKE '%ris%McKey' ;
```

will find the correct last name ("McKey") and will find the first names that contain the set of letters "ris." So this query will find "Kris" or "Chris" or "Christine."

If you wanted to find all the tuples with a last name that begins with 'McK,' then contains any single letter, and ends with "y," use the following:

```
SELECT * FROM test WHERE name LIKE '%McK_y' ;
```

This would select tuples 1, 4, and 6.

To select all the tuples that do not have a last name of 'McKey' use the NOT LIKE predicate:

```
SELECT * FROM test WHERE name NOT LIKE '%McKey' ;
```

This would select tuples 1 through 5.

If you are not sure of the case of the name entries use the UPPER function:

```
SELECT * FROM test WHERE UPPER(name) LIKE 'KRIS%' ;
```

This would select tuples 1 and 6.

If you wish to search for a string that contains a **%** or a _ then you must use the escape clause of the LIKE predicate to specify a special character that you will use to precede the **%** or _ for which you are looking:

```
SELECT * from booklist WHERE title LIKE '%he \% %' ESCAPE '\' ;
```

This would find the title "The % Method of Investment." Only the **%** immediately preceded by the escape character (\) will be taken literally. The other occurrences will be treated as a wildcard as normal.

The equals comparison (=) operator will always act with padded comparisons:

```
SELECT * FROM test WHERE name = 'Kris';
```

This will return no records as the comparison is made against "Kris   ", because 'Kris' was shorter than the name column and was padded out (with spaces) to an equal length.

Multiple conditions can be combined using the *and* or *or* connectives. To list the companies that are in Ohio and in those cities that are in the first half of the alphabet, the following statement would formulate the correct query:

```
SELECT * FROM company
    WHERE state = 'OH' AND city < 'N' ;
```

as shown in Table 20.6.

TABLE 20.6 THE QUERY RESULT SET

COMPANY	COMPANY_ID	REGION	CITY	STATE	ZIP	PHONE
D.D.E.	333	east	Cleveland	OH	12312	2162312112
C.P.P	666	midwest	Dayton	OH	23232	5132546545
Best	777	midwest	Columbus	OH	32323	3215456346
Beta	888	midwest	Akron	OH	43222	1231234534

To list the companies that are in Ohio or Indiana or New York, the following would formulate the correct query:

```
SELECT * FROM company
    WHERE state = 'OH' OR state = 'IN' OR state = 'NY' ;
```

with the result shown in Table 20.7.

TABLE 20.7 THE RESULT SET

COMPANY	COMPANY_ID	REGION	CITY	STATE	ZIP	PHONE
Tech	111	east	New York	NY	12311	1231231233
D.D.E.	333	east	Cleveland	OH	12312	2162312112
T.L.A.	555	midwest	Fort Wayne	IN	33212	3321212312
C.P.P	666	midwest	Dayton	OH	23232	5132546545
Best	777	midwest	Columbus	OH	32323	3215456346
Beta	888	midwest	Akron	OH	43222	1231234534

The IN operator offers a shorter method of expressing the same query.

```
SELECT * FROM company
    WHERE state IN ('OH', 'IN', 'NY') ;
```

The connectives can be combined as follows to list all the companies in the prior table to D in the alphabet within Ohio and all the companies after T in the alphabet in the state of New York:

```
SELECT * FROM company
    WHERE (state = 'OH' AND city < 'D') OR
        (state = 'NY' AND company >= 'T');
```

as shown in Table 20.8.

TABLE 20.8 THE QUERY RESULT SET

COMPANY	COMPANY_ID	REGION	CITY	STATE	ZIP	PHONE
Tech	111	east	New York	NY	12311	1231231233
D.D.E.	333	east	Cleveland	OH	12312	2162312112
Best	777	midwest	Columbus	OH	32323	3215456346
Beta	888	midwest	Akron	OH	43222	1231234534

The parentheses are for clarity and not required here because the *and* connective has a higher precedence than the *or* connective. This means that *and* binds the state and company restrictions on both sides before *or* is applied.

The order of precedence (from highest to lowest) within the SELECT statement is:

NOT

AND

OR

A number of column functions such as COUNT, SUM, AVG, MIN, and MAX are standard ANSI functions.

```
SELECT COUNT(ordnum) FROM cust_order ;
```

will count the number of orders in the customer order table. This will be the count of the number of rows or tuples in the invoice table. It could also be stated as:

```
SELECT COUNT(*) FROM cust_order ;
```

To count the number of unique order numbers in the customer order table where the balance is due sometime during 1994 and prior to Jan 1, 1995, we can use:

```
SELECT COUNT(DISTINCT ordnum) FROM cust_order
    WHERE date_due >= 'Jan 1 1994' AND
    date_due <= 'Dec 31 1994';
```

or

```
SELECT COUNT(DISTINCT ordnum) FROM cust_order
    WHERE date_due BETWEEN 'Jan 1 1994'
    AND 'Dec 31 1994';
```

The next example does the same thing but uses a built-in function YEAR provided by some vendors to extract the year from the date column:

```
SELECT COUNT(DISTINCT ordnum) FROM cust_order
    WHERE YEAR(date_due) = 1994;
```

To list the largest balance, the smallest balance, the total balances, and the average balance for 1994 use the following:

```
SELECT MAX(balance), MIN(balance), SUM(balance),
AVG(balance)
    FROM cust_order
        WHERE date_due BETWEEN 'Jan 1 1994'
        AND 'Dec 31 1994';
```

You can create a table as a result of a SELECT statement:

```
CREATE TABLE cust2 AS SELECT * FROM company ;
```

This creates a copy of the company customer table named "cust2."

If you wish to specify the order of the result, the ORDER BY clause allows the output to be sorted on an expression involving columns of the tables in the FROM clause. The ordering can be in ASCending (the default) or DESCending order:

```
SELECT * FROM company ORDER BY state, city, company DESC;
```

The output, as shown in Table 20.9, will be sorted first by state (in ascending order), then within each state it will be sorted by city (in ascending order);

within each city the records will be sorted by company, but in descending order. Note the difference between Tables 20.6, 20.7, 20.8 and Table 20.9 where the first three were in database retrieval order and were not sorted.

TABLE 20.9 ORDERED BY STATE, CITY AND COMPANY

COMPANY	COMPANY_ID	REGION	CITY	STATE	ZIP	PHONE
T.L.A.	555	midwest	Fort Wayne	IN	33212	3123124512
Alpha	444	east	Mills	NJ	12312	1222297312
Tech	111	east	New York	NY	12311	1231231233
Beta	888	midwest	Akron	OH	43222	1231234534
D.D.E.	333	east	Cleveland	OH	12312	2162312112
Best	777	midwest	Columbus	OH	32323	3215456346
C.P.P	666	midwest	Dayton	OH	23232	5132546545
ACME	222	midwest	Cincinnati	WA	45040	5135551234

RELATIONSHIPS

The feature that gives the relational model most of its character and a great deal of its power is the way in which relationships between tables are established. A relationship between two tables is established by correlating fields from one table to fields in another table. The technique of dynamically relating two tables by column values is a fundamental feature of the relational model and is called a *join*.

A logical interrelation between tables is expressed by the *join expression* in the SQL SELECT statement. In a join expression a column from each related table is specified. The tables are linked dynamically by the comparison of the column values in two tables, which are compared on a row-by-row basis based on one of the relational operators such as =, < >, <, or >. The joining columns are usually related in some manner, as are the tuples in the two tables.

A join is almost always used when data from more than one table are being referenced.

The column and value relationships between these tables are shown here.

COMPANY:

COMPANY	COMPANY_ID	REGION	CITY	STATE	ZIP	PHONE
ACME	222	midwest	Cincinnati	WA	45040	5135551234
Tech	111	east	New York	NY	12311	1231231233
D.D.E.	333	east	Cleveland	OH	12312	2162312112
Alpha	444	east	Mills	NJ	12312	1222297312
T.L.A.	555	midwest	Fort Wayne	IN	33212	1231231245
C.P.P	666	midwest	Dayton	OH	23232	5132546545
Best	777	midwest	Columbus	OH	32323	3215456346
Beta	888	midwest	Akron	OH	43222	1231234534

REP_SSN	CREDIT_LIMIT	LAST_ORDER_DATE	ADDRESS	ACTIVE
111223333	1500000.5	9/9/94	123 Main	y
222334444	0.55	10/10/94	1122 Apple	y
333445555	25000	10/20/94	123 Winters Lane	y
111223333	55000	10/11/94	91287 First St.	y
222334444	125000	10/14/94	302 Second St.	y
333445555	123123.5	9/11/94	110 Third St.	y
111223333	90125	9/28/94	9 Chris Court	y
333445555	500125	9/29/94	991 Kyle Lane	y

COMMENT

This is our best customer. Take special care to provide the best service to this company.

continued on next page

COMMENT

This company must pre-pay for all future orders.

Alice is taking over this account, use her as the sales rep for all future sales.

CUST_ORDER:

ORDNUM	CUSTNUM	DUEDATE	BALANCE	DATE_DUE
12121	111	19940901	4001	9/1/94
12123	222	19940901	3416.25	9/1/94
12345	777	19940901	5515.75	9/1/94
54322	888	19941029	2802	10/29/94
56788	111	19941029	1401	10/29/94
57002	222	19941029	1765	10/29/94
57009	777	19941029	5920.25	10/29/94
58990	888	19941029	5788.75	10/29/94
6111	111	19941002	1200	10/2/94
6134	222	19941002	6442.5	10/2/94
6167	333	19941002	5363.75	10/2/94
74321	444	19941022	4753	10/22/94
76901	555	19941022	7021.75	10/22/94
7777	666	19941022	400	10/22/94
8888	777	19941123	2000	11/23/94
8892	777	19941123	650.25	11/23/94
9900	111	19941212	400	12/12/94
99001	222	19941212	3767	12/12/94
9901	333	19941212	627.3800049	12/12/94
9902	444	19941212	600	12/12/94
9903	555	19941212	600	12/12/94
123123	111	19941212	123	

In this example, two tables, COMPANY and CUST_ORDER, have a relationship that is expressed by the joining value, which represents the customer's ID in each table. COMPANY.custnum and CUST_ORDER.company_id are two columns that have the same type and the same meaning. Both tables are referring to the same entity when they refer to 777 as a particular customer's ID for the company. In order to find the ORDERs that have been placed by 'Best' company, we look for the matching values of company_id (777) in the CUST_ORDER.custnum column, and we find four orders: 12345, 57009, 8888, and 8892. This is expressed by the following SQL statement:

```
SELECT ordnum FROM company, cust_order
    WHERE company.company ='BEST' AND
        company.company_id = cust_order.custnum;
```

If we wish to select a range of customers with COMPANY.company_id between '777' and '888' inclusive and to list information about those customers and all the invoices they have generated, this requires that a join be executed between COMPANY and CUST_ORDER on the customer ID columns of each table.

The SQL SELECT statement needed to return the desired result is:

```
SELECT cust.company_id, cust.company, ord.ordnum,
    ord.date_due
    FROM company cust, cust_order ord
    WHERE cust.company_id BETWEEN 777 AND 888 AND
        cust.company_id = ord.custnum
    ORDER BY cust.company, ord.ordnum;
```

Table 20.10 shows the result:

TABLE 20.10 THE QUERY RESULT SET

COMPANY_ID	COMPANY	ORDNUM	DATE_DUE
777	Best	12345	9/1/94
777	Best	57009	10/29/94

continued on next page

COMPANY_ID	COMPANY	ORDNUM	DATE_DUE
777	Best	8888	11/23/94
777	Best	8892	11/23/94
888	Beta	54322	10/29/94
888	Beta	58990	10/29/94

CARTESIAN PRODUCT

The Cartesian product of two tables is a new table having each tuple in the first table joined with every tuple in the second table. This is conceptually important to understand. The Cartesian product operation is expressed in the SQL SELECT statement by listing two or more tables in the FROM clause without a join condition expressed in the WHERE clause.

Again, consider the two tables COMPANY and CUST_ORDER shown in the previous section. The result of

```
SELECT cust.company_id, cust.company, ord.ordnum, ord.date_due
FROM company cust, cust_order ord
ORDER BY cust.company, ord.ordnum;
```

would be a 176-row table since company has 8 rows and cust_order has 22 rows. Due to the size of this table, only the beginning and end of the table are shown in Table 20.11.

TABLE 20.11 THE RESULT SET

COMPANY_ID	COMPANY	ORDNUM	DATE_DUE
222	ACME	12121	9/1/94
222	ACME	12123	9/1/94
222	ACME	123123	

continued on next page

COMPANY_ID	COMPANY	ORDNUM	DATE_DUE
222	ACME	12345	9/1/94
222	ACME	54322	10/29/94
222	ACME	56788	10/29/94
222	ACME	57002	10/29/94
222	ACME	57009	10/29/94
222	ACME	58990	10/29/94
222	ACME	6111	10/2/94
222	ACME	6134	10/2/94
222	ACME	6167	10/2/94
222	ACME	74321	10/22/94
222	ACME	76901	10/22/94
222	ACME	7777	10/22/94
222	ACME	8888	11/23/94
222	ACME	8892	11/23/94
222	ACME	9900	12/12/94
222	ACME	99001	12/12/94
222	ACME	9901	12/12/94
222	ACME	9902	12/12/94
222	ACME	9903	12/12/94
444	Alpha	12121	9/1/94
444	Alpha	12123	9/1/94
444	Alpha	123123	
444	Alpha	12345	9/1/94
444	Alpha	54322	10/29/94
444	Alpha	56788	10/29/94
444	Alpha	57002	10/29/94

continued on next page

COMPANY_ID	COMPANY	ORDNUM	DATE_DUE
444	Alpha	57009	10/29/94
444	Alpha	58990	10/29/94
444	Alpha	6111	10/2/94
444	Alpha	6134	10/2/94
444	Alpha	6167	10/2/94
444	Alpha	74321	10/22/94
444	Alpha	76901	10/22/94
444	Alpha	7777	10/22/94
444	Alpha	8888	11/23/94
444	Alpha	8892	11/23/94
444	Alpha	9900	12/12/94
444	Alpha	99001	12/12/94
444	Alpha	9901	12/12/94
444	Alpha	9902	12/12/94
444	Alpha	9903	12/12/94
777	Best	12121	9/1/94
777	Best	12123	9/1/94
777	Best	123123	
777	Best	12345	9/1/94
777	Best	54322	10/29/94
777	Best	56788	10/29/94
777	Best	57002	10/29/94
777	Best	57009	10/29/94
777	Best	58990	10/29/94
777	Best	6111	10/2/94
777	Best	6134	10/2/94

continued on next page

COMPANY_ID	COMPANY	ORDNUM	DATE_DUE
777	Best	6167	10/2/94
777	Best	74321	10/22/94
777	Best	76901	10/22/94
777	Best	7777	10/22/94
777	Best	8888	11/23/94
777	Best	8892	11/23/94
777	Best	9900	12/12/94
777	Best	99001	12/12/94
777	Best	9901	12/12/94
777	Best	9902	12/12/94
777	Best	9903	12/12/94
888	Beta	12121	9/1/94
888	Beta	12123	9/1/94
888	Beta	123123	
888	Beta	12345	9/1/94
888	Beta	54322	10/29/94
888	Beta	56788	10/29/94
888	Beta	57002	10/29/94
888	Beta	57009	10/29/94
888	Beta	58990	10/29/94
888	Beta	6111	10/2/94
888	Beta	6134	10/2/94
888	Beta	6167	10/2/94
888	Beta	74321	10/22/94
888	Beta	76901	10/22/94
888	Beta	7777	10/22/94

continued on next page

COMPANY_ID	COMPANY	ORDNUM	DATE_DUE
888	Beta	8888	11/23/94
888	Beta	8892	11/23/94
888	Beta	9900	12/12/94
888	Beta	99001	12/12/94
888	Beta	9901	12/12/94
888	Beta	9902	12/12/94
888	Beta	9903	12/12/94
666	C.P.P	12121	9/1/94
666	C.P.P	12123	9/1/94
666	C.P.P	123123	
666	C.P.P	12345	9/1/94
666	C.P.P	54322	10/29/94
666	C.P.P	56788	10/29/94
666	C.P.P	57002	10/29/94
666	C.P.P	57009	10/29/94
666	C.P.P	58990	10/29/94
666	C.P.P	6111	10/2/94
666	C.P.P	6134	10/2/94
666	C.P.P	6167	10/2/94
666	C.P.P	74321	10/22/94
666	C.P.P	76901	10/22/94
666	C.P.P	7777	10/22/94
666	C.P.P	8888	11/23/94
666	C.P.P	8892	11/23/94
666	C.P.P	9900	12/12/94
666	C.P.P	99001	12/12/94

continued on next page

COMPANY_ID	COMPANY	ORDNUM	DATE_DUE
666	C.P.P	9901	12/12/94
666	C.P.P	9902	12/12/94
666	C.P.P	9903	12/12/94
333	D.D.E.	12121	9/1/94
333	D.D.E.	12123	9/1/94
333	D.D.E.	123123	
333	D.D.E.	12345	9/1/94
333	D.D.E.	54322	10/29/94
333	D.D.E.	56788	10/29/94
333	D.D.E.	57002	10/29/94
333	D.D.E.	57009	10/29/94
333	D.D.E.	58990	10/29/94
333	D.D.E.	6111	10/2/94
333	D.D.E.	6134	10/2/94
333	D.D.E.	6167	10/2/94
333	D.D.E.	74321	10/22/94
333	D.D.E.	76901	10/22/94
333	D.D.E.	7777	10/22/94
333	D.D.E.	8888	11/23/94
333	D.D.E.	8892	11/23/94
333	D.D.E.	9900	12/12/94
333	D.D.E.	99001	12/12/94
333	D.D.E.	9901	12/12/94
333	D.D.E.	9902	12/12/94
333	D.D.E.	9903	12/12/94
555	T.L.A.	12121	9/1/94

continued on next page

COMPANY_ID	COMPANY	ORDNUM	DATE_DUE
555	T.L.A.	12123	9/1/94
555	T.L.A.	123123	
555	T.L.A.	12345	9/1/94
555	T.L.A.	54322	10/29/94
555	T.L.A.	56788	10/29/94
555	T.L.A.	57002	10/29/94
555	T.L.A.	57009	10/29/94
555	T.L.A.	58990	10/29/94
555	T.L.A.	6111	10/2/94
555	T.L.A.	6134	10/2/94
555	T.L.A.	6167	10/2/94
555	T.L.A.	74321	10/22/94
555	T.L.A.	76901	10/22/94
555	T.L.A.	7777	10/22/94
555	T.L.A.	8888	11/23/94
555	T.L.A.	8892	11/23/94
555	T.L.A.	9900	12/12/94
555	T.L.A.	99001	12/12/94
555	T.L.A.	9901	12/12/94
555	T.L.A.	9902	12/12/94
555	T.L.A.	9903	12/12/94
111	Tech	12121	9/1/94
111	Tech	12123	9/1/94
111	Tech	123123	
111	Tech	12345	9/1/94
111	Tech	54322	10/29/94

continued on next page

COMPANY_ID	COMPANY	ORDNUM	DATE_DUE
111	Tech	56788	10/29/94
111	Tech	57002	10/29/94
111	Tech	57009	10/29/94
111	Tech	58990	10/29/94
111	Tech	6111	10/2/94
111	Tech	6134	10/2/94
111	Tech	6167	10/2/94
111	Tech	74321	10/22/94
111	Tech	76901	10/22/94
111	Tech	7777	10/22/94
111	Tech	8888	11/23/94
111	Tech	8892	11/23/94
111	Tech	9900	12/12/94
111	Tech	99001	12/12/94
111	Tech	9901	12/12/94
111	Tech	9902	12/12/94
111	Tech	9903	12/12/94

The result table from a Cartesian product is of limited use, except as a basis for further restrictions. It contains some random associations between columns. It most often occurs when you forget to include a join condition between the tables. Remember that the result set can be very large since it is a Cartesian product.

MORE ON JOINS

Consider the following SELECT with a join condition between the tables COMPANY and CUST_ORDER (see Table 20.12):

```
SELECT cust.company_id, cust.company, ord.ordnum, ord.date_due
FROM company cust, cust_order ord
WHERE company_id = custnum
ORDER BY cust.company, ord.ordnum;
```

TABLE 20.12   THE JOIN RESULT

COMPANY_ID	COMPANY	ORDNUM	DATE_DUE
222	ACME	12123	9/1/94
222	ACME	57002	10/29/94
222	ACME	6134	10/2/94
222	ACME	99001	12/12/94
444	Alpha	74321	10/22/94
444	Alpha	9902	12/12/94
777	Best	12345	9/1/94
777	Best	57009	10/29/94
777	Best	8888	11/23/94
777	Best	8892	11/23/94
888	Beta	54322	10/29/94
888	Beta	58990	10/29/94
666	C.P.P	7777	10/22/94
333	D.D.E.	6167	10/2/94
333	D.D.E.	9901	12/12/94
555	T.L.A.	76901	10/22/94
555	T.L.A.	9903	12/12/94
111	Tech	12121	9/1/94
111	Tech	123123	
111	Tech	56788	10/29/94
111	Tech	6111	10/2/94
111	Tech	9900	12/12/94

The RESULT table (Table 20.12) presents a list of all the customers with the order numbers for all their orders. This certainly represents more significant information than the PRODUCT1 table. The join condition is on two columns that have the same meaning and therefore produce a meaningful result.

The format of the SELECT join expression is:

```
TABLE1.COLUMN1 h TABLE2.COLUMN2
```

where the symbol h is the join-operator, one of the comparison operators such as {=, ==, <, <=, >, >=,]}; TABLE1 is the name of one table; TABLE2 is the name of another table; COLUMN1 is a column from TABLE1; and COLUMN2 is a column from TABLE2.

COLUMN1 and COLUMN2 must have the same data types or be converted to similar types with a column function. In the next example, suppose that the CUST_ORDER table has a customer number that is a character string. In the COMPANY table the customer company id is a numeric value. It cannot then be directly compared to the CUSTNUM column.

COMPANY:

COMPANY	COMPANY_ID	REGION	CITY	STATE	ZIP	PHONE
ACME	222	midwest	Cincinnati	WA	45040	5135551234
Tech	111	east	New York	NY	12311	1231231233
D.D.E.	333	east	Cleveland	OH	12312	2162312112
Alpha	444	east	Mills	NJ	12312	1222297312
T.L.A.	555	midwest	Fort Wayne	IN	33212	1231231245
C.P.P	666	midwest	Dayton	OH	23232	5132546545
Best	777	midwest	Columbus	OH	32323	3215456346
Beta	888	midwest	Akron	OH	43222	1231234534

REP_SSN	CREDIT_LIMIT	LAST_ORDER_DATE	ADDRESS	ACTIVE
111223333	1500000.5	9/9/94	123 Main	y

continued on next page

222334444	0.55	10/10/94	1122 Apple	y
333445555	25000	10/20/94	123 Winters Lane	y
111223333	55000	10/11/94	91287 First St.	y
222334444	125000	10/14/94	302 Second St.	y
333445555	123123.5	9/11/94	110 Third St.	y
111223333	90125	9/28/94	9 Chris Court	y
333445555	500125	9/29/94	991 Kyle Lane	y

COMMENT

This is our best customer. Take special care to provide the best service to this company.

This company must pre-pay for all future orders.

Alice is taking over this account, use her as the sales rep for all future sales.

CUST_ORDER:

ORDNUM	CUSTNUM	DUEDATE	BALANCE	DATE_DUE
12121	111	19940901	4001	9/1/94
12123	222	19940901	3416.25	9/1/94
12345	777	19940901	5515.75	9/1/94
54322	888	19941029	2802	10/29/94
56788	111	19941029	1401	10/29/94
57002	222	19941029	1765	10/29/94
57009	777	19941029	5920.25	10/29/94
58990	888	19941029	5788.75	10/29/94
6111	111	19941002	1200	10/2/94
6134	222	19941002	6442.5	10/2/94
6167	333	19941002	5363.75	10/2/94
74321	444	19941022	4753	10/22/94

continued on next page

ORDNUM	CUSTNUM	DUEDATE	BALANCE	DATE_DUE
76901	555	19941022	7021.75	10/22/94
7777	666	19941022	400	10/22/94
8888	777	19941123	2000	11/23/94
8892	777	19941123	650.25	11/23/94
9900	111	19941212	400	12/12/94
99001	222	19941212	3767	12/12/94
9901	333	19941212	627.3800049	12/12/94
9902	444	19941212	600	12/12/94
9903	555	19941212	600	12/12/94
123123	111	19941212	123	

A function such as VAL() is therefore required to convert CUSTNUM to a numeric value for the join condition. This is expressed in the following SQL statement:

```
SELECT * FROM company, cust_order
    WHERE company_id = VAL(custnum) ;
```

Sometimes you will want to join a table with itself. Correlation names are necessary in this case to clarify the occurrences of column references. For example, consider a table EMPLOYEE with the schema:

```
EMPLOYEE(SSN, NAME, ADDRESS, ZIP, DEPT, SPOUSE)
```

where a column, spouse, is used to store the ssn of the spouse if the spouse is employed by the same company.

If you wished to produce a list of all the employees that have a spouse employed by the same company, we could use the following query:

```
SELECT emp1.name, emp2.name
    FROM employee emp1, employee emp2
    WHERE emp1.spouse = emp2.ssn ;
```

This query would list each pair of married employees twice. To avoid the duplicate listing the query can be modified to:

```
SELECT emp1.name, emp2.name
    FROM employee emp1, employee emp2
    WHERE emp1.spouse = emp2.ssn AND emp1.ssn < emp1.spouse ;
```

SUBQUERIES

Queries may be nested; inner queries are called *subqueries*. The inner query can only return a one-column table. The subquery must be placed inside parentheses. Suppose we wish to find information in the company table about the company that placed order number 123123.

```
SELECT * FROM company WHERE company_id =
    (select custnum FROM cust_order WHERE ordnum=123123);
```

The result set is shown in Table 20.13.

TABLE 20.13 THE RESULT SET

COMPANY	COMPANY_ID	REGION	CITY	STATE	ZIP	PHONE
Tech	111	east	New York	NY	12311	1231231233

The subquery is executed first to find the customer number, custnum, that was on order 123123. Then the outer query finds the company.company_id column value that matches that cust_order.custnum. When the outer query is joined to the inner with a comparison operator, as in this example, the subquery must return at most one custnum value.

If the subquery returns more than one value an error will occur.

Subqueries may return a set of values, against which the outer query compares a value for membership in the inner query result set. This is done using the IN operator. If we wish to list all the company information from the COMPANY table on companies that have placed orders with balances more than $1000.00, the following would produce the correct set of tuples:

```
SELECT * FROM company
    WHERE company_id IN
    (SELECT custnum FROM cust_order WHERE balance > 1000.00) ;
```

The result set is shown in Table 20.14.

TABLE 20.14 THE RESULT SET

COMPANY	COMPANY_ID	REGION	CITY	STATE	ZIP	PHONE
ACME	222	midwest	Cincinnati	WA	45040	5135551234
Tech	111	east	New York	NY	12311	1231231233
D.D.E.	333	east	Cleveland	OH	12312	2162312112
Alpha	444	east	Mills	NJ	12312	1222297312
T.L.A.	555	midwest	Fort Wayne	IN	33212	1231231245
Best	777	midwest	Columbus	OH	32323	3215456346
Beta	888	midwest	Akron	OH	43222	1231234534

The subquery is executed first to produce a set of customer id numbers, custnum, for any order that has a balance more than $1000.00. Then the outer query checks the company.company_id column values for membership in the set of cust_order.custnum values returned in the result set of the inner query (subquery).

Another way to obtain that same result would be with the following query, which avoids the use of the subquery:

```
SELECT company.* FROM company, cust_order
    WHERE company_id = custnum AND
    balance > 1000.00;
```

The result of this SELECT is shown in Table 20.15.

TABLE 20.15 THE RESULT SET

COMPANY	COMPANY_ID	REGION	CITY	STATE	ZIP	PHONE
Tech	111	east	New York	NY	12311	1231231233
ACME	222	midwest	Cincinnati	WA	45040	5135551234
Best	777	midwest	Columbus	OH	32323	3215456346
Beta	888	midwest	Akron	OH	43222	1231234534

continued on next page

COMPANY	COMPANY_ID	REGION	CITY	STATE	ZIP	PHONE
Tech	111	east	New York	NY	12311	1231231233
ACME	222	midwest	Cincinnati	WA	45040	5135551234
Best	777	midwest	Columbus	OH	32323	3215456346
Beta	888	midwest	Akron	OH	43222	1231234534
Tech	111	east	New York	NY	12311	1231231233
ACME	222	midwest	Cincinnati	WA	45040	5135551234
D.D.E.	333	east	Cleveland	OH	12312	2162312112
Alpha	444	east	Mills	NJ	12312	1222297312
T.L.A.	555	midwest	Fort Wayne	IN	33212	1231231245
Best	777	midwest	Columbus	OH	32323	3215456346
ACME	222	midwest	Cincinnati	WA	45040	5135551234

Note that there are multiple rows returned for a company. This is due to there being more than one row in the cust_order table where the balance is more than $1000.00 for a given custnum. To return only one company row for multiple cust_order.custnum rows having the same company customer number, the following query can be used:

```
SELECT distinct company.* FROM company, cust_order
    WHERE company_id = custnum AND
        balance > 1000.00
    ORDER by company_id;
```

This query will produce the results that were shown in Table 20.14.

In general, people find the first query (with the subquery) to be a more natural way of formulating this query. It is easy to see that the subquery produces a set of company numbers (custnum) from orders where an outstanding balance of more than $1000.00 exists. Then the companies (from the COMPANY table) whose company_id are found in the set of customer numbers that resulted from the subquery will be listed .

To list all the company information from the COMPANY table on companies that who have not placed orders with balances more than $1000.00, the NOT IN will be used, as in the following query:

```
SELECT * FROM company
    WHERE company_id NOT IN
    (SELECT custnum FROM cust_order WHERE balance > 1000.00) ;
```

The result set is shown in Table 20.16.

TABLE 20.16 THE RESULT SET

COMPANY	COMPANY_ID	REGION	CITY	STATE	ZIP	PHONE
C.P.P	666	midwest	Dayton	OH	23232	5132546545

In this example, the subquery is executed to create a set of CUST_ORDER.custnum for all the companies with balances more than $1000.00. Then the outer query is executed and the tuples for each company whose company_id is not found in the result of the subquery will be listed. In other words, the companies that have NOT placed an order that has a balance greater than $1000.00 will be listed.

CORRELATED SUBQUERIES

One of the least understood and most underused features of the SELECT statement is the correlated subquery. In the next example, notice which tables are being referenced in the WHERE clause of the subquery. Also note which tables are listed in the subquery's FROM clause.

```
SELECT * FROM cust_order WHERE 2 <=
    ( SELECT count(*) FROM line_item
        WHERE cust_order.ordnum = line_item.ordnum) ;
```

The subquery in this example has a reference to a table that is not listed in its FROM clause. The REP table belongs to the outer query. This outer reference is know as a *correlated reference*, making this a *correlated subquery*. When the outer table is referenced from inside the query, it means that the subquery should be executed repeatedly, once for each outer tuple that meets the search conditions specified in the outer WHERE clause.

The result of the subquery is then used to evaluate the expression that joins the inner query to the outer one (2 <= count(*) in this case), and if that expression is evaluated as true, then that outer tuple will be projected into the result table.

CUST_ORDER:

ORDNUM	CUSTNUM	DUEDATE	BALANCE	DATE_DUE
12121	111	19940901	4001	9/1/94
12123	222	19940901	3416.25	9/1/94
12345	777	19940901	5515.75	9/1/94
54322	888	19941029	2802	10/29/94
56788	111	19941029	1401	10/29/94
57002	222	19941029	1765	10/29/94
57009	777	19941029	5920.25	10/29/94
58990	888	19941029	5788.75	10/29/94
6111	111	19941002	1200	10/2/94
6134	222	19941002	6442.5	10/2/94
6167	333	19941002	5363.75	10/2/94
74321	444	19941022	4753	10/22/94
76901	555	19941022	7021.75	10/22/94
7777	666	19941022	400	10/22/94
8888	777	19941123	2000	11/23/94
8892	777	19941123	650.25	11/23/94
9900	111	19941212	400	12/12/94
99001	222	19941212	3767	12/12/94
9901	333	19941212	627.3800049	12/12/94
9902	444	19941212	600	12/12/94
9903	555	19941212	600	12/12/94
123123	111	19941212	123	

continued on next page

LINE_ITEM:

ORDNUM	LINE_NO	PARTNAME	PRICE	QUANTITY	EXTENDED_PRICE
12345	1	hardware	400	2	800
58990	1	hardware	400	2	800
8888	1	hardware	400	5	2000
12121	1	hardware	400	1	400
56788	1	hardware	400	1	400
57002	1	hardware	400	1	400
7777	1	hardware	400	1	400
54322	1	hardware	400	2	800
6111	1	hardware	400	3	1200
6134	1	hardware	400	4	1600
6167	1	hardware	400	5	2000
74321	1	hardware	400	6	2400
8892	1	hardware	400	1	400
99001	1	hardware	400	2	800
12123	1	hardware	400	2	800
76901	1	hardware	400	7	2800
57009	1	hardware	400	8	3200
99001	3	software	123.5	7	864.5
12123	3	software	123.5	7	864.5
76901	3	software	123.5	20	2470
57009	3	software	123.5	20	2470
12345	2	consulting	250.25	7	1751.75
58990	2	consulting	250.25	15	3753.75
12121	2	consulting	250.25	6	1501.5
56788	2	consulting	250.25	4	1001

continued on next page

ORDNUM	LINE_NO	PARTNAME	PRICE	QUANTITY	EXTENDED_PRICE
57002	2	consulting	250.25	2	500.5
54322	2	consulting	250.25	8	2002
6134	2	consulting	250.25	8	2002
6167	2	consulting	250.25	9	2252.25
74321	2	consulting	250.25	2	500.5
8892	2	consulting	250.25	1	250.25
99001	2	consulting	250.25	10	2502.5
12123	2	consulting	250.25	7	1751.75
76901	2	consulting	250.25	7	1751.75
57009	2	consulting	250.25	1	250.25
12345	3	software	123.5	24	2964
58990	3	software	123.5	10	1235
9900	1	consulting	400	1	400
12121	3	software	123.5	17	2099.5
9901	1	hardware	127.38	1	127.38
57002	3	software	123.5	7	864.5
9901	2	consulting	500	1	500
9902	1	consulting	400	1	400
9902	2	software	200	1	200
6134	3	software	123.5	23	2840.5
6167	3	software	123.5	9	1111.5
74321	3	software	123.5	15	1852.5
9903	1	consulting	600	1	600
123123	1	software	123	1	123

For these CUST_ORDER and LINE_ITEM tables, the subquery is executed for each order number, ordnum. If the order has two or more line items in the LINE_ITEM table, then the order number will be in the resultant set of tuples:

```
SELECT * FROM cust_order WHERE 2 <=
    ( SELECT count(*) FROM line_item
        WHERE cust_order.ordnum = line_item.ordnum) ;
```

The result is shown in Table 20.17.

TABLE 20.17 THE RESULT SET

ORDNUM	CUSTNUM	DUEDATE	BALANCE	DATE_DUE
12121	111	19940901	4001	9/1/94
12123	222	19940901	3416.25	9/1/94
12345	777	19940901	5515.75	9/1/94
54322	888	19941029	2802	10/29/94
56788	111	19941029	1401	10/29/94
57002	222	19941029	1765	10/29/94
57009	777	19941029	5920.25	10/29/94
58990	888	19941029	5788.75	10/29/94
6134	222	19941002	6442.5	10/2/94
6167	333	19941002	5363.75	10/2/94
74321	444	19941022	4753	10/22/94
76901	555	19941022	7021.75	10/22/94
8892	777	19941123	650.25	11/23/94
99001	222	19941212	3767	12/12/94
9901	333	19941212	627.38	12/12/94
9902	444	19941212	600	12/12/94

The next query adds a further restriction to the outer query that limits the order number to being more than 6000. This restriction prevents any tuples in the LINE_ITEM table with a CUST_ORDER.ordnum value less than 6000 from being selected.

```
SELECT * FROM cust_order WHERE ordnum > 6000 and 2 <=
    ( SELECT count(*) FROM line_item
        WHERE cust_order.ordnum = line_item.ordnum) ;
```

TABLE 20.18 THE RESULT SET

ORDNUM	CUSTNUM	DUEDATE	BALANCE	DATE_DUE
6134	222	19941002	6442.5	10/2/94
6167	333	19941002	5363.75	10/2/94
74321	444	19941022	4753	10/22/94
76901	555	19941022	7021.75	10/22/94
8892	777	19941123	650.25	11/23/94
99001	222	19941212	3767	12/12/94
9901	333	19941212	627.38	12/12/94
9902	444	19941212	600	12/12/94

The EXIST operator is used often with correlated subqueries. The EXIST operator tells the subquery to return TRUE if any tuples are produced by the subquery and FALSE otherwise. A query to list all the orders that have at least one line item would be:

```
SELECT * FROM cust_order WHERE EXISTS
    ( SELECT * FROM line_item
        WHERE cust_order.ordnum = line_item.ordnum) ;
```

The query steps through each customer order tuple, passes the value of the customer order number to the subquery, and then executes the subquery. If the subquery returns a TRUE value (meaning at least one tuple was found in the invoice table), then the tuple in the outer query will be output. Note that in the case of a correlated subquery using EXIST (or NOT EXIST), there is only a TRUE or FALSE result for the subquery. Since there is not an actual column of data being returned, "SELECT *" can be used instead of listing a particular column.

The following would produce the same result:

```
SELECT * FROM cust_order WHERE EXISTS
    ( SELECT ordnum FROM line_item
        WHERE cust_order.ordnum = line_item.ordnum) ;
```

A query to list all the orders that do not have line items would use the NOT EXIST as in the following example:

```
SELECT * FROM cust_order WHERE NOT EXISTS
    ( SELECT ordnum FROM line_item
        WHERE cust_order.ordnum = line_item.ordnum) ;
```

The subquery or the outer query may also involve joins. To find the orders that are greater than the average extended price dollar amount for all the line items, the subquery is used to calculate the average amount of a line-item extended price. The individual extended prices are then compared against the average in the outer query. If an extended price amount is found to be greater than the average, the line-item tuple will be joined to the customer order table to provide the order information.

Since each order may have more than one line item that has an extended price greater than the average extended price of $1325.68, the DISTINCT function is used to eliminate the redundant listing of the order information as shown in Table 20.19.

```
SELECT DISTINCT cust_order.* FROM cust_order, line_item
    WHERE cust_order.ordnum = line_item.ordnum AND
        line_item.extended_price >
    (SELECT AVG(extended_price) FROM line_item);
```

TABLE 20.19 THE RESULT SET

ORDNUM	CUSTNUM	DUEDATE	BALANCE	DATE_DUE
12121	111	19940901	4001	9/1/94
12123	222	19940901	3416.25	9/1/94
12345	777	19940901	5515.75	9/1/94
54322	888	19941029	2802	10/29/94

continued on next page

ORDNUM	CUSTNUM	DUEDATE	BALANCE	DATE_DUE
57009	777	19941029	5920.25	10/29/94
58990	888	19941029	5788.75	10/29/94
6134	222	19941002	6442.5	10/2/94
6167	333	19941002	5363.75	10/2/94
74321	444	19941022	4753	10/22/94
76901	555	19941022	7021.75	10/22/94
8888	777	19941123	2000	11/23/94
99001	222	19941212	3767	12/12/94

The quantifiers ANY, SOME, and ALL are also useful with subqueries (SOME is a synonym for ANY). The quantifiers are used with the comparison operations when used with a set of values in a subquery:

```
SELECT * FROM line_item WHERE extended_price > ALL ;
    (SELECT extended_price FROM line_item
        WHERE ordnum = 12345);
```

This query will list all the line items that have an extended price greater than every extended price found on a line item for order number 12345. This is equivalent to

```
SELECT * FROM line_item WHERE extended_price >
    (SELECT MAX(extended_price) FROM line_item
        WHERE ordnum = 12345);
```

The ANY quantifier is used in the next example:

```
SELECT * FROM line_item WHERE extended_price > ANY
    (SELECT extended_price FROM line_item
        WHERE ordnum = 12345);
```

This query will list all the line items that have an extended price greater than any extended price found on a line item for order number 12345. This is equivalent to:

```
SELECT * FROM line_item WHERE extended_price >
    (SELECT MIN(extended_price) FROM line_item
        WHERE ordnum = 12345);
```

THE GROUP BY AND HAVING CLAUSES

The output of the SELECT statement can be divided into groups that have one or more common attributes. This technique uses the SQL GROUP BY clause. The results of a SELECT can be grouped by one or more columns. The GROUP BY clause allows you to output one tuple for each group; it is usually used with some of the column functions to gather statistics on the groups. Consider the LINE_ITEM in Table 20.20.

TABLE 20.20 THE LINE_ITEM TABLE

ORDNUM	LINE_NO	PARTNAME	PRICE	QUANTITY	EXTENDED_PRICE
76901	3	software	123.5	20	2470
12345	1	hardware	400	2	800
58990	1	hardware	400	2	800
8888	1	hardware	400	5	2000
12121	1	hardware	400	1	400
56788	1	hardware	400	1	400
57002	1	hardware	400	1	400
7777	1	hardware	400	1	400
54322	1	hardware	400	2	800
6111	1	hardware	400	3	1200
6134	1	hardware	400	4	1600
6167	1	hardware	400	5	2000
74321	1	hardware	400	6	2400
8892	1	hardware	400	1	400

continued on next page

ORDNUM	LINE_NO	PARTNAME	PRICE	QUANTITY	EXTENDED_PRICE
99001	1	hardware	400	2	800
12123	1	hardware	400	2	800
76901	1	hardware	400	7	2800
57009	1	hardware	400	8	3200
99001	3	software	123.5	7	864.5
12123	3	software	123.5	7	864.5
76901	3	software	123.5	20	2470
57009	3	software	123.5	20	2470
12345	2	consulting	250.25	7	1751.75
58990	2	consulting	250.25	15	3753.75
12121	2	consulting	250.25	6	1501.5
56788	2	consulting	250.25	4	1001
57002	2	consulting	250.25	2	500.5
54322	2	consulting	250.25	8	2002
6134	2	consulting	250.25	8	2002
6167	2	consulting	250.25	9	2252.25
74321	2	consulting	250.25	2	500.5
8892	2	consulting	250.25	1	250.25
99001	2	consulting	250.25	10	2502.5
12123	2	consulting	250.25	7	1751.75
76901	2	consulting	250.25	7	1751.75
57009	2	consulting	250.25	1	250.25
12345	3	software	123.5	24	2964
58990	3	software	123.5	10	1235
9900	1	consulting	400	1	400
12121	3	software	123.5	17	2099.5

continued on next page

ORDNUM	LINE_NO	PARTNAME	PRICE	QUANTITY	EXTENDED_PRICE
9901	1	hardware	127.38	1	127.38
57002	3	software	123.5	7	864.5
9901	2	consulting	500	1	500
9902	1	consulting	400	1	400
9902	2	software	200	1	200
6134	3	software	123.5	23	2840.5
6167	3	software	123.5	9	1111.5
74321	3	software	123.5	15	1852.5
9903	1	consulting	600	1	600
123123	1	software	123	1	123

If we wish to group by the order numbers (ordnum) to compute the total extended sale price for each order, the SELECT statement:

```
SELECT ordnum, SUM(extended_price) AS total
    FROM line_item GROUP BY ordnum ;
```

would produce the following result.

TABLE 20.21 THE RESULT TABLE

ORDNUM	TOTAL
12121	4001.00
12123	3416.25
123123	123.00
12345	5515.75
54322	2802.00
56788	1401.00
57002	1765.00

continued on next page

ORDNUM	TOTAL
57009	5920.25
58990	5788.75
6111	1200.00
6134	6442.50
6167	5363.75
74321	4753.00
76901	7021.75
7777	400.00
8888	2000.00
8892	650.25
9900	400.00
99001	4167.00
9901	627.38
9902	600.00
9903	600.00

In general, you will wish to project the column(s) that you are grouping by; otherwise you cannot see the groups that have partitioned the result. It usually makes sense to include only column functions in the SELECT list, with the grouping columns as arguments of the functions. The one exception is where there is a column that has a one-to-one relation with the grouping columns (such as EMP# and SSN).

The HAVING clause allows you to restrict which groups are allowed in the output set of tuples. If we modify the previous query to be:

```
SELECT ordnum, SUM(extended_price) AS total
    FROM line_item GROUP BY ordnum HAVING COUNT(*) > 1;
```

we are specifying that only groups with more than one tuple are to be included in the output set. Since ORDNUM '8888' only occurs once in the LINE_ITEM table (Table 20.20) it will not be in the output set, and the query would produce the following result.

Table 20.22 The Result Set

ORDNUM	TOTAL
12121	4001.00
12123	3416.25
12345	5515.75
54322	2802.00
56788	1401.00
57002	1765.00
57009	5920.25
58990	5788.75
6134	6442.50
6167	5363.75
74321	4753.00
76901	7021.75
8892	650.25
99001	4167.00
9901	627.38
9902	600.00

If we wish to see only reps that have produced a total of $2000.00 or more and we wish to see the number of invoices, then the query would be:

```
SELECT ordnum, COUNT(*), SUM(extended_price)
    AS total FROM line_item
    GROUP BY ordnum HAVING SUM(extended_price) > 6000.00 ;
```

Table 20.23 The Result Set

ORDNUM	COMPUTE_0002	TOTAL
12345	3	5515.75
57009	3	5920.25

continued on next page

ORDNUM	COMPUTE_0002	TOTAL
58990	3	5788.75
6134	3	6442.50
6167	3	5363.75
76901	3	7021.75

Earlier we gave the example query:

```
SELECT * FROM cust_order WHERE 2 <=
    ( SELECT count(*) FROM line_item
        WHERE cust_order.ordnum = line_item.ordnum)
    ORDER BY ordnum ;
```

An equivalent query using GROUP BY and HAVING is:

```
SELECT cust_order.* FROM cust_order , line_item
    WHERE line_item.ordnum = cust_order.ordnum
    GROUP BY cust_order.custnum, cust_order.ordnum,
        balance, duedate, date_due
    HAVING count(*) > 1 ;
```

Note that all the columns are specified in the GROUP BY clause. This is required in many RDBMS implementations and by WATCOM SQL. You may want to check your particular RDBMS SQL manual for restrictions on the GROUP BY clause.

The union operator combines the result of two or more queries into one result set. The result of each query must have the same number of columns with exactly the same format.

```
SELECT ordnum FROM cust_order UNION
    SELECT ordnum FROM line_item ;
```

This will produce a list of all order numbers that are found in the customer order or the line item tables. Duplicate order numbers will be eliminated by default, as shown here.

TABLE 20.24 THE RESULT SET

ORDNUM
12121
12123
123123
12345
54322
56788
57002
57009
58990
6111
6134
6167
74321
76901
7777
8888
8892
9900
99001
9901
9902
9903

If this is not desired, insert ALL after the UNION, as in:

```
SELECT ordnum FROM cust_order
    UNION ALL SELECT ordnum FROM line_item ;
```

Combined with a report, the SELECT statement can quickly and easily produce great-looking and informative reports. Even by itself, the SELECT statement can provide a great deal of information.

INSERT

The INSERT statement is used to add rows to a table. The format of the INSERT statement is:

```
INSERT INTO tablename (column_name1, column_name2 ...)
    VALUES (value1, value2 ......);
```

The INSERT statement includes a table name, a column list, and a value list. For example, to insert a new row into the company table:

```
INSERT INTO company (company_id, company, address, zip)
    VALUES (1223, 'Acme Inc.', '123 Main St.', '45040')
```

This INSERT statement will create a new row in the company table. It will assign to each column specified the corresponding value from the VALUES clause.

If you are inserting a value for every column in the table, you may omit the column list. For example, for the customer order (cust_order) table.

TABLE 20.25 THE CUST_ORDER TABLE

ORDNUM	CUSTNUM	DUEDATE	BALANCE	DATE_DUE
12121	111	19940901	4001	9/1/94
12123	222	19940901	3416.25	9/1/94
12345	777	19940901	5515.75	9/1/94
54322	888	19941029	2802	10/29/94

continued on next page

ORDNUM	CUSTNUM	DUEDATE	BALANCE	DATE_DUE
56788	111	19941029	1401	10/29/94
57002	222	19941029	1765	10/29/94
57009	777	19941029	5920.25	10/29/94
58990	888	19941029	5788.75	10/29/94
6111	111	19941002	1200	10/2/94
6134	222	19941002	6442.5	10/2/94
6167	333	19941002	5363.75	10/2/94
74321	444	19941022	4753	10/22/94
76901	555	19941022	7021.75	10/22/94
7777	666	19941022	400	10/22/94
8888	777	19941123	2000	11/23/94
8892	777	19941123	650.25	11/23/94
9900	111	19941212	400	12/12/94
99001	222	19941212	3767	12/12/94
9901	333	19941212	627.3800049	12/12/94
9902	444	19941212	600	12/12/94
9903	555	19941212	600	12/12/94
123123	111	19941212	123	

You can insert a new row as follows:

```
INSERT INTO cust_order
    VALUES (1022, 777, '19941010', 3693.96, 'Oct 10 1994');
```

You must list the values in the sequence that matches the order of the columns in the table.

You can also use a SELECT statement as a source for an INSERT statement. For example:

```
INSERT INTO ohio_customers
    (CUST_NO, COMPANY, ADDRESS, ZIP, STATE)
```

```
SELECT company_id, company, address, zip FROM company
    WHERE state = 'OH';
```

UPDATE

You can change the value of one or more columns in one or more rows of a table with the UPDATE statement. The new values can be constants, expressions, or data selected from another table. The format of the UPDATE statement is:

```
UPDATE table_name SET column_name1 = expression1,
    column_name2 = expression2 ...
    WHERE <search condition>;
```

For example, to change the address of a customer, you could use the following:

```
UPDATE company SET address = '1223 Main St.', zip = '45041'
    WHERE company_id = 111;
```

This statement will update the row in the company table where the company_id = 111. You can update multiple rows as shown in the following statement:

```
UPDATE company SET state = 'OH' WHERE zip LIKE '45%';
```

This will update the state to 'OH' for any rows that have a zip code starting with '45.'

The update statement can also be used to ensure integrity between two tables as in the following example:

```
UPDATE cust_order SET custnum =
    (SELECT company_id FROM company WHERE company='Best')
    WHERE ordnum = 8888 OR ordnum = 8892;
```

Here we want to make sure that the customer number in the customer order table is the same as the company identification number in the company table for two orders, 8888 and 8892, that have been placed by the 'Best' company. This is done by setting the value of cust_order.custnum = to 'Best' company's identification number for cust_order.ordnum 8888 and 8892.

DELETE

You can remove rows from a table using the DELETE statement. The format of the DELETE statement is:

```
DELETE FROM table_name WHERE <expression>;
```

If you omit the WHERE clause, every row would be deleted from the table. For example:

```
DELETE FROM company;
```

will delete every row from the company table. To delete the nonactive customers, you could use the following:

```
DELETE FROM company WHERE active = 'N';
```

CURSORS

A cursor is a special type of SQL construct that provides a method of handling sets of records, as you do in a record-oriented computer language. As we have seen, some SQL SELECT statements can return exactly one row of data, such as:

```
SELECT count(*) from company;
```

whereas most SELECT statements will return multiple rows in the result set, such as:

```
SELECT * from company;
```

To process the result set a row at a time, as you would typically process records from an ASCII file, a cursor is required. A cursor is a symbolic name associated with the SELECT statement through a DECLARE cursor statement. The cursor consists of two distinct parts: the result set, which is the set of rows returned by the RDBMS when the SELECT statement is executed, and a position indicator, or pointer, that keeps track of the current row that is being returned to you from the result set. In this respect, cursors act like file pointers.

In most RDBMSs, cursors only support forward row-by-row traversal through the result set. This is accomplished by the FETCH statement, which returns one or more rows and changes the cursor position in the result set. The cursor must be uniquely named in a DECLARE cursor statement, opened with an OPEN cursor statement, and the row fetched into host variables with a FETCH statement before the application can process the row. Host variables are application variables defined with :variable_name as shown in the following example:

```
int :nCount

SELECT count(*) INTO :nCount FROM images;
```

Once the result set is processed, the cursor is closed. Note that the entire result set does not need to be retrieved before a cursor can be closed. The cursor can be closed at any point during traversal of the result set.

As stated above, a cursor is associated with a SELECT statement by a DECLARE cursor statement. When the DECLARE statement is executed, the cursor is closed. The cursor must be opened before it can be used. The OPEN statement allows the result set rows to be read with a FETCH statement or updated through an UPDATE or DELETE statement. You cannot insert rows into a table using a cursor. A cursor can be closed and reopened without another DECLARE. When a cursor is closed and another OPEN cursor is issued, the result set is re-created and the cursor is positioned at the first row in the re-created result set.

Let us now look at each cursor statement in more detail using PowerBuilder statements and global variables. We will first define the PowerBuilder global variables as:

```
//global vars>  > string sImage, sType, sPath
//integer nVersion.
```

Now we can define the cursor, cursor1, which will associate a SELECT statement with cursor1:

```
DECLARE cursor1 CURSOR FOR
    SELECT "images"."image", "images"."type",
  "images"."version", "images"."path"
    FROM "images"
        ORDER BY "images"."image" ASC;
```

This DECLARE statement creates the cursor structure for 'cursor1,' compiles the query (SELECT statement), and defines the relationship between the query and the named cursor, 'cursor1.' The DECLARE statement MUST occur before any other cursor statement that uses 'cursor1.' Since an ORDER BY clause is specified in the SELECT, cursor1 is a read-only cursor. Cursors can be opened for read only or update. If the DECLARE statement does not specify 'read only,' the cursor is implicitly defined as updatable unless the select statement contains DISTINCT, GROUP BY , an aggregate function such as SUM, AVG, MIN, or MAX or the UNION operator. DECLARE statements containing DISTINCT, GROUP BY , an aggregate function such as SUM, AVG, MIN, or MAX, or the UNION operator cause the cursor to be defined as nonupdatable (read only). Including ORDER BY in the SELECT causes the cursor to be defined as read only.

Cursor1 is then opened with:

```
OPEN cursor1;
```

and the open status is checked with:

```
fw_db_status ( sqlca.sqlcode, sqlca.sqldbcode, &
                sqlca.sqlerrtext )
```

The OPEN statement causes the RDBMS to execute the SELECT statement:

```
SELECT "images"."image", "images"."type", "images"."version",
    "images"."path"
```

```
FROM "images"
    ORDER BY "images"."image" ASC;
```

that was specified with the DECLARE cursor statement and to create the result set. The cursor points to the first row in the result set. No row is returned to the application when the OPEN statement is executed. The fields in the result set are in the order specified in the select list of the SELECT statement.

The data is retrieved into the PowerBuilder application with the statement:

```
FETCH cursor1 INTO :sImage, :sType, :nVersion, :sPath;
```

and the fetch status is checked with:

```
fw_db_status ( sqlca.sqlcode, sqlca.sqldbcode, &
               sqlca.sqlerrtext ).
```

This places the first row of the result set into the specified host variables; the first field ("images"."image") will be returned into host variable :sImage, the second field ("images"."type") into host variable :sType, etc. The FETCH statement moves the cursor position one or more rows, returns the data into the host variables, and stores the position of the cursor. There must be a one-to-one correspondence between the items specified in the select list of the SELECT statement and the host variables specified in the FETCH statement. The datatypes must also be compatible between each item in the select list and the corresponding host variable in the fetch list. Once a row is fetched from the result set, it cannot be fetched again unless the cursor is closed and reopened and the result set refetched to the location of the row needed. If this is required, it is the application's responsibility to keep track of the count of the row being returned so that the same row can be located when rows from the result set are refetched. By definition, rows are fetched from the RDBMS on a row-by-row basis. Some vendors allow multiple rows to be retrieved with a single FETCH. Refer to the SQL manual for your database system for additional details on the FETCH statement and multiple-row fetches.

Usually a result set is processed in a loop until there is no more data. Each row in the result set is retrieved into the application program by the FETCH statement. A FETCH statement is therefore placed into the result set processing loop. Once the end of the result set is reached, the SQLCA.SQL-CODE will become nonzero. SQLCA.SQLCODE is therefore typically used as the loop termination condition.

```
FETCH Cursor1 INTO :sImage, :sType, :nVersion, :sPath;
DO WHILE SQLCA.SQLCODE = 0
    Handle(sImage, sType, nVersion, sPath)
    FETCH Cursor1 INTO :sImage, :sType, :nVersion, :sPath;
END DO
CLOSE Cursor1;
```

The statement:

```
CLOSE cursor1;
```

closes the result set; and:

```
DEALLOCATE cursor1
```

causes the query plan for 'cursor1' and the cursor 'cursor1' to be purged from the RDBMS. Since the cursor name must be unique and 'cursor1' is now purged from the database system, any references to 'cursor1' are invalid. To use the name 'cursor1' further, it must be redefined with a DECLARE cursor statement.

Updatable Cursor Statements

After issuing a cursor FETCH statement, you can update the rows that meet the SELECT criteria defined in the DECLARE cursor statement by using another form of the UPDATE statement. The format of the UPDATE statement is:

```
UPDATE table_name
    SET column_name1 = expression1, column_name2 =
    expression2 ...
    WHERE CURRENT OF cursor_name;
```

where the contents of 'expressionN' can be a constant, a computed value, NULL, or a SELECT statement.

The following set of SQL statements:

```
DECLARE cursor1 CURSOR FOR
    SELECT * FROM images WHERE version is NULL;
OPEN Cursor1;
UPDATE images SET version = 1 WHERE CURRENT OF Cursor1;
```

declares cursor1, opens cursor1 as an updatable cursor, and assigns a value of 1 to the version field of all rows where version is NULL.

The UPDATE table ... WHERE CURRENT OF ... statement allows you to change a column in the select list or any other column in the table as long as the column being updated has not been specified in the FOR UPDATE column list of the SELECT statement. Since the update statement updates the row, to which the cursor is currently pointing, the cursor position is unchanged by the update.

Rows can also be deleted from a table based on a cursor selection. The format of the DELETE statement is:

```
DELETE FROM table_name WHERE CURRENT OF cursor_name;
```

The 'table_name' specified in the DELETE FROM ... WHERE CURRENT OF ... statement must be the table or view that was specified in the first FROM clause of the SELECT statement that defined 'cursor_name.' In the case where the cursor is to be used to delete rows, the SELECT statement specified in the DECLARE cursor statement cannot contain a join.

In the following example:

```
DECLARE cursor1 CURSOR FOR
    SELECT * FROM company WHERE active = 'N';
OPEN Cursor1;
DELETE FROM company WHERE CURRENT OF Cursor1;
```

Cursor1 is implicitly declared as an updatable cursor, cursor1 is opened, and all the inactive customers are deleted from the company table.

Since the delete statement removes one or more rows from a table, the cursor position changes. After a delete is executed the cursor points to the row just prior to the deleted row. In the preceding example, the cursor would point to the last active customer found ahead of the last inactive customer that was deleted.

STORED PROCEDURES

Stored procedures are blocks of SQL statements and flow of control statements that are assigned a name, compiled, and then stored in the database. A stored procedure is executed by name. It runs on the database server, accepting parameters from the client, and can return status values indicating success or failure of the procedure, as well as parameter values to the caller.

Different RDBMSs implement stored procedures in different ways.

The Oracle 7 syntax is:

```
CREATE PROCEDURE proc_name (argument list)
    AS BEGIN
    .. SQL statements
    END;
```

This is shown in the following example:

```
CREATE PROCEDURE s_transaction    (order IN NUMBER(6),
                amount IN NUMBER(11,2))
AS BEGIN
    UPDATE cust_order SET balance = balance - amount
        WHERE ordnum = order
END;
```

The Sybase syntax is:

```
CREATE PROCEDURE proc_name
        @parameter1 datatype, ..., @parameterN datatype
    AS
    .. SQL statements
```

The same example in Sybase format is:

```
CREATE PROCEDURE s_transaction @order char(10), @amount float
    AS
        UPDATE cust_order SET balance = balance - @amount
            WHERE ordnum = @order
```

These examples would cause a procedure named 's_transaction' to be stored in the RDBMS. This procedure has the arguments 'order' and 'amount.' The procedure, when it is executed by the application, will update the cust_order table and decrease the balance for order number, 'order,' by the dollar amount specified by 'amount.'

To execute the procedure, the following EXECUTE statement is used:

```
EXECUTE s_transaction @order=12345, @amount=100.00;
```

In this case, execution of procedure 's_transaction,' would deduct $100.00 from the current balance of order 12345 in the customer order, 'cust_order,' table. When the procedure is executed, amount is replaced with the value 100.00 and order is replaced with the value 12345. The SQL statement that is actually executed by the RDBMS then becomes the statement:

```
UPDATE cust_order SET balance = balance - 100.00
    WHERE ordnum = 12345
```

that we saw earlier in this chapter.

Stored procedures are compiled and the query plan determines when the procedure is stored into the RDBMS. However, database tables tend to change. This means that the original query plan or optimization plan can become obsolete and may need to be reoptimized. Most RDBMS vendors provide a mechanism to do this. For example, Sybase allows you to place a with recompile option in the CREATE procedure statement. This causes reoptimization of the query path each time the stored procedure is executed. This may not be desired. Sybase also allows the use of the with recompile option in the EXECUTE procedure statement. When with recompile is encountered on the EXECUTE procedure statement, a new plan is determined. This new plan is then used in further executions of the stored procedure. The frequency of re-optimizing the query should be a function of the number of changes that occur in the tables accessed by the stored procedure and the frequency of execution of the procedure. If the tables do not change frequently, frequent reoptimization of the query is not needed. However, if the tables do change frequently, you may want to reoptimize the stored procedure every time it is used.

Currently, details of stored procedures vary between vendors. See the SQL manual for your database system for more details.

APPENDIX A

USING THE EXAMPLE APPLICATIONS

This appendix describes the setup process for installing the example files. There is also a discussion about setting up and connecting to the example database (Image.db). Table A.1 lists the example applications, and tells which examples go with which chapters of the book.

TABLE A.1 THE EXAMPLE APPLICATIONS

APPLICATION	APPLICATION LIBRARY (.PBL)	CHAPTER
CopyFile	COPYFILE.PBL	2
FirstApp	FIRSTAPP.PBL	4
FirstWin	FIRSTWIN.PBL	5
Controls*	CONTROLS.PBL*	7
DirNav	DIRNAV.PBL	7
SQLApp	SQLAPP.PBL	8
FirstDW	FIRSTDW.PBL	11
ChildDW	CHILDDW.PBL	11
ImageDB	IMAGEDB.PBL	11
BlobDb	BLOBDB.PBL	11 (8)
DwStyles	DWSTYLES.PBL	11
Menus	MENUS.PBL	12
MDIApp	MDIAPP.PBL	13
UO	UO.PBL	15
UP_CBs	UO.PBL	15
UO_Toggle	UO.PBL	15
UO_Button_List	UO.PBL	15
UO_With_STructures	UO.PBL	15
Inherit	INHERIT.PBL	16
Client	CLIENT.PBL	17
Server	SERVER.PBL	17
TestDLL	TESTDLL.PBL	17
OLEDemo	OLEDEMO.PBL	17
Distrib	DISTRIB.PBL	18
HelpDemo	HELPDEMO.PBL	18

Your example directory may not contain CONTROLS.PBL. If this is the case, use the HELPDEMO.PBL program. HELPDEMO is the CONTROLS application with a Help system added.

INSTALLING THE EXAMPLE FILES

The disk that came with this book contains approximately 90 files for the example applications. The example files include a Watcom database consisting of the files IMAGE.DB and IMAGE.LOG. Many of the examples use this database and require that you have installed the Watcom database engine and the Watcom ODBC driver on your system. If you did not install the Watcom database engine, do so before proceeding with the setup of the example applications.

Installing to a Nondefault Directory

If you install the example files to a directory other than C:\PB4\CLASS, you will have to make a number of changes to the applications. For example, in the Application Open event for many of the example applications, you may find a reference to an initialization (INI) file for the application. Usually there will be a statement that defines the path and file name such as:

```
sInitFile = "c:\pb4\class\imagedb.ini"
```

You will need to modify the path to match the directory where you installed the example files. Some PowerBuilder objects, such as PictureButtons or Picture controls, may also contain the path for the associated image. You will need to open the Style dialog box for those objects and modify the path. The setup for the example database may also need to be changed.

The best solution is to accept the default directory for the installation. If you install to a different directory and cannot connect to the database, you can use the alternate installation technique presented at the end of this appendix.

Run the Setup Program

The files are in compressed format on the disk and must be installed on your hard disk using the **SETUP.EXE** program. The SETUP program must be run from Windows. Start up Windows and insert the disk in the disk drive (assumed to be **A:** for this example).

From the Windows' Program Manager select the **Run** option on the File menu. In the Run dialog box, enter **A:SETUP** as show in Figure A.1.

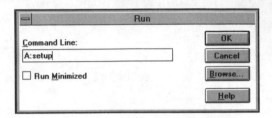

FIGURE A.1 THE RUN DIALOG

Click **OK** to launch the SETUP program. The SETUP program will present an opening dialog box as shown in Figure A.2.

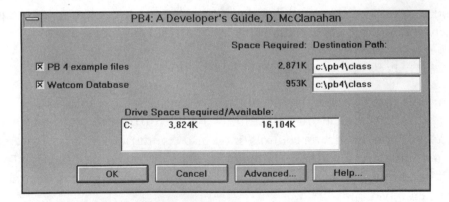

FIGURE A.2 THE INITIAL **SETUP** SCREEN

The files will be installed to the directory **C:\PB4\CLASS** by default. You may change the destination path for the example files, but it is highly recommended that you use the default. If you change the destination path, you will have to adjust some of the references in the example applications to the new path.

Click **OK** in this dialog box to proceed with the installation. The second stage of the SETUP will update the ODBC.INI file located in your WINDOWS directory. This stage will present the dialog box shown in Figure A.3.

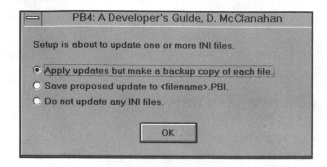

FIGURE A.3 THE SECOND STAGE SETUP DIALOG

The first option will apply the update directly to the ODBC.INI file. In most cases, this is the option you should choose. The second option will insert the proposed update to a file ODBC.PBI (in the WINDOWS directory). The third option will skip this step.

This step will update the ODBC.INI file for the example database, IMAGE.DB. The following lines will be added to the ODBC.INI file:

```
[WATCOM SQL 4.0]
DRIVER=c:\windows\system\WOD40W.DLL

[ODBC Data Sources]
IMAGE=WATCOM SQL 4.0

[Image]
AUTOSTOP=YES
DATABASE=C:\PB4\CLASS\IMAGE.DB
DATABASEFILE=C:\PB4\CLASS\IMAGE.DB
DATABASENAME=Image
DESCRIPTION=EXAMPLE DATABASE
DRIVER=C:\WINDOWS\SYSTEM\WOD40W.DLL
```

```
PWD=SQL
START=DB32W -d
UID=DBA
```

If you have installed the example file to a directory other than C:\PB4\CLASS, you will have to edit the ODBC configuration to match that directory. Chapter 19 provides instructions on how to create an ODBC configuration and database profile. You can also follow these instructions to edit the ODBC configuration and the PowerBuilder database profile for the Image database. Just choose to edit the configuration and profile rather than creating them. (You could also edit ODBC.INI in a text editor.)

Run the LibList Application

After you have completed the setup for the example files, you must run one of the example programs to complete the process. Start up PowerBuilder and run the **LIBLIST** application. This application is in the LIBLIST.PBL library, which is in the C:\PB4\CLASS directory (or the directory where you installed the example files).

To run this application, click on the **Application painter** icon on the PowerBuilder toolbar (this is the left-most icon). This will open the Application painter. Select the **File|Open** menu option, then select the **LIBLIST.PBL** library in the Select Application Library dialog box, and click **OK**. In the Select Application dialog box select **LibList** and click **OK** (this will open the application). Select the **File|Run** menu option to run the LIB-LIST application. You will see the main window (shown in Figure A.4).

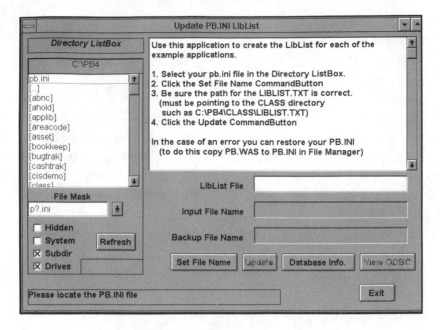

FIGURE A.4 THE LIBLIST APPLICATION

This application will update your PB.INI file (the PowerBuilder initialization file) so that the example applications will run properly. This application will also add the Image database profile to your PB.INI file. The following is the Image profile:

```
[PROFILE Image]
DBMS=ODBC
Database=Image
UserId=dba
DatabasePassword=
LogPassword=
ServerName=
LogId=
Lock=
DbParm=Connectstring='DSN=Image'
Prompt=0
```

The LibList program will also turn off the DashesInIdentifiers PowerBuilder option. This will disallow the dash (–) as a character in PowerScript identifiers, which is necessary for the example code to execute successfully. In the PB.INI file that change is:

```
[PB]
DashesInIdentifiers=0
Running LibList
```

The first step is to locate your PB.INI file in the Directory ListBox. Do this by navigating to the correct directory, such as **C:\PB4** and selecting **PB.INI** from the list of files in the ListBox. When you have completed this step, click on the **Set File Name** command button. The display should now look like Figure A.5.

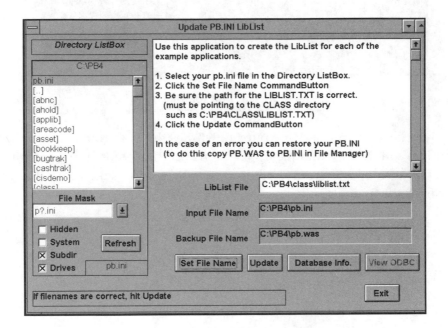

FIGURE A.5 THE LIBLIST APPLICATION

In the LibList File field, you must enter the path and file name for the LIB-LIST.TXT file. This is a file that was installed by the SETUP program. The default is **C:\PB4\CLASS\LIBLIST.TXT**. If you installed to a different directory, you will have to edit the path to the file in this field. When you are sure that the LibList reference is correct, click the **Update** button.

The Input file is the PB.INI file that is to be updated. The LibList application will backup the PB.INI file (to PB.WAS), so you may restore the PB.INI file if an error should occur.

After the backup file is created, the application will update the PB.INI file. At this point the installation is complete. For these changes to take effect you must exit and restart PowerBuilder.

If you wish to test the installation, run the **IMAGEDB** application in the IMAGEDB.PBL library. You will see the status field text change from *connecting to database...* to *connected* if everything is working. If you receive an error message, the connection was not successful. In that case go to Chapter 19 and follow the instructions on setting up the ODBC configuration and the PowerBuilder database profile.

Viewing the ODBC Configuration

You may also use the LibList application to display the ODBC.INI references to the IMAGE.DB database. To do this, click on the **Database Info** command button. The instructions will tell you to select the **ODBC.INI** file in the Directory ListBox. You will find this file in your WINDOWS directory, usually C:\WINDOWS. In the LibList File field, enter the path and filename for the ODBCINIT.TXT file, which was installed to the examples directory by the SETUP program, i.e., **C:\pb4\class\odbcinit.txt**. If everything looks okay, click **View ODBC**. You should see a display similar to the one in Figure A.6.

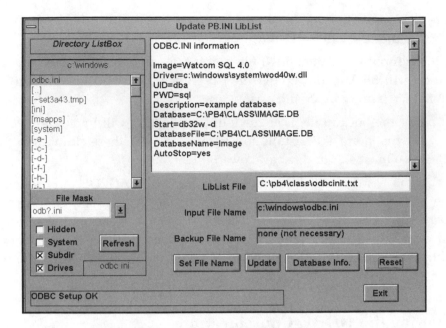

FIGURE A.6 VIEWING THE ODBC CONFIGURATION

AN ALTERNATE INSTALLATION TECHNIQUE

If you cannot connect to the IMAGE database and have followed the instructions in Chapter 19 on setting up the configuration and profile, you can use the following technique to install the examples.

If you *are* able to connect to the Image database successfully, skip this section.

NOTE

You must have installed the Watcom database engine with the PowerBuilder installation program for this technique to work. The directions in the following section will tell you how to temporarily delete the example files and create a new Image database in the Examples directory using PowerBuilder's Database painter. Creating a new Image database in the

Database painter will automatically set up the ODBC configuration and the database profile. Once the creation of the new Image database is completed, you will delete the newly created Image database and reinstall the example files to your example library. But during the reinstall, it is important that you do not allow the SETUP program to update the INI files since they will have been set up correctly in the previous step of this procedure.

Temporarily Delete the Example Files

Delete all the files from the Examples directory (such as C:\PB4\CLASS). Check to be sure that you have actually removed the database files (IMAGE.DB and IMAGE.LOG) from the example directory. The file attributes for both files are set to mark these as system files, and Windows will prompt you to be sure that you want to delete them. The directory itself must remain on the drive, so if you deleted the directory in the process, re-create it before proceeding.

Delete the Old ODBC Data Source

Next run PowerBuilder. Go to the Database painter and connect to any database other than Image (such as the PowerBuilder Examples database). Select the **Configure ODBC...** option from the File menu; this will open the Configure ODBC dialog box shown in Figure A.7.

In this dialog box you must select the appropriate driver for the database. Our sample database uses the **WATCOM SQL 4.0** driver, so select that entry in the Installed Drivers ListBox. If WATCOM SQL 4.0 does not appear in the Installed Drivers List Box, then that is the problem, and you must install the Watcom engine using the PowerBuilder installation program.

After selecting WATCOM SQL 4.0, select **IMAGE** in the Data Sources List Box. Then click on the **Remove** command button. This will delete the old nonfunctional ODBC data source. If IMAGE does not appear in this list, skip this step and continue with the next. In any case, click on **Done** to return to the Database painter.

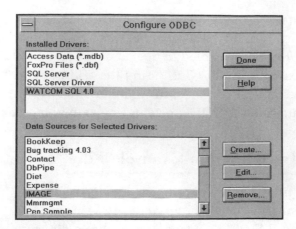

FIGURE A.7 THE CONFIGURE ODBC DIALOG

Delete the Old Database Profile

In the Database painter select the **Connect** option from the File menu to open the cascading menu shown in Figure A.8.

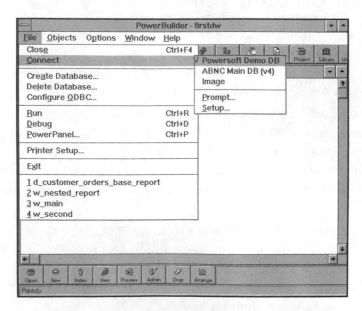

FIGURE A.8 SELECT THE SETUP OPTION FROM THIS CASCADING MENU

Select **Setup**. This will open the Database Profiles dialog box shown in Figure A.9.

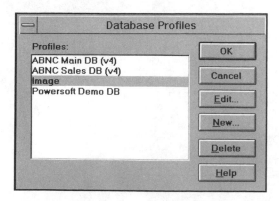

FIGURE A.9 THE DATABASE PROFILES DIALOG

In this dialog box select the **Image** profile and click on **Delete**. This will remove the PowerBuilder Image database profile from the PB.INI file. If Image is not listed (it may have been deleted by the previous step) in the Profiles listbox, skip this step.

Create the Image Database

Now you will create a new Watcom database. This will also create the ODBC data source (ODBC.INI configuration), and the PowerBuilder database profile automatically. You are creating an empty database that will be replaced with the example database in the final step of this procedure.

In the Database painter, select the **File|Create Database...** menu option (Figure A.10).

This will open the Create Local Database dialog box. Enter the disk drive letter, full path, and database name (**Image**) as shown in Figure A.11. (Adjust the path as you wish, but the directory you enter must exist on the disk.)

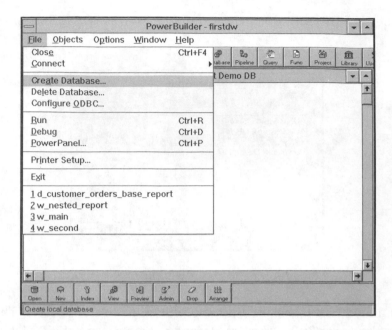

FIGURE A.10 SELECT THE CREATE DATABASE OPTION

FIGURE A.11 CREATE THE IMAGE DATABASE

The password for the Watcom database is SQL. Click **OK** to create the database. If this operation completes successfully, the Database painter will also connect to the new Image database (watch the Database painter status line for this information). When this step is complete, close the Database painter and exit PowerBuilder. This step will have created the

Image database (temporarily used), the ODBC data source definition, and the PowerBuilder database profile. All you need to do now is to install the example database (only) from the diskette that came with this book.

Delete the Newly Create Image Database Files

Now go to the Windows' File Manager, and delete the newly created files IMAGE.DB and IMAGE.LOG. Again check to be sure that they have actually been removed from the Examples directory. At this stage, the ODBC configuration and the database profile have been correctly created. You will now reinstall the example files (including IMAGE.DB and IMAGE.LOG) and skip the step that would update the ODBC configuration and database profile.

Exit PowerBuilder

Now you must exit PowerBuilder and be sure that the Watcom database is also closed. If you see the minimized Watcom icon on the Windows desktop, click on it and select **Close** from the popup menu.

Run the Setup Program

Insert the example diskette in the disk drive (assumed to be **A:** for this example) and rerun the **SETUP.EXE** program.

From the Windows' Program Manager select the **Run** option on the File menu. In the Run dialog box, enter **A:SETUP** as shown in Figure A.12.

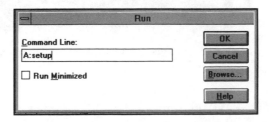

FIGURE A.12 THE RUN DIALOG

Click **OK** to launch the SETUP program. The SETUP program will present an opening dialog box as shown in Figure A.13. Change the destination path if necessary for both the example files and the Watcom database.

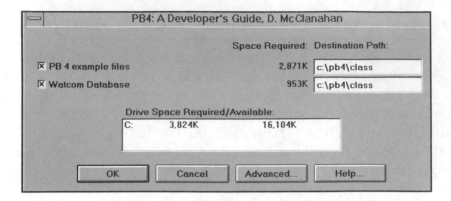

FIGURE A.13 THE INITIAL SETUP SCREEN

Click **OK** on this dialog box to proceed with the installation.

The second stage of the SETUP will present the dialog box shown in Figure A.14.

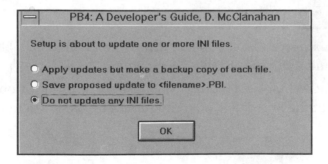

FIGURE A.14 THE SECOND-STAGE SETUP DIALOG

Select the third option so that this step does not update the INI files.

WARNING

858

The next time you run PowerBuilder, you will be able to successfully connect to the example database (IMAGE.DB). This technique must work if you have correctly installed the Watcom database engine.

Run the LibList Application

Now run the LibList application as described earlier in this appendix.

AutoStop

You can set an option in the ODBC configuration that will tell the Watcom engine to close the database when you exit PowerBuilder. Otherwise, the database remains open (you will see the minimized icon on the desktop after you close PowerBuilder). To set this option, select the **Configure ODBC** menu option from the Database painter's initial menu (Figure A.15). Select **WATCOM SQL 4.0** for the driver and **Image** as the data source. Select the **Edit** option to open the ODBC Configuration dialog box.

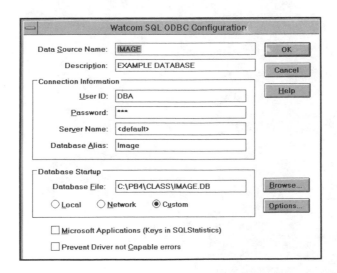

FIGURE A.15 THE ODBC CONFIGURATION FOR THE IMAGE DATABASE

Click on the **Options** command button to open the Startup Options dialog box (Figure A.16).

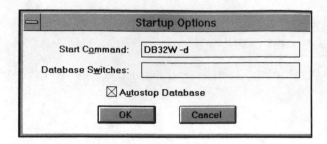

Figure A.16 The options

In this dialog box click the **Autostop Database** check box.

INDEX

PowerSource™ is your monthly guide to mastering PowerBuilder!

First FREE

You're invited to examine a free issue of the newsletter and companion disk exclusively for PowerBuilder™ users!

Congratulations on choosing PowerBuilder. You now own a powerful client/server development tool that will serve your needs for years to come.

Like any good programming system, PowerBuilder offers a vast range of capabilities—more than you could ever learn on your own. That's why you need *PowerSource* from Pinnacle Publishing.

The serious newsletter for serious PowerBuilder users

PowerSource is a monthly newsletter and companion disk exclusively for users of PowerBuilder. It's packed with tips, shortcuts, and time-saving PowerBuilder techniques—all designed to help you develop better applications faster.

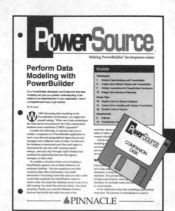

Companion disk each month

The monthly companion disk makes *PowerSource* amazingly easy to use. Each disk contains code, runnable programs, test data, even utilities and shareware. You can put each issue's PowerBuilder information to work right away!

Your first issue is FREE

Return the card below (or call us) and we'll send you the next issue of *PowerSource* and its companion disk FREE. If you don't agree that *PowerSource* will help you develop better applications, just return the invoice marked "Cancel." You'll pay nothing, and the free issue will be yours to keep.

To get your FREE issue of PowerSource, mail or fax the form below or call toll-free

800/788-1900

206/251-1900 ▲ Fax 206/251-5057

- -

☑ **Yes!** Rush my FREE issue of *PowerSource* and its companion disk. If I agree that *PowerSource* will help me save time and develop better applications with PowerBuilder, I'll pay my invoice for just $199* for 11 more issues and disks (12 in all). If I don't think so, I'll return the invoice marked "Cancel" and pay nothing!

NAME

COMPANY

ADDRESS

CITY   STATE/PROVINCE   ZIP/POSTAL CODE

COUNTRY (IF OTHER THAN U.S.)

(   )   (   )

DAYTIME PHONE   DAYTIME FAX

WJJ   *Outside the U.S.: Add $15 to Canada, $20 to other countries. Washington state residents add 8.2% sales tax. Prices subject to change.

"If you ever decide you're not satisfied with *PowerSource*, you may cancel your subscription and get a full refund on the entire subscription cost."

Susan J. Harker, Publisher

Method of payment:*

❏ Check enclosed (payable to Pinnacle)
❏ VISA   ❏ MasterCard   ❏ AmEx
❏ Bill me later

CREDIT CARD NUMBER   EXP. DATE

SIGNATURE

Pinnacle Publishing, Inc.
18000 72nd Ave. S. #217 ▲ Kent, WA 98032
206/251-1900 ▲ Fax 206/251-5057